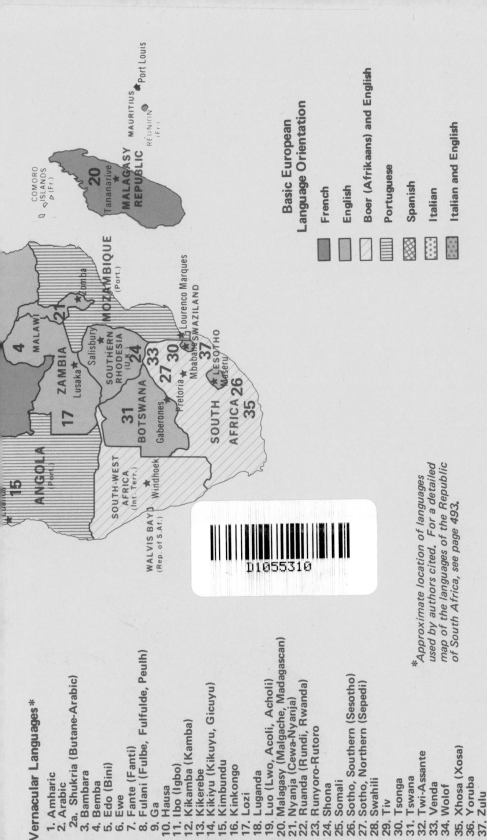

Port Louis

MAURITIUS
★ Port Louis

COMORO
ISLANDS
(Fr.)

MALAGASY
REPUBLIC
★ Tananarive

20

RÉUNION
(Fr.)

MOZAMBIQUE
(Port.)

Zomba ★

21

4

MALAWI

ZAMBIA
Lusaka ★

17

Salisbury ★

SOUTHERN
RHODESIA
(U.K.)

Lourenco Marques ★

24

SWAZILAND

33

Mbabane ★

30

27

Pretoria ★

31

BOTSWANA

Gaberones ★

37

LESOTHO
Maseru ★

26

SOUTH
AFRICA

35

15

ANGOLA
(Port.)

SOUTH-WEST
AFRICA
(Int. Terr.)
Windhoek ★

WALVIS BAY
(Rep. of S.Af.)

D1055310

Basic European
Language Orientation

French

English

Boer (Afrikaans) and English

Portuguese

Spanish

Italian

Italian and English

Vernacular Languages*

1. Amharic
2. Arabic
2a. Shukria (Butane-Arabic)
3. Bambara
4. Bemba
5. Edo (Bini)
6. Ewe
7. Fante (Fanti)
8. Fulani (Fulbe, Fulfulde, Peulh)
9. Ga
10. Hausa
11. Ibo (Igbo)
12. Kikamba (Kamba)
13. Kikerebe
14. Kikiyu (Kikuyu, Gicuyu)
15. Kimbundu
16. Kinkongo
17. Lozi
18. Luganda
19. Luo (Lwo, Acoli, Acholi)
20. Malagasy (Malgache, Madagascan)
21. Nyanja (Cewa-Nyanja)
22. Ruanda (Rundi, Rwanda)
23. Runyoro-Rutoro
24. Shona
25. Somali
26. Sotho, Southern (Sesotho)
27. Sotho, Northern (Sepedi)
28. Swahili
29. Tiv
30. Tsonga
31. Tswana
32. Twi-Assante
33. Venda
34. Wolof
35. Xhosa (Xosa)
36. Yoruba
37. Zulu

*Approximate location of languages
used by authors cited. For a detailed
map of the languages of the Republic
of South Africa, see page 493.

AFRICAN AUTHORS

AFRICAN AUTHORS

A COMPANION TO BLACK AFRICAN WRITING
Volume I: 1300-1973

By

DONALD E. HERDECK

Contributors
Abiola Irele, Lilyan Kesteloot, Gideon Mangoaela

A Black Orpheus Press/Inscape Book

INSCAPE Corporation
Washington, D.C.
1974

AFRICAN AUTHORS
A COMPANION TO BLACK AFRICAN WRITING
Volume I: 1300–1973
Second Edition

This volume represents the first of a series of biennial reference companions to Black African writing. Future volumes will update and perfect the entries of previous years, add more authors, and include new critical essays by recognized authorities on a variety of aspects of African literature. About every six years all previous volumes will be corrected, revised, cumulated, and published in a single volume. A NOTE ON THE SECOND EDITION: Through a corporate reorganization, Black Orpheus Press, Inc., the company that published the first edition of *African Authors* in 1973, has become a series imprint of INSCAPE Corporation. For this second edition, there have been numerous corrections and changes as well as the substitution of line drawings for some of the photos of the first edition. Stronger and more durable end sheets and book cloth have also been used in production.

Copyright © 1974 by INSCAPE Corporation.

Printed in the United States of America. All rights reserved. No part of this book may be used or reproduced in any manner whatsoever without written permission except in the case of brief quotations embodied in critical articles and reviews. For information address INSCAPE Corporation, 1629 K Street, N.W., Washington, D.C. 20006.

Library of Congress Catalog Card Number: 73-172338

International Standard Book Number: 0-87953-008-1

Library of Congress Cataloging in Publication Data

Herdeck, Donald E.   1924–
        African authors.
(Dimensions of the Black intellectual experience)
Includes bibliographies.
1. African literature—Bio-bibliography.
I. Title.   II. Series.
PL8010.H38   809'.89'6 [B]   73–172338
        ISBN 0–87953–008–1

Acknowledgment is hereby made to the following
for permission to reprint from their works:

Africana Publishing and Andre Deutsch Ltd.—"To Prince Magena" from *Zulu Poems*, by Mazisi Kunene.

Africana Publishing and Heinemann Ltd.—"The Stars Have Departed" from *Labyrinths with Path of Thunder*, by Christopher Okigbo, 1971.

Atheneum Publishers—*Selected Poems*, by Léopold Sédar Senghor, translated and introduced by John Reed and Clive Wake © Oxford University Press, 1964.

Oliver Bernard—For his translation of Paulin Joachim's "Enterrement." George Borchardt, Inc.—"Femme Noire" and "Prière aux masques" by Léopold Sédar Senghor.

Dennis Brutus—"Midnight," "Transition," "Immigrant," and "Autopsy" by K. A. Nortje.

Dennis Brutus and Bernth Lindfors—"And I am Driftwood" from *Poems from Algiers*, by Dennis Brutus © 1970.

The Clarendon Press, Oxford—F. W. Parsons' discussion in *A Selection of African Prose*, compiled by W. H. Whiteley, Vol. 2, 1964.

Rosica Colin Ltd.—*Mission to Kala*, by Mongo Beti.

Commonweal—Linda Kuehl's interview with Yambo Ouologuem © June 11, 1971.

John Cushman Associates, Inc.—*Long Drums and Cannons*, by Margaret Laurence © 1968.

John Day Company and Heinemann Ltd.—*A Man of the People*, by Chinua Achebe © 1966.

Andre Deutsch Ltd.—*The Gab Boys*, by Cameron Duodu. *Danda*, by Nkem Nwankwo. *The Interpreters*, by Wole Soyinka.

Diogène—"The Social and Economic Background of Portuguese Negro Poetry," by Alfredo Margarido, published in *Diogènes* No. 37, 1962.

Doubleday and Company and Heinemann Educational Books Ltd.—*God's Bits of Wood*, by Ousmane Sembène © 1962, 1970.

E. P. Dutton and Company and Barrie and Jenkins Ltd.—Preface to *Familiarity Is the Kingdom of the Lost*, by Dugmore Boetie. Ed. by Barney Simon. Preface by Nadine Gordimer.

East African Publishing House—Prologue to *Orphan*, by Okello Oculi.

Guy Flatley and *The New York Times*—Interview (November 9, 1969) with Ousmane Sembène, *The New York Times* © 1969.

Grove Press, Inc. and Faber and Faber Ltd.—*The Palm-Wine Drinkard*, by Amos Tutuola © 1953 by George Braziller.

Heinemann Educational Books Ltd.—"Kabeke's Return" in *Eating Chiefs*, by Taban Lo Liyong. Preface to *Seven South African Poets*, by Cosmo Pieterse. Arthur Ravenscroft's introduction to *The Voice*, by Gabriel Okara.

David Higham Associates—*The Truly Married Woman*, by Abioseh Nicol.

Hill and Wang (A division of Farrar, Strauss and Giroux, Inc.) and Methuen Co. Ltd.—"Death in the Dawn," "In Memory of Segun Awolowo," "Idanre," and preface from *Idanre and Other Poems*, by Wole Soyinka © 1967.

Houghton Mifflin Company—*The Beautyful Ones Are Not Yet Born*, by Ayi Kwei Armah.

Humanities Press, Inc. and Longman Group Ltd.—*Sundiata: An Epic of Old Mali*, by D. T. Niane.

Paulin Joachim—"Enterrement."

Joseph Kariuki—"New Life."

S. A. Konadu and Anowuo Educational Publications—*Don't Leave Me MERCY*, by Asare Konadu (K. A. Bediako).

Bernth Lindfors—"The Beginnings of French African Fiction," by Fredric Michelman, published in *Research in African Literature*, II, 1, Spring.

Longman Green Ltd.—"Ibadan" and "Three Moods of Princeton" from *A Reed in the Tide*, by John Pepper Clark.

Monthly Review Press and Heinemann Educational Books Ltd.—*Consciencism*, by Kwame Nkrumah © 1970.

Gerald Moser—*Essays in Portuguese-African Literature*, Penn State Studies 26.

Ezekiel Mphahlele—"Song of the Drum," by Jean Baptiste Mutabaruka.

Ezekiel Mphahlele and Doubleday and Company—*African Writing Today* and *Down Second Avenue*, by Ezekiel Mphahlele.

Thomas Nelson and Sons Ltd.—*The Forest of a Thousand Daemons*, by D. O. Fagunwa, translated by Wole Soyinka.

Northwestern University Press—"Yoruba Theatre," by Ulli Beier, article by W. S. Merwin, and untitled poem by António Neto translated by W. S. Merwin, from *Introduction to African Literature*, by Ulli Beier. *This Africa*, by Judith Gleason.

The Third Press-Joseph Okpaku Publishing Company—"The Journey," by R. Egudu, "J. B. Danquah: Evolué Playwright," by Anthony Graham-White, and "Changing Themes in the Nigerian Novel," by John Povey. Reprinted from *Journal of the New African Literature and the Arts*, © 1968, 1970.

Editions Pierre-Jean Oswald—"Tavern by the Sea," by A. Fonseca. "Hino a Minho terra," by José Craveirinha, translated by Gerald Moser.

Peter Owen—*African/English Literature* by Anne Tibble.

Oxford University Press—*Writing in French from Senegal to Cameroon*, by Birago Diop and A. C. Brench. *The Gods Are Not to Blame*, by Ola Rotimi © 1971. *The Strong Breed, The Swamp Dwellers* and *The Dance of the Forests*, by Wole Soyinka.

Penguin Books Ltd.—"Song of a Common Lover," by Flavien Ranaivo, trans. by Alan Ryder, from *Modern Poetry From Africa*, Gerald Moore and Ulli Beier (eds.). "The Vultures," by David Diop, trans. by Moore and Beier.

Poésie Vivante—"To the Poets," by Bernard Dadié.

Philadelphia Tribune Company, Inc. Pub.—"Creation," by Gladys Casely-Hayford © October 14, 1937.

Praeger Publishers, Inc. and Routledge and Kegan Paul Ltd.—*Child of Two Worlds*, by Mugo Gatheru.

Présence Africaine—*L'Harmattan*, by Sembène Ousmane (1965). "Pâcques 48," by Jacques Rabémananjara (1961). *Au*

Tchad sous les étoiles, by Joseph Brahim Seid (1962). Following poems from No. 57 of the review of *Présence Africaine* entitled *Nouvelle Somme de Poésie du Monde Noir* (1966): "O Terre," by Siriman Cissoko; "Le sens du cirque," by Youssouf Guèye; "A David Diop," by Paulin Joachim; "A Mon Mari," by Yambo Ouologuem; "Ou sont-ils donc allés?" by Alfred Sow; "Les Vautours" from *Coups de Pilon*, by David Diop.

David Rubadiri and Pergamon Press Ltd.—"The Tide that from the West Washes African to the Bone" and "Black Child," from *Pergamon Poets 2-Poetry from Africa*.

Sagerep-*L'Afrique Actuelle—Liaison d'Un Eté*, by Olympe Bhêly-Quénum.

Time, The Weekly Newsmagazine—Melvin Maddocks' review "Brotherhood of Victims" on Yambo Ouologuem's novel *Wages of Violence*, March 15, 1971 © Time Inc., 1971.

The author has made every possible effort to communicate with all firms and authors holding rights to quoted material: in those very few cases where this effort proved fruitless the author would be pleased to communicate with the holders of the rights.

Grateful acknowledgment is also made to the following for the use of the photographs reprinted herein:

Black Orpheus magazine
Andre Deutsch Ltd.
Doubleday and Co., Inc.
East African Publishing House
Edit. Pierre-Jean Oswald
Edit Renée La Coste
Edit. Seghers
Faber and Faber Ltd.
Fawcett World Library
Gerald W. and Charlotte M. Hartwig
Heinemann Educational Books Ltd.
Joseph E. Kariuki
Henry S. Kimbugwe
R. G. Leitch
Libraire Fernand Nathan et Cie.
Longman Group Ltd.
Manuel Lopes
Mme. René Maran
Ali A. Mazrui
James McNamara and *The Washington Post*
Methuen and Co. Ltd.
Gerald Moser
Jordan Ngubane
Nouvelles Editions Latines
Okike magazine and Nwamife Publishers Ltd.
Oxford University Press
Panther Books Ltd. and Granada Publishing Limited.
Penguin Books Ltd.
Présence Africaine
Research in African Literature
Routledge and Kegan Paul Ltd.
Mme. F. J. Tenreiro
Samuel Samkange
Third World Press
Rems N. Umeasiegbu
University of California Press
West African Review
Zuka magazine and Oxford University Press (Eastern African Branch)

Drawings by Munson Design

CONTENTS

Acknowledgments

My old friends, Harold and Rose Marie Ames, first suggested I consider a special study of African literature. Dr. Joseph Applegate, who as Acting Director of African Studies at Howard University gave me the opportunity to teach African literature, also deserves special thanks. Léon Gontran Damas, one of the pioneers of twentieth century African literature and a notable poet and critic, was very helpful and sympathetic in more ways than I can say here during the difficult early stages of the project. Randal Everts, a close friend and collaborator early in the project, provided invaluable help in the area of South African vernacular authors, a specialty in which his competence is matched by few scholars. We had originally planned this as a joint work and I regret that he was unable to continue his work on the project. Gideon Mangoaela, poet and scholar, was kind to consider many of the biographical and bibliographical problems I could not otherwise have resolved, and to make a very valuable contribution. Professor Gerald M. Moser of the Pennsylvania State College helped me a great deal in his responses to my queries on African writers using Portuguese, and his two studies of Portuguese-African writing are frequently cited in this work. Professor Eric Sellin of Temple University, Professor Bernth Lindfors of the University of Texas, Professor John Povey of UCLA, and the African writers Ezekiel Mphahlele and Dennis Brutus have also been very helpful and encouraging. Mrs. Ellen Conroy Kennedy, noted translator of French and francophone African works, introduced me to many African writers and scholars at various times in her Georgetown home in Washington and otherwise was helpful at various stages of my work. Professor Brian Weinstein of Howard University generously shared his knowledge of African colonial history and his fine biography, *Eboué*, sharpened and deepened my understanding of the experiences and traumas of Africa in the pre-independence period. Dorothy Porter, curator of the Moorland-Spingarn Collection at Howard University and her husband, Dr. James Porter, were at many points encouraging and helpful on this project.

Many of my students in African literature courses at Howard and Georgetown have fruitfully debated my ideas on Africa. Mr. David Ganz, carrying out a special independent study project at Georgetown under my direction, has brought to my attention a great deal of material and anthologies I would not otherwise have come to know, and has developed the information summarized in Appendix P to this volume which should be very useful to teachers and librarians seeking certain types of writers or writing for their courses or their library collections.

Mrs. Judy Toth began to type the first version of this work as early as 1966, and Mrs. Carol Roth, who worked more recently on the South African and Portuguese-language writers, did yeoman service.

Mr. Robert Greene served as copy-editor for five months, reading and re-reading two long drafts, and deserves my strongest appreciation for his general suggestions on format as well as for his tact and care in helping me prepare the final draft for the printer.

Jesse Winch was extremely helpful with photographic problems and Diana Munson did beautiful work in rendering the drawings printed here of many of the early writers.

My experiences and travels in Africa between 1962 and 1964 and my friendships since with African scholars, students, and writers in the United States have strengthened my interest in African affairs and African culture, and to all of these unnamed colleagues and friends I would like to express my thanks.

I would also like to thank my publisher who encouraged me to complete my research and present it in book form some three years ago, and who worked closely with me as I struggled with basic questions regarding the parameters and content of the study.

Finally, I wish to thank Margaret who has helped edit much of my copy, compiled many of the appendices and generally made the work easier, faster, and better.

Spring/1973

Donald E. Herdeck
School of Foreign Service
Georgetown University

AFRICAN AUTHORS

INTRODUCTION

This volume contains biographical information on 594 authors and bibliographical information on some 2,000 works in a wide variety of genres. The authors are primarily from sub-Saharan Africa, or what is generally now called Black Africa, but Malagasy and Mauritius are also included because of the very clear cross-fertilization between the mainland and island cultures and their similar colonial experience. The emphasis in genres is on standard Western categories, the novel, poem, play, and short story, but other types of literature more appropriate to African folk-oral traditions are also dealt with, including the tale, proverb, and legend. Biographic, autobiographic, critical and journalistic works and their authors are also treated when the work is historically early, or otherwise of interest in the context of the country or language literature concerned.

A total of 37 African vernacular languages, including Arabic and Amharic, are represented by 233 authors and some 500 published volumes or major titles as well as hundreds of poems, plays, stories, and other minor works, both published and unpublished. The major Western European languages, English, French, Portuguese, and Latin, as well as Afrikaans, are represented by 400 authors. (Figures add to more than the total of 594 authors dealt with because some authors work, or worked, in two or more languages.)

Sixteen appendices, including four critical essays and three bibliographies, and two maps are provided to give the reader basic tools for surveying and studying the literature of Africa from a variety of analytic and descriptive perspectives.

Purposes of the Work

With the post-World War II explosion of creative works by African writers, the need for a biobibliographical companion to African writing, including as many of the precolonial authors as possible, has become increasingly evident. Such a work is needed not only to furnish the general public with a basic reference guide to a major world literature which is little known and even less appreciated in the West, but also to provide the student and scholar in African studies a kind of base line of information of what is now known of the African literary tradition and its most contemporary productions.

A basic premise of this volume is that it is not sufficient to say that a work should stand on its own—to be a "world in itself." That might be a good test to apply to a work coming from a known tradition reflecting familiar cultural values and expressing sociological patterns and historical experiences reasonably close to those of the Western world. But this is certainly not yet the general case for creative works from Africa, even those apparently cast in European modes, and it is even less true for works springing from precolonial experiences or which are highly steeped in the African sensibility or cast in African forms.

African novels, poems, and plays may seem to be European. They come to the reader in their American, British, French, or Portuguese covers, and are usually expressed in a familiar language. But Black African writing is never completely Western and sometimes it is hardly Western at all. It comes from a world in some ways as alien to most readers in the West as the literature of China or even ancient Egypt. Further, it speaks of an agrarian world for the most part and often reflects concerns and occupations now increasingly rare in Europe and America. Finally, African literature is often complex, ambiguous, and full of ethical values which are not necessarily akin to those held by non-African peoples. We are all of mankind, but there are differences—and those differences ought to delight and enlighten the reader rather than disturb, mystify, or amuse him.

Accordingly, to understand African writing, we need to know more about African authors. A companion to African writing needs to help the reader perceive some of the hardships these writers have encountered both in their personal lives and in the labors of their craft as verbal artists. Such a companion needs to show how these writers combine their African heritage and sensitivity with the demands of the written word and European artistic genres which to some degree remain exotic forms to them. Possibly even more important is a knowledge of the writer's attitude toward the African past as well as his views on the major issues facing the new Africa.

Selection of Entries

Most of the entries in this volume concern creative literature written since the early twentieth century, though an effort has also been made to include authors whose journalistic and historical studies, or work in folklore and oral literature, provided later writers with needed inspiration or materials. Though most of the earliest writers thus covered were not creative artists in the Western sense, and did their writing during the pre-independence period, there is a small body of important artists, mostly poets working in Arabic, who in or outside of Africa, were important writers. Five writers are dealt with who lived earlier than the 15th century and twenty are treated who worked before the advent of the 18th. Though it is unlikely we shall ever know much more about these very early writers than we do now, their work is proof that African literature is not only a rich one in its traditional oral forms, but also that there exists an ancient written record of high achievement.

Needless to say, the long period of oral literature, still very much alive in most of Africa today, underlies almost all of the written literature produced in the past century. A great deal of research remains to be done in this fascinating area to establish the inter-connections between the vernacular-oral traditions and the work largely conceived in Western forms and designed for literate audiences.

Somewhere between strictly oral literary traditions and the published literature of the Western-educated elites of Africa is the popular, so-called "market" literature of Onitsha, Nigeria and such centers as Accra and Nairobi, and the pamphlet and newspaper novels of such writers as Félix Couchoro of Togo. These brassy, vivid novelettes and plays aimed at the growing number of Africans who have elementary skills in an European language have been the middle ground between the old folk literatures and the more classical European inspired fiction, drama and verse. A few of the most prolific and interesting of the authors producing works in this popular field are included in this volume.

Finally, in some cases, men who have made their reputations primarily as politicians are included if they have done interesting translations or if their biographies and political works are of high intellectual quality or provocative for their picture of African problems and the contemporary African scene. Readers seeking coverage of the political scene as such, however, should consult such works as *Reuter's Guide to the New Africans* or Ronald Segal's *Political Africa: A Who's Who of Personalities and Parties*.

Most works discussed are the product of artists who have both African and European educations. Only a few works are strictly historical or ethnological in the narrow sense or otherwise the result of a purely "African" culture. Only a few authors working in Amharic, Swahili, and Arabic were untouched by European influences. Even such well-known and brilliantly captured tales as those of Birago Diop's in his *Stories of Amadou Koumba* must be read in the French language and recognized to have been influenced and subtly changed by Diop's own European education and his need to please a primarily French audience.

A few authors not widely read or now remembered are included to give some coverage to young writers, to provide exposure to artists coming from countries with only the newest written literatures, or to rescue from undue neglect authors important historically. No attempt has been made to eliminate writers as undeserving of attention on Western literary grounds although only a few of the writers producing "market" literature, as noted, have been dealt with.

Format of a Typical Entry

The capsule biography: The author's name is provided on the first line with any variants or pseudonyms presented in parenthesis. On the second line is birth and death data including the name of the natal village, city, region, and modern name of the country. On the third line is the citation of the genre or genres of the works cited in the entry, plus the author's profession, such as scholar, journalist, teacher, which may be relevant in considering the writer's training and intellectual experiences. When no reliable birth year could be discovered, a year usually 30 years before the date of the author's first publication was assigned arbitrarily but shown to be an approximate one. In some cases, the approximative date is believed accurate to within one or a few years but otherwise not further discoverable because of the ancient period concerned or because an oral literature is involved.

The main biography: The first paragraph is usually devoted to the author's schooling, degrees, professional training, travel, jobs and positions held, honors won, and general statements, if called for, of the author's relative importance and literary reputation. One or more works may be cited and briefly discussed in the opening paragraph.

For minor or young writers, a single paragraph usually suffices. For a major author, the career history, the works he has composed, his friendships, influences, and other matters may be spun out over several pages with comparatively detailed discussion given to individual works.

In addition to giving the facts of each author's life, I have attempted in many cases to give a "taste" of the author's work by offering brief extracts or quotations from the work concerned. Extracts are also used to provide examples of style, or of a particularly interesting emphasis in handling a theme or rhythm. No attempt has been made to offer selections from each major author, but the hope has been to furnish some insight into the qualities of a few authors and to whet the reader's interest. These selections are taken directly from the original works whenever possible and only when the originals were unavailable or especially difficult to obtain by purchase or loan or consultation in a library have I gone to a secondary source. Translations of quoted material are referenced in the text of the essays; some of the translations are mine.

Although the size of any entry, relative to others in this volume, obviously reflects to some degree my conception of the author's importance, the space devoted to any one author does not necessarily suggest just how important he may be on some abstract scale of excellence. In some cases I have chosen to devote relatively little space to one work and much more to another. Sometimes a given work, though of general interest, is not noticeably better than others of its sort; it may be to some degree unoriginal or not particularly well written, and it is given only passing attention. In contrast, some fairly detailed attention may be devoted to a work which I find is provocative, or original, or in some manner calling for more concentrated consideration. Again, one author may have published many works, all or most of which demand some comment, while another author, very possibly quite important for one or more reasons, has only one or a very few works to be discussed. Though the latter author may, by contemporary judgment, be the more significant, he possibly has received less "treatment" at my hands than a more prolific, but lesser, artist.

The case of statesmen who are also authors is a special problem. To ignore a man's prestigious political career to a greater or lesser extent in favor of what in fact may only be a minor aspect of his life's work may seem to misplace the emphasis. Yet, to provide political or other information in great detail or a list of political works more or less complete on persons only marginally "creative writers" would be excessive. Accordingly, I have attempted to provide relevant political information only in general outline. Where the statesman is as much creative artist as politician, the information provided might often be equally focused on each aspect of the man's life. For such pre-eminent artists as Léopold Sédar Senghor of Senegal, or Jean-Jacques Rabemananjara of Malagasy, the intermingling of political, social, and artistic facts and concerns was unavoidable, even productive, of a better comprehension of their life goals and literary aspirations.

My major effort, then, beyond remedying, where possible, the factual, interpretative, or critical inadequacies, of previous scholarship, is to furnish a panoramic overview of each of the more important authors and to give a reasonably complete summary of his achievements both in and outside of literature.

Writings: Following each main biography is a systematic listing of the author's works broken down by genre, and including details on dates of publication. Where possible, the publisher is also listed, since works on Africa are often difficult to procure and bibliographic information scanty. In addition, an effort has been made to list all the English-language editions and all editions of the work in the language in which it was originally published. Since this information reflects the literary history and importance of each title, an effort has been made to make this sub-section capable of standing on its own, and a reader may use it without reference to the main biography. Translations of a work into languages other than English are cited only in special cases when an important work may not have an English edition, or, the extent and frequency of a work's being translated serves to indicate its importance or popularity beyond the area and language of its original appearance.

Biographical/Critical Writings: This sub-section is included only on writers that have generated some secondary commentary on their lives and/or their works. No claim is made that all possible relevant studies on a given author have been provided, but an effort has been made to cite the most important, detailed, and up-to-date studies available. An effort also has been made in this and the "Writings" sub-section to spell out most terms and other bibliographic data to eliminate the usual eye-straining and sometimes confusing abbreviations so common in reference works.

Technical Points

The languages used by the authors: The language in which the author habitually writes and/or in which he is usually published is not specifically stated for those writers working in English, French, or Portuguese. The author's name in some cases and the citation of the works in the original titles I believe is sufficient indication of the language used. However, some writers, particularly the collectors of folkloric materials, often publish in the vernacular language concerned, and then, subsequently, in one of the European languages. In such cases, although the main biographic essay on the author makes such practices clear, the African language or languages generally used is specifically given on line three of the capsule biography along with other languages used.

Translation of titles: Immediately after the citation of the original title of a work, I offer in parenthesis an informal and unofficial translation (or a Roman script version of the title). Where I offer no such translation I am confessing my ignorance and/or that of my sources. I have been able to double-check most of the translations of the titles from Botswanan, Lesothan and South African vernacular works with Professor Gideon Mangoaela of Howard University, but I have not been able to obtain equally valuable assistance from scholars in other vernacular languages.

When a work has been translated into English, I generally provide the title in its published British or American version as the case may be, unless the English-language title is considerably different from a literal rendering of the original. In the case of works in Amharic, I have in all cases provided an English rendering, italicized, for the original citation of each work, not wishing to employ a script few outside Ethiopia can read and which few printers can furnish. My sources generally did not provide Romanized versions of the Ethiopian (Amharic) titles and I saw no utility in doing so myself.

Arabic, Swahili and Somali titles are given in Roman letters, and where possible they are followed by the general sense of the title in English. No attempt has been made to provide titles in Cyrillic or other non-Roman scripts when Russian or other titles are cited.

Capitalization of titles: Works in English are capitalized according to general American practice; works in French and Portuguese have only the first word, often the article, capitalized, and words invariably capitalized, such as proper nouns. Titles in African languages follow the sources.

Dates and dating: Arabic and Ethiopian dates are generally translated into the modern Western calendar. In some cases, however, my source may offer a double date (ex: 1796/97) to indicate that the unreformed Julian calendar or its Ethiopian equivalent provides one date which would be a year later in the reformed Gregorian calendar of the West although the exact month and day have not been computed.

The problem of names, pseudonyms, and similar difficulties: I have chosen to cite first the name of the author by which I believe he is most commonly known or which a preponderance of my sources indicate is well-known. For example, the entry on the fine Cameroonian writer, Alexandre Biyidi, is found under BETI, Mongo, his long-used *nom-de-plume,* with his "actual" name and his discarded first pseudonym, Eza Boti, being provided as simple cross-reference entries. In some cases an author appears to have written poetry under one name, fiction under another, and possibly to have signed his legal papers under a third. In that case, I chose the name for his most highly regarded body of work if I could, and furnished the other names as cross-references.

Because the Portuguese practice is to employ a wife's family surname along with a married man's family name, something some of my sources do not recognize or otherwise fail to distinguish, I have been forced to seek out a generally recognized and common variant of the writer's name in question and to provide other versions of his name as cross-references.

The problem of dealing with Arabic, Swahili, Amharic and Somali writers

7

was of a much more complex nature. When possible, I offered the bio-graphic entry under the most commonly known name which may be anything from one to six or seven, no one of them being a surname in the Western sense. Again, to obviate too long a search for any of these authors, I have cross-referenced as many of the variant names as seemed reasonable.

In most cases when there seemed a commonly used name, I designated it arbitrarily as the "surname" but occasionally had to employ a more com-plex name of many elements without trying to establish a Western-type family or surname.

Female writers are generally to be found under their married names if they published under those names and any maiden names used in publica-tions are given as cross-references even if much of the author's work in question saw print under the name used before marriage.

How to Use the Appendices

The appendices are divided into four parts. Part I is primarily for the general reader who is unfamiliar with African literature. Appendix A therefore provides historical background and a general overview of con-temporary African literature; Appendix B traces the interrelationship between African writers and their writings and the intellectual and political revolution against colonialism which has characterized twen-tieth-century Africa; Appendix C discusses the large body of badly neglected vernacular writings by black South Africans; and Appendix D gives background on three Afro-Caribbean writers who have been ex-tremely influential in shaping the themes and tone of contemporary African writing. While they cannot substitute for more detailed surveys, they hopefully will provide a starting point for further reading and should be very helpful to the non-specialist in placing the individual biographies in a broader framework.

By employing the information offered in the various lists of Part II as to date of first work, or genre of work, or country of origin, or language or lan-guages used, the interested reader can arrive at some idea of the achieve-ment of a particular country, region, or language group. Appendix E provides a chronological approach to the authors covered, citing the first significant work produced, usually one that saw publication. Even a cursory glance at this list will show not only the long tradition of literature in Africa but the growing pace of writing in the modern period. Appendices F through J furnish other needed information in list or tabular form concerning the genres in which the authors have written, their linguistic and post-independence national origins, and, in the case of Appendix J, the fact that they are women and contributing a new source of intelligence and experience to the stream of African creative writing.

Let us take a special area, that of Yoruba drama, for our first specific example of what can be done with the lists of Part II as guides to carrying out a brief study of the field of drama, poetry, or any of the other genre employed, or of a language, or national, or regional group the reader might be interested in pursuing. In Appendix H we find a list of writers working in the various African languages and by consulting the list of Yoruba writers and checking it against the names on Appendix F (the author by genre list) we can quickly determine which of the Yoruba writers are dramatists. Such artists as Duro Ladipo, Obotunde Ijimere, Hubert Ogunde, E. Kolawole Ogunmola, Wale Ogunyemi and Olawale Rotimi are identified and by reading the entries concerned we shall learn how they helped and stimulated each other and how they gradually came to create a distinguished corpus of plays both in English and Yoruba. The entries on these writers will also lead the reader to such writers as Wole Soyinka, a Yoruba dramatist who writes in English, and to Amos Tutuola, whose famous *The Palm-Wine Drinkard,* written and published in English, has been turned into a play in Yoruba and staged with success. We shall also learn of Chief Fagunwa, a major Yoruba novelist, and even of non-Yoruba playwrights such as John Pepper Clark who works in Ijaw and English but who has made a major contribution to Nigerian drama.

Appendix E will provide chronological data should the interest be in reading about the authors in a specific language-literature, from the earliest to the most recent. This list should be particularly useful in getting some idea of the development of a given body of writers by country, or language employed, or in such special areas as short fiction or folklore.

Similarly, if one wishes to have some idea of the development of vernacular writings in South Africa, he might turn back to Appendix C which offers a brief survey of the beginnings of South African vernacular writing and then turn to Appendices F and H again to compile the names of Sotho or Xhosa or Zulu writers working in particular genres, etc. on whom there are detailed essays.

A reader wishing to make a survey of poetry from West Africa could, by using Appendix E and F, compile a list of poets in the period at issue. The entries concerned would furnish career and bibliographic details and, should the reader wish to read the poetry, he could consult the anthologies analysed in Appendix P or otherwise cited in the appropriate bibliography at the end of this volume.

One could compile a list of novelists from one or several countries from East Africa and, by turning to Appendix E (the chronological list) read the biographies in order so that the general evolution of themes from the first glimmerings of a written literature to the latest could be seen. One might also select from Appendix E Ghanaian writers, 1900 to 1957, for instance, and by reading the appropriate biographic entries have a capsulized version of the early movements and influences on writers at the turn of the century, and procede then step-by-step through the colonial era to the year of independence. In doing the same for that country's writers since independence one could gain a clear idea of the different themes, methods of treatment, and the quality of language used in the earlier Gold Coast period as contrasted to the days of Kwame Nkrumah and after.

Part III is included to give background and basic information on those publishers, both of books and journals, who have played and are playing important roles in the area of African literature. Bookshops and book distributors specializing in African literature are also listed to aid the librarian or general reader in the often difficult task of acquiring Africanist books. Addresses are included which will hopefully serve prospective authors, other publishers, librarians, and the general reading public.

Part IV is designed to point the reader toward additional books on Africa and African literature. In addition to listing bibliographies and general and critical works, considerable attention is devoted to anthologies of African writings.

Mainly for the teacher, scholar, and librarian, the bibliographies of anthologies are designed to alert the careful student to possibilities of varied readings in reasonably accessible works. Many librarians, teachers, or readers will not wish to, nor even be able to obtain, many of the individual works of a particular writer or kind of writing, but most libraries with a modest African literature collection should have some of the anthologies, at least those in English.

Teachers and librarians may wish to determine which anthologies should be put on the reserve shelf for required or optional readings, and in the case of recent anthologies, to consider whether one or more might not be used as a general text. Further, Appendix P, which analyzes the anthologies as to type of genre covered, the number of pages devoted to various genre and the breadth of coverage, should facilitate the task of deciding what basic works should be ordered to fill gaps in the teacher's or the school's library of African literature. Though a few of the titles cited are out of print, most of them are comparatively recent and may easily be obtained. Many African creative works quickly go out of print and are frequently expensive, and a good collection of anthologies may be the best method to ensure a broad coverage of the varied production of all geographic areas and of most languages used in African writing.

Introduction

Only the reader's interests or lack thereof should limit the nature and range of information available by an imaginative use of the critical apparatus available at the end of this volume.

Sources and Special Problems

Scholars of African literature are well aware of how difficult it is to find, identify, and record writings often produced in limited numbers in Africa or published in scores of languages in Africa or elsewhere. Many African works do not carry dates and the various editions or printings are often not indicated. To make matters worse, major libraries in the United States and elsewhere have generally incomplete collections of African literature, even the most recently published. The Library of Congress is very weak in this area, and even Howard University's Spingarn and Moorland collections have decided gaps and fail to keep up with the now prolific production of creative literature from the continent. The Bibliothèque Nationale in Paris is good only in francophone works and British and Portuguese libraries similarly concentrate on their own cultural-political areas and slight African works produced by writers from other language and culture areas.

Even modern publishers of African writers are not as helpful as they might be. Where one could expect on book jackets or covers, or in prefaces etc., fairly detailed and reliable bio-bibliographic data concerning their own writers, there is sometimes nothing at all, or only vapid, inaccurate, and sometimes downright deceptive information or puffery. Even new works coming from Africa itself often fail to provide more than a thin sketch of a writer's career and works. The paper editions of Heinemann's African Writers Series are the notable exceptions in this area.

Possibly more surprising is the lack of meaningful and detailed information on publishing and biographical date in many critical essays on a given writer or group of writers. Even the finest scholars can be faulted for mentioning many writers in their sweeping essays without once pausing to give more than a title or two along the way or a date or publisher. Worse, many articles appear to reflect knowledge of only a few works by the author or authors concerned and little awareness of similar works produced in the same region or country. The same works and translations are studied over and over and little new information is turned up, either of a scholarly or critical-esthetic nature, because the same "major" writers and their works appear the only ones worth scrutiny.

Many of my letters to authors have gone unanswered, and publishers and literary agents have usually nothing to say biographically or otherwise about their authors beyond the facts of publication. One digs where one

11

can, and of course for a few of the major artists such as Senghor, Achebe, Soyinka, and Tutuola there are major biographies now in print, but even these have lacunae and inaccuracies.

If current bibliographies, publishers, and libraries fail us, one must begin anew: first collating the available sources, then checking all dates against the actual publications by personally handling the volumes concerned whenever possible, and then, where necessary, choosing between two or more dates or biographical facts on the basis of "likelihood," or the relative fidelity to accuracy demonstrated by the several sources at issue. Appeals to the authors themselves, to their publishers, and other sources such as embassies, as noted, have been helpful but not as much as might have been expected. In doing this work of collation I have discovered weaknesses in well-esteemed reference works where once I thought there were only strengths, and petty but numerous errors in other well-known scholarly studies.

There will be errors and misinterpretations in any work of this sort, but I have endeavored to control all dates and facts against the best available sources. In most cases, the information is "primary," that is, it comes from the published works themselves, the actual volumes, or journal numbers, or newspaper issues, from obituaries, etc., presumed to be the final evidence of validity. To the degree possible, critical comments are based on a personal reading of the works analyzed and the opinions of Africans and other scholars, critics, and creative artists.

A Request to Writers, Scholars, and Publishers Specializing in African Literature

Though every effort has been made to make this volume as complete and accurate as possible, and as broad in its coverage in time and space as seems practicable at this moment in African studies, the student and scholar engaged in the study of this literature will be painfully aware of how much more work needs to be done. Future research will undoubtedly unearth many more writers of African origin in pre-20th century history. Some writers just now breaking into print or who are now relatively neglected will call for greater treatment in the future. New bibliographic research will eliminate many of the confusing contradictions concerning editions, titles, contents, and even, in some cases, the genres, of African creative writings.

The essence of scholarship is to produce a work which stimulates efforts to produce a more perfect work. To facilitate this on-going process, my publisher has agreed to record and maintain the entire first edition of

African Authors on special photo-composition tape. What this means in practice is that any future additions, corrections, or other modifications of the original text can be made quickly and easily and incorporated into future editions. Accordingly, I encourage scholars and others specializing in African literature to offer suggestions of authors and works deserving initial or more extensive treatment than received in this first edition. Reactions to this work by African authors with their comments and corrections will be particularly gratifying and helpful. Finally, anyone who finds errors of fact or interpretation is encouraged to write to point out how I have gone wrong. Send all information to the publisher whose address may be found on the verso of the title page.

A Final Word

I have dealt with works which a substantial body of opinion, African and Western, has found valuable. Most if not all bibliographies, specialized studies, critical volumes, major periodicals devoted to African literature and hundreds of volumes of poetry, fiction, and folk literature have been consulted. Quite obviously I have depended on my sources very heavily when the original works were not available or out of my reach linguistically, but ultimately any errors of fact and understanding are mine to rectify.

My aim for the most part has been *descriptive*. It is far too early to attempt to differentiate most of the contemporary authors on esthetic grounds which are themselves under debate. Of course, a few writers, Soyinka, Achebe, Dadié, Beti, Senghor, Laye, David Diop, and Rabéarivelo, seem clearly to be major talents, but time alone will allow the winnowing process to be complete.

African writing has not been produced in isolation from the pressure of events, remembered in history or legend, or experienced personally. The time has come for all readers of imagination and good will to recognize especially the range of contemporary writing, its antecedents, problems, and successes, and the world or worlds in which these works have come to life. This volume will have served its purpose if it turns the reader who has consulted its pages back to the original creative work with renewed interest and a broader appreciation of the qualities and significance of both text and artist.

BIOBIBLIOGRAPHICAL
ENTRIES, A–Z

A

ABDILE, Hasan
(See MAHAMMED, Sheikh 'Abdille
Hasan)

ABDILLAAHI, Muuse
b. 1880, Somalia; d. unknown.
Somali oral poet.

Abdillaahi is especially known for his
didactic poetry and for poems composed
to celebrate special events. A folk
philosopher, he is remembered in
Somalia for his sayings and maxims
summing up the everyday wisdom of the
people. One of his best known aphorisms
is "He who speaks to termite hills will
not get any sense out of them." Abdillaahi was given the honorific title of
Sheikh for having memorized the
Koran.

Writings: Poem: "An Elder's Reproof to
his Wife" in *Somali Poetry,* Andrzejewski
and Lewis, editors, Oxford, Clarendon
Press, 1964.

ABDULLA, Muhammed Said
(MUHAMMED, Said Abdulla)
b. ca. 1940, Kenya.
Swahili prose writer.

Abdulla's first novel, *Mzimu wa Watu wa
Kale* (The Home of the Spirits of the
Ancestors), "takes Sherlock Holmes as
its model, but provides an original plot
with an authentic Zanzibar background," according to English critic W.
H. Whiteley. The novelist has completed
a second work, *Hisima cha Giningi* (The
Well of Giningi), and is working on a
third. Abdulla's novels are among the
very few contemporary works available
to Swahili readers and they may be the
harbinger of a new growth in Swahili
writing. They have not been translated.

Writings: Novels: *Mzimu wa Watu wa Kale,*
The East African Literature Bureau,
1960; *Hisima cha Giningi.*

*Biographical/Critical Sources: A Selection of
African Prose,* W. H. Whiteley, editor,
Oxford, The Clarendon Press, 1964;
"The Future of Swahili Literature" by
Whiteley, in *East Africa's Cultural
Heritage,* Nairobi, East African Institute
of Social and Cultural Affairs, 1966.

ABEDI, Sheikh Kaluta bin Amri
b. 1924, Ujiji, Tanganyika, now
Tanzania; d. Oct. 15, 1964.
Swahili poet, government official.

Abedi attended the Tabora Secondary School (1937–41) and the following year enrolled in a one-year training program in the Post Office. From 1944 until 1953 he studied to be a missionary. After working in that field for a year, he entered Rabwath College in West Pakistan where he did additional study for two years. He returned to Tanzania, won a parliamentary seat in 1959, and the next year was elected mayor of Dar es Salaam. In 1962 he became Regional Commissioner, and in 1963 was appointed the Minister of Justice for Tanzania, a position he held until his death. His one collection of poems, *Sheria za Kutunga Mashairi, na Diwani ya Amri (The Rules of Versification and the Poems of Amri)*, was published in 1954.

Writings: Poetry: *Sheria za Kutunga Mashairi,* Dar es Salaam, East African Literature Bureau, 1954; an enlarged edition, 1966.

ABRAHAMS, Peter Lee
(pseudonym: Peter Graham)
b. 1919, Vrededorp, outside
Johannesburg, South Africa.
Novelist, poet, short story writer,
journalist.

A man of mixed heritage, Abrahams' father was an Ethiopian and his mother was a "Cape Coloured," a South African racial category. Left fatherless at the age of five, Abrahams went to live with his aunt and uncle in the Transvaal village of Elsburg. Some of his experiences from this period appear in a semi-autobiographical novel published in 1954, *Tell Freedom.* Still illiterate at nine, he began work as a tinsmith's helper earning two and one half shillings (about fifty US cents) per week. Fortunately, a

young South African Jew became interested in the youth and read stories to him from Lamb's *Tales From Shakespeare.*

Stimulated and encouraged, Abrahams resolved to learn to read and write, but he frequently had to interrupt his schooling for long stretches at menial jobs such as kitchen helper, dishwasher, market porter and clerk. The writer Ezekiel Mphahlele, a contemporary, remembers Abrahams at St. Peter's Secondary School in Johannesburg as a shy, dreaming boy who wrote verse modelled on the poetry of Marcus Garvey and Langston Hughes.

In 1935, at the age of 16, he gave up formal schooling to wander about South Africa. He tried to start a school with a friend for the poor Africans of Cape Flats near Cape Town but the venture failed. Unemployed in 1939 he took a job as a stoker. After two years at sea, he worked his way to England. *The London Observer* assigned him to South Africa in 1952 for a series of articles which drew widespread attention, especially after they were rerun in the *New York Herald Tribune's* Paris edition. He also wrote several radio scripts for the BBC's Third Programme in the early 1950's. In 1955 the British government asked him to go to Jamaica to do a book for the Corona Library Series. The result was *Jamaica: An Island Mosaic.* In 1957, Abrahams emigrated to Kingston, Jamaica where he now lives with his wife and three children, working as a radio broadcaster-commentator for the program, West India News, and as a freelance writer. He also has worked as editor of the *West Indian Economist.*

During World War II, Abrahams wrote short stories, published as *Dark Testament* (1942) and his first novel, *Song of the City* (1945). Also dating from this period is a rare and little-known 21-page collection of verse, *A Blackman Speaks of Freedom.*

Abrahams' second novel, *Mine Boy* (1946), did much to establish him as one of the leading African novelists. It was one of the earliest books to dramatize the plight of black South Africans and was only the second novel by a black South African to be published in English since Solomon Plaatje's *Mhudi* in 1930.

The work describes the life of Xuma, an illiterate but kindly man from the "reserves" (areas outside the cities restricted to Blacks), who undergoes brutal experiences when he goes to work in the mines. Xuma, however, refuses to be brutalized by his ordeals. At the novel's end he prepares to turn himself in to the authorities, primarily as a gesture of solidarity with his white foreman, Red, who has befriended him and has himself been arrested. Here Abrahams dramatized his hope that, despite racial barriers, strong men of good will could act to help one another.

Abrahams' third novel, *The Path of Thunder* (1948), deals with the apartheid laws and the South African system of racial segregation. The book details the illicit love between the "Coloured," Swartz and a white Afrikaaner girl, Sarie, and their eventual destruction. The handling of sub-plots and minor characters in the novel show a growth in Abraham's craft. Translations into close to 30 foreign languages have been made of this novel.

Mphahlele believes that Abrahams' best book is *Wild Conquest* (1951). The novel picks up certain themes from Plaatje's *Mhudi*—Zulu resistance to the encroaching Boers, for example, but introduces such characters of a period some 20 years earlier than *Mhudi's,* as Chief Mzilikazi and Gubuza. Among the additional characters also not in *Mhudi,* are the fictional Mkomozi, a witch doctor, who resembles a similar character, Isanusi, in Thomas Mofolo's novel, *Chaka,* and Dabula, a sentimentalist.

In *A Wreath for Udomo,* (1956) the central figure, a charismatic leader named Udomo, returns to his homeland, the fictional Panafrica, and wrests the country from its British rulers. However, what might be termed the "nativist" faction in the new country turns against Udomo and has him assassinated, for in his efforts to get investments from a neighboring white-controlled country (obviously patterned on South Africa) he has soft-pedalled the blacks-only policy advocated by the hard liners in Panafrica. The novel is prescient, for although written before most African countries obtained independence, Udomo faces many of the problems of new rulers of states attempting to escape the colonial or neo-colonial situation.

The poem, "The Negro Youth," was

19

published in the *Bantu World* newspaper (Johannesburg), when Abrahams was only 17 years old. Although the verse is awkward it speaks of his early ambitions, of the pain suffered by all black Africans in South Africa, and the burden of much of his later work.

> *He stood alone,*
> *A Negro youth.*
> *What of his future?*
> *His cap was worn,*
> *This Negro youth.*
> *Why was he born?*
> *Born to lead an empty useless life,*
> *Born to mar the record of his race,*
> *Or born to lead his race?*
> *Locked are the doors,*
> *Locked–the doors of his future.*
> *His burden to bear,*
> *To suffer the pain of life's cruel ways,*
> *That is why he was born.*

Writings: Novels: *Song of the City,* London, Dorothy Crisp, 1945; *Mine Boy,* London, Dorothy Crisp, 1946; reissued by Faber and Faber, 1954, 1966; Knopf, New York, 1955; London, Heinemann African Writers Series, 1963, reprinted in 1965, 1966 and 1968; *The Path of Thunder,* New York, Harper, 1948, also London, Faber, 1948, 1952; *Wild Conquest,* London, Faber and Faber, 1951; first published in United States by Harper, 1950; London, Penguin, 1966; *Tell Freedom,* New York, Knopf, 1954, New York, Colliers, 1970; *A Wreath for Udomo,* London, Faber and Faber, 1956; New York, Knopf, 1956. *A Night of Their Own,* London, Faber, 1965; New York, Knopf, 1965.

Short stories: *Dark Testament,* London, Allen and Unwin, 1942.

Poetry: *A Blackman Speaks of Freedom,* Durban, Universal Printing Works, 1941.

Travel: *Jamaica: An Island Mosaic,* London, Her Majesty's Stationery Office, 1957; *Return to Goli,* London, Faber, 1953, 1957; *This Island Now,* London, Faber, 1966; Knopf, 1967; *The Quiet Voice,* Philadelphia, Dorrance, 1966.

Biographical/Critical Sources: Michael Wade, *Peter Abrahams,* London, Evans, 1971; James Gecau, "The Various Levels of Betrayal in *A Wreath for Udomo,*" *Busara,* II, 1, Nairobi, 1969.

ABRUQUAH, Joseph Wilfred
b. ca. 1940, Ghana.
Novelist.

Educated at Wesley College, Kumasi, Ghana, a local high school, Abruquah received his B.A. (Honors) and Teacher's Certificate at King's College and Westminster College, London. After returning to Ghana, he taught at Keta Secondary School and later became headmaster at Mfantsipim School in Cape Coast. After the fall of the Busia government in January 1972, Abruquah lost his position. His first novel was *The Cathechist,* probably the first autobiographical novel written in Ghana. His second, *The Torrent,* portrays the difficulties faced by an African boy, Joshia Afful, who is sent to an African school but one that is run according to Western educational principles.

Writings: Novels: *The Catechist,* London, Allen and Unwin, 1965; *The Torrent* London, Longmans, Green, 1968.

ABU DULAMA IBN AL-DJAUN (or ABU DULAMA ZAND B. AL-DJAWN)
b. ca. 720, Baghdad (?); d. 777 or 787. Arabic-language poet.

Abu Dulama, by most accounts a pure black African, was a court poet for Al-Saffah, a wealthy merchant of Baghdad, and later of the Caliphs al-Mansur and al-Mahdi, both of the Abbasides dynasty. Though dismissed by his contemporaries as a court-jester with no literary talent, he was witty and some of his verse is memorable. His humor was extremely earthy even for the tastes of the day, and he did not hesitate at the grossest of flattery. He also had, however, a barbed tongue that spared no one, particularly if he were speaking as the mouthpiece of an important member of the court seeking to ridicule another. Abu Dulama, in his role as jester, even dared take liberty with Islamic law.

As a poet he ranged over the entire life of the court and could be both serious and frivolous. His first important poem was his elegy on the death of Abu Muslim (d. 754 or 755).

Writings: Poems and praise-songs, in Arabic manuscript collections.

Biographical/Critical Sources: Encyclopaedia of Islam, London, 1934; Carl Brockelmann, *Geschichte der arabishen Literature,* Volume I, second edition, Leiden, 1943.

ABUBAKAR, Iman (also Alhaji Abubakar Imam Kagara)
b. ca. 1920, Hausa country, northern Nigeria.
Hausa story writer.

His first published works, a volume of travel tales, *Tafiya mabudin ilmi* (Traveling, Key of Knowledge), and *Ruwan Bagaja* (Water of Bagaja) appeared in 1952 and 1955, respectively. In 1960 he published a 73-page collection of Hausa

tales, *Tarihin annabi Muhammadu* and, a year earlier, another collection of stories, *Magana jari ce* (Speech is Gold) appeared.

Writings: Travel: *Tafiya mabudin ilmi,* Zaria, Gaskiya, 1952.

Stories: *Ruwan Bagaja,* Zaria, North Regional Literature Agency, 1955; illustrated edition by Gaskiya, 1968; *Magana jari ce,* Zaria, Norla, 1959; *Tarihin annabi Muhammadu,* Zaria, Nigeria, Gaskiya Corp. 1960.

ABUBAKAR, (Alhaji) Sir Tafawa Balewa
b. 1912, Bauchi Province, northern Nigeria; d. January, 1966.
Story writer, politician, statesman.

Educated in Nigerian schools, he attended Katsina Higher College (1928–33) and the London School of Education (1945–46). After London, he returned to Nigeria as an education officer.

Shortly after entering politics he was appointed to the first Northern House of Assembly and was elected to the Federal House of Representatives in Lagos. He was appointed Chief Minister of Nigeria in 1957 and with independence in 1960 became the first Federal Prime Minister. He remained in that office until 1964 and then became chancellor of Ibadan University. He was assassinated in January, 1966, in a military coup against the Federal officials.

His *Nigeria Speaks*, a polemic, was a dynamic declaration of his country's hopes and purposes. His little fable, *Shaihu Umar*, has been popular. A mother and son are carried into slavery at the end of the 19th century, but after separation and many adventures and much suffering, they find each other again. Patterned on Hausa folk tales of the marvelous, the work is a tale of death,

violence, and virtue sorely tried and partially rewarded. The 79-page work well depicts three Hausa institutions of the late 19th century: the court, slavery, and the Muslim system of education.

Writings: Polemics: *Nigeria Speaks*, London, Longmans, Green, 1964.

Novel: *Shaihu Umar*, Zaria, Nigeria, Gaskiya Corp. 1955; translated from Hausa into English with notes by Mervyn Hiskett, London, Longmans, 1967.

Biographical/Critical Source: Ronald Segal, *African Profile*, London, Penguin, 1963.

ACHEBE, Chinua
b. 1930, Agidi, Ibo country (a few miles east of the Niger River, in eastern Nigeria).
Novelist, short story writer, poet, critic, teacher, diplomat.

Son of one of the first Ibo Mission teachers, Achebe first studied in a school of the Church Missionary Society. He completed his secondary education at Government College in Umuahia, a town which figures prominently in his novels, and later took his B. A. at Ibadan University.

He began work in broadcasting for the Nigerian Broadcasting Company (N.B.C.) in 1954 and in 1961 became the company's first director of external broadcasting. In intervals between 1954 and 1961 he worked for the BBC in England. He quit his N. B. C. job in 1966 to write full-time.

During the Biafran struggle for independence (1967–69) he served as a diplomat for the break-away state, a position which enhanced his reputation abroad. His writing on the Biafran struggle includes an article in the London *Sunday Times,* June 9, 1968, on the horrors of the war and a piece in *Transition,* a short-lived east African intellectual journal, in which he discusses Biafra's plight and his attitude toward the Federal Government of Nigeria.

His first novel, *Things Fall Apart* (1958), has become, with the possible exception of Amos Tutuolo's *The Palm-Wine Drinkard,* the most famous novel written in English by an African. By 1969, *Things Fall Apart* (the title is from Yeats' poem "The Second Coming") had sold 300,000 copies in the Heinemann imprint alone. A stage version of the novel was presented in Lagos, in the mid-1960's by Eldred Fiberesima Productions.

The novel centers on Okonkwo, a sullen, ambitious and physically overpowering leader who has a fatal flaw—in moments of crisis he stutters and strikes out in wrath and frustration at his loss of expression. Unable to think out his problems, he takes refuge in action. This causes him to break the laws of his people and, finally, leads him to murder a messenger sent by the British, an act that drives him to commit suicide after he sees that it has not roused his village to rebel. Okwonkwo's flaws would not have destroyed him had the Europeans not broken in upon the peaceful agricultural society of the Ibos at the end of the 19th century, but with conditions changed, his formerly approved bravery and power are dangerous to his own people and ultimately to himself.

His second novel, *No Longer At Ease,* picks up Obi Okonkwo, grandson of the hero of *Things Fall Apart,* as he returns to Nigeria in the 1950's with an English university degree and high expectations for job, salary and prestige and all that goes with them. Instead, everything falls to ashes. The frame of the book is a trial for bribery which opens and closes the novel. But the real story is what happens to the idealistic Europeanized Obi as his family, his village, his lover, and the demands of his English type civil service job, pull him in opposite directions and lead to his destruction.

The third novel, *Arrow of God,* picks up the middle generation of Ibos of the 1910–20 colonial period. It follows the head priest Ezuele through a series of increasingly important psychological victories over the British District Commissioner. Ultimately, however, he ends in total defeat and madness. The similarities with *Things Fall Apart* are readily apparent. Both Okwonkwo, the athlete-warrior, and Ezuele, the intellectual-religious leader, fall victim to British power as it erodes both the political and religious traditions of Ibo life.

If the first three novels may be consid-

Achebe

ered a trilogy, Achebe's latest novel, *A Man of the People* is a coda with a somewhat changed emphasis and a new set of characters who up-date Okonkwo's and his grandson's experiences.

Though conflicts between village and the capital (Lagos) are important themes, the focus of this work is on independent Nigeria and what it has become as rival politicians struggle for personal aggrandizement, for public works for their home villages and for favors for their sons and daughters. But Achebe's anger and bitterness are not really directed at the politicians; rather, he indicts his whole people.

Some political commentators have said that it was the supreme cynicism of these transactions that inflamed the people and *brought down the Government. That is sheer poppycock. The people themselves, as we have seen, had become even more cynical than their leaders and were apathetic into the bargain. "Let them eat," was the people's opinion, "after all when white men used to do all the eating did we commit suicide?" Of course not. And where is the all-powerful white man today? He came, he ate and he went. But we are still around. The important thing then is to stay alive; if you do you will outlive your present annoyance.*

And at the novel's end, he has his protagonist, Odili, deliver one last attack on the Nigeria of the mid-1960's. His words were prophetic of the moral rot of the village and nation in the immediate prelude to the Biafran civil war:

My father's words struck me because they were the very same words the villagers of Anata had spoken of Josiah, the abominated trader. Only in their case the words had meaning. The owner was the village, and the village had a mind; it could say no to sacrilege. But in the affairs of the nation there was no owner, the laws of the village became powerless.... For I do honestly believe that in the fat-dripping, gummy, eat-and-let-eat regime just ended—a regime which inspired the common saying that a man could only be sure of what he had put away safely in his gut or, in language ever more suited to the times: "you chop, me self I chop, palaver finish."

In 1962, Achebe published a 32-page booklet of stories, *The Sacrificial Egg*. In 1971 appeared his most recent volume, *Girls at War and other Stories*, a book which reflects his experiences in the Biafran war. Also recently, Achebe has increasingly turned to poetry to express himself. One of the earliest of his poems to be published in the United States was "Mango Seedling," dedicated to Christopher Okigbo, the fine Ibo poet killed during the war (see *New York Review of Books,* May 22, 1968). The 150-page volume, *Beware, Soul Brother,* (1971), contains his poetry of the tragic Biafran War.

Achebe, who has lectured widely in Europe and North America and in the late 1960's taught at the University of Colorado at Boulder, has written scores of articles, and a widely-known children's tale, *Chike and the River.* In 1971 he assumed the editorship of the new literary journal, *Okike,* published in Enugu, Nigeria by Nwanko–Ifejika, and became the director of African Studies at the University of Nigeria at Enugu.

Writings: Novels: Things Fall Apart, London, Heinemann, 1958; New York, McDowell, Obolensky, 1959; *No Longer At Ease* Heinemann, 1960; Obolensky, 1961; *Arrow of God,* Heinemann, 1964; first United States edition, New York, John Day Co., 1967; Anchor Books, 1969; *A Man of the People,* Heinemann, 1966; John Day, 1966. Fawcett Publications, Inc. has also published in paperback *Things Fall Apart* and *No Longer at Ease.*

Poetry: *Beware, Soul Brother,* Enugu, Nigeria, Nwanko–Ifejika, 1971.

Collections of short stories: *The Sacrificial Egg,* Onitsha, Etudo Ltd., 1962; *Girls at War and other Stories,* Heinemann, London, 1971.

Children's story: *Chike and the River,* Cambridge, Cambridge University Press, 1966.

Articles on Biafra: *London Sunday Times,* June 9, 1968; *Transition,* Kampala, Uganda, Vol. 7, No. 36.

Biographical/Critical Sources: The most complete critical biography is *The Novels of Chinua Achebe,* G. D. Killam, New York, Africana Publishing Corp., 1969. Arthur Ravenscroft's *Chinua Achebe,* London, Longmans, Green, 1969, is also a good study of this most important of the anglophone novelists. *Seven African Writers,* Gerald Moore, London, Oxford, 1962; *Long Drums and Cannons,* Margaret Lawrence, London, Macmillan, 1968; *This Africa,* Judith Gleason, Evanston, Northwestern University Press, 1965.

ACQUAH, Gaddiel Robert
(or ACQUAAH)
b. 1884, the Gold Coast; d. 1954 in the present Ghana.
Novelist (in English), Fante language scholar, Fante poet.

G. R. Acquah was the editor of the *Fante Grammar of Function,* prepared for use in the lower schools of the former Gold Coast (now Ghana). Other Fante language studies were didactic poems in

Oguaa Aban (Cape Coast Castle); *Nsem a Wonyin* and *Mbofraba asorye ndwom* (Hymns for Children). A novel, *The Morning After*, was published posthumously in 1961.

Writings: Novel: *The Morning After*, London, Goodwin, 1961, published posthumously.

Poetry: in *Oguaa Aban*, Methodist Book Depot, 1939; Longmans, London, 1939, 1943, 1946, 1968; *Nsem a Wonyin*, London, Longmans, 1939; *Mbofraba asorye ndwom*, Cape Coast, Atlantis Press, 1929.

Language studies: Editor, *Fante Grammar of Function*, Cape Coast, Methodist Book Depot, 1942.

ADALI-MORTTY, Geormbeeyi
b. ca. 1920, Gbogame, Northern Eweland, former British Togo, now Ghana.
Poet, educator, administrator, anthologist.

After studying at Achimota College in Accra, and Cornell University, Adali-Mortty taught for many years, specializing in adult education. A government administrator, he served until 1968 as special commissioner for redeployment of labor. He is now a professor of business management at the University of Ghana (Legon). He has travelled widely in both Americas, Europe, and has visited Ceylon.

His poetry covers a wide range, from nostalgic verse on African themes to meditations about places of sojourn abroad. Some of his early work was published in *Voices of Ghana*. Adali-Mortty is considered by most Ghanians the "senior" poet of the country. He joined with Kofi Awoonor in editing the valu-

able volume, *Messages: Poems from Ghana* which includes 14 of his own poems along with those of Joseph de Graft, A. Kayper Mensah, Ayi Kwei Armah, Kwesi Brew, Amu Djoleto, and other important Ghanaian poets.

Writings: Edited with Kofi Awoonor and contributed poems to: *Messages: Poems from Ghana*, London, Heinemann, 1970; *Voices of Ghana*, Accra, Ministry of Information, 1958.

ADEMOLA, Frances
(née Quashie-Idun)
b. ca. 1930, Ghana.
Critic, journalist.

Educated in Ghanaian schools in her early years, Mrs. Ademola attended Achimota College in Accra, Westonbirt (a British girls' high school) in Gloucestershire, England, and University College, Exeter, England where she received an honours degree in English. She married a Nigerian and went to Lagos with him where, for several years, she was "Head of Talks" of the Nigerian Broadcasting Corporation. She then headed the N.B.C.'s West Regional Programs until 1961.

Mrs. Ademola edited an anthology on African prose and verse, *Reflections: Nigerian Prose and Verse*.

Writings: Editor, anthology of prose and verse, *Reflections: Nigerian Prose and Verse*, Lagos, African Universities Press, 1962.

ADOKI, G. E.
b. ca. 1910, Nigeria.
Short story writer.

Educated in Nigerian schools, he served

as a plantation manager on an experimental farm and then studied library science with the help of the British Council in Lagos during the 1940's. Some of the stories of this early writer have been published and broadcast, including "Emergency," which appears in *African New Writing*.

Writings: Short story: "Emergency," in *African New Writing*, London, Lutterworth Press, 1947.

ADUAMAH, Enos Yao
b. ca. 1940, Ghana.
Novelist, scholar.

Aduamah is now a professional staff member in the research department at the University of Ghana. He has studied local customs and has published several studies on African culture in the Accra review, *West Africa*. An excerpt from his novelette, *Nothing Happens for Nothing*, appeared in the journal, *African Arts*, Spring, 1971, after having won the 1970 *African Arts* literary competition.

Writings: Excerpt from novelette; "Nothing Happens for Nothing," *African Arts*, Spring, 1971.

AFAWARK, Gabra Iyasus
b. July 10, 1868, Zagé peninsula, Lake Tana, Ethiopia; d. Sept. 25, 1947, Jimma, Ethiopia.
Amharic novelist, poet, scholar, diplomat, painter.

Born into an aristocratic family, Afawark was related to Queen Taytu, wife of the Ethiopian king, Menelik II. He was a member of the delegation Menelik sent to Italy in 1887 and was permitted by the Ethiopians to study painting at the Albertina de Belle Arti in Turin. Returning to the court at Shoa, he was asked to decorate a recently built church in the old capital of Entoto. By 1894 he was back in Switzerland working with Walter Ilg, Menelik's Swiss adviser. He married a relative of Ilg's and after a brief stay in Eritrea returned to Italy. His second marriage, to Eugenia Rossi, an Italian, took place in 1904. He had studied by that time at the Collegio Internazionale in Turin and in 1902 was hired as an assistant to Professor Francesco Gallina in the Istituto Orientale in Naples.

From 1902 to 1912 he wrote three Italian works on the Amharic language, including *Il Verbo Amarico* (The Amharic Verb). He also published a French and Amharic guide, *Guide du Voyageur en Abyssinie* and an Amharic novel, *Wallad Tarik* (A Fictional Story), published in 1908. During that period he also issued an early edition of psalms, and a biography, *Menelik II*.

A warm supporter of things Italian, Afawark left Ethiopia, transferring himself and his family to Asmara, then in Italian Eritrea, in 1912 to set up a business. He almost immediately felt called upon to defend the Italians attacked in a poem by Egzi'abeher which protested Italy's war with Turkey over Libya. Afawark's response was an anonymous work published in Asmara in 1912.

In 1918, Afawark headed a trade mission to the United States for Queen Zawditu, and in 1922 he became director of customs at Dire Dawa. In 1931 he went to Italy as the Ethiopian Ambassador, being recalled in October, 1935, when Italy invaded his country. Afawark was a member of the group negotiating a settlement with Italy in Djibouti in 1936, and he agreed to serve as chief of the Ethiopian local courts with the

27

title of Afa-Qesar under the Italians. When Haile Selassie returned from exile in 1941, Afawark was exiled and imprisoned in Jimma. He died there in 1947, totally blind, at the age of 79.

Though he was deeply conscious of European, and specifically Italian culture, Afawark remained deeply patriotic toward Ethiopia. One of the early supporters of modernization, he felt change was necessary if Ethiopia were to avoid further domination and disintegration.

His novel, *Wallad Tarik* (1908), was one of the earliest to reach print in any African language and the very first in Amharic. Exploiting every possible resource of a complex language and culture, the work, in Western terms, is ornate, overly-precious, and full of improbable disguises and coincidences. It portrays the victory of love, generosity, and honor. Where his *Guide de Voyageur* had revealed the dark side of the Ethiopian reality of his day, the novel presents the ideal in the complex, devotional tradition of ancient Ge'ez Church literature, here for the first time rendered in Amharic instead of the ancient Ge'ez language.

Other works about which there is little specific information are the novelettes, *Anthony and Cleopatra, When the Serpent was Reigning*, and *Midas*.

Writings: Novels: *Wallad Tarik* (A Fictional Story), Rome, 1908; *Tobbya,* an English translation of *Wallad Tarik* published by Tadese Tamrat, *Ethiopia Observer,* VII, 1964.

Novelettes: *Anthony and Cleopatra, When the Serpent Was Reigning, Midas.*

Language studies: *Il Verbo Amarico,* Rome, 1911.

Travel: *Guide du Voyageur en Abyssinie,* Rome, 1908.

Biography: *Menelik II,* Rome, 1909.

Translation, Poetry: An early edition of psalms, Rome, 1902.

Biographical/Critical Sources: Four African Literatures (Xhosa, Sotho, Zulu, Amharic), Albert S. Gérard, Berkeley, University of California Press, 1971; Richard Pankhurst, "The Effects of War in Ethiopian History," *Ethiopian Observer,* VII (1963), and "Misoneism and Innovation in Ethiopian History," *Ethiopian Observer,* VII (1964); Enrico Cerulli, "Recente publicazione abisine in amarico," *Oriente Moderno,* VI (1926).

AFRICANUS, Equiano Olaudah
(see VASSA, Gustavus Olaudah)

AGGREY, James Emman Kodwo Mensa Otsiwadu Humamfunsam Kwegyir
b. Oct. 18, 1875, Anambu, in old Gold Coast (now Ghana); d. July 30, 1927, in the United States.
Polemical writer, social worker.

James Aggrey, son of a king's chief counselor, was educated in a Mission School in the Gold Coast. At the age of fourteen he was converted to the Christian religion, remaining a fervent believer the rest of his life. When he was 23 he journeyed to the United States to complete his studies at Livingston College, North Carolina (B.A. in Classics, 1902). He also studied agriculture and spent almost two decades with rural blacks in the Carolinas as a preacher and social worker. In 1921, after twenty years abroad, he returned to the Gold Coast for three years before going to South Africa.

Both in America and Africa, Aggrey, a compelling orator, worked hard in the field of race relations. Returning to the United States after several years in South Africa, he died in 1927 after completing his doctorate at Columbia University, New York.

His works are contained in various studies of his career, including *Aggrey of Africa* by Edwin W. Smith; *Aggrey of Achimota* by N. Musson; and *Dr. Aggrey* by William McCarthey.

Biographical/Critical Studies: The following include excerpts from Aggrey's writings: *Aggrey of Africa,* Edwin W. Smith, New York, Doubleday, 1929; *Aggrey of Achimota,* N. Musson, London, United Society for Christian Literature, Lutterworth Press, 1944; *Dr. Aggrey,* William McCarthey, London, SMC Press Ltd., 1949. Also see *The Origins of Modern African Thought,* Robert W. July, New York, Praeger, 1967.

AGUNWA, Clement
b. ca. 1940, Ibo-land, Nigeria.
Novelist.

More Than Once, a boisterous and uninhibited novel, is the story of a struggling businessman, Nweke Nwakor, who almost makes a fortune. J. P. Clark, the well-known poet and playwright, called the work "familiar and fantastic, farcical and bizarre . . . a breath of the hot, loud, broad wind that blows in the face of the visitor when he crosses the river Niger to Onitsha."

Writings: Novel: *More Than Once,* London, Longmans, 1967.

AIDOO, Christina Ama Ata
b. 1942, Abeadzi Kyiakor, near

Dominase in the center of Ghana. Poet, playwright, short story writer.

Educated in Ghanaian schools, she graduated from the University of Ghana (Legon) with a B.A. with honors in 1964. Upon her graduation, she was appointed research fellow of the Institute of African Studies at the same university. She also studied creative writing at Stanford University (Palo Alto, California). She is now an English Professor at the University of Ghana, Cape Coast branch.

Christina Aidoo became seriously interested in writing when a short story of hers won a prize in a competition sponsored by Mbari Press (Ibadan University, Nigeria). Since then she has had a number of stories published in *Black Orpheus* (Ibadan) and *Okyeame* (The Spokesman) (Ghana) of which she has been editor. Her first play, *Anowa,* was published in 1970.

Her works include the poems, "Last of the proud ones" and "Sebonwoma," and a play, written after *Anowa, The Dilemma of a Ghost,* 1965. Her story, "No sweetness here," won a prize from *Black Orpheus* magazine and was the title work of a recent collection of eleven short stories, all set in Ghana.

Writings: Short stories: *No Sweetness Here,* London, Longmans, 1969, and New York, Doubleday, 1970; individual stories in *Black Orpheus* (Ibadan); and *Okyeame* (Ghana); "The Message" in *African Writing Today,* London, Penguin, 1967; "A Gift from Somewhere" in *New African Literature and the Arts I,* Joseph Okpaku, ed., New York, Crowell, 1970.

Plays: *Dilemma of a Ghost,* London, Accra, Longmans, 1965; *Anowa,* Longmans, 1970.

Poetry: in *New Sum of Poetry from the Negro World,* Paris, Présence Africaine, Vol. 57, 1966.

AIG–IMOUKHUEDE, Frank
b. 1935, Edunabon, near Ife in Yoruba country, west Nigeria.
Poet, playwright, journalist.

He attended a score of primary schools before studying at Igbobi University College, Ibadan, where he contributed early poetry to John Pepper Clark's review, *The Horn.* He was a journalist for a period for a Lagos daily and at present he is working for the Nigerian Federal Government as an Information Officer and is writing plays for radio and television.

He has written poems in pidgin English, has appeared in *Black Orpheus,* the literary journal published at Mbari Press, University of Ibadan, and is being increasingly anthologized.

In his "One Wife for One Man," the poet, in pidgin English, pokes fun at the missionaries' zeal in spreading monogamy.

I done try go church, I done go for court
Dem all day talk about de "new culture":
Dem talk about "equality," dem mention
"divorce"

Dem holler am so-tay my ear nearly cut;
One wife be for one man.

His two performed plays are *Ikeke* and *Day of Sasswood.*

Writings: Poetry: in the journal *Black Orpheus,* Mbari Press; "One Wife for One Man," republished in *The African Assertion,* Austin J. Shelton, editor, New York, The Odyssey Press, 1968.

Plays: *Ikeke,* performed, Lagos; Theatre Workshop, Nigerian Museum, 1964; *Day of Sasswood,* performed, Lagos, Eldred Fiberesima Productions, 1965.

AKAR, John Joseph
b. May 20, 1927, Sierra Leone.
Playwright, short story writer, journalist.

Akar's play, *Valley Without Echo,* unpublished, was one of the first African plays to be produced in Europe (with the support of the British Council, 1954). It was reviewed by *West African Review* in an issue which also carried his second play, *Cry Tamba,* a work that won the "Independence Competition," conducted by the Congress for Cultural Freedom in 1961.

Writings: Plays: *Cry Tamba* published in *West African Review,* July, 1954; *Valley Without Echo,* produced abroad by British Council, 1954.

Biographical/Critical Source: Review of play, *Valley Without Echo,* in *West African Review,* July, 1954.

AKIGA, Benjamin (also, SAI, B. Akiga)
b. 1898, northern Nigeria.

Autobiographer, historian, journalist-editor, statesman (wrote in Tiv, published in English).

One of the first of the Tiv people to receive a missionary education, Akiga spent twenty years collecting and recording his nation's history and traditions. His work, translated by Rupert M. East, his mentor, was published as *Akiga's Story*. Literally "given" to the missionaries of the Dutch Reformed Church Mission, Akiga underwent intensive training. As he puts it, while wandering "round through every part óf Tivland, preaching the gospel of Jesus Christ and, at the same time seeing and hearing the things of Tiv," the "idea of this 'history' took shape in my mind."

In his later years, B. Akiga Sai, as he is also known, has served as editor of a Tiv-language newspaper and as a member of the House of Assembly in Northern Nigeria.

Writings: Autobiography: *Akiga's Story,* Rupert M. East, translator, London, Oxford University Press, 1939.

Biographical/Critical Source: African Heritage, Jacob Drachler, New York, Collier Books-Macmillan, 1964.

AKINSEMOYIN, Kunle
b. ca. 1930, Yoruba-land, western Nigeria.
Poet, short story writer.

His poems have appeared in several publications, including *An Anthology of West African Verse.* He has also published three short volumes of children's stories: *Twilight and the Tortoise, Twilight Tales,* and *Stories at Sundown.*

Writings: Poetry: in *An Anthology of West African Verse,* Ibadan, Ibadan University Press, 1957.

Children's stories: *Twilight and the Tortoise,* Lagos, African Universities Press, 1963; *Twilight Tales,* Lagos, African Universities Press, 1965; *Stories at Sundown,* London, Harrap, 1965.

AKPAN, Ntieyong Udo
b. ca. 1940, Ibo country, eastern Nigeria.
Novelist, political pamphleteer.

The Wooden Gong (1965) is his only novel to date. It remains possibly the best fictional treatment of the secret societies, the groups that ruled their villages through ritual warnings, and, if necessary, through punishments of various severity. In the old chief, the Imam of Mbiabong, Akpan has created a warm and humane portrait of a wise man trying to hold together both his secret society and the people he rules in a period of rapid change. Akpan's style is lucid and always diverting though naive at times. His contribution is in revealing the traditional inner workings of an Ibo village, badly eroded by Christianity and British rule.

Two of Akpan's other works are *Epitaph to Indirect Rule: A Discourse on Local Government for Africa* and *Ini Abasi and the Sacred Ram,* a children's story book.

Writings: Novel: *The Wooden Gong,* London, Longmans, Green, 1965.

Children's book: *Ini Abasi and the Sacred Ram,* London, Longmans, Green, 1966.

Non-fiction: *Epitaph to Indirect Rule: A Discourse on Local Government for Africa,* London, Frank Cass, 1967.

ALBASINI, João
b. ca. 1890, Mozambique; d. 1925.
Novelist, journalist.

Born of an "assimilated" (mixed Portuguese-African) father, João Albasini and his brother, José, founded the first press for black Africans in Mozambique in 1918, the *O Brado Africano* (The African Call). Published bi-weekly in Portuguese and Xironga, the paper tried to support whatever cultural efforts the small but growing cities of Lourenço Marques and Beire could muster. João published one small work of fiction, *O livro da dor* (The Book of Sorrow), in 1925, which is of historical rather than literary interest since it was one of the earliest works of African literature in Portuguese.
Writings: Story: *O livro da dor,* 1925.

ALCANTARA, Osvaldo
(pseudonym for LOPES da Silva, Balthasar)
b. 1904, São Nicolau, Cape Verde Islands.
Novelist, poet, story writer, teacher, lawyer.

Alcântara was educated in Cape Verde schools before taking his professional training (law and Roman philology) in Portugal at the University of Lisbon. He is both a lawyer and school principal on Liceu de S. Vincente, Cape Verde. Two of his poems, "Maman," and "Ressaca," appeared in Mário de Andrade's *Antologia da poesia negra de espressão portuguesa.* He has four tales in the collection he edited, the *Antologia da ficção cabo-verdiana contemporânea.* His little novel, *Chiquinho,* was first published in São Vicente, Cape Verde, in 1947, and is now considered a classic of Cape Verdean literature. He publishes his poetry

under the name Alcântara, and his prose under his actual name of Lopes.

Unlike most of his generation, Alcântara studied the literary possibilities of native speech. His research resulted in a monograph on the dialect, *O dialecto crioulo* (The Creole Dialect) in 1958, the first produced on this subject. However, he published as early as 1940 a folktale in the Creole of Fogo Island, "João que mamou na bourra" (João, Who Was Suckled by a She-Ass).

His verse often employs images similar to those in T.S. Eliot's "The Waste Land," images of sterility, drought, rain, symbolizing spiritual exile and physical isolation. This theme of alienation is an increasingly common one for the islanders who feel marooned in the Atlantic and lost in a European culture that only grudgingly accepts them. Alcântara's work expressing such concerns began to appear in 1936 in *Claridade* (Clarity), a journal founded to publish the work of writers of African ancestry, most of whom, however, wrote in Portuguese rather than the island Creole.

Writings: Novel: *Chiquinho,* São Vicente, Cape Verde, Edições Claridade, 1947; a second edition, Lisbon, Prelo, 1961.
Story: "João que mamou na bourra," 1940, place and publisher not known.
Prose: Four tales in *Antologia da ficção cabo-verdiana contemporânea* Praia, Cape Verde, Imprensa Nacional, 1962.
Poetry: in *Antologia da poesia negra de espressão portuguêsa,* Mário de Andrade, editor, Paris, 1958.
Monograph: *O dialecto crioulo* (The Creole Dialect), Lisbon, 1958.

ALEGRE, Caetano da Costa (also COSTA ALEGRE, Caetano)
b. 1864, São Tomé; d. Lisbon, 1890.
Poet.

Born into an old family of landowners of mixed blood, Alegre's poetry, written mostly between 1882 and 1889 while he was a medical student in Lisbon, expressed homesickness for his island home and his disappointments at his unhappy experiences in Portugal. Some of his poems deal with his African heritage, and exalt black women.

Despite the melancholy and feeling of alienation in his work, he was a popular figure in Portugal. After his death over 1,000 people followed his coffin to the grave through the streets of Lisbon.

Alegre's work was the first in Portuguese which clearly dealt with Africans and their isolation in white society. His one volume of poetry, *Versos,* published in 1916 by one of his old classmates, Cruz

Magalhães, in Lisbon, contains his best work. Norberto C. N. Costa Alegre edited the 1951 new edition of his *Versos.*

Writings: Poetry: *Versos,* edited and with introduction by Cruz Magalhães, Lisbon, Libraria Ferin, 1916; reprint, Lisbon, Papelaria Fernandes, 1950; 2nd edition, Lisbon, Livraria Ferin, 1951; poems in *Literatura africana de expressão portuguêsa,* Vol. I. Poesia, Mário de Andrade, editor, Algiers, 1967; *Poetas e contistas de expressão portuguêsa,* J. Neves, editor, São Paulo, Editôra Brasiliense, 1963.

Biographical/Critical Source: *O Livro de Costa Alegre: O Poeta de São Tomé e Príncipe.* Lopes Rodrigues, Lisbon, Agência-Geral do Ultramar, 1969.

ALHAJI, Abubakar Imam Kagara
(see ABUBAKAR, Imam)

AL HARDALLO (see HARDALLO, El or Al)

ALI, Abdullah Gureh
b. ca. 1940, Somalia.
Somali poet.

His poem "To Arms," commenting on
the clash in 1962 and 1963 between
Somalis and Kenyans over areas of
Kenya's Northern Frontier District,
appears in *The African Assertion.* It
begins:
> *The British have forcibly taken our land!*
> *They have murdered our women and chil-*
> *dren!*
> *Rise up, all you Somalis, rise up together,*
> *Take up your arms for battle*
> *To recover the land and restore our people!*

The poem exhorts the Somalis to fight
for land where they had traditionally
lived and which had been "turned over"
to Kenya by the British on Kenya's accession to independence. "To Arms" was
collected "in the field" by Colin Legum
whose "Somali Liberation Songs" offers
other Somali irridentist poems of the
post-colonial period.

Writings: Poetry: "To Arms," in *The Afri-
can Assertion,* Austin J. Shelton, editor,
New York, The Odyssey Press, 1968;
also in Colin Legum's "Somali Liberation
Songs," in *Journal of Modern African
Studies,* I, No. 4 (1963).

further work at Government College,
Ibadan. He studied civil engineering and
town planning at Lagos University and
at London University (1946–50). From
1950–1956 he worked as an engineer,
and in 1956 he became Town Engineer
at Lagos for four years. In 1960 he
became director of public works for
Nigeria's Western Region, a post he held
for many years. He now teaches
engineering at the University of Lagos.

ALMEIDA, José Maria (see de
ALMEIDA, José Maria)

ALUKO, Timothy Mofolorunso
b. 1918, Ilesha, Yoruba country,
western Nigeria.
Novelist.

After elementary and secondary schooling at Ilesha primary and Yaba Higher
College (a high school), Aluko did

His first three novels are *One Man, One
Wife; One Man, One Matchet;* and *Kinsman
and Foreman.*

Aluko began to write as a young man
in his 20's and some of his early stories
were published in *West African Review*
and broadcast on "Calling Africa," a
B.B.C. program. His first novel, *One
Man, One Wife,* satirizes the quarreling
factions in a village: the Christianized
element with its puritanical and officious
pastors; the old chiefs with their age-old

wisdom which fails to meet contemporary problems. But Aluko's emphasis is always on the people, their foibles, problems and private victories and defeats. As Margaret Laurence says in her useful *Long Drums and Cannons:*

> These villagers of Isolo are portrayed lovingly, with all their concentration on gossip and triviality, all their irritating irrationality and their continuing concern with the things which ultimately matter the most—children, and the onward-going of life under whatever circumstances.

Aluko's second novel, *One Man, One Matchet,* deals with the efforts of Udo Akpan, a well-trained Nigerian official, to effect social and economic changes from the supposedly prestigious position of District Officer in the pre-independence Nigeria of 1947. The local cocoa trees are diseased and Akpan must convince the farmers of Ipaja that some trees must be cut down and burned to save the others. The Africans, aghast not only at destroying life which seems healthy but at the idea of destroying their money crop as well, resist. Benjamin Benjamin, a wily and imaginative demagogue, seizes the opportunity to enflame the villagers against the program. Things go from bad to worse; the village's ancient wisdom and its good old leadership grow more and more confused. The British government moves in forcibly to cut down the diseased trees. The old chief, Momo, just cannot believe that trees have diseases, leads his household against the move and is jailed for his pains. Benjamin, adapting Lincoln's Gettysburg Address, organizes a drive to free Momo and recites the overwhelming lines, " . . . government of the people of Ipaja by the people of Ipaja for the people of Ipaja shall not perish from the earth." The plot becomes even more complex, and at the same time

genuinely enjoyable. Udo Akpan, the first black district commissioner, weathers all the storms, but disillusioned with the British system he once admired, the local Yoruba culture he had meant to respect, and with himself, he resigns.

The third novel, *Kinsman and Foreman,* has as its protagonist, Titus Oti, an English trained engineer. He returns to his native village in 1950 as head of public works, but the demands of his relatives make success in improving local conditions all but impossible. This novel has less life than the first two. It is clearer in concept and marches to its purposes much more coherently but it lacks a certain power. It does, however, vividly portray, as did the other books, the dilemmas facing Africa—how to get on with necessary changes without destroying irrevocably the very fabric and meaning of African life.

In 1970, his fourth novel, *Chief the Honourable Minister,* appeared. It deals with the problems of modern Nigerian officials several notches higher on the political scale than the heroes of the earlier novels. The action takes place in Afromacoland, much like Nigeria, as the hero, Alade Moses, returns from London to become his country's Minister of Works. The tale ends in violence, corruption, and an "inevitable" army takeover.

Through all the books, Aluko's writing is less than supple and his dialogue often stiff, but he is direct and his portraits of village heroes and common people are beguiling. These books give a vivid picture of real people and their problems in the confusing clash of cultural values that is Africa today.

Writings: Novels: *One Man, One Wife,* Lagos, Nigeria, Nigerian Printing Company, 1959; *One Man, One Matchet,* London, Heinemann, 1964; *Kinsman and Foreman,* London, Heinemann, 1966; *Chief, the Honourable Minister,* Heinemann, 1970.

Biographical/Critical Source: Long Drums and Cannons, Margaret Laurence, London, Macmillan, 1968.

AMADI, Elechi

b. 1934, near Port Harcourt, eastern Nigeria.
Novelist, teacher.

Amadi attended high school at Government College, Umuahia, and took his B.A. in physics and mathematics at University College, Ibadan. He worked as a land surveyor for a time, taught, and in the middle 1950's was commissioned in the Nigerian army and attached to the Military School in Zaria, northern Nigeria. Resigning in 1965, he returned to teaching in Port Harcourt. He is married, has several children, and is a good sportsman and musician.

His novels are *The Concubine,* published in Heinemann's African Writers Series (1958), and *The Great Ponds* (1969). The first work, set in an African world before the intrusion of Europeans, is unusual for modern African fiction. Its atmosphere is totally African, though obviously presented in the form and structure of the European novel. To some extent the author adopts a European point of view, and the actions are managed so as to produce a pace of increasing speed. Certain high points are also developed as dramatic denouements. However, the characters are always seen from the inside and there is no attempt to relate the actors or their acts to contemporary events.

The overwhelmingly beautiful hero-ine, Ihuoma, though good and rich in dignity, one by one destroys all the men who come to love her. The village priest informs her she is the wife of the sea-god and that though she may be a concubine she never can be a wife. Fate then has the lead role in this novel and the story, though an African one, is the universal one of man trying to satisfy his gods and to move safely through life. This same story is told by Flora Nwapa in her novel *Efuru.*

Margaret Laurence in *Long Drums and Cannons* does justice to the book in these perceptive sentences: "Amadi, like Soyinka, does not ever suggest that man is improving every facet of his life. On the contrary, *The Concubine* expresses the mystery at the centre of being."

Amadi's second novel, *The Great Ponds,* pits two groups against each other for the ownership of a pond and the right to fish in it.

Alastair Nivins delivered a paper, "The Achievement of Elechi Amadi," at the Aarhus Conference on Commonwealth Literature, April, 1971, which is probably the first detailed study of his work.

Writings: Novels: *The Concubine,* London, Heinemann, 1966; *The Great Ponds,* London, Heinemann, 1969.

Biographical/Critical Sources: Long Drums and Cannons, Margaret Laurence, London, Macmillan, 1968; *An Introduction to the African Novel,* Eustace Palmer, New York, African Publishing Corporation, 1972; "The Achievement of Elechi Amadi," Aarhus, University of Aarhus, Denmark, % Anna Rutherford, English Department, 1971.

AMO, Antonius Guilielmus
b. 1703, probably in or near Axim, Gold Coast, now Ghana; d. 1750's (?).
Philosopher, scholar (in Latin).

Captured as a child along the old Guinea coast, Amo was fortunate in being put into the hands of the Dukes of Brunswick-Wolfenbrittel, Germany. After being educated by his masters, he became professor of philosophy at the University of Wittenberg and Halle. At Halle in 1738, he published his Latin tract, *Tractatus de arte sobrie et accurate philosophandi* (A Study of the Art of Philosophizing Soundly and Truthfully), a work which has been compared to that of Christian Wolff and Immanuel Kant. An earlier Latin tract, *Dissertatia inauguralis philosophica . . .* (Inaugural Philosophical Dissertation . . .) is cited in Jahnheinz Jahn's *Bibliography of Creative African Writing.*

Upon the death of his patrons, Amo, unlike most Europeanized Africans of this period, returned to his native land to drop out of Western history.

Writings: Philosophy: *Tractatus de arte sobrie et accurate philosophandi . . .,* Halle, 1738; *Dissertatio inauguralis philosophica . . .,* Wittenberg, 1734.

Biographical/Critical Sources: Bibliography of Creative African Writing, Jahnheinz Jahn, editor, Nendeln, Switzerland, Kraus-Thompson; and J. Jahn, *Neo-African Literature,* New York, Grove Press, 1968.

ANAHORY, Terêncio (also SILVA, Terêncio Casimiro Anahory)
b. 1934, on the Island of Boa-Vista, Cape Verde.
Poet.

Though born in Cape Verde, Anahory has spent most of his life on mainland Portuguese Guinea (Bissau). He worked for awhile on the newspaper, *Bulletin of Cape Verde* (Boletim de Cabo-Verde e Bolaneuse published in Bissau. He studied law in Lisbon. He is represented in *New Sum of Poetry from the Negro World* and *Poetas e contistas africanos de expressão portuguêsa.* He has published one collection of verse, *Caminho longe* (The Long Road).

Writings: Poetry: *Caminho longe,* Lisbon, Sagitario, 1962; in *New Sum of Poetry from the Negro World,* Paris, Présence Africaine, Vol. 57, 1966, and in *Poetas e contis-*

tas africanos de expressão portuguêsa, São Paulo, Editôra Brasiliense, 1963.

ANANG, Dei (see DEI-ANANG, M.F.)

ANANOU, David
b. ca. 1930, Togo.
Novelist.

Le fils du fétiche (The Charm's Son), published in 1955, is Ananou's contribution to francophone African fiction. This work, though trying to show African life, skirts certain "true" pictures to avoid offering the European reader the chance to confirm his ideas of African "primitiveness." Though written, as the author maintains, because "Africa is often misunderstood," it is only an early effort to break down the stereotyped, European way of seeing the African reality.

Writings: Novel: *Le fils du fétiche,* Paris, Nouvelle Editions Latines, 1955.

ANDRADE, Costa (also da COSTA ANDRADE, Fernando, and pseudonym SILVESTRE, Flávio)
b. 1936, Lepi, Angola.
Poet, story writer.

Costa Andrade studied architecture in Yugoslavia in the 1950's; then, after a period in Italy, he emigrated to Brazil where, politically active in leftist politics, he was arrested after the fall of President Goulart. Earlier, he had been an activist in student groups in Lisbon and a member of the M.P.L.A. (Movement for the Liberation of Angola).

Now living in Zambia, in exile from his native Angola, Andrade has published three volumes of verse: *Terra de acácias rubras* (Land of the Red Acacias), 1961, *Tempo angolana em Italia* (Angolan Days in Italy), 1963, and *Un ramo de miosótis* (A Spray of Forget-me-nots), 1970. The latest work appeared informally in a mimeographed volume.

His stories have appeared in various journals and collections. The story, "Um conto igual a muitos," (A Story Worth Many), appeared in *Contistas angolanos* (Angolan Stories) in 1960.

Writings: Poetry: *Terra de acácias rubras,* Lisbon, Edição da Casa dos Estudantes do Império, 1961; *Tempo angolana em Italia. Poemas,* São Paulo, Felman Rêgo, 1963; *Un ramo de miosótis,* Lusaka, 1970.
Story: "Um conto igual a muitos," in *Contistas angolanos,* F. Mourao, editor, Lisbon, Casa dos Estudantes do Império, 1960.

ANOZIE, Sunday Ogbonna
b. 1942, Owerri, eastern Nigeria.
Critic, scholar (writes and publishes in both English and French).

Anozie was educated in Nigerian schools and took his B.A. at the University of Nsukka in 1963. He continued his studies in Paris on a UNESCO scholarship, obtaining his doctorate in sociology at the Sorbonne with a "trés honorable." He founded and was managing editor of the Biafran journal *Conch* which began publication in Paris in 1969 and was devoted to African culture and literature. He has contributed many book reviews to *Présence Africaine* and other journals. At the present time he is a visiting professor of English at the University of Texas in Austin, where *Conch* is now published.

His *Sociologie du Roman Africaine* offers a "structuralist" analysis of French and English African creative literature, which deals with the ever-changing political and social setting and environment of the novelists and their novels as well as providing new readings of important works. The book's three major sections are: I: Theoretic Explication (a consideration of the African novel from the points of view of tradition, of social change, of alienation, and of the new urban and politicization of the people, II: Realism and Determinism in the West African novel (Tutuola and the "Realism" of Folklore, the Individual of the Traditional Past, Existential Realism and Psychological Realism); here most of the well-known African writers are dealt with, and III: Conclusion: The Perspectives of the West African Novel (Tradition and Modernism, The Instability of the Socio-Economic Structures, Independence and Disillusion, and Messianic Tendencies).

In 1970, Anozie published *Christopher Okigbo*, a study of the Nigerian poet, who, in his early Mbari Press collection, *Limits* (1962) had warmly thanked Anozie for helping him refine his poems into their "present form."

Writings: Criticism: *Sociologie du Roman Africaine,* Paris, Aubier-Montaigne, 1970; *Christopher Okigbo,* London, Evans, 1970.

ANTAR (or ANTARAH Ibn Shaddah el 'Absi)
b. ca. 550, in or near Medina, Arabia;
d. 615, Arabia.
Arabic-language poet, chief, warrior.

Antar (the Lion) was son of an important Arab chief, Shaddah, and a black African mother, Zabiba or Zebeeba, a slave in his father's household. He became the most gifted and famous of the pre-Islamic poets of the Arabic language. He lived a great part of his life in the desert region between el-Hejr and the capital city of Medina. A great warrior of legendary exploits and possessed of a golden tongue, Antar loved and married Abla, became chief of the Abs, the strongest nomadic tribe in Arabia, and lived a violent, successful life. He died in battle against the tribe of the Taiyi through the treachery of Wizr b. Djabir.

As the author of one of the seven *mo'allaqâ* (The Seven Golden Odes) which were hung in honor on the walls of the Kaaba at Mecca, Antar was highly praised by the Prophet Mohammed who declared him to be "the only famous Bedouin warrior that I have wished I could have known." Further, the Prophet Mohammed declared that Antar's feats were to be told to Islam, "for thus will their hearts be steeled harder than stone."

Possibly even more famous than his *mo'allaqâ* were the thousands of poems ascribed to him which are scattered through the *Sirat Antarah,* or Antar Romance, which includes the work of many of his literary followers and imitators. His poems were considered so great and beautiful that a broad and long-lived school of poets began to work in his tradition and became known as the *Antareeyeh.* Antar's works and those of his school were handed down relatively accurately and completely for centuries. First written down by Asma'i (740–830), this work is no longer extant, but Ibn al-Mujalla al-Antari (the supreme Antareeyeh), a physician living in a city on the banks of the Tigris, wrote another version of the Antar poems in the mid-12th century which is still extant. From the latter version have been made modern transcriptions into Arabic and other languages, including a story in Russian by Senkosky which influenced Nikolai Rimsky-Korsakov's Antar Symphony, his ninth work, afterwards called the Oriental Suite. Asma'i had made his written collection at the request of Abdallah al-Ma'moun, son of an African mother and the famous Haroun al-Rashid.

Cedric Dover in his study of Antar in *Phylon* notes frequent references in Antar's work to the poet's blackness and his pride in his ancestry and desire to vindicate his mother's race, concluding that it is the first "classical work concerned with colour prejudice." Dover discusses the long neglect of this greatest of all Arabic poems in the West because, as he argues persuasively, racial prejudice in the 18th and 19th centuries intimidated scholars from making the necessary effort to translate and then popularize poems written by or in imitation of the work of a half-black poet. Even the first English translator, Terrick Hamilton, in his preface to his 1819 edition of the *Sirat Antarah* thought it necessary to question both Antar's mother's slavery and her African origin. The European shipping and colonial interests were still horrified by the revolution in Haiti and slave revolts elsewhere, and the publication of a major work by a talented black, himself a mighty soldier, could only be looked on as dangerous in the extreme. Only a third of Hamilton's translations, scheduled for complete publication in 12 volumes, were printed, the first volume in 1819 and the last three in 1820. Even today, there is no complete or full translation of the

Sirat Antarah, despite the fact that the Romance is the base of most of the folk stories told throughout the Islamic world today and of the tales which reached Europe through medieval Spain and gave birth to chivalry and the Christian romances.

Claude McKay, the Jamaican-American poet, was delighted to learn during his stay in North Africa in the 1930's that "even the illiterate Moor is acquainted with the history of Antar." Whenever McKay visited coffee-houses and was introduced as a poet, he would be greeted, he reports, with the welcome, "Our greatest poet, Antar, was a Negro."

Writings: Poetry: Antar's ode, or *mo'allaqâ,* with the other six, was first translated by Sir William Jones as *The Moallakât, or Seven Arabian Poems Which Were Suspended on the Temple at Mecca,* London, 1782, reprinted by W. A. Clauston in *Arabian Poetry for English Readers,* Glasgow, 1881; A. Blunt and W. S. Blunt, *The Seven Golden Odes of Pagan Arabia,* London, 1903; *The divans of the six ancient Arabic poets,* London, 1870, contains the Arabic text and an English translation; and the Arabic text with German translation is in Friedrich Rückert's *Hamâsa oder Die ältesten arabischen Volkslieder,* Stuttgart, 1846. *Sirat Antarah,* first published in Arabic, Beirut, 1865 and 1869–77 in ten volumes, and again in six volumes, 1883–85; again in Bulak, Syria, 1866–1870 in 32 volumes, possibly from an expanded version of Asma'i's original by Abu Muwajjid Muhammad ibn al-Mujalla al—'Antari; Terrick Hamilton's translation into English appeared in London, 1819–20 in four volumes as *Antar, a bedoueen romance,* one third of the total translation; L. M. Devic, *Les aventures d'Antar, fils de Chaddad, roman Arabe des temps anté-Islamique,* Paris, 1864, 1878, 1898, offers fairly complete translation of the *Sirat Antarah;* A. T. De Vere, *Antar and Zara, an Eastern Romance,* London, 1877; Arabic manuscripts; two versions of the Antar poems *(The Sirat Antar)* are: 1) the recension of *Hidjaz (al-Sira al-hidjaziya),* chief edition: Cairo, 1306–1311 in 32 parts; and 2) the briefer Syrian recension, (the *al-Sira al-shamiya),* considered identical to the "Babylonian" recension (the *al-Sira al-irakiya):* published in the Beirut editions of 1865 and 1869–77, cited above.

Biographical/Critical Sources: Encyclopaedia of Islam, London, Leiden, 1934; Carl Brockelmann, *Geschichte der arabishen Literature,* 2nd edition, Leiden, 1943; J. Jahn, *Neo-African Literature: A History of Black Writing,* New York, Grove Press, 1968; Joseph Freiherr von Hammer-Purstall, "On Arabian poetry, especially the romance of Antar," *New Monthly Magazine,* XIII, 1820; Cedric Dover, "The Black Knight," *Phylon,* XV, Nos 1/2, Atlanta, Ga., 1954; Claude McKay, *A Long Way from Home,* New York, 1937.

ANTONIO, Mário (pseudonym for de OLIVEIRA, Mário António Fernandes)
b. 1934, Luanda, Angola.
Poet, story writer, scholar, teacher.

Although António is a trained meteorologist, he works as a research sociologist in the Portuguese-held territories in Africa. In his early days he was a leader of the Movement of New Poets of Angola. He now lives in Lisbon but grew up in Luanda; he has remained close to his natal sources for inspiration for his poetry and stories.

He has published in Portuguese and Angolan journals, including *Tavola Redonda* (Round Table). His works of verse are: *Poesias* (Poems), published in 1956; *Era, tempo de poesia* (Era, The Time for Verse); *Amor: poesias* (Love: Poems); *Poemas e canto miúdo* (Poems and Small Songs); *Chingufo: poemas angolanos* (Chingufo: Angolan Poems); *100 poemas* (100 Poems); *Rosto de Europe* (The Face of Europe); and *Nossa Senhora da Vitória de Messangano* (Our Lady of Vitória de Messangano).

This prolific writer also has four volumes of stories: *Gente para romance: Alvaro, Lígia, António* (People for Adventure . . .); *Farra no fim de semana* (The Wild Week-end); and *Crónica da cidade estranha* (Chronicle of the Strange City) which contains the long title story and nine sketches. There is also a collection of freely adapted folk stories: *Mahezu:*

Antonio

Tradições angolanas (Mahezu: Angolan Folk Tales), published in 1966.

António has done research in early Angolan poetry, most of which was originally published in the old Lisbon journal, the *Almanach de Lembranças* (The Almanac of Lembranças) between 1879 and 1893. (See António's "Colaborações angolanas no *Almanach de Lembranças*, 1851–1900," in the *Boletim do Istituto de Investigação Científica de Angola*, III, 1 1966. Much of this material is also elaborated upon in his scholarly works.)

Two mimeographed essays are: "Influências da literatura brasileira sôbre as literaturas portuguêsas do Atlântico Tropical, Conferência." (The Influences of Brazilian Literature on the Literature of the Tropical Atlantic), and "Situação da literatura no 'espaço português. Conferencia" (The Situation of Literature in Portuguese Territory. Conference Report.)

A 17-page linguistic study published in the specialized journal, *Boletim da Sociedade de Geografia de Lisboa*, Jan–March, 1968, was "Unidade e diferenciação linguísticas na literatura ultramarino portuguêsa" (Linguistic Similarities and Differences in Overseas Portuguese).

A long comment on the future of Angolan writing appeared in English in G. M. Moser's *Essays in Portuguese-African Literature*, drawn from the Lisbon journal, *Colóquio*, No. 9. There Antonio assessed past efforts of African writers in Portuguese and the very problematical future. António's poem, "O amor e o futuro" (Ah, Love and the Future), appears in Moser also, in the original Portuguese and in Moser's English translation. António is also represented in *New Sum of Poetry from the Negro World*.

Writings: Poetry: "O amor e o futuro,"

in Portuguese and English, G. M. Moser's *Essays in Portuguese-African Literature*, University Park, Penn State Studies 26, 1969, *Poesias* (16 pages), Lisbon, 1956. *Era, tempo de poesia*. Sá de Bandeira, Imbondeiro, 1966; *Amor; poesias*. Lisbon, Casa dos Estudantes do Império, 1960; *Poemas e canto miúdo*. Lisbon, 1960, and Sá da Bandeira, Publicações Imbondeiro, 1961; *Chingufo; poemas angolanos*. Lisbon, Agência-Geral do Ultramar, 1962; *100 (cem) poemas*. Luanda, Edições ABC, 1963 or 1964; *Rosto de Europe*. Braga, Editôra Pax, 1968; *Nossa Senhora da Vitória de Messangano*. Luanda, 1968; in *New Sum of Poetry from the Negro World*. Paris, Présence Africaine, 1966.

Stories: *Gente para romance: Alvaro, Lígia, António*. Sá da Bandeira, Imbondeiro, 1961; *Mahezu. Tradições angolanas*. Lisbon, Serviço de Publicações Ultramarinas, 1966; *Farra no fim de semana*. Braga, Editôra Pax, 1965; *Crónica da cidade estranha*. Lisbon, Agência-Geral do Ultramar, 1964.

Scholarly works: "A sociedade angolana do fim do século XIX e um seu escritor. Ensaio." Luanda, Nós, 1961, an essay on Joaquim Dias Cordeiro de Mata (1857–1894); "Influências da literatura brasileira sôbre as literaturas portuguêsas do Atlântico Tropical. Conferência." Lisbon, 1967; "Colaborações angolanas no *Almanach de Lembranças*, 1851–1900," *Boletim do Istituto de Investigação Científica de Angola*, III, 1, 1966; "Situação da literatura no 'espaço português,' Conferência." Lisbon, 1967; "Francisco Tenreiro, poeta," in Francisco José Tenreiro's *Obra Poética*, Lisbon, 1967; five essays in *Luanda, 'ilha' crioula*, a 163-page collection containing: "Luanda, ilha crioula," "Um intelectual angolense do século XIX," "O roman-

cista angolense António Assis Júnior," "Tomas Vieira da Cruz, poeta," and "A obra literária de Oscar Ribas," Lisbon, Agência-Geral do Ultramar, 1968; "Unidade e diferenciação linguísticas na literatura ultramarina portuguêsa," *Boletim da Sociedade de Geografia de Lisboa,* Jan–March, 1968; "African Writers in Portuguese," *African Arts,* III, 2, Los Angeles, Winter, 1970.
Translation: extract from *Colóquio,* No. 9, June 1960, in G. M. Moser's *Essays in Portuguese-African Literature,* University Park, Pennsylvania, Penn State Studies 26, 1969.

Biographical/Critical Source: Elementos para uma bibliografia da literatura e cultura portugêsa ultramarina contemporânea, with Amândio César (Pires Monteiro), Lisbon, Agência-Geral do Ultramar, 1968, which is a bibliography of poetry, prose fiction, memoirs, and essays.

APRONTI, Jawa
b. 1940, Ghana.
Poet, critic.

Apronti studied English literature at the University of Ghana in Legon and later at Leeds University, Yorkshire, England. He first published in *Transition* magazine (Kampala, Uganda) and appears in Moore and Beier's *Modern Poetry from Africa.* He is now teaching at the University of Ghana. At one time he was an editor of *Okyeami,* Ghana's leading literary journal.

Writings: Poems in *Transition* Magazine, Kampala, Uganda; *Modern Poetry from Africa,* Moore and Beier, eds., rev. ed., Baltimore, Penguin, 1968.

ARKHURST, Frederick S.
b. ca. 1920, Ghana.
Poet, commentator, diplomat.

Arkhurst was graduated from Aberdeen University, Scotland and saw army service in Australia. He was First Secretary of the Ghanaian Permanent Mission to the U.N. and more recently was attached to the U.N. Economic Commission for Africa. He is represented in Langston Hughes' *An African Treasury* with the article "Renascent Africa."

Writings: Article, "Renascent Africa," *An African Treasury,* Langston Hughes, ed., New York, 1965.

ARMAH, Ayi Kwei
b. 1938, Ghana.
Novelist, poet, short story writer, journalist.

Armah was educated in local Ghanaian schools, but as a young man travelled to America and completed his secondary schooling at Groton and took his B.A. at Harvard. He also studied at Achimota College and the University of Ghana at Legon. He has been a script writer and teacher in Ghana and was for a time an editor and translator on the staff of *Jeune Afrique,* Paris. One of his short stories, "Yaw Manu's Charm," appeared in the *Atlantic,* May, 1968, and another, "The Offal Kind," was published in *Harper's Magazine,* January, 1969. Armah has worked on an advanced degree in English for some years in New York City on a fellowship, but he calls Paris his home base.
Armah has published three novels: *The Beautyful Ones Are Not Yet Born,* (1968); *Fragments,* (1970); and *Why Are We So Blest?* (1971). The first two works

attack the corrupt politicians in Ghana and offer little optimism that things may change for the better in the foreseeable future.

In the *Beautyful Ones* (the author saw the unique phrase and spelling on a "mammy" wagon or truck converted into a bus for transporting country people), Armah is almost violent in his repudiation of the cruelties and corruption of Nkrumah's Ghana. He attacks not only post-independence Ghana, but all of the African "Black Colonialists" who, having replaced the Europeans, take to themselves the power, luxuries, and arrogance of the displaced whites. The flavor of Armah's prose and his treatment of corruption is caught here in a passage in which attacks Koomson, the rags-to-riches minister in Nkrumah's cabinet:

Ideological hands, the hands of revolutionaries leading their peoples into bold sacrifices, should these hands not have become even tougher than they were when their owner was hauling loads along the wharf? And yet these were the socialists

of Africa, fat, perfumed, soft with the ancestral softness of chiefs who have sold their people and are celestially happy with the fruits of the trade.

One of Armah's rare poems, "Aftermath," appears in *Messages: Poems from Ghana.* Half-bitterly, half resignedly the narrator says goodbye to a lover who has not been able to keep their love pure and independent of racial and other pressures. The poem ends forcefully:

Do not torture your mind
Searching for justification
I need none.
Enjoy your freedom.
Leave me,
Go.

He could well be addressing these words, too, to the African leaders who have forgotten their origins and have betrayed the trust of the masses who had hoped for "beautiful" men to lead them toward a new Africa.

Writings: Novels: *The Beautyful Ones Are Not Yet Born,* Boston, Houghton Mifflin Co., 1968; Heinemann, 1969; Macmillan, New York, 1969; *Fragments,* Boston, Houghton Mifflin, 1970; *Why Are We So Blest?* New York, Doubleday, 1971.

Short Stories: "Yaw Manu's Charm, *Atlantic,* May, 1968; "The Offal Kind," *Harper's Magazine,* Jan. 1969.

Poetry: "Aftermath," in *Messages: Poems From Ghana,* London, Heinemann, 1971.

ARMATTOE, Raphael Ernest Grail Glikpo
b. August 13, 1913, in former British Togoland, now a part of Ghana; d. December 21, 1953, in Germany.
Poet, historian.

At 13, Armattoe was sent by his father to England to begin his long foreign studies. He became a medical doctor, anthropologist and poet. His work, though now dated in its treatment of the dignity and suffering of Africans under colonialism, was original for its times—the 1930's and 1940's. On his return to the Gold Coast (now Ghana) he became active politically and was a good friend of Kofi Abrefa Busia, the recent President of Ghana. He moved to Ireland in 1943, staying for ten years, except for one brief trip home in 1950.

In Ireland he wrote the poems represented in two volumes: *Between the Forest and the Sea* (1950) and *Deep Down the Black Man's Mind,* (1959), both privately printed. He has published many works in other fields.

Most of his poetry is pedestrian, usually lacking in passion, and prosaic in tone and imagery. However, the short poem "Servant-Kings," published with four others from his second volume in Donatus Ibe Nwoga's *West African Verse* (1967), has its charm and power. Armattoe attacks the bickering puppet-kings and chiefs, or politicians, who were so easily managed by their colonial masters:

Leave them alone,
Leave them to be
Men lost to shame,
To honour lost!
Servant Kinglets,
Riding to war
Against their own,
Watched by their foes
Who urge them on,
And laugh at them!
Leave them alone,
Men lost to shame,
To honour lost.

In 1953, he was the leader of a delegation to the United Nations seeking international support for a union of French and British Togo as an independent state. Returning to Ghana by way of Ger-

many, he came down with acute pneumonia and died suddenly in a Hamburg hospital, December 21, 1953.

Writings: Poetry: *Between the Forest and the Sea,* Londonderry, Ireland, Lomeshie Research Centre, 1950; *Deep Down the Blackman's Mind,* Ilfracombe, N. Devon, England, Stockwell, 1954; Five poems, including "Servant-Kings," *West African Verse,* Donatus Ibe Nwoga, editor, London, Longmans, Green, 1967.

Biographical/Critical Source: Obituary, *Ashanti Pioneer,* January 4, 1954.

ASALACHE, Khadambi
b. 1934, Western Kenya.
Novelist, poet, teacher.

Growing up as a herdsman, Asalache heard the tales of tribal feuds which later figured in his writings. Locally educated, he struggled hard to get to high school and despite extreme poverty went on to study art and architecture at the Royal College, Nairobi. While attending an international students' conference in Tunis, he decided to travel, visiting

Rome, Geneva, Vienna and then London in 1960 instead of returning home. He has since remained in London, worked at a variety of jobs, and written TV scripts for the B.B.C. His first novel, *A Calabash of Life,* concerns precolonial Kenya and recounts the days of tribal war, love, and intrigue.

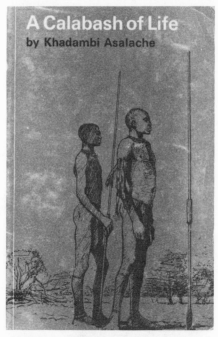

Writings: Novel: *A Calabash of Life,* London, Longmans, 1967.

ASARE, Bediako
b. ca. 1930, the Gold Coast (now Ghana). Novelist, journalist.

Born in the Gold Coast, Asare was a journalist on various papers and an assistant editor on the *Ghanaian Times.* In 1963 he went to Dar es Salaam to establish with other non-Tanzanian staff the journal, *The Nationalist.* After local schooling, his first job had been on the *Ashanti Sentinel* in Kumasi, 1952, followed by work with the Ghana Trade Union Congress and service as editor of the *Worker* and *Ghana Labor.*

Asare's first novel, *Rebel,* was completed in Dar es Salaam, in 1968. First published in 1969, it was reprinted in 1970 with illustrations by Taj Ahmed. Dramatic and well-written, the work exploits the theme of the struggles between the modern generation of African leaders and the conservative, not always benign, older leadership of priests and village elders. In the fictional tribal area of Pachanga, the protagonist, Ngurumo, fights a brutal battle for control of his people caught in the "superstitious" coils of Mzee Matata, the powerful priest who hates change and any challenge to his paramount authority in matters secular and divine.

Writings: Novel: *Rebel,* London, Heinemann, 1969; reprinted in Heinemann African Writers Series, London, 1970, with illustrations by Taj Ahmed in both editions.

ASARE, Konadu (pseudonym for KONADU, Samuel Asare, as is the name BEDIAKO, Kwabena Asare)

ASHENAFI, Kebede
b. May 7, 1937, Bulga, Shoa, Ethiopia. Novelist in English, composer and musical scholar, educator, government official.

Grandson of an Ethiopian who had attended an Italian university in the late 19th century under Menelik II, Ashenafi attended the Haile Selassi I School in the nation's capital, and later went on to Harar Teaching Training School.

Having taught for two years at home, he then studied music at the Eastman School of Music, University of Rochester, New York State, receiving the B.A. in 1962. After teaching for one summer at Georgetown University in Washington, D.C. he taught at Tafari Makonnen School in Ethiopia. In 1964 he was appointed to the Ministry of Education and Fine Arts, and at present is director of the National School of Music.

One product of Kebede's experiences in America was his semi-autobiographical novel, *Confession,* published in English. Like several new African novels published elsewhere in the continent, it details the often painful course of a young African's love affair with a white girl. In this work, the girl is American and she dies in a riot in Shreveport, Louisiana during the early days of the civil rights movement initiated by Freedom Bus Riders. Beyond the inter-racial elements of the story there is the recognition by the author of a common bond between black Africans and their descendants everywhere, both in and out of Africa.

Ashenafi has a growing list of scholarly monographs in Amharic on Ethiopian music, and has also written music and texts for choral works.

Writings: Novel: *Confession,* Addis Ababa, 1965.

ASSIS JUNIOR, António de
b. ca. 1870, Luanda, Angola;
d. Portugal, 1960 (?).
Novelist, journalist, lawyer.

Trained as a lawyer in Portugal, Assis Júnior was active in literary-nationalist movements in Angola. He was exiled to Portugal where he died in the early 1960's, after a long period under surveillance. His one novel, *O segredo da morta* (The Dead Girl's Secret), published in 1934, presents a picture of the Luandan society of the 1890's in which he lived as a man of mixed European-African blood. The central character is a pathetic young woman who goes insane after suffering from a severe case of sleeping sickness. The work is not successful artistically and reflects the indecisions and sterilities of the hybrid, colonial creole culture of the period.

Assis Júnior was arrested for unknown reasons after the novel appeared, but his preface to his work may carry a hint of what led to his exile in Portugal: "The Angolan's life which civilization has not totally obliterated—that civilization which is imposed rather through command and fear than through persuasion and reasoning . . . that still represents a problem today for which there is no easy solution. . . ." (as quoted in G. M. Moser's *Essays in Portuguese-African Literature).*

Writings: Novel: *O segredo da morta. Romance de costume angolenses,* Luanda, A Luzitana, 1934.

Biographical/Critical Sources: Essays in Portuguese-African Literature, G. M. Moser, University Park, Pennsylvania, Penn State Studies 26, 1969; *A Tentative Portuguese-African Bibliography: Portuguese Literature in Africa and African Literature in the Portuguese Language,* G. M. Moser, Bibliographic Series, No. 3, University Park, Pennsylvania, The Pennsylvania State University Libraries, 1970.

AWOLOWO, Obafemi Awo
b. March 6, 1909, Ijebu-Remo,

Awolowo

Yoruba-land, western Nigeria.
Autobiographer, journalist, politician.

Awolowo was a farmer's son, and with great sacrifice to himself and his family studied at Anglican and Methodist mission schools in Ikenne and the Methodist School and Baptist Boys High School, Abeokuta. On his father's death, he left school to work as a student-teacher in nearby schools, then went to Wesley College, Ibadan, for teacher training. Clerking for a German firm in Lagos from 1932–34, he trained himself as a journalist and trader. In the late 1930's he became the secretary of the Nigerian Motor Transport Traders Association which he had earlier organized. While working as an editor of the *Nigerian Worker* he studied for five years and received his B.A. in commerce in 1944. He is married and the father of three children.

He was secretary of the Ibadan branch of the Nigerian Youth Movement in June 1940 and led efforts for the reform of the Ibadan Native Authority Administration Council which resulted in the formation of the Native Authority Advisory Board two years later. He became co-founder of the Trades Union Congress of Nigeria in 1943, and the following year traveled to England to study law, a long-cherished ambition. In London he helped establish a Yoruba cultural and political group, the Egbe Omo Oduduwa. He published *Path to Nigerian Freedom* which stated his hope that Nigeria would adopt the "Federal" system which, he argued, would offer the highest possible autonomy to each ethnic group while providing a coherent national government.

Taking his law degree in 1947, Awolowo returned to Ibadan to practice law and to continue his efforts on behalf of the Egbe Omo Oduduwa of which he became General Secretary in 1948. From the stimulation of the Egbe, Awolowo and his associates moved on to form the Action Group in 1951, an openly political party. This group swept the Western Region elections that year with Awolowo being elected to represent his home region of Ijebu-Remo. From 1951–54 he was a minister in the cabinet of the local government, and in 1954 he became premier of the Western Region, a position of strength from which he sought to broaden the Action Group into an all-Nigerian party. Despite his energetic and often innovative efforts, he failed to carry any seats in the Federal Parliament from areas outside the Western Yoruba-dominated part of the country, but he did go to Lagos the capital to become head of the opposition in 1959.

Though he and his party were initially moderate and generally pro-Western in their orientation, they moved left in the next years to accommodate the generally more radical younger intellectuals and to create a more viable "opposition" role in the national legislature. Awolowo even travelled to Ghana to visit Nkrumah in June 1961 and returned to urge his government to join the Ghana-Guinea-Mali Union, the most socialist and anti-Western grouping of new African states.

In 1960 he published *The Autobiography of Chief Obafemi Awo-lowo*. His political life became the raw material for a new autobiography with the turbulent events of 1961–63 when Awolowo broke with the number two man in the Action Group, Chief Samuel Akintola, the Premier of the Western Region who was dismissed May 21, 1962, by the Region's Governor, Sir Adesoji Aderemi. Akintola challenged the dismissal in the courts and a general free-for-all ensued, with charges flying between Akintola and his supporters on the one hand and Awolowo and his allies on the other. The Federal government became involved, a Federal Commission was named, and the upshot was that Akintola joined the opposition and Awolowo's group won most of the seats to the Lagos Municipal Council in October, 1962. Awolowo himself and 30 associates were charged with treasonable felony because explosives had been found in a house in Lagos occupied by one of the Action Group circle and by persons allegedly trained in the use of weapons outside of Nigeria for revolutionary acts in Nigeria.

Increased dissension between the various parties was the consequence and led to Awolowo's being imprisoned. He remained incarcerated in Calabar Prison until being released in 1966 by the military regime which took over the Federal and Regional governments under Major General J. T. U. Aguiyi Ironsi, an Ibo. On August 12, 1966, he was unanimously elected leader of the Yoruba-dominated Western Region (population: ten million) and head of the Region's delegation to the All-Nigeria Constitutional Conference which was to deliberate on the future of the strife-torn country. During his prison days at Calabar, he wrote *Thoughts on the Nigerian Constitution*, in which he argues for a confederal constitution as "probably the only way out of the present impasse in Nigeria," and *My Early Life* which went through three printings the first year of publication, 1968.

Writings: Autobiographies: *My Early Life*, Lagos, John West Publications Ltd., 1968; *Awo: The Autobiography of Chief Obafemi Awolowo*, London, New York, Cambridge University Press, 1960.

Political: *Path to Nigerian Freedom*, London, Faber and Faber, 1947, 1966; *Thoughts on the Nigerian Constitution*, London, New York, Oxford University Press, 1967; *The Peoples' Republic*, Ibadan, Oxford University Press, 1968; *The Strategy and Tactics of the People's Republic of Nigeria*, London, Macmillan, 1970.

Biographical/Critical Sources: Mother is Gold: A Study in West African Literature, Adrian A. Roscoe, Cambridge, Cambridge University Press, 1971; *The New Africans*, New York, G. P. Putnam's Sons, 1967.

AWOONOR-WILLIAMS, George
(See AWOONOR, Kofi).

AWOONOR, Kofi (also
AWOONOR-WILLIAMS, George)

Awoonor

b. 1935, Wheta, Keta district, Volta Region, Ghana.
Poet, novelist, playwright, teacher.

Kofi Awoonor, son of a Sierra Leonean father and a Togolese mother, was educated in Ghanaian schools, including the Achimota Secondary School. He specialized in vernacular poetry at the University of Ghana's Institute of African Studies. On a Longman Fellowship, he later studied at the University College of London where he received his M.A. in 1968.

As editor of *Okyeame*, an important, but irregularly-issued Ghanaian literary journal begun in 1961, he encouraged a number of unknown young writers by publishing their works. He served for a time as associate editor of *Transition*, published in Kampala, Uganda. In addition, he has written for radio, acted on the stage and been managing director of the Ghana Film Corportation. Currently he teaches African literature and is chairman of the comparative literature program at the Stony Brook campus of the State University of New York.

His first volume of poetry was *Rediscovery and other poems,* published in 1964. In his second volume of poetry, *Night of My Blood,* Awoonor uses the form of traditional Ewe songs to lament the neglect of old Africa's gods and shrines and the perverting influence of Western culture. An awareness of the omnipotence of death stalks his work along with a concern for the effort of one man to know another. He is represented in many anthologies including *New Sum of Poetry from the Negro World* and Moore and Beier's *Modern Poetry from Africa.* He has also edited with G. Adali-Mortty a collection of poetry by Ghanaians, *Messages: Poems from Ghana* which includes the work of such poets as Joseph de Graft, Kayper Mensah, Ayi Kwei, Cameron Duodu, Frank Kobina Parkes, Efua Sutherland, and E. A. Winful.

In June 1968 he was invited to read along with the poets Herbert of Poland and Guitlev of France at the Poetry Center in New York.

Awooner's first collection of plays, *Ancestral Power,* appeared in 1970.

His recent novel, *This Earth, My Brother . . . ,* deals with the corruption and degradation of much of African life today, a condition that the author sees as partly the legacy of colonialism, partly the product of African selfishness and egotism. The novel indicts the African political elite as being sordid and inefficient. Amamu, the protagonist, a European-trained lawyer, suffers a nervous breakdown as he confronts the complex world of newly independent Ghana. The bribery and violence in his society are too much for him. The reader is left to ponder the question: if a man like Amamu fails, who will succeed?

Writings: Poetry: *Rediscovery and other Poems,* Ibadan, Mbari Press, 1964; *Night of My Blood,* New York, Doubleday, 1971; poems in *New Sum of Poetry from the Negro World,* Paris, Présence Africaine, 1966; *Modern Poetry from Africa,* Moore and Beier, editors, London, Penguin, 1970; Edited, with G. Adali-Mortty, *Messages: Poems from Ghana: Poems from Ghana,* London, Longmans, 1970.

Plays: *Ancestral Power,* London, Longmans, 1970.

Novel: *This Earth, My Brother,* New York, Doubleday, 1971, No. 108 in Heinemann's African Writers Series, London, 1971.

Criticism: *The Breast of the Earth. A Study of the Cultures and Literatures of Africa,* New York, Doubleday, 1972.

Journalism: "Kwami Nkrumah: symbol of emergent Africa," *Africa Report,* June, 1972.

AZEVEDO, PEDRO Corsino de
b. 1905, São Nicolau, Cape Verde Islands; d. 1942.
Poet.

A member of the pioneering writers' movement associated with the journal *Claridade,* founded by Jorge Barbosa and others in the mid-1930's, Azevedo early adapted the Cabo-Verdean islanders' oral traditional poetry for his Portuguese verse. His one volume of collected poems, "Era de ouro. Poesias." (The Age of Gold: Poems), is being prepared for publication.

One poem, "Terra distante" (The Faraway Land), appears in Mário de Andrade's *Literatura Africana de expressâo Portuguêsa.* His work appeared in *Claridade* from 1947 till his death.

Writings: Poetry: "Terra distante," *Literatura africana de expressâo portuguêsa.* Mário de Andrade, editor, Algiers, 1967; *Claridade,* São Vicente, Cape Verde; in manuscript, "Era de ouro. Poesias."

AZIKIWE, Benjamin Nnamdi
b. November 16, 1904, Zungeru, northern Nigeria.
Autobiographer, publisher, journalist, politician.

Azikiwe's father, an Ibo from Onitsha, was a clerk in the Nigerian Regiment at Zungeru in the far north and young "Zik" was born there in 1904. He was educated at mission schools in Onitsha, Lagos, the Hope Waddell Institute in Calabar and later at the Methodist Boys' High School, Lagos. He worked for four years (1921–25) as a clerk of the Treasury at Lagos. He then stowed away on a ship to America where he attended Storer College, West Virginia, Howard University in Washington, D.C. and took a B.A. in political science at Lincoln College, Pennsylvania.

Azikiwe suffered racial slights while in the United States and was influenced by the Marcus Garvey movement. Later he studied journalism and did graduate work in political science and history at the University of Pennsylvania. He also lectured at Lincoln College. By 1934, he was in London and there published *Liberia in World Affairs.* He then moved to the Gold Coast (now Ghana) where he became editor for three years of the

Azikiwe

Africa Morning Post. In 1937, Azikiwe returned to Nigeria where he joined the Nigerian Youth Movement's executive committee and quickly became the leading spokesman for Ibo interests. He started a chain of newspapers, among them the important *West African Pilot,* and four provincial journals in Ibadan, Onitsha, Port Harcourt, and Kano. During these years he wrote *Renascent Africa.*

Azikiwe was Governor-General of Nigeria between 1959 and 1963. When

Nigeria became a republic in October, 1963, he was unanimously elected the first President. With the first military coup against the Federal Government, Azikiwe went into isolation at his home in Nsukka where he had been instrumental in establishing the University of Nigeria at Nsukka. In July, 1966, he agreed to serve as political advisor to the military regime which had taken over the Eastern Region. Then the Ibo-dominated Eastern Region seceded from the nation, Azikiwe exiled himself to London to teach and to write. With the fall of the short-lived Biafran state, he returned to help in the establishment of a unified government.

Writings: Political: *Liberia in World Affairs (1934),* reprinted as *Liberia in World Politics,* Westport, Conn., Negro Universities Press, 1970; *Renascent Africa,* Lagos, 1937, and London, Cass, 1969, and New York, Negro Universities Press, 1970; *My Odyssey,* London, Hurst, 1970; *Zik, A Selection from the Speeches of Nnamdi Azikiwe,* London, New York, Cambridge University Press, 1961.

Biographical/Critical Sources: African Profiles, Ronald Segal, London, Penguin, 1962, revised 1963; *The New Africans,* New York, Putnam's Sons, 1967.

B

BA, Mallam Amadou Hampaté
b. ca. 1920, southern Mali.
Story-teller, theologian, scholar.

Known as the "sage" of Bamako throughout West Africa, Bâ has published many works in the field of Islamic theology and Africa religions, particularly those of the Bambara and Fulani peoples. He worked for a long period for the *Institute Français d'Afrique Noire* in Dakar, and was a director of Radio Bamako's Cultural Programs. His *Kaidara* presents both the original "oral", text from Fulani and Bâ's French translation of a long, traditional, allegorical poem.

Hampaté Bâ developed a satisfactory Arabic script for the modern Fulani language. Two of his scholarly works are: *L'empire peul du Macina 1818–53* (The History of the Peul Empire of Macina) and a biography, *Tierno Bokar—Le Sage de Bandiagara*. An English version of Ba's printing of a Bambara tale, "The Valiant Knights Kala N'dji Thieni and Kala N'dji Korobba" appeared in *Black Orpheus* magazine, No. 6, November 1959. He collaborated with G. Dieterlen in *Koumen; texte initiatique des pasteurs peuls* (Sacred Texts of Initiation of the Fulani Shepherds). See also Ba's article, published in English, "On Animism (studied) through the Myths of Negro Africa," *Second Congress of Negro Writers and Artists.*

Writings: History and biography: *L'empire peul du Macina 1818–53*, Dakar,

I.F.A.N., 1955; —*Le Sage de Bandiagara* (written with Marcel Cardaire), Paris, Présence Africaine, 1965.

Poetry: *Koumen: texte initiatique des pasteurs peuls* (with G. Dieterlen), Paris, Mouton, 1961; *Kaidara*, Paris, Présence Africaine, 1965.

Article: "On Animism (studied) Through the Myths of Negro Africa," *Second Congress of Negro Writers and Artists*, Paris, Présence Africaine Vol. XXIV–XXV, 1957.

English version of Bambara tale: "The Valiant Knights Kala N'dji Thieni and Kala N'dji Korobba," *Black Orpheus Magazine*, No. 6, November, 1959.

BA, Oumar

b. ca. 1900, Mauritania.
Poet (in Fulani and French), scholar, linguist, editor, administrator.

Locally educated, Oumar Ba is one of the outstanding scholars of Fulani or Peul traditions and verse. He was the long-time head of I.F.A.N. (Institut Fondamental d'Afrique Noire) in Saint-Louis, Senegal.

Eighteen of his Peul language poems have been published in "Dix-huit poémes peuls modernes, présentés par Pierre F. Lacroix" in *Cahiers d'Etudes Africaines*, later republished in his modest volume of 45 pages, *Poèmes peuls modernes* (Modern Peul Poems).

The 24-page collection, *Dialogue ou D'une rive à l'autre* (Dialogue, or, From One Bank to the Other), presents French works of modern sensibility in the same epigrammatic form as his Peul verse.

*Writings:*Poetry: *Poèmes peuls modernes,* Nouakchott, Imp. Mauritanienne, 1965; *Dialogue ou D'une rive à l'autre,* Saint-Louis, Senegal, Etudes Mauritanienne, 1966; eighteen Peul language poems in "Dix-huit poèmes peuls modernes prèsentés par Pierre F. Lacroix," *Cahiers d'Etudes Africaines,* II, 8 (1962), with translations by author.

Scholarship: Fulani-French glossaries and linguistic papers, studies of Toucouleur society, published by I.F.A.N.

BABA, Ahmad al-Tinbukhti

b. 1556, Timbuktu, Mali; d. 1627.
Arabic language Koranic scholar.

Baba was the author of many legal commentaries, 13 of which are still in use in West Africa. Captured in the Moorish invasion of Mali in 1591, Baba refused to serve his captors and was taken in chains to Marrakesh across the Sahara. Only much later in his life was he allowed to return to his home in Timbuktu. His excellent library was famous for years after his death and the general decline of his natal city.

His most important literary work was *Dhail al-Dibadj,* a collection of legends built upon by his greatest student, Abdulrahman Sadi in his *Tarikh al-Sudan.*

His work, *al-kashf wa'l-bayan,* deals with the law concerning the taking of slaves in the Sudan (now Mali). The study is cited in Mervyn Hiskett's introduction to Sir Abubakar Tafawa Balewa's *Shaihu Umar.* Though Islam unequivocally accepted the institution of slavery, Ahmad Baba even at that time appeared fully conscious of the inhumanity of slavery in general and the contradiction of a religious sanction for it. Abubakar's *Shaihu Umar* similarly exploits a situation where the moral-ethical ambiguities of slavery are seen in dramatic situations involving the capture and sale of a mother and her son, Umar. Their long journey ends in death, for her and eventual freedom and honor for the son as a Koranic scholar.

Writings: Legends: *Dhail al-Dibadj.* History: *al-kashf wa'l-bayan.*

Biographical/Critical Sources: Introduction by Mervyn Hiskett to Sir Abubakar Tafawa Balewa's *Shaihu Umar,* London, Longmans, 1967; *Encyclopaedia of Islam,* London, 1934.

BABALOLA, Solomon Adeboye Q.
b. ca. 1930, Yorubaland, Nigeria.
Yoruba-language playwright, scholar, teacher.

Primarily a scholar and teacher, Babalola's major work is *The Content and Form of Yoruba Ijala* which deals with the poems generally sung by female beggars or trained male bards associated with the worship of Ogun. The *ijala* takes one of three forms: the verbal salute, random comment, and, as Babalola puts it, "hearty benediction." This form of poetry served the Yorubas as a political and social commentary of a public nature playing much the same role as newspapers and other organs of opinion and mass communication in the west.
His one play, published in Yoruba in 1958, is *Pàsán sìnà* (The Whip Fell on the Wrong Person).

Writings: Play: *Pàsán sìnà,* Ibadan, Ministry of Education, 1958.
Scholarship: *The Content and Form of Yoruba Ijala,* Oxford, The Clarendon Press, 1966.

BADIAN, Seydou Kouyaté
(formerly known as KOUYATE, Seydu, or Saïdou)
b. April 10, 1928, Bamako, Mali.
Novelist, poet-playwright, economist, government official.

Seydou Badian received his elementary and high school education in Bamako at the Lycée Terrasson de Fougéres, and his university education in France (Montpelier), including a medical degree with the dissertation, "Nine African treatments of yellow fever." On Mali's accession to independence, 1960–61, Badian became his country's Minister of Rural Development and the Plan in the old Senegalese-French Sudan union called Mali. In the succeeding administrations of Mali as it is now constituted with its capital in Bamako, he continued in a ministerial post until 1966 when he took up private medical practice in Koulouba, a suburb of Bamako.

Badian has published one novel, *Sous l'orage* (Under the Storm), published in Avignon (1957), and a French-language poetic work in dramatic form (five acts), *La mort de Chaka* (The Death of Chaka) which treats anew the Zulu hero dealt with in African literature by Thomas Mofolo in his novel *Chaka*. The novel, originally entitled *Kany*, was begun at Montpelier and was nine years in the writing. The life described is that of a large unnamed city (no doubt Bamako) and the surrounding villages along the Niger River in the 1930–50 period.

In 1964, there appeared Badian's Marxist-oriented study of the Africans' conflicting goals and hopes as they try to secure a genuine independence from the West, *Les dirigeants Africains face a leur peuple* (African Leaders and Their People), which won the Grand Prix Littéraire de L'Afrique Noire.

Writings: Novel: *Sous l'orage,* Avignon, Les Presses universelles, 1957.

Poetic drama: *La mort de Chaka,* Paris, Présence Africaine, 1962.

Political science: *Les dirigeants africains face à leur peuple,* Paris, François Maspero, 1964.

BAHELELE, Jacques N.
b. 1911, near Banza Manteke, Congo (Zaïre).
Kikongo novelist, poet, story writer, minister, teacher.

Trained as a teacher at Kimpese mission school from 1937–1941, Bahelele worked at Matadi in the early 1930's, then at Mukimbungu from 1934–37, and at Kimpese school from 1941–46. It was during the last period that he began to write. Receiving his ordination in 1946, Bahelele served as a pastor from 1946–60 at Sundi-Lutete and from 1961–68 as director of the Sundi-Lutete mission. Since 1968 he has served as director at Kinkenge where he is preparing a study of local magic (called *kindoki* in the Bakonga area) for the press.

Bahelele's first work was *Kinzonzi ye ntekolo andi Makundu* (Kinzonzi and his Grandson Makundu), written in 1946 but not published until 1948. Makundu, the young man, learns his peoples' wisdom by studying some 360 proverbs and other traditional lore from his grandfather, but he does not try to give them a Christian significance as had been the case in so much of the earlier Kikongo works dealing with folk material. The author is zealous in his efforts to preserve the authenticity of the stories and sayings. Bahelele's continuing interest in folk materials bore fruit in a second work, *Bingana bia nsi a Kongo* (Congo Country Stories), published in 1953 though completed two years earlier.

In 1954, with a colleague, Joseph Samba from the Congo, Brazzaville, Bahelele published his last work, *Nsamununu za mambu Nzambi* (The Art of Preaching the Word).

During his life Bahelele wrote many hymns, two of which found their way into the collection *Minkunga mia Kinwadi*, which contained the works of many Kikongo poets.

Writings: Novel: *Kinzonzi ye ntekolo andi Makaundu,* Matadi, Imprimerie de la S.M.F., 1948.

Stories: *Bingani bia nsi a Kongo,* Matadi, Impr. de le S.M.F, 1953.

Preaching Manual: *Nsamununu za mambu Nzambi,* with Joseph Samba, 1954.

Poetry: in various journals; two in

Minkunga mia Kintwadi, Léopoldville, LECO, 1956.

Biographical/Critical Sources: Mbololo ya Mpiku, "Introduction à la littérature kikongo," *Research in African Literatures,* African and Afro-American Research Institute, The University of Texas, III, 2, (Fall 1972), pp. 117 ff, with many extracts of poetry in Kikongo and accompanying French translations.

BALOGUN, Ola (Olatunbosun)
b. 1945, Aba, Nigeria.
Playwright, diplomat (writes and publishes in French and English).

Balogun, a Yoruba, after completing high school at King's College in Lagos went on to attend Dakar University in Senegal in 1962–63, and then travelled to France to study for his "licence" in modern literature at the University of Caen, earning that degree in 1966. For the next two years he studied at the Institut des Hautes Études Cinématographiques before returning to Nigeria in 1968 to work with the Film Service of the Ministry of Information. In 1969 he was named press attaché at his country's embassy in Paris. He is married, with one daughter, Delphine Omolara.

His first published volume contains two plays, *Shango,* three acts, and *Le roi-éléphant,* three scenes, 1968. The former works out two contradictory myths of Shango, the rain and storm god of the Yorubas; and the latter employs the African fable of talking animals to make its points about contemporary Africa. In *Le roi-éléphant* an elephant and cock argue and discuss matters until they bring disaster to themselves as a wise old tortoise comments on their foolishness.

The elephant is the greed which leads to hunger and the cock is the greed which leads to fighting and the arrival of soldiers, both destructive of peace, justice and prosperity. At play's end the tortoise ruminates whether the young animals visiting China will come back with the knowledge of how to avoid both starvation and soldiers.

Writings: Plays: *Shango,* followed by *Le roi-éléphant,* in one volume, Paris, P.-J. Oswald, 1968.

Criticism: review of Amos Tutuola's *Ajaiyi and his inherited poverty,* in *Présence Africaine,* No. 65, Paris, 1968.

BAMBOTE, Pierre Makambo
b. April 1, 1932, Ouadda, Central
African Republic.
Poet.

Bamboté's earliest poetry is in the volume published in 1960, *La poésie est dans l'histoire* (Poetry is Inside History). His three succeeding collections of verse are: *Chant funèbre pour un héros d'Afrique. Précédé d'un chant populaire adapté par Sembene Ousmane* (Funeral Dirge for an African Hero, preceded by a popular song adapted by Sembene Ousmane); *Le grand état central* (The Great Central State); and *Le dur avenir* (The Hard Future). His poems, "L'homme qui joue," (The man who plays), "Vous voyez," (You see), and "A Paris," (In Paris), appear in *New Sum of Poetry from the Negro World*.

Bamboté also has published a 160-page illustrated romance, *Les randonnées de Daba (de Quaddà à Bangui)* (The Trip of Daba from Quaddà to Bangui).

Writings: Poetry: *La poésie est dans l'histoire,* Paris, Pierre-Jean Oswald, 1960; republished by Kraus Reprint, Nendeln, Liechtenstein; *Chant funèbre pour un héros d'Afrique. Précédé d'un chant populaire adapté par Sembène Ousmane,* Tunis, Société Nationale d'Edition et de Diffusion, 1962; *Le grand état central,* Goudargues, Gard, France, Editions de la Salamandre, 1965; *Le dur avenir,* Bangui, 1966; three poems, "L'homme qui joue", "Vous voyez", and "A Paris", appear in *New Sum of Poetry from the Negro World,* Paris, Présence Africaine, Vol. 57, 1966.

Illustrated romance: *Les randonées de Daba (de Quaddà à Bangui),* Paris, Eds. La Farandole, 1966.

BANKS–HENRIES, Mrs. A. Doris
(see HENRIES, Mrs. A. Doris
Banks)

BANKOLE, Timothy (or TIMOTHY, Bankole)
b. ca. 1920. Freetown, Sierra Leone.
Poet, journalist, scholar.

After attending schools in Sierra Leone he took his B.A. from London University. As a staff member of the *London Daily Express,* Bankole was the first black African journalist to work for a London newspaper. In 1951, he joined the *Daily Graphic* in London as assistant editor and later went to the Gold Coast (now Ghana) as correspondent for the *London Observer* and the *Ceylon Daily News.* He wrote stories and poems during this period, some of which were broadcast or dramatized on BBC's Overseas and African "Voices" programs.

Bankole's *Kwame Nkrumah—His Rise to Power* shows him to be a perceptive and wide-ranging reporter of the African scene.

Writings: History: *Kwame Nkrumah—His Rise to Power,* London, Allen and Unwin, 1955.

BARBOSA, Domingos Caldas (also CALDAS)
b. ca. 1738, on board a slave ship destined from Angola to Brazil;
d. November, 1800, in Lisbon.
Poet.

Son of a Portuguese father, a merchant, and a black Angolan mother, Barbosa received his education at the Jesuit College in Rio, served in the local military forces in the frontier province of Sacramento, Brazil, and fled to Lisbon after the Spanish took over Sacramento in the 1770's. Caldas published his first verse in 1775 and subsequently founded in Portugal, with his fellow poets, the Academy of Fine Arts, later called the Nova Arcádia (The New Arcadia), becoming the Academy's first president.

Though Caldos wrote many poems in the conventional metrics of the day, his popularity was due to the success of the *modinhas* and *lundás*, forms introduced from Brazil which employed African (Angolan) tonalities, rhythms and moods. The *modinhas* were languid, limpidly passionate songs, considered dangerously voluptuous and enervating by William Beckford, a British visitor to the Portuguese court at the height of their popularity. The *lundás* were less ambiguous and resembled the *batuque* and *samba* of later fame and were frank celebrations of erotic love. The uninhibited dancing which accompanied the original Angolan "lundás" was eliminated in Brazilian and later Portuguese performances, becoming naturalized and somewhat stylized. The *lundás* retained, however, a lively and broadly sexual flavor, becoming the first African music and poetry to be completely accepted by any European culture.

Writings: Poetry: *Collecção de poesias feitas,* Lisbon, 1775; *A doença,* Lisbon, 1777; *Os viajantes ditosos,* Lisbon, 1790; *A saloia namorada, ou O remedio e casar,* Lisbon, 1793; *A escola dos ciosos,* Lisbon, 1795; *Viola de Lereno,* 2 volumes, Lisbon, 1798, and Rio de Janeiro, 1944; *Poema mariano,* Vitoria, Brazil, 1854.

Biographical/Critical Sources: William Beckford, *Italy, Spain, and Portugal,* New York, 1845; Oneyda Alvarenga, *Música*

popular brasilēna, Mexico, 1947; J. Jahn, *Neo-African Literature,* New York, Grove Press, 1968.

BARBOSA, Jorge (also VERA–CRUZ)
b. 1902, Santiago Island, Cape Verde.
Poet, story teller, customs official.

Born into an educated Creole family, Barbosa early employed the local vernacular of Portuguese in his free verse which was influenced by the Brazilian poets of his day. His *Arquipélago* (1935) dealt with the poverty and suffering of his fellow islanders. He helped found the early cultural journal, *Claridad* (Clarity) in 1936 which has given space to two generations of regional poets who have developed the local color and vernacular possibilities of Caboverdean writing.

Barbosa's second volume of verse, *Ambiente* (The Circle), a 98-page work issued in 1941, and his third collection, *Caderno de um ilheu* (An Islander's Notebook), some 98 pages, was published in 1956. The latter volume won the Overseas Literary Prize in 1956 awarded by the publishers, Agência-Geral do Ultramar. Individual poems have appeared in numerous reviews and anthologies.

Writings: Poetry: *Arquipélago,* 1935; *Ambiente,* Praia, Cape Verde, Minerva de Cabo Verde, 1941; *Caderno de um ilheu,* Lisbon, Agência–Geral do Ultramar, 1956; poems in *Claridad,* Praia, Cape Verde; *Antologia da ficção cabo-verdiana contemporânea,* Praia, Cape Verde, 1960; *Modernos poetas contemporâneos,* Praia, Imprensa Nacional de Cabo Verde, 1961; and *Poetas e contistas africanos do expressão portuguêsa,* Sâo Paulo, Editôra Brasiliense, 1963.

BARRETO, Rui Moniz (see NOGAR, Rui)

BART–WILLIAMS, Gaston
b. 1938, Sierra Leone.
Playwright, poet, short story and radio feature writer.

Bart–William's works include poems published in *Pergamon Poets–2,* a BBC play, *A Bouquet of Carnations,* and features for the BBC, the Canadian Broadcasting Corporation as well as for radio stations in Sweden, Germany, and Norway. He has won several prizes including the "All African Short Story Award" (sponsored by the Congress for Cultural Freedom) and the Michael Karolyi International Award (France). His poems appeared originally in such journals as *The London Magazine* and *Studio Du Mont* (Mountain Studio). His one mimeographed volume of verse, *Poems* (Cologne, 1964) and a mimeographed play, *Curse Your God and Die* (Cologne, 1965) are his only major works "in print." Two radio plays, *In Praise of Madness* and *Uhuru,* the latter produced on West German radio, December 13, 1969, remain in manuscript.

Writings: Poems in *Pergamon Poets–2, Poetry from Africa,* Oxford, Pergamon Press, 1968; *Commonwealth Poems of Today,* London, John Murray, 1967; and *Black Orpheus,* London, Longmans, 1964; *The London Magazine; Studio Du Mont.*
Plays for radio: "A Bouquet of Carnations" (BBC), "Uhuru" (West German Radio), "In Praise of Madness."

Mimeographed volume of verse: *Poems,* Cologne, 1964;
Mimeographed play: *Curse Your God and Die.*

BEBEY, Francis
b. July 15, 1929, Douala, Cameroon.
Poet, novelist, short story writer, composer, guitarist.

Educated through high school in Cameroon schools, Bebey attended the Sorbonne where he studied French literature and music. He has worked with the African Service of the French National Radio, Cameroon Radio, and Radio Ghana, and has been serving with the Information Office of UNESCO in Paris since the early 1960's. He is the author of *La Radiodiffusion en Afrique Noire* (Broadcasting in Black Africa), and his poetry is represented in Clive Wake's *An Anthology of African and Malagasy Poetry in French.*

In 1968, Bebey published *Embarras et Cie* (Embarrassed and Co.), a collection of nine stories, each followed by a poem. His novel, *Le fils d'Agatha Moudio* (Agatha Moudio's Son), was published in Yaoundé, 1967, but has recently been issued in the Heinemann African Writers Series, London, 1971. A very amusing work, it concerns the complications of being in love with the "wrong" woman in a society not changing fast enough to allow a man to marry his true love without getting the whole village, and his loving mother, involved. Translated into Italian, Dutch and German, and winner of the Grand Prix Littéraire de l'Afrique Noire, this tale of the very strong and somewhat wily fisherman from Wouri (on the Cameroonian coast below Douala) should become very popular. The protagonist, Mbenda, is a modern man in a complex African setting.

At last report, Bebey's new novel, *La poupée ashanti* (The Ashanti Doll), was ready for publication by CLE, Yaoundé.

Writings: Stories and poems: *Embarras et Cie, nouvelles et poèmes,* Yaoundé, Eds CLE, 1968; poems in *An Anthology of African and Malagasy Poetry in French,* Clive Wake, editor, Oxford, Three Crowns Press, 1965.

Novel: *Le fils d'Agatha Moudio,* Yaoundé, CLE, 1967, 2nd edition, 1968; translated as *Agatha Moudio's Son* by Joyce A. Hutchinson, London, Heinemann, 1971.

Music: Recordings: *Spirituals du Cameroun; Pièce pour guitare seule,* Paris, Disque Ocora, 1965; *Concerts pour un vieux mosque,* and *Le chant d'Ibadan: Black Tears,* place and company not known.

Musicology: *La musique africaine moderne,* Paris, Présence Africaine, 1967; *Musique de l'Afrique,* Paris, 1969.

Study: *La radiodiffusion en afrique noire,* Paris, 1963.

BEDIAKO, Kwabena Asare (see KONADU, Asare)

BEMBA, Sylvain
b. ca. 1930, Congo, Brazzaville.
Short story writer.

Bemba's first success was the story, "La Chambre Noire" (The Black Room), which won first prize for the Best African Story in French sponsored by the magazine *Preuves* in 1964. This story in English translation is in Ezekiel Mphahlele's *African Writing Today.* Recently Bemba has been Chief-Editor of

L'Agence Congolaise d'Information, Brazzaville.

Writings: Story, "La Chambre Noire," *Preuves* magazine, Paris, 1964; in English translation, *African Writing Today,* Ezekiel Mphahlele, editor, London, Penguin, 1967.

BENGANI, Redvus Robert
b. ca. 1899, Gordon Memorial Mission Station, near Pomeroy, Msinga, District of Natal, South Africa.
Zulu novelist, educator.

Bengani was enrolled in Gordon Memorial Mission School where he passed Standard VI, roughly equivalent to eighth grade, in 1916. He went on to St. Chad's College where he obtained his Teachers' Certificate in 1918, and from 1918 until 1920 he was head teacher at the Ngonyama and Douglas Mission Schools. In 1921 he enrolled at Amanzimtoti (Adams) College where he obtained the Higher Teachers' Certificate. He was head teacher at several other institutions, including Blaauwbosch School, Edendale School, and Machibise School. In 1952 he was appointed supervisor of schools for the Dundee Circuit. At the end of 1961 he retired from public service.

His two novels are *Uphethani* (What Do You Decide?), and *Wozuyithathe,* (Will You Begin The Story?).

Writings: Novels, *Uphethani,* 1939; *Wozuyithathe,* 1940, both published by Shuter and Shooter, Pietermaritzburg.

BESSA–VICTOR, Geraldo (also Vítor, Geraldo Bessa)

61

Bessa–Victor

b. 1917, Luanda, Angola
Poet, short story writer, essayist, lawyer.

Son of an assimilated Black African family, Bessa–Victor received an excellent education, including training as a lawyer in Lisbon. Though he has not identified with any "independence" or "African" movement, his verse does defend the African and his culture while tipping a hat to Portuguese culture. He now practices law in Lisbon and is a-political.

Bessa–Victor's *Ecos dispersos* (Scattered Echoes) of 1941 reflected his readings in an already dated Portuguese poetry. His *Ao som das marimbas* (To the Sound of the Marimbas), his second volume of verse, published two years later, demonstrated his search for more African themes.

As he became aware of the francophone writers involved in the "Négritude" movement, his poetry became more intensely evocative of his African past, as seen in *Mucanda*. His next two volumes, *Debaixo de céu* (Under the Sky), and *Cubata abandonada* (The Abandoned Vat), show him continuing to enrich his poetry with African themes and a more original treatment of language. The latter volume received the Camilo Pessanha Prize. His last three volumes of poetry are now available from Kraus Reprint. French translations of some of the poems in three collections by Gaston-Henry Aufrère appeared in 1967 in *Poèmes africains*.

Nostalgia for the vanishing Creole days is reflected in his 27-page collection of stories, *Sanzala sem batuque* (The Slave House with Gaiety).

Writings: Poetry: *Ecos dispersos,* Lisbon, Imprensa Portugal Brazil, 1941; *Ao som das marimbas*, Lisbon, Livraria Portugália, 1943; *Mucanda*, Braga, Editôra Pax, 1946, 1964, second edition, 1965; *Debaixo de céu*, Lisbon, Editoriale Império, 1949, 1958; 2nd ed., Editôra Pax, 1966; *Cubata abandonade. Poesias de motivos negro-africanos*, Lisbon, Agência–Geral de Ultramar, 1958; 2nd ed., editôra Pax, 1966; French translations of poems in last three volumes by Gaston–Henry Aufrère in *Poèmes africains*, Braga, Editôra Pax, 1967.

Stories: *Sanzala sem batuque*, Braga, Ed. Pax, 1967.

Essays: *Minha terra e minha dama. Ensaios sôbre temas literários de África* (My Land and My Lady: Essays on Literary Themes of Africa), Lisbon, 1952; and *A poesia e a política* (Of Poetry and Politics), Luanda, 1937.

BETI, Mongo (favorite pseudonym for Alexandre Biyidi; also wrote one novel under pseudonym, BOTO, Eza)
b. June 30, 1932, Mbalmayo, near Yaoundé, Cameroon.
Novelist, short story writer, teacher.

Alexandre Biyidi was educated in local schools in and around Mbalmayo until his expulsion at the age of 14. Accepted by the lycée at Yaoundé, he took the French B.A. in 1951. He went to France the same year, studying first at the Faculty of Letters at the University of Aix-en-Province, and later at the Sorbonne in Paris, taking the "Licence," or the "B.A." (Honors). Beti, the pseudonym Biyidi has used in writing three of his four novels, is, along with Camara Laye, the most famous and well-regarded of all the francophone writers from Black Africa with Beti the professional critic's usual favorite.

Beti wrote and published his first novel, *Ville cruelle* (Cruel City), while he was still a student at Aix, under the pseudonym of Eza Boto. Though repudiated by its author along with the nom de plume, this work strongly exploits the bewilderment, tension and hostility felt by many rural Africans pushing into work at industrial sites set up by European firms in the African world. The novel is set in Tanga, the capital of "the kingdom of logs," with its giant saw mills, rail yards, massive machinery, and men from many different villages and even different linguistic groups. Here the men and their equally confused families are hurried into a proletarian world that threatens and attracts them at the same time. Weakly structured and often melodramatic, the novel is obviously a first effort, but it foreshadows the humor, intelligence, and cutting satirical thrust so evident in the later works.

Possibly the greatest flaw in *Ville cruelle* is in the rambling, seemingly pointless monologues of the central character, but the second novel, *Le Pauvre Christ de Bomba* (The Poor Christ of Bomba), demonstrates Beti's sure handling of the "exclamatory" monologue in the mind of the acolyte Denis to indict both the Church and France. Serving the well-meaning but usually obtuse Reverend Father Superior Drumont, Denis, naive and trustful, has one experience after the other which educate the reader if not himself to the baser, though sometimes humorous, aspects of religious and colonial life in the Cameroons of the 1930's and early 1940's.

Drumont constantly runs into small disasters and telling "non-comprehensions" and never understands his wily, lecherous cook, Zacharie, whose uproarious amours offer Beti almost a Rabelaisian variety of weapons to puncture the countless, if often petty, cruelties of colonialism. He mocks subtly, occasionally brutally, the so-called Christian mission in Africa and the civilizing role the French proclaimed to justify their rape of African wealth and independence. French communists delighted in the attacks, and the Soviet Union hurried to seek publication, though reports have it that the Russians found Zacharie's lubricious exploits too frank and ribald for their puritanic tastes. This vivacious novel has appeared in the Heinemann African Writers Series in a translation by Gerald Moore. It has also been re-issued in its original French format by Kraus Reprint.

Mission terminée (winner of the Sainte–Beuve Prize, 1948) for many readers is the most clever and articulate of his works. Humorously and ironically, Beti manipulates his naive hero, Medza, in and out of bizarre situations which gradually build up an indictment of the European school-system which unsettled two generations of Africans, alienating them from their own culture and giving most of them little more than the rudiments of Western culture. Medza, newly failed in his exam for the "Bac," returns to his father's village just in time to be appointed a special envoi to the distant town in the "brush" whence his uncle's wife has fled with her lover. Accepted as a paragon of learning, the young man goes off reluctantly to seek out the fast-moving, errant wife. Encountering his heroic-sized first cousin, Zambo, the hero goes through trial after trial of his manhood in the rustic, rambunctious setting of Zambo's cronies, conniving relatives, and seductive girls. Zambo becomes a sort of Sancho Panza to Medza's Quixote and at book's close the two wander off into "the world"—neither Africa nor Europe in any realistic sense, but rather into a realm of experience in a post-colonial world. At the least, Medza has learned "that the tragedy which our nation is suffering today is that of a man left to his own devices in a world which does not belong to him, which he has not made and does not understand." This novel, translated by Peter Green as *Mission to Kala* has been extremely popular with English readers of African literature.

Beti's last novel, *Le Roi Miraculé, Chronique des Essazam*, was translated as *King Lazarus*. The novel sets up a confrontation between the good-natured, permissive pagan king of a traditional community and the missionary ardours of Le Guen, Drumont's old vicar from *The Poor Christ of Bomba*. Though considering himself more sensitive and modern than the "bumbling" Drumont, Le Guen in his zeal to Christianize the court of the king stirs up a hornet's nest

of confusion and anger. The French Colonial Office, depite its official interest in the good of the Church, loves order and decorum more and sees to it that Rome and Paris have Le Guen recalled.

Though not polemical, Beti leaves no doubt as to the harm European values and the Christian religion, imposed in ignorance and often in violence, have done to the African's soul and his total society.

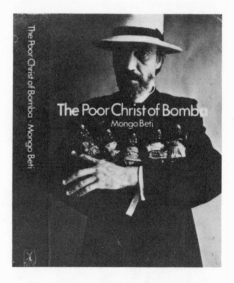

Despite three extremely well-received novels and increasing sales of his works in French and other languages, Beti has been forced to fall back on teaching to support himself and his growing family. Taking the Aggregation (akin to the American M.A.) in 1966 from the University of Paris, he has taught first in the small Bretagne village of Lamballe, and since his last degree, at a lycée in the Norman city of Rouen where he teaches classical Greek, Latin, and French literature.

A convinced Marxist even today, and unable to accept the Yaoundé regime of

President Ahidjo, Beti wrote articles for the anti-colonial journals *Tumultueux Cameroun* and the *Revue Camerouaise* and otherwise allied himself with the opposition to those in control of his home-land and to the Gaullist government of France. Married to a Normandy wife, father of three children, and unwelcome in Yaoundé, he lives in relative isolation from African events and intellectual currents. Though Beti declares himself to have works in progress, he has not returned to the Cameroon for ten years. In a recent unpublished letter he wonders when, if ever, the vein so joyously discovered and exploited in the five-year creative surge from 1953 to 1958 when he wrote four novels and the story, "Sans amour et sans haine" (Without Love or Hate), will be found again.

Writings: Novels: *Ville cruelle,* Paris, Editions Africaines, 1954; originally in *Présence Africaine 16, Trois écrivains noirs,* Paris, Présence Africaine, 1954; re-issued in paperback, Paris, Présence Africaine, 1971; *Le pauvre Christ de Bomba,* Paris, Laffont, 1956; re-issued in original French format, Kraus Reprint, Nendeln, Liechtenstein, 1970; and in English translation by Gerald Moore as *The Poor Christ of Bomba,* London, Heinemann, 1971; *Mission terminée,* Paris, Ed. Buchet Chastel/Corrêa, 1957; translated by Peter Green as *Mission to Kala,* London, Frederick Muller, 1958; New York, Macmillan, 1958; Heinemann African Writers Series, London, 1964; *Le roi Miraculé. Chronique des Essazam,* Paris, Buchet Chastel/Corrêa, 1958, translated as *King Lazarus,* London, Muller, 1961; now in Heinemann paperback, London, 1970.

Biographical/Critical Sources: Thomas Melone, *Mongo Béti: L'homme et le destin,* Paris, Présence Africaine, 1971, also: Anne Tibble, *Africa/English Literature,* London, Peter Owen, 1965; *Mongo Beti; écrivain camerounais,* text selected and discussed by Roger Mercier and Monique and Simon Battestini, Paris, Nathan, 1964.

BHALO, Ahmad Nassir bin Juma
(see NASSIR, Ahmad)

BHELY–QUENUM, Olympe
b. September 26, 1928, Donukpa (now Cotonou), Dahomey.
Novelist, journalist, short story writer.

Born into the ruling nation of the Quénum, Olympe enjoyed a certain amount of family prosperity, his father being a school-teacher. From 1938 to 1942 he attended the Ecole des Pères, and finished secondary schooling before beginning three years of wandering through Dahomey, neighboring Togo, Nigeria and the Gold Coast (now Ghana). Learning English, he went to work for the British firm of John Walkden and Co., staying from 1945 to 1948.

Having saved a modest sum, he went to France to study for the French "Baccalauréat classique" in the Collège Littré at Avrance in Normandy after a year of serious sickness in Marseilles. He passed the first part (Latin and Greek) of the "bachot" in 1952 and after winning the Zellidja scholarship in 1954, he was able to travel widely through French Equatorial Africa in the summer, returning to France to pass the second part of the bachelor's degree in philosophy the next year. After more study he won a Certificate in General Literature at Caen University in Normandy in 1957

Bhêly-Quénum

and then began teaching at Paul-Langevin Lycée at Suresnes in north central France.

The Institut des Hautes Etudes d'Outre-Mer awarded him a certificate in diplomatic studies in 1962, and he then began his studies in sociology at the Sorbonne. He also has studied at the Academy of International Law at The Hague and has served in the French consular service at Consulates General at Genoa, Milan, Florence and at the French Embassy in Rome. Having learned Italian in the early 1950's and having served in Italy, he was inspired to write his *Reactions de la presse Italienne devant les événéments Africains* (The Italian Press' Reaction to African Events). Though he is a close student of African and Islamic beliefs, Olympe is a fervent Catholic.

Bhêly-Quénum is presently editor and managing director of *La Vie Africaine* and works for UNESCO in Paris, as a full-time journalist. He is married and has four children.

His stories have appeared in French, Italian, Swiss and Canadian journals, including the Dakar review *Bingo*, which is devoted to African writing. He has also collaborated with S.A.M. Pratt on a seven-volume *Practical French*.

Bhêly-Quénum's first novel, *Un piège sans fin* (The Endless Trap), begun at Caen University, deals with the feelings and tribulations of being black in Europe and colonial Africa. It was widely hailed in France and well received in other European countries. His second novel, *Le chant du lac* (The Song of the Lake) won the Literary Grand Prize for Black Africa in 1966. Driss Chraibi, the well-known Moroccan writer, quickly adapted it for a one-hour presentation on French television. His third work, a novelette, *Liaison d'un été* (The Summer Affair), appeared in book form in 1968, but originally saw print in *Bingo* (April, 1961). (J. A. Ramsaran in *New Approaches to African Literature* states *Liaison d'un été* also was published by Stock, Paris, 1961, but other bibliographic sources do not confirm this.)

In the introduction to *Liaison d'un été*, Bhêly-Quénum recalls the day 20 years before, about 1948 or 1949, when he met the famous surrealist André Breton and fell under his influence. He writes of how Breton asked him whether he was writing anything and of his reply that he had not—that he had only a recent dream. Breton encouraged him "to tell" the dream and tell it he did for 15 minutes. He still remembers Breton's response: "It's weird, but it's a dream of the primitive state. I see that you have not yet encountered Freud, but you ought to write out this dream, before becoming a writer."

The dream was put down on paper, entitled "Promenade dans la forêt," as the first of eight "histoires" in the book. It is dated "Avranches, Octobre–decembre 1949." Each of the other tales or fragments are also dated: "Les lois de la forêt," "Cotounou–Abomey, Aout, 1954," "Les Brigands, Paris 1963," etc. The title story "Liaison d'un été" is dated "Domville-les-bain, été, 1959."

Bhely–Quénum's first articles generally were published anonymously in Norman and Parisian journals between 1956–1959. The first signed article appeared in 1957 as a lively response to a Normandy Deputy of Parliament's article, "Le feu couve en Afrique" (Curfew in Africa), which had sneered at the independence movements in Africa. There was some fear for his position as a teacher at the Lycée de Coutance when the article was published, but his fellow professors supported him. Moving to Paris in 1958, Bhêly–Quénum wrote for the short-lived journal La Vie Africaine which he edited from 1962 to 65. Three months after the journal's demise he and his Norman-French wife began to publish L'Afrique Actuelle, the first bilingual (French and English) journal devoted to African writing and affairs.

The French have always been inordinately proud of their language. Accordingly, the comments of André Retif concerning Bhêly–Quénum's second novel, Chant du lac are of importance, for they could be said of all of his work: "A master of the French language to which he acts as if it were his religion. The writing is crafted, elegant, aristocratic." (trans, D.H.). And as for the "flow" or narrative power, an unnamed critic in the review Dialogues wrote of the same work: " . . . in its continuous action it can be named in the same breath as Hemingway's The Old Man and the Sea."

Two of his novels remain unpublished: La vague déferlée (The Combers), his first novel which was considered too "ferocious" in its picture of Paris slum life and French provincial mores to see print; and Forces obscure (Mysterious Force), on a Dahomean theme. Jahnheinz Jahn in his Bibliography of Creative African Writing, 1971, also lists two other novels in manuscript: Les amazones du roi (The King's Amazons) and Une grande amitié (A Great Friendship).

Two of his published stories are: "Les brigands" (The Thieves), appearing in Fraternité–Matin (Ivory Coast), and "La reine au bras d'or" (The Queen with the Golden Arm), published in France–Eurafrique (1964).

Writings: Novels: Un piège sans fin, Paris, Edition Stock, 1960; Le chant du lac, Paris, Présence Africaine, 1965; adapted for French television.

Novelette: Liaison d'un été, Paris, Sagerep, 1968; originally in the journal Bingo, Dakar, April, 1961, possibly also Paris, Stock, 1961.

Stories: "Les brigands," in Fraternité–Matin, Ivory Coast; "La reine au bras d'or," in France–Eurafrique, 1964.

Unpublished novels: La vague déferlée; Forces obscures; other novels in manuscript listed by Jahnheinz Jahn in Bibliography of Creative African Writing, Nendeln, Kraus–Thomson, 1971: Les amazones du roi; Une grande amitié.

Biographical/Critical Source: Olympe Bhêly–Quénum, écrivain dahoméen (Olympe Bhêly–Quénum, Dahomean Writer), text, chosen and discussed by Roger Mercier, and Monique and Simon Battestini, Paris, Nathan, 1964.

BIKOUTA–MENGA, Gaston-Guy (see pseudonym, MENGA, Guy)

BIYIDI, Alexandre (pseudonyms: BETI, Mongo and BOTO, Eza; see BETI, Mongo)

BLAY, J. Benibengor
b. ca. 1900, Ghana.
Novelist, poet, dramatist.

Blay was educated in Ghana and has traveled and studied in Europe and the United States at the university level. He has been a member of the Ghanaian parliament, and has published 19 works in various categories and many radio scripts, many of them issued by his own company, Benibengor Book Agency.

Blay's five novelettes are: *Emilia's Promise and Fulfilment* (Ghana, n.d., but 1944 and still in print), *Dr. Bengta Wants a Wife*, and a sequel, *After the Wedding* (1967 and still in print), *Coconut Boy*, 1970, a work of 134 pages, and *Alomo*, also 1970, a briefer work of 72 pages.

Four collections of his verse are published: *Immortal Deed*, 1940; *Memoirs of the War*, 1946; *King of the Human Frame. A Tale in Verse*, 1947, and *Ghana Sings*, 1965, which carried an introduction by Kwame Nkrumah. The first three collections appear in the single volume, *Thoughts of a Youth*. A volume of his early stories, *Be Content with Your Lot* (1947), introduction by J. Abedi Boafo, had its recent third edition in 1969.

Though Blay's fiction is pedestrian and derivative of outdated works by European or American standards, he has found readers in Ghana's "penny" press and among juveniles in school. His poetry is uninspired but does deal with the usual problems of change and pain in the evolving Africa of the preindependence year.

Writings: Novelettes: *Emilia's Promise and Fulfilment*, probably first edition, Accra, 1944, second edition, Accra, Waterville Publishing House, 1967; *Dr. Bengta Wants a Wife*, London, Blackheath Press, 1953; *After The Wedding*, Accra, Waterville Publishing House, 1967; *Coconut Boy*, Accra, West Africa Publishers, 1970; *Alomo*, Accra, West African Publishers, 1970.

Poetry: *Immortal Deeds*, London, Stockwell, 1940; *Memoirs of the War*, Ilfracombe, Devon, Stockwell, 1946; *King of the Human Frame. A Tale in Verse*, Ilfracombe, Stockwell, 1947; *Ghana Sings*, Accra, Waterville Publishing House, 1965; first three in single volume, *Thoughts of A Youth*, Aboso, Ghana, Benibengor Book Agency, 1967.

Stories: *Be Content with Your Lot*, 1947; third edition, Aboso, Ghana, Benibengor Book Agency, 1961; *Parted Lovers*, Accra(?), 1948, second edition, Aboso, Benibengor Books Agency, 1968; *Operation Witchcraft*, Accra(?), 1956, second edition, Aboso, Benibengor, 1968; *Love in a Clinic*, Aboso, Benibengor, 1957, many later editions; *Stubborn Girl*, Accra, Guinea Press, 1958, new ed., 1968, Aboso, Benibengor; and *Folk Tales* (also called *Tales for Boys and Girls*), London, Macmillan, 1966, and Aboso, Benibengor, 1966.

BOETIE, Dugmore
b. ca. 1920; d. November, 1966; South Africa.
Novelist.

Dugmore Boetie came to letters the hard way; by his own confession, he lived the life of a tramp, jail-bird, cripple, and con man. As his editor Barney Simon explains in his epilogue, the work published as *Familiarity Is the Kingdom of the Lost: The Story of a Black Man in South Africa* is not a biography. But, he goes on, "I don't know what it is. A book certainly . . . covering years (early 'thirties to early 'fifties) that he (Boetie) knew, and set mostly in places that he knew." As "Duggie" *bled* Barney Simon for money for pages that only slowly got written, so the book, a first person narrative, offers the imagined revenges and victories of the hero, Dugmore, who goes to war, loses a leg, goes in and out of prisons, becomes a dope peddler, etc. He is constantly in trouble and just about to get out of it with a clever trick when he gets caught again.

Chapter 14 of *Familiarity* first appeared in *The Classic*, the South African literary magazine edited by Nat Nakasa and afterwards by Barney Simon. Nadine Gordimer did the preface to the complete work that explains the "truth" of the book. She writes, "there is an accusation to be read in the fantasy of the people, too. Dying, still lying, Dugmore Boetie produced his 'true, hot book,' that nothing could kill inside him."

Writings: Novel: *Familiarity Is the Kingdom of the Lost: The Story of a Black Man in South Africa,* London, Cresset Press, 1969, New York, Dutton, 1970; paperback, Greenwich, Connecticut, Fawcett, 1970.

BOGNINI, Joseph Miezan
b. 1936, Grand-Bassam, Ivory Coast.
Poet.

Bognini was educated in secondary schools in the Ivory Coast and then attended the School of Architecture in Paris beginning in 1958.

He is represented in Clive Wake's *An Anthology of African and Malagasy Poetry in French* and in *New Sum of Poetry from the Negro World.* Ellen Conroy Kennedy translated a few of his poems in "Four African Poets" in *African Forum,* Summer, 1966. His two collections in the original French are the verse volumes: *Ce dur appel de l'espoir* (The Hard Call of Hope) and *Les âmes vives* (Live Souls).

Writings: Poetry: *Ce dur appel de l'espoir,* Paris, Présence Africaine, 1960, 1962; *Les âme vives,* Présence Africaine, 1962; poems in *An Anthology of African and Malagasy Poetry,* Clive Wake, editor, Oxford, Three Crowns Press, 1965; *New Sum of Poetry from the Negro World,* Présence Africaine, Vol. 57, 1966; poems in "Four African Poets," translated by Ellen Conroy Kennedy, *African Forum,* Vol. 2, No. 1, Summer, 1966.

BOKWE, John Knox
b. March 15, 1855, at Ntselamanzi, near Lovedale; d. February 22, 1922; South Africa.
Xhosa poet, song-writer, musician, teacher, preacher.

Son of a former teacher at Lovedale, the famous mission school, John Knox Bokwe was born at Ntsalamanzi, near Lovedale, where he received his early education from 1865 to 1869, studying under William Daniel Msindwana and William Kobe Ntsikana, a son of Ntsika the "prophet." During the next three years he was under the tutelage of the historian George McCall Theal of

Bokwe

Lovedale's College Department, and for a while served as private secretary to the school's principal, James Stewart. In 1873 he took charge of the local telegraph and post office and also served as bookkeeper and cashier for Lovedale, continuing in this service for twenty years. He contributed articles to and helped edit William Gqoba's journal, the *Isigidimi SamaXosa* (The Xhosa Courier), published at Lovedale.

Introduced to Western music by Mrs. Stewart, Bokwe became a good pianist and began to write the words and music for hymns. The hymnbook *Amaculo ase-Rabe* (Presbyterian Hymns), published in 1885, contained the work of several leading Xhosa clergymen, among them, Tiyo Soga, and several of Bokwe's own works, including "I-culo lika Ntsikana" (Ntsikana's hymn) and "Vuku Deborah" (Arise Deborah). Years later, in 1947,

these two hymns were specially sung at Lovedale for the British Royal Family. Others of his compositions appeared in the *Isigidimi* paper. The best of these was "Intlaba-mKosi yakwaTixo" (The Battle Cry of the Lord) with words by William Kobe Ntsikana set to solfa music by Bokwe. He translated many sermons from English to Xhosa, conducted and took important parts in the Lovedale Choir, and in 1879 translated and published some of the sermons of the then famous C. H. Spurgeon. In 1874, and again in 1892, he toured the United Kingdom performing his own and others' hymns in Xhosa.

In 1897, Bokwe left his regular position as chief of the Postal-Telegraph office for an editorial position in King William's Town on the successful paper *Imvo zabantsundu* (Opinion of the Blacks), joining John Tengo Jabavu as a partner. Writing both in English and Xhosa, Bokwe stayed only a year. His very first article is believed to have been published on January 6, 1898, entitled "Build a good house and keep a good fire."

Leaving his partner Jabavu, Bokwe was ordained a minister in late 1899 or early 1900 and took over at Ugie where he helped construct a new church building and 13 new mission stations in the Ugie, Maclear and Tsolo districts. During this period his biography in Xhosa and English, *Ibali lika Ntsikana* (The Story of Ntsikana) was published in 1904. Ten years later, having gathered much new material from friends and children of the prophet Ntsika, and such authorities as John Muir Vimbe (1808–1898), he brought out a large, augmented edition.

One of Bokwe's most significant actions was to help found the South African Native College at Fort Hare which became the great center of university training for Africans in that area. The new college opened in 1916 with Bokwe's being encharged with opening ceremonies featuring the South African Prime Minister, General Louis Botha, as guest of honor.

At the time of his death, Bokwe was working on a metrical translation of the psalms into Xhosa. He left his widow Leta Ncheni, four sons, and two daughters. One son, Rosebery Thandw'efika Bokwe (1900–1963), became famous as a medical doctor. One of his daughters, Frieda Debora Nobusi Bokwe, married Zachariah Keodirelang Matthews (1901–1968) who became an important politician and writer. Bokwe's strong mind but small stature earned him the sobriquet "Umdengetenga," or "Tall-with-the-stick."

Writings: Biography: *Ibali lika Ntsikana,* Lovedale, 1904, augmented second edition, 1914.

Hymns: in *Amaculo ase Rabe* (or *Lovedale),* Lovedale, 1885.

Biographical/Critical Source: Albert S. Gérard, *Four African Literatures,* Berkeley, University of California Press, 1971.

BOLAMBA, Antoine–Roger
b. 1913, Boma, Zaïre.
Poet, journalist.

Bolamba serves as editor of *La Voix du Congolais* in which he has published numerous articles and poems. He has published one study of the evolution of African woman under colonialism, *Etudes sociales. Les Problèmes de l'évolution de la femme noire* (Social Studies: The Problems of the Evolution of Black Women).

His first volume of poetry, published in 1947, *Premier essais* (First Tries), and his second, *Esanzo: chants pour mon pays* (Esanzo: Songs for my Country), 1956, mark him as one of the earliest published Congolese poets. He is represented in Moore and Beier's *Modern Poets from Africa.*

Bolamba's poetry is often slack and full of trite expressions. Though intensely patriotic, his work generally is not impressive, for it offers neither genuine passion nor visions of a convincing reality. There is some evidence of the influence of the great poet from Martinique, Aimé Césaire, on Bolamba's work.

Writings: Poetry: *Premier essais,* Elisabethville, Congo, Eds. de l'Essor du Congo, 1947; *Esanzo: chants pour mon pays,* Paris, Présence Africaine, 1956; poems in *Modern Poets from Africa,* Moore and Beier, eds., London, Penguin, 1963.

Social history: *Etudes sociales.Les Problèmes de l'évolution de la femme noire,* Elisabethville, Eds. de l'Essor du Congo, 1949–50.

BOLOMBO, G. (but possibly only a pseudonym for an unknown author)
b. ?, Zaïre.
Novelist (in French).

Although Jahnheinz Jahn in his *Bibliography of Creative African Writing* for undisclosed reasons brands Bolombo's supposed novel *Kavwanga* a "forgery," Judith Gleason writes eloquently of this work in *This Africa.* The novel deals with a subject surprisingly rare in African fiction, the psychological difficulties of an African lad who rejects his family's traditional beliefs for Christianity and becomes a Catholic priest.

Kavwanga, the hero, lives in a small village of 35 huts and some 150 persons.

Bolombo

The Belgians are firmly in control when the book begins, but are disliked and feared. Kavwanga's uncle, a more powerful and feared person in the Congolese family than the father, after listening to ancestral voices, refuses to pay the Belgian-imposed head-tax, and as a result is sent to a forced labor camp. Kavwanga's older brother, just 18, is then obliged to try to earn the tax by working for a European company. At this critical juncture in the lives of the family and the village, and when everyone feels the weight of the colonial regime, Sitefani, a catechist of the Christian faith, comes to the area to teach the stories of the New Testament.

The sensitive Kavwanga, then eleven, is attracted to the new teachings and slowly moves toward a full acceptance of Christianity, despite the hostility of his father and his uncle. After many spiritual crises, the most important occurring in a football accident in secondary school, Kavwanga, long since christened Jean, returns to his village as L'Abbé Jean. But he has had almost daemonic struggles in his psyche to accept this role and to exercise authority outside the traditional world of belief.

As his village's secret societies strike out to hold the people in line against the Belgian world, so Jean, himself bruised earlier by the Belgians, must struggle to reorganize his being into the semblance of a Christian with a new set of pieties and a new set of fears. His priestly robes are his outward protection against violence but inwardly he must struggle with his remaining ancestral beliefs, for he is still young and the village and the forest still press closely around.

Though considered a "minor" novel by Gleason because of its structural weaknesses and its relatively weak plot, the work probes into the darker and more sensitive parts of the African soul more honestly than most works. A stronger objection to the novel is that the viewpoint is exclusively Christian: nowhere does the dying African culture merit more than a menacing role as devil or evil spirit.

Gleason notes the somewhat similarly handled theme of the South African writer, Mopeli-Paulus, in *Turn to the Dark* (1956), written with Miriam Basner:

> But the colonial condition, the use of magic and terror to fortify the spirits of the group against that which is destroying their way of life are treated with critical understanding by the author of a very different sort of "village" book. The case for reversion is far more difficult to make than the case for submission or for forced conversion although one wonders why this must inevitably be so. A maimed body is more difficult to look at than a maimed spirit. But is an account of the excesses of various recidivistic organizations really more frightening than accounts of "lonely Africans" maimed by excesses of missionary zeal?

Writings: Novel: *Kavwanga,* Namur, Ed. Grand Lac, possibly 1954; information is disputed (see above).

Biographical/Critical sources: Bibliography of Creative African Writing, Nendeln, Switzerland, Kraus-Thomson 1971; *This Africa,* Judith Gleason, Evanston, Northwestern University Press, 1965.

BOMELA, Bertrand M.
b. December 25, 1928, Duff Mission, Idutywa, Transkei, South Africa.
Xhosa novelist, teacher.

Bomela passed his Standard VI examination in late 1943, finishing first in his district. Early the next year he entered Lovedale School, obtaining his Junior Certificate in 1945. He entered Langa High School in 1947, and in late 1948, passed his Senior Certificate with a first class pass in Xhosa and Latin. He hoped to enter Fort Hare, but family debts prevented this, so he enrolled in a teaching course at Healdtown Institution in 1949, studying under the Rev. Seth Nokitimi. He qualified as a teacher in 1950 and the following year, went to work at the Ncambele Secondary School in Umtata. In 1952 he took a position at Good Hope School, Idutywa, and in 1953 began teaching at Duff Mission School in Idutywa, his present position.

Bomela won second prize in 1956 in the Afrikaanse Pers-Boekhandel literary competition for his novel *Umntu akanambulelo* (A Person Has No Gratitude).

Writings: Novel: *Umntu akanambulelo,* Johannesburg, Afrikaanse Pers-Boekhandel, 1959.

BONNE, Nii Kwabena III
b. January 26, 1888, Ghana; d. ca. 1960. Autobiographer.

Bonne, the son of a chief, achieved Standard V (Junior High) at the Wesleyan School and worked as a clerk, contractor, builder, merchant and finally as a chief. He travelled widely on business and pleasure and was well known for the parties he gave at various European hotels. He gives a very vivid picture of his life in his autobiography *Milestones in the History of the Gold Coast: An Autobiography of Nii Kwabena Bonne III.*

Writings: Autobiography: *Milestones in the History of the Gold Coast: An Autobiography of Nii Kwabena Bonne III,* London, Diplomatist Publications, 1953.

BONI, Nazi
b. 1910, Bwan, Upper Volta; d. 1969. Novelist, teacher, politician.

Boni was a chief in the Bwa or Bwanu group, and one of the first to get European schooling, first at the local école supérieure, and then at the famous l'Ecole Normale William Ponty for his lycéen studies in Dakar. He taught from 1931–41 in Ouagadougou (Upper Volta) and in other schools. In 1941 he was named Directeur de l'Ecole Primaire de Treichville at Abidjan and during this time placed first in the competitions in oral and practical teaching leading to the "concours supérieure" for experienced teachers.

He supported Félix Houphouet-Boigny, leader of the Rassemblement Démocratique Africaine (R.D.A.), who sought a united government for the African francophone states, but Boni was eventually forced to work for the ultimate separate independence of Upper Volta. He was elected deputy in 1948, 1951, and 1956 for Upper Volta in the French parliament while also serving as a member of the Upper Volta Assembly (1947–1960). In 1955 he founded Le Mouvement Populaire Africaine, which had a Pan-African program that went unrealized. In 1958 he became president of the Territorial Assembly and helped found the Mouvement du Regroupement Voltaique, a local section of the regional Parti du Regroupement Africain (the PRA), later to be called the Parti de la Fédération

Africaine (the PFA). Boni was increasingly in opposition to the majority parties eventually led by Maurice Yaméogo who was President of the Republic of Upper Volta (1959–1965). Boni's final political efforts as head of the Parti Republicain de la Liberté led to the proscription of the PRL and his own forced exile to Mali. He died in an automobile accident in 1969.

Boni published one novel, *Crépuscule des temps anciens* (Twilight of the Ancient Days), which celebrated an African reality untouched by the European world and is the product of much research on the Bwanu people.

The April 1965 issue of *Afrique* offered a detailed examination of his political career and a full discussion of his novel. See also the discussion of recent (1950–1970) developments in Upper Volta in *Protest and Power in Black Africa*.

Writings: Novel: *Crépuscule des temps anciens*, Paris, Présence Africaine, 1962.

Biographical/Critical Sources: Afrique, No. 46, April 1965; *Protest and Power in Black Africa*, Rotberg and Mazrui, eds., New York, Oxford University Press, 1970.

BOTO, Eza (pseudonym for BIYIDI, Alexandre, but see BETI, Mongo)

BRAND, Dollar
b. ca. 1935, Cape Town, South Africa. Poet, jazz musician.

He attended primary school in Cape Town and graduated from Trafalgar High School in Cape Town's District Six. A professional jazz pianist and composer, he has played widely in Cape Town, Johannesburg, and in 1960 made a tour with his group to Switzerland and Scandinavia, remaining for some six years. He earlier had spent two years in the United States before returning in 1958 to South Africa where he now resides. He is married to the singer Bea Benjamin.

Brand has been writing poetry since the mid–1960's and had his first considerably body of verse published in *The Journal of the New African Literature and Arts*. That group of poetry has been republished in Cosmo Pieterse's *Seven South African Poets* and is called "Africa, Music and Show Business (An analytical survey in twelve tones plus finale)." Some of the poems such as poem V are very short,

> *rhythm afrique*
> *joey had the biggest feet*
> *so he played tenor*

and others are pictorial, as is poem VI:

> *blues for district six*
> *early one new year's morning*
> *when the emerald bay waved its clear waters*
> *   /against the noisy dockyard*
> *a restless south easter skipped over slumber-*
> *   /ing lion's head*
> *danced up hanover street*
> *tenored a bawdy banjo*
> *strung an ancient cello*
> *bridged a host of guitars*
> *tambourined through a dingy alley*
> *into a scented cobwebbed room*
> *and crackled the sixth sensed district*
> *into a blazing swamp fire of satin sound*

which is vaguely reminiscent of T.S. Eliot's "Preludes." The finale is angry and vulgar:

> *but alas, it was too late*
> *for when they touched the spring,*
> *   /there occurred a terrifying explosion*

and the whole monkey kingdom was
                              /blown to bits
the resultant itch woke up TIME
and she scratched vaguely under her
                              /armpit

Writings: Poems in *The Journal of the New African Literature and Arts;* republished as "Africa, Music and Show Business (An analytical survey in twelve tones plus finale)" in *Seven South African Poets,* Cosmo Pieterse, editor, London, Heinemann, 1971.

BREW, Osborne Henry Kwesi
b. 1928, Cape Coast, Ghana.
Poet, short story writer.

Kwesi Brew, born of a Fanti family, was educated in local schools, and was brought up by a warm-hearted guardian, the Education Officer, K. J. Dickens of England, after the poet's early loss of both of his parents. Brew credits Dickens with his love of books and says he "owes everything" to this generous man. Brew took his B.A. at the College of the Gold Coast (now the University of Ghana, Legon) and was one of the first to do so.

While a student, he won a poetry competition established by the British Council and took part in college dramatics. Later he acted in serveral Gold Coast (Ghana) Film Unit productions.

Upon leaving school, Brew served as Assistant District Commissioner and later as a Commissioner in his own right, seeing duty in Krachi, British Togoland (now the Volta Region of Northern Ghana). More recently, as a member of the Ghanaian Diplomatic Corps, he has served in England, France, India, Germany, the U.S.S.R. and as Ambassador to Mexico and Senegal after a period at home as Chief of Protocol in Ghana's Ministry of Foreign Affairs.

Brew's poetry has appeared in *Okyeame* (Ghana); *Pergamon Poets–2* (1968); *Voices of Ghana* (1958); a radio anthology edited by H. Swanzy; Reed and Wake's *A Book of African Verse;* Moore and Beier's *Modern Poetry from Africa;* and *Messages: Poems from Africa,* edited by Awoonor and Adali-Mortty. Brew's one volume of poetry, *Shadows of Laughter,* 1968, has most of his better poems.

One of the most tightly-knit is "The Search" which begins:
The Past
Is but the cinders
Of the present;
The future
The Smoke
That escaped
Into the cloud-bound sky.
and ends with these lines:
The rain came down,
When you and I slept away
The night's burden of our passions;
Their new-found wisdom
In quick lightning flashes
Revealed the truth
That they had been
The slaves of fools.

In general, Brew's theme, very unusual for an African, is that of the value of the individual as contrasted to that of his society as a whole. Stylistically, he is tender and lyrical, with brief lines and broken phrases.

Writings: Poetry: *Shadows of Laughter,* London, Longmans, 1968; poems in *Messages: Poems from Africa,* Awoonor and Adali-Mortty, editors, London, Heinemann, 1971; *Modern Poetry from Africa,* Moore and Beier, editor, London, Penguin, 1963; *A Book of African Verse,* Reed and Wake, editors, London,

Heinemann, 1964; a radio anthology edited by H. Swanzy, *Voices of Ghana,* Accra, Ministry of Information and Broacasting, 1958; *Pergamon Poets–2,* Oxford, Pergamon, 1968; *Okyeame,* Accra, Ghana.

BRUTUS, Dennis
b. November 28, 1924, Salisbury, Southern Rhodesia.
Poet, teacher.

The son of South African "coloureds" who were both teachers, Dennis Brutus was educated in Port Elizabeth whence his parents had returned after his birth. He took a B.A. in English in 1946 at Fort Hare University College and studied law at the University of Witswatersrand, 1962–63. His early years were extremely difficult because financial hardship caused his parents to separate.

Brutus taught English and Afrikaans in several South African high schools from 1948 to 1962. In the late 1950's he traveled by car, by foot and by "4th Class rail" (in cattle cars) through Rhodesia and Mozambique. During this period he began to take an active part in organizing opposition to apartheid, particularly in sports in which he took a personal interest. The South African government retaliated, firing him from his teaching job in 1961, and banning him from writing. He was further ordered to avoid any political or social meetings and was arrested in 1963 for being present at a sports meeting. Freed on bail, the author first sought refuge in nearby Swaziland. Then, while on his way clandestinely to Baden–Baden on a Rhodesian passport to protest apartheid before the Olympic Executive Committee, he was picked up by Portuguese police and turned over to the South African police at the border. While being returned to prison, he tried to escape, only to be shot in the back in a street of Johannesburg. After convalescence, he was sentenced to 18 months at hard labor on Robben Island, the "Devils Island" of South Africa.

Finishing his sentence in 1965, Brutus was permitted to leave South Africa in 1966 with his wife and seven children with an "exit permit" which provides for his imprisonment should be return.

Brutus went to London where he worked from 1966 to 1970 at a variety of teaching and journalistic assignments. During this period he also served on the International Defence and Aid Fund for the victims of apartheid. After three months at the University of Denver in the United States, he returned to England after visiting New Zealand, Australia, and India. By September, 1971, he was back in America as Lecturer in the English Department of Northwestern University, Evanston, Illinois. He has attended many conferences in the United States and other countries concerned with literature or with racial prejudice in sports. He has recently begun working on the development of a Ph.D. program in African literature at Northwestern.

He has served as director of the World Campaign for the Release of South African Political Prisoners and is also currently president of SANROC (South African Non-Racial Olympic Committee), the group that was successful in having South Africa excluded from the Olympic Games in 1964 and 1968. In 1967 he toured the U.S. on behalf of the International Defense Aid Fund for South Africans for which he is now the representative in the U.S., and accredited as such to the United Nations.

On March 21, 1972, Brutus helped launch in New York City another pressure group, I.C.A.R.I.S., the International Campaign Against Racism in Sport, and is acting chairman of the new organization. The banning of the Rhodesian team from the 1972 Olympics in Munich was due in part to the efforts of I.C.A.R.I.S. and associated groups. The United Nations has published a pamphlet featuring Brutus entitled *Special Committee on Apartheid Hears Mr. Dennis Brutus*. In March, 1972, he took a leading part in the conference, "The United States and Southern Africa," in Washington, D.C., designed "to share information and plan action strategies with special focus on (1) U.S. corporate involvement, and (2) support for liberation movements."

Brutus has testified three times before U.S. congressional committees on apartheid and other aspects of racial cruelty since 1966. In 1971 he appeared with Arthur Ashe, the black U.S. tennis player, who was himself banned from play in South Africa, before a congressional committee. Earlier, in August, 1967 *The Washington Post* (Washington, D.C.) carried an interview with Brutus on apartheid conditions during his first visit to the United States for SANROC.

Brutus's poetry has been widely published and translated. His first collection, *Sirens, Knuckles, Boots* (1963) was published while the poet was in prison on Robben Island. His captors were sufficiently interested in it to procure a copy and to interrogate him about it. Surprisingly, despite his poems' strong language against the regime, he was shortly thereafter released and allowed to leave the country. The work won an Mbari Prize (University of Ibadan, Nigeria) for poetry in 1962.

His prison experiences, including the severe wound inflicted while he was attempting to escape, furnished the substance for his second volume, *Letters to Martha and Other Poems from a South African Prison* (1968). The poems are "letters" to Martha, his sister-in-law, because he was forbidden to write anything, including poems, which might be of interest to publishers.

Many of his occasional poems and extracts from his volumes appear in popular anthologies including *New Sum of Poetry from the Negro World, Seven African Writers,* and Moore and Beier's *Modern Poetry from Africa.*

In 1970, the University of Texas published his *Poems from Algiers* which ponders the meaning of his attendance and the presence of various African artists at the "Premier Festival Culturel Panafricain," Algiers, July 21–August 1,

Brutus

1969. The poems are beautifully reproduced in the quasi-Carolingian holograph of Brutus himself. In a prose afterward Brutus comments on the circumstances attending the writing of the poems.

He has much to say and his work, full of a personal force combined with a sense of troubling unease and "voluptas," mixes erotic statement with acrid political memories. He employs a rugged, often swinging, impassioned line.

The first poem in *Poems from Algiers* concerns the query as to just where is the African's place at the table of modern civilization:

And I am driftwood
on an Algerian beach
along a Mediterranean shore.

and I am driftwood.

Others may loll in their carnal pool
washed by tides of sensual content
in variable flow, by regulated plan

but I am driftwood.

And the tides devour,
lusts erode the shelving consciousness
fierce hungers shark at the submerged mind

In *Letters to Martha*, Brutus imagines having to commit an act of violence to break free of the cruel world of apartheid, but how, he asks, shall he be judged guilty, for it is God, permitting all this, who forces him "along the knife-blades/till I choose/perdition."

Brutus is preparing a new collection of his poems, *A Simple Lust*, which will contain all of *Sirens, Knuckles, Boots*, long out of print in its now prized Mbari Press edition; all of *Letters to Martha;* and most of *Poems from Algiers;* and a few new works. It will be issued by Heinemann

of London in hardcover in the general poets' series, with a paperback edition in the African Writers Series shortly thereafter.

Another recently published work which concerns Brutus is the Heinemann volume, *African Writers Talking*, which features taped interviews with sixteen authors, including Christopher Okigbo, Alex La Guma, Chinua Achebe, and Brutus. Issue No. 4 of Texas' *Occasional Publication of the African and Afro-American Research Institute: Palaver: Interviews with Five African Writers in Texas* (1972) offers taped interviews, one of which is a recent one with Brutus. The other writers are John Pepper Clark, Ezekiel Mphahlele, Kofi Awoonor, and Chinua Achebe. A small collection of Brutus' poems have appeared in translation into Russian, published recently in Moscow.

Nominated "poet laureate of South Africa" in Horizon Press' *A History of Africa* (which carries an article on Brutus), the poet is a modest, warm man, an introspective scholar-poet. Having suffered oppression, shooting, imprisonment, and now exile, he lived for two years in Evanston, Illinois, with three of his older children while his wife and the five younger children remained in England. They have now joined him in America.

Brutus' three volumes of poetry move from the strained life in South Africa, through the prison days and nights of the 1963–65 period, to an overview, which, if not calm, shows his having come through to a new determination to use art to fight for human dignity. In "Nightsong City" from *Sirens*, he had written:

Sleep well, my love, sleep well:
the harbour lights glaze over restless docks,
police cars cockroach through the tunnel
/streets;

78

In an untitled poem dated "2 July 1966" in *Letters to Martha,* we find:
yeast in me
waiting for the time of achievement
which will come if God wills
when I flog fresh lashes across these thieves.
And, moving from his own predicament, and those of the men of his continent, he wrote for all artists in the poem, "for Chris Okigbo/Wole Soyinka: 29.7," in *Poems from Algiers:*
A wrong-headed bunch we may be
but the bodies of poets will always be
the anvils on which will be beaten out
a-new, or afresh, a people's destiny.

Writings: Poetry: *Sirens, Knuckles, Boots,* Ibadan, Mbari Press, 1963; *Letters to Martha and Other Poems from a South African Prison,* London, Heinemann, 1968; *Poems from Algiers.* No. 2, *Occasional Publication of the African and Afro-American Research Institute,* The University of Texas, Austin, 1970; poems in *New Sum of Poetry from the Negro World,* Paris, Présence Africaine, 1966; *Seven South African Poets,* Cosmo Pieterse, editor, London, Heinemann, 1966; *Modern Poetry from Africa,* revised edition., Moore and Beier, editors, London, Penguin, 1966. Interviews: *The Washington Post,* August, 1967; *Palaver,* No. 3 *Occasional Publication of the African and Afro-American Research Institute,* Austin, Texas, The University of Texas, 1972; *African Writers Talking,* D. Duerden and C. Pieterse, editors, London, Heinemann, 1972. Pamphlet: *Special Committee on Apartheid Hears Mr. Dennis Brutus,* United Nations Unit on Apartheid, Department of Political and Security Council Affairs, No. 7/70, New York, March, 1970.

Biographical/Critical Sources: A History of Africa, New York, Horizon Press, 1971; Profile in *The Bitter Choice,* Colin Legum, editor, New York, Excalibur Books, World Publishers; *Introduction to African Literature,* Ulli Beier, editor, Evanston, Illinois, Northwestern University Press, 1967.

BUD–M'BELLE, Isaiah (see MBELLE, I. B.)

BUKENYA, Augustine S.
b. 1944, Masaka, Uganda.
Playwright, poet, novelist, teacher.

Bukenya attended primary school at Masaka, high school in Kampala, Uganda's capital, and University College, Dar es Salaam, Tanzania, where he studied literature, language, and linguistics. His play *The Secret* appears in Cook and Lee's *Short East African Plays in English.*

While an undergraduate, Bukenya founded the college literary journal, *Darlite.* He took the B.A. in 1968, and was the first student at University College to pass with First Class Honors. His M.A. in Traditional African Literature at Makerere University followed. Presently he teaches English at Makerere.

His verse has appeared in various journals and anthologies, including *Poems from East Africa,* 1971. His first novel, *The People's Bachelor* saw print in Nairobi, 1971.

Writings: Play: *The Secret,* in *Short East African Plays in English,* Cook and Lee, eds., Nairobi and London, Heinemann, 1968.
Poetry: in *Poems from East African* London, Heinemann, 1971.
Novel: *The Peoples' Bachelor,* Nairobi, East Africa Publishing House, 1971.

BUNSEKI, A. Fukiau kia (also
FUKIAU)
b. 1934, near Banza Manteke,
Congo (Zaïre).
Kikongo poet, folklore collector,
essayist, scholar.

He studied at the middle and high
school at Kimpese mission from 1954–
58 and taught there from 1958–60
while completing a correspondence
course given by the Institut Pelman de
Psychologie in France which awarded
him a diploma in 1963. Beginning in
1960 he was a teacher in Kinshasa while
studying at the extension school of the
University of Lovanium in the capital.
During this time he began writing and
published a collection of proverbs
analyzed for their philosophical content, *Mampinda ma Nkongo wakedika*; an
essay on Kikongo poetry, *Wazola zinga
mokina ye bafwa;* a grammatical study; a
political essay, *Twaduswa ye twadisa*
(Being Governed and Governing), and
several other grammatical or scholarly
works.

In 1964 Bunseki entered his most
active period, establishing an advanced
school at Manianga near the Sundi-
Lutete mission which he called Skûlu kia
Minsoniki (The School of Authors) and
also Kinkîmba kia Kôngo (The Congolese Academy). Here a great effort was
made to encourage creative writing in
various African languages, particularly
Kikongo, Lingala, Swahili, and
Tshiluba. He himself wrote many works
during this period, two of which were
of special interest: *Nkongo ye nza yakun-
zungidila. Nza-Kongo* (The Mukongo and
the World In Which He Takes His
Being. Congo Cosmogony), published
in 1966, and *Dingo-Dingo* (The Cycle of
Life), also 1966. *Dingo-Dingo* is considered possibly the finest of Kikongo

volumes of poetry. In it Bunseki inter-
wove oral poetry, proverbs, and songs into a long narrative philosophical specula-
tion about life. The seven poems in the
work are unusually long, therefore, by
traditional Kikongo standards. Mbololo
ya Mpiku in his essay, "Introduction à
la littérature kikongo," gives extensive
extracts from the prologue to the collection, "Mamo dingo-dingo kwandi," with
French translation. Fukiau, as Bunseki
is also known, has been very active in
submitting articles to the journals *Moyo*
and *Minsamu Miayenge*.

Writings: Poetry: *Dingo-Dingo*, 1966;
Imeni mu nding'andi, essay on poetry
followed by his verse, 1966.
  Literary-critical essays: *Wazola zinga
mokina ye bafwa,* essay on Kikongo poetry,
1961; *Dodokolo Tâta*, 1962.
  Philosophy: *Nkongo ye nza yakun-
zungidila. Nza-Kongo*, 1966; repub-
lished, Kinshasa, l'Office National de la
Recherche et du Developpement, 1969,
with a French translation by C.
Zamenga-Batukenzanga; *Mampinda ma
Nkongo wakedika* (The Philosophy of
The True Mukongo), 1960, a collection
of proverbs and philosophical analysis
of their content.
  Grammars and Linguistic Studies:
Dîngu kia uding'a kikongo, 1961;
Nding'a kikongo, 1962; three works in
French: *Etudier le verbe congolais*, 1963;
Les affixes (du kikongo), 1963; and *La
momification Kôngo*, 1967.
  Political essays: *Twaduswa ye twa-
disa*, 1961; *Tambula nsengo*, 1966, a
treatment of the theme of labor.
  Ethnography: *Kimpodi ye Kinganga-
Mpodi*, an essay, 1967.

Biographical/Critical Source: Mbololo ya
Mpiku, "Introduction à la littérature
kikongo," *Research in African Literatures,*

African and Afro-American Research Institute, the University of Texas, III, 2, (Fall 1972), with extract in Kikongo of "Mamo dingo-dingo kwandi" from *Dingo-Dingo*, with French translation.

BURNS–NCAMASHE, Sipo (or Sipho) **Mangindi**
b. December 1, 1920, King William's Town, South Africa.
Xhosa poet.

He entered St. Matthew's College about 1935 where he obtained his teacher's certificate, and received his higher education at Lovedale. He took his B.A. from Fort Hare about 1941 and lectured there for two years. He obtained his B. Ed. degree from the University of Cape Town, and has worked as an interpreter and headmaster. At present he is the principal of the Kabah Secondary School, Uitenhage.

His one volume of poetry, published in 1961, is *Masibaliselane* (Let us Tell Each Other Stories).

Writings: Poetry: *Masibaliselane*, Cape Town, Oxford University Press, 1961.

BUSIA, Kofi Abrefa (also Kenneth A.)
b. 1913 or 1914, Wenchi (Brongahafo District), northwest Ghana.
Critic, scholar, statesman.

Dr. Busia came of the royal family of Wenchi in the upper northwest area of the Ashanti peoples. After studying in Ghanaian schools and earning his B.A. at Achimota College, he was a teacher at Achimota in 1939 when he earned an extension degree in history from London University and thereby won a scholarship to Oxford University.

Returning with an Oxford degree in sociology he became a professor of African studies at University College of the Gold Coast (now the University of Ghana) and in 1951 published his classic study, *The Position of the Chief in the Modern Political System of the Ashanti.*

Busia became the leader of the Ghana Congress Party (GCP) in 1952 which opposed the growing authoritarian tendencies of Nkrumah and in October, 1957 he was elected the leader of the merger of all the opposition parties to Nkrumah's Convention Peoples' Party (CPP) called the United Party (UP). In response, the Government began to arrest the leaders of the UP, accusing two of them of plotting to assassinate Nkrumah. Busia, lecturing in Holland in 1959, chose exile when the Nkrumah regime further attacked the remnant of the opposition, remaining in Europe until 1966 when Nkrumah was turned out by a military coup. Returning a month after the new regime had taken over, he was met by a tumultous crowd at Accra Airport and shortly thereafter became first Vice-Chairman and then Chairman of the National Liberation Council, the civilian committee set up to advise the military. Dr. Busia then became Prime Minister of Ghana's civilian regime.

At the time of Busia's "recall" to Ghana, he was a senior member of the Department of Sociology at Oxford's St. Anthony's College. His useful *Purposeful Education for Africa* (1964) was reissued in paperback in 1968 and is still in print.

The military take-over of the government on January 13, 1972, by Colonel Ignatius Acheampongi forced Busia, who was receiving medical treatment in London, out of office and back into exile. He is now a lecturer in sociology at Oxford University.

Busia

Writings: Political science: *The Position of the Chief in the Modern Political System of the Ashanti,* 1951; *The Challenge of Africa,* London, Pall Mall, 1962, New York, Praeger, 1962; *Purposeful Education for Africa,* 1964; reissued in paperback, 1968; *Africa in Search of Democracy,* London, Routledge, 1967, New York, Praeger, 1967.

C

CALDAS (see BARBOSA, Domingos Caldas)

CALUZA, Reuben Tolakele
b. ca. 1900, Edendale, South Africa; d. 1965.
Zulu song writer, lyricist, musician, teacher.

Caluza attended school in Edendale, Ohlange and Mariannhill and early began to take an interest in music. Encouraged by Fr. Bernard Huss, head of the Teacher Training College at Mariannhill, Caluza wrote and published his first song, "Ixegwana" (Little Old Man), in *The Native Teachers' Journal* (January, 1921). In 1930 he went to London as the leader of a choir of ten Zulu singers (half of whom were women), sponsored by the Native Affairs Department. The group, besides giving many concerts, recorded some 120 songs, many composed by Caluza, but most based on Zulu traditional music for weddings, religious ceremonies, or dealing with patriotic feeling and humorous incidents.

Moving to the United States in 1931, Caluza studied at Hampton Institute for a B.A. and an M.A. in music and then returned home to teach, becoming chairman of the music department at Adams College in 1945. His most significant work in Western form is his "Rondo for Orchestra: Reminiscences of Africa" for string quartet.

In 1928, Caluza had published his earliest songs, the first secular lyrics ever to see print in Zulu. According to some authorities many of them became popular because they appealed to the increasingly detribalized Zulus working in the large mines of the Rand and doing domestic and factory work in the cities. To this new proletariat of *abaqhafi* who affected Western manners and clothing, Caluza's work, a new hybrid form, offered solace to a people who themselves were cultural hybrids experiencing the trials of adjustment, nostalgia, and suffering.

Writings: Musical compositions, with poetic texts: "Ixegwana," *The Native Teachers' Journal,* January, 1921; "Rondo for Orchestra: Reminiscences of Africa."

CAMARA, Laye (see Westernized, now habitual, rendering as LAYE, Camara).

CAPITEIN, Jacobus Elisa Joannes
b. 1717, place unknown in Africa;
d. Holland, ca. 1745.
Scholar, early tract writer, missionary.

Captured at an early age at an unknown place in Africa, Capitein was transported to Holland where he benefitted from an education offered by a wealthy Dutch merchant. He became so Europeanized that he came to defend the institution of slavery in a Latin treatise, *Dissertatio politico-theologica, de servitute, libertati christianae non contraria* (A Political Theological Examination of Slavery as Being Not Contrary to Christian Liberty), Leiden, 1742. He later was a missionary in Fort d'Elmina and Fort St. George in the old Gold Coast and translated part of the Bible into the coastal language.

Writings: Dissertatio politico-theologica, de servitute, libertati christianae non contraria, Leiden, 1742.

CARDOSO, António
b. 1933, Luanda, Angola.
Poet, journalist, clerk.

Locally educated, he worked on Angolan journals and the review *Mensagem* (Messenger). His one volume of verse was *Poemas de circunstância* (Angola), first published in 1953 while he was still a student. One of his poems in Portuguese, "Um Dia" (One Day), is found in *New Sum of Poetry from the Negro World.* His story, "São Paulo," also appears in the collection *Colecção Imbondeiro,* No. 14.

Active in Angolan resistance to the Portuguese colonial regime, he was arrested in 1961 and sentenced to fourteen years in Chao-Bom Prison in the Cape Verde Islands.

Writings: Poetry: *Poemas de circunstância,* Angola, Lisbon, Edição do Casa dos Estudantes do Império, 1953, 1961; "Um Dia," in *New Sum of Poetry from the Negro World,* Paris, Présence Africaine, Vol. 57, 1966.

Story: "São Paulo," in *Colecção Imbondeiro,* 14, Benúdia, ed., Sá da Bandeira, Imbondeiro, 1956, 1961.

CARDOSO, Pedro Monteiro
b. ca. 1890, Fogo Island, Cape Verde Islands; d. 1942.
Poet, folklorist, story collector.

Cardoso's first two important volumes of poetry are *Caboverdeanas* (Cape Verdean Verse) published in 1915, and *Algas e corais* (Seaweed and Coral), 1928. The latter volume is written in classical Portuguese verse forms and lines but is clearly expressive of a new realism and feeling for the local Caboverdean people and sentiments. Some other volumes of his total of ten are: *Hespéridas. Fragmentos de um poema perdido em triste e miserando naufrágio* (Hesperides: Fragments of a poem lost in a sad and miserable shipwreck), *Sonetos e redondilhas* (Sonnets and Redondillas), both 1934. The redondilha is a verse form consisting of lines of five and eight syllables.

Cardoso published one volume of traditional stories in 1933, *Folclore caboverdeano,* 120 pages.

Writings: Poetry: *Caboverdeanas,* Cape Verde; 1915; *Primícias,* 192(?); *Jardim das Hespérides,* Cape Verde, 1926; *Duas canções,* 1927; *Algas e corais,* Vila Nova de Famalição, Portugal, Tipografia Minerva, 1928; *Hespéridas. Fragmentos de um poema perdido em triste e miserando naufrágio,* Cape Verde, 1930; *Sonetos e redondilhas,* Cape Verde, 1934; *Morna e saudade,* Cape Verde, 1940; *Ritmos da morna, Versos II,* Cape Verde, 1941, *Sem tom nem som. Versos III,* Praia, Cape Verde, 1942; *É mi que é-Lha'r-Fogo. Versos I,* Praia, Cape Verde, 1941.

Stories: *Folclore caboverdeano,* Porto, Maranus, 1933.

CASELY–HAYFORD, Adelaide
(née Smith)
b. 1868, Sierra Leone; d. 1959, Ghana.
Short story writer, autobiographer.

Born of Fanti and English parentage, Adelaide Smith studied at local schools in Sierra Leone and then in England and Germany, returning to establish The Girls Vocational School in Freetown in 1897 with her sister. She married the

distinguished Gold Coast lawyer, Joseph Ephraim Casely-Hayford, and travelled widely during her long life, which included a two-year sojourn in the United States. At the age of 91 she completed her autobiography. *West African Review* published her memoirs in 1959, their first appearance in print. Her short story, "Mista Courifer," is in Langston Hughes' *An African Treasury.* Her daughter, Gladys May Casely-Hayford, became a published poet.

Writings: Autobiography: *Memoirs, West African Review,* 1959.

Short story: "Mista Courifer," in *An African Treasury,* Langston Hughes, ed., New York, Pyramid, 1961.

CASELY–HAYFORD, Gladys May
(pseudonym Aquah Laluah)
b. May 11, 1904, Axim,
Gold Coast (Ghana);
d. October, 1950, Freetown,
Sierra Leone.
Poet, story teller.

Gladys May was the daughter of the famous lawyer, Joseph Ephraim Casely-Hayford, and Adelaide Smith. Educated in local schools in the early years, she later studied in Wales. She returned to Africa to teach at the Girls Vocational School, the institution her mother and aunt had founded in Freetown, Sierra Leone. She remained in Freetown until her death from black-water fever in 1950. She had the advantages of being reared in a cultured home by parents interested in the arts, and she was the goddaughter of *Coleridge-Taylor,* a celebrated musician. At an early age she began writing the stories and poems which appeared in journals over many years. Her one exotic experience was in dancing for a brief period with a jazz group in Berlin when she was in her 20's.

Though her poetry now seems redolent of the piety and parochialisms of a bygone missionary and colonial period, it is sincere and sometimes moving. Her short tales and sketches which appeared in the *West African Review* show her determined to capture the Africa of her personal vision and reveal her sympathy for the life of the ordinary man or woman. *The Philadelphia Tribune* on October 14, 1937, published two of her little poems, "Creation" and "Art Pure and True."

The poem "Creation" has the perfume of an old valentine, but gives little hint of her mature work:

A flush, a curve, a wind that blows—
A breath of life–and 'twas called a ROSE.

A little sorrow and joy in part,
A breath of love–and 'twas called a
HEART

A Heart, a Rose,–God took these two
And wove them together, and called them
you.

Some of her poetry has recently been collected in such anthologies as Langston Hughes' *Poems from Black Africa*, Hughes' *An African Treasure* and Donatus Ibe Nwoga's *West African Verse*. Her poem, "The Serving Girl," which the author originally published in *West African Review* under a pseudonym, Aquah Laluah, has appeared in the *Atlantic Monthly* and in Hughes' *An African Treasury*. The poem clearly shows her musicality:

She brought palm wine that carelessly slips
From the sleeping palm tree's honeyed lips.
But who can guess, or even surmise
The countless things she served with her
eyes?

The calabash wherein she served my food
Was polished and smooth as sandalwood.
Fish, white as the foam of the sea,
Peppered and golden fried for me.

In 1948, six of her poems, partly in Krio, were published in a tiny volume *Take 'um so* with "the taking it" being the borrowings from Krio poetry, a language with which she increasingly experimented in occasional verse.

Writings: Poetry: In *Poems from Black Africa*, Langston Hughes, ed., Indiana University Press, 1963; *An African Treasury*, Langston Hughes, ed., New York, Pyramid, 1961; *West African Verse*, Donatus Ibe Nwoga, ed., London, Longmans, 1967; *Take 'um so*, Freetown, New Era Press, 1948; two poems: "Creation" and "Art Pure and True," in *The Philadelphia Tribune*, October 14, 1937.

Stories and sketches: *West African Review*, various volumes.

CASELY–HAYFORD, Joseph Ephraim
b. 1866, the Gold Coast (Ghana);
d. 1930.
Novelist, statesman, scholar, journalist, lawyer.

J. E. Casely-Hayford married Adelaide Smith Casely-Hayford and was the father of Gladys May Casely-Hayford. In his day he was considered the most important leader of African nationalism. His novel, *Ethiopia Unbound*, originally published in 1911 was first reissued in 1969 by F. Cass in London and by Humanities Press in New York. F. N. Ugonna of the University of Ibadan has prepared a new introduction to this new edition.

The work, primarily propagandistic in intent, centered around what was believed to be the religious and political ideas of Ethiopians, the only independent nation in the Africa of that day excepting newly settled Liberia. Obviously much of Casely-Hayford's own ideas and needs have gone into this polemical work.

Another classic work of this early leader, his *Gold Coast Native Institutions with Thoughts upon a Healthy Imperial Policy for the Gold Coast and the Ashanti* (originally published in 1903) has been reissued by African Publishing Company with an introduction by W. E. Abraham.

Casely-Hayford led the Gold Coast Africans' movement to greater independence in the first quarter of the 20th century. He performed the task so well that he won the name of the "great MOSES of West Africa" in the words of W. H. Whiteley in his *A Selection of African Prose: 2.* Whiteley's volume contains two excerpts from Casely-Hayford's famous speeches: "Speech delivered during the Budget Session of the Legislative Council, on 9 March 1928, on the Provincial Council System and Native Administration Ordinance," and the "Presidential Address delivered during the Third Session of the National Congress of British West Africa, held in Bathurst, Gambia, December 1925." Humanities Press has published many of his discourses in *Public Speeches of J. E. Casely-Hayford,* collected by M. J. Sampson.

Writings: Novel: *Ethiopia Unbound,* London, C. M. Phillips, 1911; reissued, London, F. Cass, 1969; New York, reprint, Humanities Press. 1969. Polemic: *Gold Coast Native Institutions with Thoughts upon a Healthy Imperial Policy for the Gold Coast and the Ashanti,* originally published in 1903; reissued by African Publishing Company, 1970, with introduction by W. E. Abraham. Speeches and excerpts: *A Selection of African Prose: 2,* W. H. Whiteley, editor, Oxford, Clarendon Press, 1964; *Public Speeches of J. E. Casely-Hayford,* M. J. Sampson, editor, New York, Humanities Press, 1970.

CHACHA, Tom
b. ca. 1940, Tanzania.
Short story writer.

Educated in local schools at the lower level, he took the B.A. at Makerere University in Uganda where he began to contribute to the college literary magazine, *Penpoint.* His story "The Road to Mara" appears in Neville Denny's *Pan African Short Stories.*

Chacha is now home in Tanzania where he continues to write in his spare hours.

Writings: Short story: "The Road to Mara," in *Pan African Short Stories,* Neville Denny, editor, London, Thos. Nelson, 1965.

CHAFULUMIRA, English William
b. ca. 1930, Malawi.
Nyanja-language novelist.

Chafulumira has published three short narratives in Nyanja, his mother tongue: *Kazitape* (The Rumor–Monger), *Kantini* (The Tea Room), and *Mfumu watsopano* (The New Chief) which was published in London by Macmillan in 1962.

Writings: Novels: *Kazitape,* London, Macmillan, 1950, 1959; *Kantini,* London, Macmillan, 1954; *Mfumu watsopano,* London, Macmillan, 1962.

CHIDYAUSIKU, Paul
b. ca. 1935, Rhodesia.
Shona-language story writer, novelist, playwright, journalist.

Chidyausiku

Chidyausiku has published one collection of stories *Pfungwa dzasekuru Mafusire* (Thoughts of Uncle Mafusire), all concerned with daily family problems and experiences with European culture. His three novels are: *Nhoroondo dzukuwanana* (Getting Married), *Nyadzi Dzinokunda Rufu* (Death before Dishonor); and *Karumekangu,* 1970. These three works were published by Oxford University Press in association with the Rhodesia Literature Bureau.

His one published play is *Ndakambokuyambira* (I Warned You Before).

Writings: Collection of stories: *Pfungwa Dzasekuru Mafusire,* Gwelo, Rhodesia, Catholic Mission Press, 1960; reprinted 1965.

Play: *Ndakambokuyambira,* Gwelo, Mambo Press, 1968.

Novels: *Nhoroondo Dzukuwanana,* Cape Town, Oxford University Press, 1958; reprinted 1962, 1966; *Nyadzi Dzinokunda Rufu,* Cape Town, Oxford University Press, 1962; *Karumekangu,* Salisbury, Rhodesia, Longmans Rhodesia, 1970.

Essay: "Sources of Material for Creative Writing," in *African Literature in Rhodesia,* Gwelo, Mamba Press, 1966.

Biographical/Critical Source: African Literature in Rhodesia, E. W. Krog, editor, Gwelo, Rhodesia, Mambo Press in association with the Rhodesian Literature Bureau, 1966.

CHINAKA, B. A. (possibly a pseudonym for STEPHEN, Felix N.)

CHITEPO, Herbert Wiltshire Pfumaindini
b. 1923, Southern Rhodesia, now Rhodesia.
Shona poet, lawyer.

Chitepo, a Shona speaker from Southern Rhodesia, was educated in South Africa at Adams' College in Natal, and at Fort Hare University College in the Cape Province where he received his B.A. degree about 1946. He then travelled to London to study for the bar and obtained the Barrister-at-Law at Middle Temple in 1957. Chitepo returned to practice in Southern Rhodesia, then moved to Tanzania to practice as Advocate and Director of Public Prosecution in Dar es Salaam, the position he holds today.

His one creative work is *Soko Risina Musoro* (The Tale without a Head), a long Shona epic poem based on historical events in Southern Rhodesia. The poem itself concerns a council of elders at the court of King Mutasa of the Manyika people during a severe drought. The epic is 15 pages long, but the volume contains the English translation, an extensive introduction to Shona orthography, tones, phonology, grammar, vocabulary and other linguistic matters relevant to appreciate the poem. There is also a bibliography of linguistic, sociological, and historical works in English and Shona.

Writings: Epic poem: *Soko Risina Musoro,* translated by Hazel Carter, London, Oxford University Press, 1958.

Biographical/Critical Source: African Literature in Rhodesia, E. W. Krog, Editor, Gwelo, Rhodesia, Mamba Press, 1966.

CHUM, Haji
b. ca. 1920, Kenya.

Collector of folk and epic material in Swahili.

Chum's *Utenzi wa vita vya Uhud* (The Epic of the Battle of Uhud) is available in English in a 1962 translation by H. E. Lambert. His long tale, *Kisa cha ndugu wawili* (The Story of Two Brothers), is a recent addition to contemporary Swahili literature.

Writings: Epic: *Utenzi wa vita vya Uhud,* editor and translator, H. E. Lambert, Nairobi, East African Literature Bureau, 1962.

Long tale: *Kisa cha ndugu wawili,* London, Evans Brothers, 1969, illustrated.

CISSE, Emile
b. ca. 1930, Guinea.
Novelist. teacher.

Cissé, an educator, visited the United States with a group of Guinean teachers in 1966.

Cissé is known to have published only one novel, *Faralako, roman d'un petit village africain. Liberté dans la paix* (Faralako: Novel of a Little African Village: Liberty in Peace), published in Mamou, Guinea, 1958. So far as is known, Guinea had only one small press, a missionary-owned facility in Kankan, before the East Germans established one in the early 1960's in Conakry. The Mamou imprint, therefore, probably only reflects the author's official residence. Cissé also is known to have published, again allegedly in Mamou, located some 150 miles from Conakry on the coast, the story, *Assiatou de septembre,* probably in the late 1950's. The novel *Faralako,* highly didactic and filled with pride in the new independence of Guinea, con-

tains a preface by Diallo Saifoulaye, the country's vice president.

Writings: Novel: *Faralako, roman d'un petit village africain. Liberté dans la paix,* Mamou, Guinea, 1958.
Story: *Assiatou de septembre,* Mamou, late 1950's.

CISSOKO, Siriman (see SIRIMAN, Cissoko)

CITASHE, I. W. W.
b. ca. 1845, Uitenhage, Cape Province, South Africa, of the Xhosa tribe;
d. ca. 1930.
Xhosa poet.

One of the earliest of published Xhosa poets, Citashe submitted work to the journal *Isigidimi sama Xhosa* (The Xhosa Messenger) which was printed from 1877 to 1888 at Lovedale Mission near Alice, South Africa.

His poem "Weapon," which is in Langston Hughes' *An African Treasury,* was originally published in *Isigidimi.* It prophetically calls for militant writers who are depicted as the last hope against the ever-growing oppression by the whites in South Africa:

Your cattle are gone,
My countrymen!
Go rescue them! Go rescue them!
Leave the breech loader alone
And turn to the pen.
Take paper and ink
For that is your shield..

Your rights are going!
So pick up your pen,
Load it, load it with ink,
Sit in your chair—

Repair not to Hoho,
But fire with your pen.

The Hoho of the poem was the last stronghold of Sandile, Chief of the Ngqika clan, killed in June 1878 by British forces.

Writings: Poem: "Weapon," in *An African Treasury,* Langston Hughes, editor New York, 1965; originally in *Isigidimi sama Xhosa* and later in *Africa South.*

CLARK, John Pepper
b. April 6, 1935, Kiagbodo, Ijaw country, Niger Delta, western Nigeria.
Playwright, poet, teacher, short story writer.

Clark was educated at Okrika and Jeremi, in Nigeria, then went on to Government College, Warri, in Ughelli (now the University of Ibadan) from 1955 to 1960 where he took the B.A. in English with honors. While still in college he founded a poetry magazine, *The Horn,* which published many young writers now important in Nigerian literature.

After school he worked as a journalist in Ibadan as head of features and editorial writer for the *Daily Express* group of newspapers in Lagos. He also served for a year as Information Officer for the Nigerian Federal Government, 1960–61, and did some research on the Ijaw epic at the Institute of African Studies, University of Ibadan.

In 1962, as a recipient of a Parvin fellowship, he travelled to the United States to attend Princeton University for one year. Based on his experiences in America, which were more bitter than sweet, was *America, their America,* a satirical swipe at the USA. Returning to Nigeria, he became the leading editorial writer on the Lagos *Daily Express,* and

did further work at the Institute of African Studies in 1963–64.

Since 1961 Clark has published three volumes of poetry and four widely performed plays. One of them, *Song of a Goat,* was written while he was at Princeton. *The Masquerade,* which continues to some extent the theme and story of *Song of a Goat,* and *The Raft* and *Ozidi,* (1966) which exploits Ijaw legend and culture, together make him the most important playwright after Soyinka in Black Africa. *Poems* and *A Reed in the Tide,* along with many miscellaneously published poems, also have established him as a major figure in African verse.

Clark, who bears the three small caste marks beside his eyes and four on each cheek, is deeply committed not only to general African values and themes but to local ones as well. At the same time, his verse reflects his reading in English literature and the Greek classical plays. He is very active in international conferences on literature and was a founding member of the Society of Nigerian Authors. In 1968, with Abiola Irele, he became co-editor of the new series of *Black Orpheus* magazine (called Vol. II somewhat confusingly) with publication and distribution by the *Daily Times* of Lagos, Nigeria.

Song of a Goat is Clark's most widely known and performed work, first being put on at Ibadan University by the Mbari Writers' Club in 1962. That same year it was produced in Enugu in Ibo country and has had scores of performances in Europe and the United States. It concerns an impotent husband, a frustrated wife, and the husband's virile younger brother. The themes of tension, temptation, anger, revenge and the decay of a "house" unfold in supple, sometimes tender lines of blank verse. The work has action, a constant play of emotional contrasts, and dramatic moments ending in murder.

Clark's work is austere and pointed and though his own approach is highly "classical" in the sense that his emotions are under control and his diction polished and taut, his characters are always African, speaking and acting in modes fitting for their lives. Employing an English of the most polished sort, and utilizing highly sophisticated poetic resources, he expresses his own culture and his personal anguish in a very original manner. He has been criticized for bringing unrelated sexual themes into his plays, thought to have been borrowed from the moodier nightmares of Greek dramatists or the lusty preoccupations of the Elizabethans. His blank verse, often broken into half-lines or incomplete lines, also has prompted, the charge that he is derivative and lacking in the capacity to develop a natural "African" English supple and true enough to capture the African sensitility.

His lyric poetry is purer stylistically than his dramatic poetry, fuller and richer in rhythm and texture, and full of myths and allusions to local Ijaw customs and manners. His five-line poem "Ibadan" from his volume *A Reed in the Tide* is typical of his image-making powers:

> *Ibadan,*
> *running splash of rust*
> *and gold – flung and scattered*
> *among seven hills like broken*
> *china in the sun*

and owes a partial debt to imagism, the early twentieth-century literary movement associated with Ezra Pound. His "Three Moods of Princeton" catches the shock of the African student in his first encounter with snow and the culture of snow. Here, in the second of the three "moods," we see

> *The elm trees, still*
> *Shaven bald and gaunt,*
> *In the brief buba*
> *They wear after the snow,*
> *Are a band of alufa*
> *Deployed down the neighborhood.*

Recently Clark has begun to produce works in film, including a documentary, *The Ozidi of Atazi*, an ancient Ijaw epic he had already dealt with in his last play, and *The Ghost Town*, a study of the once important Nigerian port town of Forcados.

Clark is now a professor of English at Lagos University where he also teaches African literature. He is married and has one child.

Africana Publishing Corporation issued Clark's latest volume of poetry,

Casualties: Poems 1966–68, in 1970 and Heinemann published his study of African literature entitled *The Example of Shakespeare* the same year. The five essays in the latter volume, taken from *Transition, Nigeria Magazine, Présence Africaine, African Forum* and *Black Orpheus* magazine, are "Themes and African Poetry of English Expression," "Aspects of Nigerian Drama," "The Communication Line Between Poet and Public," "The Useless Scene in Othello," and "The Legacy of Caliban." The new poetry volume deals, in Clark's own words, with "the unspeakable events that almost tore apart Nigeria." The work is a lament that grieves for the dead and suffering of both sides in the Nigerian Civil War, 1967–69, and the events leading up to it.

Writings: Plays: *Song of a Goat,* Ibadan, Mbari Press, 1961; *Three Plays* (contains *The Masquerade, The Raft,* and *Song of a Goat),* London, Oxford University Press, 1964; *Ozidi,* London, Oxford University Press, 1966.
  Poetry: *Poems,* Ibadan, Mbari Press, 1962; *A Reed in the Tide,* London, Longmans, 1965, 1967; *Casualties: Poems 1966–68,* New York, Africana Publishing Corporation, 1970, and London, Longmans, 1970.
  Satire: *America, their America,* London, A. Deutsch, 1964; Heinemann, 1968, New York, Africana Publishing Corp., 1969.
  Criticism: *The Example of Shakespeare,* London, Longman, and Evanston, Ill., Northwestern University Press, 1970. "Note sur la poésie nigérienne," *Présence Africaine;* No. 68, 1968, "Aspects of Nigerian Drama," *Nigeria Magazine,* June, 1966.
  Films: *The Ozidi of Atazi,* details un-

known; and a documentary on Forcados, *The Ghost Town.*

CLARK, Peter E. (see KUMALO, Peter E.)

CODJOE, Thomas A.
b. ca. 1925, Gold Coast (now Ghana). Popular prose and verse writer, journalist.

Codjoe has been a jack-of-all-trades publisher, writing his own articles and poems, setting up the type and running off copy on a foot-pedaled press. He has been a wholesaler of papers, a news vendor, job-printer, pamphlet-writer and homespun philosopher. For awhile in the 1950's he published a bi-weekly newspaper, *The Voice of Kushara,* which contained his better prose and poetry. His B.A. was taken with Honors at London University and he also has earned the doctorate in Science and Law.

Writings: Prose and poetry in bi-weekly newspaper, *Voice of Kushara.*

COLE, Robert Wellesley
b. October 1907, Adah, Sierra Leone. Novelist.

Cole's *Kossoh Town Boy* celebrates not only the pleasures of being young but the simple rural life of the African villager.

Writings: Novel: *Kossoh Town Boy,* Cambridge, Cambridge University Press, 1960; reprinted 1970.

CONTON, William Farquhar
b. 1925, Bathurst, Gambia.

Novelist, short story writer, teacher, government official.

Though born in Gambia, Conton has spent most of his days in Sierra Leone where he has worked for the most part as an educator. He has served as principal of the Government Secondary School in Bo, Sierra Leone, and is now Chief Education Officer of the Sierra Leone Government.

He has written one novel, *The African* (1964). The moving force in the book is the passion of its hero, Kisimi Kamara, to obtain independence for his people. Freighted with a devotion to his English sweetheart Greta, Kamara succeeds in organizing a dynamic political party that ends the worst aspects of colonialism. Victorious at home, he dies on a strangely benighted voyage to a country that could only be South Africa in his search for Greta's history. The novel, generally awkward in pacing and loaded with prosaic factual or documentary information, has one genuine merit: it does provide a useful picture of the early efforts of the young, Western-educated elites to build independence movements in their homelands once they had returned from study abroad. *The African* has been published in Arabic, Russian, and Hungarian and in two American editions.

Conton has written many short stories, one of which, "The Blood in the Wash Basin," appears in *Pan African Short Stories*. He also has written a history text on Africa which has been used widely.

Writings: Novel: *The African,* London, Heinemann, 1960, 1964; also published in Arabic (twice, 1962 and 1963), Russian (1966), and Hungarian (1963); also in two American editions; Boston, Little Brown, 1960; New York, New American Library, Signet, 1961.

Short story: "The Blood in the Wash Basin" in *Modern African Stories,* London, Faber, 1964.

COOPER, Charles Edward
(pseudonym for KARLEE, Varfelli)

COSTA ALEGRE, Caetano (see ALEGRE, Caetano da Costa)

COUCHORO, Félix
b. ca. 1905, Togo.
Novelist, journalist.

Couchoro earned his living as a letter writer and was active in work for the National Party (Comité de l'Unité Togolaise) organized by Sylvanus Olympio, later first president of independent Togo. French colonial countermeasures forced Couchoro to flee in 1951 and he took up residence in Aflao, a Ghanaian border town near Togo where he remained until 1959, the year of Togolese independence.

He assumed the assistant editorship of the Togolese Information Service and was able to republish his two earliest novels, *L'esclave* and *Amour de féticheuse*. He quickly wrote and published 16 chapbooks, or short popular novels, in serials in *Togo Presse*. All of them were specially prepared for publication because each was subsequently to be separately published by Editogo, the national publishing company. *L'heritage cette peste*, was the only chapbook, however, to be published later as a book. Accordingly, Couchoro has published in book form four novels and, as chapbooks, 16 novelettes.

Writings: Novels: *L'esclave,* Ed. de "La Dépêche Africaine," 1929; *Amour de féticheuse,* Ouidah, P. d'Almeida, 1941; *Drame, d'amour à Anecho,* Ouidah, Dahomey, P. d'Almeida, 1950; *L'heritage, cette peste,* Lomé, Impr. Editogo, 1963. Novelettes *(all in Togo Presse)*: *Max Mensah* Oct 1–Nov 14, 1962; *Béa et Marilou,* Dec 31, 1962–Feb 16, 1963; *Les secrets d'Elénore* (called *L'héritage cette peste* in book form), Feb 16–April 17, 1963; *Pauvre Alexandrine,* Oct 1–Nov 18,1964; *Sinistré d'Abidjan,* Feb 12–April 1, 1965; *La dot plaie sociale,* Feb 14–April 3, 1966; *Le passé resurgit,* April 4–June 7, 1966; *Les caprices du destin,* June 8–Aug 2, 1966; *Accusée, levez-vous,* Feb 24–April 6, l967; *Gangsters et policiers* Aug 31–Oct 20, l967; *Les gens sont méchants* Oct 21– Dec 4,1967; *Ici bas tout se paie,* Dec 5, 1967–Jan 16, 1968; *Le secret de Ramanou,* Jan 17–March 2, 1968; *L'homme á la Mercédés-Benz,* Mar 4– April 25, 1968; *Les dix plaies de l'Afrique,* Sept 26–Nov 11,1968; *Fille de nationaliste,* Feb 13–April 17,1969; *D'Aklakou á El Mina,* Jan 23–March 13,1970. Also published as serials were the previously published works: *L'esclave,* April 27–Sept 30, 1962; and *Amour de féticheuse au Togo,* July 10– Aug 30, 1967.

Biographical/Critical Source: Alain Ricard, "Francophone Chapbooks in West Africa: A Bibliographical Note," in *Research in African Literatures,* III, 1, Spring, 1972; Robert Cornevin, "Felix Couchoro," in *Dictionnaire bio-bibliographique du Dahomey,* Porto Novo, IRAD, 1969.

COULIBALY, Augustin-Sonde

b. 1933, Tin-Orodara, Upper Volta.
Poet, novelist, journalist, collector of folklore, government official.

Coulibaly completed his primary studies at Orodara in 1942, his highschool work in Abidjan, Ivory Coast, in 1946, and his university work at the Centre International d'Enseignement Supérieur de Journalisme at the University of Strasbourg, 1962. He has contributed articles and poems to such journals as *Présence Africaine* (Paris), *Dialogue et Culture* (Brussels), *Poésie Vivante* (Geneva), and *Encres-Vives* (Toulouse). From 1967 to 1969 he served as the director of the Cercle d'Activités Littéraires et Artistiques de Haute Volta of which he was the founder and has been occupied for the past decade in collecting the traditional oral literature of his country. His anthology of 12 Voltaic writers is being prepared for publication and is scheduled for release in 1973. His collection of poems published in various journals, *Minuit-Soleil,* won second prize in the *Encres-Vives* competition of 1965.

His governmental honors and posts have been: Knight of the Order of Arts and Letters of the French Republic, 1962; Director of the Cabinet of the Voltaic Ministry of Justice, 1966–71; and presently, Head of the Press in the President's Office in Ouagadougou. He is married with three sons and two daughters.

Coulibaly's poetry in French is direct and rich in the gestures and ways of his people. The objects of daily use are also brought in organically to make of his verse a thoughtful blend of the musicality of the French language and the contents and preoccupations of an African. Occasionally there are references to Christian saints, practices and holidays. All in all, the poetry is not négritudist, for there is little nostalgia for the past and only a few poems show signs of anger or racial pride of the defensive sort. There is merely statement of feeling and simplicity of tone.

The collection *Quand chante le nègre* has more poems concerned with the cruelties of colonialism than the two earlier ones, but the anger seems "historical" and almost abstract—rather than based on personal grievances. Coulibaly believes that the poet has the opportunity of reconciling his peoples' bitterness with hopes of fraternity in a future without war and oppression.

Writings: Poems: *Minuit-Soleil* (Midnight Sun), 1960; *Paradis noir* (Black Paradise), 1965; *Quand chant le nègre* (When the Black Man Sings), 1966; individual and groups of poems in various journals: collections in mimeograph.

Novels: in mimeograph: *Les rives du Tontombili* (The Shores of the Tontombili), 1955; *Enfer lune de miel* (A Hellish Honey-moon), 1956; *Les saintes erreurs* (The Holy Errors), 1958; and *Les dieux délinquants* (The Delinquent Gods), 1968.

Critical Essay: *Essai d'approche à la culture africaine,* in mimeograph.

Anthology: being prepared for the press: "Anthologie africaine voltaïque."

CRAVEIRINHA, José (pseudonym: José Gr. Vetrinha)
b. May 28, 1922, Lourenço Marques, Mozambique.
Poet, story writer, journalist.

Craveirinha is a journalist whose work is gradually appearing in various anthologies and reviews, including Moore and Beier's *Modern Poetry from Africa.* He has worked for the Portuguese language journals in Mozambique, *Brado Africano, Notícias,* and *Tribuna.* His early work made him a leader of the new nationalist poets from the country. He has spent a considerable time in various Portuguese prisons because of his work with African resistance groups.

One collection of his poetry, *Chigubo,* was published in Lisbon in 1964. Five lengthy poems, "Poema 'Africa',", "Poema Manifesto," "Poema do futuro cidadào," "Poema 'Ao Meu Pai'," and "Mamana Saquina," appear in *New Sum of Poetry from the Negro World.* Two of his poems, translated by Phillippa Rumsey into English, "Poem of the Future Citizen," and "Song of the Negro on the Ferry" also appear in Ezekiel Mphahlele's *African Writing Today.* In some of his poems he employs a Walt Whitman-like catalogue of African place names:

And I shout Inhamússua, Mutamba Mas-
/sangulo!!!
And again I shout Inhamússua, Mutamba
/Massangulo!!!

Craveirinha

And other names of my land
Come to my filial mind, sweet and proud
/names.

Some twenty lines each of his poems "Grito negro" and "N'goma" (The Big Drum), which originally appeared in *Notícias do Bloqueiro Oporto,* No. 6 (1960), are given with translation in G. M. Moser's *Essays in Portuguese-African Literature.* One long poem, "Cantico a un dio di Catrane" (A Song to a God of Catrane) appeared in the early 1960's in an Italian translation.

Writings: Poems in *Modern Poetry from Africa,* Moore and Beier, editors, revised edition, London, Penguin, 1968; *New Sum of Poetry from the Negro World,* Paris, Présence Africaine, Vol. 57, 1966; *African Writing Today,* Ezekiel Mphahlele, editor, London, Penguin, 1967; excerpts from poems, "Grito negro" and "N'goma," in *Essays in Portuguese-African Literature,* University Park, Pennsylvania, Penn State Studies, 26, 1969; *Chigubo,* Lisbon, Edição da Casa dos Estudantes do Império, 1964. Unpublished: "Manifesto. Colectânea de poesias," which won the Alexandre Dáskalos Prize in November, 1962, awarded by the Casa dos Estudantes do Ultramar, Lisbon.

Poem: "Cantico a un dio di Catrane," translated into Italian by Joyce Lussu, Milan, Lerici, 196?

CUGOANA, Ottobah

b. ca. 1745, Ajumako, near Winneba in what is now Ghana; d. ca. 1790. Tract writer.

Stolen as a child from his Fanti parents, Cugoana was eventually brought to England from America to serve in the household of an Englishman. Believed freed in 1772 or 1773, possibly because of the James Somerset case which established a precedent for liberating slaves in England, Cugoana, whose kindly master had helped him to an education and to baptism, became active in the reform movements seeking the abolition of slavery. He eventually married an English woman, had a family, and died in England.

His *Thoughts and Sentiments on the Evil and Wicked Traffic and Commerce of the Human Species* marshals the theological, humanitarian and commonsensical arguments against slavery. His major concern was to attack and reduce to absurdity once and for all the supposed Scriptural sanction of slavery. The 148-page work is written in a vivid, rhetorical, baroque style, and is full of graphic descriptions of slavery.

Writings: Tract, *Thoughts and Sentiments on the Evil and Wicked Traffic and Commerce of the Human Species* London, T. Becket, 1787; republished, Legon, Ghana, Institute of African Studies, University of Ghana, 1966 (?), New York, Africana Publishing Corporation, 1969.

Biographical/Critical Source: Robert July, *The Origins of Modern African Thought,* New York, Praeger, Inc., 1967.

D

da COSTA ANDRADE, Fernando
(see ANDRADE, Costa)

da CRUZ, Viriato
b. March 25, 1928, Porto Amboim, Angola.
Poet, journalist.

Viriato da Cruz has worked on various Portuguese–Angolan journals and was one of the founders of the movement Vamos Descrobrir Angola (We're Going to Discover Angola), and of the more activist MPLA (Movimento Popular de Libertação de Angola), of which he was once secretary general. (Since 1963 MPLA has been outlawed by the Portuguese government.) He is presently living in exile in Peking, China, after some years in exile in Algeria. In China he is a member of the Office of Afro–Asian Writers.

Da Cruz' one volume of verse is *Colectânea de poemas* (A Collection of Verse). He often works in the broken patois of Portuguese spoken by illiterate Angolan blacks called pequeno-portuguêse and scorned by white Angolans as "pretoquês" (swarthy-guese). He is represented in *New Sum of Poetry from the Negro World*. Da Cruz' poem, "Sô

Santo" (Holy Seigneur) points out the thought processes and beliefs which he shared with such writers of his generation as Mário Pinto de Andrade, Antonio Jacinto and Agostinho Neto. Da Cruz describes this group as "modern" in spirit as compared to the colonialized minds of the poets of the early 1900's.

Writings: Poetry: *Colectânea de poemas,* Lisbon Edição da Casa dos Estudantes do Império, 1961; poems in *New Sum of Poetry from the Negro World,* Paris, Presence Africaine, Vol. 57, 1966.

DADIE, Bernard Binlin
b. 1916, Assinie, Ivory Coast.
Novelist, playwright, poet.

A member of the Brafe people, a group of the Agni Ashante who had emigrated to the Ivory Coast from the old Gold Coast between 1620 and 1730, Bernard Dadié, at the age of six, went to live with his uncle, Melantchi, on a plantation near Bingerville, some miles from the capital, Abidjan. On the death of his uncle in 1929, a close friend of Bernard's father, M. Marius Gantry, offered to take him to Martinique to further his education, but the father refused, wishing to keep the boy with him. Despite this lost opportunity, the young Dadié struggled to get a French education. He succeeded in attending, first, the Catholic School in Grand-Bassam called L'Ecole du Quartier-de-France, then L'Ecole Primaire Supérieure, Binger-ville, and finally the famous Ecole Nor-male, William–Ponty, Gorée, Dakar, Senegal, where he took the Diplôme de Commis d'Administration. His student poetry was first published in the Dakar journal, *Genèse*.

Dadié worked from 1936 to 1947 at IFAN (Institut Français d'Afrique Noire) in Dakar, then served with the Ivory Coast Information Service as an officer from 1947 to 1960, leaving to become Director of Fine Arts and Research for the Ivorian Government. He is presently the Director of Cultural Affairs of his country.

His three volumes of poetry are *Afrique debout* (Africa Upright), a patri-otic work full of a love for his people; *La ronde des jours* (The Circle of Days), and *Hommes de tous les continents* (Men of Every Continent), poems and long tales. His novels and stories are *Le pagne noir: contes Africains* (The Black Cloth: African Stories), a long short story pro-viding the volume its title; and the novels, *Climbié*, which deals with the day-to-day experiences of a young Ivorian at home; and *Un nègre à Paris* (A Black in Paris), which exploits the well-known theme of the young African coming to grips with his European education and environment. In 1964, Dadié published a personal narrative, *Patron de New York*.

Seghers published his one-volume col-lection of tales, *Légendes africaines* (1954, 1966), and Présence Africaine put out his most recent play, *Monsieur Thôgô-gnini*, in 1970. Africana Publishing House in New York issued a translation of *Climbié* by Karen C. Chapman in 1971.

His play, *Assemien Déhylé, roi du Sanwi (Chronique agni)* (Assemien Dehyle, King of the Sanwi [Chronicle of the Agni]), was published in the "Album officiel de la Mission Pontificale" in 1936 and later, after performance at the Théâtre Champs-Elysées, Paris, 1937, in *L'Education Africaine*. His second play, *Les villes* (The Cities) appeared in 1939 in Abidjan, Ivory Coast, but remains unpublished. The earlier play, a dramatization of early Ivory Coast his-tory, was first performed in a student production at Lycée William Ponty in 1936. Recently published, in 1971, was a hird drama, *Béatrice du Congo* (Beatrice of the Congo), and a volume of three short plays, *Sidi Maitre Escroc; Situation difficile; Serment d'amour.* Présence Africaine has published many of his stories and collected tales as well as his articles of literary criticism and history. Seghers in Paris in 1966 published his folktales, many of his poems and the novel, *Climbié* in one large volume, *Légendes et poèmes; La ville où nul ne meurt* (The Place Where Nothing Dies), a travel record; and *Les voix dans le vent* (Voices in the Wind), a play.

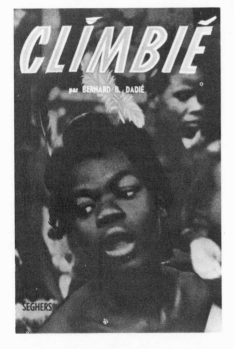

Un nègre à Paris was the first African novel since the Second World War to be set in Paris though several Black Caribbean authors had done so, and Dadié seizes the opportunity to cast a hard eye at the French on their home territory. Though Camara Laye in *L'en-* *fant noir,* and the writers Sadji and Malonga had earlier sent their heroes off to Europe, they did not choose to describe their protagonists' lives there. But following Dadié, Ak Loba in *Kocoumba, l'étudiant noir* (1960) and Sheikh Hamidou Kane in *L'aventure ambiguë* (1961), show their protagonists in the French capital.

Dadié is quoted in *Afrique*, No. 43 (1964), in the article, "Bernard Dadié, ou l'écrivain engagé" (Bernard Dadié, or the Involved Writer), as saying: "Present-day African poems must cry out encouragement to overcome our difficulties. Poets must not allow themselves the luxury of ever praising the joys of life when there are genuine problems of making a living which must be solved." In his poem "Aux Poets" (To Poets) which appears in the original French and in English translation in Austin J. Shelton's *The African Assertion* he writes:

Fishermen of the dawn
breakers of chains
in the night,
Harvesters of stars
Old paladins, roaming the world,

asserting the role and responsibilities of the new African artists, and he ends the poem with these lines:

I am sick of corners
In my steel cage
in my tumultuous silence.

Fishermen of the dawn
Harvesters of stars
Make it Day around me
day around all of my brothers.

Writings: Novels: *Climbié,* Paris, Seghers, 1956; English translation by Karen C. Chapman, New York, Africana Publishing House, 1971 and London,

Heinemann, 1971; *Un nègre à Paris*, Paris, Seghers, 1959.

Poetry: *Afrique debout*, Paris, Seghers, 1950; *La ronde des jours*, Paris, Seghers, 1956; poem, "Aux Poets," in *The African Assertion*, Austin J. Shelton, editor, New York, Odyssey Press, 1968.

Tales and poems: *Hommes de tous les continents*, Paris, Présence Africaine, 1967.

Stories: *Le pagne noir: contes africains*, Paris, Présence Africaine, 1955, 1970.

Travel: *La ville où nul ne meurt. (Rome.)*, Paris, Présence Africaine, 1968; *Patron de New York*, Paris, Présence Africaine, 1964.

Plays: *Assémien Déhylé, roi du Sanwi (Chronique agni)*, in Album officiel de la Mission Pontificale, Dakar, 1936; also *L'Education Africaine*, numero spéciale, 1937; *Les villes*, 1939, unpublished; *Monsieur Thôgô-gnini*, Présence Africaine, 1970; *Béatrice du Congo*, Paris, Présence Africaine, 1971, and *Sidi Maitre Escroc; Situation difficile; Serment d'amour*, Paris, Présence Africaine, 1971; *Les voix dans le vent*, Yaoundé, CLE, 1970.

Collection of tales: *Legendes africaines*, Seghers, 1954, 1966, introduction by Alioune Diop; *Les belles histoires de Kacou Ananzé, l'araignée*, Paris, F. Nathan, 1963?

Collection: *Légendes et poèms. Afrique debout. Légendes africaines; Climbié. La ronde des jours*. Paris, Seghers, 1967.

Biographical/Critical Sources: Bernard Binlin Dadié, C. Quillateau, editor, Paris, Présence Africaine, 1968; *Writings in French from Senegal to Cameroon*, A. C. Brench, London, Oxford Press, 1967, including excerpts from *Un nègre à Paris*, along with a Dadié bibliography and criticism; *Bernard Dadié*, a biography, Series: Littérature Africaine, Paris, Fernand Nathan, 1971; article, "Bernard

Dadié, ou l'écrivain engagé," *Afrique*, No. 43, 1964.

da GRACA, José Veira Mateus
(see VEIRA, Luandino)

da MATTA, Joaquim Dias Cordeiro
(also da Mata in modern spelling, and MATTA, Jakim Ria)
b. December 25, 1857, Angola; d. March 2, 1894, Angola.
Poet, story writer, ethnographer, linguist.

Da Matta was a scholar of Kimbundu, the Creole language of Luanda, capital of Angola, and published *Philosophia popular em provérbios angolenses* (Popular Philosophy in Angolan Proverbs) in 1891, and *Ensaios de Dicionário Kimbundo-Português* (Essays Toward a Kimbundu-Portuguese Dictionary) in 1893. The former work contained over 700 Kimbundu proverbs and riddles from the Luanda district. Under the stimulation of Héli Chatelain, the noted Swiss missionary and early collector of African folklore, da Matta also published a Kimbundu grammar in 1892 and a small Kimbundu dictionary. G. M. Moser's *Essays in Portuguese African Literature* discusses Chatelain's influence on da Matta and quotes at some length the inspirational letter of Chatelain calling for "holy zeal" in developing a budding Angolan literature. The entire letter appeared in da Matta's own first work, the *Philosophia popular*. Moser also notes that Mário Antonio's study, *A sociedade angolana do fim do século XIX e um seu escritor* (Angolan Society at the End of the 19th Century and its Writer) has an important section devoted to da Matta and his period. Moser also notes that da Matta published at least eleven poems and one folktale in *Almanach de Lembranças* between 1879 and 1894.

Despite these scholarly efforts to recognize and to develop the local language, da Matta in his own poetry turned to tried and true Portuguese in his own collection, *Delírios: Versos 1875–1887* (Raptures: Verse 1875–1887).

Writings: Poetry: *Delírios: Versos 1875–1887*, Lisbon, 1887; *Almanach de Lembranças*, Lisbon, 1879–1894, one story and eleven poems.

Linguistic studies: *Philosophia popular em provérbios angolenses*, Lisbon, Typographia e Stereotypia Moderna, 1891; *Ensaios de Dicionário Kimbundu-Português*, Lisbon, 1893; a Kimbundu grammer, 1892; a small Kimbundu dictionary, date unknown.

Biographical/Critical Sources: Essays in Portuguese African Literature, G. M. Moser, University Park, Pennsylvania, Penn State Studies, 26, 1969; Mário António, *A sociedade angolana do fim do século XIX e um seu escritor*, Luanda, 1961.

DANQUAH, Joseph Kwame Kyeretwie Boakye
1895–1965, former Gold Coast, now Ghana.
Playwright, scholar, statesman (published in English and Akuapem-Twi).

One of the earliest playwrights from Black Africa, Joseph Boakye Danquah published two five-act dramas: *Nyankonsem* (Heavenly Tales) written in 1946 in Akuapem-Twi, his maternal tongue; and *The Third Woman*, a 152-page work written in English. The latter, an allegorical play, mixes African folk elements with Shakespearean foolery in the tale of a wise "fool" who wins a throne and a beautiful woman. Danquah's second Twi play, *Biribi wo baabi* (There Is More Beyond), remains in manuscript. Anthony Graham–White, in an essay, "J. B. Danquah: Evolué Playwright," in *New African Literature and the Arts*, criticizes the play for failing to bring in much legitimate African culture or genuine concerns in its blank verse lines which are "waveringly Shakespearean," and questions its claim to follow the unities of time, place, and action. Graham-White concludes his study, "It must be added that *The Third Woman* is interesting only for the way in which its complex construction illustrates the position of the évolué; as drama it is static and literary. So far as I know, it has never been performed."

Other works of Danquah are: *Revelation of Culture in Ghana* (1961) which explores the migration of the iron-working Akan people as they move south, away from the marauding Arabs, down to the present Ghana, there to meet neolithic peoples in the forest areas; and *The Akan Doctrine of God* (1944, 1968).

A 34-page pamphlet, *Liberty: A Page from the Life of J. B. Danquah*, was published in Accra.

Writings: Plays: *Nyankonsem*, London, Longmans, 1941; *The Third Woman*, London and Redhill, Surrey, United Society for Christian Literature, 1943; *Biribi wo baabi*, unpublished.
Studies: *Revelation of Culture in Ghana*, Accra, 1961; *The Akan Doctrine of God*, 1944, 1968;
Pamphlet: *Liberty: A Page from the Life*

of J. B. Danquah, Accra, H. K. Akyempong, 1960.

Biographical/Critical Source: Anthony Graham–White, "J. B. Danquah: Evolué Playwright," *New African Literature and the Arts,* New York, Crowell, 1970.

DANQUAH, Mabel, née Dove
(also known as MENSAH, Marjorie)
b. ca. 1910, Gold Coast, now Ghana.
Short story writer, journalist, legislator.

Mabel Dove was educated in local schools and married J. B. Danquah, playwright and scholar. She did additional study in England and also travelled in Europe and the United States before returning to the Gold Coast to serve as editor of the *Accra Evening News.* She was the first woman to be elected a member of an African legislature when she became a member in 1952 of the parliament of the embryonic new state of Ghana. Under the pseudonym Marjorie Mensah she contributed a column to the *West African Times.* She is represented in Langston Hughes' *An African Treasury* and in A. J. Shelton's *The African Assertion.*

Three of her stories, "Anticipation," "Payment," and "The Torn Veil," appear in *African New Writing.* The latter tale, a ghost story, depicts the rejection by an up-and-coming merchant of his country or "cloth" wife who speaks only Ga and Twi and knows no English and few European ways. Wishing to cast her aside in favor of a modern girl, an English speaking school teacher, he repudiates his wife and sets out to marry the new girl who is nothing loathe to make such a good catch. The Church wedding solemnizes the new union, but

sleeping in his chair, ill from drink, too much food, and a bad conscience after the banquet, the husband dreams or "sees" his first wife, younger and more beautiful than ever. In an effort to catch her "wedding train" he rises in his stupor to seize her and chases the wraith around the dining room table. He falls, braining himself. The next morning the dead man is discovered, and a telegram is delivered from the father of the first wife saying that his daughter, living with him, had died the previous day at 10 a.m.

Basically a tale of new Africans lost between their old world and the new, it is a sad story of pompous pride on the part of Kwame Asante, the husband, and the righteous hurt of the faithful and lovely wife, who is intelligent and gentle, if not Western educated.

"The Torn Veil" also appears in *A Selection of African Prose: 2. Written Prose.*

"Anticipation," her tale of the twentieth anniversary celebration of the ruler Nana Aduku II's "taking of the stool" (coming to power), appears in Langston Hughes' *An African Treasury.*

Writings: Short stories: "Anticipation," "Payment," and "The Torn Veil," in *African New Writing,* London, Lutterworth Press, 1947; stories also in *An African Treasury,* Langston Hughes, editor, New York, Crown Publishers, 1960; *The African Assertion,* A. J. Shelton, New York, the Odyssey Press, 1968; *A Selection of African Prose: 2. Written Prose,* W. H. Whiteley, editor, Oxford, Clarendon Press, 1964.

DASCALOS, Alexandre
Mendonça de Oliveira (see
DASKALOS, Alexandre)

da SILVEIRA, Onésimo
b. February 10, 1935, São Vicente,
Cape Verde.
Poet, critic, government official.

Da Silveira first worked in São Tomé on
the plantations from 1956 to 1959 with
forced laborers and then as a minor official in Angola. He has contributed to the
Cape Verde review *Claridada* and is represented in the collections, *Coleccão
Imbondeiro*, and the student anthology,
Coleccão Autores Ultramarinos. He is also
in *New Sum of Poetry from the Negro World*,
(and Mário de Andrade's *Literatura
africana de expressão portuguêsa, Vol. I,
Poesia* (1967).

He has published two small collections
of verse: *Hora grande* (The Big Time)
and *Toda a gente fala: sim, senhor*
(Everybody Says Yes, Boss). The story
which gives its name to the volume is
followed by three poems. His one
political work is the 32-page essay,
*Consciencialização na literatura cabo-
verdiano* (Growing Self-Awareness in
Cape Verde Literature). Because of his
political views and Portuguese measures
taken against him, he fled his homeland
and for a time lived in exile in the
Peoples' Republic of China, where,
harshly criticizing the European absorption of the culture of the islands, he has
called for a return to Black African
values and leadership. More recently he
has sought exile in Sweden. G. M. Moser
gives a short English translation of Silveira's ideas in his *Essays in Portuguese-
African Literature*. Moser also discusses
Silveira's specific program for re-
Africanizing Cape Verdean literature.

Writings: Poetry: *Hora grande*, Nova Lisboa, Angola, Publicações Bailundo,
1962; (1967); *Toda a gente fala: sim,*
senhor, Sá da Bandeira, Angola,
Publicações Imbondeiro, 1960; poems in
Colecção imbondeiro, Angola; *Colecção
autores ultramarinos*, Lisbon, Edição da
Casa dos Estudantes do Império;
Literatura africana de expressão portuguêsa,
M. de Andrade, editor, *Vol. I, Poesia,
1967; New Sum of Poetry from the Negro
World*, Paris, Présence Africaine, Vol. 57,
1966.

Criticism: *Consciencialização na
literatura caboverdiano*, Lisbon, Casa dos
Estudantes do Império, 1963.

Biographical/Critical Source: Essays in Por-
tuguese–African Literature, G. M. Moser,
University Park, Pennsylvania, Penn
State Studies 26, 1969.

DASKALOS, Alexandre (also
DASCALOS, Alexandre Mendonça
de Oliveira)
b. 1924, Nova Lisboa, Angola; d. 1961.
Poet, veterinarian.

After local schooling, he studied veterinary medicine in Portugal and practised
his profession for some 15 years in
Angola. His poetic works which had
appeared in various journals or left in
manuscript, were organized into two
collections: *Colectânea de poemas* 1947–
1950 (A Collection of Poems 1947–
1950), and *Poesias* (Poetry), the latter
edited by Alfredo Margarido. He is represented in *Poetas e contistas africanos de
expressão portuguêsa* (African Poets and
Story-tellers of Portuguese Expression).

Writings: Poetry: *Colectânea de poemas
1947–1950*, Nova Lisboa, Angola,
Bailundo, 1961; *Poesias*. Lisbon, Casa
dos Estudantes do Império, 1961;
Anthology: *Poetas e contistas africanos*

de expressão portuguêsa. São Paulo, Editôra Brasiliense, 1963.

DAZANA, S.
b. September 1905, Tsolo District, South Africa.
Xhosa novelist.

Dazana was educated at Lovedale where he obtained the Junior Certificate in 1924 and the Primary Higher Certificate in 1926. The following year he taught at Shawhury Practising School, and in 1930 he was transferred to St. Matthew's College. In 1931 he was appointed principal of St. Cuthbert's Higher Boarding School, a post he held until 1937. In 1941 he was made a Supervisor of Schools, and in 1955 he was promoted to Sub-Inspector of Bantu Schools at 'Umtata. He had obtained his B.A. from an American university with specialized study in Xhosa language and literature.

Dazana won first prize in 1956 in the Afrikaanse Pers-Boekhandel competition for his Xhosa novel *Ukufika kukaMadodana* (Madodana's Arrival), unpublished.

Writings: Novel: *Ukufika kukaMadodana,* unpublished.

de ALMEIDA, José Maria, and
Francisco Viana (also VIANA de ALMEIDA, José Maria da Fonseca, and also ALMEIDA, José Maria da Fonseca)
b. 1903, São Tomé.
Storywriter, journalist.

Born on the small island off the coast of the Cameroon, de Almeida has joined other young intellectuals from the Cape Verde Islands and Angola in the effort to bring back the legitimate Black African heritage of the Portuguese–African writer. However, his one volume of published stories, *Maiá Póçon* (Mary from Town), published in Lisbon, 1937, and concerned with plantation life, is considered poorly written. Nevertheless, it is a pioneering and honest effort to deal with a subject beyond the Creole world of the coastal city. He published this work under the name "Viana de Almeida."

One of his tales, "O ódio de raças" (Race Hatred), exploits the rather cliché situation of the black medical doctor saving a white mother and child during a terrible delivery and the instant conversion of the white racist husband. But more important than the plot is the picture concerning the hesitant efforts of young Creole intellectuals to organize a literary group on the island. For the Portuguese authorities such efforts could only be seen as revolutionary or potentially so. This reflects the hesitant, but important work, of the young island intellectuals in the early 1960's, best represented by Onésimo Silveiro's *Consciencialização na literatura caboverdiana* (Growing Self-Awareness in the Literature of Cape Verde), 1963, which proclaims that the young writers' main task is to make the ordinary islanders highly conscious of their African past and African future.

Writings: Short stories: *Maiá Póçon, Contos africanos,* Lisbon, Momento, 1937.

de ANDRADE, Mário Coelho Pinto
b. August 21, 1928, Galungo Alto, Angola.
Poet, critic, politician (publishes in Portuguese and Kimbundu)

Educated in the early years of school in Angola, he went to high school in Luanda, in Mozambique, in Lisbon, and then to Paris for university studies in sociology. He was one of the leaders of Movimento Popular de Libertação de Angola (MPLA), founded secretly in 1957 in Luanda, an early effort to oppose Portuguese colonialism. He also took an active part in the union of the MPLA with three other groups of rebels in the Frente Revolucionãria Africana para a Independência das Colónias Portuguêsas (FRAIN), formed in Tunis, 1960, at the second All-African Peoples' Congress.

Many of the leaders of MPLA were arrested in March, 1959, by PIDE (the Portuguese Secret Police) and consequently new headquarters had to be established, first in Conakry, Guinea, and then, on October 30, 1961, in Leopoldville, now Kinshasa, Zaïre. De Andrade, then president of the organization, declared to a committee of the United Nations on August 9, 1962, that there were 50,000 card-carrying members. Despite this alleged strength, however, times were difficult and de Andrade felt it necessary to go into exile in Paris during the early 1960's, working for a time for *Présence Africaine*, the leading French language journal of African writing. He now resides in Rabat, Morocco, after stays in Guinea and Algeria.

In 1958 de Andrade helped organize the Conference of Negro Writers in Rome, and he began to publish scholarly articles in sociology reviews issued in Angola, Brazil, and Portugal. His poems have appeared in a variety of reviews and his poem, "Cancão de Sabalu" (Song of Sabalu), written originally in his mother tongue of Kimbundu, is found in *New Sum of Poetry from the Negro World*.

His story "Eme ngana, eme muene," appeared in the journal *Mensagem* (Messenger) (1952), and in *Côntistas angolanos*, 1952.

In 1958, de Andrade published in France the pioneering work, *Antologia da poesia negra de expressão portuguêsa*, 106 pages. His earlier collection of just 18 pages had been published in Lisbon and circulated clandestinely in Angola and other Portuguese colonies as *Caderno de poesia negra de expressão portuguêse*, 1953. Two large mimeographed volumes, were published in Algiers: *Literatura africana de expressão portuguêsa*, Vol. 1. *Poesia*, 326 pages, 1967, and *Vol. 2. Prosa*, 301 pages. A French translation of the volume, by Jean Todrani and André Joucla-Ruau, was published in Paris as *La poésie africaine d'expression portugaise. Anthologie précédée de "Evolution et tendances actuelles"* (African Poetry in Portuguese. An Anthology preceded by "Current tendencies and developments"), 148 pages. The *Antologia* and both the Algiers volumes have been republished by Kraus Reprint (1970) in three new clothbound volumes. De Andrade offers an introduction to the set which places the poetical and prose works in their political and cultural contexts, making of them an expression of an oppressed people fighting for their freedom and personal dignity.

Writings: Poem: "Cancão de Sabalu," *New Sum of Poetry from the Negro World*, Paris, Présence Africaine, Vol. 57, 1966.

Anthologies: with Francisco José Tenreiro, *Caderno de poesia negra de expressão portuguêsa*, Lisbon, Livraria Escolar Editôra, 1953; *Antologia da poesia negra de expressão portuguêsa, precedida de "cultura negro-africana assimilação,"* Eds., Pierre-Jean Oswald, Paris, Lisbon, 1958; *Literatura africana de expressão portuguese,*

de Andrade

Vol. 1 Poesia, Algiers, 1967: *Vol. 2, Prosa,* Algiers, 1968, both mimeographed; in French translation, *La poésie africaine d'expression portugaise. Anthologie précédée de "Evolution et tendances actuelles, in Présence Africaine,* No. 65, Paris, 1968, and Honfleur, France, P–J Oswald, 1969; *Antologia* and both Algiers volumes republished, Kraus Reprint, Nendeln, Liechtenstein, 1970.

Italian translation of two Algiers volumes: *Letteratura Negra,* Vol I: *La poesia,* Vol II, *La Prosa,* Rome, Editori Riuniti, 1961.

Story: "Eme ngana, eme muene" in *Mensagem,* Luanda, 1952; also in *Contistas angolanos,* Lisbon, Casa dos Estudantes do Império, 1960.

Biographical/Critical Source: Southern Africa in Transition, Davis and Baker, editors, New York, Praeger, 1966.

de GRAFT, Joe Coliman
b. ca. 1932, Ghana.
Novelist, short story writer, playwright, poet.

De Graft has had a widely varied career both at home and elsewhere. In the early years of Ghana's independence, he organized the Drama Program at Ghana's School of Music and Drama and published an early play, *Sons and Daughters.* The play shows the children of Aaron Ofosua a conservative struggling to realize an independent life in the new Africa. At present De Graft works for UNESCO in Kenya.

One of his popular works still in print is *The secret of Opokuwa: The success story of the girl with a big state secret.* Another of his popularly priced works from Anowuo is *Visitor from the past* (1968).

Fifteen of his poems are found in *Messages: Poems from Ghana.* The first poem in the group, "The Gene," worries about the nuclear holocaust. It ends:
Who will redeem the future?
Time is a hermaphrodite,
And the ulcer burns crimson on her
/chromosome.

De Graft's one-act play, *Through a Film Darkly,* was favorably reviewed in *African Report* (May, 1971) by Mary Robert Patterson. It was originally produced as *Visitors from the Past* by the Ghana Dance Studio, Accra, September, 1962, and later staged by the University of Ghana Drama Studio in 1966 in a slightly revised version. The play shows two Ghanaian couples, one mixed, working out their destinies in an Africa loved and misunderstood and with their racial consciousness being very raw because of recent experiences in London. The "film" of the title is a film of sputum spit at one of the protagonists in a never-to-be-forgotten incident in England. The play is jazzy, "modern," and attempts to show the over-Westernized "elites" trying to readjust to the African scale and value of things after many years abroad.

Okyeame, the Ghanaian literary review, published his short play, *Old Kweku,* in 1965.

Writings: Novel: *The secret of Opokuwa: The success story of the girl with a big state secret,* Accra, Anowuo Educational Publications, 1967; *Visitor from the past,* Accra, Anowuo Educational Publications, 1968.

Plays: *Sons and Daughters,* London, Oxford University Press, 1963; *Through a Film Darkly,* London, Oxford University Press, 1970; *Old Kweku,* in *Okyeame,* Vol. 2, No. 2, June, 1965.

Poems: in *Messages: Poems from Ghana,* Awoonor and Adali-Mortty, editors, London, Heinemann, 1971.

DEI–ANANG, Michael Francis
b. 1909, Mampong–Akwapim, Gold Coast, now Ghana.
Poet, playwright, story writer.

Educated at Achimota College, Ghana, and the University of London, he began his career as a civil servant. Since 1938 he has served in several ministries in the pre- and post-colonial Ghana, including an assignment as Principal Secretary of State in the Ministry of Foreign Affairs. He attended the Bandung Conference of Unaligned States in 1955 as a delegate of Ghana. Arrested for two months after the fall of Nkrumah, he was released and is presently heading the Secretariat for African Affairs in Accra. He has long maintained an interest in the folk poetry and legends of his people.

His poems in English were the first creative works by an African to be published in the Gold Coast. His first volumes of verse were *Wayward Lines from Africa* (1946), and *Africa Speaks,* 1959 which contain a useful introductory essay on African poetry, interesting partly because so much has happened since its publication in this area. Individual poems have appeared in the Ghanaian journal *Okyeame* and in Langston Hughes' *An African Treasury.*

Recent volumes of verses are: *Ghana semi–tones, 18 new poems,* and *Ghana Glory. Poems on Ghana and Ghanaian Life* [*with Yaw Warren and an introduction by Kwame Nkrumah*].

His one play is *Okomfo Anokye's Golden Stool,* in three acts, based on the ancient legend of the influence tribal gods had on two royal Ashanti lovers. First published in 1960, this play was produced by the University of Chicago's Masquers Theatre in 1961 in Chicago and appeared in a second edition by Waterville Publishing House; 1963.

More didactic was his earlier work *Cocoa Comes to Mampong: Brief Dramatic Sketches Based on the Story of Cocoa in the Gold Coast and some Occasional Verses* which tells of the arrival of the cocoa culture in his natal area.

A writer of the "old school," his work now seems too obviously intended to instruct and reflective of English styles and mannerisms that poorly reflect African reality.

Writings: Poetry: *Wayward Lines from*

Africa, London, United Society for Christian Literature, 1946; Kraus Reprint, Nendeln, Liechtenstein, 1971; *Africa Speaks,* Accra, Presbyterian Book Depot, 1962; *Ghana semi-tones,* Accra, Presbyterian Book Depot, 1962; *Ghana Glory. Poems on Ghana and Ghanaian Life,* London, Nelson, 1965; poems in *Okyeame; An African Treasury,* Langston Hughes, editor, New York, 1960.

Play: *Okomfo Anokye's Golden Stool,* Ilfracombe, Devonshire, Stockwell, 1960; second edition, Accra, Waterville Publishing House, 1963.

Historical sketches: *Cocoa Comes to Mampong,* Cape Coast, Methodist Book Depot, 1949; Kraus Reprint, Nendeln, Liechtenstein, 1971.

DEMBELE, Sidiki
b. ca. 1930, Mali.
Novelist, playwright.

Dembele has published one work of fiction, *Les inutiles* (The Useless Ones), and one play, *Le chant du Madhi* (The Call of the Mahdi), collected with dramas by other Africans in *Le théâtre populaire en Républic de Côté d'Ivoire* (The Popular Theatre in the Ivory Coast).

Writings: Novel: *Les inutiles,* Dakar, Ed., Bingo, 1960.

Play: *Le chant du Madhi* in *Le théâtre populaire en Républic de Côte d'Ivoire,* editors, F. J. A. d'Aby, B. B. Dadié, and G. C. Gadeau, Abidjan, Cercle Culturel et Folklorique de la Côte d'Ivoire 1965, 230 pages, illustrated.

DEMPSTER, Roland Tombekai
b. 1910, Tosoh, near Robertsport, Liberia; d. 1965.
Poet, teacher.

Dempster took his B.A. in business studies and literature at Liberia College and the University of Liberia where he taught for a period of time after employment with the government.

Some of his works are: *Echoes from a Valley,* with B. T. Moore and H. C. Thomas; *The Mystic Reformation of Gondolia,* a satire on moral philosophy; *To Monrovia Old and New,* a poem; *A Song Out of Midnight. Souvenir of the Tubman-Tolbert Inauguration,* January 4, 1960 (Monrovia, but surprisingly dated, Autumn, 1959); and *Liberia* (1961).

Dempster's work is highly derivative of English language classics of the past and employs verse forms and meters no longer in vogue.

Writings: Poetry: *Echoes from a Valley,* with B. T. Moore and H. C. Thomas, Cape Mount, Douglas Muir Press, 1947; poem, *To Monrovia Old and New,* Monrovia, 1958; *The Mystic Reformation of Gondolia,* London, Dragon Press, 1953, 1961; *A Song Out of Midnight. Souvenir of the Tubman-Tolbert Inauguration, January 4, 1960,* Monrovia, dated Autumn, 1959; *Liberia,* 1961.

de NORONHA, Rui
b. 1909, Lourenço Marques, Mozambique; d. 1943.
Poet.

Son of an Indian father and African mother, Rui de Noronha had to struggle for his education and lived the bohemian life of the poor artist. He is considered the father of modern Mozambique writing. His posthumous *Sonetos* (Sonnets) is his only book. He sees Africa as a dreaming slave who, Lazarus-like, must rise to life and power through both a modern savior and technical progress.

One early poem, "Quenguêlequêzê," appeared in the journal *Moçambique*.

Writings: Poetry: *Sonetos,* edited by D. dos Reis Costa, Lourenço Marques, Tip.Minerva Central, 1943, 1949. "Quenguêlequêzê," in *Moçambique, March, 1936.*

de OLIVEIRO, M. A. F. (see António, Mário)

DESEWO, P. M.
b. ca. 1925, Ewe country, northeastern Ghana.
Ewe–language story collector.

One of the first scholars in the Gold Coast seriously to collect Ewe folk-stories, Desewo published in 1951 his useful collection, *The Three Brothers and Other Ewe Stories.*

Writings: Collection of folk stories: *The Three Brothers and Other Ewe Stories,* London, Longmans, 1951.

DE SOUSA, Noémia Carolina Abranches (née Soares; also pseudonym, MICAIA, Vera)
b. September 20, 1927, Lourenço Marques, Mozambique.
Poet.

Noémia de Sousa worked on various journals and reviews of Mozambique and on Portuguese journals from 1951 to 1964. She is the first African woman to gain a genuine reputation for her poetry. She has published in Brazilian, Angolan and Mozambique journals, in Andrade's first anthology, *Caderno,* and

his later collections of Portuguese-African writers. Her poetry is negritudist, influenced by American and Caribbean Black writing, and, often, in its free verse measures, it reflects her hearing of records by Paul Robeson and Marian Anderson. She married a Portuguese in Lisbon and during that relatively quiet and happy period produced no work of consequence. However, after protesting the restrictive laws and actions of the Portuguese government, she eventually was forced to go into exile. She now lives in France, employs the pseudonym Vera Micaia, and is actively writing again.

Writings: Poems in the journal *Caderno* as well as other Brazilian, Angolan, Mozambique and French publications.

DHLOMO, Herbert Isaac Ernest
b. 1903, Siyamu, Natal Province, South Africa; d. October 20, 1956.
Zulu novelist, poet, editor, playwright (also wrote in English).

Son of the preacher Ezra Sigadiya ka Gcugcwa ka Luphoko ka Mlozi ka Ngongoma Dhlomo and his wife Sarah Caluza Dhlomo, and brother of Rolfus Dhlomo, Herbert studied in local schools before going on to Amanzimtoti (Adams') College, where he earned his Teacher's Certificate about 1924. An accomplished singer, he was a serious student, fond of Shakespeare's tragedies and the music of Bach, Beethoven, and Schubert.
  Herbert Dhlomo taught for many years in Natal schools before taking, because of ill health, a less taxing job as librarian in the non-European section of the Germiston Library outside Johannesburg in the late 1930's. Shortly thereafter he also accepted a position as assistant editor of *Ilanga lase Natal,* pub-

lished in Durban, remaining there for some 16 years until his death.

A prolific playwright, Dhlomo's play *Dingane* saw performance in 1954, achieving a "succes d'estime," as had *Nongqause* earlier in 1948. Other plays were: *Shaka, Cetywayo, Moshoeshoe, Ntsikana, Mfolozi,* all on Zulu heroes. His English-language plays were: *Men and Women, The Living Dead, Workers Boss Bosses, Ruby, Malaria, The Expert,* and *Bazaar. Nongqause* was published in 1935 as *The Girl Who Killed to Save (Nongqause the Liberator). Shaka* was performed, date unknown, in Johannesburg by the African Dramatic and Operatic Society.

Along with his many occasional pieces in both Zulu and English in *Ilanga lase Natal* and such journals as *Drum, South African Outlook,* and the *Native Teachers' Journal,* he wrote poetry, most of it published in *Ilanga.* Considered his poetic masterpiece is *The Valley of a thousand hills* (1941), which saw two more editions in the next three years. All of his poetry was full of anger at the plight of the native South African and this poem begins:

This beauty's not my own! My home is not
My home! I am an outcast in my land!

They call me happy while I lie and rot
Beneath a foreign yoke . . .
The same theme is struck forcefully in "The Great Question":
Would you have me as a brother?
Or a revengeful beast?
Would you have us help each other,
Or have our hates increased?
Dhlomo died on October 20, 1956, after many months in the hospital following a heart attack. He left his wife, Ethel, and several children. His father, Ezra, died a few months later in December, 1956.

Writings: Plays: *The Girl Who Killed to Save (Nongqause the Liberator),* Lovedale, Lovedale Press, 1935; *Shaka, Cetywayo, Dingana, Moshoeshoe, Ntsikana, Mfolozi; Men and Women; The Living Dead, Workers Boss Bosses, Ruby, Malaria, The Expert, Bazaar,* all in manuscript.

Poetry: *The Valley of a thousand hills,* Durban, Knox Publishing Company, 1941; poems in *Ilanga lase Natal.*

DHLOMO, Rolfus Reginald Raymond
b. 1901, Siyamu, Natal Province, South Africa.
Zulu novelist, journalist, editor (published one work in English).

Dhlomo attended local schools in Siyamu (Ohlange Institute) and Amanzimtoti (Adams Training College) from 1918 or so until graduation in the early 1920's. After a short period clerking for a mining office in the Rand near Johannesburg, he took up a job as assistant to Stephen Black, editor of *The Sjambok* to which he began to contribute tales and sketches. He served as an assistant editor from 1930–1932 on the Zulu journal, *Ilanga lase Natal.* From 1933–1942 he was assistant editor of *The Bantu World* (Johannesburg), and then editor 1942–43. Returning to the Zulu journal *Ilanga* in 1943 as editor, Dhlomo stayed on until 1960, the year of his retirement. His English language column, "Rolling Stone," became a leading feature of *Ilanga* as were his articles in English and Zulu.

His first book was *An African Tragedy* (1928), a rambling work describing the effects of the big city on the morals of simple country-folk, and is believed to be the first novel published in English by an African writer. His second novel, *Izikhali zanamuhla* (Today's Weapons), came out under the Shuter and Shooter imprint, as did all his subsequent historical novels: *U-Dingane ka Senzangakhona* (Dingane, Son of Senzangakhona) (1935) about Chaka's half-brother who killed the tryannical Zulu super-king; *U-Shaka* (1936); *U-Mpande ka Senzangakhona* (Mpande, Son of Senzangakhona) (1936); *UNomalanga ka Ndengezi* (Nomalanga, Daughter of Ndengezi) (1934, 1946, 1962); and *U-Cetshwayo* (1952), concerning the last great chief of the Zulu nation; and *UDinuzulo ka Cetshwayo* (Dinuzulo, Son of Cetshwayo) (1968).

His novels, *Idlela yababi* (The Path of the Wicked), and *Bharabha* (Barabbas) first appeared in serial publication in *Ilanga*. The former was published in a second edition in 1962 by Shuter and Shooter. Issued in 1936 was his general work, *Ukwazi kuyathuthukisa* (Knowledge Improves One).

Dhlomo was the first winner of the Vilakazi Memorial Award, given by the University of the Witwatersrand (worth 20 Rand or 28 U.S. dollars at that time), and he was honored as a Zulu masterwriter by the African Literature Committee of the Durban Y.M.C.A. In 1958 he covered the expulsion of Black African representatives from the South African Parliament by Prime Minister H. F. Verwoerd for his paper, *Ilanga*.

Writings: Biographical novels: *Izikhali zanamuhla*, Pietermaritzburg, Shuter and Shooter, 1935; by Shuter and Shooter: *U-Dingane ka Senzangakhona*, 1935; *U-Shaka*, 1936; *U-Mpande ka Senzangakhona*, 1936, 13th edition, 1965; *UNomalanga ka Ndengezi*, 1934, 1946, 1962; *U-Cetshwayo*, 1952, rev. ed.,

1967, *UDinuzulo ka Cetshwayo*, 1968; *Indlela yababi*, 1946, 1962, second edition, rev., 1966; and *Bharabha*, in *Ilanga lase Natal*.

Prose narrative: *An African Tragedy*, Lovedale, Lovedale Press, 1928.

General: *Ukwazi kuyathuthukisa*, Shuter and Shooter, 1936; in ms: novel dealing with outbreak of racial violence between Indians and Africans in Durban, 1949.

Biographical/Critical Source: Albert S. Gérard, *Four African Literatures*, Berkeley, University of California Press, 1971.

DIAGNE, Ahmadou Mapaté
b. ca. 1890, Senegal.
Novelist, grade school teacher.

Hardly anything is now known of this writer, considered by some the first black African to write a work of fiction in French. His *Les trois volontés de Malic* inspired Birago Diop as a schoolboy because it offered a story about Africans written by an African, a decided change from the French school readers which featured only European children.

Malic, the school-boy hero overcomes many difficulties: first in getting into the newly-established school in his village; later in going on to a technical high school in the distant city; and finally, as a blacksmith, starting work as a "forgeron" in his natal village, a shock to his parents and others because such work was for a special, ill-considered caste. Above all, the little hero helps eliminate caste differences in the village because he has returned from the city with the idea that honest work and economic and technical know-how are the most important things the new Africa must have. Though the little book in its time was expressive of the combined liberal (anti-caste) and pro-colonial viewpoints (the little village school was seen as an improvement over the harsh, often unkempt Koranic schools of the period), it seems quaint and highly limited today. (For an interesting two-page discussion of this rare work, including a few extracts, see Fredric Michelman's article, "The Beginnings of French-African Fiction," in *Research in African Literatures*).

Roland Lebel's essay, "Le Mouvement intellectual indigène," *La Critique Littéraire*, No. 3 (1931), cites another work, otherwise unknown of Diagne's, *Un pays de pilleurs d'épaves* (A Country of Ship Wreckers).

Writings: Novel: *Les trois volontés de Malic*, Paris, Larousse, 1920; *Un pays de pilleurs d'épaves*, le Gandiole, 1919, genre unknown, but probably a short narrative.

Biographical/Critical Sources: Fredric Michelman, "The Beginnings of French-African Fiction," *Research in African Literatures*, II, I, Spring, 1971, University of Texas; Roland Lebel, "Le Mouvement intellectual indigene," *La Critique Littéraire*, No. 3, 1931.

DIAKHATE, Lamine
b. September 18, 1928, Saint-Louis, Senegal.
Poet, playwright.

Locally educated, Diakhaté published his first verse in 1954 in the ten-page volume of *La joie d'un continent* (The Joy of a Continent) and is represented with a long poem, "Sur le tombeau de John Kennedy," in *New Sum of Poetry from the Negro World*. His play, *Sarzan*, saw print in *L'Afrique Nouvelle* March 1, 1955, in

Traits d'union, No. 7, Dakar, March-April, 1955, and was performed at the Théâtre de Palais, Dakar, 1955, by Keita Fodeba's troupe. The drama, adapted from a story of Birago Diop's, centers on the experiences of a sergeant returned to his village after many years in the French army.

His most recent volumes of verse are: *Primordial du sixième jour* (The Necessity of the Sixth Day), and *Temps de mémoire* (Time for an Accounting). Ellen Conroy Kennedy offers several pages of his poetry in English translation in "Four African Poets," in *African Forum*, Summer, 1966.

Writings: Poetry: *La joie d'un continent*, Ales, Impr. de Pab, 1954; *Primordial du sixième jour*, Paris, Présence Africaine, 1963; *Temps de mémoire*, Paris, Présence Africaine, 1967; poem, "Sur le tombeau de John Kennedy" in *New Sum of Poetry from the Negro World*, Paris, Présence Africaine, Vol. 57, 1966; poems in English translation in "Four African Poets," *African Forum*, Summer, 1966, Vol. 2, No. 1, New York.

Play: *Sarzan*, in *L'Afrique Nouvelle*, March, 1955, and in *Traits d' Union*, No. 7, March/April issue, 1955.

DIALLO, Assane Y.
b. ca. 1940, Senegal.
Poet, in Peul and French.

Locally educated, Diallo, a Peul, has published in both his mother tongue and in French. His only collected verse to date is in the 44-page volume, *Leyd'am* (My Land) of Peul (or Foulah) poems. Two poems, "Blues," and "Remords," (Remorse) in French are in *New Sum of Poetry from the Negro World*.

Writings: Poetry: *Leyd'am*, Honfleur and Paris, Pierre-Jean Oswald, 1967; poems: "Blues," "Remords," in *New Sum of Poetry from the Negro World,* Paris, Présence Africaine, Vol. 57, 1966.

DIALLO, Bakary
b. 1892, M'Bala, Senegal.
Novelist, poet, government official.

Conscripted into the French territorial army from Senegal for duty in France during the first World War, Diallo was severely wounded.

His experiences in the army at home, in Europe, and his suffering in a hospital are part of his 1926 novel, *Force-Bonté* (Good Will), which today reads embarrassingly for its willingness to accept French superiority and African childishness. Though willing to excuse most French arrogance and intolerance in his awe and respect for things European, the author still makes clear the brutalities of the colonial period.

While in a French hospital Diallo came to know Mme. Cousturier, a serious and generous friend of Africans and author of two works dealing with Africa *(Des inconnus chez moi* (The Unknown with Us), Paris, Sirène, 1920; and *Mes inconnus chez eux* (Our Unknown in Their Home), two volumes, Paris, F. Rieder, 1925). She was responsible for Diallo's work being read by Jean-Richard Bloch, director of F. Rieder et Cie., who eventually published this very early work of francophone fiction. Bakar Diallo's novel is discussed in Fredric Michelman's article, "The Beginnings of French-African Fiction," *Research in African Literatures,* II, 1, Spring, 1971. According to Michelman, the novel is written in "straightforward and simple language," and

is not "devoid of a certain lyricism which, however, often lapses into the maudlin." But, he adds, the book is possessed of "a rather artless charm, especially the first half in which the reader follows the thoughts and reactions of this shepherd boy—leaving his village for the first time at the age of eighteen." Written in the form of a journal, the reader follows the amazed progress of the naive lad as he moves from his insular village to the greater life of Africa and Europe and the horrors of the war. Michelman points out that the novel presents various episodes "both dated and recounted in the present as if to leave no doubt that they actually occurred. This approach, which endeavors to fix the protagonist in time and space, is in direct opposition to traditional African literature in which the individual is a timeless and symbolic representation of the solidarity and continuity of the group. *Force-Bonté* thus derives directly from the European novel form."

Bakary Diallo today lives near his natal village of M'Bala, after having served most of his life as a "chef de canton" or cantonal supervisor.

Diallo has also published one poem, "Mon M'Bala," a song of praise for his home village. It appears in the original Peul and in the author's French translation in *Présence Africaine,* No. 6. (1949).

Writings: Novel: *Force-Bonté,* Paris, Rieder, 1926; poem: "Mon M'Bala," in *Présence Africaine,* first series, No. 6, Paris, 1949.

Biographical/Critical Source: Fredric Michelman, "The Beginnings of French-African Fiction," *Research in African Literatures,* II, 1, Spring, 1971, University of Texas.

DIAS, João
b. 1926, Moçambique; d. Portugal, 1949.
Story-writer.

Considered a promising young writer at the time of his death at 23, João Dias, the son of Estácio Dias, editor of the bilingual journal published in Lourenço Marques, *O Brado Africano*, absorbed a strong interest in literature. He studied at universities in Coimbra and Lisbon in Portugal. His one collection of stories, *Godido e outros contos* (Little Pebble and Other Stories), reached print posthumously in 1952 with a preface by Orlando de Albuquerque, Mozambiquan and Angolan poet.

*Writings:*Poetry: *Godido e outros contos.* Lisbon, Casa dos Estudantes do Império, 1952; Anthology: *Poetas e contistas africanos de expressão portuguêsa*, São Paulo, Editôra Brasiliense, 1963.

DIOP, Birago Ismaïl
b. December 11, 1906, Ouakam, suburb of Dakar, Senegal.
Story writer, poet, veterinarian, diplomat.

Son of Ismaïl Diop, a master mason, and Sokhna Diawara, the young Birago was educated in local rural lower schools, but studied in high school in Dakar, staying there until 1921. With a scholarship he then transferred to the Lycée Faidherbe, Saint-Louis, Senegal. In 1925 he was awarded the Brevet de Capacité Coloniale and that same year took the French baccalauréat in philosophy. He travelled to France to become a veterinarian, taking the doctorate from the Toulouse School of Veterinary Medicine in 1933 following one year of military service. He met Leopold Senghor in Paris, became a close friend, and col-

laborated with him in the editing and publication of the pioneering *L'Etudiant Noir* (The Black Student), the forerunner of various negritude journals which, though short-lived, prepared the way for independent writing by African artists. Even earlier, he had contributed to *L'Echo des Etudiants*, a student journal of Toulouse University, employing the pen-names, "Max," and "d'Alain Provist."

Returning to Africa in 1937, Diop, accompanied by his young French wife, worked at his profession in various areas of the French Empire beginning in the Sudan from 1937 to 1939. In what is now Mali he met the griot (professional folksinger) Amadou Koumba N'Gom whose stories he captured in two books, *Les contes d'Amadou Koumba* (The Stories of Amadou Koumba), and *Les nouveaux contes d'Amadou Koumba* (The New Stories of Amadou Koumba), with a long preface by Léopold Senghor. Léon Gontran Damas had preserved the early manuscript of the first collection, which had failed of publication during the second World War, safe in his quarters at the Hotel Victoria until he saw to Diop's story, "L'os," (The Bone), being published in the initial number of Alioune Diop's *Présence Africaine* magazine, thereby demonstrating his importance as a story-teller. *Les contes* quickly were awarded the Grand Prix Littéraire de l'Afrique Occidentale Française. Joyce Hutchinson edited a 176 page school edition in the original text but with excellent English notes and discussion of African story tradition.

After three years at home in Senegal, Diop was assigned to wartime Paris, not returning to Africa until 1945, when he saw service in the Ivory Coast as head of the Zoological Technical Services, in Upper Volta, and in Mauritania from 1950 to 1955. There followed five years of work in Senegal, crowned with an appointment by President Senghor, his old friend, to be the newly independent nation's first ambassador to Tunis.

Diop's last volume of tales is *Contes et lavanes* (1963) which won the Prix d'Afrique Noire, 1964. His one collection of poetry is *Leurres et lueurs* (Lures and Gleams). His poetry is found in Clive Wake's *An Anthology of African and Malagasy Poetry in French* and in many other anthologies.

Three of his tales from the first volume have been adapted for the stage: "Sarzan" was used by Lamine Diakhaté for presentation by Keita Fodeba's troupe at the Théâtre de Palais, Dakar, 1955; "Maman Caïman" was performed by a student group in France; and "Les Mamelles" (The Humps, also a reference to the twin hills outside Dakar?), was performed by students at the College de Jeunes Filles, Saint-Louis, Senegal. Adapted for radio production by the students of Dakar's Ecole des Arts under the direction of Pierre Richy, 1962–63

(Emission "aux jeunes"), was the tale, "Fari l'ânesse" (Fari the She-Ass).

A. C. Brench in his *Writing in French from Senegal to Cameroon* offers a four-page discussion of Diop's work and a partial but useful list of Diop's other published stories as well as critical articles and reviews of his works. Diop, according to Brench, "was able to overcome the stresses which Islam, colonial regimentation and participation in the anticolonial struggle created for Africans..." and Diop is able to fuse "the written and the oral tradition... to create a feeling of immediacy and dramatic movement" in his work.

Writings: Stories: *Les contes d'Amadou Koumba,* Paris, Fasquelle, 1947 and Présence Africaine, 1961; Joyce Hutchinson edition of French text as *Contes choisis* with notes in English, London, New York, Cambridge University Press, 1967; *Les nouveaux contes d'Amadou Koumba,* Paris, Présence Africaine, 1958, 3rd. ed., 1967; *Contes et lavanes,* Paris, Présence Africaine, 1973. story: "L'os," in first number, *Présence Africaine* magazine.

Translation: *Tales of Amadou Koumba,* translation and introduction by Dorothy S. Blair, London, Oxford University Press, 1966.

Poetry: *Leurres et lueurs,* Paris, Présence Africaine, 1960; poems in *An Anthology of African and Malagasy Poetry in French,* Clive Wake, editor, Oxford, Three Crown Press, 1965.

Plays: Three stories adapted for the stage, versions in ms. only: "Sarzan," performed Dakar, 1955, "Maman Caïman," France, date unknown; and "Les Mamelles," Saint-Louis, Senegal, date unknown.

Biographical/Critical Sources: A. C. Brench, *Writing in French from Senegal to Cameroon,* London, Oxford Press, 1967; R. Mercier, Monique and Simon Battestini, *Birago Diop, écrivain sénégalais,* Paris, F. Nathan, 1964 (both works offer extracts); Mohamadu Kane, *Birago Diop,* Paris, Présence Africaine, 1970.

DIOP, David Mandessi
b. July 9, 1927, Bordeaux, France;
d. August, 1960, Dakar, Senegal.
Poet, teacher.

Born of a Senegalese father (a medical doctor) and a Cameroonian mother, Diop lived most of his life in France. Once almost completely assimilated to French culture, Diop fought his way back to a feeling for Africa and an identification with its sufferings. Accordingly, his forceful negritude poems protest the violent break-in of European culture on Africa and the consequent alienation of such Africans as himself from the ancestral home.

His one volume of verse, *Coups de pilon* (Poundings) in 1956, has served as the source of much of his fame, though Senghor's *Anthologie* has given him his best showcase. In the British work of Clive Wake, *An Anthology of African and Malagasy Poetry in French* and in Moore and Beier's *Modern Poetry from Africa,* he is well represented.

A teacher from 1957–58 at the Lycée Maurice Delafosse in Dakar, he moved on to Guinea for two years to serve as principal of a lycée in the town of Kindia, 60 miles inland from Conakry the capital. In August, 1960, returning from a holiday visit to Paris, his plane crashed on the approach to the Dakar airport, killing Diop and his family. All his unpublished manuscripts were destroyed in the burning plane.

Diop's "The Vultures" as given in English in various anthologies, comes from *Coups de pilon* (1956), and is as uncompromising as any anti-colonial poem ever written:

> In those days
> When civilization kicked us in the face
> When holy water slapped our cringing
> /brows
> The vultures built in the shadows of their
> /talons
> The bloodstained monument of tutelage.
> In those days
> There was painful laughter on the metallic
> /hell of the roads
> And the monotonous rhythm of the pater
> /noster
> Drowned the howling on the plantations.
> O the bitter memories of extorted kisses
> Of promises broken at the point of a gun

Writings: Poetry: *Coups de pilon*, Paris, Présence Africaine, 1956; poems in *An Anthology of African and Malagasy Poetry in French*, Clive Wake, Editor, Oxford, Three Crowns Press, 1965; *Modern Poetry from Africa*, Moore and Beier, editors, London, Penguin, revised edition, 1968; L. S. Senghor, *Anthologie de la nouvelle poésie nègre et malgache*, Paris, Présence Africaine, 1947.

Biographical/Critical Sources: Gerald Moore, *Seven African Writers*, London, Oxford University Press, 1962; Paulette Trout and Ellen Conroy Kennedy, "Profile of an African Artist. David Diop: Negritude's Angry Young Man," *Journal of the New African Literature and the Arts*, Spring and Fall, 1968.

DIOP, Massyla
b. ca. 1886, Senegal; d. 1932.
Novelist, journalist.

Half-brother of the well-known Birago Diop, Massyla Diop, in 1925, published what may well have been the second francophone novel after Ahmadou Mapaté Diagne's *Les trois volontés de Malic* (The Three Wishes of Malic). Diop's work, *Le reprouvé—roman d'une sénégalaise* (The Outcast—the Novel of a Senegalese Girl), which appeared in *La Revue Africaine Artistique et Littéraire*, July 1925, was obviously the product of a sophisticated writer. Fredric Michelman in his article, "The Beginnings of French-African Fiction," *Research in African Literatures*, Spring, 1971, discusses the early novels of Massyla Diop, Diagne and Bakary Diallo, and finds Massyla Diop's work, though only available to him in a fragment, far superior to the work of the others. Jahnheinz Jahn offers, however, the information that Joseph Mbelolo ya Mpiku prepared a dissertation for the Licence in Roman Philology at Liège entitled "Le roman sénégalaise de langue française: la période de formation (1920–1952)," submitted in 1969. It discusses Massyla Diop in some detail and seems based on additional material (cf. Jahn's *Bibliography of Creative African Writing*).

Diop, an accountant by training, became a journalist and took over the direction of the Dakar political journal, *Le Sénégal Moderne*, and later served as editor-in-chief of *La Revue Africaine Artistique et Littéraire* which had earlier published his novel.

Writings: Novel: *Le réprouvé—roman d'une sénégalaise*, in *La Revue Africaine Artistique et Littéraire*, Dakar, July, 1925.

Biographical/Critical Sources: Fredric Michelman, "The Beginnings of French-African Fiction," *Research in African Literatures*, II, 1, Spring, 1971, University of Texas; Jahnheinz Jahn, *Bibliog-*

raphy of Creative African Writing, Nendeln, Switzerland, Kraus-Thomson, 1971.

DIOP, Ousmane Socé (see SOCE, Ousmane Diop)

DIPOKO, Mbella Sonne
b. 1936, Missaka, near Douala, Cameroon.
Novelist, poet.

Dipoko grew up on his father's farm in Missaka on the Mungo River in the Western Cameroon and as a child he also lived for a time in Eastern Nigeria. He was educated in these areas from 1952 to 1956, going out to work for a short period as a clerk for the Development Corporation, Tiko, Cameroon, before joining the news staff of Radio Nigeria in Lagos in 1957. Working as a reporter from that time until 1960, he took an assignment in Paris, staying there until 1968.

While in Paris he studied law at the University of Paris, worked for Présence Africaine publishing house, and wrote his first novel in English, *A Few Nights and Days* (1966). This work, part of an announced trilogy, was followed by *Because of Women* (1969), with the third volume still in progress. *A Few Nights and Days* is a very frank, and often very crisp, treatment of a love affair between an African student, Doumbe, and a bourgeois girl, Thérèse, in Paris. The girl's father, horrified at his daughter's plan to marry an African, forces her to break off the engagement. She commits suicide while Doumbe, who really had loved her, was worrying about Bibi, Thérèse's Swedish girlfriend, pregnant with his child from a casual, almost scornful

coupling one hot night. The survivors are horrified at their own callousness and frivolity, but now Thérèse is gone. Doumbe returns to Africa at book's end, chastened and vaguely alarmed at his Paris experiences of love and death.

Dipoko's second novel, *Because of Women,* also has the erotic theme of an active male, Ngoso, and two women, Njale, pregnant with his child, and the seductive, modern Ewudu. Both women truly love Ngoso, who dies leaving Ewudu also with child. She must enter a sad "marriage" with the man who had loved her and, who, despite her betrayal, still will have her as his wife.

Dipoko's poetry has appeared in *United Asia* (Bombay), *Présence Africaine* and various other journals. He is also included in Moore and Beier's *Modern Poetry from Africa* and *New Sum of Poetry from the Negro World.*

Although raised in the strict Protestant world of his uncle's family, Dipoko did not abandon his peoples' dances, songs, and religious expressions and ideas. His anti-colonial poem, "Pain," shows his power and anger in these lines:

All was quiet in this park
Until the wind, like a gasping messenger,
/announced
The tyrant's coming.
Then did the branches talk in agony.

The poem ends with an identification of human limbs with the first stanza's "branches":

Mutilated our limbs were swept away by
/the rain
But not our blood;
Indelible, it stuck on the walls
Like wild gum on tree-trunks.

Writings: Novels: *A Few Nights and Days*, London, Longmans, 1966; a paperback edition, London, Heinemann, 1970; *Because of Women*, London, Heinemann, 1969.

Poems: in *United Asia* (Bombay), *Présence Africaine*, Paris; *Modern Poetry from Africa*, Moore and Beier, London, Penguin, 1966; *New Sum of Poetry from the Negro World*, Paris, Présence Africaine, Vol. 57, 1966.

DISENGOMOKO, A. Emile
b. 1915, near Banza Manteke, Congo (Zaïre); d. 1965.
Kikongo novelist, poet, essayist, teacher.

Son of a Christian minister, and educated in a protestant mission from 1921 to 1928, the young Disengomoko began his studies at the Kimpese Mission school of Mbanaa Manteka, an American-run institution. After French studies at the school of Madzia in Congo, Brazzaville in the early 1930's, he returned to Kimpese from 1934–37 for advanced training and again in 1941, this time to prepare himself in theology. The Second World War interrupted and

Disengomoko became director of a primary school at Thysville from 1942–49. He began to work for the publishing firm LECO in 1949 in Kinshasa (then Léopoldville) while continuing his studies, and from 1951–54 he studied at the Ecole Normale d'Etat at Nivelles, Belgium, earning a diploma in literature (the diplôme de regent littéraire). He returned home to become director of a school at Ngombe-Lutete from 1955–58, then professor at the Athenée de Ngiri-Ngiri in Kinshasa from 1960–61, and dean of students at the schools at Ngiri-Ngiri and Kalima the same year. He was director-general of the Congolais Polytechnic Institute from 1961–65, and a member of the Administrative Council of the Free University of the Congo at Kisingani.

His first published work was an ethical tract, *Ku Ntwala,* a translation of an American work; but his first volume of creative writing was a novel, *Kwenkwenda* (Where Shall I Go?), published the next year, 1943. Kwenkwenda the hero must carve out a life for himself between the competing demands of his newly acquired Christian values and the traditional ones that retain their power. He decides he will indeed remain a Christian, however, without repudiating the finer traditions of his own people. The work won the Margaret Wrong prize in 1948, an award of increasing prestige in Africa. His third work, composed while he was at Thysville, was *Luvuvamu mu nzo* (Peace in the House), an essay about contemporary conditions of the Congolese family, and he began to publish articles in French in *La Voix du Congolais,* published in Kinshasa and edited by Antoine-Roger Bolamba. Some 15 of his hymns also saw print in *Kinkunga mia Kintwadi* and others were published in various Kikongo journals. Much of Disengomoko's work continues to be used in the Protestant schools of Zaïre, or their successors.

Writings: Novel: *Kwenkwenda,* first edition, probably 1943, third edition, Léopoldville, LECO, 1957, fourth edition, also Leco, 1965.

Poetry: in *Minkunga mia Kintwadi,* Léopoldville, LECO, 1956.

Ethical Tract: *Ku Ntwala,* (Kikongo translation of O. R. Winstedt's *Right Thinking and Right Living,* first edition, Kimpese, EPI, 1942, second edition, 1944, third edition, Léopoldville, LECO, fourth edition, LECO, 1965.

Sociology: *Luvuvamu mu nzo,* second edition, Thysville, 1950, third edition, Léopoldville, LECO, 1952, fourth edition, 1957.

Articles and essays: in French in *La Voix du Congolais* (Kinshasa) and in other journals.

Biographical/Critical Source: Mbololo ya Mpiku, "Introduction à la littérature kikongo," *Research in African Literatures,* African and Afro-American Research Institute, The University of Texas, III, 2, (Fall 1972); the biography in Kikongo written by André Massaki: *A. E. Disengomoko. Zingu kiandi: 1915–1965,* Kinshasa, LECO, 1968.

DJOLETO, Amu
b. 1929, Ghana.
Novelist, poet.

Djoleto attended Accra Academy and St. Augustine's College, Cape Coast. He studied English at the University of Ghana and, later, problems of textbook production at the University of London's Institute of Education. Afterwards, he returned to Ghana to become editor of Ghana *Teacher's Journal* and presently is in charge of the Education Ministry's new publishing program.

Djoleto's poem, "The Lone Horse," appeared in *Voices of Ghana,* but a considerable body of his poetical work, "A Passing Thought," "The Good Old Motto," "Why is it?," "The Quest," and "The Search," appeared in *Messages: Poems from Ghana.*

His one novel, *The Strange Man,* published in 1967, recounts the growing pains of Mensa, who is always in trouble, as, for example, on the day he tried to capture an old "billy-goat." Even as a grown man in the civil service, married and the father of a beautiful daughter, Odole, he is put into a nervous strain by her scandalous behavior. At the novel's end, Odole, suffering horribly from a hemorrhage (possibly caused by an abortion), bleeds to death and Mensa has a heart attack. Close to death himself, he is carried off to the hospital.

Writings: Novel: *The Strange Man,* London, Heinemann, 1967; New York, Humanities Press, 1968.

Poems, in *Voices of Ghana,* London, Heinemann, 1971.

do ESPIRITO SANTO, Alda
(see ESPIRITO SANTO)

DOGBEH–DAVID, Richard G.
b. ca. 1935, Dahomey.
Poet.

Dogbeh-David is well represented in his two collections of verse, *Les eaux du Mono* (The Waters of Mono); and *Rives mortelles* (The Mortal Shores) which have been republished by Kraus Reprint along with the first volumes of the poets: Basile-Juléat Fonda (Cameroon), Pierre Bamboté (Central African Republic), Maurice Koné (Ivory Coast), Jean-Paul Nyanai (Cameroon), and Job Nganthojeff (Cameroon). In 1969, Edition C.L.E. published his third volume of poetry, *Cap Liberté* (Cape Liberty).

His travel book, *Voyage au pays de Lénine. Notes de voyage d'un écrivain en URSS* (Journey to the Country of Lenin. Notes of a Voyage of an African Writer to the USSR), appeared in 1967.

Writings: Poetry: *Les eaux du Mono*, Vire, Calvados, France, Société Lec-Vire, 1963; *Rives mortelles*, Porto-Novo, Dahomey, Eds. Silva, 1964; republished by Kraus Reprint, Nendeln, Liechtenstein, 1970; *Cap Liberté*, Yaoundé, Edition C.L.E., 1969.

Travel: *Voyage au pays de Lénine. Notes de voyage d'un écrivain en URSS*, Yaoundé, Ed. C.L.E., 1967.

DOMINGUES, Mário
b. 1899, São Tomé.
Novelist.

Author of very many works, long a resident of Portugal, only his *Menino entre gigantes* (Child among Giants) touches on Black African culture.

Writings: Novel: *Menino entre gigantes*, Lisbon, Prelo, 1960.

DONGMO, Jean Louis
b. ca. 1945, Douala, Cameroon.
Poet.

Locally educated, Dongmo is a young poet whose best early work "Prostitution," "Pacification," and "Depart en France," has appeared in *New Sum of Poetry from the Negro World*. He completed his university education at Yaoundé in the late 1960's.

Writings: Poems in *New Sum of Poetry from the Negro World*, Paris, Présence Africaine, Vol. 57, 1966.

DOS SANTOS, Marcelino
(pseudonyms: KALUNGANO, and MICAIA, Lilinho)
b. May 20, 1929, near Lumbo, Mozambique.
Poet.

A former labor-union leader, dos Santos was one of the leaders of the independence movement, FRELIMO. He has been forced to flee and now uses the pseudonym "Kalungano" in Dar es Salaam where he presently resides. He studied in Paris at the Institute des Science politique and at l'Ecole pratique des Hautes Etudes, the Sorbonne.

Dos Santos has published two volumes of his poetry, both of which were translated into Russian by Lidiya Nekrasova, a 31-page collection, published in 1959, and a 92-page collection in 1962. There has also been a Chinese translation but information is lacking. Individual poems have appeared in various Mozambique journals and in *New Sum of Poetry from the Negro World*. The poem, "Dream of the Black Mother," translated by Philippa Ramsey, was published in Mphahlele's *African Writing Today*. A few of his poems, first published in the review, *Africa*, appear in Langston Hughes' and Christiane Reygnault's *Anthologie africaine et malagache*.

Writings: Poetry: Two volumes in Russian: both Moscow, Pravda: one in 1959

121

and the second in 1962; poems in *New Sum of Poetry from the Negro World,* Paris, Présence Africaine, 1966; *African Writing Today,* Ezekiel Mphahlele, editor, London, Penguin, 1967; *Anthologie africaine et malagache,* Langston Hughes and Christiane Reygnault, editors, Paris, Seghers, 1962.

DOVE–DANQUAH, Mabel (see DANQUAH, Mabel, née Dove)

DUARTE, Fausto Castilho
b. 1903, Santiago, Cape Verde Islands; d. Portugal, 1953.
Novelist, government official.

A long-time resident of Guinea (Bissau) where he was a government administrative officer, Duarte was one of Africa's earliest novelists. His first work, *Auá (novela negra),* published in 1934, won a prize in the Portuguese competition for "Colonial Literature." This novelette exploits his experiences in Guinea where he tried to understand the local peoples, but some critics of African literature in Portuguese find the work too full of exoticisms, too much the product of an alien temperament to be a satisfactory "African" work. It does, however, as is also the case with his later novels, attempt to picture the daily lives of the Fulah or Fulani peoples of the area in and around Bissau. His three other works of long fiction are: *O negro sem alma* (O Blackman Without Soul) of 1935, *Rumo ao degrêdo* (The Line to Exile) of 1939, and *A revolta* (The Revolt) of 1945.

Duarte's stories were collected in the volume, *Foram estes os vencidos* (Some Defeated Besides These), published in 1945. His scholarly interest in the litera-

ture of the Cape Verdes produced the 19-page lecture published as "Da literatura colonial e da 'morna' de Cabo Verde," (Colonial Literature and the Cabo–Verdean 'Morna', published in 1934.

Writings: Novels: *Auá (novela negra),* Lisbon, Livraria Clássica, 1934, 3rd. edition, Lisbon, Editôra Marítimo-Colonial, 1945; *O negro sem alma,* Lisbon, Livraria Clássica, 1935; *Rumo ao degrêdo,* Lisbon, Guimarães, 1939; *A revolta,* Porto, Livraria Latina, 1945.

Stories: *Foram estes os vencidos,* Lisbon, Inquérito, 1945.

Criticism: "Da literatura colonial e da 'morna' de Cabo Verde," *Conferência,* Porto, I° Exposição Colonial Portuguêsa, 1934.

DUBE, John Langalibalele
b. February 22, 1871, near Inanda Mission Station, South Africa; d. 1946.
Zulu novelist, collector of folk tales, educator, statesman.

Son of the Rev. James and Elizabeth Dube, and the sixth of nine children, John Langalibalele Dube received his early education at Inanda Mission, which was run by the American Board Mission and later at Amanzimtoti (Adams') College. The first of three brothers to make the trip to America, John arrived at Oberlin College in 1889, where he remained for ten years. He took his B.A. from Oberlin in 1893, did further study, taught, was ordained in 1897, and published his first work, "A Talk Upon My Native Land" in 1892. During this period, Dube met most of the leading American black intellectuals of the day: Booker T. Washington, W.E.B. du Bois and John Hope of Atlanta University.

After marrying Nokuthela Mdima, he returned to South Africa for a brief period, hoping to establish a school of industrial arts along the lines of Washington's Tuskeegee Institute, but the Boer War made fund-raising impossible. Virtually penniless, he returned to the United States with his wife who helped him raise a sufficient sum to return to South Africa to establish the new Zulu Christian Industrial School in Natal. Situated on a crest of the Inanda Hills fifteen miles from Durban and facing the Indian Ocean, the school opened in July, 1901. Renamed the Ohlange Institute, it grew to include a girls' school after a second fund-raising trip to the United States by Dube and his wife.

Joining Ngazana Luthuli (ca. 1870–1951) a leading Zulu journalist, Dube founded the *Ilanga lase Natal* (The Natal Sun), the first Zulu-language newspaper (some English articles were carried) with the initial copies appearing on June 3, 1903. During its early years, the Government closed down the paper for awhile when Dube vigorously supported Chief Bambata in his protess in support of Zulu rights. The "Bambata Rebellion," as it was called by the whites, put Dube under severe pressure but he held firm. Again, in 1908, Dube was in hot water when Commissioner Marwick became aware of the paper's pun on Marwick's Zulu nickname, "Muhle," or "The Good One." The journal employed "Mubi, or "The Bad One." Marwick easily won a suit for libel. Undaunted, Dube published in 1909 his historically important *The Zulu's Appeal for Light and England's Duty* and the next year he sought out former Prime Minister Gladstone to argue for restoring the fast eroding rights of black South Africans. At Bloemfontein, January 8, 1912, Dube was elected the first President-General of the South African Native National Congress, the forerunner of the African National Congress. Remaining in this office till 1917, Dube led a group to London in 1914 to protest the Land Act of 1913. The press was by and large sympathetic but the government, and most of the members of Parliament were either contemptuous or unreachable. Defeated, the delegation, except for Solomon Plaatje, returned home to be greeted on arrival by the news of the outbreak of World War I. Though Dube and the Congress loyally offered their support to the Government in the war effort, their help was refused in polite but consciously, and explicitly, racial terms. The war was a matter for the whites to settle themselves.

Growing oppression on the one hand and increasing bitterness on the other made such moderate efforts as Dube's more and more suspect to the more militant Africans. With the establishment of the Industrial and Commercial Workers' Union (the I.C.U.) and the fiery rivalry of Allison George Wessels Champion (b. 1897), Dube's own leadership seriously began to wane.

In literature and scholarship Dube had produced an early collection of Zulu folk songs and dance songs to help pay for a trip to the United States. He also wrote *Isita esikhulu somuntu omnyama nguye uqobo lwake* (The Greatest Enemy of the Black Man is Himself), published in 1922, a work considered the first clearly masterful use of Zulu in written form; and an English work, (with Archdeacon Lee), *Clash of Colour*. His great historical novel, *Ujeqe insila ka Tshaka* (Ujeqe, Servant to Chaka) is a graphically imagined life-story of Ujeqe, which depicts the daily life of much of Chaka's court and the great Zulu king himself. A work of some 80 pages, Dube's novel was eventually translated into English by J. Boxwell as *Jeqe, the Bodyservant of King Tshaka* (1951). The year 1935 saw the publication of Dube's last two works: *U-Shembe*, a biography of Isaiah Shembe, the famous Zulu prophet; and *Ukuziphatha kahle* (Good Manners).

In the last twenty years of his life many honors came to Dube. In August, 1926, he was a participant at the International Conference of Christian Missions at Le Zoule, Belgium, which dealt with religion, race relations, and related matters. In 1936 he received a Ph.D. from the University of South Africa (to which few Blacks were ever admitted), and from 1942 on he was Natal's elected representative at the Native Representative Council which met twice yearly and of which he became senior spokesman of the twenty-two man committee. Terribly ill, he had to be carried into the first meeting on a stretcher.

The hard-working Dube, called the "Mafukuzela" or "Trail-Blazer," died at the age of 75. Taking Dube's seat in the Native Representative Council was Chief Albert John Mvumbi Lutuli (1898–1967), winner of the Nobel Peace Prize in 1960.

Writings: Novel: *Ujeqe insila ka Tshaka*, Mariannhill, Mission Press, 1933; in English translation, *Jeqe, the Bodyservant of King Tshaka*, Lovedale, Lovedale Press, 1951.

Biography: *U-Shembe*, Pietermaritzburg, Shuter and Shooter, 1935, *Ukuziphatha kahle*, Mariannhill, Mariannhill Mission Press, 1935.

Polemics: *The Zulu's Appeal for Light and England's Duty*, London, Unwin Brothers, 1909; *Isila esikhula somuntu omnyama nguye uqobo Lwake*, Marrianhill, Mariannhill Mission Press, 1922; *Clash of Colour* Durban, Robinson and Col. Ltd. 1926.

DUBE, Violet (see mention in NXUMALO, Natalie)

DUODU, Cameron
b. 1937, Asiakwa (or Akyem Abuakwa), Ghana.
Novelist, journalist, poet.

Duodu received some local schooling but is largely self-taught. He worked as a radio journalist for five years (1956–1960) for the Ghana radio station and from 1960 to 1965 served as the editor of *Drum*, the Ghanaian magazine organized in emulation of the famous review of the same name in South Africa which featured black writers. Losing his early fervor for president Nkrumah,

Duodu went into self-exile in 1965 and moved to London. He returned to Ghana in 1966 after the military coup which overthrew Nkrumah.

Deeply troubled by the modern and "modernized" African's need to find or to establish a culture of his own, Duodu wrote *The Gab Boys* (1967). It reflects his own frustrations with growing up in an African state. One is free but not free, Duodu says, free of England but still permeated with England's values, free of tyranny but increasingly oppressed by Nkrumah's police, spies, and informers. His novel's young men and women are flighty, imitative, seemingly loose and disrespectful but underneath they seek genuine causes to serve, values to believe in, a modern Africa they can work and live in with joy and freedom. At book's end, the hero, Kwasi Asamoa, is in Accra, Ghana's capital, with "B," his most modern and intelligent sweetheart who has reformed him—for the better, he hopes. He will no longer be a Gab-Boy, rootless and prone to wildness, and even to violence. The title of the novel comes from the "gabardine" or "blue-jean" material used for trousers all over the world.

Though the language often seems stilted, particularly the "dialogue" of ideas contrasting African and European values—as enunciated at the novel's close by Kwasi and B., Duodu's work does succeed in getting to the concerns of the uprooted as they try to make a new life in post-independence Accra. Duodu also interweaves the songs of his own people in the vernacular, often joinng African to English text in an organic fashion. The book, too, is one of the first to deal with the cynical regimes which gradually developed as the years of political independence offered opportunities for graft and oppressive power to the new elites. The last brooding lines are these:

B. " . . . And we will have rain, for the rain loves a people like us who are fertile in soul . . ."

Kwasi: "We shall have rain, I repeated to myself, adding the prayer, 'Make it fast, oh lord. Otherwise, we shall sweat blood! Blood! . . .'"

Two of Duodu's infrequent poems, "Return to Eden," and "The Stranded Vulture," appear in *Messages: Poems from Ghana.*

Writings: Novel: *The Gab Boys*, London, André Deutsch, 1967; in paperback, London, Fontana–Collins, 1969.

Poems: "Return to Eden" and "The Stranded Vulture" in *Messages: Poems from Ghana*, London, Heinemann, 1971.

DUUH, Ali
b. mid-19th century in Somali;
d. ca. 1910.
Somali oral poet.

Considered an important poet by Somalis, his work has been written down and is in several private collections in Somalia, one of his works having been translated into English.

Duuh employed his poetry for personal purposes in factional quarrels within his clan, and his known works demonstrate polemical wit, epithets of force, and an attacking, biting style.

DZOVO, Emmanuel Victor Kwame
b. ca. 1915, Ho, Northern Ghana.
Novelist, educator.

Educated in Ho primary schools, Dzovo later trained to be a teacher in Akropong Presbyterian Training College and visited many countries in Europe to broaden his experience. Returning to the Gold Coast, now Ghana, he served as a teacher for 21 years in various schools before entering his country's civil service in 1961.

Dzovo has written one novel, designed for junior and senior high school, *Salami and Musa*. The story concerns a northern Ghanaian boy who, discouraged with his task of herding the family's stubborn cattle, runs off to seek his fortune. After many adventures, he settles down with a wife, raises a son, Musa, who, well guided by his father, grows up to be a medical doctor.

Writings: Novel: *Salami and Musa*, London, Longmans, 1967.

E

EASMON, Raymond Sarif
b. ca. 1930, Sierra Leone.
Novelist, short story writer, playwright, medical doctor.

Locally educated except for his medical training in Europe, Easmon has practiced medicine in Freetown, the capital of Sierra Leone, while writing his novel, short stories, and plays. His two plays are *Dear Parent and Ogre* which won the prestigious prize offered by *Encounter Magazine*, and *The New Patriots*, a work in three acts. The latter play was published in April, 1966, though the book bears an earlier date. *Dear Parent and Ogre* was first produced by Wole Soyinka's play-troupe, the 1960 Masques, in mid-1960 at the Arts Theatre in Ibadan. Soyinka directed the play and performed the lead role of Dauda Touray, a politician. Easmon's one novel is *The Burnt-out Marriage*.

Easmon's powerful story, "Bindeh's Gift," appears in Ezekiel Mphahlele's *African Writing Today*. In this tale, the author finds a heroic African in the world of Kai Borie, a Chaka-like king (see Thomas Mofolo's *Chaka*). The redeeming, more humane qualities of Kai Borie come to the surface too late,

however, to avoid tragedy. The King kills three snakes dropped on him by Bindeh, a woman trying to avenge her husband, a defeated general who has been sentenced to death by Borie. Bindeh plunges into a deadly waterfall, and Kai Borie dies, too, but before his breath fails, the once all-vengeful warrior king appoints the aghast Bensali his heir and new king.

Writings: Novel: *The Burnt-out Marriage*, London, Nelson, 1967.

Plays: *Dear Parent and Ogre*, London, Oxford University Press, 1964; *The New Patriots*, London, Longmans Green, 1965 (actually released, April, 1966).

Story: "Bindeh's Gift," in *African Writing Today*, London, Penguin, 1967.

ECHERUO, Kevin
b. 1946, Okigwi, East Central State, Nigeria; d. October, 1969.
Poet, painter.

Born in Ibo-land, Kevin Echeruo did his early schooling in local towns, but went to Nsukka University to study fine arts. The Biafran war interrupted his studies, but he continued to paint. He died at age of 23. His pictures won 13 medals and certificates, including the All Africa Student Art Context in 1964.

Although little of his poetry had appeared before his death, one of his best poems appeared in the April 1971 *Okike,* a journal edited by Chinua Achebe.

Writings: Poem in *Okike,* Chinua Achebe, editor, Enugu, Nigeria, I, 1 April, 1971.

ECHERUO, Michael J. C.
b. 1937, Okigwi, Owerri Province, Ibo-country, Western Nigeria.
Poet, play producer, teacher.

Educated in local schools, he attended Stella Maris College in Port Harcourt and University College, Ibadan, where he majored in English. He was a professor of English at Nsukka University until 1967. During the Biafran war he studied in the United States, taking the M.A. and Ph.D in English at Cornell University, Ithaca, New York.

Echeruo directed the first production of John Pepper Clark's *Song of a Goat* at Enugu in 1962.

His early poems were first published in *Black Orpheus,* No. 12, and his first collection, *Mortality,* was published in 1968. Poems also appear in *New Sum of Poetry from the Negro World,* as well as in other anthologies. His dedicatory poem for the Ibo poet killed in the Biafran war, "For Christopher Okigbo," appears in *New African Literature and the Arts.*

Writings: Poetry: *Mortality,* London, Longmans, 1968; poems in *Black Orpheus,* No. 12 *New Sum of Poetry from the Negro World,* Paris, Présence Africaine, Vol. 57, 1966; *New African*

Literature and the Arts, Joseph Okpaku, editor, New York, Crowell, 1970.

EDYANG, Ernest
b. ca. 1935, Nigeria.
Playwright.

Edyang's three-act play *Emotan of Benin* appeared in the March 1963 edition of *Nigeria Magazine,* No. 76, Lagos.

EGBUNA, Obi Benue
b. ca. 1942, Nigeria.
Playwright, novelist, short story writer.

Oxford Press published his play, *The Ant Hill,* in 1965 about African students in London. A year earlier Faber and Faber had brought out his novel, *Wind Versus Polygamy.* The novel concerns an over-amorous chief who, asked to decide whom the voluptuous Elina should marry, decides to make her his 31st wife. Brought into court for having ignored the new anti-polygamy law, the virile chief makes a strong defense of the old ways of living and loving. Without condescension to his own people, Egbuna pulls all stops in developing the humorous aspects of the conflict between African elites trying to introduce new ways.

Oxford University Press published Egbuna's collection of stories, *Daughters of the Sun and Other Stories* in 1970. Two of them, "Divinity," and "The Medics," pit modern, trained men in losing conflict against the older, traditional world. "The Scarecrow of Nairobi" dramatizes the clash between a right-wing white settler and a new leader of the local Africans. The title story is a traditional tale told in a somewhat modern manner and from a modern viewpoint. His play,

"The Agony," was performed in the Unity Theatre, London, February, 1970. "Divinity, A Radio Play," adapted from the short story "Divinity," appeared in *The New Africa*, IV. *The Gods are not to Blame*, his most recent play, appeared in 1970.

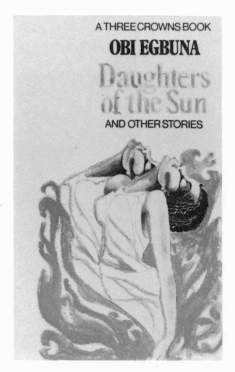

A THREE CROWNS BOOK

OBI EGBUNA

Daughters of the Sun

AND OTHER STORIES

Writings: Novel: *Wind Versus Polygamy*, London, Faber, 1964.

Plays: *The Ant Hill*, London, Oxford Press, 1965; *The Agony*, performed in London, 1970; "Divinity, A Radio Play" in *The New Africa*, IV, Nos. 6 and 7, August and September, 1965; *The Gods are not to Blame*, London, Oxford University Press, 1970.

Stories: *Daughters of the Sun and Other Stories*, London, Oxford University Press, 1970.

EGHAREVBA, Chief Dr. Jacob Uwadiae
b. ca. 1920, Benin Coast, Southern Nigeria.
Edo-language poet, collector of tales, anthropologist.

Chief Egharevba was educated locally through the university level but he took his doctorate in a British university in anthropology. His *Some Stories of Ancient Benin* provide a valuable retelling in English of these old tales. Companion volumes, *The City of Benin, Benin Law and Custom* and *Some Tribal Gods of Southern Nigeria* offer a thorough anthropological, legal, and cultural history of the Nigerian coastal people. All the volumes have recently been reissued by Kraus Reprint. His 26-page collection of traditional poems appears in *Ihum-an Edo* (Edo Songs).

Writings: Some Stories of Ancient Benin, Benin City, Nigeria, 1950; second edition, 1951; *The City of Benin*, 1952; *Benin Law and Custom*, third edition, Benin, 1949; *Some Tribal Gods of Southern Nigeria*, Benin, 1951; all volumes reissued by Kraus Reprint, Nendeln, Liechtenstein.

Poetry: *Ihun-an Edo*, Benin City, 1950.

EGUDU, Romanus
b. ca. 1930, Ibo-country, eastern Nigeria.
Poet, critic.

Egudu was educated locally in lower schools and at Nsukka University,

Egudu

Nigeria where he later served as Professor of English and African Literature until 1967 when the Biafran war broke out. He has recently taken the Ph.D. at Michigan State University in Lansing, Michigan. His post-graduate studies include detailed examination of Ibo traditional poetry. His verse has appeared in *Black Orpheus* magazine and other journals.

His poem, "The Journey", which appeared in *New African Literature and the Arts:* I, is metaphysical and tinged with T. S. Eliot's Christian despair and questioning. In Section I of the 60-line work he ponders:

> *If the journey ends so quick and sharply,*
> *if at that end no further end is in view,*
> *no hope of another light of another day,*
> *no hope of retreat, but one concluding*
> *   /night,*
> *then why at all the watery formation of*
> *   /a shadow*
> *in the inside of another shadow?*
> *why the break of the initial light so tantaliz-*
> *   /ing,*
> *leading but from the dark to the thicker*
> *   /dark?*
> *and why was the latch ever lifted to let*
> *   /out*
> *the prospective victim through the natural*
> *   /door-way?*

Writings: Poem: "The Journey" in *New African Literature and the Arts: I,* New York, Crowell 1970; other poems in *Black Orpheus* magazine (Ibadan), and *Okike,* Nsukka, Nigeria.

EKWENSI, Cyprian Odiatu Duaka
b. September 26, 1921, Minna, Nigeria.
Novelist, short story writer, pharmacist.

Born of Ibo parents working in Northern Nigeria, Ekwensi has been less rooted in the village life of his people than his famous colleague, Chinua Achebe, for he grew up in an area which was Moslem rather than Christian or pagan, and from the beginning was oriented to the hurly-burly of the new African cities. He attended Ibadan University and after his B.A. he went to Ghana University and then to the Chelsea School of Pharmacy, the University of London, where he took a professional degree.

After returning home, he taught science at Igbobi College, Lagos after service with the School of Forestry, Ibadan. More recently he has lectured in English, biology, chemistry, pharmacognosy and pharmaceutics. His long career has also included work for several African corporations, including the Nigerian Broadcasting Corporation, where he was head of features; service as director of information in the Federal Ministry of Information, Lagos; and a period as chairman of the Bureau for External Publicity in Biafra during the Ibos' effort to break away from Lagos, 1967–69. During the Biafran War he made at least one trip

130

to the United States to seek money for Biafra and to purchase radio equipment for the independent Biafran radio station of which he was director. His latest novel, *Africhaos*, completed in 1969 but unpublished, concerns the plight of the surrounded Ibos during the last days of the Biafran War. At present he is working as a chemist for a plastics firm in Enugu, Nigeria.

Ekwensi is possibly the most skillful writer in Africa in depicting the feelings and dilemmas of rural Africans who have pushed into the developing urban centers, often outside their tribal areas, to face both the excitements and the terrors of a strange and complicated new way of life. His writing, though warm and vivid, is often weak in characterization and plotting. He is at his best when he has the rich panorama of the city to paint. His novel, *People of the City* (1954) and *Jagua Nana* (1961) were the first good treatments of the varied peoples of modern Lagos. In *Jagua Nana* there is the most convincing and vivacious handling of the theme of the crowded, corrupt, but dynamic metropolis.

Ekwensi began his career by writing three "penny dreadfuls" or Onitsha market novelettes, or chapbooks. They are produced for the large number of Nigerians with only rudimentary abilities to read English, but with a strong hunger for books of any sort. *When love whispers, The leopard's claw,* and *Ikola the wrestler* all appeared in 1947 or 1948 in Onitsha, although the books themselves indicate no dates. *Ikolo* has appeared in a British edition and *The leopard's claws* came out under Longman's imprint in 1950. There seems not to be any clear record of whether he turned out other titles for this popular market, but his later work, even the best of it, shows some influence from the breezy, impres-sionistic style and hardly-thought-out characters of the chapbooks. From this period also came five of his short stories, "Banana Peel," "The Tinted Scarf," "Land of Sani," "The Cup was Full," and "Deserters' Dupe," published in *African New Writing,* which won an award of the British Council. One of these stories had earlier appeared in *Wide World Magazine.*

His novels, *Burning Grass* (1962), which tells the story of the Fulani herding people of the grassy savannas of Northern Nigeria, and *Beautiful Feathers,* which recounts the career of a pharmacist turned party-organizer, crowd-pleaser, and, finally, delegate to a Pan-African Congress in Dakar, are well known. Less known is his novel *Iska* (1966) which portrays an Ibo heroine who marries a Hausa official, becomes a model in Lagos, and otherwise leads an exciting life full of love and tragedy.

The little Heinemann volume, *Lokotown* contains nine stories, including "Fashion Girl" which is the original version for the most popular and critically acclaimed of his works, *Jagua Nana.* Five volumes of his stories for children are: *The Drummer Boy,* (1960), *The Passport of Mallam Ilia* (1960), *An African Night's Entertainment* (1962), *The Rainmaker and Other Stories* (1965), and *Juju Rock* (1966). These works are extremely attractive readers, produced in durable paper covers, and handsomely illustrated by African artists.

Other works are *Yaba Roundabout Murder,* a novella; *Great Elephant-bird,* folklore; *Trouble in Form VI,* a school-novelette, and *The Boa Suitor,* folklore.

Ekwensi's best work, *Jagua Nana,* concerns a lusty, bright heroine of that name, so called because the British car, the Jaguar (or Jahg-wah), is expensive, wanted, ostentatious. Nana was chosen because Ekwensi no doubt was thinking of Emile Zola's flesh-pot heroine of the Second Empire in France. Ekwensi's Jagua moves through all levels of society and the reader gets to know through her the hurly-burly of the new Lagos, filled with country hustlers and city sophisticates.

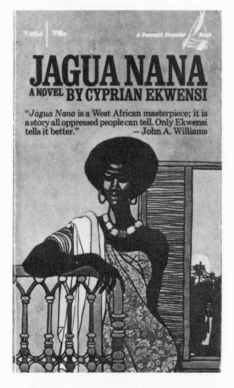

Ekwensi is not an accomplished stylist, but he writes with vivacity and can paint a scene quickly and convincingly. His work expresses a very warm sensuality and there is little preciosity or primness in his work, characteristics of many of the less accomplished African writers.

Writings: Novels: *People of the City,* London, Andrew Dakers, 1954; paperback, London, Heinemann, 1963; Evanston, Northwestern University Press, 1967; revised edition, Greenwich, Connecticut, Fawcett, 1969; *Jagua Nana,* London, Hutchinson, 1961; paperback, London, Panther, 1963; Greenwich, Conn., Fawcett, 1969; *Burning Grass,* London, Heinemann, 1962, reprint in Heinemann's African Writers Series, 1968; *Beautiful Feathers,* London, Hutchinson, 1963; *Iska,* London, Hutchinson, 1966, London, Panther Books, 1968; *Africhaos,* 1969.

Novelettes: *When Love Whispers,* Yaba, Nigeria, Chuks, 1947, and Onitsha, Tabansi Bookshop, 1956(?); *The Leopard's Claw,* and *Ikola the Wrestler,* both Yaba or Onitsha, 1947 or 1948; also, *The Leopard's Claw;* London, Longmans, Green, 1950; *Ikola,* Nelson, 1947, 1954; *Great Elephant Bird,* London, Nelson, 1965; *Yaba Roundabout Murder,* Lagos, Tortoise Series Books, 1962, 1964.

Short Stories: "Banana Peel," "The Tinted Scarf," "Land of Sani," "The Cup Was Full" and "Deserters' Dupe" in *African New Writing,* London, Lutterworth Press, 1947; "Fashion Girl" in *Lokotown,* London, Heinemann, 1966; *Lokotown and other stories,* London, Heinemann, 1966.

Childrens books: *The Drummer Boy,* London, Cambridge University Press, 1960; *The Passport of Mallam Ilia,* London, Cambridge University Press, 1960; *An African Night's Entertainment,* 1962; *The Rainmaker and Other Stories,* 1965; *Juju Rock,* 1966, the last three all by African Universities Press; also *Trouble in Form VI,* Cambridge, Cambridge University Press, 1966; *The Boa Suitor,* London, Nelson, 1966.

Biographical/Critical Sources: Bernth Lindfors, "Cyprian Ekwensi—an African popular novelist," *African Literature Today,* No. 3, London, 1969; Robert W. July, "The African Personality in the

African Novel," in *Introduction to African Literature*, Ulli Beier, editor, Evanston, Ill., Northwestern University Press, 1967; Hans Zell, editor, *A Reader's Guide to African Literature*, New York, Africana Publishing Corp., 1971.

EKWERE, John
b. ca. 1930, near Calabar, Eastern Nigeria
Poet, playwright, short story writer.

Educated locally, he studied drama in England after taking a B.A. at Ibadan University, Nigeria. He has written many poem, plays, and stories, mostly unpublished, and was, in the 1960's, Director of Programs for Eastern Nigerian Television Services. He is presently the Director of Information, South-Eastern State, Calabar, Nigeria.
His poem "Rejoinder" with its surprise last line early made a point which became a major theme in African fiction:
Now no more the palefaced strangers
With unhallowed feet
The heritage of our fathers profane;
Now no missioned benevolent despots
Bull-doze an unwilling race;
No more the foreign hawks
On alien chickens prey—
But we on us!

Writings: Poem: "Rejoinder" in *Reflections: Nigerian Prose and Verse*, F. Ademola, Lagos, African Universities Press, 1962.

EL HARDALLO (see HARDALLO)

ELMI, Bownderi (see ILMI, Bownderi)

EPANYA–YONDO, Elolongué
b. March 8, 1930, Douala, Cameroon.
Poet.

Epanya–Yondo's one volume of collected verse, *Kamerun! Kamerun!* (Cameroon! Cameroon!), published in 1960, offers poems in various of the Cameroonian languages followed by French translations. The work was translated into Russian by Aleksandre Revich in 1963. He is represented by a long, three-page poem, "Souviens-toi" (Remember), in *New Sum of Poetry from the Negro World.*

Writings: Poetry: *Kamerun! Kamerun!*, Paris, Présence Africaine, 1960; a Russian translation, Moscow, 1963; poem: "Souviens-toi," in *New Sum of Poetry From the Negro World*, Paris, Présence Africaine, Vol. 57, 1966.

EQUIANO, Africanus Olauda(h)
(see VASSA, Olaudah Gustavus)

ESPIRITO SANTO, Alda de (also de Espírito Santo, Alda)
b. April 30, 1926, São Tomé.
Poet, journalist, teacher.

Alde de Espírito Santo has worked as a teacher and published poetry in Portuguese and has appeared in Andrade's *Cadorno* and his anthology *(Antologia da poesia negra de espressão portuguesa)*. She is also represented in Moore and Beier's *Modern Poetry from Africa*, London, and in *New Sum of Poetry from the Negro World*. In her poem, "Descendo o meu bairro" (Walking Down Through My Part of Town), she sympathizes with the day laborers toiling on the large Portuguese plantations. Her other verse also is full of African sentiment. Her poem, "Lavandeiras do Agua Grande" (The Washerwoman of Agua Grande), is a not too veiled allegory of the quasi-enslavement of the African by the Portuguese settler. The poem, "Onde estâo os homens cacados neste vente de lourura" (Where Are the Men Swept by this Wind of Folly?), is clearly concerned with the massacre of Creoles by the Portuguese army and white settlers of Angola in February, 1953.

She was accused in late 1965 of taking part in nationalist politics in Saõ Tomé, and arrested. She was released in January, 1966 and has returned to teaching.

Writings: Poems in de Andrade's *Cadorno de poesia negra de expressão portuguêsa*, Lisbon, Livraria Escolar Editôra, 1953, and *Antologia da poesia negra de espressão portuguesa*, Paris, P-J Oswald, 1958; *Poetas de S. Tomé e Príncipe*, 1963; *Modern Poetry from Africa*, Moore and Beier, editors, Revised edition, London, Penguin, 1968; *New Sum of Poetry from the Negro World*, Paris, Présence Africaine, Volume 57, 1966.

EUBA, Femi
b. ca. 1935, Nigeria.
Playwright, actor.

Born and educated in Nigeria, Femi Euba went to England to study drama and has performed leading roles in several London productions of Wole Soyinka's plays, and has also appeared on various B.B.C. broadcast dramas. His short play, *The Game*, has been performed on B.B.C.'s "African Theatre" series (December 29, 1965), and has been published in Cosmo Pieterse's *Ten One-Act Plays*. Other performed but unpublished plays of Euba's are: *The Telegram, The Union, Who is the Devil*, and *The Yam Debt. Abiku* is a screen play in manuscript.

Writings: Plays: *The Game*, in *Ten One-Act Plays*, Cosmo Pieterse, editor, London, Heinemann, 1968; performed but unpublished, *The Telegram, The Union, Who is the Devil, The Yam Debt, Abiku*.

F

FAARAH, Nuur
b. ca. 1850, Somali-land; d. ca. 1930.
Somali oral poet.

Leader of his clan, Faarah used his poetry to argue his people's case in their disputes with a more powerful clan (the Iidegale) to which tribute had to be paid. His poetry also deals with the European invasion of his homeland and its subsequent partition. His poem, "The Limits of Patience," seems to demonstrate his recognition of the plans of the British, Ethiopians and Italians to divide the Somali country. The text is in *Somali Poetry*.

Writings: Poem: "The Limits of Patience," in *Somali Poetry*, Andrzejewski and Lewis, editors, Oxford, Clarendon Press, 1964.

FAFUNWA, A. Babs
b. September 3, 1923, Lagos, Nigeria.
Journalist, teacher.

Fafunwa was educated locally in Nigeria and later at Bethune–Cookman College, Florida. During his undergraduate years and afterwards he wrote articles concerning his experiences in Africa and in the United States. He took an M.A. (1951) and a Ph.D. (1955) at New York University. He became Deputy Vice-Chancellor, Univ. of Ife, 1970.

Writings: Articles: "An African's Adventures in America," *An African Treasury*, Langston Hughes, editor, New York, Pyramid Books, 1961, and many scholarly essays in professional journals.

FAGUNWA, Chief Daniel Olorunfemi
b. 1910, Yoruba-land, West Nigeria;
d. December 9, 1963.
Novelist in the Yoruba language.

Educated and trained as a teacher, Fagunwa for a long while worked for the Ministry of Education in Ibadan.

He exploited Yoruba folk tales and legends and became probably the most widely-known writer in Nigeria who employed a vernacular language. His first work was *Ogboju ode ninu igbo Irunmale* (The Skillful Hunter in the Forest of Four Hundred Spirits). He has published many other works since, among them: *Igbo Olodumare* (Forest of the Lord), part II to *Ogboju*, probably his most popular; *Adiitu Olodumare* (God's Secret); *Alaye fun Oluko Nipa Lilo Iwe*

Fagunwa

Taiwo ati Kehinde; Ireke-Onibudo (The Guard's Cane); *Irinago apa Kini; Irinkerindo Ninu igbo Elegbeje: Apa keta* (Adventures in the Forest of Elegbeje); *Obbuju Ode Ninu Igbo Irunmale;* and *Asayan itan* (Selected Stories).

These and other works were first published in Yoruba in Nigeria before being translated and/or published in English. The first work cited above has recently been rendered into English as *The Forest of a Thousand Daemons* by Wole Soyinka, Africa's most important dramatist. Soyinka wrote of Fagunwa in the introduction to his adaptation-translation:

> *Fagunwa's style fluctuates, for he is both the enthusiastic raconteur and pious moralist, and the battle of the inventive imagination with the morally guided is a constant process in much of his work. His total conviction in multiple existences within our physical world is as much an inspiration to some of the most brilliant fiction in*

Yoruba writing as it is a deeply felt urge to 'justify the ways of God to man.'

Soyinka goes on to discuss Fagunwa's special qualities:

> *The experience of sheer delight in his verbal adroitness is undoubtedly a great loss in translation, but it is not reason enough to limit Fagunwa to the readership of Yoruba speakers only. As Fagunwa himself would put it, 'onisango di kiriyo, o l'oun o jo bata, ijo o gbo duru, ejika ni kōtu fa ya.' (The Christian convert swore never again to dance to Sango drums; when he heard the church organ, his jacket soon burst at the seams . . .)' Let the story-teller himself persuade us.*

Fagunwa was only 53 when *The Daily Express,* (Lagos, December 10, 1963) announced his death in the town of Bida: "Fagunwa dies in crash. The well-known Nigerian writer Chief, D. O. Fagunwa, died yesterday in a motor accident, a few days after he submitted what could be called his last literary work to the *Daily Express.*" Fagunwa left a wife and five children.

Writings: Novels: *Ogboju ode ninu igbo Irunmale,* London, Nelson, 1939, 1950, 1958; English translation, *The Forest of a Thousand Daemons,* London, Nelson 1968; Part II of *Obgoju* entitled *Igbo Olodumare,* London, Nelson, 1946, 1949, 1961; *Adiitu Olodumare,* Edinburgh, Nelson, 1961; *Alaye fun Oluko Nipa Lilo Iwe Taiwo ati Kehinde,* London, Oxford University Press, 1949; *Ireke–Onibudo,* Edinburgh, Nelson, 1948, 1949, 1961; *Irinago apa Kini,* London, Oxford University Press, 1949; *Irinkerindo Ninu igbo Elegebeje: Apa keta,* Edinburgh, Nelson, 1954, 1961; *Obbuju Ode Ninu Igbo Irunmale,* Edinburgh, Nelson, 1954, 1956, 1961.

Stories: *Asayan itan,* London, Edinburgh, Nelson, 1959.

Biographical/Critical Sources: Introduction by Wole Soyinka to Fagunwa's *The Forest of a Thousand Daemons,* London, Nelson, 1968; Ulli Beier, "Fagunwa—a Yoruba novelist," *Black Orpheus,* No. 17, Ikeja, June 1965; A. Olubummo, "Fagunwa—a Yoruba novelist," *Odù,* No. 9, September, 1963.

FARAH, Nuruddin
b. 1945, Baidoa, Southern Region, Somalia.
Novelist, story writer, playwright, teacher.

The fourth son in a family of ten, Farah attended local schools where he studied Italian and English along with the usual European subjects. He took his first job with the Ministry of Education of the new Republic of Somalia, remaining for several years before going to India to study philosophy and literature at the University of Chandigarh. While studying for the B.A. he married an Indian woman and at present is teaching in a high school in Mogadishu, Somalia's capital. His first novel, *From a Crooked Rib* is the first work of fiction to be published by a Somali writer in English.

The work takes its title from the old Somali proverb: "God created Woman from a crooked rib; and any one who trieth to straighten it, breaketh." The little novel (179 pages) concerns Ebla, a country-girl who slowly travels from rural innocence to town knowledge (in Belet Wene) to city wisdom and pain (in Mogadishu). Along the way she is cheated and learns to cheat. She survives and after many years of trouble comes to rest in the arms of her lover Awill.

Writings: Novel: *From A Crooked Rib,* London, Heinemann, 1970.

FERREIRA, António Baticã
b. ca. 1938, Guinea (Bissau).
Poet, medical doctor.

After local schooling, Ferreiro studied in Lisbon, Dakar, and in the School of Medicine at Geneva during the early 1960's. Son of a chief, he is a Roman Catholic and is a practicing physician.

Ferreiro has contributed to various journals and is represented by the poem, "Infancia," in *Poetas e contistas africanos de expressão portuguêsa* (African Poets and Story-tellers of Portuguese Expression).

Writings: Poetry: "Infancia," *Poetas e contistas africanos de expressão portuguêsa,* São Paulo, Editôra Brasiliense, 1963.

FERREIRA, José da Silva Maia
b. ca. 1825, Benguela, Angola;

Ferreira

d., after 1850.
Poet.

Probably born to an African mother and a Portuguese father, Ferreira's collection of poems, *Espontaneidades da minha alma* (Spontaneous Outpourings of My Soul), published in 1850, appears to have been the first volume of Portuguese verse to have been printed on the Portuguese government's press set up in 1845 in Luanda. (The book shows the date 1849, but two poems in the collection are dated 1850.) The poems, mostly written in Rio de Janeiro in the 1840's, celebrate the handsome Benguele women and express a naive patriotism and religious sentiment. Ferreira's work, though graphically describing African fevers and other diseases, rapacious merchants and the unknown and feared jungles outside Benguele and Luanda, nevertheless is more romantic than realistic—not touched by the new literary currents of Europe.

Writings: Poems: *Espontaneidades da minha alma. As senhoras africanas. Poesias I.,* Luanda, Imprensa do Govêrno, 1849 (but probably issued in 1850); poem, "Amor e Loucura" (Love and Madness), in *Almanach de Lembranças,* Lisbon, 1879.

FODEBA, Keita (see KEITA, Fodeba)

FONSECA, Aguinaldo Brito
b. 1922, Cape Verde Islands.
Poet, clerk.

An active member of the literary group centered around the journal *Claridade* from 1945 on, Fonseca now lives in Lisbon where he works as an administrative clerk. He has contributed to many literary reviews, including *Seara Nova, Atlântico,* and *Mundo Literário* and is represented in Mário de Andrade's *Antologia de poesia negra de expressão portugêsa.* His one volume of poems is *Linha do horizonte* (The Horizon Line), published first in 1945. His diction is terse and his mood often acrid as in this excerpt from "Tavern by the Sea" as translated by Moore in *New Poetry from Africa:*

> *A distant glimmer*
> *And a beacon spitting light*
> *In the black face of night.*
> . . .
> *Love passionate and brutal*
> *Amidst the open knives*
> *And the abandon*
> *Of a prostitute's embrace.*

Writings: Poetry: *Linha do horizonte,* Lisbon, Grafica Modala, 1945; 1951 second edition is Lisbon, Casa dos Estudantes do Império; "Cancao dos rapazes da ilha," (Songs of the Boys of the Island) poem in *Poetas e contistas africanos de expressão portuguêsa,* São Paulo, Editôra Brasiliense, 1963; poems also in *Literatura africana de expressão portuguêsa,* Algiers, 1957, and *Modern Poetry from Africa,* revised edition, Moore and Beier, eds., Baltimore, Penguin, 1970.

FONSECA, Mário Alberto
b. 1939, near Praia, Santiago Island, Cape Verde.
Poet, journalist.

Fonseca has been a journalist both at home and in Lisbon where he worked for the journal *Mensagem* (Messenger). He is now in exile in Europe, unable to return home or to Portugal because of his work with the African Party of Independence for Guinea and Cape Verde (the P.A.I.G.G.). He is represented by one poem, "Quando a vida nascer" (When Life begins), in the original Portuguese in *New Sum of Poetry from the Negro World* and has been collected in other anthologies.

Writings: "Quando a vida nascer," *New Sum of Poetry from the Negro World,* Paris, Présence Africaine, Vol 57, 1966.

FONTES–PEREIRA, José de (see PEREIRA, José de Fonte)

FREIRE, Albuquerque
b. ca. 1935, Mozambique.
Poet.

Freire has published three volumes of verse and has appeared in various reviews. His works are: *O livro dos sonetos* (A Book of Sonnets), 1960; *Canção negra e outros poemas* (Negro Songs and Other Poems), 1961; and *Cântico da paz e do desespero* (Canticles of Peace and Despair), published in 1963.

Writings: Poetry: *O livro dos sonetos,* Lourenço Marques, 1960; *Canção negra e outros poemas,* Lourenço Marques, Tip. Minerva, 1960; *Cântico da paz e do desespero,* Lourenço Marques, Minerva, 1963.

FUKIAU (see BUNSEKI, A. Fukiau kia)

FULA, Arthur Nuthall
b. May 8, 1908, East London, South Africa; d. May 20, 1966.
Afrikaans language novelist, poet, teacher, civil servant.

In 1910 Arthur Fula's parents moved from East London to the Rand, then occupied by the Boers and he consequently came into close contact with Afrikaans, a language he later used exclusively in his writing, a unique event in Bantu literature. He first attended the Siemert Coloured School, Doornfontein, where Afrikaans was the school language, and then the Eurafrican Normal College in Vrededorp, obtaining the Standard IV certificate in 1930. Fula also studied French at the Alliance Française. He taught for several years, and worked as a clerk and later in a hospital. Appointed interpreter in the Johannesburg Magistrate's Court, he dealt with the Xhosa, Zulu, Sotho, Tswana and Pedi languages in addition to Afrikaans and English.

Fula published two novels. The first was *Jôhannie giet die beeld* (Johannesburg Molds the Shape) (1954) in which a young man comes to the city from the country and is overwhelmed and corrupted by Johannesburg life. The theme was increasingly popular with the new African writers such as Cyprian Ekwensi in his *People of the City* and *Jagua Nana* and the Zulu writer Rolfus Dhlomo with his *African Tragedy*. Fula's second novel, *Met Erbarming, O Here* (With Pleasure, Dear Sirs) appeared in 1956. Here, Dr. Adriana Maledi Tsukudu strives to deal with, if not overcome, the superstitious fears of the poor in the slums of Johannesburg; the story is based on the author's own extensive acquaintance with such conditions.

Some of Fula's verse appeared in random journals and a few of his poems were collected in the anthology *Suid-*

Fula

Afrikaanse Erzahlen edited by Peter Sulzer.

After a sudden heart attack, Fula died in his home outside Johannesburg on May 20, 1966, leaving his wife and five children.

Writings: Novels: *Jôhannie giet die beeld,* Johannesburg, Afrikaanse Pers-Boek-handel, 1954; *Met erbarming, O Here,* Johannesburg, Afrikaanse Pers-Boek-handel, 1956.

Poems: In *Suid-Afrikaanse Erzahlen,* Peter Sulzer, editor, Switzerland, 1963.

FUTSHANE, Zora Z. T. (see mention in SWAARTBOOI, Victoria)

FUZE, Magema ka Magwaza
b. ca. 1845, Zululand, South Africa;
d. 1922?
Zulu folklore collector and commentator.

A student of Bishop John Colenso who had published the first English language study of Zulu, the *Elementary Grammar of the Zulu Kafir Language* (1855), Fuze wrote the first book to appear in print by any Zulu author, *Abantu abamnyama lapha bavela ngakhona* (Black People: Where They Come From), though it had to await publication until 1922. Colenso's daughter had encouraged Fuze to recapture the past and he sought without precedent or much guidance to trace the history and customs of his people. The work had strong influence on later writers: the exaltation of the Zulu nation and its proud sense of power and identity; the nostalgic memorial to the eroding customs and beliefs of the Zulu; and the growing feeling of a pan-Bantu loyalty and solidarity. This last aspect was reflected in the efforts of the leaders of the South African Native Congress during the World War I years to bring the Bantu Africans together in a meaningful alliance. (See entry for Jordan Ngubane, grandson of one of Fuze's daughters.)

Writings: History-Folklore: *Abantu abamnyama Lapha bavela ngakhona,* Pieter-maritzburg, City Printing Works, 1922.

Biographical/Critical Source: Albert S. Gé-rard, *Four African Literatures,* Berkeley, University of California Press, 1971.

G

GABRA, Egzi'abeher
b. early 1860's, Tigré, Ethiopia;
d. ca. 1914.
Amharic poet, government official.

Considered possibly the first poet to
write in Amharic, Gabra spent his youth
in Sada Krestian (Hamesien), Eritrea,
and attended school there. He was
imprisoned at Nocra during the Italian
War with King Menelik II and also spent
time in jail in 1902 at Harar for asserting
that the earth circles the sun. Working
as a court jester of sorts for Menelik,
he soon demonstrated his wit and courage by satirizing leading courtiers. He
later issued his work in handwritten
copies. Political and modernist in
thought, these "poems" in the oral tradition of older court poetry, drew attention and earned him a certain amount
of fame.

He published anonymously in 1897
the pamphlet *Advice for Seeking and
Grasping the Best Way to Strengthen the State
for the Benefit of People and Country.*

Four of Gabra's poems, with English
translation, have appeared in *An Amharic
Reader.* None of his poetry reached print
in his lifetime including the one in which
he attacked Italy during its war against
Turkey over Libya. It was this poem that
provoked the pro-Italian poem released
anonymously by Afawarq Gabra Iyasus
in 1912.

Though honored with the title of
"*Blatta,*" an honorific similar to "Sir," he
eventually lost favor at court and died
in relative obscurity about 1914.

Writings: Poems in *An Amharic Reader,*
J. I. Eadie, editor, Cambridge, Cambridge University Press, 1924.

Pamphlet: *Advice for Seeking and Grasping the Best Way to Strengthen the State for
the Benefit of People and Country,* published
outside Ethiopia, 1897.

GABRE–MEDHIN, Tsegaye (see
TSEGAYE, Gabre–Medhin)

GALAAL (see MUSA, Hajji Ismail
Galaal)

GALVAO, Duarte (see LEMOS,
Virgílio de)

GATANYU, James
b. 1945, Londiani, Kenya.
Playwright.

Gatanyu

Educated at Alliance High School, Gatanyu is presently studying development economics at the University of Sussex, England.

He took several leading roles in plays while at Alliance and became chairman of the school's dramatic society.

Gantanyu's play, the *Battlefield*, was first performed in March, 1966, at the Kenya Schools' Dramatic Festival where it won the prize for the greatest originality. It deals with the tense political atmosphere of pre-independence Kenya of the late 1950's.

Writings: Play: *The Battlefield*, Nairobi, East African Publishing House, 1968.

GATHERU, Reuel John Mugo
b. 1925, Kikuyu-land, Kenya.
Autobiographer.

Mugo Gatheru's *Child of Two Worlds,* written while the author was a student at Lincoln College in Pennsylvania and Roosevelt College in Chicago, Illinois, provides scholarly background on the culture of his people and deals with his own experiences in Africa and America. Though the work is somewhat derivative of Kenyatta's *Facing Mt. Kenya,* it does offer new material and insights concerning the interplay of Western and African values.

The son of an important "medicineman" or priest ("Mugo" means "medicine," or more literally, "Man of God"), Gatheru writes in his first paragraph: "I come from a long line of men who have borne this name, a line stretching far, far back into time. They were highly respected men among their own people, the Kikuyu. My people are Africans, reddish-brown and chocolate-brown men, women and children, living in the highlands of Kenya, East Africa." In the introduction he recounts how during the hey-day of "McCarthyism" the U.S. Immigration Service sought to expel him because the Mau Mau (rebels against British rule in Kenya) were considered Communists and, ergo, he, Gatheru, must also be a Communist. He fought the expulsion order for three years with the help of friends, finally winning his case in 1957. The autobiography, then, is not only a personal record, but a vindication of his people's humanity, culture, and right to struggle against the government of Great Britain, something still shocking to most Western minds as late as the 1950's.

Accordingly, he wrote:

In 1952, when the Mau Mau crisis broke out in my country, I was in school in the United States. I was there throughout a four-year war in my country which cost the British Government some £ 55,585,424, and during which over 15,000 of my people died and another 100,000 were placed in concentration camps. During all this time I was studying and reading and thinking and brooding.

The road to America and to higher education was long. Beginning his schooling in Kahuti-Weithaga, Kambui, later at the Medical Training School in Nairobi, he was blocked from further education by the British authorities in Kenya because he wrote a letter to a local newspaper complaining of racial discrimination against the Kenyans. In 1949 he traveled to India to study at Allahabad University. In 1950, after a trip from Bombay to England and six weeks in London, he sailed to New York City, arriving in America on April 30th, to begin an eight years' sojourn. He took the B.A. at Lincoln in 1954, and the M.A. at New York University in 1958. In November, 1958 he left for England to

142

begin his law studies. The book ends with Mugo sitting in his flat at Hammersmith, June 1, 1963, picturing in his mind Jomo Kenyatta as he "stands . . . on a platform draped in scarlet" taking from Queen Elizabeth the power to lead his country into independence.

Shortly thereafter, Gatheru finished his legal studies and left for Kenya with his white American wife, whom he had married in 1958, and their infant son, "Gatheru, Gatheru-son-of-Mugo."

Writings: Autobiography: *Child of Two Worlds,* London, Routledge and Kegan Paul, 1964; London, Heinemann, 1966.

GBADAMOSI, Bakare A.
b. 1930, Oshogbo, Western Nigeria.
Yoruba short story writer, poet, ethnographer.

Locally educated, Gbadamosi is presently assistant ethnographer for the Nigerian Museum in Lagos and has been a professional letter writer for the illiterate or semi-literate, a professional magician and an actor. He has published *Oriki,* traditional Yoruba poems, and a book of short stories, *Oro pelu idi re* (Words and Their Meaning), both in Yoruba, and three books of folk-lore in collaboration with Ulli Beier, a German professor who was helpful to young Nigerian writers at the University of Ibadan in the late 1950's and early 1960's in organizing the Mbari Club, an organization that encouraged new writing.

Gbadamosi and Beier's *Not even God is ripe enough* is a particularly enjoyable volume of 58 pages. The little "stories" bear such titles as "Kindness won't kill you, but it can give you a lot of worries," or "When life is good for us, we become

bad," or the "Not even god is ripe enough to catch a woman in love."

In 1959, Gbadamosi, with Ulli Beier, published "Yoruba Poetry in Translation," in *Black Orpheus* magazine.

Writings: Poetry: *Oriki,* Ibadan, Mbari, 1961.

Short Stories: *Oro pelu idi re,* Oshogbo, Mbari Mbayo, 1965. Folklore: With Ulli Beier, *Not Even God is Ripe Enough,* London, Heinemann, 1968.

Article: with Beier, "Yoruba Poetry in Translation," *Black Orpheus* magazine, Special Number, Ibadan, Mbari Press, Ibadan University, 1959.

GERMACAW, Takla Hawaryat
b. 1915, Ethiopia.
Amharic novelist, playwright, government official.

Son of the early playwright, Takla Hawaryat, Germacaw studied in local schools, then went on to France for his high school training. At home during the Italian invasion, he just missed execution in the massacre of Ethiopian intellectuals in 1937 ordered by Marshall Graziani. He was taken to Italy and remained there till 1943. By 1945, he was director general of the Press and Information Office and in the next few years produced the novel, *Ar'aya* (Good Example) and the play, *Tewodros.* Though the novel has much of the traditional moralistic tone of earlier fiction in Amharic, it does have highly descriptive passages of local scenery and the emphasis is on improved agriculture. Though not a Soviet "tractor–drama," the work was quickly translated into Russian and Chinese, the first Amharic work to be so honored. The play deals with the early centralizing efforts of Tewodros II (Theodore II) who, though unsuccessful in his policies, pointed the way for Menelik II and Emperor Selassie, both of whom sought to rein in the nobles and to modernize the state.

In 1950, Germacaw took on a series of demanding diplomatic assignments: Councillor and Chargé d'affaires at Stockholm; work in the Embassy at Rio de Janeiro (1954); official of the Ministry of Foreign Affairs (1956); Ambassador to Rome (1958) and to Bonn (1960). In 1961, he was Minister of Information and Governor General of Ilubabor Provinces; in 1966 he was named Minister of Agriculture; and in 1960, Minister of Health. During this twenty-year span he seems not to have written or published.

Writings: Novel: *Ar'aya*, Asmara, Imp. Pietro Silla, 1941–42, Addis Ababa, 1948–49.

Play: *Tewodros*, Addis Ababa, 1942–43, 1949–50.

Biographical/Critical Source: Pierre Comba, "Le roman dans le littérature Ethiopienne de langue amharique," in *Journal of Semitic Studies* (Spring 1964), IX, 173–186.

GICARU, Muga
b. 1920, Kikuyu country, Kenya.
Autobiographer, novelist.

Educated at a mission school and later at a night school in Nairobi, Gicaru showed promise enough to be encouraged to go to England for further training. Returning to Kenya in his 30's, he began his autobiographical novel, *Land of Sunshine. Scenes of Life in Kenya Before Mau Mau*. In the book, set primarily in the Kenya before the Mau-Mau uprising, Gicaru romanticizes the African past

but develops the needed contrast to the violence and terror of the revolt that came later.

Writings: Novel: *Land of Sunshine. Scenes of Life in Kenya Before Mau Mau*, Introduction by Trevor Huddleston, London, Lawrence and Wishart, 1958; Russian edition, Moscow, 1961.

GONÇALVES, António Aurélio
b. ca. 1920, São Vicente, Cape Verde Islands.
Story writer, novelist, critic, teacher.

Gonçalves did his university studies (art and letters) in Portugal and has been a high school teacher in the Cape Verde Islands. He is considered one of the best critics and scholars from his home islands and his stories are among the most sensitively written in Portuguese-African literature. His 94-page novelette, *Pródiga* (The Prodigal Girl), first published in 1956, was one of the earliest works of longer fiction from the islands. He became a leading contributor to the literary journal, *Claridade*, founded in the 1930's

His short story of 43 pages, "O entêrro de nhâ Candinha Sena" (The Funeral of "Aunt" Candinha Sena) was first published in 1957, but was republished along with *Pródiga* in the volume, *Colecção Imbondeiro 35/36* in 1962, with a preface by Manuel Ferreira.

One of his best-known critical essays is "Problemas da literatura romanesca em Cabo Verde" (Problems of Romanesque Cabo-Verdean Literature), 1956.

Writings: Story: "O entêrro de nhâ Candinha Sena," in *Colecção Imbondeiro 35/36*, Sá da Bandeira, Angola, Imbondeiro, 1962; in *Poetas e contistas africanos*

de expressão portuguêsa, São Paulo, Editôra Brasiliensa, 1963; originally in booklet form, Praia, Cape Verde, Imprensa Nacional, 1957.

Novel: *Pródiga.* Praia, Cape Verde, 1956.

Scholarly works: Editor of *Antologia da ficção cabo-verdiana contemporânea,* Praia, Cape Verde, 1960, in which appeared his essay, "Problemas da literatura romanesca em Cabo Verde."

GQOBA, William Wellington

b. August, 1840, Gaga, Chumie Valley, Cape Province, South Africa;
d. April 26, 1888.
Xhosa poet, journalist (in Xhosa and English), preacher.

Born into Chief Ngqika's clan of the Xhosa speaking peoples, Gqoba attended mission school at the Chumie Mission Station and then at the age of 13, entered the junior class at Lovedale in September 1853, remaining until May, 1856. For the next ten years he worked as a wagonmaker, but in 1863 he began work as an interpreter and teacher at Gwali for the Rev. Tiyo Soga, staying until 1867. In 1867–68 he taught at Lovedale, returned to Gwali for the period 1868–70 and then became school master and interpreter in King William's Town. He married about 1870. In January, 1873, the Rabula Church called Gqoba as their preacher, keeping him until 1877. During the next three years he directed the school at Peelton for the Rev. R. Birt, and then, after a short period at Rabula, he took up teaching at Lovedale.

In the early 1880's he began contributing poems and articles to the newspaper, the *Isigidimi sama–Xosa* (The Xhosa Courier). After four years in the Kimberley diamond fields, he returned to Lovedale to become editor of the *Isigidimi sama–Xosa* and to teach courses in translation. His articles often dealt with historical topics such as the Mfecane Wars or the experiences of the Mbo people. His article "Ibali laseMbo" had a section devoted to the great Zulu chief, Chaka. His Xhosa poems, didactic for the most part, dealt with the unsettled lives of the Xhosa peoples who were gradually being westernized. Many of his articles, never published in his lifetime because they were too critical of colonialism and related matters, later were published by Walter Benson Rubusana in *Zemk' inkomo magwala ndini.*

Gqoba died suddenly on April 26, 1888, and his newspaper ceased publication. Though his work was of a lower level than Tiyo Soga's, it helped prepare the way for a more comprehensive vernacular literature in Xhosa.

Writings: Poems and articles in *Isigidimi sama–Xosa,* a newspaper; *Zemk' inkomo magwala ndini,* Walter Benson, editor, carried many of his political articles.

GRAHAM, Peter (see ABRAHAMS, Peter)

GUEYE, Youssouf

b. May 8, 1928, Kaédi, Mauritania.
Poet.

Represented in *New Sum of Poetry from the Negro World,* Guèye's extremely beautiful poems employ long and musical lines with frequent run-overs. His "Le sens du Cirque," an anti-colonial poem, begins:

Carillons lointains de la Grande Horloge
/de cuivre

échos voilés des clairons et des chants
/de foules (choeurs de
grande agapes, applaudissements syncopés
/descendus
aux profondeurs le long des vertes abysses),
nous remontons les SONGES à hauteur
/bleue d'étoile
tout au haut des gradins du Cirque sonore
et éblouissant de lumières.

Far away bells of the Great Clock of copper
veiled echoes of bugles and the songs of
/the mobs (choirs of
great intimate feasts, applause, syncopat-
/edly dropping
into the depths of the long green abysses),
we climb up the ranks of DREAMS to
/the top blued by stars
high above the arena-seats of the Circus
and the noisy, dazzling light.)
and ends by joining European colonial
villains to African heroes:
. . . Smith et N'Komo, Salazar
et Roberto, Verword et Luthuli, grandes
/flaques de nuit dans
les clairières du Kivu, miaulement de fusées
/complices de retours
de moussons de violence.

(. . . Smith and N'Komo, Salazar
and Roberto, Verword and Luthuli, great
/pools of the night
in the clearings of Kivu, howling of guilty
/fuses,
the revenge of the tornadoes of violence.)
(trans. D. H.)
This poet deserves greater recognition.

Writings: Poems in *New Sum of Poetry from
the Negro World*, Présence Africaine, No.
57, 1966.

GULUBE, D. N. (see mention in last
paragraph NYEMBEZI)

GUMA, Enoch Stephen
b. ca. 1901, Ncembu, South Africa;
d. 1918.
Xhosa novelist.

Born to poor, Christian parents, Guma
studied at St. Matthew's in Keiskama
Hoek, graduating with a Teacher's Certificate in mid–1918. Legend has it that
one day he vanished into the rural
reaches surrounding the school,
remained invisible for some days, then
reappeared with a miscellaneous collection of papers in a handwritten manuscript. Father Clement of St. Matthew's
to whom Guma presented the bundle
saw the merits of the narrative and got
it published by Lovedale Press as
*U–Nomalizo okanye izinto zalomhlaba
ngamajingiqiwu* (Nomalizo, or, "The
Things of This Life Are Sheer Vanity").
The short novel carried a foreward by
the Rev. Godfrey Callaway. The Sheldon
Press later published the 64-page work
in English and a Swahili version in 1965.
This brilliant young man died at 17 in
the influenza epidemic of October, 1918.

Writings: Novel: *U-Nomalizo okanye izinto
zalomhlaba ngamajingiqiwu*, Lovedale
Press, 1918; in English, London, Society
for Promoting Christian Knowledge,
1923; London, The Sheldon Press, 1928,
1951; in Swahili, London, Sheldon Press,
1965.

GUMA, Samson Mbizo
b. ca. 1923, South Africa.
Southern Sotho poet, novelist.

Samson Guma has published two historical novels: *Morena Mohlomi, mor'a
Monyane* (Chief Mohlomi, Son of

Monyane), 1960, and *Tshehlana tseo tsa Basia* (The Light-colored Basia Girls), 1962, and one collection of poems, *Dikoma* (Initiation Songs), 1966.

The first novel deals with the conflicts in Chief Mohlomi's village, one part of which refuses to accept the usual killing of one of the twins born to Mohlomi and secedes from the group. The second novel dramatizes a crisis caused by the death in war of the great chief and the work of two bold women to hold the people together in a time of indecision and confused leadership.

Guma has also translated two versions of the popular Sotho legend about Senkatana, the hero often associated with Christ by Christianized Zulus, in his *Form, Content and Technique of Traditional Literature in Guma's Work in Southern Sotho Literature.*

Writings: Novels: *Morena Mohlomi, mor'a Monyane,* Pietermaritzburg, Shuter and Shooter, 1960; *Tshehlana tseo tsa Basia,* Pietermaritzburg, Shuter and Shooter, 1962.

Poetry: *Dikoma,* Pietermaritzburg, 1966.

History: *The Form, Content and Technique of Traditional Literature in Southern Sotho,* Pretoria, Van Schaik, 1967.

Biographical/Critical Source: Four African Literatures, A. S. Gérard, Berkeley, University of California, Press, 1971.

GUREH, Ali Abdullah (see ALI, Abdullah Gureh)

H

HAJI, al-Ghassaniy (see MUYAKA)

HARDALLO (AL or EL HARDALLO)
b. ca. 1860, the Sudan; d. 1919.
Arabic oral poet.

Considered the greatest poet of the
Shukria Arabic speaking peoples of the
south-eastern Sudan, El Hardallo's
works are known to most educated
Sudanese and recited in the country's
schools. Many of his Shukria-Arabic
poems were collected by scholars and,
rendered into classical Arabic, were published in 1960. No version of any of his
verse is known in English or other Western languages. For a discussion of El
Hardallo and other Shukria poets see
Anne Tibble's *African/English Literature:
A Survey and Anthology.*

Biographical/Critical Source: Anne Tibble,
African/English Literature. London, Peter
Owen, 1965.

HASAN, Mahammed Abdille (see
MAHAMMED, Abdille Hasan)

HAYFORD, Gladys May (see
CASELY–HAYFORD, Gladys May)

HAYFORD, J. E. (see CASELY-
HAYFORD, Joseph Ephraim)

HAZOUME, Paul
b. April 16, 1890, Porto Novo, Dahomey.
Novelist, biographer, ethnologist.

Locally educated except for university
training in France as an ethnologist,
Hazoumé worked as a scholar and
sociologist in Dahomey. He is now
retired.

Hazoumé's one work of fiction is
Doguicimi, a 510-page novel which sets
out to recapture Dahomeyan life under
King Ghezo (1818-1858). At about the
beginning of the Christian era the Fon
people, along with the Yoruba, whose
vassals they were, crossed the Niger into
the present territories north of the Bay
of Benin between modern Togo and
Nigeria. By the 18th century the Fon
had fought their way to the coast to begin
their monopoly of the flourishing slave
trade in that area.

The Fon kings by remote control from
their capital dominated the slave traffic
and their people prospered. Hazoumé's
novel concerns the period immediately
following the abolition of legal slaving
thanks to British efforts. During this

149

period, Dahomey suffered a drastic decline in power and wealth, though not in social organization.

Writing in the late 30's, Hazoumé, a trained ethologist, was obviously seeking to convince his French readers that despite the corruptions and barbarisms of the slave trade, his Fon people had their heroism and humanity. His heroine, Doguicimi ("Distinguish me"), however, criticizes her country's regime as a bloody one. The work is generally a prosaic vehicle of protest against the excesses of her people as seen from the 20th century. King Ghezo, though surrounded by male and female plotters is better than his times and most of his people. Ghezo even extends the boundaries of his nation and in 1827 finally breaks the yoke of servitude to the Yorubas though this interesting latter fact is not discussed by Hazoumé.

Though trying to justify his people, the author seems too eager to show barbarisms which, though explicable, are not exactly matters for praise—such events as immolations, the killing of a slave in honor of the king's good sleep every morning, and similiar minor atrocities. At book's close, Hazoumé's "mouthpiece," Dee, an old storyteller, seems to represent a world the author would like to see revived. This of course seems fantasy, but for Europeanized Africans like Hazoumé, who could not in the 1930's discern the end of colonialism, this might have been the only intellectual "solution" available.

Writings: Novel: *Doguicimi*, Paris, Larose, 1938; stage version by Felix Morisseau-Leroy in mimeographed volume, Accra, 1961.

Scholarship: *Cinquante ans d'apostolat au Dahomey. Souvenirs de Mgr. Fr. Stein-metz,* Lyons, France, no date; *Le pacte de sang au Dahomey,* Paris, 1956.

Biographical/Critical Source: This Africa, Judith Gleason, Evanston, University of Northwestern Press, 1965.

HEAD, Bessie
b. 1937, Pietermaritzburg, S. Africa.
Novelist, teacher.

Bessie Head has published two novels, *When Rain Clouds Gather,* and *Maru.* In the latter work she treats of the relationship between the Masarwa or the Bushmen and the African villagers. Central in the story is the love story of the young Chief Maru and Margaret, a Masarwa girl and a product of a Christian mission training.

Writings: Novels: *When Rain Clouds Gather,* New York, Simon and Schuster, 1968; London, Gollancz, 1969; *Maru,* London, Gollancz, 1971, and London, Heinemann, 1972.

HENRIES, A. Doris Banks
b. ca. 1930, Liberia.
Poet, critic, biographer, anthologist.

Doris Banks Henries has been one of the most active Liberian writer.

Her comments on her own writing as well as on that of Liberian writing in general appear in "Survey of Liberian literature" in *Liberian Writing. Liberia as seen by her own writers as well as by German authors.* In 1966, she published her pioneering anthologies of Liberian writers: *Poems of Liberia* (1836–1961)and *Liberian Folklore.* She is represented by the poem, "Pageant of Modern Africa" in *New Sum of Poetry from the Negro World.*

Writings: Poem: "Pageant of Modern Africa," *New Sum of Poetry from The Negro World*, Présence Africaine, Volume 57, 1966.
Anthologies: *Poems of Liberia (1836-1961)*, London, Macmillan, 1966. *Liberian Folklore*, New York, Macmillan, 1966.
Criticism: Selection in *Liberian Writing. Liberia as Seen By Her Own Writers as Well as by German Authors*, Tübingen, Erdmann, 1970.
Biography: *A Biography of President William V. S. Tubman*, London, 1967; and *Heroes and Heroines of Liberia*, illustrated, New York, 1962.

HENSHAW, James Ene
b. 1924, Calabar, eastern Nigeria.
Playwright, medical doctor.

A member of a well-known family, Henshaw attended Christ the King College, Onitsha, and took his M.D. from National University, Dublin.
His first volume of plays was, *This Is Our Chance: Three Plays from West Africa*, which includes the title play, *The Jewel of the Shrine* and *A Man of Character*, 1956. So popular was this volume that it went through ten printings by 1970. *The Jewel of the Shrine* won the Henry Carr Memorial Cup, 1952, in the All-Nigeria Festival of the Arts, held in Lagos, and is in Litto's *Plays from Black Africa*. Henshaw's next volume, *Children of the Goddess and Other Plays*, contains *Companion for a Chief*, *Magic in the Blood*, both one act, and *Medicine for Love*, a comedy in three acts. His most recent play is *Dinner for Promotion*, 1967. This volume includes

an introduction by the author, entitled "The African Writer, the Audience and the English Language," and notes on production of the play.

Writings: Plays: *This Is Our Chance*, London, University of London Press, 1956; *Children of the Goddess and Other Plays*, London, University of London Press, 1964; *Dinner for Promotion*, London, University of London Press, 1967; the play, *The Jewel of the Shrine*, in Fredric M. Litto's *Plays from Black Africa*, New York, Hill and Wang, 1968; and separate edition of *Medicine for Love*, London, University of London Press, 1964.

HERUY, Sirek Walda Sellase
b. May 7, 1878, Den, Shoan province of Marhabété, Ethiopia;
d. September 19, 1938, in Bath, England.
Amharic novelist, biographer, didactic tale-writer, statesman.

Heruy is considered the father of modern Amharic literature. The facts of his life before 1917 are not known though he is believed to have translated the Bible into Ge'ez, to have married in 1902, and to have visited Cairo, Athens and Western Europe. With the regency of Räs Täfari in 1917, Heruy was asked to assume many posts, including the Directorship of the National Printing Shop (the Imprimerie Ethiopienne) which soon began an augmented program in Ge'ez and Amharic devotional works. The same year he initiated the first literary journal, *Goha Sebah* (Dawn) which in its few issues presented mostly poems of praise for the new regent. However, the press continued to publish other books and modern Amharic literature and gradually widened its production into a small stream of new work.

Honored by the title "Blatta" in 1920, he became head of the new consular court of justice in 1922, travelled abroad a great deal and wrote the reports of the regent's wife's trip to Palestine and Egypt and of the Regent's visit to Europe and the Middle East in 1924 which opened Ethiopian eyes to the fast changing outer world.

Heruy's first work was a catalogue of books in Ge'ez and Amharic physically available in Ethiopia. Early published works in these languages often had been published abroad with few copies returning to Ethiopia. Updated in 1927–28, the work included many more items, an indication of the improvement in the local literary situation. Heruy also republished in 1917–18 his early biography of Emperor John (Yohannes of Ethiopia); a collection of funeral chants; and moral and philosophical "pensées." Reprinted in 1922 was a series of parables illustrating the character and actions of men: *My Friend, My Heart*. This popular work saw its fourth printing in 1956–57.

In 1919, he brought out a collection of extracts from the Bible and from various national and local histories, given the title he earlier had used for his journal, *Goha Sebah*. The same title was also given to the press he established the next year, an independent one free of the subsidy and control exercised over the government-owned Imprimerie Ethiopienne. In 1934, Heruy founded the journal, *Atbiya Kobab* (Morning Star).

His two important Amharic novels are: *Thought of the Heart: The Marriage of Berhane and Seyon Mogasa,* and *The New World*. The earlier work is a simple study of two lovers who wisely defer marrying for some years and when they do are blessed by a large family. This was advice to the numerous Ethiopians who rushed into early marriage and then, as quickly into divorce. Some 60% of all marriages ended in divorce according to one estimate in the 1930's. The second work which became quite popular shows a French-trained young man, Awwaga, returning to a backward part of his country to celebrate, despite the scorn of relatives and former friends, a more honest and less rowdy funeral for his father than custom dictates. Later he celebrates without drunkeness his marriage to the woman of his own choice. This book ends with an Utopian vision of a national church council deciding on certain long-needed reforms. It is instructive to compare this work of the 1920's with all its hopes for change with the poem "Home-Coming Son" of Tsegaye Gabre Medhin, published forty years later. That poem begins: "Look where you walk, unholy stranger," and is addressed to the foreign-trained Ethiopian returned home. In this verse Tsegaye urges the young man to "walk free, walk naked," and to let his "naked skin absorb the home-sun and shine ebony." in an assertive proclamation of "negritude" and the need to return to the life of the people.

Named Minister of Foreign Affairs in 1931, Heruy followed the Emperor into exile in England, and died in Haile Selassie's palace at Bath, England, in 1938.

A few of his many works are worth noting: *Ethiopia and Matamma: A Short Biography of Emperor Yohannes; Biographies: Information for the Generations to Come;* and *Book of Hymns by the Ancient and Modern Doctors and Masters of Ethiopia.* All titles are English version of Amharic.

Writings: Catalogue: *Catalogue of Books Written in Ge'ez and Amharic, to be found in Ethiopia,* revised edition, 1927.

Parables: *My Friend, My Heart,* Addis Ababa, 1915 and 1922; Biblical excerpts, etc; *Goha Sebah,* 1926; *Poems of Funeral Songs: Their Meaning in Harmony with the Scriptures,* Addis Ababa, 1910.

Novels: *Thought of the Heart: The Marriage of Berhané and Seyon Mogasa,* Addis Ababa, 1923, 1930-31; *The New World,* Addis Ababa, 1925, 1932.

Biography: *Ethiopia and Matamma: A Short Biography of Emperor Yohannes,* Addis Ababa, 1910, 1917; *Information for the Generations to Come,* Addis Ababa, 1915.

General: *Goha Sebah: Dawn Has Come: Estracts from the Holy Writ From History and from Various Other Books.* Addis Ababa, 1919; *Virgil: To Celebrate Tomorrow: the History of the Kings of Ethiopia,* Addis Ababa, 1921; *The House of Light: The Japanese Country,* Addis Ababa, 1924; *The Book of the Astrolabe,* Addis Ababa, 1924.

Biographical/Critical Source: Four African Literatures, Albert S. Gérard, Berkeley, University of California Press, 1971.

HIGO, Aig
b. ca. 1942, Nigeria.
Poet.

Higo studied English at Ibadan University and did post-graduate work at Leeds University, Yorkshire, England. Presently working as a publisher's representative in Nigeria, his poem "One Wife for One Man," written in pidgin English, is in Moore and Beier's *Modern Poetry from Africa.* Five of his poems also appear in *New Sum of Poetry from the Negro World.*

Writings: Poem: "One Wife For One Man" in *Modern Poetry from Africa,* Moore and Beier, editors, revised edition, 1968; five poems in *New Sum of Poetry from the*

Negro World, Présence Africaine, Vol. 57, 1966.

HIHETAH, Robert Kofi
b. ca. 1935, Ghana.
Novelist, teacher.

Hihetah is a high school teacher in Upper Ghana, known for his one novel, *Painful Road to Kadjebi.*

Writings: Novel: *Painful Road to Kadjebi,* Accra, Anowuo, 1966.

HINAWY, Sheikh Mbarak Ali (The Honorable)
b. 1896, Kenya.
Swahili scholar.

Sheikh Hinawy was educated privately and at a British school in Mombasa. He served with the King's African Rifles in World War I and returned to the British territorial army in World War II. In 1918 he entered the civil service and later was appointed Liwali (Governor) of Mombasa. An authority on Swahili literature and history, he has done much to bring to light old East African manuscripts. He was named Liwali of the Coast in 1942, was a member of the Kenyan Legislative Council and served before independence as the personal advisor on Arab affairs to the Governor. He is represented in Peggy Rutherford's *Darkness and Light.*

Writings: Story: "The Cunning of Suua," In Peggy Rutherford, *Darkness and Light: An Anthology of African Writing,* Johannesburg, Drum Publications, 1958; London, Faith Press, 1958, published as *African Voices,* New York, Grosset, 1959, 1970.

HOLOGOUDOU (see OLOGOUDOU, Emile)

HONWANA, Luís Bernardo (also Augusto Manuel)
b. November, 1942, Lourenço Marques, Mozambique.
Short story writer, journalist.

Son of an interpreter employed by the Portuguese government, Honwana was one of eight children and grew up in poverty in a village outside the capital. He had to continue his secondary schooling part-time and took on jobs as cartographer and as contributor to the literary section of the capital's newspaper, before completing his courses. He became a reporter and later an editor of two papers in Beira, Mozambique's second largest city. For his nationalist ideas he has been imprisoned by the Portuguese authorities.

Honwana has had short stories and reviews issued in various local journals and a volume of his stories, *Nos Matámos o Cão-Tinhosa*, was published by Publicações Tribuna, in 1964. It deals with African peasants and black proletariats in and around the Portuguese cities of Africa.

His extremely dark and brutal story, "Dina," appears in Ezekiel Mphahlele's *African Writing Today*. The story is not brutally told, but rather, it is about the almost unendurable work the peonized workers in the colony must perform, the power of violence exercised by the Portuguese overseers and the loss of self-respect by the Africans who are herded together for the long labors in the blazing hot fields.

Writings: Short Stories: *Nos Matámos o Cão-Tinhosa*, Lourenço Marques, Publicações Tribuna, 1964; in English as *We Killed Mangy Dog and Other Stories*, London, Heinemann, 1960; Story: "Dina" in *African Writing Today*, London, Penguin, 1967; the story "We Killed Mangy Dog," was published with the story, "Argo," by Andreas Embiricos in London, A. Ross, 1967.

HORATIO-JONES, Edward Babatunde Bankole (also, JONES, Edward Babatunde Bankole Horatio)
b. January 9, 1930, Lagos, Nigeria.
Short story writer, novelist, film maker.

Horatio-Jones, a Yoruba born in Lagos, was locally educated through high school in Sierra Leone in 1943, and then went on to the London University in 1951 to study literature and philosophy. In 1957 he went to Paris to enroll in the Ecole Normale Superiéure, and from 1958 to 1959 he studied at the Institut des Hautes Etudes. The following year

Horatio-Jones enrolled in the Ecole Photo et Cinema in Paris, and in 1961 he moved to Berlin to study cinema where he lived for some time. He is presently working with Carlo Ponti in Italy.

He has one published short story, in German, "Der Leichenzug," (The Funeral Procession) which appears in J. Jahn's *Das Junge Africa*, and two as yet unpublished novels, *The Africans*, and *The Finer Side of Death*. He is represented in *Africa in Prose*, edited by Dathorne and Feuser.

Writings: Short Stories: "Der Leichenzug" in *Das Junge Africa*, J. Jahn, Vienna, Munich, Basel, Kurt Desch Verlag, 1963; "Mourner's Progress," in O. R. Dathorne and Wilfred Feuser; editors, *Africa in Prose*, Harmondsworth, Middlesex, England, Penguin, 1969.

Novels: "The Africans;" "The Finer Side of Death," unpublished.

HORTON, James Africanus Beale
1832–1883, Sierra Leone.
Pamphleteer, medical doctor, statesman.

Horton was born of Ibo parents living in Sierra Leone, and, educated there and later in England. He practiced medicine in Cape Coast, Gold Coast (now Ghana), and took an interest in advancing the liberty and dignity of Africans and expressed opinions and ideas that were ahead of his time. In some ways he was the opposite of Edward Wilmot Blyden, a conservative African thinker of the period. He published in 1868 his important work, *West African Countries and Peoples, British and Native. With the requirements necessary for establishing that self-government recommended by the committee of the House of Commons; and a vindication of the African race.*

Writings: Pamphlet: *West African Countries and Peoples, British and Native,* London, W. J. Johnson, 1868; Edinburgh, Edinburgh University Press, 1969; Nendeln, Liechtenstein, Kraus Reprint, 1970.

Letters: in *Letters on the Political Condition of the Gold Coast,* New York, Humanities Press, 1970; London, Cass, 1970.

Biographical/Critical Sources: Africanus Horton, 1835–1883: West African Scientist and Patriot, by Christopher Fyfe, New York, Oxford University Press, 1972; *Africanus Horton: The Dawn of Nationalism in Modern Africa,* Davidson Nicol, editor, London, 1970.

HUTCHINSON, Alfred
b. 1924, Hectorspruit, eastern Transvaal, South Africa; d. October 14, 1972, in Nigeria.
Autobiographer, playwright, short story writer, teacher.

His maternal grandfather was a Swazi chief, his other grandfather an Englishman, and both of his grandmothers were Swazi. Educated in local schools, he attended St. Peters School and Fort Hare University College where he graduated with a B.A. He later earned an M.A. from the University of Sussex. Hutchinson then started work as a high school teacher in Johannesburg but lost his job because of his involvement in the 1952 Defiance Campaign. He later taught at Central Indian High School.

In 1956 South African authorities had Hutchinson arrested on the charge of high treason. Temporarily freed when the prosecution withdrew the original indictment, he fled without a passport to Ghana hoping his English fiancée, Hazel Slade, could join him. On the slow train moving across Southeastern Africa, he thought out his life, the "treason trials," and the whole growing miasma of apartheid in his homeland. Memorialized in *Road to Ghana*, the book laments the broken Africans, exults in the unconquered and the even rarer unconquerables. An excerpt from the book appears in Jacob Drachler's *African Heritage*. Dennis Brutus, himself an exile from apartheid, considered the work was possibly the finest study of the experience of living under the racist regime in South Africa then published.

His play, *The Rain-killers*, also appears in Fredric Litto's *Plays from Black Africa* and another play, *Fusane's Trial*, is in Cosmo Pieterse's *Ten One-Act Plays*. His short story, "High Wind in the Valley," has been anthologized.

Hutchinson lived in England for almost a decade, separated in his last lonely years from his English wife. He taught in various schools in London before moving to Nigeria in late 1971.

He died there of a heart attack in the fall of 1972. Dennis Brutus, an old friend since college days at Fort Hare, wrote the following for a special memorial service: "The pressures of ghetto existence in South Africa, and the agonies and anxieties of exile prevented his talent from coming to full fruition. He is one of the long list of talented black writers driven into exile by the inhumanities of Apartheid, and doomed to die there."

Writings: Autobiography: *Road to Ghana*, London Gollancz, 1960; New York, John Day, 1960; and excerpt in *African Heritage*, Jacob Drachler, New York, Collier Books, 1964.

Plays: *The Rain-Killers*, London, University of London Press, 1964; collected in *Plays from Black Africa*, New York, F. Litto, editor, Hill and Wang, 1968; *Fusane's Trial, a Radio Play*, first published in *The New African*, IV, 4, London, (January 1965), and in *Ten One-Act Plays*, London, Heinemann, 1968.

I

IBUKUN, Olu
b. ca. 1945, Yoruba country,
western Nigeria.
Novelist.

Now living in Kenya, Ibukun is an official of UNESCO. He exploited in a relatively prosaic style in his first novel, *The Return*, the familiar theme of the conflicts within a protagonist who is pulled between his African past and the new Western religion, culture and lifestyle.

Writings: Novel: *The Return*, Nairobi, East African Publishing House, 1970.

IJIMERE, Obotunde (pseudonym for Ulli BEIER)

Ulli Beier, a German national, has lived for many years in Nigeria and has assumed a Yoruba "persona" and a biography which follows.

For some time Obotunde was an actor in Duro Ladipo's company which produced Yoruba language plays, but he soon turned to writing. His best known play, *Eda*, is a Yoruba adaptation of *Everyman* and has been performed all over the world. *Born with the fire on His Head* is adapted from *The History of the Yorubas* by the early Yoruba historian, Samuel Johnson (Lagos, 1921) and appears in *Three Nigerian Plays* with *Moremi* of Duro Ladipo and *The Scheme* by Wale Ogunyemi. All the plays are in English. He is also the author of *The Imprisonment of Obatala and Other Plays*. The other plays in this volume are *Everyman* (the English of the Yoruba play, *Eda*) and *Woyengi*, based on an Ijaw myth written down by Gabriel Okara.

The Suitcase. A Plaything In One Act, by Sebastian Salazar Bondy, was an adaption of Ijimere's for Theatre Express, and published by that theatre in Oshogbo in 1966. His farce, *The Bed*, appeared the next year (1967) under the imprint of the Theatre Express in Oshogbo.

Writings: Plays: *Eda*, adapted with songs and music by Duro Ladipo, Oshogbo, Nigeria, Mbari, 1965; *Born with the Fire on His Head* in *Three Nigerian Plays*, Ulli Beier, editor, London, Longmans, 1967; *The Imprisonment of Obatala and Other Plays*, adapted into English by Ulli Beier, London, Heinemann Educational Books, Ltd, 1965, 1966; *The Suitcase*, adapted by Ijimere from Bondy's play of that name, Oshogbo, Theatre Express, 1966; *The Fall of Man,* Oshogbo, Theatre Express, 1966; *The Bed,* Oshogbo, Theatre Express, 1967.

Biographical/Critical Sources: Paper, "Yoruba Folklore and Drama: Obàtálá as a Case Study," by Joel Adedeji, delivered at African Folklore Conference, Bloomington Indiana, July 16–18, 1970, available from Indiana University. Background: Samuel Johnson. *The History of the Yorubas,* Lagos, C.M.S. Bookshop, 1921; *Mother is Gold: A Study in West African Literature,* Adrian A. Roscoe, ed., Cambridge, England, Cambridge University Press, 1971.

IKE, Vincent Chukwuemeka
b. 1931, Ibo country, Eastern Nigeria.
Novelist and teacher.

Locally educated, Ike took his B.A. at Ibadan University. He has written two novels, *Toads for Supper* and *The Naked Gods.* Both of his works are concerned with Nigerian life. The first deals with student hi-jinks, love affairs and other growing pains of Ibadan University. Reviews have agreed that his second novel, dealing with the college-town intrigues attendant on the selection of a new Vice-Chancellor, is far more mature and just as humorous as his first. Both novels light-heartedly describe Nigerian life.

Ike is married and has several children.

Writings: Novels: *Toads for Supper,* London, Harvill Press, 1965, and London,

Collins (Fontana), 1965; *The Naked Gods,* London, Harvill Press, 1970.

IKELLE–MATIBA, Jean
b. April 26, 1936, Song–Ndong, Cameroon.
Novelist, essayist, poet.

After local studies he went to Paris to study law and since 1963 he has worked in West Germany as a representative of *Présence Africaine,* the French-language journal based in Paris which specializes on African writing. He has also contributed to *Aeropag* and the *Journal* of *Modern African Studies* and has spoken in many European countries for the Society of African Culture.

Ikellé-Matiba's first major work, the novel *Cette Afrique-là!* (This Particular Africa), won the Grand Prix Littéraire de l'Afrique Noire in 1963. It recites the career of Franz Momha in the late 19th century during the German occupation. Translated only into German at the present time, it is the first of a planned trilogy, the other two volumes to be called *Transition* and *La Solitude.*

As a poet he admits being influenced by Aimé Césaire, the famous poet from Martinique, and by Senghor, and Birago Diop. His generally simple poems are critical of much of the new Africa but still bitter about the colonial past and frequently contrast the "cold" qualities of Europe with the "warm" human values of Africa. Twelve of his poems in French appear in *New African Literature and the Arts* 2.

Writings: Novel: *Cette Afrique-là!* Paris, Présence Africaine, 1963; Twelve French-language poems in *New African Literature and the Arts 2,* Joseph Okpaku, editor, New York, Thomas Y. Crowell Co., 1968, 1970.

IKIDDEH, Ime
b. April 11, 1938, Uyo, South Eastern State, Nigeria.
Playwright, anthologist.

Ikiddeh received his early education at home but took his B.A. at Legon University (Ghana) in English and did graduate work (M.A.) at the University of Leeds, returning to teach at Legon (University of Ghana) in October, 1966. He has written several plays, one of which, *Blind Cyclos,* first broadcast by the B.B.C., appears in *Ten One-Act Plays.*

Writings: Plays: *Blind Cyclos,* in *Ten One-Act Plays,* Cosmo Pieterse, editor, London, Heinemann, 1968. He has translated many African stories and edited the volume, *Drum Beats, An Anthology of African Narrative Prose,* Leeds, E. J. Arnold & Son, 1968.

ILMI, Bownderi (also ELMI, Bownderi and other variations)
b. ca. 1903; d. ca. 1938, Somalia.
Somali oral poet.

The poet, "Bownderi" or "Bonderii" or "Boderii," all corruptions of the English word "boundary," was born on the frontier between Ethiopia and Somaliland, and thus his name, Elmi the Borderman. He never married but fell deeply in love with a fifteen-year old beauty, Hodan Abdillahi, whom he called "Baar" in his famous poem "Qaraami." For six years he continued to love her though her family prevented a marriage because of the poet's poverty. When he was on his deathbed, Hodan,

married by then, paid him a visit, another incident that helped keep the love affair a legend.

Many of Ilmi's poems have been gathered by private Somali collectors in the northwest of the country where the poet's reputation is greatest. In English some texts are available in "The Life of Ilmi Bownderi, A Somali Oral Poet Who is Said to Have Died of Love," *(Journal of the Folklore Institute),* and *A Tree for Poverty: Somali Poetry and Prose* by Margaret Laurence.

Writings: Poems in "The Life of Ilmi Bownderi, A Somali Oral Poet Who is Said to have Died of Love," *Journal of the Folklore Institute,* Bloomington, Indiana, Indiana University Press, 1967; *A Tree for Poverty: Somali Poetry and Prose,* Margaret Laurence, Kampala, Nairobi, Dar es Salaam, The Eagle Press 1954.

IROAGANACHI, J. O.
b. ca. 1940, Nigeria.
Short story writer, educator, civil servant.

Iroaganachi studies at the Uzuakoli Methodist Secondary School in Eastern Nigeria were followed by a year at the School of Oriental and African Studies in London, where he analyzed the spelling of his native Igbo tongue for his major study. He was later appointed to the Igbo Translation Bureau in Eastern Nigeria and subsequently was named African Assistant at the School of Oriental and African Studies. He took his B. A. degree eventually in history at London University.

He studied and traveled for one year in the United States, followed a course in visual aids, and obtained an advanced degree. He was employed in the Education Department in Eastern Nigeria in the middle 1960's and is active in the program of teaching written Igbo in the Ibo lands of Eastern Nigeria.

He has translated stories by other authors into Igbo. His short story, "I'm Afraid of the Night," translated into English by M. M. Green, appears in the UNESCO-sponsored *A selection of African prose II*. He has articles on various subjects in Igbo which are as yet unpublished.

Writings: Story: "I'm Afraid of the Night," English translation by M. M. Green in *A Selection of African Prose,* W. H. Whiteley, editor, Oxford, Clarendon Press, 1964.

ISHAK
b. 13th century, Ethiopia.
Story-teller.

Ishak, called "The Poor Man," lived in Ethiopia in the 1200's and is remembered for his Amharic version of the *Kebra Nagast* (The Glory of Kings), which tells the story of Solomon and the Queen of Sheba at a time when Solomon's line of successors to the Ethiopian throne had been restored.

Writings: Kebra Nagast, 13th century.

ISMAA'IIL, Mire (see
MIRE, Ismaa'iil)

ITAYEMI, Phebean
b. 1928, Yoruba-land, western Nigeria.
Short story writer.

Itayemi's story, "Nothing So Sweet," which won the first prize in the British Council's competition in 1946, appears in *African New Writing*. When only 15 years old she began a novel and has been writing since. She was a student teacher at Queen's College, Lagos and has studied in England.

"Nothing So Sweet" is a fairly long story with a heroine who resists by seven days of fasting and little sleep becoming the 16th wife of a rich farmer-merchant who probably had purchased her when she was two years old. At story's end, she finds protection with an English woman doctor and her husband at their clinic. The story is of the new African woman who no longer will suffer the power and arrogance of either suitor or parents in an unwished-for marriage.

Writings: Story: "Nothing So Sweet" in *African New Writing*, London, Lutterworth Press, 1947.

J

JABAVU, Davidson Don Tengo
b. October 20, 1885, Healdtown,
South Africa; d. 1959.
Xhosa and English-language poet,
journalist, scholar, statesman.

Eldest son of John Tengo Jabavu, Davidson became an excellent linguist and
scholar, developing skills in Sotho,
Tswana, and English and mastering the
grammar and writing of his mother
tongue, Xhosa. After lower schooling in
local institutions, and being barred from
all-white Dale College in King William's
Town, Davidson was sent to England in
1903, taking his B.A. with honors in
1912 at the University of London. In
England Davidson became a fine pianist
and violinist, and studied singing and
choir conducting as well as journalism.
He spent some time in the United States,
visiting Tuskegee Institute and Hampton University to learn more about
higher education for Blacks in America.
By 1913 he was back in England, where
he took a teacher's degree from Bir-
mingham University the next year.

Returning to South Africa in 1915 he
became the first lecturer at the Native
College at Fort Hare (now Fort Hare
University College) in 1916, remaining
there until 1946 as a teacher of Bantu
languages (Xhosa, Zulu, Sotho, Tswana),
English, Latin and history. He was married September 2, 1916, to Florence Nolwandle Tandiswa. For a long while he

served as secretary of the College Senate and for some time was warden of one of the men's dormitories. He was officially designated Professor (akin to full professor in the U.S.) in 1942.

On the death of his father in 1921, Davidson Tengo, with his brother Alexander Macauley Jabavu, took over the editing and publishing of *Imvo zabantsundu* (Opinion of the Blacks), the important newspaper founded by his father. Many of Davidson's occasional travel pieces first appearing in *Imvo* later were published by Lovedale Press: *E-Jerusalem* (To Jerusalem) (1928); *E-Amerika* (To America), 1932, telling of his days in that country, and *E-Indiya nase-East Afrika* (To India and East Africa), 1951, concerning his trip to the East.

Most of Davidson Tengo's works were written and published in English except for his collection of poems, *Izidungulwana* (Twigs), which appeared posthumously, and the earlier *Izithuko* (Abuses), an 1954 volume of praise poems.

Some of his many other works in English were: *The Black Problem* (1920); *Bantu Literature* (1921); *The Life of John Tengo Jabavu* (1922), a biography of his father; *What Methodism has done for the Natives* (1923); *The Segregation Fallacy* (1928); *The Influence of English on Bantu Literature* (1943). He also edited various works including *I-bali lama Mfengu* (The Story of the Mfengu People), by Richard Tainton Kawa, and *U-Kayakhulu*, by Chief Shadrach Fuba Zibi.

Major activities during his career included his membership, from 1920 to 1930, in the Native Conferences sponsored by the Government under the Native Affairs Act; the organization and leadership, with others, of the Non-European Conference seeking to unite all non-white people in South Africa to oppose the Hertzog Bills and the repressive Government policies of 1925. With Pixley ka Izaka Seme, then Secretary of the African National Conference, he called the first All-African Convention on December 16, 1935, and became its first president, a post he held for thirteen years. He worked with the Joint Councils of Europeans and Natives, and the South African Institute of Race Relations, of which he was vice president from 1932 until his death. He received the Ph.D degree from Rhodes University after his retirement in 1946 and a medal was struck in his honor by the Royal African Society. In May, 1954, he was presented the "Freedom of New Brighton" award in Port Elizabeth. Shortly before his death from cancer, Davidson Tengo established the All-African Insurance Company.

Earlier, in 1951, Davidson's wife, Nolwandle Jabavu, died. Their three children were Helen Nontan-o Jabavu who later wrote under the name Noni; Alexandra Nothemba Jabavu, and Tengo Max Jabavu, murdered in 1955. In 1961 money was raised by popular subscription to erect a memorial stone on Davidson Jabavu's grave at Middlerift, Cape Province.

Writings: Poetry: *Izithuko*, Lovedale, Lovedale Press, 1954; *Izidungulwana*, Cape Town, Maskew Miller, ca. 1960.

Travel: *E-Jerusalem*, 1928; *E-Amerika*, 1932; *E-Indiya nase-East Africa*, 1951; all Lovedale, Lovedale Press.

All Non-fiction: *The Black Problem*, 1920, second edition, 1921; *Bantu literature*, 1921; *The Life of John Tengo Jabavu*, 1922; *What Methodism has done for the Natives*, 1923; *The segregation fallacy*, 1928; *The Influence of English on Bantu Literature*, 1943; all Lovedale,

Lovedale Press. Edited: *I bali lama Mfengu*, by Richard Tainton Kawa, Lovedale, Lovedale Press, 1929; *U' Kayakhulu*, by Chief S. F. Zibi, Rustenberg, Lovedale Press, 1930.

JABAVU, Helen Nontando (see JABAVU, Noni)

JABAVU, John Tengo
b. January 11, 1859, Healdtown, South Africa; d. September 10, 1921.
Xhosa journalist, teacher, publisher, politician.

Eldest son of Christian parents, Ntwanambi and Mary Jabavu, John Ntengo herded cattle until his tenth year when his mother was able to send him off to school at Healdtown. At the age of 16, now called John Tengo, he received the Government's Teacher's Certificate and in 1876 began teaching at Somerset East, remaining there until 1881. During this period he learned the printer's trade, journalism and the newspaper business. He also had himself taught Greek and Latin and began writing articles for newspapers, especially the *Cape Argus*.

He was named editor of Lovedale's Xhosa-language newspaper, *Isigidimi sama-Xosa* in July, 1881 for a three-year period. On July 26, 1883, Jabavu became the second African to enter the University of South Africa in Cape Town, having passed the matriculation examination (ranking 76th of 88). When his contract as editor with Lovedale expired in September, 1884, he found financial backing from R. W. Rose–Innes, brother of James Rose–Innes, a candidate for the South African Parliament for whom

he had once campaigned, and J. W. Weir, that enabled him to establish a new paper, the *Imvo zabantsundu* (Opinion of the Blacks), at King William's Town. It was the first newspaper to be established and run completely by an African. Jabavu wrote some 2,000 articles of all sorts for this journal, often a one-man operation, where he was reporter, editor, composer, advertising salesman, clerk, and copyreader.

Always a religious man, Jabavu in 1883 became a member of the Wesleyan Conference. In 1885 he married Elda Sakuba, daughter of a minister, and in 1891 he founded a night school for adults in King William's Town.

Because Cecil Rhodes could not buy Jabavu's support, Rhodes helped Allan Kirkland Soga start a rival paper, the *Izwi labantu* (1897–1909), edited by Chief Cyril Nathaniel Mhalla (ca. 1850–1920). Jabavu threw his journal's support to the Afrikaaner Bond candidates led by Hofmeyr, a serious error of judgment, for the action lost him a great deal of trust in the African community. On January 5, 1895, the journal became *Imvo neliso lomzi* (Opinion and Guardian of the Nation), but on April 6, 1898, shortly after the arrival of John Knox Bokwe as co-editor, it became *Imvo zontsundu (neliso lomzi)*, (Black Opinion [and Guardian of the Nation]). It soon reverted to its original title of *Imvo zabantsundu*, however, by which name it is known today.

Active in public affairs, he attended conventions at Lovedale in 1905 and 1908 to establish a Native College (later to be Fort Hare). He raised funds in Cape Colony, the Orange Free State, the Transvaal, and Lesotho in support of the scheme; and in 1909 and 1911 he travelled to London. The first time he went to protest the clauses in the projected Constitution of the Union of South Africa which would exclude blacks from most citizen rights and duties. On the second trip he attended the Universal Races Congress to gain support for a black college. In February, 1916, the University College at Fort Hare, near Lovedale, opened, with Jabavu's son, Davidson, the first teacher. So unsparing had been his efforts that in the early days the new school was called "I-Koleji ka Jabavu," or "Jabavu's College."

Despite his efforts for better African education, Jabavu lost all of the African support in politics by supporting the Land Act of 1913 which prohibited blacks from acquiring land. Introduced into parliament by J. W. Sauer, a close friend of Jabavu's, the act was severely attacked by Solomon Plaatje, a leading black writer and statesman, but Jabavu persisted in supporting it. Worse, he ran in 1914 against the incumbent Walter Benson Rubusana, thus splitting the black vote and ensuring the loss of the one seat in the South African parliament held by a black South African. Consequently, until his death seven years later, he was a pariah in black South African politics. He remained active, however, as a member of the College Executive and its Governing Council and in 1920 became a member of the Cape Provincial Commission on Native Education.

Prime Minister Jan Christian Smuts eulogized him at his death on September 10, 1921. His reputation remains controversial, though his major works in journalism and education were milestones in the African absorption of European culture and technology in South Africa.

Writings: Numerous editorials and articles in *Imvo zabantsundu; Imvo neliso lomzi; Imvo zontsundu.*

JABAVU, Noni Helen Nontando
also (Mrs. Cadbury, also JABAVU, Alexandra Nothemba)
b. August 20, 1919, Cape Province, South Africa.
Novelist.

The daughter of Davidson Don Tengo Jabavu, she went to England in her fourteenth year where she studied until 1939.

During the war she discontinued her musical studies at the Royal Academy to become a film technician. She married the English film director, Michael Cadbury Crosfield, and travelled in Mozambique, Kenya and South Africa. She resided with her husband for a period in Uganda, but they now live in England.

Her first novel, *Drawn in Colour, African Contrasts*, details the impact the West had on the peoples of East and South Africa. In 1963, her second novel, *The Ochre People: Scenes from a South African Life*, also autobiographical, deals with a different geographical area in each of its three sections. One commentator has said that her too frequent use of Xhosa words disturbs the flow of the work. This might be true for the European or American reader, but if her novel is to be considered for South Africans, particularly for her own kinsmen, the Xhosa might actually enhance the book's basic English medium.

Writings: Novels: *Drawn in Colour, African Contrasts*, London, John Murray, 1960, 1963; New York, St. Martin's Press, 1962; *The Ochre People: Scenes from a South African Life*, London, John Murray, 1963; New York, St. Martin's Press, 1963.

JACINTO, António do Amaral Martins (also used pseudonym TAVORA, Orlando)
b. 1924, Luanda, Angola.
Poet, story writer, businessman.

One of the leaders of the brief surge of literary nationalism in the 1950's, Jacinto worked for the Angolan journal, *Imbondeiro*, and, taking part in anti-Portuguese activities, was arrested along with two other young poets, António Cardoso and Luandino Vieira, and imprisoned with them at Tarrafal on the Cape Verde Islands in 1961 with a 14-year sentence. Earlier, he had worked for a time as a manager for a small firm.

Jacinto attacks the forced labor system on the Angolan plantations in the poem "Já quer e já sabe" (You Ask a Question and You Know the Answer):

My poem is my white self
Mounted on my black self
Riding through life
and he calls for revolt.

Jacinto's poems have appeared in Andrade's Portuguese language anthology and his earlier collection of 1953, *Caderno*. In translation he is represented in Moore and Beier's *Modern Poetry from Africa*. A short volume of his verse, *Colectânea de poemas*, was published in Lisbon. His poem, "Monangamba," is found in *New Sum of Poetry from the Negro World*.

The poem "Monangamba" also appears in *Poetas e contistas africanos de expressão portuguêsa* (African Poems and Stories of Portuguese Expression) and in Mário de Andrade's *Literatura africana de expressão portuguêsa, Vol. I, Poesia*, 1967. The story, "Vôvô Bartolomeu," appears in *Novos Contos d'Africa* (New Stories from Africa). Because of his imprisonment, his poems and stories date back to the late 1950's, and most of his work remains in manuscript or, if published, uncollected.

Writings: Poetry: *Colectânea de poemas*, Lisbon, Edição da Casa dos Estudantes do Império, 1961; poems in *Modern Poetry from Africa*, Moore and Beier, editors, revised edition, London, Penguin, 1968; poem: "Monangamba" in *New Sum of Poetry from the Negro World*, Paris, Présence Africaine, Vol. 57, 1966, and also in *Poetas e contistas africanos de expressao portugûesa*, São Paulo, Editôra Brasiliense, 1963; also represented in *Caderno*, Lisbon, 1953, and *Literatura*

Jacinto

africana de expressão portuguêsa, Vol. I. Poesia, Algiers, 1967.

Prose: Story: "Vôvô Bartolomeu," *Novos contos d'Africa,* Sá da Bandeira, Angola, Imbondeira, 1961.

Biographical/Critical Source: Alfredo Margarido, "The Social and Economic Background of Portuguese Negro Poetry," *Diogenes,* XXXVII, (1962).

JEBODA, Joshua Ofuwafemi (also Femi)
b. ca. 1930, Nigeria.
Yoruba novelist.

His three works, in Yoruba, are the novels *Olowolaiyemo* (The World Knows Only the Wealthy), *Ikeja,* and the novelette *Afinju adaba* (Beautiful Pigeon). The first and third works concern the excitements and vices of city life in the new cities of Yorba-land. *Olowolaiyemo* won first prize in the competition for realistic novels sponsored by the General Publications Department of the Ministry of Education at Ibadan in celebration of independence, October 1960.

Writings: Novels: *Olowolaiyemo,* Ibadan, Longmans, Green, 1961; *Ikeja,* Ibadan, Longmans, 1964.
Novelette: *Afinju adaba,* Ibadan, Ministry of Education, 1964.

Biographical/Critical Source: "A Survey of Modern Literature in the Yoruba, Efik, and Hausa Languages," by Adeboya Babalola, in *Introduction to Nigerian Literature,* Bruce King, ed., New York, Africana Publishing Corp., 1972.

JOACHIM, Paulin
b. 1931, Cotonou, Dahomey.
Poet.

Joachim received his early education in Dahomey and Gabon. He attended the Catholic University of Lyon where he studied law and received a Diplôme de l'Ecole Supérieure de Journalisme in Paris. He was political editor of *France-Soir* for three years and now lives in Paris, where he is editor-in-chief of the Dakar review *Bingo: Black World Review.*

His two collections of poems are: *Un nègre raconte* (A Black Narrates), first published in 1954, and *Anti-grâce,* 1967. He is represented in *New Sum of Poetry from the Negro World,* which includes the poem written in Paris, 1964, "A David Diop," killed in a plane crash in August, 1960. It begins with the striking lines:
et il est vrai que nous sommes blessées
au plus bas de l'espoir

and it is true we are wounded to the
very depths of hope
(trans. D. H.)

His poem "Burial," translated by Oliver Bernard, in Ezekiel Mphahlele's *African Writing Today* is more hopeful, ending:
But because time heals those wounds and
softens angles
I wish to rear up a monolith to time
I ejected by time and exiled by former ages
now reintegrate time
and become its sacred aorta
see how my territory widens
my land of shadows awakening
/hollowing itself out
like a limitless reservoir for the ages to
/come

Writings: Poetry: *Un nègre raconte,* Paris, Eds. des Poètes, 1954, Paris, Editions

Bruno Durochor, 1961; *Anti-grâce*, Paris, Présence Africaine, 1967; poem: "Burial," *African Writing Today*, Ezekiel Mphalele, editor, London, Penguin, 1967; also poems in *New Sum of Poetry from the Negro World*, Paris, Présence Africaine, Vol. 57, 1966.

JOHNSON, Lemuel
b. ca. 1935, Nigeria.
Poet, short story writer and novelist.

Johnson returned to Sierra Leone at a young age with his parents, who were Sierra Leoneans, and received his lower education there. He took a Ph.D. in comparative literature at the University of Michigan. His novel, *First Glimpses*, won the Hopwood Award for Major Fiction awarded by the University of Michigan. A short story of the same name, the first chapter of the novel, appeared in *New African Literature and the Arts* in 1970. Another story, "Amy's Case," and his poem, "In Memory of Ayodele: II," also appear in the volume as do his free translations from the Spanish: "Night-time and War in the Prado Museum," from Raphael Albert's "Noche de guerra en el museo," and "The People's Dreamer," based on Albert's "Un sonador par un pueblo."

Writings: Novel: *First Glimpses,* unpublished; stories: "First Glimpses," "Amy's Case."
Poems: "In Memory of Ayodele: II"; and translations: in *New African Literature and the Arts,* Joseph Okpaku, editor, New York, Crowell, 1970.

JOLOBE, James James Ranisi
b. July 26, 1902, Indwe, Thembuland, Cape Province, South Africa.
Xhosa poet, novelist, playwright, teacher, scholar, preacher.

Son of a Presbyterian minister, James James Jolobe grew up at Matatiele in the Springdale Mission Station, and entered St. Matthew's Training College in 1916. Graduating in 1919 with a teacher's certificate, he began a career which took him to various mission schools until 1927 when he entered the Native College at Fort Hare. After graduating in 1931 following study in theology and the arts and being ordained a minister, he moved to the Lovedale Training School as a teacher. In the mid-1950's he left Lovedale to become the minister of the St. Patrick Presbyterian Church. He is a member of the Advisory Council of Fort Hare University College, a member of the Lovedale Press Committee which provides editorial guidance for the *South African Outlook,* and a member of the Department of Education's Xhosa language and literature committee. He married Jeanne Buthelwa Nongogo in 1937 and has two children.

His first creative work was the collection of poems *Omyezo,* which, in the words of Benedict Vilakazi, were full of the spirit of "experimentation and innovation," backed by his knowledge of history and of European literature "which generates poetic poise."

Jolobe's later works of poetry are *U-Mthuthula,* published in 1937, and winner of the 1936 Esther May Bedford Competition Award; *Lovedale Xhosa Rhymes (Izicengcelezo zaseDikeni),* 1952, children's verse; *Ilitha* (Stream of Light), 1959, which, while still in manuscript, won the 1954 poetry prize offered by Afrikaanse Pers-Boekhandel. A collection of his poems, including a shortened version of "U-Mthuthula," appeared in English as *Poems of an African*. His collection, *Indyebo yesihobe* (Harvest of Songs), Vols. I and II, was recently brought out by Afrikaanse Pers-Boekhandel.

His one novel is *Elundini loThukela* (On the Shores of the Thukela River). He has published Xhosa translations of W. Bonsel's novel in Africaans, *Die biene Maya* (Maya the Bee) as *uMaya, amahla-ndinyuka enyosi,* 1957; H. Rider Haggard's *King Solomon's Mines* as *Imigodi kakumkhani USolomon,* 1958; Aesop's fables as *Iintsomi zika-Aesop,* 1953; and in. 1955, with Eliphalet Thandiwe Makiwane (b. ca. 1920), he translated from English the *Work Guide to Health for Adults* by N. Fletcher into Xhosa, the work entitled *Impilo-ntle* (Good Health). His play, *Amathunzi obomi umdlelo wokulinganiswa* (The Shadows of Life), is based on imagination rather than on an historical event. Published in 1957, it won the Afrikaanse Pers-Boekhandel prize for plays in 1954. In 1952 Jolobe was awarded the Vilakazi Memorial Prize for his writings. His earlier collection of essays, *Amavo* (Traditions), appeared in 1945 as Volume V of the Bantu Treasury Series.

In 1951, with Jackson Tinise Arose (b. 1900), he composed a small grammar called *Xhosa grammatical terminology,* and the same year saw publication of his Xhosa version of *Up from Slavery* by Booker T. Washington, called *Ukuphakama ukusuka ebukhobokeni.*

Jolobe's earliest writings, homiletics or religious commentaries, were *U-Zagula,* 1923, written when he was in Matatiele; *Iindlela ezahlukeneyo* (Different Paths), 1930; and *U-Myezo* (The Vineyard), 1936, selected as Volume II of the Bantu Treasury Series, but also later separately republished by the University of the Witwatersrand in 1961.

Writings: Poetry: *U-Myezo,* or *Omyezu,* Johannesburg. University of the Witwatersrand, 1936 (Vol II of Bantu Treasury Series), 1961, 1965, translated by author into English, London, Stockwell, 1938; *U-Mthuthula,* 1936; in English, London, 1937; *Izicengcelezo zase-Dikeni,* Lovedale, Lovedale Press, 1952; *Ilitha,* Johannesburg, Afrikaanse Pers–Boekhandel, Bona Press, 1959; *Poems of an African,* Lovedale, 1946; *Indyebo yesihobe,* Volumes I and II, Afrikaanse Pers–Boekhandel, late 1960's.

Novel: *Elundini loThukela,* Afrikaanse Pers–Boekhandel. 1958.

Play: *Amathunzi obomi; umdlelo wokulinganiswa,* Afrikaanse Pers–Boekhandel, 1957.

Essays: *Amavo,* Volume V of Bantu Treasury Series, University of the Witwatersrand Press, 1945.

Translations into Xhosa: *uMaya, amahla-ndinyuka enyosi,* Afrikaanse Pers–Boekhandel, 1957; *Imigodi kakumkhani USolomon* (King Solomon's Mines), Afrikaanse Pers–Boekhandel, 1958; *Iintsomi zika-Aesop* (Aesop's Fables), Lovedale, Lovedale Press, 1953; *Impilo-ntle,* Lovedale, Lovedale Press, 1955; *Ukuphakama ukusuka ebukhobokeni (Up from Slavery,* Booker T. Washington), Johannesburg, Afrikaanse Pers–Boekhandel, 1951.

Religious works: *U-Zagula,* Lovedale, Lovedale Press, 1923; *Iindlela ezahlukeneyo,* Lovedale, 1930.

English essay: "The Prospects for a Native of South Africa After Completing a Course of Work and Service Among His Own People," in *South African Outlook,* 1931.

JONES, E.B.B.H. (see HORATIO-JONES, E.B.B.)

JORDAN, Archibald Campbell
b. October 30, 1906, Mbokothwane,
Tsolo District, Cape Province,
South Africa; d. Madison,
Wisconsin, October 20, 1968.
Xhosa novelist, short story writer,
poet, scholar, teacher.

A. C. Jordan's early schooling from 1913
to 1921 was at Mbokothwane Higher
Mission School and in 1922 at St.
Cuthbert's Higher Boarding School.
The next two years he was a student at
St. John's College, Umtata (1923–25);
then, after four years of work, he studied
at Fort Hare University College (1929–
30). He took his B.A. and his M.S. from
the University of South Africa through
Fort Hare. His master's thesis was "Some
Features of the Phonetic and Grammatical Structure of Baca."

For eight years Jordan was a teacher
at the Bantu High School, Kroonstad,
in the Orange Free State (1936–1944).
Then, having earned his M.A., he was
appointed Lecturer at the University of
Cape Town, remaining there until 1961.
He took his Ph.D. in 1956 at that university with the dissertation, "A Phonologi-
cal and Grammatical Study of Literary
Xhosa." In 1962, he left South Africa
for good, taking a position as visiting lecturer at the University of California at
Los Angeles, and one year later took a
position at the Institute for Research in
Humanities at the University of Wisconsin, Madison. In 1964, he was named
full professor in the Department of African Languages and Literature, remaining at Wisconsin until his death after
long illness at his home in Madison in
1968.

A. C. Jordan's first novel, *Inggoumbo
yeminyanya* (The Wrath of the Ancestral
Spirits), is considered the classic of modern Xhosa writing. Encouraged to write
by his white missionary friends, Jordan's

work is tragic and full of the deep sor-
rows of an oppressed people. His second
and third novels, still in manuscript in
Madison, are historical works about the
Mpondomise people. They are *Ulubhelu-ndongana,* and *Ookhetshe babhazalele*
(The Hawks Abroad). Those Xhosa
scholars who have seen these works in
typescript regret their not having been
published.

A fine poet also, Jordan published in
a number of journals. His militant poem
"Uthi mandiyeke" (You Tell me to Sit
Quiet), begins:

You say, sit there, just stay quiet
(when you know I've been unmanned)
I've nowhere to go, you've taken all I had
Here, there, I stumble, hungry
My house, bare-bones, only the locust's cry.
(trans. Everts and D. H.)

This poem and others, including the
even more bitter "Umngeni" (Open the
Door), remain in the unpublished manuscript of verse, *Imihobe* (Songs).

An unpublished collection of short
stories is entitled *Kwezo mpindo zeTsitsa*
(Along the Bends of the Tsitsa). The
journal, *Africa South,* carried Jordan's
long essay, "Towards an African Literature," in 12 installments between 1957
and 1960. Also worth noting is Longman
Green's publication in 1965 of Jordan's
Practical Xhosa Course for Beginners.

Dr. Jordan is survived by Phyllis P.
Jordan, herself a writer and scholar, who
publishes her fiction under the name
Phyllis P. Ntantlala), and four children.

Writings: Novel: *Inggoumbo yeminyanya,*
Lovedale, Lovedale Press 1940; unpub-
lished: *Ulubhelu-ndongana; Ookhetshe
babhazalele.*
Poetry: *Imihobe,* Unpublished.
Short story: "Kwezo mpindo ze-
Tsitsa."
Essay: "Towards an African Litera-
ture," *Africa South,* 1957–1960.

Jordan

Other: *Practical Xhosa Course for Beginners*, Cape Town, 1965.

JORDAN, Phyllis P. (see NTANTLALA, Phyllis P.)

K

KA, Abdou Anta (see MOFOLO entry for mention of KA)

KABBADA, Mika'el (also KEBEDE, Mikael)
b. November 2, 1915, Ethiopia.
Amharic playwright, poet, diplomat, statesman.

Kabbada's formal education ended with high school because of the Italian invasion, but he continued to read and study French and English and when he was 18 he began to write poetry. He was a contributor to Yilma Darassa's pioneering anthology, *In Praise of Independence* (1941–42). His first published volume was *The Light of Intelligence* (Addis Ababa, 1933–1934, 1942–43), a collection of poems reflecting both Western literature and folktales. Emperor Haile Selassi brought to his attention the novel, *Beyond Pardon*, by the once popular 19th century American novelist, Bertha M. Clay, and suggested he translate it. Choosing an original approach, he rendered the novel into 1500 lines of Amharic verse with a detailed introduction (in 1936–1937), and, unlikely as it might seem, the work proved popular and influential. Kabbada received appointments to high-level positions in the Ministry of Education and the Ministry of Foreign Affairs, and was ambassador to the Vatican in the early 1950's.

Drama was Kabbada's major form. His first play, *Prophecy Fulfilled* (1933–34), was performed in the Theatre of the Lycée Tafari Makonnon. The play dealt with predictions of the future and was full of the traditional "spiritual" message. Kabbada used more realistic and dramatic language in revising the play for its second edition of 1954–55. Here there is more action and livelier dialogue and it is this version that Stephen Wright translated into English. His second play, *The Storm of Punishment,* attacks materialistic atheism. In the protagonist, Balay, a poor man, and the Devil, Qalil, Kabbada dramatizes stereotyped ethical confrontations in a somewhat more fluid manner than in his first play. The Devil argues the Marxist, utilitarian philosophy of the modern world and Balay humbly struggles to support the old pious virtues, the rule of God, etc.

Kabbada's third play was *Hannibal* (1948–49), which earlier had been performed in the Haile Selassie I Theatre during the celebrations of the Emperor's 25th year in power in 1945. The work shows the jealousy of the Carthaginian nobles of Hannibal and the resultant defeat of Carthage by the less divided Romans. Other plays are *Kaleb* (1956–57, 1965–66), set in the ancient kingdom of Axum of the 5th century, and *Achab* (1960–61), both issued in Addis Ababa as were all his books. All the plays are austere, philosophical treatments of moral and ethical themes, akin to the dramas of Racine and Calderón, and have failed to achieve the popularity of the more "bourgeois" dramas written by a younger generation of Ethiopian playwrights.

Writings: Plays: *Prophecy Fulfilled*, Addis Ababa, 1933–34; English translation by Stephen Wright, 1953; *The Storm of Punishment*, Addis Ababa, 1948–49; *Hannibal*, Addis Ababa, 1948–49, 1955–56; translation into French by author: *Annibal, tragédie en cinq actes*, 1964; *Kaleb*, 1956–57, 1965–66; *Achab*, 1960–61; 1967–68.

History: *Ethiopia and Western Civilization*, 1941–42, 1947–48; published in Amharic, French and English; *Great Men*, 1943–44, 1950–51; *History of the World*, Part I, 1941–42; Part II, 1954–55; *The Modernization of Japan*, 1953–54; *Alexander the Great*, 1947–48; *Old Ethiopian Paintings*, 1961–62, in Amharic, French and English, 1961; *Story and Parable*, Part III, 1935–36; *How Did Japan Modernize Itself?*, 1946–47; *Civilization*, no date.

Poetry: *The Light of Intelligence*, 1933–34, 1941–42; Amharic Verse version (of 1500 lines) of B. M. Clay's *Beyond Pardon* 1936–37, 1943–44, 1951–52. *Poetry*, 1956–57. Translation: Shakespeare's *Romeo and Juliet* 1946–47, 1953–54.

Biographical/Critical Source: Albert S. Gérard, *Four African Literatures*, Berkeley, University of California Press, 1971.

KACHINGWE, Aubrey
b. 1926, Malawi.
Novelist, journalist.

Kachingwe was educated in Malawi and later in Tanganyika, (now Tanzania) and travelled to London to study journalism. In 1950 he joined the *East African Standard* newspaper group in Nairobi, Kenya, and then worked for the *Daily Herald* on the foreign desk. He worked from 1960 to 1963 for the Department of Information in Malawi, and then went back to London to work in BBC's African Service and News Department. Moving to Africa again, he was employed by the Ghana Broadcasting Service in Accra, and finally returned home to work for the Malawi Broadcasting Corporation, where he is now head of the news program staff.

His one novel, *No Easy Task*, is a documentary-like study which focuses on one African family whose problems reflect those of all peoples in a nation on the uneasy path to political independence.

Writings: Novel: *No Easy Task*, London, Heinemann, 1966.

KAGAME, Abbé Alexis (or Alegisi)
b. 1912, Kiyanza, Chieftainship of Buriza, Rwanda.
Rwanda language poet, historian, ethnographer (also publishes in French).

Son of Pierre Bitahurwina, the deputy-chief of the Tutsi people, Alexis was sent to the state-run school in Ruhengeri and later to the Kabgayi seminary school, where he studied theology and philosophy. He was ordained a priest in

1941 and took a doctorate some years later at the Pontifical Gregorian University in Rome.

His first work, a history published in 1943, *Inganji Karinga* (The Victorious Drums), recounts the story of the ancient Rwandans. His poetic epic, published in three parts, *Isoko y'ámäjyambere* (Sources of Progress), deals with the Christianization of Rwanda. He has translated portions of the epic into French as *La divine pastorale* in three volumes. Volumes I and II were republished in 1952 as *Veillées* (The After Dinner Hours) and Volume III in 1955, as *La naissance de l'univers* (The Birth of the Universe).

His first critical studies of his country's poetry were the 30-page *Bref aperçu sur la poésie dynastique du Rwanda* (A Brief Look at the Dynastic Poetry of Rwanda), 1950, and *La poésie dynastique au Rwanda* (Dynastic Poetry of Rwanda), a work of 240 pages, published in 1951.

Other works are: *Iyo wiliwe nta Rungu* (1949); *Umuliribiya wa nyili-ibiremwa* (The Lord's Creation Song) (1952–53); and *Indyohesha-birayi* (The Seasoner of the Potatoes) (1949). In 1970, Kagame published his *Introduction aux grands genres lyrique de l'ancien Rwanda* (Introduction to the Great Lyrical Poems of Ancient Rwanda).

Abbé Kagame, while continuing his church duties, is devoted to research in the history, culture, and literature of his people and has been instrumental in getting support for some ten serious studies from the Belgian Académie Royale des Science d'Outre-mer of which he is a corresponding member. The Abbé is also an associate of the Institut pour la Recherche Scientifique en Afrique Centrale.

Writings: Poetry: *Isoko y'ámäjyambere*, 3 volumes, Kabgayi, Editions Morales, 1949–51; in author's translation, *La divine pastorale*, Brussels, Eds., du Marais, Volumes I and II as *Veillées*, 1952, Volume III as *La naissance de l'univers*, Other: *Iyo wiliwe nta Rungu*, Nyanza, Rwanda Editions, Royale de Nyanza, 1949; *Umuliribya wa nyili-ibiremwa*, Astride, Rwanda, 1952–53; *Indyohesha-birayi*, Kabgayi, Editions Royale, 1949; *Introduction aux grands genres lyrique de l'ancien Rwanda*, Butare, Edition Universitaires de Rwanda, 1970; *Bref aperçu sur la poésie dynastique du Rwanda*, Brussels, Ed. Universitaires, 1950; *La poésie dynastique au Rwanda*, Brussels, Institut Royal Congo Belge, 1951.

History: *Iganji Karinga*, Kabgayi, 1943.

Biographical/Critical Sources: Literature de cours au Rwanda, A. Coupez, T. Kamanzi, reviewed by François-savier Gasana, who also reviewed Kagame's *Introduction aux grandes genres*, in *Research in African Literature* II, 2, Fall, 1971, University of Texas, Austin.

KAGARA, Malam Abubakar Imam
b. ca. 1910, northern Nigeria.
Hausa story writer, journalist, biographer, travelogue-writer.

Younger brother of Malam Muhammadu Bello Kagara, he is considered the father of modern Hausa literature and for an important period was editor of the Hausa language paper, *Gaskiya to fi kwabo*. He has authored many stories and a life of the prophet Mohammed.

KAGARA, Malam Muhammadu Bello
b. ca. 1905, Northern Nigeria.

Kagara

Biographer, novelist, in the Hausa language.

Malam Muhammadu Bello Kagara, Chief Alkali of Katsina, published his important *The Life of the Emir of Katsina, the Late Alhaji Muhammadu Dikko, C.B.E. (1865–1944)* in 1951.

In 1934, Kagara published a novel, *Gandoki,* which was one of five novels chosen in a competition by the Translation Bureau, the forerunner of the Gaskiya Corporation. The work was recently reprinted in the original Hausa in 1952 and 1965. Written in a bombastic, heroic style, in keeping with its lionhearted hero, a soldier of the last generation of pre-colonial Hausas, the story is told in the words of Gandoki himself. Proverbs, idiomatic phrases and highly graphic passages mark this interesting work.

The biography of Dikko, in contrast, is simple and marches along in a manner befitting the subject, the Emir of Katsina. Frequent anecdotes from the subject's life lighten the tone. Everywhere attention is focused on the Emir, a person of great character and accomplishments. F. W. Parsons, who translated the selection, "The Death of Alhaji Muhammadu Kikko, C.B.E." in W. H. Whiteley's *A Selection of African Prose.* Vol. 2, wrote in his introduction: " . . . in these final pages describing the death and funeral of the emir, the author rises to a height of simple but emotive writing which—to me at any rate—has the same sort of impact as have some of the great narrative passages of the Authorized Version in English. Hausas themselves I know share my views as to the greatness of this passage as literature by any standards."

Writings: Biography: *The Life of the Emir of Katsina, the Late Alhaju Muhammadu*

Dikko, C.B.E. (1856–1944), Zaria, Nigeria, Gaskiya Corporation, 1951.

Novel: *Gandoki,* Zaria, Nigeria, Gaskiya Corporation, 1934, 1952, 1965.

Biographical/Critical Source: F. W. Parsons in *A Selection of African Prose,* W. H. Whiteley, editor, Oxford, Clarendon Press, 1964.

KAHIGA, Samuel
b. ca. 1940, Kenya.
Short story writer.

Samuel, with his brother, Leonard Kibera, collaborated on the volume of short stories, *Potent Ash.* Samuel's stories are "God's Water," "Esther," "Departure at Dawn," "The Last Breath," "Father

Comes Back," "The Wind," and "The Clerk." Most of the stories concern protagonists who struggle for life in the whirlpool of danger during the revolt against British rule in Kenya by the Kikuyu (the Mau-mau period of the middle 1950's).

Writings: Stories in *Potent Ash,* Nairobi, East African Publishing House, 1968.

KAKAZA, Lillith
b. ca. 1885, South Africa; d. 1950.
Xhosa story-writer.

Her two published volumes are: *Intyatyambo yomzi* [The Flower in the Home], a 31-page novelette, and *UTandiwe wakwa Gcaleka* [Tandiwe, a Damsel of Gaikaland], a long tale published in 1914.

Writings: Stories: *Intyatyambo yomzi,* Gcuwa, 1913, and *UTandiwe waka Gcaleka,* Cape Town, Methodist Book Room, 1914.

KALUNGANO, (see DOS SANTOS, Marcelino)

KANE, Sheikh (or Cheikh)
Hamidou
b. April 3, 1928, Matam, Senegal.
Novelist, government official.

Born in the Fouta Djalon area of the Fula people (northern Guinea, Guinea-Bissau, and Senegal), Kane's thought is richly impregnated with Islamic cultural and religious feeling. He spoke only Peul (or Fulani) the first years of his life and attended a Koranic school. However, at 10, he was sent to a French school, suc-

cessfully passed the examination for the C.E.P. diploma, 1941, and took the B.A. in Dakar in 1948. He later studied for the license in law at the University of Paris and received his license (akin to the American M.A.) in philosophy from the Ecole Nationale de la France d'Outre-mer in 1959. He returned home to be appointed an official of the French colonial regime in Senegal, serving as deputy director of development, and then as Chef du Cabinet to the Minister of Development and Planning after Senegal became independent.

He served as governor of the district of Thiés from 1960 to 1963, and concurrently served as Commissioner-General of Senegal's first five-year plan of development. He is presently an official of the United Nations Emergency Fund (UNEF) in Lagos, Nigeria, working on problems left by the Biafran war.

His 1961 novel, *L'aventure ambiguë,* published in English as *Ambiguous Adven-*

ture, is a moving study of the emotional, intellectual, and theological breakdown of a Koranic trained man of mystical bent who undergoes a thorough Western education. For the young protagonist, harshly introduced to the austerities and beauties of the Islamic faith by his fanatical but highly spiritual teacher, the philosophical and social underpinnings of Western civilization are destructive, inhuman, and too involved with the immediate and sensual. The work won the Grand Prix Littéraire de'Afrique Noire d'Expression Française in 1962.

As in Mongo Beti's *Mission to Kala*, there is a "twin" relationship in Kane's novel. Samba, royal, educated, highly sensitive, is balanced at the end of the work with an illiterate, obtuse, but deeply suffering former Senegalese soldier who has become the protector of the old Koranic scholar and one-time teacher of Samba. The two men, of roughly the same age, are both friends and foes at the side of the dying holy man. And in a dreamlike moment, mythical in intention, the half-insane tramp mystic slays the already spiritually lost Samba, who has returned to an Africa he can neither accept nor repudiate.

Kane has contributed two essays to journals which are of interest: "L'Islam en Afrique noire," in *L'Etudiant d'Afrique Noire*, and "Comme se nous nous étions donnés rendez-vous" (It is as Though We were Given an Appointment), in *Esprit*, October, 1961.

A. C. Brench in his *Writing in French from Senegal to Cameroon*, offers an excerpt from the novel and a fairly extensive biography and bibliography. Certainly Kane's novel is one of the most intelligent and poetic of the francophone novels.

Writings: Novel: *L'aventure ambiguë*, Paris, Juilliard, 1961; in English translation by Katherine Woods as *Ambiguous Adventure*, New York, Walker and Company, 1963, New York, Collier Books-Macmillan, 1969.

Essays: "L'Islam en Afrique noire," *L'étudiant d'Afrique noire;* "Comme se nous nous étions donnés rendez-vous," *Esprit*, October, 1961.

Biographical/Critical Sources: Writing in French from Senegal to Cameroon, A. C. Brench, London, Oxford Press, 1967; *Cheikh Hamidou Kane*, Roger Mercier and M. and S. Battestini, Paris, Fernand Nathan, 1964, 1967.

KARIM, Ahmed Awad
b. ca. 1890, The Sudan.
Shukria (Butana-Arabic) oral poet.

Karim wrote in the old "dobeit" form, a loosely linked four-line stanzaic narrative sung poetry. His work was collected in 1963 on tape, translated into classical Arabic by Sheikh Ahmed Khalid and then into English by Ali Sayed Lufti for publication in Anne Tibble's *African/English Literature*.

Writings: Oral poetry collected in *African/English Literature*, Anne Tibble, London, Peter Owen, 1965.

KARIUKI, Joseph E.
b. August 25, 1931, Banana Hill, near Nairobi, Kenya.
Poet.

Kariuki received his local schooling and secondary training at Alliance High School, and then went on for four years at Makerere College, Uganda, where he received his B.A. in 1953 and a teaching diploma in 1954. He taught English for several years in Kenya at two different high schools (Alliance High School, 1955–1956, Kangaru School, 1957–60) before traveling to England on a scholarship to study English at King's College, Cambridge, where he graduated with honors in 1965. He did broadcasting for BBC, including reading his poetry which he had written in his spare time on the air.

In 1962, he returned to Kenya where he is became principal of the Institute of Public Administration. In 1968–69 Kariuki was Head of the Training Unit of the United Nations Economic Commission for Africa; in 1969 he was named the Director-General and Manager of the U. N. Project CAFRAD in Morocco. His wife Susan and he have one son and three daughters.

His poetry has appeared in various reviews and collections, including Moore and Beier's *Modern Poetry from Africa,* which includes his "Come Away, My Love." The poem "New Life" appears in Ezekiel Mphahlele's *African Writing Today.* It tells the ancient story of a villager waiting for his lover to slip to his side during a storm. Kariuki joins the fertility of man and the fields in the last lines; as men to women, so women to the waiting fields:

It comes heaving, tearing, bearing down,
Surging in impatient billows to drain its
source,
Till unable to bear its own forces
It settles to a timeless steady flow
Endless.

There is calm in the air,
And greater calm by my side.

Tomorrow the village women go planting
Their seed in the hungry ground:
And life is born anew.

Kariuki's *Ode to Mzee,* a five-page poem, was printed in 1964.

Writings: Poem: *Ode to Mzee,* Nairobi, Chemchemi Cultural Center, 1964; poems in *Modern Poetry from Africa,* Moore and Beier, editors, London, Penguin, revised edition, 1968; *African Writing Today,* Ezekiel Mphahlele, editor, London, Penguin, 1967.

KARLEE, Varfelli (pseudonym COOPER, Charles Edward)
b. ca. 1900, Liberia.
Novelist.

Born and educated in Liberia, Karlee's novels are among the rare works dealing with the hinterland of Liberia, inhabited by Africans native to the area rather than those who were transplanted from America to occupy the coastal areas north and south of Monrovia. His only novel was *Love in Ebony: A West African Romance* (1932).

Writings: Novel: *Love in Ebony: A West African Romance*, London, Murray, 1932; Kraus Reprint Series, Nendeln, Liechtenstein, 1970.

KATI, Mahmud
b. ca. 1468, Timbuktu; d. after 1570.
Collector of legends and tales
in Arabic, scholar.

As a young man in his 20's, Kati became a member of the personal staff of Askia Muhammad the Great who had seized the throne of Songhai, and accompanied the emperor to Mecca. He began writing about 1519 and is believed to have continued collecting legends of the older empires in this area, as did the later Abd al-Rahman as-Sadi (1596– 1656), until his death sometime late in the century. Some sources claim Kati lived 125 years.

Kati's *Tarikh al-Fattash* (The Chronicle of the Seeker After Learning), probably mostly composed in the period 1519–1560, primarily tells the story and legends of the ancient Ghana empire. Some of the tales reach back to the 7th century and to the era of one of the greatest of Ghana's kings, Kanissa'ai. Kati's work, carried on by several successors, including sons and grandsons, was completed about 1655.

Works: Legends and tales: *Tarikh al-Fattash,* in Arabic manuscript; translated into French by O. Houdas and M. Delafosse, Paris, 1913.

KAY, Kwesi
b. ca. 1940, Ghana.
Playwright, actor.

Educated in Ghana, Kay has been active in English theatre since 1963 in repertory, television, films, and radio. He has done many reviews and poems for BBC radio. He has written several plays, among them, *The Treasure Chamber,* published in 1970, and *Maame,* published in 1968 in Cosmo Pieterse's *Ten One-Act Plays. The Treasure Chamber* is about ancient, pharaonic Egypt.

Writings: Plays: *Maame,* in *Ten One-Act Plays,* London, Heinemann, 1968, and *The Treasure Chamber,* London, Heinemann Secondary Educational Books, 1970.

KAYIRA, Legson
b. ca. 1940, formerly Nyasaland,
now Malawi.
Novelist, autobiographer.

Kayira received secondary schooling at a mission. Then, lacking funds for further study, he walked 2500 miles to Khartoum, Sudan, where he made friends with the American consul who helped him. Later he was admitted to Skagit Valley Junior College in Washington State which raised the money for his airplane ticket to the United States. He went on to the University of Washington in Seattle, and then won a two-year scholarship to Cambridge. He now lives in England.

Kayira's first novel, *The Looming*

His second novel, *Jingala,* takes its name from the old villager, a retired tax collector, who opposes his son's wish to become a Catholic priest. In the battle of generations, the pain and anger suffered because of the disruption of the immemorial patterns of life is again dramatized.

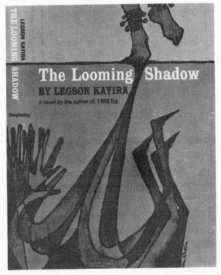

Kayira's third novel, *The Civil Servant,* reached print in 1971.

Shadow (1967), exploits the rivalries of villagers, one of whom, Matenda, accuses the protagonist, Musyani, of bewitching him and making him ill. The novel ends with the conviction of three men who have burned Musyani's house after the village has been inflamed with fear and violence by the feud. The wise chief, Mwenimuzi, administers the best justice he can, nullifying the efforts of the wily medicine man, Simbwindimbwi, to support Matenda's charge of witchcraft. Though the work has some general interest, it is hardly the "first authentically African novel by a native African" as claimed by Doubleday in the dust jacket.

Earlier, Kayira had written of his extraordinary "walk" for education and his subsequent studies in *I Will Try,* which won the Northwest (U.S.) Non-Fiction Prize in 1966.

Writings: Novel: *The Looming Shadow,* Garden City, New York, Doubleday, 1967; London, Longmans, 1968; paperback edition, New York, Collier Books-Macmillans, 1970; *Jingala,* London. Longmans. Doubleday, 1969; *The Civil Servant,* London, Longmans, 1971.

Autobiography: *I Will Try,* Garden City, New York, Doubleday, 1965; London, Longmans, 1966.

KAYO, Patrice

b. ca. 1940, Cameroon.

Poet, folklorist, teacher.

Locally educated, Kayo now teaches at Bafoussam, Cameroon. His two volumes of verse are *Chansons populaire Bamiléké* (1969), and the next year, *Hymnes et sagesse* (Hymns and Wisdom). Kayo is represented in Moore and Beier's anthology, *Modern Poetry from Africa* and in *New Sum of Poetry from the Negro World*.

Writings: Poetry: *Chansons populaire Bamiléké*, Yaoundé, 1969 (?); *Hymnes et sagesse*, Honfleur, Paris, P. J. Oswald, 1970; poems in *Modern Poetry from Africa*, Moore and Beier, editors, revised edition, 1968; *New Sum of Poetry from the Negro World*, Paris, Présence Africaine, Volume 57, 1966.

KAYPER-MENSAH, Albert William
(also MENSAH, Albert William Kayper)
b. 1923, Secondi, Ghana.
Poet, playwright, diplomat, teacher.

Kayper-Mensah studied at Mfantsipim School, Wesley College, Achimota, all in Ghana, then at Cambridge, where he took a B.A. in Natural Science. He did later work at the graduate level in education at London University. After returning home, he taught for several years before joining Ghana's new diplomatic service, serving in Bonn and London. He began his poetry while a student in England and has published in *Branta, Okyeame, Ghanaian Times, Neues Afrika* and *Afrika Heute*. He is also represented in several important anthologies, including *Messages: Poems from Ghana*.

In 1957, he was awarded the Margaret Wrong Literary Prize for a volume of poems published in 1970 as *The Dark Wanderer*. More recently he received a British Council prize for one of his plays,

and he has four others in manuscript awaiting publication.

Writings: Poetry: *The Dark Wanderer*, Tubingen, Horst Erdmann Verlag, 1970, poems in *Messages: Poems from Ghana*, London, Heinemann, 1971.

Plays: all in manuscript: *Hearts That Have Loved; Kisses for a Stone;* and *The Rescue*.

KEBEDE, Mikael (see KABBADA, Mika'el)

KEITA, Fodeba (also FODEBA, Keita)
b. 1921, Siguiri, Malinké area, upper part of Guinea.
Poet, songwriter, choreographer, playwright, government official
(also writes in Malinké)

Educated in Guinea and Senegal (the Lycée William Ponty, Gorée, Dakar), Keita later studied law in Paris. He opened several nightclubs there featuring African dance and music and later organized the world-famous Ballet Africaine, which since the independence of Guinea in 1957, has become a National Dance Troupe that has entertained all over the world. Keita himself has composed much music and poetry. His strongly Marxist and nationalist poems were banned in French West Africa in 1951 and remained so until Guinean independence in 1957.

Employing his homeland's rich musical resources, vivacity, and creativity, he has composed songs and music which celebrate the recent past and the arrival of independence. His published works are *Poèmes africains* (African Poems), *Le Maître d'école* and *Minuit* (The Schoolmaster and the play Midnight), *Le Théâtre africain* (African Theatre), no date, and *Aube africaine* (African Dawn). His poems are also found in various anthologies.

Though Keita has composed songs in his mother-tongue, Malinké, his works are known to the non-Guinean world only in French.

Because of his griot background (the griot were professional musicians and singers) and his musical training in Paris, he was asked to do the introduction to Michael Huet's *Les hommes de la danse* (Dancing People), a critical study of African dance. Keita's early play, *Grain de sel* (A Grain of Salt), mixes European with African elements and contains the line, "if to our salt a little of that of others is added we will be enriched."

Returning to Guinea at the request of President Sekou Touré in 1957, Keita served in a variety of cabinet posts in the new government, including Minister of Economic Affairs and the Minister of National Defense. Because of plots and counter-plots in Guinea during the period from 1968 to 1971, Touré turned against many of his former close collaborators. At last report, Fodeba Keita was imprisoned, or, even secretly executed. There is no reliable word as to the fate of this talented man.

Writings: Poetry: *Poèmes africains*, Paris, Seghers, 1950; *Le maître d'école* and *Minuit*, Paris, Seghers, 1953; *Le Théâtre africain*, no date; *Aube africaine*, Paris, Seghers, 1965.

Play: *Grain de sel,* unpublished.

Scholarship: Introduction to *Les hommes de la danse,* Lausanne, Ed. Clairefontaine, 1954.

KENYATTA, Jomo (pseudonym for Kamaua Ngengi)
b. ca. 1893, Ichaweri, Kenya.
Statesman, anthropologist, lawyer, writer.

Grandson of an important medicineman priest, orphaned at ten, Kamaua Ngengi, as his name appears on early medical and school records, never gave up his Kikuyu culture though he lived for many years abroad. Receiving his earliest education at the Church of Scotland Mission, where the teaching was in Kikuyu, he was called Johnstone Kamau wa Ngengi. While employed in Nairobi by the water department, he was given the nickname 'Kenyatta' because of the beaded belt he usually wore *(Mucibi wa kinyata* in Kikuyu). Later, as the leader of the fight for independence, he was called "Burning Spear."

Kenyatta has stated he does not know the date or year of his birth though he has cited specific dates at various times.

Kenyatta

Beginning in the 1920's, Kenyatta took a leading role in fighting for greater freedom for his people and the return of the expropriated land to its original owners. During this period he published a newspaper in Kikuyu, *Muigwithania,* and in 1929 he testified before the Hilton Young Commission which was investigating the land situation. Later he traveled for the first time to England as a member of a Kikuyu delegation that was petitioning the government for permission to run Kikuyu language schools, a request which was granted. In 1931 he returned to Britain, this time to stay for fifteen years of intensive study, writing and political activity. At Quaker College, Woodbrooke, Selly Oak, he studied English, and later he moved to London where he shared an apartment with the American black singer, Paul Robeson and later with Peter Abrahams, the South African author who was then just beginning to write. These men, both deeply hurt by racial injustices, helped shape his political thinking and stimulated, he sought in his studies the language and ideas necessary to the analysis of his peoples' dilemmas.

In 1933 he began work at the School of African and Oriental Studies as an assistant in phonetics and in 1936, working under Bronislaw Malinowski, he took a graduate diploma in anthropology at the London School of Economics. A product of his work with Malinowski was his valuable *Facing Mount Kenya* (1936), a moving but balanced study of the customs, beliefs and landholding traditions of the Kikuyu.

He traveled widely in Europe and attended for awhile the University of Moscow. During World War II, he was back in England, married Edna Clark an Englishwoman, in 1943, and held a variety of jobs, ranging from work in the fields to lecturing for the Workers Educational Association. He continued to work for African rights and with George Padmore, Kwame Nkrumah, and several others, organized the Pan-African Federation, and held the Fifth Pan-African Congress. He ended this period with the publication in 1945 of *Kenya–Land of Conflict,* in which he predicted that unless there were radical changes in Kenya, revolution would be inevitable.

In 1946 he returned to Africa after a decade and a half in Europe and became, in June 1947, the president of the Kenya African Union (K.A.U.), an organization made up mostly of his fellow-Kikuyus. By 1951 the K.A.U. claimed 150,000 members, and under the leadership of Oginga Odinga the Luo people began to join the Kikuyu. Kenyatta became principal of the independent Teachers' Training College and from this position extended his influence throughout the colony. Disorders broke out and British settlers began to demand that the colonial government arrest Kenyatta and his colleagues. Kenyatta strongly denied the K.A.U. was responsible and disclaimed any connection with what was becoming known as the Mau-mau. However, he was detained on October 22, 1952, along with five associates, and charged on November 18 with leading the Mau-mau. Despite defense efforts by the English lawyer, D. N. Pritt, and other attorneys from Nigeria, India and the West Indies, he was found guilty on April 8, 1953, and sentenced to seven years' imprisonment. Meanwhile terrorism erupted at isolated places and guerrilla bands openly challenged British rule. The Mau-mau battle had begun.

Though his friends and fellow K.A.U. leaders sought in many ways to free him, it was not until April 15, 1961, that Kenyatta was finally released. However, he was banned from participating in the fast-developing movements working for total independence. Again disavowing any connection with the terrorists, Kenyatta said in his first press conference (August 11, 1961), reported by the *London Times*, that "the Corfield Report, which sought to establish such a connection, was a pack of lies and a one-sided document aimed at one purpose—to crush Kenyatta."

Kenyatta was still in prison when the Kenya African National Union, successor to the K.A.U., was formed in March, 1960, and elected him its president. Eventually released, Kenyatta took an active part in new deliberations with the British. Entering the Legislative Council in January, 1962, as leader of the opposition, he led his party to victory in the 1963 elections. On December 11, 1963, at midnight, the new Kenyan flag was raised and Kenyatta became Prime Minister. The next year he became President of the Republic of Kenya.

Known to his people today as *Mzee* (the "Grand Old Man"), Kenyatta has been married for some twenty years to Ngina, the daughter of a Kikuyu chief. They have four children.

Writings: Autobiography and anthropology: *Facing Mount Kenya;* London, Martin Secker & Warburg, 1938; New York, Vintage, Random House, 1962.

Scholarship: *Kenya–Land of Conflict*, London, 1945; *Harambee: The Prime Minister of Kenya's Speeches 1963–1964*, Nairobi and London, Oxford University Press, 1964; *Suffering Without Bitterness: The Founding of the Kenya Nation*, Nairobi, East African Publishing House, 1968.

Biographical/Critical Sources: The New Africans, New York, G. P. Putnam's Sons, 1967; *African Profiles*, Ronald Segal, Baltimore, Penguin, 1963, revised edition.

KGOSITSILE, William Keorapetse
b. 1938, Johannesburg, South Africa.
Poet.

Educated locally, Kgositsile left South Africa while in his early 20's to travel to Dar es Salaam, Tanzania, where he wrote for *Spearhead* magazine. Since 1962 he has been in the United States working on graduate degrees at Lincoln University, the University of New Hampshire, Columbia University, and the New School for Social Research in New York City. He is widely published in poetry journals featuring African and Black American poets, including *Présence Africaine, Transition,* and *The New African Literature.* He published *My Name is Africa* (1971), which, despite its title, mostly concerns the "Black Scene" in the United States, but his work attempts to bring black men everywhere together.

Two earlier volumes of his verse, both published in the U.S., are: *Spirits Unchained: Paeans* and *For Melba: Poems.* He recently has served on the staff of *Black Dialogue Magazine* in New York City.

Writings: Poetry: *My Name is Africa,* New York, Doubleday, 1971; *Spirits Unchained: Paeans*, Detroit, Broadside Press, 1969; *For Melba: Poems*, Chicago, Third World Press, 1970; poems in *Présence Africaine, Transition, The New African Literature.*

KHAKETLA, Bennett Makalo
b. 1913, Makhaleng, Qacha's Nek District, Lesotho.

Khaketla

Southern Sotho poet, playwright, journalist, scholar, teacher.

Bennett Makalo Khaketla, the sixth of seven children of peasant parents, first entered a mission school in 1924 at the age of eleven. Making rapid progress, he graduated five years later with a Standard VI certificate. He then studied at Mariazell Institute, Matatiele, earning his Teacher's Certificate in 1932. That same year he became a teacher at St. Patrick's School, Bloemfontein, and successfully studied for the Junior Division Music Examination from Trinity College, London which he passed with honors, and took the Junior Certificate in 1936.

Resigning his teacher's job in 1939, he worked as a clerk-typist for a few months and then began to study for the Matriculation Examination. He taught at Heilbron, Orange Free State, in 1940 and there met Anthony Muziwakhe Lembede, already noted for his interest in Bantu affairs. Stimulated, Khaketla, through private study, took the B.A. at the University of South Africa in 1942, concentrating in Southern Sotho studies and international affairs. He taught from 1944 to 1946 at Betshabelo High School in Middleburg and from 1946 to 1949 at Bantu High School, Maseru, Lesotho.

Returning to South Africa in 1949, he founded the outspoken journal *Mohlabani* (The Soldier) in 1956 with Ntsu Mohhehle. By this time Khaketla had already begun to take a part in politics aimed at stirring the British Government to take measures protecting the rights of the Africans.

Elected in 1957 to the executive council of the Basutoland African Congress, he quickly was elected Deputy President of the newly changed Congress, now called the Basutoland Congress Party. Respected both by the chiefs and the less traditional Basotho, he was elected a member of the Legislative Council of Lesotho in 1960 and shortly thereafter a member of the Executive Council. On December 29, 1960, he resigned from his party in a quarrel over policy and leadership, and launched his own party, the Basuto Freedom Party, aimed to obtain independence from Great Britain.

Khaketla's first play, *Moshoeshoe le baruti* (Moshoeshoe and the Missionaries), was published in 1947. His later plays were: *Tholoana tsa sethepu* (The Result of Polygamy), 1954, and *Bulane*, 1958, which won first prize in the Southern Sotho group of over 241 manuscripts submitted for Afrikaanse's competition. A fourth play, *Tholoana tsa boikakaso* (The Result of Pride), awaits publication.

His novels are: *Meokho ea thabo* (Tears of Joy) and *Mosali a nkhola* (The Woman Who Hurt Him), published in 1960. He collected one volume of traditional praise songs as *Likenkeng* (A Grab-Bag) and his own verse in *Lipshamate* (Titbits) (1954).

Always interested in the structure and grammar of his native Sotho, Khaketla published the product of his research in the grammar *Sebopheho sa puo* (The Grammar of the [Sotho] Language) in 1951. A second volume intended to be a supplement to the grammar awaits publication as *Thapholiso ea Sesotho* (Sesotho Stories).

Khaketla's wife, Caroline Ntseliseng Khaketla, is also an author, having written two plays and one volume of poetry.

Writings: Plays: *Moshoeshoe le baruti*, Morija, Morija Sesuto Book Depot, 1947, second edition, 1954; *Tholoana tsa sethepu;* Afrikaanse, 1954; *Bulane,* Johannesburg, Afrikaanse Pers-Boekhandel, 1958; *Tholoana tsa boikakaso,* Afrikaanse, 1954.

Novels: *Meokho ea thabo,* Afrikaanse, 1951; *Mosali a nkhola,* Afrikaanse, 1960.

Poetry: *Lipshamate,* Johannesburg, Afrikaanse, 1954, also Bona Press, 1963.

Song: *Likenkeng,* Afrikaanse, n.d.

Grammar: *Sebopheho sa puo,* 1951; *Thapholiso ea Sesotho,* a supplement, in manuscript.

KHAKETLA, Caroline Ntseliseng 'Masechele Ramolahloane
b. ca. 1918, Lesotho.
Southern Sotho novelist, poet.

Caroline Khaketla, wife of the Sesotho writer and statesman Bennett Makalo Khaketla, received her education in local schools. Her first play, *Mosali eo u 'neileng eena* (The Woman You Gave Me), was published in 1956, and she has one play in manuscript, *Mahlopha-a-senya* (Both Good and Bad at The Same Moment), which won the 1954 play competition of the Johannesburg publisher, Afrikaanse Pers-Boekhandel.

Her one volume of poetry, *'Mantsopa,* contains the bitter poem, "Mmalesehlana le Mmamotshwanyane," (Mrs. White and Mrs. Black), which begins:

When I leave, white mama, slaughter the
*   fat steers;*
Glut your man and children, fine meat and
*   juices*
Flowing so that even the dogs get their
*   share,*
And with the extra, make a cargo
For your kindred across the oceans.

But you, dark mama, don't give up;
Someday a great thing will happen
And your eyes will flame up,

When time comes in full course
And the chased bird will peck the off-limits
*   corn.*

(*trans.* R. Everts)

Writings: Plays: *Mosali eo u 'neileng eena,* Morija, Morija Sesuto Book Depot, 1956; *Mahlopha-a-senya,* 1954, unpublished.

Poetry: *'Mantsopa,* Cape Town, Oxford University Press, 1963.

KHUMALO, J. M. (see mention last paragraph NYEMBEZI)

KIBERA, Leonard
b. ca. 1940, Kenya.
Short story writer, novelist, playwright.

With his brother, Samuel Kahiga, Leonard Kibera published eighteen stories in the volume *Potent Ash* (1968). All the stories are dramatic and mostly deal with the days of the "emergency" in the middle 1950's when Kenyans in the so-called Mau-mau revolt sought to throw off British colonial rule.

In 1970, Kibera's first novel appeared, *Voices in the Dark,* a tightly expressed vision of modern post-independence Kenya's tensions and problems. The chapters swing the reader back and forth in time, but the disjointed approach to reality makes the strain of the new Africa all the more compelling.

A short play called *Potent Ash* was published in *New African Literature and the Arts* 2. Based on the short story of the same name, which gave its name to the first volume of stories he published, the play won third prize in the B.B.C. African Drama Contest in 1967, and was produced in June, 1967, in London on the B.B.C.'s African Service.

Writings: Short stories: *Potent Ash,* Nairobi, East African Publishing House, 1968.

Story: "The Spider Web," Paris, *Présence Africaine,* 2nd trimester, 1972.

Novel: *Voices in the Dark,* Nairobi, East African Publishing House, 1970.

Play: *Potent Ash,* in *New African Literature and the Arts* 2, Joseph Okpaku, editor, New York, Thomas Y. Crowell, 1968, 1970.

KIMBUGWE, Henry S. (see SERUMA, Eneriko)

KIMENYE, Barbara
b. ca. 1940, Uganda.
Short story writer, journalist.

Locally educated, Miss Kimenye is now a widely-known columnist for a Nairobi newspaper. Her three volumes of short stories are: *Kalasanda,* published in 1965; *Kalasanda Revisited* (1966); and *The Smugglers.* Her story, "The Winner," included in her first volume, appears in Neville Denny's *Pan African Short Stories.*

Writings: Short stories: *Kalasanda,* London and New York, Oxford University Press, 1965; *Kalasanda Revisited,* Oxford and New York, Oxford University Press, 1966; *The Smugglers,* London, Nelson, 1966, 1968; "The Winner," in *Pan African Short Stories,* Neville Denny, editor, London, Nelson, 1965.

KINYANJUI, Peter
b. ca. 1940, Kenya.
Playwright.

Educated in Kenya, Kinyanjui went on to Makerere University College in Kam-

pala, Uganda, for a B.A. in English in 1965. Later he went to the United States and took an M.A. at Syracuse University in New York State in 1967. He has recently been staff tutor at the Institute of Adult Studies, University College, Nairobi. Since his college days he has been active in writing, producing, and performing in plays.

His play, *Third Party Insurance,* concerns a silly girl who, pregnant by her soldier-lover, finds safety and honor in marriage with the less-than-heroic schoolteacher who long has loved her silently and from a distance. Though similar to Soyinka's more interesting and well-done *The Lion and the Jewel,* Kinyanjui's work has some freshness and no doubt would draw many laughs from a rural audience in Kenya. The play, which is in Cook and Lee's *Short East African Plays,* was first performed by the Makerere Travelling Theatre in Kampala, Uganda, in 1965.

Writings: Play: *Third Party Insurance,* in *Short East African Plays,* Cook and Lee, editors, Nairobi, London, Heinemann, 1968.

KIRONDE, Erisa
b. ca. 1940, Uganda.
Playwright.

Erisa Kironde took his schooling, including college-level study, at home to prepare himself to be a teacher. Recently, however, he has been working for the central electrical works in Kampala, Uganda. He has been active in assisting in the writing and producing of locally-composed plays and has also helped get some of them published. His play, *The Trick,* an Africanization of the Irish playwright J. M. Synge's *The Shadow of the Glen,* is successful. It has become completely naturalized as an Ugandan work, without any wooden or derivative aspects. Only Synge's general psychology and thematic structure remain and these are organically absorbed in the tissue of the new play. The work has been published in Cook and Lee's *Short East African Plays in English.* Julius Nyerere's adaptation of Shakespeare's *Julius Caesar* into an African language is an outstanding example of what Kironde has sought to do in this difficult area. He has also done a volume, *Four Plays for School* (1969).

Writings: Play: *The Trick,* in *Short East African Plays in English,* Nairobi, London, Heinemann, 1968; *Four Plays for School,* Kampala, Uganda Publishing House, 1967.

KITEREZA, Aniceti
b. ca. 1900, Bukerebe Island,
northwestern Tanzania.
Kikerebe-language novelist,
collector of folklore, scholar,
teacher (also uses Swahili).

After primary schooling at the Catholic mission school on the island of Bukerebe (Ukerewe) where he still lives, Kitereza went on to a seminary at Bukoba, a northwestern port on Lake Victoria where his teachers were Dutch, French, and German priests of the order of White Fathers. After one year teaching at the Bukerebe school in 1919, he worked for two decades, 1919–1939, for an Italian merchant, Signor Bonini at Mwanza. For the next five or six years Kitereza worked with Father Simard, a Canadian, collecting the stories and poetry and other traditional materials of the area. Descendant of the Sese leadership group of the once all-powerful Silanga clan, and grandson of Machunda (ca. 1835–1869), the *omukama,* or Chief, of Bukerebe, Kitereza, a devout Christian, has nontheless sought to preserve the ancient values of the mixed populations of the island and the sometimes conflicting customs of the Silangi, Jita, Kara, and Subuma peoples who have come into the area over the centuries.

Accordingly, he has concentrated on the practices and ideas reaching back to his grandfather's period, hoping to instill "pride in the common traditions of all Kerebe" by his works primarily designed for students at the local school. At first Kitereza, encouraged by Father Simard, sought merely accurate description and cataloguing of local folklore, but urged to do more, he began to weave stories, poems, observations, riddles, and songs into a consecutive narrative. The novel, *Bwana Myombekere na Bibi Bugonoka na Ntulanalwo,* was the result. Some 300 pages in the original, single-spaced typescript, it was the first work ever composed in Kikerebe in long, narrative form. Completed in 1945, Father

Simard planned to translate the work into French during a sabbatical in Canada but he could not finish the task and he was unable to find a publisher for an extensive work in a language of small diffusion. At Simard's death in 1952 or thereabouts there seemed little hope the work would ever see print.

Finally, at the age of 72, and after 15 months of work hampered by severe rheumatism of the hands and feet, Kitereza completed a new version in Kiswahili which, hopefully, would have a greater audience and could be rendered into English with less difficulty. Heinemann is preparing an English edition of *Bwana* for release in its African Writers Series and there is a possibility of a Swahili version, though not the cheap school text envisioned three decades ago by the author. English readers will find the work divided into two parts, *Bwana Myombekere na Bibi Bugonoka* (A Man and His Wife) which deals with village law and the various relationships governing social roles in the community, including duties and rights of husbands and wives; and *Ntulanalwo na Bulihwali* (The Children—or, A Boy—and a Girl) which deals with the new generation and its need to learn the wisdom of the past.

Writings: Novel: *Bibi Bugonoka na Ntulanalwo*, in Kikerebe manuscript, also called *Bwana Myombekere na Bibi Bugonoka na Ntulanalwo*, translated into Swahili by the author and being prepared for publication in English by Heinemann, London. An extract from the novel, in English, appears in *Natural History* as "How Men and Women Came to Live Together," Volume 79, 1970, with introduction and editing by Charlotte and Gerald Hartwig.

Biographical/Critical Source: Charlotte M. and Gerald W. Hartwig, "Aniceti Kitereza: A Kerebe Novelist," *Research in African Literature,* African and Afro-American Research Institute, The University of Texas, III, 3 (Fall 1972).

KOFFI, Raphaël Atta
b. ca. 1935, Ivory Coast.
Novelist, playwright.

In 1961, Koffi published his first work, a novel, *Les dernières paroles de Koime* (The Last Words of Koime). Eight years later, his television play, *Le trône d'or* (The Golden Stool), was published in Paris by Office de Radiodiffusion-Télévision Française.

Writings: Novel: *Les dernières paroles de Koime,* Paris, Debresse, 1961.
Television play: *Le trône d'or,* Paris. the Office de Radiodiffusion-Télévision Française, 1969.

KOMEY, Ellis Ayetey
b. 1927, Accra, Ghana; d. 1972.
Poet, editor.

Komey was educated in local schools and at Accra Academy. He has served as the African editor of the review *Flamingo,* and his poetry has appeared in *Black Orpheus, West African Review* and in Moore and Beier's *Modern Poetry from Africa.* He helped edit a recent collection of African short stories with Ezekiel Mphahlele, *Modern African Stories.* Most recently, six of his poems, "The Change," "Oblivion," "Lost Sanity," "Acceptance," "Domination," and "Farewell to Europe," appeared in *Messages: Poems from Ghana.* His article, "Wanted: Creative Writers," appeared in the *West African Review* of November, 1961.

Writings: Poetry in *Messages: Poems from Ghana*, London, Heinemann, 1971; poems in *Black Orpheus; West African Review; Modern Poetry from Africa*, revised edition, London, Baltimore, Penguin, 1968.

Article: "Wanted: Creative Writers" in *West African Review*, London, November, 1961.

KONADU, Samuel Asare (also pseudonyms BEDIAKO, Kwabena Asare and ASARE, Konadu)
b. 1932, Asamang, Ashanti, central Ghana.
Novelist, short story writer.

Educated in local primary schools, Konadu attended Abuakwa State College in Southern Ghana and studied journalism in London and Strasbourg from 1956 to 1957 on a government scholarship. He began work for the Ghana Information Service as a reporter in 1951, worked for the Gold Coast Broadcasting Service, and later joined the Ghana News Agency. He has also been a reporter on several government newspapers and has traveled widely in Africa and Europe.

Since 1963 he has devoted himself to researching traditional customs and in writing novels. He now owns a publishing firm, Anowuo Publications, which turn out his own works. They deal mostly with village life in rural Ghana. The books are in unsophisticated English, but, designed for the mass audience, they offer more information and analysis of contemporary dilemmas than does the popular press. His short stories,

too, are mostly concerned with the local Ghanaian customs and the problems of country folk.

His works include: *A Woman in Her Prime* which relates the troubles of a childless woman; *Ordained By the Oracle*, the story of a man who begins to doubt the traditional customs of his people; *Come back Dora!* which is, in Konadu's own words, about the hero Boateng's "intimate confessions, . . . pity, duty and the shattering impact of the traditional custodians of their culture who would stop at nothing to see that Boateng is taken through the rituals, . . ."; and *Shadow of wealth* which dramatizes the corruption and power plays in high places in the Ghanaian government. According to Konadu, this work has sold 30,000 copies in two years. He has four other novels, including *Wizard of Asamang, The lawyer who bungled his life* and *Night Watchers of Korlebu*.

Under the pen-name of Kwabena Asare Bediako, Konadu has also published many other little novels for the popular market of new English readers. Published by Anowuo Educational Publications, also, they include *Don't leave me MERCY*, first issued in May, 1966, and reprinted in June in 15,000 additional copies, and *A husband for Esi Ellua*, 1967.

The earlier work begins:
Mercy Birago tied the tuft of hair in a little handkerchief and walked across the row of compound houses into the street. It was nine o'clock in the evening and time to see the medicine man who had promised to prepare her a charm to "turn her husband's head." She looked around and stepped into the road.

The novel's red cover offers this information: "*Echoes (sic) from Owosu's marriage life. Richly entertaining and educative.*" The book's many trials for James Owosu and Mercy Birago in the marriage bonds serves as a written "marital counsellor" to the reader presumably equally tried by spouse and in-laws.

Writings: Novels: *Wizard of Asamang*, Accra, Waterville Publishing, 1964; *The lawyer who bungled his life*, Accra, Waterville Publishing, 1965; *Come Back Dora!*, 1966; *Shadow of wealth*, 1966; *A Woman in Her Prime*. 1967; *Night Watchers of Korlebu*, 1968; these four in Accra, Anuwuo Publications. Novels published under the name Kwabena Asare BEDIAKO: *Don't leave me MERCY*, 1966, and *A husband for Esi Ellua*, 1967, both Accra, Anowuo.

KONE, Maurice
b. 1932, Ivory Coast.
Poet, novelist.

Born to a Lebanese father and an Ivorian mother, Koné entered school at nine, and after many interruptions, he finished primary school in 1961. He worked in many jobs in Bouaké and Abidjan, as apprentice mechanic, cargreaser, plumber, ambulant bread salesman and boxer. He finally obtained a stable job in the City Hall of Abidjan. He began working in television in June, 1964, where his work won a second prize for Ivorian poetry that same year.

Koné captured his early life in the Ivory Coast in his autobiographical novel of 1963, *Le jeune homme de Bouaké* (The Young Man from Bouaké).

His early poetry was collected in the volume *La guirlande des verbes* (A Garden of Words), 1961, and later reprinted along with poems by Basile-Juléat Fouda, Pierre Bamboté, Jean-Paul Nyunai, Job Nganthojeff, and Richard G. Dogbeh-David in one collection. His

second volume was *Au bout du petit matin* (At the Start of the Morning), 1962, which won the first prize for Ivorian poetry in 1963, and his most recent was *Au seuil du crépuscule* (At the Threshold of Evening), 1965.

Two of his poems, a letter, and a autobiographical sketch appeared in *Poésie Vivante*.

Writings: Novel: *Le jeune homme de Bouaké*, Paris, Grassin, 1963.

Poetry: *La guirlande des verbes*, Paris, Grassin, 1961; republished Kraus Reprint, Nendeln, Liechtenstein, in *African Poems in French*, 1971; *Au bout du petit matin*. Bordeaux, Germain, 1962; *Au seuil du crépuscule*, Rodez, Subervie, 1965; two poems in *Poésie Vivante* (Sept.-Oct. 1965).

KOUADIO-TIACOH, Gabriel
b. ca. 1920, Ivory Coast.
Story-teller, collector of legends and tales.

In *La Légende de N'zi le Grand, Guerrier d'Afrique*, Kouadio-Tiacoh retells the Akan-Ashanti story of the great hero N'zi, who, though born in slavery, grew to be a powerful soldier who saved his adopted people. The Baoulé of the modern Ivory Coast have also preserved this legend because an Akan Queen, in exile from the Akan empire of the 16th century, took refuge with the Baoulé and helped found a new empire called N'Zipri, or "the tribe of N'zi the great."

The little work of 99 pages is extremely well illustrated with original drawings by M. Abauzet. The work has been adapted and simplified in this version for a French school reader for African children by Helène Gauvenet.

Writings: Folk tale: *La Legende de N'zi le Grand, Guerrier d'Afrique,* Paris, Didier, 1967; illustrated by M. Abauzet.

KOUYATE, Seydou (see BADIAN, Seydou Kouyaté)

KUMALO, Peter E. (now CLARKE, Peter E.)
b. 1929, South Africa.
Short story writer, painter, poet.

Kumalo works as a manual laborer on the docks of Simon's Town, Cape Province, South Africa, and writes in his free hours. Twice he has won *DRUM* magazine's short story contest. He is represented in Langston Hughes' *An African Treasury* with "Death in the Sun," one of his stories from *DRUM* magazine, and the poem, "Play Song."

Writings: Story: "Death in the Sun," and other stories in *DRUM* Magazine.
    Poem: "Play Song," in *An African Treasury,* Langston Hughes, editor, New York, Crown, 1960.

KUNENE, A. A. S. (see mention last paragraph NYEMBEZI)

KUNENE, Mazisi Raymond
b. 1930, Durban, South Africa.
Zulu poet, playwright.

Kunene took his M.A. at Natal University with a study of Zulu poets, "An Analytical Survey of Zulu Poetry both Traditional and Modern." He also studied at the School of Oriental and African Studies, University of London in 1959. Actively engaged in political work, he has written an epic, still unpub-

lished, which recaptures the spirit and cosmology of the Zulu nation. He has also written several plays and many poems in Zulu, some of which he has translated into English. He won the Bantu Literary Competition in 1956 and is represented in various South African journals and in Moore and Beier's *Modern Poetry from Africa, New Sum of Poetry from the Negro World,* and Ezekiel Mphahlele's *African Writing Today.*

In 1970, Kunene published a collection, *Zulu Poems,* which includes his recreation in English of his own Zulu poems. His introduction is not only a fine introduction to his poetry and the problem of translation but extremely useful for an understanding of some aspects of the vernacular poetry of the Zulu people. The poems deal with a wide range of subjects, including peace and war, the poet's role in traditional and modern Zulu society, and Joan Baez, the popular American folk singer. If the poems must be characterized in one phrase, possibly the term Yeatsian suggests something of Kunene's spareness yet occasional lyrical "spring." In the poem "To Prince Magena," there are the lines:

> *In that moment of your downfall*
> *You were as beautiful as red iron thongs.*
> *You were like an ancestral spirit,*
> *Your eyes sparked with lightning*

In the three next verses he recalls the once mighty chief's pride and noisy followers but the poem ends:

> *Then I knew*
> *Even the weeds that grow in the field*
> *Flower and emit their scent,*
> *Like you, you who are the shell of your*
> *power.*

Writings: Poetry: *Zulu Poems,* London, André Deutsch, 1970; poems in *Modern Poetry from Africa,* Moore and Beier, editors, revised edition, London, Penguin, 1968; *New Sum of Poetry from the Negro World,* Présence Africaine, Volume 57, 1966; *African Writing Today,* London, Penguin, 1967.

KUPONA, Mwana (see MWANA, Kupona)

KYEI, Kojo Gyinaye
b. 1932, Ghana.
Poet, painter, architect.

Kyei completed his university studies in the United States, including training as an architect, and published his first poetry in 1963 in *Day Dreaming and Experience; some original poems.* He had an exhibition of his paintings in London in 1968 where he is presently living and continuing his sculptural work in wood. In 1969 his second book of poetry, *The Lone Voice,* appeared. He is well represented by 11 poems in *Messages: Poems from Ghana,* many of them reflecting his experiences in America, including his days in the southern state of Mississippi.

Writings: Poetry: *Day Dreaming and Experience: some original poems,* Lawrence, Kansas, University of Kansas, 1963, *The Lone Voice,* Accra, Ghana Universities Press, 1969; poems in *Messages: Poems from Ghana,* London, Heinemann, 1971.

L

LADIPO, Duro
b. ca. 1930, Yoruba-land, Nigeria.
Yoruba-language playwright,
producer, actor.

After receiving his primary education in local schools through form six, Ladipo became an elementary school teacher for several years. Working under his headmaster, Alex Peters, he developed an interest in Yoruba dance-drama, and followed Peters north to Kaduna where he acted in the latter's amateur Yoruba dramatic presentations.

Ladipo returned to his native Oshogbo in 1956 to teach. In 1960 he picked up his interest in music and drama, composed music for All Saints' Church in Oshogbo, and then started to write plays for production by children and young teachers-in-training. In 1962, inspired by the example of the Mbari Club at Ibadan started by Ulli Beier, Wole Soyinka and others, he helped found the Mbari Mbayo Club in Oshogbo. His play, *Oba Moro*, was first produced on the day the group was founded, March 17, 1962. *Oba Koso* was presented on the first anniversary of the founding in 1963, and *Oba Waja* on the same day in 1964. The three plays have become classics of the Yoruba stage and

have introduced Yoruba dramatic ideas and conventions to a world audience through a growing list of international productions and/or literary discussion and criticism.

Ladipo has sought to bring both traditional and adapted dance-drama to the people in Oshogbo and elsewhere by performing plays on specially equipped wagon-stages. Dance and music function organically in his work, as a dramatic "voice" and not merely to accompany or to provide atmosphere.

He has composed many Yoruba folk operas and staged many of them himself. Among the favorites are: *Enia Sora* (The Unreliable), a story of royal love; and the above mentioned: *Oba Kosa* (The King Does Not Hang), a dramatization of the battle between two leaders of the army of the Raingod, Shango, which includes the suicide by hanging of the King who can no longer control his generals; and *Oba Moro* (The Ghost King). Possibly his best-known and most frequently played work is *Oba Waja* (The King is Dead) which laments the loss of the older patterns of Yoruba life.

Ladipo's production of *Eda*, a Yoruba adaptation by Obotunde Ijimere of the European medieval *Everyman*, is proof that Nigerian drama can exploit the

193

comic form with "borrowed" substance. *Oba Kosa* was presented at the Berlin Theatre and Music Festival in September, 1964, and was acclaimed, along with a Stravinsky concert and Jean Genet's *The Blacks*, as one of the major attractions. In the late 1960's, Ladipo toured Europe and Israel with his Yoruba theatrical group, performing *Eda* and *Oba Koso* and appearing at the Commonwealth Festival.

Mbari Press has published translations-adaptations by Ulli Beier of *Oba Koso, Oba Moro,* and *Oba Waja* in *Three Yoruba Plays.* (These three plays are also written as Oba Kò So, Oba M'Orò, and Obá W'Ajà.) Beier's volume, *Three Nigerian Plays,* offers Ladipo's *Moremi, The Scheme* by Wale Ogunyemi, and *Born with Fire on His Head* by Obotunde Ijimere, a former member of Ladipo's theatre group.

Writings: Plays: *Oba Koso, Oba Moro, Oba Waja,* in *Three Yoruba Plays,* English adaptation by Ulli Beier, Ibadan, Mbari Press, 1964; *Moremi,* in *Three Nigerian Plays,* London, Longmans, 1967; *Enia Soro,* unpublished. *Oba Koso* was transcribed and translated (from a tape of a live performance recorded by the musicologist, Curt Wittig) by the American scholar, R. G. Armstrong and the Nigerian scholars, Robert L. Awijoola and Val Olayemi. They produced texts in both Yoruba and English in mimeograph at the University of Ibadan's Institute of African Studies in 1968. Earlier, in 1966, Armstrong published *Selections from Oba Koso,* providing English excerpts of the most interesting parts of the long Yoruba original published in an 147 page, illustrated edition, Lagos, 1970.

LA GUMA, Alex
b. February 20, 1925, Cape Town, South Africa.
Short story writer, novelist.

Alex La Guma is the son of a former president of the South African Coloured Peoples' Congress, Jimmy La Guma. Alex La Guma was at one time a coloured member of the Cape Town City Council, but was imprisoned for his struggles against apartheid and accused in the South African "Treason Trials." He was for years confined to his house in Athlone, Cape Town, and later imprisoned and spent much time in solitary confinement. He finally managed to go to London with his family where he now resides.

Though he had briefly worked for a Cape Town newspaper, his real writing dates from his incarceration, for he produced three novels in those years: *A Walk in the Night* (1962), *And a Threefold Cord* (Berlin, 1964) and *The Stone Country* (1967). He may not be quoted or published in South Africa. He is represented in Richard Rive's *Quartet* which features his work and that of three other South African writers. From 1960–62 he worked on the journal *New Age*.

Black Orpheus magazine has published two stories: "A Glass of Wine" and "Slipper Satin," both of which concern mixed marriage in South Africa. *Africa South* published "Out of Darkness," a story of a long-term prisoner "Old Cockroach" who committed a murder because of the tensions of interracial love. His story, "Tattoo Marks and Tails," is a similar tale of prison life. La Guma's symbolic tale, "Blankets," published in *African Writing Today*, focuses on the various blankets under which the protagonist Choker must sleep. Choker is first seen trying to sleep under a vermin-ridden rag, then under a used torn blanket, and finally, as he lies dying in a hospital, he finds peace of a sort under a clean coverlet. The hopeless poverty and violence of life in the apartheid slums of South Africa is starkly told in this brief story.

La Guma's novelette, *A Walk in the Night*, once again tells a tale of interracial love and violence leading to murder. It is told in harsh, spare language which "celebrates" the cruelty of night and the city in which African man can find no peace. With the addition of short stories, this 90-page novelette in its first

edition from the Mbari Press, saw a second edition as *A Walk in the Night and Other Stories* in 1967 in London.

The Stone Country deals with the brutal day by day life in South African jails. All jails may be brutal, but the men in La Guma's novel are doubly damned, for as blacks or Kaffirs they are doomed to struggle against oppression and cruelty both in and out of prison. The author dedicated his work to "the daily average of 70,351 prisoners in South African gaols in 1964."

Writings: Novels: *A Walk in the Night,* Mbari Press, Ibadan, 1962; *A Walk in the Night and Other Stories,* London, Heinemann, 1967; *And a Threefold Cord,* Berlin, Seven Seas, 1964; *The Stone Country,* Berlin, Seven Seas, 1967. Stories: "A Glass of Wine," "Slipper Satin," "Tattoo Marks and Tails," in *Black Orpheus,* Ibadan; "Out of Darkness" in *Africa South;* "Blankets" in *African Writing Today,* Ezekiel Mphahlele, editor, London, Penguin, 1967; also in *Quartet: New Voices from South Africa,* New York, Crown Publishers, 1963, and London, Heinemann, 1965, 1968 (La Guma edited this volume).

Biographical/Critical Sources: Lewis Nkosi, "Alex La Guma—the Man and His Work," *South Africa: Information and Analysis,* No. 59, special: South African Authors, Paris, January, 1968.

LALUAH, Aquah (see CASELY-HAYFORD, Gladys)

LARA FILHO, Ernesto (also Pires Barreto de Lara Filho)
b. 1932, Angola.
Poet, journalist.

Lara Filho

Lara Filho attended university in Portugal and is a trained agronomist. He has, however, worked for a period as a journalist in Angola. He has published one volume of poems, *Picada de Marimbondo* (The Sting of Marimbondo).

Writings: Poetry: *Picada de Marimbondo,* Nova Lisboa, Angola, Publicações Bailundo, 1961.

LATINO, Juan (or LATINUS, Ioannes)
b. ca. 1516, probably Guinea;
d. Spain, 1606.
Poet, scholar (employed Latin).

Brought to Spain as a child of 12, Juan Latino and his mother, both slaves, worked in the house of Doña Elvira, the daughter of Spain's most famous general at that time, Gonzalo Fernández, "el gran Capitán." Moving from Baena to Granada with Doña Elvira a few years later, Juan's job was to carry the school books of her son, and his young master, Don Gonzalo Fernández, six years old at that time. Juan, then 14, began to read the books himself, joined in the lessons, and showing much promise, he became the young Don Gonzalo's tutor, learning Latin and Greek at the Cathedral School with him and eventually attending the University of Granada with his young companion.

Renouncing his slave name of Juan de Sessa, he named himself Juan Latino, taking the B.A. in 1546. Along with his studies in classical literature he became an excellent player of the organ, guitar and lute.

His romantic life was equally dramatic, for, while teaching Latin to Doña Ana, daughter of Don Carlobal, they fell in love, as the story has it, while conjugating *amo, amos, amat, amamus.* Doña Ana bore a daughter, Juana, in 1549. The couple subsequently married and had three more children in 1552, 1556, and 1559.

Juan Latino became a professor at Granada University in 1557 and in 1565 delivered the Latin address to open the academic year, the highest honor a professor could be given. In 1569, Don Juan of Austria, soon to be victor against the Turks at Lepanto, joined Juan Latino and his now grown friend, Don Gonzalo, the fourth Duke of Sessa. The three played cards and became well-acquainted. After the Battle of Lepanto, Juan Latino composed his famous poem, *Austrias,* in Latin to celebrate Don Juan's victory over the Turks. Other Latin works appeared in 1573, 1576 and 1585. He resigned his academic post for health reasons at the age of 70 in 1586. He is believed to have died some time in his ninetieth year, about 1606.

Juan's Latin was extremely refined, full of clever sophistries and linguistic plays, so much so that Cervantes memorialized him in *Don Quixote.* More important possibly are these lines in which he vigorously rejects racial stereotypes:

Quod si nostra tuis facies Rex nigra minis
/tris
Displicet, Aethiopum non placet alba viris.

If our black face, O King, seems ugly to
/your ministers,
Black men find your egg-white faces equally
/so.

On his tombstone, beneath which he lies with his beloved Doña Ana, is his own Latin inscription stating his pride in his scholarship, oratorical abilities, teaching, his poem on Don Juan of Austria, his wife and his being "Filius Aethiopum, prolesque nigerrima patrum," ("Ethiopia's offspring and deep black son of African ancestors.")

Writings: Poem: "Austrias" which begins, "Ad catholicum pariter et invictissimum Philippum dei gratia hispaniarum regem, de foelicissima . . . ," Granada, Hugo de Mena, 1573.

Biographical/Critical Sources: Valaurez B. Spratlin, *Juan Latino, Slave and Humanist,* New York, Spinner Press, 1938; Janheinz Jahn, *New-African Literature,* London, Faber and Faber, 1968; New York, Grove Press, 1969.

LAYE, Camara (The family name is Kamara; Laye is his personal name)
b. January 1, 1928, Kouroussa, Guinea.
Novelist, short story writer.

Considered one of the most important of the francophone novelists from Africa, Camara Laye's first work, *L'enfant noir,* 1953, quickly established him as the leader of the new African literature. The eldest son of the twelve children of Kamara Komady, a goldsmith, and Daman Sadan, the daughter of a goldsmith, Laye early became aware of the beauties and mysteries of his father's craft. To the forge came all the villagers at one time or another, and the father, able to establish strange empathies with bird and beast, lived in a world that was fast receding under the impact of Western ways. This old life, recalled nostalgically but not sentimentally in the novel, showed that a new day was dawning for African expression. Rendered into English as *The Dark Child* in 1955, the work became, with Chinua Achebe's first novel, *Things Fall Apart,* standard fare for African literature and culture courses.

Born in Kouroussa in Upper Guinea, in the center of the Malinké country along the Niger River, where his people were the inheritors to some extent of the ancient culture of the old empires of Ghana, Mali, and Songhai, Laye writes with the consciousness of a rich and proud past. His work does not bespeak the nervous and embittered seeking for roots of a writer such as David Diop of Senegal, who, born and reared in Bordeaux, France, had to struggle to recapture his past. Nor has Laye felt the pull of doctrinaire communism as the solution to his peoples' colonial or postcolonial position. Instead, he observes his native land and Africa in general with undogmatic eyes. Not anti-colonial enough, however, for some, his first work was condemned as a wistful exercise of nostalgia, or even as an apology for French colonialism.

197

Although his family was Islamic, his Father's trade, that of gold smith, meant some of the old animist beliefs still tinged the workshop and the lives of the family. Each metal had its soul and there were special procedures and prayers for the working of the material in the glowing hearth. Though early subjected to the teachings of a "Karamoko," or Islamic religious teacher, and pressured into memorizing Koranic verses, Laye still felt the pull of the ancient days when powers and spirits were sensed everywhere. Both of Laye's first two novels are full of this mysterious impression of a spirit world enclosing the everyday world.

Laye's formal French education began in local schools and he then went on to the Collège Poiret in Conakry, a technical high school. He finished first in his class and with the grudging approval of his parents left for France on a government scholarship for advanced training in engineering in Paris. Assigned to the Automobile Mechanical School at Argenteuil, he found the weather horribly cold and the European world, including Paris, strange in the extreme. Finishing with a Professional Certificate but with a horror of the profession, he sought relief and began a new line of study in Paris with his own resources. Eight months of struggling as a self-supporting student at night school at the Conservatoire des Arts et Metiers was supported by part-time work in the brawling market, Les Halles. Forced by poverty to seek full-time employment, he secured a job as a "specialized" worker in a Simca factory in the industrial suburbs outside Paris. He continued as best he could with his studies, and moved to other jobs, but what sustained him in these difficult days was his writing. Locked in his cold, bare room, he captured on paper the sunshine, the great flame trees, the waterfalls, and green hills of his native Guinea.

Moving to the Technical School for Aeronautics and Automotive Construction to prepare for the examination in engineering, he continued with his writing, producing the The African Child in the fall of 1953 and winning the important award, *Prix Charles Veillon,* in 1954. Stimulated by this unexpected success and the financial support which came with it, Laye produced in 1954 what he termed a Kafkaian novel, his *Le regard du roi (The Radiance of the King* in James Kirkup's translation).

L'enfant noir recounts his early memories at the age of four or five and follows his gradual maturation and estrangement from his village as he receives a French education. By the book's end, as he heads off to Paris, he knows what he has grown away from but he can do no more than regret. There is a new world for him and Africa and it must be entered. There are many vivid scenes in the novel but one of the finest is the harvest of wheat in December when "the whole world is in flower and the air is sweet . . ." and the men "would line up at the edge, naked to the loins, their sickles at the ready." This Africa has not gone, nor is it likely to for a long time and Laye makes it glow before us.

The second novel, *Le regard du roi,* is a Kafkaian wandering of a white Ishmael in the heart of the burning, pungent Africa of the Sudan. Clarence, a starveling Frenchman adrift in a black world, sifts downward in poverty and pain, to the point where he is used as a slave-stud in the harem of a jaded husband. Clarence in the last pages of the work falls into the arms of the boy king, a gesture that spells his total surrender to the most naked of feelings, love. Stripped of his European superiority, of his pride, of his body, of his will, and totally alone, he is absorbed into the mystical black king to perish, or to be reborn a new man.

Laye's successes with these two novels did not go unnoticed and in 1955 he was named Attaché at the Ministry of Youth in Paris, but he soon left that post and his tiny apartment on the rue Molière to return to Guinea in 1956. For almost two years he was employed in a technical capacity by the French colonial regime. In 1958, with the establishment of an independent Guinea, Laye was sent to a number of African countries including Liberia and Ghana on diplomatic missions. Returning to Guinea he was named Director of the Study and Research Center in the Ministry of Information in Conakry. Laye was frequently outside the capital and had to leave off writing his draft of a work tentatively named, after Aimé Cesairés poem, translated as *Return to One's Native Country.*

He did succeed in publishing the rather obscure short story, "The Eyes of the Statue," in 1959. Gerald Moore, whose chapter on Laye in *Seven African Authors* (1962) is good though inaccurate in some biographical and bibliographical details, criticizes the story as having a narrative "so baffling that we can get no further." He allows for the possibility that the story in its English translation is cliché ridden and otherwise wooden, but he argues, still, that it seems "a mistake to write an entire story in this somewhat consciously mysterious manner. The mind is nowhere diverted, as it is by the sinister comedy of the trial or many other episodes in *The Radiance of the King.*" He then compares the story to the unsuccessful, in his opinion,

episode of the Fish Women in that novel, "which is the least satisfactory in the whole book."

Laye himself was undergoing a traumatic experience in Guinea, along with other young intellectuals who had hoped independence would mean greater personal freedom. The reverse was true. Laye fell into disfavor with President Sekou Touré, and from 1960 on he was more or less under house arrest and unable to travel or work effectively. In the summer of 1964 he became poisoned from eating tainted meat and his body swollen, he sought an exit visa to seek an emergency cure. The American Public Affairs Officer sought to have him flown to the Leahy Clinic in Boston, but President Touré would not permit him to leave the country. In 1965 he took advantage of a rare opportunity and left the country with his wife and four children.

Because of his experiences, his long promised work, *Return,* turned out to be the bitter, nightmarish *Dramouss,* called *A Dream of Africa* in translation. This novel brings the first person narrator back to his homeland after six years in Europe to find a savage political party in complete control, with the new rulers heedless of both African traditional values and the few French values which might serve the new country. Most French-writing Africans in their attacks choose to invent names and a mythical history and geography for their natal countries. Not so, Camara Laye. He calls his country Guinea and though he does not employ actual politicians' names, he dubs the dictator-president of his nightmare Guinea the Big Brute possibly a borrowing from George Orwell's Big Brother in *1984.* Coming down from a dream flight, Fatoman the narrator declares:

Yet everything was somewhat different from all I had formerly known. It was Samakoro, but the men and women living there were less numerous than when I had left the place ... Many of them must have run away to escape persecution and famine. After all, did not Samakoro now form an integral part of the 'Big Brute's' domain? And did not the Big Brute amuse himself by starving and terrorizing his subjects?

At novel's end, Fatoman has his hut burned around his ears because he has summoned up the powers of the goddess Dramouss while bedded with his wife, Marie. Jealous, the goddess has given him feverish dreams and then chastened him with flames. Reality and dreams are interchangeable in this book and though there is an expressed hope in the last pages that things will finally be honest and peaceful in Guinea, life and sleep there are both nightmares.

Gerald Moore ended his study of Laye with "It is now six years since Camara Laye's last book *(Radiance,* 1954) and it seems unlikely that he will return to the symbolical manner, or to the nostalgic lyricism of *The Dark Child....* Or the exciting and catastrophic events of contemporary Africa may force him to abandon the disengaged and apolitical manner of his books so far, for he is rumoured to have become deeply interested in Guinea's political revolution." There is some remarkable prescience in Moore's comment and a very ironic inaccuracy. Laye still is a-political in the sense that he neither wishes a leadership role nor involves himself in plots. Nonetheless, he has earned President Touré's enmity.

In an unusual forward to *Dramouss* Laye stated he writes "in order that African ways of thinking ... may be a new force—not aggressive, but fruitful." In an interview in the Abidjan (Ivory Coast) newspaper *Fraternité–Matin* Laye was asked, "Your last novel is not totally a work of fiction. Dramouss, that dream-phantom who terrorized Guinea, seems to resemble certain personages well and clearly?" Laye replied " ... fiction and reality are not incompatible things; rather, they are the two faces of the same truth. Each complements the other, each clarifies the other."

This last work, unequivocal as it is about the author's horror at the situation in Guinea, did not imply Laye was joining other Guineans in exile in sterile anger. Living for a time in the Ivory Coast and more recently in Senegal, he has not become embittered or a carping critic of the Touré regime, though he wrote a few articles for several African journals, including *Dakar–Matin* (formerly *Le Soleil)* which made his philosophical and personal position clear.

He has been in exile since 1965 and now works with the Dakar–based Institut Francais d'Afrique Noire (I.F.A.N.), collecting and editing the folk tales and songs of his Malinké people. Recently he published an article, "The Black Man and Art," in the Autumn, 1970 issue of *African Arts.* Laye's personal tragedy these days is his wife's imprisonment in Conakry, Guinea. She returned to Conakry by air with the visiting Senegalese football team in 1970 to visit her ill mother, was seized in the autumn of 1970, and has been incarcerated as an enemy of the state ever since.

Indeed, *Dramouss* was neither idle fancy nor hysteria. Today Laye, an ill man, lives in Dakar, with his four children.

Writings: Novels: *L'enfant noir,* Paris, Plon, 1953; as *The Dark Child* in translation by James Kirkup, London, Collins,

1955; as *The African Child,* also Collins, (Fontana books) 1959; as *The Dark Child,* translated by James Kirkup, Ernest Jones, Elaine Gottlieb, New York, Noonday Press, 1954; as *The African Child,* New York, Farrar, Straus and Giroux, 1969; *Le regard du roi,* Paris, Plon, 1954, as *The Radiance of the King* in James Kirkup's translation, London, Collins, 1956; Collins' Fontana Books, 1965; and New York, Collier Books-Macmillan, 1965; *Dramouss,* Paris, Plon, 1966; as *A Dream of Africa* in Kirkup's translation, London, Collins, 1968.

Story: "The Eyes of the Statue," (translation of French title) in *Présence Africaine,* No. 5, 1959.

Interview: in *Fraternité–Matin,* Abidjan, Ivory Coast, September 22, 1966.

Article: "The Black Man and Art," *African Arts,* Autumn, 1970.

Biographical/Critical Sources: "Camara Laye's symbolism: an interpretation of 'The Radiance of the King," J. A. Ramsaran, and "Camera Laye's symbolism: a discussion," Jahn and Ramsaran, in *Introduction to African Literature,* Ulli Beier, editor, Evanston, Northwestern University Press; *Camara Laye,* Paris, Fernand Nathan, 1964, No. 2, in Littérature Africaine Series; *Seven African Authors,* Gerald Moore, editor, London, New York, Oxford University Press, 1962.

LEMOS, Virgílio de (pseudonym GALVAO, Duarte)
b. November 29, 1929, Lourenço Marques, Mozambique.
Poet, journalist, critic.

Lemos has worked on many journals of his homeland, including *Brado Africano, Notícias, Tribuna, Itenerio* and has appeared in such anthologies as *New Sum of Poetry from the Negro World* and *Antologia de poesia de Moçambique.*

His one volume of poetry, *Poemas do tempo presente,* was published in 1960, the year he was arrested by the Portuguese authorities for working with the nationalists. He now lives in exile, having left Mozambique in January, 1964, and, using the pseudonym Duarte Galvão, writes for various international journals. His *Angola et Mozambique. Esclavage et révolution* (Slavery and Revolution in Angola and Mozambique), was translated into French and published in Paris in 1966.

Writings: Poetry: *Poemas do tempo presente,* Lourenço Marques, Mozambique, 1960; poems in various journals, including *Brado Africano, Notícias, Tribuna, Itenerio* and collections such as *New Sum of Poetry from the Negro World,* Paris, Présence Africaine, No. 57, 1966, and *Antologia de poesia de Moçambique,* Orlando de Albuquerque and Víctor Evaristo, editors, Lisbon, Casa dos Estudantes do Império, 1951 (offprint from journal, *Mensagem,* No. 12).

Essay: *A juventude e o império,* Porto Amélia, Mozambique, 1961, 16 pages.

Critical Reviews: Of Luís Romano's *Famintos,* in *Présence Africaine,* No. 54, 1965; of Romano's *Clima,* in *Présence Africaine,* No. 54, 1965; of Luís Honwana's *Nós matamos o ção tinhoso,* in *Présence Africaine,* No. 55, 1965; of Luandino Vieira's *Luuanda,* in *Présence Africaine,* No. 58, 1966.

Scholarly Paper: published in *The Writer in Modern Africa,* Per Wästberg, editor, Uppsala, Sweden, The Scandinavian Institute of African Studies, 1968, New York, Africana Publishing Corporation, 1969.

Polemic: *Angola et Mozambique. Esclav-*

age et révolution, Paris, Présence Africaine, 1966.

LESHOAI, Benjamin Letholoa
(also Bob)
b. July 1, 1920, Bloemfontein, Orange Free State, South Africa.
Story writer, playwright (in English).

Believed to be his people's first creative writer in English, Leshoai does not publish in his native Sotho. Educated locally, he obtained his Teacher's Certificate at Healdtown Missionary Institution, 1944, and took his B.A. at Fort Hare in 1947 in English and Native Administration. He taught English in a Pretoria high school for ten years after graduation, becoming headmaster in 1957, keeping that position until 1960 when he resigned.

Moving to Johannesburg, Leshoai joined the Bantu players, Union Artists, as assistant manager. This group had earlier done the jazz opera *King Kong.* Going into exile in Zambia in 1963, he taught English in Ndola, studied for one year in the United States where he got an M.A. in speech and theatre at the University of Illinois in 1964. He then became a teacher of English at Mufulira Teachers' College, Zambia, in 1965 and stayed three years. Since 1968 he has been a teacher in the Department of Theatre Arts, the University College, Dar es Salaam, Tanzania.

Leshoai's collection of freely adapted traditional tales is *Masilo's Adventures and Other Stories.* One story in the collection received special attention by A. S. Gérard in his *Four African Literatures.* It deals with the legendary ruler Senkatana who in various Sotho works has been portrayed as a prototypical Christ–figure. He appears in Sophonia M.

Mofokeng's *Senkatana,* 1952, in Thomas Mofolo's *Moeti oa bochabela*; and S. M. Guma's two short versions in his *Form, Content and Technique of Traditional Literature in Southern Sotho,* 1967. Because Leshoai wrote his story in English, and was possibly influenced by African writers elsewhere on the continent, he felt compelled, in order to reach an audience mostly outside Africa, to add details of culture obviously not needed by the original, vernacular legend. Moreover, according to Gérard, the "optimistic" treatment of many European fairy tales permeates Leshoai's handling. But it is a beginning, and Gérard believes it may be the harbinger of a new English-Lesotho literature exploiting Sotho themes but moving toward the mainstream of Afro-English writing.

Leshoia has gone on with his English writing to produce a play, *The Wake,*

which saw publication in *New Writing from Zambia*, (1968).

Writings: Stories: *Masilo's Adventures and Other Stories*, London, Longmans, 1968. Play: *The Wake*, in *New Writing from Zambia*, No. 2, Lusaka, 1968.

Biographical/Critical Sources: Albert S. Gérard, *Four African Literatures*, Berkeley, University of California Press, 1971; earliest written version of the Senkatana story was Edouard Jocottet's *Litsomo tsa Basotho* (Myths and Legends of the Sotho), Morija, 1909, 1911.

LESORO, Ephraim Alfred Shadrack
b. March 18, 1929, Flatkop, Ficksburg District, Orange Free State, South Africa.
Southern Sotho novelist, poet, playwright, short story writer, educator.

The son of Christian parents, Shadrack Gentle and Evodia Lesoro, Ephraim began school at age ten when he entered the Ficksburg Bantu United School. He passed the Standard VI in 1943 and he graduated from Lovedale Training Institution in 1948 after receiving the Junior Certificate at Kroonstad Bantu High School in 1946. He has taught at various schools and most recently has served as principal of Waterfall Bantu School.

A prolific writer, Lesoro's novels are: *Leshala le tswala molara* (Charcoals Makes Ashes) and *Pere ntsho Blackmore* (Black Horse Blackmore). His dramatic works are: *Tau ya ha Zulu* (The Zulu Lion), a stage version of Robert Louis Stevenson's *Treasure Island*, entitled *Sehlekleka sa letlotlo* (unpublished), and many radio

plays broadcast by the Sotho Service of Radio Bantu. Also unpublished is his Sotho rendering of Shakespeare's *King Henry IV, Part I*, entitled *Morena Henry wa bone.*

Lesoro's more important works are probably his poetry which includes the modest collection of child's nursery rhymes, *Raneketso tsa bana* and four other volumes: *Dithothokiso tsa sejwalejwale* (Modern Poems); *Mathe–malodi* (Nice Words); *Makodilo a bana* (Children's Flutes); and *Mmitsa* (Lucky Charms), which won the Samuel Edward Krune Mqhayi prize for Bantu literature, date not known. Still in manuscript is his last collection of verse, *Mophutso wa Mqhayi le dithothokiso tse ding* (Mqhayi's Bundle and Other Poems).

Lesoro has also contributed short stories and miscellaneous news items to Radio Bantu for its Sotho programs and he won a Radio Bantu Poetry Competition in 1965, celebrating the fifth year of South Africa's life as a republic.

Writings: Novels: *Leshala le tswala molara,* publishing data unknown; *Pere ntsho Blackmore,* Johannesburg, Bona Press, 1968.

Plays: *Tau ya ha Zulu,* Johannesburg, Afrikaanse-Bona Press, 1964; *Sehlekleka sa letlotlo,* unpublished: dramatic version of R. L. Stevenson's *Treasure Island;* and *Morena Henry wa bone,* based on Shakespeare's *Henry IV, Part I;* and many unpublished radio plays.

Poetry: *Raneketso tsa bana,* Cape Town, Via Afrika, 1959; *Dithothokiso tsa sejwalejwale,* Johannesburg, Afrikaanse, 1960; *Mmitsa,* Johannesburg, Afrikaanse, 1961; *Makodilo a bana,* Johannesburg, Afrikaanse, 1963; *Mathe–malodi,* Cape Town, Via Afrika, 1964; *Mophutso wa Mqhayi le dithothokiso tse ding,* unpublished.

Lima

LIMA, Manuel
b. 1935, Angola.
Poet.

Manuel Lima has published one volume
of poetry, *Kissange; poemas* (Kissange,
poems), 1961.

Writings: Poetry: *Kissange; poemas,* Lisbon, Casa dos Estudantes do Império,
1961.

LIYONG, Taban Lo
b. 1938, northern Uganda.
Story writer, poet, novelist.

Locally educated at Gula High School
and the Sir Samuel Baker School, Liyong
took the B.A. at National Teachers' College, Kampala. He also studied political
science at Howard University, Washington, D.C., and at Knoxville College, Tennessee. He was the first African to
receive an M.A. in Fine Arts from the
Writers' Workshop at the University of
Iowa, (1968) and then returned to East
Africa after many years abroad. He
joined the Cultural Division of the
Institute for Development Studies at the
University College, Nairobi, Kenya.
Aided by a Tutorial Fellowship, he concentrated on research into Lwo (or Luo)
and Masai vernacular literature. At present, he is teaching English at the University College, Nairobi, and editing the cultural journal, *Mila.*

Liyong's collection of stories, *Fixions,*
appeared in Heinemann's African Writers Series in 1969, and in 1971 he published a collection of poetry, *Franz
Fanon's Uneven Ribs: Poems, More and
More.* The East African Publishing
House issued a collection of his literary
criticism in 1969: *The Last Word. Cultural*

Synthesism, which included studies of
Amos Tutuola and Okot p'Bitek along
with essays on negritude and the changing African culture.

Stimulated by his research into Lwo
vernacular literature, Liyong has recast
tales from that language in the volume,
*Eating Chiefs: Lwo Culture from Lolwe to
Malkal,* 1970. He has taken the old
stories, for the most part originally transcribed by anthropologists, and redone
them in a swinging Lwo-English line
which is a staccato free verse. An example from the poem–tale "Kabeke's
Return" is illustrative of his method and
style:

But for fractionalization itthey manand-
/woman again and again
The factors can manwoman in test tubes
/too.
Manandwomanandotheranimalsandthings
/broke off a tree;

204

The tree broke off humid ground.
Wait for this hot chemical to reach your
/chemicals.

In his acknowledgements in this volume, Liyong states the "idea of writing this [work]" came to him in the home of Dr. Okot p'Bitek, the author of the early Lwo novel, *Lak Tar Miyo Kinyero Wi Lobo,* and the well-known *Song of Lawino.* He also thanks J. P. Crazzolara for his "unorthodox" and yet detailed, research of Lwo tales. The prose poem, "To you Crazzolara," shows the refugee Patiko people outwitting a selfish ruler who only grudgingly has permitted them to hunt on his lands. Dedicated to Crazzolara, the poem seems to indicate Liyong's admiration for the original ways of the older scholar who no doubt had to circumvent a lot of red tape to get his work done.

Liyong elsewhere has written, "To live, our traditions have to be topical; to be topical they must be used as part and parcel of our contemporary contentions and controversies." His 148-page *Eating Chiefs* is a fresh and delightful work, weaving the old and new together in a contentious way.

The publication figures on one of his works as of mid-1972 show the typical readership pattern of African works: *Fixions* sold 2,500 copies in the United States, mostly to libraries on automatic orders, 1,000 in Great Britain, and only 500 in Africa.

Writings: Stories: *Fixions,* London, Heinemann, 1969.
Poetry: *Franz Fanon's Uneven Ribs,* London, Heinemann, 1971.
Criticism: *The Last Word. Cultural Synthesism,* Nairobi, East African Publishing House, 1969.
Folktales: *Eating Chiefs: Lwo Culture from Lolwe to Malkal,* London, Heinemann, 1970.

LOBA, Aké
b. August 15, 1927, Ababo Baoulé, near Abidjan, Ivory Coast.
Novelist, diplomat.

One of twelve children, Aké Loba assisted his father on the family farm until his eighteenth year. Then his father sent him to France to learn more of European crops and farming methods adaptable to Africa. The work, day labor in the fields of Brittany and Beauce, was hard, and not academic, and it was impossible to continue when his father died. Taking a menial job in a Paris factory, he began to take night classes. His stay in France lasted fifteen years during which time he married, fathered two children and wrote three novels: *Kocoumbo; l'étudiant noir* (Kocoumbo, Black Student); and *Les Fagaies sous les fleuves* (The Fagaies Under Water). Extracts from the autobiographical *Kocoumbo* appears in Ezekiel Mphahlele's *African Writing Today,* and in A.C. Brench's *Writing in French from Senegal to Cameroon,* along with a brief bibliography on him and his works. His third novel is *Les fils de Kouretcha* (Kouretcha's Sons), 1970.

He returned to his homeland in the early '60's and became Director of the Information Service for Private Farms in the Ministry of Agriculture. Recently he has served in the Ivory Coast's Embassy in Bonn.

Writings: Novels: *Kocoumbo, l'étudiant noir,* Paris, Flammarion, 1960; extract from *Kocoumbo,* entitled "Without a breath or a murmur," translated by William Feuser, appeared in *The New African*, September, 1966, London; *Les Fagaies sous les fleuves*, Paris, Flammarion, 1962; *Les fils de Kouretcha*, Nivelles, Belgium, Editions de la Francité, 1970.

Excerpts in anthologies: *African Writing Today*, E. Mphahlele, editor, London, Penguin, 1967; *Writing in French from Senegal to Cameroon*, A. C. Brench, editor, London, Oxford Press, 1967.

LOMAMI-TSHIBAMBA, Paul
(sometimes LOMAMI OR
LOMANI-TCHIBAMBA, Paul)
b. 1914, Brazzaville, former French Congo (of Zaïre, former Belgian-Congo, parentage.
Novelist, journalist.

Son of a Leloua father and a Mongvaidi mother, Paul Lomami-Tshibamba, after eight years in Brazzaville, went with his parents to Leopoldville in 1922. He studied at various mission schools in the Congolese capital and in 1928 he entered the Catholic seminary of Bala-Kiéla in Mozambique. On finishing his seminary studies he entered the field of journalism.

For a long period he served as editor of the journal, *Liaison*, and later became its manager. He has also served as editor of *La Croix de Congo*, a journal issued in Leopoldville, now Kinshasa. His historically interesting editorial, "L'occidentalism," dealing with hoped for independence for the then Belgian Congo, appeared in No. 48 (1955) of *Liaison*.

His novel, *N'gando* (The Crocodile), 1948, a work of 117 pages, was the first novel in French by a Congolese and was republished by Kraus Reprint in 1971. The work weaves the dream-like qualities of old Congolan myths with bits of the old and the new life along the Congo river. No work of fiction has come from his pen since the 40's and one critic, Léonard Sainville, has stated that Lomami–Tshibamba has not participated with the young writers of the Congo in the work of developing a literature looking forward to freedom and post-independence in a new Africa. (For discussion of younger Zaïre writers see entries for Samuel A. Nsimba, A. E. Disengomoko, J. Ngangu, R. Malutama, J. Bahelele, and others from the Congo-Zaïre.)

Writings: Novel: *N'gando*, Brussels, Deny, 1948; reprint by Kraus, Nendeln, Liechtenstein, 1971; extract in *Anthologie africaine noirs d'expression française*, Paris Institut Pédagogique Africaine, 1962.

Editorial: "L'occidentalism," *Liaison*, No. 48, 1955.

Biographical/Critical Sources: Review: "L'auteur de 'Ngandu' [sic] nous parle, "Paris, *Présence Africaine*," No. 7, 1949; Review by Jean Caillens in *Présence Africaine*, No. 12, Paris, 1951; Biographical sketch, *Romanciers et conteurs négro–africains*, II, Léonard Sainville, Paris, Présence Africaine, 1968.

LOPES, Balthasar (see ALCANTARA, Osvaldo, pseudonym for LOPES)

LOPES da SILVA, José (see LOPES, José da Silva)

LOPES, Henri
b. September 12, 1937, Leopoldville (now Kinshasa), Zaïre.
Poet.

Lopes is represented by two poems: "Du Cote du Katanga" and "Dipenda!" in *New Sum of Poetry from the Negro World.*

Writings: Poems in *New Sum of Poetry from the Negro World,* Paris, Présence Africaine, Volume 57, 1966.

LOPES, José da Silva
b. 1872, São Nicolau, Cape Verde Islands; d. São Vincente, Cape Verde, 1962.
Poet, teacher.

Lopes, who lived some years in Angola, but spent most of his life on his home islands, was influenced by the French Parnassian poets of the mid-19th century in the verse he belatedly published in 1916: *Jardim das hespérides* (Garden of Hesperides). This volume was later republished in a second edition in Lisbon in 1929, with *Sonetos do livro "Hesperitanas,"* (Sonnets from the volume "Hesperitanas"). The *Sonetos* [had] themselves had first appeared in the first literary journal of the Islands, *Almanach Luso-Africano,* published by the Catholic Seminary of São Nicolau.

The poet's 1920 publication was *O berço e a campa* (The Cradle and Tombstone), an eight-page poem, and his second collection, which contained poems written between 1895 and 1929 and showed movement away from the French Parnassian poets, was *Hesperitanas: Poesias* (Hesperides: Verses), issued first in 1928.

Later volumes of this prolific writer are: *Mussolini,* 1937; *O vandalismo hispano-russo* (Spanish-Russian Vandalism), attacking the Loyalist side in the Spanish Civil War, 1937; *Braits. Sonetos,* 1945; *Alma arsinária,* 1952; *Saudades da patria* (Home Sickness), 1952; *Meu preito*

(My Homage), Praia, 1957; and *Helvétia* (Switzerland), São Vincente, 1958. In 1952 he published a three-page discussion of poetry, "Ainda os nossos poetas" (They Yet Are Our Poets).

Writings: Poetry: *Jardim das hespérides,* 1916; second edition: with *Sonetos do livro "Hesperitanas,"* Lisbon, J. Rodriguez, 1929; *Sonetos,* published earlier in *Almanach Luso-Africano,* São Nicolau, date unknown; *O berço e a campa,* Praia, Cape Verde, 1920; *Hesperitanas: Poesias,* Lisbon, J. Rodriguez, 1928, 1933; *Mussolini,* Rio de Janeiro, 1937; *vandalismo hispano-russo,* Rio de Janeiro, 1937; *Braits. Sonetos,* Lisbon, 1945; *Alma arsinária,* 2 volumes, Lisbon, 1952; *Saudades da patria,* São Vicente, 1952; *Meu preito,* Praia, Cape Verde, 1957; *Helvétia,* São Vicente, 1958.

Criticism: "Ainda os nossos poetas," in *Cabo Verde,* September 1, 1952.

LOPES, Manuel (António)
b. 1907, São Vicente, Cape Verde Islands.
Poet, novelist, painter.

After long service with the state telephone and telegraph company in various parts of Portuguese territory, Lopes retired in Portugal. He is considered one of the leading Cape Verdean writers in both prose and poetry; most of his work celebrates his home islands.

His first long work appeared in 1932 as *Paúl,* a study of the paúl, or marshes, of the island of Santo Antão. His next prose work was the novel, *Chuva braba, Novela cabo–verdiana* (The Savage Downpour), issued in 1956. In 1960 he published a second novel, *Os flagelados do vento leste* (Scourged by the Eastwind), and the story, "Aódesamparinho" (In the Wasteland). Possibly his earliest published story was "Visão da madrugada" (The Dawn Spectre), published in 1928. He also published a few works of criticism.

Lopes' two poetry collections are: *Poemas de quem ficou* (Poems of Those Who Stay), 1949, and *Crioulo e outros poemas* (Creole Songs and Other Poems), 1964.

Writings: Essay: *Paúl*, São Vicente, Cape Verde, 1932.

Novels: *Chuva braba, Novela cabo-verdiana*, Lisbon, Edição do Instituto de Cultura e Fomento de Cabo Verde, 1956; *Os flagelados do vento leste*, Lisbon, Ulisseia, 1960; *Chuva braba* appeared in second edition, Lisbon, Ulisseia, 1965; a translation into Russian by Elena Ráusova of *Chuva braba* as *Yarostni Livernh*, appeared in Progress (English trans. of Russian title), Moscow, 1972.

Stories: "Visão da madrugada" in *Novo almanach de lembranças luso-brasileiro*, Lisbon, 1928; "No terreiro do bruxo Baxenxe (On the Terrace of the Sorcerer Baxenxe), in *Poetas e contistas africanos de expressão portuguêsa*, São Paulo, Editôra Brasiliense, 1963; "Aódesamparinho" from the collection "O Galo que cantou na baía" (The Cock Who Crows in the Bay), published in the *Antologia da ficção cabo-verdiana contemporânea*, Praia, Cape Verde, Imprensa Nacional, 1960; the collection, "O Galo . . ." was earlier published as "O galo que cantou na baia e outros contos cabo-verdianos," in *Colecção Hoje e Amanhã*, No. 1, Lisbon, Orion, 1958, 221 pages.

Poetry: *Poemas de quem ficou*, Angra do Heroísmo, Azores, 1949; *Crioulo e outros poemas*, Lisbon, 1964.

Criticism: *Os meios pequenos e a cultura* (Little Means and Culture), Horte, Azores, 1951; "Reflexões sobre a literatura cabo-verdiana ou literatura dos meios pequenos," in *Colóquios cabo-verdianos*, Lisbon, 1959; "A literatura caboverdiana," in *Cabo Verde*, October 1, 1959.

LUFTI, Ali Sayed
b. 1930, The Sudan.
Poet, translator (from Shukria–Arabic to English), teacher.

The son of a Western-educated father who introduced new teaching methods into the Rufaa region, Ali Sayed Lufti had English schooling in the Sudan, and is himself a schoolmaster. He has collected many of the shepherd songs, or dobeits, of his people and translated them into English.

The common *dobeit*, a sung poem in four lines, loosely linked into a narrative pattern, is chanted more than sung around the evening campfire, usually accompanied by the *zumbara,* a five-stop pipe, or the *zithr,* the ancient African guitar. Six groups of dobeits in Lufti's translation of traditional Shukria shepherds' songs (as well as five modern Shukria poems by Wad Hadad Rabu) appear in Anne Tibble's *African/English Literature.*

Writings: Poems in *African/English Literature,* with discussion of the dobeit, Anne Tibble, London, Peter Owen, 1965.

LUTULI, (Chief Albert John Mvumbi; a variant spelling is LUTHULI)
b. 1898, near Bulawayo, Southern Rhodesia; d. 1964, on his farm in Natal, South Africa.
Autobiographer, statesman, educator.

Lutuli, the grandson of a Zulu chief, was educated locally at Groutville Mission School, then at Adams College and the American Mission Secondary School where he qualified as a teacher. He grew up in the Vryheid district of Northern Natal and then in the Groutville Reserve. His father had been a congregationalist Mission interpreter and the nephew of the ruling chief of the Abasemakholweni Zulu. Lutuli was a local chief when, in 1952, he became president of the African National Congress (ANC) which was the leading organization of the blacks in South Africa until 1960 when it was banned.

He taught Zulu history and literature at the American Mission School for seventeen years until he took up the chieftanship of the Christianized Zulus in the Groutville area, a position formerly held by his uncle and grandfather. Summoned to Pretoria in October of 1952 in connection with his support of the Defiance Campaign, he was requested to resign either his chieftanship or his leadership of the African National Congress. Lutuli refused to do either. In November, 1952 the Government expelled him from the chieftanship, but the membership of the ANC elected him president which made him a far more important figure, and extended his influence far beyound the Groutville area.

After a two-year restriction to his village, Lutuli flew to the capital of Johannesburg to protest the Western Areas Removal Scheme through which Africans lost their last property rights in and around the capital, and were forced to relocate on a distant reserve. Lutuli was forbidden to address his followers and was restricted for two years to his modest farm. In December of 1956 he was charged with high treason but, along with 64 others, was released after one year and the charges dropped.

In May 1959, he began an extremely successful speaking tour of the Western Cape and began to reach whites as well as non-whites. Quite obviously he was provoking many to conceive of a new kind of South Africa. The Government banned further travel and speeches, again restricting him to his farm. However, on March 26, 1960, when he was again in Johannesburg to testify at his treason trial he burned his pass book and called for a national day of mourning on March 28 in memory of those killed at a peaceful protest meeting at Sharpeville. He was again arrested and physically assaulted by a policeman on March 30.

The Nobel Peace Committee awarded

him the Nobel Prize for 1960, and, surprisingly, he was permitted to travel to Oslo to accept the award on December 10, 1961. His autobiography *Let My People Go,* first published in 1962, recounts the long history of his efforts to help his people. As a leader, Lutuli had argued moderately for a multiracial society with justice for all, but his writings were finally his only way to address the world. Confined by the police to his farm, he wrote until his death.

Writings: Autobiography: *Let My People Go,* London, Collins, 1962; New York, McGraw Hill, 1962; and New York, World Publishing House, 1969, in paperback (Meridian).

M

MABOKO, F. M.
b. ca. 1920, South Africa.
Tsonga-translator.

Maboko is the principal of the Mbokota
Primary School in the Zoutpansberg in
the Northern Transvaal. In 1963 he
organized the Bantu Library Service of
the North. His one important work is
a translation of Edwin W. Smith's *Aggrey
of Africa* into the Tsonga language as
Aggrey wa Afrika, 1956.

Writings: Translation: *Aggrey wa Afrika,*
from E. W. Smith's *Aggrey of Africa,* Swiss
Mission, South Africa, 1956.

MACAULEY, Jeanette
b. 1943, Freetown, Sierra Leone.
Critic, teacher.

Jeanette Macauley studied in Freetown
schools until 1961 when she went to England to study French. In 1964 and 1967
she was able to go to Paris to deepen
her knowledge of French literature and
language and to specialize in the francophone novels of black African writers.
Presently teaching at the University of
Sierra Leone, she is helping to set up
an African Studies Department.

Her essay, "The Idea of Assimilation,"
concerned with Mongo Beti and Camara
Laye, is included in *Protest and Conflict
in African Literature.*

Writings: Essay: "The Idea of Assimilation" in *Protest and Conflict in African
Literature,* New York, Africana Publishing Company, 1969.

MACHADO, Pedro Félix
b. ca. 1865, Angola, d. ca. 1940?
Story writer.

Machado's first work, *Scenas d'Africa* (African Scenes), a romance written in 1892
in the vein of Portuguese works then
popular in Lisbon, dealt with black Africans in an aloof, vaguely satiric fashion.
First published as a serial in the Lisbon
Gazeta de Portugal, it saw print as a special
volume in 1892, the only year any work
of his seems to have been published. He
is a precursor of writers, braver and
more aware of the need to portray their
fellow Africans in Portuguese-language
literature than he could have been in
his era. Only in his *O segredo da morta*
(The Secret of the Dead Woman) published in Luanda in 1934 did he face
the problem of treating Creole society

211

and the black world of his ancestral Angola.

Writings: Romance: *Scenas d'Africa. Romance íntimo,* serially published in *Gazeta de Portugal,* Lisbon, 1892; second edition, Lisbon, Ferin, 1892, in two volumes; *O segredo da morta,* Luanda, 1934.

Play: *Os beijos. Monólogo,* in manuscript; probably never published.

Poetry: *Sorrisos e desalentos. Sonetos,* in manuscript, probably never published.

MACHAKA, Samson Rasebilu Mfoka
b. May 31, 1932, Phakene, South Africa.
Northern Sotho poet, educator.

Born into the Batlokwa clan of the Tswana-speaking people, grandson of Chief Ntwamala Puledi Masenyane Machaka and son of the heir apparent, Masilo Malebogo Machaka, Samson Machaka attended Sekonye Mission Station school where he earned the Standard VI Certificate in 1944. He studied at the Lemana Training College (1945–49), taking the Junior Certificate, and at Wilberforce Institute (1951–52), winning the Teacher's Certificate. By early 1953, Machaka was the principal of the Westphalia School, remaining for three years. After a short period as a clerk in Kilnerton Normal College and in the Department of Bantu Education he went on to the University College of the North where he became an administrative clerk, his present position.

His first published work, a collection of poems, *Mehlodi ya polelo* (The Flavor of the Language) appeared in 1962 and was awarded the Samuel Edward Krune Mqhayi prize for poetry for 1965. Later

volumes of poetry were *Thereŝo* (The Truth) and *Naledi* (Stars).

Writings: Poetry: *Mehlodi ya polelo,* Johannesburg, Afrikaanse Pers Boekhandel, 1962; *Thereso,* Pretoria, Van Schaik, 1966; *Naledi,* Pretoria, Van Schaik, 1967.

MADDY, Pat (also Abisodu and Amadou)
b. 1936, Sierra Leone.
Playwright, poet.

Educated in Sierra Leone, Pat Maddy worked for a short period for the Sierra Leone Railways before traveling to England. He resided in Denmark during the middle 1960's where he lectured on contemporary African literature. His plays have been televised in Denmark and England and his poetry has appeared in Danish, English, and various African journals. His *Yon Kon* appears in Cosmo Pieterse's *Ten One-Act*

Plays, 1968. Returning to Sierra Leone in 1969, he became a producer of radio plays and then went to Zambia for a period to train that country's National Dance Troupe for Expo 70, the Montreal World's Fair.

Heinemann published his volume of four plays, *Obasai and other plays,* in 1971. The title play, *Obasai,* was broadcast originally on the BBC's African Service and the plays in the volume have had stage performances. *Obasai* and *Gbana-Bendu* combine African dance and song with satirical dialogue in an original mix of European and African drama. *Allah Gbah* tells the tale of Joko Campbell's life, his imprisonment for murder, and his last hours in jail. *Yon Kon* is also about prison life and how in Yon Kon's case at least, jail is better than unemployment on the outside.

Maddy's one published volume of poetry, *Ny afrikansk prosa,* (1969), has appeared only in Danish.

Writings: Plays: *Yon Kon* In *Ten One-Act Plays,* Cosmo Pieterse, editor, London, Heinemann, 1968; *Obasai and other plays,* London, Heinemann, 1971.

Poetry: *Ny afrikansk prosa,* translated by Ulla Ryum, Copenhagen, Stig Vendelkaers Forlag, 1969.

MADE, Emmanuel H. A.

b. ca. 1905, Natal Province, South Africa.
Zulu poet, novelist, biographer.

Emmanuel Made, considered one of the greatest of contemporary Zulu poets, attended local schools through high school but did not enter college until he was in his 30's. Encouraged by the scholar, Professor B. W. Vilakazi, he finally did attend Amazimtoti (Adams')

Training College in the early 1940's to study history and literature. His reputation is based primarily on one collection of verse, *Umuthi wokufa nezinye enkondlo* (The Tree of Death and Other Songs), published in 1950. His poems celebrate the past, bitterly consider the future, or elegize his friends. His long poem in praise of Vilakazi (1906–1947), *UBambatha kaMakhwatha* (Bambatha, Son of Makhwatha), begins:

Bambatha, how close you were;
Now, even dearer in my memory,
I sing my songs to you.
You held my heart to the fire
(When I was full of toys
Not yet ready for a man's joys)
And told me sing—as did the old
Praise-poets of the Golden Past.

Earlier prose works of Made's were: *Amaqhawe omlando* (Heroes of Other Lands); a long novel, *Indlafa yase-Harrisdale* (The Man Who Owned Harrisdale), warmly praised by Professor Vilakazi; and *Ubuwula bexoxo* (The Folly of a Frog), moral essays, appearing in 1945.

Writings: Poetry: *Umuthi wokufa nezinye enkondlo,* Pietermaritzburg, Shuter and Shooter, 1950; *UBambatha kaMakhwatha,* Johannesburg, Witwatersrand University, 1950.

Novel: *Indlafa yase-Harrisdale,* Shuter and Shooter, 1940.

Biographies: *Amaqhawe omlando,* Volume I, 1938; Volume II, 1940.

Essays: *Ubuwula bexoxo,* 1945, all three by Shuter and Shooter.

MADIBA, Moses Josiah Sekxwadi

b. 1909, Polokwane, Pietersburg District, Transvaal, South Africa.
Northern Sotho novelist, poet, educator.

Madiba began school in Setotolwane, did his high school work at Moshashane, and from 1926 to 1929 studied at the Kilnerton Training Institute. He took his Junior Certificate in 1930, the B.A. from Fort Hare in 1941 and the University Education Diploma the next year. He taught at Makanspoort Primary School (1929–30), served as principal at Malkspruit United School (1930–35) and the Kratzenstein Higher Primary School (1935–36). Other jobs in education have included Supervisor of Bantu Education, Pietersburg West Circuit (1936–1946); Warden and teacher at the then new Pretoria Bantu Normal College, Atteridgeville, Pretoria (1947–48); principal, Mokopane Training School (1948–1958); and Sub-Inspector of Schools, Potgietersrust Circuit (1958 to the present). In 1960 he was named chairman of the Advisory Council seeking to establish the University College of the North.

Madiba's two novels are: *Tsiri* (1942) and *Nkotsana, khudu ga a lahle legapi la yona* (Nkotsana, the Tortoise, Doesn't Lose His Shell) which went through five editions from 1955 to 1968. His one volume of verse to date is *Direto tša Sesotho*, Vols. I and II.

Madiba also published his two series of Sepedi (Northern Sotho) readers: *Thuto ya polelo* (The Teaching of the Language) and *Mahlontebe*.

Writings: Novels: *Tsiri*, Pretoria, Van Schaik, 1942, 1960; *Nkotsana, khudu ga a lahle legapi la yona*, Pretoria, Van Schaik, 1955.

Poetry: *Direto tša Sesotho*, Volumes I and II, Pretoria, Van Schaik, 1960.

Language Readers: *Thuto ya polelo*, Pretoria, Union Books, 1941; *Mahlontebe*, Pretoria, Union Books, 1952–54.

MAHAMMED, Sheikh 'Abdille Hasan (or SAYYID, Mahammed 'Abdile Hasan)
b. April 7, 1864, Somalia; d. 1920.
Somali oral poet.

Born at a small watering place between Wudwud and Bohotle, the Dulbahante country in eastern Somaliland (later to become a British protectorate), Mahammed began to learn the Koran at age seven. By his tenth year he was the teacher's assistant and at 15 he was a teacher of the Koran in his own right. Four years later he was given the honorific "sheikh" by his people in recognition of his learning. He traveled widely in adjoining areas, particularly the Sudan and Kenya, during his early years.

While visiting Mecca he met Sayyid Muhammad Saalih, a religious reformer, and was led to join Saalih's religious fraternity, the Saalihiya. Upon returning to Somalia in 1891, he married a woman of the Ogaadeen clan. In 1894 he journeyed once again to Mecca, Hejaz and Palestine. The establishment of a French Catholic mission in his country and its apparent success in converting some children to Christianity angered him and he began a lifelong struggle to purify the Islamic faith in his country and to oust the Christians, particularly the British who gradually obtained control of the area. Accused of stealing a rifle, Mahammed led a revolt against the British which went on for years, ending only in 1920 with his defeat and exile to Ethiopia. He died from influenza at the town of Guano Imi shortly after capture by the British. He had married 12 times and left nine sons and one daughter.

Considered the founder of the modern independence and nationalistic movement in Somalia, Mahammed Hasan also composed highly alliterative poems which quickly made their way into vernacular popularity, and were told and retold over the years. The inflammatory verse was marked by puritanical religious fervor and patriotism. He was a gifted writer with a strongly developed pictorial imagination which fills his verse with vivid scenes of the desert and the arid plains of his country. He also composed some poems and religious hymns in classical Arabic but they are less well known than his Somali verse. His poems were collected by Sheikh Jama Umar Ise and Musa H. I. Galaal, both of Somalia's capital, Mogadishu.

Mahammed's poem, "The Death of Richard Corfield," celebrates the fate of a British officer, Corfield, who, like the American General Custer, got his camel detachment into a tight spot fighting Abdille's forces, and died with his men, August 9, 1913. Composed in the *gabay* form, a short narrative poem of 50 to 150 lines of 14–18 syllables with the caesura between the 6th and 7th syllables of each line, the poem in English translation appears in Austin J. Shelton's *The African Assertion*. The poem originally appeared in *Somali Poetry*.

Five other poems of his also appear in that collection: "Hiin Finiin, the poet's favorite horse," "The Sayyid's reply," "The road to damnation," "The path of righteousness," and "A message to the Ogaadeen."

Writings: Poem: "The Death of Richard Corfield," in English translation in *The African Assertion*, Austin J. Shelton, editor, New York, The Odyssey Press, 1968; originally, with five other poems, in *Somali Poetry*, Andrzewski and Lewis,

editors, Oxford, Clarendon Press, 1964.

Biographical/Critical Sources: R. L. Huss, "The 'Mad Mullah' and Northern Somalia," *Journal of African History*, V, No. 3, 1964; D. Jardine, *The Mad Mullah of Somaliland*, London, 1923.

MAHTAMA, Sellase Walda Masqal
b. October 29, 1905, Addis Ababa, Ethiopia.
Amharic poet, biographer, scholar, statesman.

Coming from a family originally from Bulga, Shoa, and son of a former Minister of the Pen (Head of Emperor's Executive Staff), Mahtama graduated from Menelik II grade and high school in Addis Ababa, then went on to the French lycée in Cairo, took further studies in southern France, and received a certificate from the Institut National Supérior d'Agronomie in Nogent-sur-Marne, France. He established a high school in 1930 at Ambo and was private secretary to the Crown Prince in 1934. Deported to Italy in 1937, he remained in Europe for two years. When Emperor Haile Selassie returned to power, Mahtama was given the first of a long series of important government posts: Secretary-General for the Provinces of Wallo, Gondar, and Tigre (1939–46), Director General in the Ministry of Agriculture (1947–49), Vice Minister of Agriculture (1949–54), Minister of Agriculture (1954–58), Minister of Finance (1958–60), and was honored with the title of Balambaras in 1958. He was Minister of State for Art and Education in 1960 when the revolt against the Emperor broke out. He

215

remained loyal and was named Minister of Public Works and Communications (1961–65). In May, 1966, he was awarded the title Blattengeta and made a member of the Crown Council.

Winner of the Haile Selassie I Prize in Amharic literature in 1965, Mahtama is primarily a collector of folk poetry and proverbs. His first works, however, were *Memories* (1942–43), a study of Ethiopian society and social and political institutions from the time of Menelik II to the present, and *The Greatness of God*, religious meditations written in Italy during his enforced exile in that country.

Mahtama's first work of poetry was the collection of some 3,000 proverbs in verse form gathered in *The Spirit Is Immortal* (1951–52). His *Selected Tales* contains 60 fables, and in 1948–49 he published *Amharic Poems*, written in the traditional religious style. This collection includes works by Sahla Sellase (king of 19th century Shoa), and Hayla Malakot (father of Menelik II).

Writings: Poetry: *The Spirit Is Immortal*, Addis Ababa, 1951–52; expanded edition, 1953–54; *Amharic Poems*, 1948–49; 1955–56.

Other works are: *Great Marvel* (1943), *Remains of the Fathers* (1943), *Land Property in Ethiopia: A Survey* (1957); and *The Name Above the Grave: A Short Biography of Tesfahe Taezaz Walda Masqal* (1956), all published in Addis Ababa; *Memories*, Addis Ababa, 1942–43; *Selected Tales; The Greatness of God*, details not known.

MAILE, Mallane Libakeng

b. July 31, 1895, Hermone,
Mafeteng District, Lesotho.
Southern Sotho novelist, playwright, collector of folk-lore, minister.

The son of Libakeng and Delina Maile, Mallane Maile first attended school at Hermona (1908–11) where he won his Teacher's Certificate. He began teaching at Morija in 1916 and at the age of 40, entered the Dutch School in Stofberg to study for the ministry, where, after eight years, he earned the doctorate in theology in 1943 after earlier receiving the bachelor of theology degree. His doctoral dissertation compared African religion and the related ceremonies and scripture with the Christian scriptures and practices. Ordained in the Dutch Reformed Church, he began preaching at Bothaville, Orange Free State, where he is today still active in church matters.

Maile's first novel, *Ramasoabi le Potso* (Ramasoabi and Potso) appeared in 1928 and was a popular success among Sotho readers. Other short novels were *Morui le Lazaro* (The Rich Man and Lazarus), 1947; *Ngoanana ha a botsa telejane* (An Unhappy Young Wife), *Barapeli ba Morija* (The Preachers of Morija), 1950, all religiously oriented; and the novelette, *Mohokolli* (The Persistant One). More recently, longer novels have appeared: *Moiketsi* (The Self-Made Man) and *Boiphetetso* (Get Revenge!).

His first play, *Pitso ea diphoofolo* (The Animals' Meeting), was published in 1957 and a second, *Ba ntena ba nteka* (They Bore and Seduce Me), in 1965. His collections of original hymns are *Koli'a malla* (Laments), 1947, and *Mantloa a kajeno* (Modern Improvisations). Three of his religious tracts may be mentioned: *Sefapenong sa Jesu* (At Christ's Cross), *U se kena* (You May Still Enter) and *Ho tloha lehlaheng ho isa* (From Birth On).

Writings: Novels: *Ramasoabi le Potso*, Morija, Morija Sesuto Book Depot, 1928; *Morui le Lazaro*, 1947; *Ngoanana ha a botsa telejane,* 1947; second edition, 1955; *Barapeli ba Morija,* 1950; *Moiketsi,* Cape Town, Via Afrika, 1958; *Boiphetetso,* Via Afrika, 1965.

Novelette: *Mohokolli,* Bloemfontein, N. G. Sending Pers, 1953.

Plays: *Pitso ea diphoofolo,* Johannesburg, Afrikaanse Pers-Boekhandel, 1955; *Ba ntena ba nteka,* Cape Town, Via Afrika, 1965.

Collections of hymns: *Koli'a malla,* Morija, Morija Besuto Book Depot, 1947; *Mantloa a kajeno,* Morija, date unknown.

Religious tracts: *Sefapenong sa Jesu; U se kena; Ho tloha lehlaheng ho isa;* dates for these works unknown.

MAIMANE, J. Arthur
b. 1932, South Africa.
Short story writer, playwright, journalist.

Educated in local schools Maimane became a journalist on various newspapers in South Africa, but from 1958 on he has lived in exile, first as Reuter's correspondent in East Africa, then briefly in Ghana. Reuters then brought him back to London where he still resides and works for the B.B.C. as a current affairs commentator.

Most of Maimane's stories concern black-white tensions, often those of a sexual origin or those that stem from the apartheid restrictions. Some of his tales are "Just a Tsotsi," "The Hungry Boy," and "The Madness," in which an aging white woman commands her servant to make love to her. His reward for obliging her is to be hanged for rape. In "A Kaffir Woman," a white farmer takes an African woman to bed and, dis-

covered by his white neighbors, commits suicide. Maimane's stories also have appeared in *Transition, The New African,* and *Drum.*

Maimane has written several plays and his *The Opportunity,* was published in Cosmo Pieterse's *Ten One-Act Plays.*

Writings: Stories: "Just a Tsotsi," "The Hungry Boy," in *Following the Sun,* Berlin, 1960; "A Kaffer Woman," Ibadan, *Black Orpheus* magazine; stories also in *Transition, The New African,* and *Drum;*

Play: *The Opportunity* in *Ten One-Act Plays,* London, Heinemann, 1968.

MAIMO, A. O. (also 'Sankie)
b. ca. 1940, West Cameroon (former English part of Cameroon, now Cameroon).
Playwright, poet (in English).

Maimo's play, *I Am Vindicated* (1959) was the first to be written and published by a Cameroonian. A revised edition, including the addition of some poems from his verse collection *Twilight Echoes* (details not known) has been republished by Kraus Reprint. His most recent play, *Sov-Mbang, the Soothsayer,* was published in 1968. This satirical work exploits folkloric elements, Biblical legends, and the conflicts between the older, traditional generations, and the young, Westernized one.

Writings: Plays: *I Am Vindicated,* Ikenne, Nigeria, 1959; revised edition including poems from *Twilight Echoes,* in *Early West African Poetry and Drama,* Nendeln, Liechtenstein, Kraus Reprint, 1970; *Sov-Mbang, the Soothsayer,* Yaounde, Editions CLE, 1968.

MAKGALENG, Mamagase Macheng
b. ca. 1930, Natal, South Africa.

Makgaleng

Sepedi (Northern Sesotho)
playwright.

Locally educated, Makgaleng has published one work, a play, *Tswala e a ja* (Growing Pains), in 1964. The 45-page work was republished by Van Schaik in a revised edition in 1969.

Writings: Play: *Tswala e a ja*, Pretoria, Van Schaik, 1964; revised edition, 1969.

MAKIWANE, Tennyson Xola
b. 1930, South Africa.
Journalist, political commentator.

Educated in South Africa, Makiwane now lives in exile in London. His article, "African Work Songs," appears in Langston Hughes' *An African Treasury*. The brief story originally entitled "They Call Us Jim," later included in "African Work Songs," first appeared in the South African journal, *Fighting Talk*.

Writings: Article: "African Work Songs" in *An African Treasury*, New York, Pyramid, 1961; Story: "They Call Us Jim," first published in the journal, *Fighting Talk*, date unknown but late 1950's.

MAKONNEN, Endalkacaw (also MAKWANNEN)
b. 1892, Ethiopia; d. February 27, 1963.
Amharic novelist, playwright, autobiographer, story writer, statesman, painter.

Born into the powerful family of the Addisgé from Tagulat, Makonnen was educated at court and was a close friend all his life of Emperor Haile Selassie. He visited London in 1924, was honored with the O.B.E., and on his return to Ethiopia was named to many important posts, including comptroller of the Addis-Jibouti Railway (1924–26), Minister of Commerce (1926–1931), Ethiopian envoy to England and to the League of Nations (1931–33), Mayor of Addis Ababa (1933–34), and Governor of Ilubabor Province (1935).

Named a general during the Italian invasion he fled to Jerusalem when the Emperor left for Britain and earned a living selling his own religious paintings. At the Emperor's request he also worked with the many Ethiopian refugees in Palestine. In 1942 he was named Ethiopia's first Prime Minister and in 1957 became President of the Senate with the honorific title of Ras Bitwadded, a title that can only once be awarded by an Emperor. Makonnen then, was of the highest eminence, power, and aristocratic origin.

His literary works, unlike those of most of the earlier writers, were conservative, traditional, and looked back to older political and religious verities. His first novel, *The Inconstant World* was published in Addis Ababa in 1940–41. Portraying the tribulations of the heroine, Yayné Ababa, and her family, the work's message is that the world's only justification is to test the pure and just in heart. His second published work, a play, *The Voice of Blood* (1941–42), celebrated the martyrdom of Abuna Pétros, head of the Ethiopian church who was killed by the Italians during their occupation of the country. A second novel, *Do Not Say I Am Not Dead*, originally published in 1945–46, later appeared in the collection, *Advise Me*. Its humble hero, Ato Tamaccu, whose life and home are broken by the war, serves as a symbol of the good man who suffers. Though the book attacks European colonialism, it is primarily a tract urging patience under the twin yokes of injustice and poverty. Published in *Advise Me* also was the play, *The City of the Poor,* which showed the struggle of the wealthy businessman, Habteh Yemar, to resist the spiritual urgings of his foreboding dreams and the advice of the good man, Abba Sawbakantu.

One of Makonnen's most recent works, the novel, *Sahay Masfen* (1949–50, 1956–57), deals with young lovers in modern Addis Ababa, is, like all his works, didactic and moralistic.

The major theme in his writing is obviously the idea of the ascendancy of the old feudal lords and of the good old ways. To further this view, Makonnen's novelette, *David III: A Historical Novel* (1942–43), obliquely criticizes the centralizing efforts of Emperor Haile Selassie by describing the frivolities and unorthodox beliefs of the eighteenth-century Ethiopian king, David. Later turned into a play, and then translated into English by Lij Endalkacaw Makonnen, the author's son, *David III,* with *The Voice of Blood* and *The City of the Poor* appeared in one volume, *Three Plays.*

Makonnen's last two novels were *The Bloody Era* (1947) and *Taitu Bitul* (1950–51), both historical novels. His writing career ended with the autobiographical volumes, *The Good Family* and *The Course of Dreams* both originally published in 1949, which also memorialized the rights and responsibilities of the old ruling classes.

Writings: Novels: *The Inconstant World,* Addis Ababa, 1940–41, 1947–48; *Do Not Say I Am Not Dead* 1945–46; also in collection, *Advise Me,* 1952–53; *Sahay Masfen,* 1949–50, 1956–57; *The Bloody Era,* 1947; *Taitu Bitul,* 1950–51.

Novelette: *David III: A Historical Novel,* 1942–43; later turned into a play, *King David the Third.*

Plays: *The Voice of Blood,* 1941–42, 1947–48; *The City of the Poor,* also in collection, *Advise Me; King David the Third.*

Autobiography: *The Good Family, The Course of Dreams,* Asmara, 1949; Addis Ababa, 1956–57.

Genre unknown: *Man and His Thoughts,* Addis Ababa, 1943.

The City of the Poor, was translated into English by K. M. Simon, and *The Voice of Blood,* was rendered into English by Stephen Wright.

Biographical/Critical Source: Albert S. Gérard, *Four African Literatures,* Berkeley, University of California, 1971.

MAKOUTA-MBOUKOU, Jean-Pierre
b. 1929, Congo, Brazzaville.
Short story writer, critic, novelist, poet, teacher.

Trained in local schools and later at the University of Grenoble, he taught from 1963 to 1969 in the Congo and then came to the United States to study for a doctorate in linguistics at Georgetown University, Washington, D. C. His first works were long stories or novelettes, "Les initiés" (The Initiated) and "En quête de la liberté, ou Une vie d'espoir" *(The Search for Freedom: or, A Life of Hope),* published in the early 1960's. Makouta-Mboukou's *Introduction à la littérature noire* appeared in English in 1973 as *Black African Literature: An Introduction* under the imprint of Black Orpheus Press, Washington, D. C. All these works originally appeared in French under the imprint of edition C.L.E. in Yaoundé, Cameroon.

Les initiés is an autobiographical novelette of 85 pages, where *En quête* is more imaginative and departs from the life of the author more freely.

His first collection of poetry, *L'âme bleue* (The Blue Soul), was published by CLE in Yaounde, 1972.

Writings: Novels: *Les initiés; En quête de la liberté, ou Une vie d'espoir,* both Yaoundé, CLE, 1970, earlier as stories.

Criticism: *Introduction à la littérature noire,* Yaoundé, Cameroon, *C.L.E.* 1970; published in English translation as *Black African Literature: An Introduction,* Washington D.C., Black Orpheus Press, 1973.

Poetry: *L'âme bleue,* Yaoundé, CLE, 1971.

MAKUMI, Joel
b. ca. 1945, Kenya.
Novelist.

An excellent student of English, Makumi was educated in local schools. He has published two works in English, *End of the Beginning* and an earlier novelette, *The Children of the Forest.*

Writings: Novels: *End of the Beginning,* Nairobi, East African Publishing House, 1970; *The Children of the Forest,* London, MacMillan, 1961.

MAKWALA, Silpha Phaladi Ngwako
b. ca. 1930, South Africa.
Sepedi (Northern Sesotho) playwright, novelist.

Locally educated, Makwala has written several plays in Sepedi, but only one, *Kgašane,* (1962) has been published. His one novel, *Tselakgopo* (The Devious Way), also appeared in 1962.

Writings: Play: *Kgašane,* Pretoria, Van Schalk, 1962.

Novel: *Tselakgopo,* Johannesburg, Cape Town, Afrikaanse Pers-Boekhandel, 1962.

MAL'AKU, Baggosaw
b. ca. 1900, Ethiopia; d. Cairo, Egypt, 1940.
Amharic playwright.

Locally educated, Mal'aku was appointed to the Menelik II Lycée in Addis Ababa as a dramatist in residence. None of his plays reached publication but Yilma Darasa, in the 1941 anthology, *In Praise of Independence,* cited Mal'aku as an excellent author and example for younger playwrights to follow. His greatest success was *The Great Judge* which concerns Solomon, produced in November 1934 at the Menelik II School Theatre, and which ran twice weekly for four months in the capital. His second most acclaimed play, *Zannabac,* a lesser success, dramatized the plight of a young girl enduring the frivolous marriages and divorces of an erratic mother.

Self-exiled after the Italian invasion, Mal'aku lived in a monastery in Jerusalem for some years, but died of tuberculosis in Cairo before being able to return with Emperor Haile Selassie to Addis Ababa.

Writings: Plays: *The Great Judge,* produced in 1934; *Zannabac,* produced mid 1930's.

Biographical/Critical Sources: Mal'aku's plays were discussed in *In Praise of Independence,* Yilma Darasa, editor, Addis Ababa, Marha Tebab Press, 1941; Albert S. Gérard, *Four African Literatures,* Berkeley, University of California, 1971.

MALANGATANA, Valente (see VALENTE, Malangatana Gowenha)

MALEMBE, Timothée
b. ca. 1935, Zaïre.
Novelist.

Malembe's novel, *Le mystère de l'enfant disparu* The Mystery of the Vanished Child) exploits folkloric material from his people in a work that is more mythical than realistic. It was republished in 1970 by Kraus Reprint, along with two other early Congolese novels, *Ngando* (1948) by Paul Lomami-Tshibamba and *Victoire de l'amour* (Love's Triumph) (1953) by Dieudonné Mutombo.

Writings: Novel: *Le mystère de l'enfant disparu,* Leopoldville, 1962; Kraus Reprint, Nendeln, Liechtenstein, 1970, along with *Ngando* by Paul Lomami-Tshibamba and *Victoire de l'amour,* by Dieudonné Mutombo.

MALONGA, Jean
b. February 25, 1907, Brazzaville, Congo.
Novelist, statesman.

Malonga was educated at a church school in Brazzaville and later at a teacher-training institution there. He went on to France in 1946 as a deputy for the Congo in the French National Assembly, remaining until 1951.

His publications are: *La légende de M'Pfoumou Ma Mazono* (The Legend of M'Pfoumou Ma Mazono), a novel published in 1954; *Coeur d'Aryenne* (Aryenne's Heart), a novelette, 1954. A portion of the latter work is given in the original French, along with a commen-

tary on the novelette by A. C. Brench in his *Writing in French from Senegal to Cameroon.*

Writings: Novel: *La légende de M'Pfoumou Ma Mazono,* Paris, Edition Africaines, 1954.

Novelette: *Coeur d'Aryenne,* in *Trois écrivains noirs,* Paris, Présence Africaine, No. 16, 1955; an excerpt in *Writing in French from Senegal to Cameroon,* London, Oxford University Press, 1967.

MALUTAMA, Rémy
b. ca. 1915, near Kimpese, Congo (Zaïre); d. May 27, 1956, Nsona Mpangu (or Mbanza Manteke), Zaïre.
Kikongo hymn writer, teacher.

Malutama first studied at the mission school at Mbanze Manteke and at Kimpese mission where he completed a four year course in two years. There followed three years (1946–49) at the Institut des Mission Evangelique de Likamba in the Cameroon and then travel to Brussels in 1948 to attend the 70th anniversary of the founding of Protestant missions in the Congo. He remained in Belgium for four years to study at the Ecole Normale de l'Etat at Nivelle where he joined a fellow Congolese, A. Emile Disengomoko. Receiving his diploma in 1955, he returned to the Congo to be named director of the secondary school at Nsona Mpangu, but falling ill, died after only a few months at his new post.

He composed many hymns, five of which appear in the collection *Minkunga mia Kintwadi.*

Works: Hymns (poems): five in *Minkunga mia Kintwadi,* Léopoldville, LECO, 1956.

Malutama

Biographical/Critical Source: Mbololo ya Mpiku, "Introduction à la littérature kikongo," *Research in African Literatures,* African and Afro-American Research Institute, The University of Texas, III, 2, 1972.

MAMA, Goodwill Soya
b. 1925, Cape Province, South Africa.
Xhosa poet, scholar.

Mama attended local schools and Paterson High School in the Cape where he was encouraged by the Reverend James James Ranisi Jolobe to write poetry. In 1940, his first published verse, "Ode to the Royal Air Force," appeared in an African-language newspaper. Ten years later 42 of his poems appeared in a collection, *Amaqunube (imihobe yesiXhosa),* translated as "Blackberries: Songs in Xhosa." His former teacher, the Rev. Jolobe, edited the volume which also contained eleven poems by A. Z. T. Mbebe (b. ca. 1920).

Contributing poems to such Xhosa journals as *Imvo zabantsundu* (The Opinion of the Blacks) and *Umthunywa* (The Delegate) and traveling about in the Xhosa language area collecting idiomatic and colloquial expressions and old praise-poems, Mama increased his command of the traditional vernacular literature. This research resulted in a collection of praise-songs, *Indyebo kaXhosa* (Xhosa Harvest), published in 1954. About 1945, Mama took a clerk's position in New Brighton, Cape Province, on the coast of South Africa, where he lives and works today.

Writings: Poetry: *Amaqunube (imihobe yesiXhosa),* London, Oxford University Press, 1950; *Indyebo kaXhosa,* Johannesburg, Afrikaanse Pers-Boekhandel, 1954; the latter also contained works by others which he edited.

MANGOAELA, Gideon (see last paragraph MANGOAELA, Zakea entry)

MANGOAELA, Zakea Dolphin
b. February, 1883, Hohobeng, near Palmietfontein, Herschel District, Cape Province, South Africa;
d. October 25, 1963.
Southern Sotho poet, teacher, scholar, translator.

The son of Christians, Zakea Mangoaela was baptized by the Rev. D. F. Ellenberger in Masitise, Lesotho, where he grew up. An excellent student, he studied at local schools, passing the Standard IV examination in 1895 at the unusually early age of twelve. After waiting for two years to enter the Basutoland Training College, he received his Teacher's Certificate in 1902 and began to teach in the Moloti Mountains of Lesotho (the Drakenberg), then an isolated area. He also worked in the ministry and produced three graded readers including *Lipaliso tsa Sesotho* (1903). In 1907 he began teaching at Koeneng Mission School and became a fast friend of the Rev. Everitt L. Segoete, the mentor of Thomas Mofolo, the novelist. At this time, Mangoaela began to submit articles on local history, and short stories to the journal *Leselinyana* (The Little Light). During this period he married the daughter of the Rev. Bethuel Sekokotoana at Koeneng.

Beginning in 1910, Mangoaela began to teach at Morija and to work as a bookkeeper and translator for the Book Depot, as well as overseeing the publication of the Depot's journal, *Leselinyana.*

His study *Tsoelopela ea Lesotho* (Lesotho's Progress) appeared in 1911 followed in 1912 by a collection of tales and folklore, *Har'a libatana le linyamat'-sane* (Among the Wild Beasts, Large and Small). In 1921 his praise poems of the Basotho chiefs, *Lithoko tsa marena a Basotho* appeared, the first Southern Sotho praise songs ever to be published.

During this period he worked with E. Jacotett on the latter's grammar of Sesuto, and turned out tracts and religious pamphlets. In 1937 he was named a member of the Regional Literature Committee for Sotho and from 1954 to 1958 he was chief editor of the journal *Leselinyana*. Mangoaela's funeral in 1963 was attended by more than 600 mourners.

His nephew, Gideon Lebakeng Mangoaela (b. 1915), writes poems in the four major languages of South Africa, Xhosa, Zulu, Sotho, and Tswana, and is now lecturer in the vernacular literatures of South Africa at Howard University in Washington, D.C. A volume of his verse with accompanying English translation is being prepared for publication in the United States.

Writings: Study: *Tsoelopela ea Lesotho,* Morija Sesuto Book Depot, 1911.

Tales and folklore; *Har'a libatana le linyamatsane,* 1912.

Poetry: *Lithoko tsa marena a Basotho,* 1921.

Others: *Grammar of the Sesuto Language,* 1932, with E. Jocotett; *Likhomo tsa ha Khumalo,* Morija, 1944, a translation of E. Roux's *The Cattle of Khumalo; Sebopheho sa bokreste,* 1960, translation of H. Stephen's *Christian Character.*

MARANGWANDA (see WEAKLY, John)

MARGARIDO, Maria Manuela
(née da Conceição Corvalho)
b. 1926, São Tomé (or Príncipe).
Poet, journalist.

Married to the Portuguese poet and novelist, Alfredo Margarido, Maria Manuela has contributed to various journals. Her poem, "Memoria da Ilha do Príncipe" (Remembrance of the Isle of Príncipe), appears in *Poetas e contistas africanos de expressão portuguêsa,* and two of her poems, "Socopé," and "Vosque Ocupais a Nossa Terra" (Take Care of Our Land), appear in *New Sum of Poetry from the Negro World.* Her one volume of verse, some 36 pages, is *Alto como o silêncio* (Loud as Silence), 1957. She has worked on *Mensagem* (Messenger), Angola, and the review *Estudos Ultramarinos,* Lisbon.

223

Margarido

Writings: Poetry: *Alto como o silêncio,* Lisbon, Publicações Europa-America, 1957; poems in: *New Sum of Poetry from the Negro World,* Paris, Présence Africaine, Vol. 57, 1966; *Poetas e contistas africanos de expressão portuguêsa,* São Paulo, Editôra Brasiliense, 1963; *Antologia da poesia de São Tomé e Príncipe,* Lisbon, 1963.

Criticism: "Inquetação e serenidade. Aspectos da insularidade na poesia de Cabo Verde" (Disquiet and Serenity: Aspects of Insularity in Cabo-Verdean Poetry), in *Estudos Ultramarinos, Literatura e Arte,* No. 3; *Uma introdução à poesia de Jorge Barbosa,* Praia, Cape Verde, Minerva, 1964; *Poetas de Cabo Verde,* Lisbon, Casa dos Estudantes do Imperio, 1960 or 1961 (which he edited).

MARIANO, Gabriel
b. April , 1928, São Nicolau, Cape Verde Islands.
Poet, journalist, story writer, critic, public official.

Trained as a lawyer in Lisbon, Mariano now serves as a judge in Cape Verde. He has worked on the Cabo-Verde review, *Claridade* and has had many of his works published in it. He has also worked as a lawyer in Mozambique and has been collected in international anthologies of poetry. His first volume of verse, *Capitão Ambrosia* (Captain Ambrosia) and one collection of stories, *O rapaz doente* (The Sickly One) established him as one of the better young writers in Potuguese Africa. He has also written some criticism.

Writings: Poetry: *Capitão Ambrosio,* Sà da Bandeira, Angola, Publicações Imbondeiro, date unknown; *12 poemas de circumstância,* Praia, Cape Verde, 1965; poems in *New Sum of Poetry from the Negro World,* Paris, Présence Africaine, Volume 57, 1966; *Literatura africana de expressão portuguêsa,* Volume I, *Poesia,* Algiers, 1967.

Stories: *O rapaz doente,* Sà da Bandeira, Publicações Imbondeiro, 1963; story in *Poetas e contistas africanos de expressão portuguêsa,* São Paulo, Editôra Brasiliense, 1963.

MARKWEI, Matei
b. ca. 1925, Ghana.
Poet.

Educated in the old Gold Coast (now Ghana) and later at Lincoln University in Pennsylvania, he went on to Yale for advanced study in theology. He is now an ordained minister, serving at home. Markwei is represented in Langston Hughes' *An African Treasury* with his poem "Life in Our Village."

Writings: Poem: "Life in Our Village," *An African Treasury,* Langston Hughes, editor, New York, Crown, 1960.

MARTINS, Ovídio de Sousa
b. 1928, São Vicente, Cape Verde Islands.
Poet.

Martins studied law at the University of Lisbon after local schooling and in 1962 published a volume of poetry, *Caminhada* (The Walk). A collection of stories, *Tutchina,* appeared the same year. He was part of the younger group gathered around the review, *Claridade,* and has contributed to the journals *Cabo Verde* and *Suplemento Cultural* and *Vertice.* His poem "Para Alem do desespêro" appears in *Poetas e contistas africanos de expressão Portuguêsa.*

Writings: Poetry: *Caminhada,* Lisbon, Edição da Casa dos Estudantes do Império, 1962; poem, "Para alem do desespêro," in *Poetas e contistas africanos de expressão portuguêsa,* São Paulo, Editôra Brasiliense, 1963.

Stories: *Tutchina,* Sà da Bandeiro, Publicações Imbondeiro, 1962.

MASONDO, Titus Z.
b. ca. 1907, Natal, South Africa; d. March 25, 1949.
Zulu novelist, collector of folk tales, teacher, historian.

Masondo's early schooling was at Amanzimtoti (Adams') Training College (1923–26), where he graduated with the Teacher's Certificate. He began his professional career at the Imfume Primary School in 1927 as an assistant teacher and later that same year was named principal of the Adams' Intermediate School. Appointed principal of the Mhlangomkulu Primary School in 1928, he remained until 1930 when he took a similar position at Edendale Practising School, staying there until 1939. He was an assistant teacher at the Ladysmith Government School in 1939 and from 1940 to 1942 served again as principal, this time at the Impolweni Government School. He was a supervisor of schools, from 1942 to 1946, and then, because of ill health, he resigned to become first a teacher and then principal at the Newscastle Government School (1946) and at the Pietermartizburg Village Government School, (1947) where he worked until his death on March 25, 1949.

His one original work was a novel, *UVulindlebe* (The Close Listener) published in 1939. His first work, *Ezomdabu wezizwe zabantsundu nezokufika nokubusa kwabelungu* (The History of the Bantu Races and the Coming of the Whites), written with Arthur Molefe, appeared in 1933. In 1939 his collection of folk tales *Ezekethelo* (Choice Stories), was printed. His second book of folklore appeared the next year as *UQamunda* (Mr. Doubletalker) and in 1945 his *Amasiko osiZulu* (Zulu Customs).

Writings: Novel: *UVulindlebe,* Pietermaritzburg, Shuter and Shooter, 1939.
History: *Ezomdabu wezizwe zabantsundu nezokufika nokubusa kwabelungu,* with Arthur Molefe, Pietermaritzburg, Shuter and Shooter, 1933.
Folklore: *Ezekethelo,* 1939, *UQamunda,* 1940; *Amasiko esiZulu,* 1945; all by Shuter and Shooter.

MASSAKI, André
b. ca. 1915, Angola.
Kikongo poet, essayist, biographer, journalist.

Moving to the congo (Zaïre) to work as a journalist in the 1930's, Massaki helped edit the French language journal *Envol,* founded in 1957 at Léopoldville with help from Protestant missionaries. In 1958 he became the editor of *Sikama,* founded to be the Kikongo sister-journal to *Envol.* He published an autobiograhical novel in *Sikama* in 1959 entitled *Nsamu a Nsiamiudele* (The Life of Nsiamiudele), republished in book form in 1960 as *Mwan'Ansiona* (The Orphan). Set in the 1920–30 period, the young hero's father emigrates to the Congo near Kimpese mission from Angola in 1920 but dies soon after arriving. His wife, still in Angola, is arrested and beaten so badly that she and her infant

Massaki

daughter in her arms are killed. Nsiamiudele swears to kill his sister's murderer but is brought to Matadi in the Congo by his uncle and he begins his studies with the protestant missionaries. Although obsessed with his idea of vengence for many years, he is dissuaded when the murderer comes to Matadi and is seen by the hero who decides not to commit a crime against man and God. From then on Nsiamiudele is at peace with himself and he goes on to a useful life.

Massaki has published many other works in various genres and translations. Since 1963 he has edited a monthly, *Moyo*, published in the Kikongo-Kituba language at Kinshasa.

Writings: Novel: *Nsamu a Nsiamiudele,* serialized in *Sikama,* Léopoldville, Congo, 1959, republished in book form as *Mwan'Ansiona,* Léopoldville, LECO, 1960, second edition, 1965.

Moral essays: *Luzingu lwa nkento ye bakala mu nzo,* Léopoldville, LECO, 1960; and *Nzambi muna nkia kanda kavwilu e?* (To What Race Does God Belong?), Léopoldville, LECO, 1961.

Biography: *A. E. Disengomoko. Zingu kiandi: 1915–1965,* Kinshasa, LECO, 1968.

Translation:*Nzambi ye muntu,* Kikongo translation of the American work, *God and the Man,* by Mervyn Temple.

Biographical/Critical Source: Mbololo ya Mpiku, "Introduction à la littérature kikongo," *Research in African Literatures,* African and Afro-American Research Institute, The University of Texas, III, 2 (Fall 1972).

MATHIEU, Jean
b. ca. 1930, Zaïre.
Novelist.

One of the early writers from the old Belgian Congo, Mathieu has published three works: *La consultation de midi* (The Meeting at Noon), 1955; *Deux chômeurs* (Two Unemployed), 1957, and *Les hommes de l'aube* (Men of the Dawn), 1956.

Writings: Novels: *La consultation de midi,* Brussels, Impr. de Science, 1955; *Les hommes de l'aube,* Brussels, 1956; *Deux chômeurs,* Brussels, 1957.

MATHIVHA, Matshaya Edward Razwimisani
b. December 24, 1921, Sibasa, South Africa.
Venda novelist, playwright, scholar, educator.

The son of pastoral Venda-speaking people, the young Matshaya Mathivha herded cattle and did not begin school until 1935 when he was almost 14. He attended the Sinthumule Primary School from 1935 to 1937 and then the Mapata Primary School, and the Beuster Primary School where he passed Standard VI in 1940. He earned the Junior Certificate at the Tshakhuma Secondary School (today the Vendaland Institute) in 1943 after three years' study. With a scholarship he attended the Botshabelo Institute where he received the Native Teacher's Certificate in 1945. He earned the B.A. in 1951 from the Universtiy of South Africa and a second B.A. with honors in 1961 from Turfloop University. In 1957 he had earned a University Education Diploma.

His professional career saw him in various posts. From 1951 to 1959 he was principal of Mphaphuli High School where he helped set up advanced classes. He has lectured in the Bantu language department of the University College of the North where he also served as senior lecturer and departmental head of the Venda language department from 1961 to 1969. Since 1969, Mathivha has served as a member of the Bantu Advisory Board.

His only novel to date is *Tsha ri vhone* (Let's See), published in 1952. His play in the Venda language, *Mabalanganye,* appeared in 1963, and in 1966 his Venda grammar, *Thahuelelea luVenda* (Perfect Your Venda), written with J. T. Makhado, was published.

Writings: Novel: *Tsha ri vhone,* Johannesburg, Afrikaanse Pers-Boekhandel, 1952.

Play: *Mabalanganye,* Johannesburg, Afrikaanse, 1963.

Grammar: *Thahuelelea luVenda,* with J. T. Makhado, Pretoria, Unie-Boekhandel, 1966.

MATIP, Benjamin

b. May 15, 1932, Eseka, Cameroon.
Novelist, poet, playwright, biographer, lawyer.

Following his education in local schools and the study of political economy and law at the University of Paris, Matip entered law practice in Paris in 1955. He was a delegate from Cameroon to the Afro-Asian Writers' Conference in 1958, and in 1959 he was a member of the permanent staff of the Afro-Asian Writers at the Colombo Conference in Ceylon.

Matip has published one novel, *Afrique nous t'ignorons* (Africa, We Don't Pay Attention to You), 1956, and fables in *A la belle étoile* (At the Beautiful Star), 1963. His play, *Le jugement suprème* (The Highest Judgment), published in 1963, was performed in December 1969 in the Cameroon.

His scholarly-political studies are *Afrique, ma patrie,* (Africa, My Homeland), 1962 and *Les relations Europe-Afrique dans l'histoire* (African-European Relations Through History), 1959.

In the late 1960's, Matip began collecting the materials for a biographic study of African intellectuals and artists scheduled for publication in 1972.

His novel, *Afrique nous t'ignorans,* deals with the Cameroons of the 1930's and the turbulence occasioned by the outbreak of the Second World War. The work is an exploration of the hopes and fears of three representative leaders of modern Africa: the Christian priest, the medical doctor, and the village chief. The first two are obviously highly Westernized, while the third is less so and fighting for some of the more traditional ways of doing things. The three are close neighbors and men of good will but their tensions show much of what is good and difficult to balance—in the post-colonial world.

Matip

Matip left Paris for legal work in Douala, main port of the Cameroon in the 1960's. He now considers himself primarily a professional writer and his work was recognized in 1961 by *Présence Africaine* when he won the first prize for African literature.

Writings: Novel: *Afrique nous t'ignorons,* Paris, Ed. Renée Lacoste, 1956.
Fables: *A la belle étoile,* Paris, Présence Africaine, 1963.
Play: *Le jugement suprème,* Yaoundé, Collection Lipaf, 1963.
Political works: *Afrique, ma patrie,* Yaoundé, Col. Lipaf, 1962; *Les relations Europe-Afrique dans l'histoire,* Paris, Ed. la Nef, 1959.

MATSEPE, Oliver Kgadine
b. 1932, Transvaal, South Africa.
Tswana novelist, poet, businessman.

Oliver Matsepe was born into the royal household of Chief Monamudi of the Bakopa clan of the Tswana-speaking peoples in the Transvaal. After local schooling he enrolled at the Kilnerton Training School, graduating in 1952. While at Kilnerton he wrote his first novel, *Sebata–kgome* (The Spotted Cow—a praise name meaning A Fine Man), published in 1962 after a lapse of ten years. After working for seven years as a clerk in the Department of Bantu Administration and Development, he opened a retail grocery store in the Groblersdal District, a business he operates today.

Matsepe's second novel, *Kgorong ya Mosate* (At the Chief's Court), won the Samuel Edward Mqhayi Encouragement prize for Bantu Literature in 1964. The prize was a modest 200 Rand, about $280. His third work of fiction, *Lesita-phiri* (The Big Problem) saw print in

1963. His publisher, Van Schaik, has also issued four volumes of his poetry: *Kgotla a mone* (Taste Something Sweet), 1968, *Molodi wa thaga* (The Song of the Weaver Bird), also 1968, and *Todi ya dinose* (The Nectar of Honey), 1969. His most recent verse is in *Molodi wa mogami* (The Milkers Whistle), 1970.

He has published one volume of essays in *Megokgo ya bjoko* (Thought's Harvests), 1969.

Writings: Novel: *Sebata-kgome,* Johannesburg, Afrikaanse Pers-Boekhandel, 1962; *Kgorong ya Mosate,* Pretoria, Van Schaik, 1962; *Lesita-phiri,* Pretoria, Van Schaik, 1963.
Poetry: *Kgotla o mone,* 1968; *Molodi wa thaga,* 1968; *Todi ya dinose,* 1969; *Molodi wa mogami,* 1970; all by Van Schaik.
Essays: *Megokgo ya bjoko,* Johannesburg, Bona Press, 1969.

MATSHIKIZA, Todd
b. 1922, Queenstown, South Africa;
d. 1968, in Lusaka, Zambia.
Playwright, musician, teacher.

Matshikiza was educated in Queenstown and at Lovedale Institute where he became a teacher after graduation. He was an instructor at St. Peter's and worked for awhile for the broadcasting system of South Africa and at various journalistic jobs. He wrote a daily column in *Drum* called "With the Lid Off," noted for its ironic, crisp style.

The son of an excellent church organist, Todd learned music early and became a fine pianist. In 1956 he received a commission to write a choral work with orchestra for the Johannesburg Festival. His greatest success, however, was in writing the music for the popular and critically acclaimed musical *King Kong* in 1960. He traveled to London on the company's first foreign road trip. In 1965, he collaborated with Alan Paton on another musical, *Mkhumbhane,* staged in South Africa. For several years he wrote for local South African papers as a jazz critic and social columnist.

His first published volume was *Chocolates For My Wife,* a lively account of his life in Africa and England.

Selections of three of his bitter-sweet pieces from *Drum* appear in Langston Hughes' *An African Treasury* under the title, "With the Lid Off."

After work with the Malawi national radio system, he moved to Lusaka to work for Radio Zambia. At his early death he left a wife and several children.

Writings: Score and book: for *King Kong,* a musical; with Alan Paton, *Mkhumbhane,* staged in South Africa; both unpublished.

Autobiography: *Chocolates for My Wife,* London, Hodder and Stoughton, 1961.

Journalism: many articles in column, "With the Lid Off," in *Drum,* popular illustrated news magazine published in Johannesburg; selections from *Drum,* republished in *An African Treasury,* New York, Pyramid, 1961.

MATTHEWS, James
b. 1929, Cape Town, South Africa.
Novelist, short story writer,
journalist.

Locally educated, Matthews worked as a newsboy, messenger, and telephone operator to support himself, and devoted his free time to writing for *Drum,* the leading journal open to black writers in South Africa. He has con-

tributed stories to various magazines and is in many anthologies, including Richard Rive's *Quartet,* 1965. Each of the four writers in the volume, Rive, Alex la Guma, Alf Wannenburg, and Matthews, have four stories apiece.

A volume of stories, *Azikwelwa,* has appeared in Sweden in the Swedish language, as has his one novel to date *Mary, Bill, Cyril, John and Joseph.*

Writings: Stories: *Azikwelwa,* translated into Swedish by Pelle Fritz-Crone, Malmö-Lund, Bo Cavefors Bokforlag, 1962; stories in *Quartet: New Voices from South Africa,* London, Heinemann, 1965; "The Party" in *Pan African Short Stories,* London, Nelson, 1965.

Novel: *Mary, Bill, Cyril, John and Joseph,* translated into Swedish by Aida Törnell, Malmö-Lund, Bo Cavefors, 1963.

MAUNICK, Edouard J.
b. September 23, 1931, Mauritius.
Poet, television director.

During the 1960's, Maunick served as Director of Cultural Programs for the Office of Cooperation of the French national radio and television in Paris. His long and complex poem, "Sept Versant Sept Syllable" (Seven Slope Seven Syllable), dedicated to Aimé Césaire and Pierre Emmanuel, was originally published in a verse collection, *Les manèges de la mer* (Taming the Sea) in 1964. Présence Africaine publishing house issued in 1966 three long poems in *Mascaret ou le livre de la mer et de la mort* (Tidal Wave or the Book of the Sea and Death). They have the intriguing titles: "cet étrange calcul des racines" (This Strange Rule of Roots), "dire les limites du plain-chant" (To Give the Limits of Plainsong), and "pro memoria" (Pro Memoria), all taken from his earlier volume, *Les oiseaux du sang* (The Birds of Blood), 1954. *Mascaret* received the Prix des Mascareignes in 1966.

Présence Africaine published his newest volume in 1970, stimulated by the Nigerian Civil War, *Fusillez-moi: Un poème sur la tragédie de Nigeria* (Shoot Me: A Poem on the Nigerian Tragedy).

Writings: Poetry; *Les oiseaux du sang,* Ile Maurice, Regent Press, 1954; "Sept Versant Sept Syllable" in his verse collection, *Les manèges de la mer,* Paris, Présence Africaine, 1964; *Mascaret ou le livre de la mer et de la mort,* Paris, Présence Africaine, 1966; *Fusillez-moi: Un poème sur la tragédie de Nigeria,* Paris, Présence Africaine, 1970.

MAZRUI, Ali Al'Amin
b. February 24, 1933, Mombasa, Kenya.

Novelist, critic, editor, teacher, political scientist.

After local schooling, Mazrui studied at the University of Manchester in England for his B.A. After graduate work in political science at Columbia University in New York and at Oxford, Mazrui returned to Africa to teach. He is now head of the Department of Political Science, Makerere University. For awhile in the 1960's he was an associate editor of *Transition* magazine, published in Kampala, and later of *Mawazo,* successor to the *Makerere Journal,* also in Kampala.

Though primarily a political scientist, Mazrui has recently published his first novel, *The Trial of Christopher Okigbo.* A philosophical work, it deals with the problems of the engaged artist in the African context of social change, independence, and war. Okigbo, the fine Nigerian poet, dead in the Biafran war, was first an Ibo and only secondarily a Nigerian, and the novel's "Judges" examine, rather, try, Okigbo on a double charge: 1 (that he had taken a parochial or "tribal" position rather than a pan-Nigerian one, and 2 (that he sacrificed his art to the role of soldier and patriot. Okigbo's poetry is quoted and his work and life are threaded through the semi-dream-like events of the novel. The charges against Okigbo and Biafra, are left "Not Proven." The Court, operating in a metaphysical time and land, agrees that the poet and Biafra had a right to be afraid, but no right to secede from Nigeria, or "to dismember the embryo of political Africa."

At book's end, in a symbolic banishment, Hanusi, a Moslem from Kenya and the protagonist of the novel, with his sweetheart, Salisha Bemedi, are permitted to live in a limbo of sorts in a baobab tree in Gabon, there to wail for centuries. Hanusi, too, had not thought "largely enough" of the new Africa, so, he cries out every evening, in words strangely like Okigbo's, " . . : without name or audience,/Making harmony among the branches." This sometimes confusing work probably drew on some of the author's ideas as developed in his essay, "The Patriot as Artist," and in other literary essays cited below.

Writings: Novel: *The Trial of Christopher Okigbo,* London, Heinemann, 1971.
Articles: "Meaning vs Imagery in African Poetry," Paris, *Présence Africaine,* No. 66, 1968; "Some Socio-political Functions of English Literature in Africa," in *Language Problems of Developing Nations,* Fishman, Ferguson, da Gupta, editors, New York, John Wiley and Sons, 1968; "Abstract Verse and African Traditions," *Zuka,* No. 1, Nairobi, September, 1967; "The Patriot as Artist,"

Black Orpheus, II, 3, Lagos 1969; "The United Nations and Some African Political Attitudes," *International Organization,* XVIII, 1964; "The Soldier and the State in East Africa: Some Theoretical Conclusions on the Army Mutinies of 1964," with Donald Rothchild, in *The Western Political* Quarterly, XX, 1967.
Scholarship: *Towards a Pax Africana,* Chicago, University of Chicago, 1967; *The Anglo-African Commonwealth,* Oxford, University of Oxford Press, 1967; *On Heroes and Uhuru-Worship,* London, 1968; *Violence and Thought,* London, 1969; and co-editor with Robert I. Rotberg of *Protest and Power in Black Africa,* New York, Oxford University Press, 1970.

M'BAYE, Annette (Mme.)
b. ca. 1940, Senegal.
Poet.

Locally educated, Mme. M'Baye has two collected volumes of verse: *Poèmes africains,* 1965, and the privately printed *Kaddu,* possibly 1967. She has also published in various journals and is represented by three poems in the original French: "Témoignage" (Testimony), "Sablier" (Hour-Glass), and "Silhouette," in *New Sum of Poetry from the Negro World.*

Writings: Poetry: *Poèmes africains,* Paris, Toulouse, Centre d'Art National Français, 1965; *Kaddu,* Impr. A. Diop, 1967?; poems in *New Sum of Poetry from the Negro World,* Paris, Présence Africaine, Volume 57, 1966.

MBEBE, A.Z.T. (see first paragraph MAMA, G.S.)

MBELLE, Isaiah Budlwana (also
BUD-M'BELLE, I.)
b. June 24, 1870, Burgersdorp,
Cape Province, South Africa;
d. July 16, 1947.
Folk literature collector, scholar,
civil servant.

Mbelle attended the Wesleyan Methodist Primary School in Burgersdorp, and then, from 1886 to 1888 studied at Healdtown for the Teacher's Certificate, passing with honors. He began teaching in Herschel and Colesberg, staying for five years (1888–93) and at the same time studied to be a Xhosa-English interpreter. Appointed Bantu Interpreter in the High Court of Griqualand West, Kimberley, on July 1, 1895, he remained there for the next twenty-five years. He married Maria Johanna Smouse in Colesburg on April 24, 1897.

In 1896 he passed an examination as a lower-bench magistrate but because he was not white he was not appointed a judge. He did serve as an examiner in Native Languages for the Education Department and Public Commission of the Cape Province Government. After a trip to England and Wales in 1908, he was also appointed interpreter for the Superior Courts of the Cape Province in Kimberley, a post he held from 1909 to 1920. Moving to Pretoria in 1920, Mbelle became interpreter for the head office of the Native Affairs Department. He served as interpreter for Edward, Prince of Wales, in 1925 on his visit to South Africa. A faithful member of the Methodist Church, he worked with various religious groups, helped found the Bantu Advisory Board in Pretoria, was a member of the African National Congress, and a cricket-loving sportsman.

Mbelle's one literary work, written and published in English, was *Kafir Scholar's Companion*, a 200-page compendium of history, customs, and folk literature with bibliographies of the Xhosa language, an important source for later scholars. The work bears his nickname "I. Bud-M'belle."

Retiring in 1930, he lived quietly at his home in Pretoria. Attendance at the funeral after his death on July 20, 1947, is said to have been the largest to that date in the capital city.

Writings: History and folklore: *Kafir Scholar's Companion*, Lovedale, Lovedale Press, 1903.

MBIA, Guillaume Oyônô (see OYONO-MBIA, Guillaume)

MBITI, John Samuel
b. November 30, 1931, Kitui, Kamba country, Kenya.
Kikamba poet, story teller, scholar, teacher.

Mbiti was educated at Alliance High School, Makerere College, Uganda, and studied theology at Barrington College, USA, where he was ordained a minister in 1960. The next year he entered Cambridge University in England to begin work leading to the doctorate at Westminster College. Since 1964, he has taught religious studies at Makerere and is head of the department of religious studies and philosophy at that college. He has written several books and many articles on African religion and philosophy. He is married and has two children.

A member of the Akamba people where every person is expected to learn to tell stories skilfully, Mbiti collected some 1500 folk tales of which 78 appear in his collection, *Akamba Stories*, 1966. He also writes original poems and stories in both his mother tongue, Kikamba and in English. His collection of verse, *Poems of Nature and Faith*, 1969, was found by one reviewer to be unimaginative except in a few more personal poems or in those dealing with tales from folklore. His work has appeared in various periodicals in Europe and in *Modern Poetry from Africa*. His first volume was semi-autobiographical, *M. and His Story*, 1954.

Mbiti has translated Kenyan folktales into English, and has published his autobiography as a vernacular work, *Mutunga na ngewa yaka* (Mutunga and His Story), 1954, and a prose work of unknown genre, *Over the Fence*, also 1954. He has also contributed a scholarly piece to *Présence Africaine*, "Reclaiming the Vernacular Literature of the Akamba Tribe."

Writings: Autobiography: *Mutunga na ngewa yaka,* the Kikamba version of *M. and His Story,* both London, Nelson, 1954, 1958.

Stories: *Akamba Stories,* London, Oxford University Press, 1966.

Poetry: *Poems of Nature and Faith,* Nairobi, East African Publishing House, 1969; poems in *Poems from East Africa,* Cook and Rubadiri, editors, London, Heinemann, 1971, and *Modern Poetry from Africa,* revised edition, Moore and Beier, editors, London, Penguin, 1966.

Religion and Philosophy: *African Religions and Philosophy,* New York, Doubleday-Anchor, 1969, 1970; *Concepts of God in Africa,* 1970; *New Testament Eschatology in an African Background,* 1970.

Literary Criticism: "L'éveil de la littérature indigène de la tribu akamba," Paris, *Présence Africaine,* Nos. 24–25, 1959; "Reclaiming the Vernacular Literature of the Akamba Tribe," *Présence Africaine.*

Genre unknown (possibly autobiographical): *Over the Fence,* 1954.

MEDEIROS, António Alves Tomás
b. 1931, São Tomé.
Poet, medical doctor.

After local schooling, Medeiros took his degree in medicine at the State Medical School of the Crimea (USSR). He is a member of the outlawed Committee of Liberation of São Tomé and Príncipe. A student of local culture and art, Medeiros has contributed poems to various journals and is preparing a study of the beginnings and evolution of poetry in São Tomé.

His poem, "Meu Canto Europa" (My European Song), appears in *Poetas e contistas africanos de expressão portuguêsa* and he is represented as well in *Literatura africana de expressão portuguêsa,* edited by Mário de Andrade.

Writings: Poetry: "Meu Canto Europa," in *Poetas e contistas africanos de expressão portuguêsa.* São Paulo, Editôra Brasiliense, 1963; poems in *Literatura africana de expressão portuguêsa.* Vol I, *Poesia.* Algiers, 1967.

MEDHIN, Tsegaye Gabre (see TSEGAYE, Gabre-Medhin)

MEDOU, R. G. M. (see MVOMO, R. G. Médou)

MENGA, Guy pseudonym for BIKOUTA-MENGA, Gaston-Guy)
b. ca. 1940, Congo, Brazzaville.
Playwright, novelist.

This successful young playwright has published two plays: *La marmite de Koka-Mbala* (The Pot of Koko-Mbala), a two-act work published in 1966, and *L'oracle. Comédie en 3 actes* (The Oracle), 1969. The latter play won the "Grand Prix" of the Interafrican Theatre Competion, Paris, 1967–68, and *La marmite* received its première at the first World Festival of the Arts, Dakar, 1966.

Menga's one novel to date is *La palabre stérile* (The Worthless Palaver), which deals with the adventures of a young man leaving his home village just before the independence of the Congo. Published in 1968 in Yaoundé, the work won the Grand Prix Littéraire de l'Afrique Noire the next year.

Writing: Plays: *La marmite de Koka-Mbala*, Monte Carlo, Monaco, Editions Regain, 1966; republished, Paris, Office de Radiodiffusion Française, Direction des Affaires Extérieures et de la Coopération, 1969; *L'oracle,* Paris, Office de Radiodiffusion . . . , 1969.

Novel: *La palabre stérile*, Yaoundé, CLE, 1968.

MENSAH, Albert William Kayper
(see KAYPER-MENSAH, Albert William)

MENSAH, Marjorie (see DANQUAH, Mabel, née DOVE)

MENSAH, Toussaint Viderot (also VIDEROT, "Mensah," Toussaint)
b. ca. 1935, Togo.
Poet, novelist.

Mensah's first poems were collected in *Courage; poèmes* a volume of 93 pages published in 1957. Three years later, augmented to 158 pages, this work was published under the title, *Courage, si tu veux vivre et t'épanouir, fils de la grande Afrique!* (Courage, if You Wish to Live and Flourish, You Son of Africa!).

His only novel to date is *Pour toi, nègre mon frère . . . "Un homme comme les autres."* (For Thee, Blackman my brother . . . "A Man Like All the Rest."), issued 1960.

Writings: Poetry: *Courage; poèmes*, Paris, Ed. Hautefeuille, 1957; *Courage, si tu veux vivre et t'épanouir, Fils de la grande Afrique!,* Monte Carlo, Eds. Regain, 1960.

Novel: *Pour toi, nègre mon frère . . . "Un homme comme les autres,"* Monte Carlo, Regain, 1960.

MESATYWA, Ezra Whillemus Mginyimvubu Malashe
b. November 29, 1909, Shawbury, near Healdtown, South Africa;
d. December 1, 1960.
Xhosa folk literature collector, educator.

Mesatywa attended primary school in Shawsburg, then entered Healdtown Institute about 1926 and earned his Junior Certificate in 1930. Graduating from Lovedale in 1935 with a B.A., Mesatywa taught at Healdtown Institute for twenty years, leaving in 1955 to serve as sub-inspector of Bantu (African) Education for the Queenstown Region, remaining in that position until his death in 1960.

Izaci namaqhalo esiXhosa (Idioms and Proverbs in Xhosa) was his only work though he did co-author with H. W. Pahl a series of readers, the *Ulwini lwesiXhosa* (The Xhosa tongue). With A. C. Jordan, Mesatywa compiled a second collection of Xhosa proverbs but it remains unpublished.

Writings: Collection: *Izaci namaqhalo esiXhosa,* Cape Town, Longmans, Green, 1954; Collection of proverbs, with A. C. Jordan, unpublished. Readers: *Ulwini lwesiXhosa,* with H. W. Pahl, Johannesburg, Pers-Boekhandel, 1957.

MEZU, Sebastian Okechukwu
b. April 30, 1941, Emekuku, Owerri, Nigeria.
Critic, poet, novelist, teacher.

An Ibo, educated in Roman Catholic schools, The Holy Ghost at Owerri, and the Upper School of the Holy Family at Abak, Mezu early turned to writing and was president of the Nigerian students' magazine, *Voice,* published at the University of Ibadan. He taught for six months at the Saint-Rosary College in Port Harcourt after taking his B.A. at Ibadan. In 1961 he came to the United States to study at Georgetown University in Washington, D.C., and then at The John Hopkins University in Baltimore, Maryland. He later earned a doctorate from the Sorbonne in Paris with a dissertation on Léopold Sédar Senghor, published in 1968.

Mezu's one collection of poems, *The Tropical Dawn,* 1966, was republished recently by Black Academy Press. His essay, "The Origins of African Poetry," appeared in *New African Literature and the Arts,* 1970.

In 1971 he published a novel on the Biafran War in Nigeria, entitled *The Rising Sun.*

Writings: Poems: *The Tropical Dawn,* Baltimore, Md., 1966; Buffalo, N.Y., Black Academy Press, 1970.

Novel: *The Rising Sun,* London, Heinemann, 1971.

Biographical/Critical Study: *Léopold Sédar Senghor et la défense et illustration de la civilisation noire,* Paris, Didier, 1968 (from Mezu's doctoral dissertation).

Essay: "The Origins of African Poetry," in *New African Literature and the Arts,* Joseph Okpaku, editor, New York, Crowell, 1970.

MICAIA, Lilinho (see dos SANTOS, Marcelino)

MICAIA, Vera (see de SOUSA, Noémia)

MILHEIROS, Mário (pseudonym TORRES, Farinha)
b. 1916, Angola.
Novelist, poet, story writer, scholar, ethnographer, government official.

Milheiros has published one novel, *Entre negros e corsários* (Between the Blacks and the Pirates), issued in 1957; a collection of stories, *Muata Maiende. "O Crocodilo,"* published in 1950; and a volume of verse, *Não! ... (No! ...),* which appeared in 1960. His story, "O imbondeiro maldito," was collected in the 1948 volume, *Colecção aventuras africanas,* (African Adventure Collection), but published under his pen name, Farinha Tôrres.

An important scholarly work is *Etnografia angolana. Esbôçe para um estudo etnográfico das tribos de Angola* (Angolan Ethnography: A Sketch for an Ethnographic Study of the Angolan Tribes), first edition in 1951.

Milheiros

Writings: Novel: *Entre negros e corsários, Romance histórico,* Luanda, Edições Mondego, 1957.

Stories: "O imbondeiro maldito," in *Colecção aventuras africanas,* Porto, 1948, later republished as "*O imbondeiro*" in *Contos portuguêses do Ultramar,* II, Porto, 1969; *Muata Maiende.* "*O Crocodilo,*" Porto, 1950.

Poetry: *Não!* . . ., Luanda, ABC, 1960.

Ethnography: *Etnografia angolana,* etc., Luanda, Mensário Administrativo, 1951; second edition, revised, as *Notas de etnográfica angolana,* Luanda, Instituto de Investigação Científica de Angola, 1967.

MIRANDA, Nuno de
b. ca. 1930, Cape Verde Islands.
Poet, story writer, scholar.

Miranda has published two volumes of verse: *Cais de ver partir* (The Wharf of Goodbye) of 1960, and *Cancioneiro da ilha* (Island Song Book), issued in 1964. In 1961 his 91-page collection of stories appeared, *Gente da ilha* (People of the Island) and in 1966 he published a 125-page collection of essays as *Epiderme em alguns textos* (The Skin on Some Texts). He has also edited two volumes and written many studies of Cabo-verdean literature.

Writings: Poetry: *Cais de ver partir,* Lisbon, Orion Distribuidora, 1960; *Cancioneiro da ilha,* Braga, Pax, 1964.

Stories: *Gente da ilha,* Lisbon, Agência-Geral do Ultramar, 1961.

Essays: *Epiderme em alguns textos,* Lisbon, Panotama, 1966; two volumes with Manuel Ferreira: *Colóquios cabo-verdianos,* Lisbon, Junta de Investigações do Ultramar, 1959; *Regionalismo cabo-verdiano,* Lisbon, 1962; "Comentário em torno do bilinguismo cabo-verdiano," in *Colóquios cabo-verdianos*; "Morna, expressão de lirismo," in *Antologia de ficção cabo-verdiana contemporânea,* Praia, Cape Verde, 1960.

MIRE, Ismaa'iil (also ISMAA'IIL Mire)
b. 1884, Somaliland; d. ca. 1950.
Somali oral poet.

A member of the Ali Geri section of the Dulbahante clan, Mire was a close relative and supporter of Sheikh Mahammed Abdille Hasan. As Hasan's advisor and military leader, he led the unsuccessful Dervish attack on the British Camel Constabulary in the battle of Dul Madoobe, August 9, 1913. In his poem "Rewards of success" he seems to have risen above the bitterness of the loss to the British. He was considered an authority on Somali history and custom and his poems constitute a history of North Somaliland. The poem, "Rewards of success," composed in 1921 shortly after the collapse of the holy war, appears in *Somali Poetry.*

Writings: Poem: "Rewards of success" in *Somali Poetry,* Andrzejewski and Lewis, editors, Oxford, Clarendon Press, 1964.

MKHIZE, C. S. (see last paragraph NYEMBEZI)

MKIZE, E. E. N. kaTimothy (see last paragraph NYEMBEZI)

MNCWANGO, Leonhard L. J.
b. October 28, 1926, Thokazi, near Nongoma, Natal Province, South Africa.

Zulu playwright, novelist, librarian, (also writes in English).

Leonard Mncwango attended primary school in Ngomoma, Natal Province, and then studied at Christ King School, St. Francis School in Mahlabatini, and, in 1944, at Inkamana High School. He graduated from Mariannhill's St. Francis School in 1948.

A rather isolated figure at Sesotho-speaking Pius XII University College in Roma, Lesotho, and estranged from his own Zulu people, he turned inward and began to write. His first play, *Manhla iyokwendele egodini* (The Day of Going Down Into the Grave) appeared in 1951.

He left Pius XII University College in late 1949 to study first at Thokazi and then at Durban in the University of Natal, working as a day laborer to support himself. Later he was a clerk in the Durban Corporation's Non-European Affairs Department. Appointed an assistant librarian in the Durban Library in the early 1950's he finally had the job stability he needed to write and he has remained in that position.

Mncwango's first and only published fiction is his novel *Kusasa umngcwabo wakho nami*, (Tomorrow is Your Funeral—and Mine), published in 1958. The work dramatizes the plight of tuberculosis-stricken slum-dwellers crowded into the outskirts of the South African cities. When written, half a decade earlier, this highly realistic novel had trouble finding a publisher. Encouraged by the final publication of *Kusasa*, he wrote two more novels in English: *This Madness in the Blood,* and *The Prodigal Daughter,* which remain in manuscript. The former treats of an African girl caught in the Zulu-Indian race riots in Durban in 1949, and the latter deals with the return to the country of a girl who

underwent terrible experiences in the city where she had dreamed of finding a better life. A third work, an unpublished mystery *Umbulali* (The Killer) was completed in 1960.

In 1959, the year in which his second work was published, and two more novels were written, his second play, *Ngenzeni?* (What Did I Do?), also appeared. This work treats of life during the reign of the famous Zulu King, Shaka.

Writings: Novel: *Kusasa umngcwabo wakho nami,* Pietermaritzburg, Shuter and Shooter, 1958; *This Madness in the Blood; The Prodigal Daughter; Umbulali,* unpublished.

Plays: *Manhla iyokwendele egodini,* Pietermaritzburg, Shuter and Shooter, 1951; *Ngenzeni?,* Shuter and Shooter, 1959.

MOCKERIE, Parmenas Githendu
b. ca. 1910, Kikuyu country, Kenya.
Sociologist.

Locally educated except for his English training begun in 1932, Mockerie's *An African Speaks For His People* was an early and vigorous attack on the colonial system in Africa and a severe critique of the destruction of the African cultural community. When most Africans were just lifting their heads to look around them, and when "negritude" was just getting its start, Mockerie's book spoke bluntly of the need for change. Leonard and Virginia Woolf who owned Hogarth Press engaged Julian Huxley to do the foreward to the book.

Writings: Sociology: *An African Speaks For His People,* London, Hogarth Press, 1934.

MODISANE, ("Bloke"), William
b. August 28, 1923, Sophiatown,
African suburb of Johannesburg,
South Africa.
Poet, short story writer, autobio-
grapher, novelist, journalist.

Educated in local schools taught by
whites, Modisane became a reporter on
the *Golden City Post,* a Johannesburg
newspaper. Resigning in 1958, he
worked on *Drum* magazine but then fled
South Africa and now lives in London
where he works as a writer, actor, and
broadcaster for the BBC and the Royal
Court Theatre. In 1963, he visited the
USA to lecture on African music and
general culture. He took a leading role
in Genet's *The Blacks* during its London
production.

His autobiographical novel, *Blame Me
on History,* depicts in vivid language the
plight of the black man in the world of
apartheid. Though bitter at South
Africa's racial policies, he also felt guilty
in fleeing the country. His article, "Why
I Ran Away," showing the strain of fear-
ing the oppressor and guilt in not staying
to fight, was originally published in the
New Statesman and appeared again in
Langston Hughes' *An African Treasury.*
His ironic story "The Dignity of Begging" first was published in 1951 and later appeared in *Come Back, Africa* in 1968.

Bloke Modisane's many stories,
including, "The Situation," deal with one
man's response to the social and political
horrors of South Africa. Other stories
recently appearing in collections are
"The Professional Beggar," "All Langa
Was Quiet," which concerns a strike, and
"The Situation," describing the educated
African's plight in a land where he has
no freedom and is cut off from his own
past.

Modisane's poetry, mostly about the
racial situation, lacks distinction.

Recently he has been in Africa and
Germany doing historical research in
preparation for a study of the Maji Maji
Rebellion.

Writings: Autobiographical novel; *Blame
Me on History,* London, Thames and
Hudson, 1963; New York, Dutton, 1963.

Article: "Why I Ran Away," originally
in *New Statesman; An African Treasury,*
Langston Hughes, editor, New York,
Pyramid, 1961.

Story: "The Dignity of Begging,"
1951; in *Come Back, Africa,* 1968.

Biographical/Critical Source: Critical discussion on Modisane: "Modisane et les
masques," Paris, *Présence Africaine,* No
65, 1968.

MODUPE, Prince (see PARIS,
Prince Modupe)

MOFOKENG, Sophonia Machabe
(or Machebe)
b. April 1, 1923, near Fouriesburg,
Orange Free State, South Africa;
d. June 6, 1957.
Southern Sotho playwright, story writer,
educator, scholar.

Mofokeng's early schooling was at the
Dutch Reformed Church in Fouries-
burg, the Stofberg Gedenk School and,
from 1935, Adams' Mission High
School, Natal, where he received a dip-
loma in 1939 with a major in botany and
Southern Sotho. Fort Hare University
College awarded him the B.A. and the
University Education Diploma. He took
a second B.A. (Honors) in history at the

University of the Witwatersrand in 1944 with private and part-time study. He earned a third B.A. (Honors) from Witwatersrand in Bantu Languages and took his M.A. in 1951 with the thesis, "A Study of Folktales in Sotho." Mofokeng's Ph.D. in March, 1955, was the first doctorate ever awarded to an African by Witwatersrand. His dissertation, written for the Bantu Studies Department, was entitled "The Development of Leading Figures in Animal Tales in Africa."

His teaching began at the Johannesburg Bantu High School (1942–1944); he continued at Witwatersrand (1944–47) as a junior language assistant, as language assistant (1947–1954), and as senior language assistant (1954–57).

Mofokeng used his first long stay in the hospital (1947–49) to write a play, *Senkatana,* dealing with the legendary material of Senkatana and the monster Kgodumodumo; and a volume of stories, *Leetong* (On The Road). The play was issued as Volume XII of Witwatersrand's Bantu Treasury series. His second volume of fiction was published in 1961 as XV in that series under the title, *Pelong ya ka* (In My Heart), a novelette.

While working with Professor Clement Martyn Doke on a textbook of Southern Sotho Grammar, Mofokeng died of tuberculosis after a painful month in the hospital, leaving a wife and children, and the grammar in incomplete manuscript.

Writings: Play: *Senkatana,* Johannesburg, Witwatersrand University Press, 1952, 1962, both editions as Volume XII in Witwatersrand University's Bantu Treasury Series.

Stories: *Leetong,* Johannesburg, Afrikaanse Pers-Boekhandel, 1954;

Pelong ya ka, Johannesburg, 1961, as Volume XV of the Bantu Treasury Series.

Grammar: "Textbook of Southern Sotho Grammar," with C.M. Doke, 1957.

MOFOLO, Thomas Mokopu
b. August 2, 1875, Khojane,
Mafeteng District, Lesotho;
d. September 8, 1948.
Southern Sotho novelist,
businessman.

The son of Christian parents, Thomas Mofolo, who became known as the greatest of South African Vernacular novelists with his *Chaka* (1925), grew up in the Qomoqomong Valley, Quthing District, Lesotho. Baptized by the Rev. Hermann Dieterlen of the Paris Evangelical Missionary Society (French Protestant Church), Thomas went to school whenever he could, took part in hunts for leopards, deer, or chimpanzees, and, like most boys, listened to old hunters' tales of the heroic deeds of bygone days. He proved a good student at the Paris Evangelical Society school in Qomoqomong, and under the tutelage of Everitt Segoete made exceptional progress.

He also studied at Masitise under the Rev. Frederick Ellenberger, the Morija Bible School from 1894 to 1896, and the Basuto Training College, where he earned the Teacher's Certificate in 1898. For the next year he worked at Morija's Printing Works and Book Depot under the Rev. Casalis, but the Boer War interrupted the publishing program, and he went off to Lelealeng Technical School, Cape Province, to study carpentry for a year. He taught for several years at various schools, including Maseru Mission School.

Mofolo

Returning to work at the Morija Book Depot, he served as a proof-reader and secretary. Encouraged by the Rev. Casalis, S. Duby and Edouard Jacottet of Morija, he began to write his own material for the press. The first published product of these efforts was a novel, *Moeti oa bochabela* (The Traveller to the East) which was serialized in the journal *Leselinyana* (The Little Light) in 1906, and appeared in book form in 1907. The work details in missionary tract fervor the search for wisdom which led its hero to East Africa, where he met mysterious strangers (Christian missionaries), and then to the Biblical East. *The Traveller to the East* reached print in English in 1934.

Mofolo's second narrative work, never published, was *L'ange déchu* (The Fallen Angel). It was written in Sesotho as were all of his works, but it bears the French title in a Mission list; his quarrel with several aspects of the then popular British author, Marie Corelli (1855–1924), said to be Queen Victoria's favorite novelist, provoked the book.

Pitseng (In the Pot, the exotic name of a village), first serialized in *Leselinyana* in 1910, and published as a book the same year, is highly autobiographical. It draws on the author's days as a student and contains a warm portrait of his teacher, Everitt Segoete, who appears in the work as the preacher Katse. Mofolo's love for the women who was to become his first wife also figures in this interesting novel. This 433-page work had reached its ninth printing by 1960 in the original text.

As early as 1909, Mofolo was doing the traveling and research necessary for the creation of his greatest novel, *Chaka*, based on the life and works of Shaka, the greatest of all Zulu chiefs and organizer of the great Zulu power in what is now Natal Province. Feted at Mgungundlovu (now Pietermaritzburg) the old capital of the Zulus, Mofolo visited the grave of Shaka (the Zulu name as rendered in English orthography as compared to the "ch" sound used by the Sesotho writer) and otherwise sought to absorb the atmosphere, the feel of the Zulu places, and their customs, mannerisms, and social organization.

At some time in late 1911 or early 1912, he was ready to submit a newly finished manuscript to Morija Press for consideration. Though written from a Christian point of view (the superstitious or witch-prone Shaka is decidedly seen as influenced to evil), Mofolo's characterization of the great king and his people is strongly sympathetic and obviously permeated with a respect for the old Zulu values and way of life. Though the manuscript was warmly supported by Jacottet and Casalis, the Morija authorities refused to publish the work, and it was only because of Casalis' persistent efforts that it finally, with some excisions, appeared in 1925.

Translated by F. H. Dutton and published by Oxford University Press in 1931, and then into French, German and other languages including Ibo, King Chaka has become the "culture hero" of many Black African intellectuals and increasingly is the subject of poems and plays written by artists far from Zululand. Léopold Senghor has a long poem dedicated to the personality and exploits of "The Black Napoleon." Others are: Abdou Anta Ka's *Les Amazoulou; épopée inspiré du "Chaka" du Thomas Mofolo* (The Amazulus: An epic play inspired by Thomas Mofolo's Chaka), produced in Dakar's Théâtre Daniel-Sorano, date unknown; Fwanyanga M. Mulikita's play, *Shaka Zulu*, 1967; Seydu Badian's *La Mort de Chaka*, 1962; Charles Nokan's *Les malheurs de Tchakô*, 1968; and Condetto Nénékhaly-Camara's *Amazoulou*, 1970; and Djibril Tamsir Niane's *Chaka*, 1971 (?).

Though E. A. Ritter's biography of Shaka has established a more detailed and professional historian's account of the king, and apparently influenced Mulikita's *Shaka Zulu*, it is Mofolo's early novel that has captured much of the world's attention and it is the novel's portraitures and elevated prose style which is at the center of our conception of Shaka and his reign. Rider Haggard's *Nada the Lily* (1892) may in its day have influenced Mofolo's conception and handling of the theme, for Haggard makes Shaka a powerful figure in his novel, but Mofolo's "African" sympathies and relative closeness to his hero make his work the outstanding one in all the literature on the subject.

Turning to another heroic subject, Moshoeshoe, the founder-king of the Basotho nation, Mofolo, it is believed, produced another major work but the manuscript, "Moshoeshoe" was tragically consumed in a fire at Morija Press and the historical novel never saw print through Mofolo later tried to rewrite it from memory. In ill health and discouraged by business reverses, he turned away from literature for good when the attempt to reconstruct "Moshoeshoe" failed. A manuscript exists but it never has received serious consideration for publication nor been found worthy of careful study.

For a time Mofolo lived in Lealui in Barotseland, then in Northern Rhodesia, later in Johannesburg on the Rand. By 1912 he was in Northern Lesotho employed by the Eckstein Group of the Central Mining-Rand Mines and managing a thirty-mile postal route between Ficksburg and Teyateyaneng. In 1916, Mofolo purchased a modern steam engine and milling plant, becoming one of the earliest African businessmen in the area. Having lost his wife, he remarried and in 1919 he joined the Basutoland Progressive Association and began to take an active political role in trying to have members of the Basutoland National Council elected rather than designated by the hereditary paramount chief.

Setting himself up as an independent Labor Agent in 1922, Mofolo, leaving Eckstein, recruited workers for the diamond mines, sugar plantations and the large farms in the area. Three years later he opened a branch of the Labor Office at Teyateyaneng with Ben Mofolo, his brother, in charge, 1927 was a bad year, for Ben resigned, Mofolo's second wife died, he sold his mill, gave up his recruiting office and invested in a trading store in the Maloti Mountains in Bokong in 1928. From that time until 1937 he did well in his business, married a third time in 1933, but had to leave the high elevation of Bokong for health reasons.

For a short period he was at Port Elizabeth, but soon moved on to Griqualand East District among his own people. Purchasing a farm from a white farmer at Matatiele he ran afoul of the Land Act of 1914 which limited sales of land to Africans to plots contiguous to land already owned by Bantu Africans. Mofolo's new farm touched one farm at a narrow edge owned by another African but the courts took Mofolo's land from him and he lost a great deal in the lawyers' costs and the suit in the courts. Impoverished and ill, he bought and sold increasingly poor farms, and for awhile ran a boarding house at Matatiele, a venture that failed.

Receiving a monthly pension of three pounds sterling after his complete physical breakdown in 1940, he lived on in poverty till his death at Teyateyaneng. He was survived by his third wife, two sons, Ovid Khera Mofolo, teacher and writer, and Mofolo Thomas Mofolo, now president of the Lesotho Senate, and three daughters, one of whom was married to the noted scholar, Gladstone Llewllyn Letele.

Writings: Novels: *Moeti oa bochabela*, serialized in *Leselinyana*, 1906; book form, Morija, Morija Sesuto Book Depot, 1907; English translation of *Moeti oa bochabela*, entitled *The Traveller to the East*, translation by H. Aston, London, Society for Promoting Christian Knowledge, 1934; French translation of part of *Moeti oa bochabela*, as "Georgiques et voyage du chrétien au Lessouto, Fokesi," in *Le Monde non-chrétien*, No. 11, 1949; *L'ange déchu*, unpublished, so listed in the *Livre d'or de la Mission du Lessouto*, Paris, 1912; *Pitseng*, Morija, 1910; in serial form in *Leselinyana*, 1910; ninth printing by 1960, and in book form, Morija, Morija Sesuto Book Depot, 1910; *Chaka*,

Morija, 1925; English translation of *Chaka* by F. H. Dutton, Oxford University Press, 1931; abbreviated, school text of *Chaka*, London, Oxford University Press, 1949, illustrated; first edition in "official" orthography of Sesuto used in Republic of South Africa, illustrated, Morija, 1962; "Moshoeshoe," unpublished.

Biographical/Critical Sources: O. R. Dathorne, "Thomas Mofolo and the Sotho Hero," *The New African*, September, 1966; Daniel P. Kunene, *The Works of Thomas Mofolo—summaries and critiques. A forerunner of 'A digest of African Vernacular Literatures.'* Los Angeles, African Studies Center, University of California, Occasional paper No. 2, 1967; Daniel Kunene, "Retention of Indigenous Literary Features in Thomas Mofolo's Writings in Dutton's Translations," unpublished paper; Works (plays and fiction) dealing with Chaka by South African and Sesotho writers: *Ngenzeni* by L. Mncwango; *UShaka* by H. I. E. Dhlomo; *Ukufa kukuShaka* by Elliot Zondi; *UJeqe insila kaShaka* by John L. Dube; *UShaka* by R. R. R. Dhlomo; and poems dealing with Chaka in: *Inkondlo kaZulu* by B. W. Vilakazi. A general approach to this subject is Robert E. McDowell's "The Brief Search for an African Hero. The Chaka–Mzilikazi Story in South African Novels," in *Discourse*, XI (1968).

MOHAPELOA, John, and Joshua P. and Moeketsa (see last paragraph MOHAPELOA, Josias)

MOHAPELOA, Josias Makibinyane
b. May 23, 1914, Modumong,

Lesotho.

Southern Sotho poet, teacher.

The youngest child in a family of writers, Josias Mohapeloa started primary school in Modumong, Lesotho, went on to the Basuto Training Institute in Morija where he won his Teacher's Certificate, and then to the Fort Hare University taking the B.A. in 1937 and the M.A. in 1941. He then studied privately for an English degree, and was graduated a fellow of the College of Preceptors, New College, Oxford in 1948.

Mohapeloa's teaching career began at the Peka Primary School (1933–35) and Morija Bible School (1935–37). He taught at Modderpoort (1940–41), at Basutoland High School, Maseru (1942–44), again at Modderpoort School (1944–47), and Basutoland High School (1947–1950), where he was a principal as well as teacher. In 1951 he was appointed education officer for the Lesotho Government, a position he holds today.

His one published work of verse is *Mosikong oa thabana ea Borata* (At the Edge of Mt. Borata), published in 1954. In 1945 he published an English language pamphlet, *Africans and their Chiefs: Should Africans be Ruled by their Chiefs or by Elected Leaders?*.

Josias' father, the Rev. John Mohapeloa, wrote *Mating a pheheang* (Brewed Beer), a moralistic work, and his older brothers are noteworthy authors. Moeketsa Daniel Mohapeloa (b. 1912) is a published poet and editor of the excellent anthology of Sesotho poetry and accompanying biographies, *Letlole la lithoko tsa Sesotho* (The Treasury of Sesotho Language Poetry). His oldest brother, Joshua Pulumo Mohapeloa (b. ca. 1910) is a musician and hymn writer whose works are collected in the three-volume *Meloli le lithallere tsa Afrika* (Tunes and Songs from Africa), and is the author of the stirring "Morija," a hymn sung throughout South Africa.

Writings: Poetry: *Mosikong oa thabana ea Borata,* Morija, Morija Sesuto Book Depot, 1954.

Pamphlet: *Africans and Their Chiefs: Should Africans Be Ruled by Their Chiefs or By Elected Leaders?* Cape Town, African Bookman, 1945.

Works by other members of the Mohapeloa family: *Mating a pheheang* by John Mohapeloa, Morija, 1924; *Letlole la lithoko tsa Sesotho,* Johannesburg, Afrikaanse Pers-Boekhandel, 1950, by Moeketsa Daniel Mohapeloa; and hymns of Joshua Pulumo Mohapeloa in *Meloli le lithallere tsa Afrika,* three volumes, Morija, and the hymn, "Morija."

MOHAPI, Michael Molelekoa
b. June 23, 1926, Mafeteng, Mafeteng District, Lesotho.
Southern Sotho playwright, poet, journalist, businessman.

The son of Ephraim and Anna Mohapi, both Christians, Michael attended Mafeteng Controlled School and Basutoland High School, Maseru (1941–1945), which awarded him his senior certificate or diploma. He worked as a typist and translator from 1945 to 1948 for the Department of Information. In 1948 he was assigned as a translator and sub-editor for the journal *Tswelopele* (Progress), a Sotho-language magazine supported by the South African government. Remaining with *Tswelopele* until 1967, Mohapi moved up to assistant editor and contributed many book reviews and articles to that journal as well as to the *Bantu Education Journal* and

Zonke magazine, a popular monthly in Sotho, similar to the English-language *Drum*. Since 1967, Mohapi has been engaged in private business in Mafeteng and with his writing.

His one volume of poetry is *Sebobolane* (Little Noises or The Loudspeaker) published in 1955 and his one play is *O jeloe ka makhala* (He Feels He's Inferior) (1957).

His most recent work, *Nako lia khutsufala* (The Seasons Grow Short), is being prepared for the press. Morija Sesuto Book Depot published his historical-technical study of old methods of agriculture based on his interviews with elderly farmers in *Teme eo boholeholo Lesotho* (Lesotho Agriculture in the Old Days), 1956.

Writings: Poetry: *Sebobolane,* Johannesburg, Afrikaanse Pers-Boekhandel, 1955.

Play: *O jeloe ka makhala,* Afrikaanse Pers-Boekhandel, 1957.

Agriculture: *Temo ea boholeholo Lesotho,* Morija, 1956.

Other: "Nako lia khutsufala," unpublished.

Reviews and articles: in *Tswelopele* magazine, *Bantu Education Journal,* and *Zonke.*

MOIKANGOA, Cornelius E. Rakhosi
b. 1877, Lesotho; d. 1949.
Southern Sotho short story writer, novelist, teacher.

Moikangoa as a youth worked as a cattle herder and not until the age of 12 did he begin school at Morija, Basutoland. He later became the first African principal of the Lovedale Practising School and one of the first two African Inspec-

tors of Native Education, remaining in that position until he retired in 1937. He took an active role in the African National Congress, the Federation of South African Teachers Association and similar groups.

He has written many stories, one of which, "Sobolelo Comes Home," a tale of sorcery, has been collected in *African New Writing.* A 97-page story, "Sebogoli sa Ntsoana-tsatsi" (The Guardian of Ntsoana-tsatsi) appears in a volume with the same title. "Sebogoli" won second prize in the first May Esther Bedford competion, 1935.

Writings: Stories: "Sobolelo Comes Home" in *African New Writing,* London, Lutterworth Press, 1947; "Sebogoli sa Ntsoana-tsatsi," and two other stories in volume *Sebogoli sa Ntsoana-tsatsi,* Maseru, Lesotho, Mazenod Institute, 1943.

Biographical/Critical Source: Albert S. Gérard, *Four African Literatures,* Berkeley, University of California Press, 1971.

MOILOA, James Jantjies
b. June 6, 1916, Wepener, Orange Free State, South Africa.
Southern Sotho poet, playwright, teacher.

Moiloa earned his teacher's certificate about 1935, taught in Bradfort for 12 years, and then went to teach in Bloemfontein for 14 years. Since the early 1960's he has been lecturer in Bantu languages at the University of the Orange Free State and is also the principal of the Lereko Secondary School in Bloemfontein.

His works are: *Dipale le metlae* (Tales and Jokes); the poetry volume, *Mohahlaula dithota* (Roamer of the Heights),

1965; *Jaa o siele motswalle* (Eat but Leave Something for a Friend), 1966, a play; and one novel, *Paka-Mahlomola*, 1965.

Writings: Poetry: *Mohahlaula dithota*, Cape Town, Via Afrika, 1965.
    Play: *Jaa o siele motswalle*, Cape Town, Via Afrika, 1966.
    Novel: *Paka-Mahlomola*, Cape Town, Via Afrika, 1965.
    Stories: *Dipale le metlae*, Cape Town, Via Afrika, 1963.

MOKGATLE, Monyadioe Moreleba Naboth

b. 1911, Phokeng, District of Rustenberg, Transvaal Province, South Africa.
Autobiographer.

Naboth Mokgatle underwent hardships as a child and a young man, working as a herdsboy, houseboy, shop clerk, day-laborer, and part-time student. Later he did political work with a small Communist group in Pretoria and Johannesburg. His work, issued in 1971 by The University of California Press, is *The Autobiography of an Unknown South African.* The English edition, *Naboth Mokgatle of Phokeng: An Autobiography,* appeared in 1970.

Frequently arrested, known for awhile only as No. 1082386, he finally abandoned his unsympathetic wife ("She was always trying to pull me down, urging me to be like everyone else . . .") and fled to London. The book ends in 1954 and the publisher is evasive in providing any specific information about the author's further experiences or whereabouts since that time.

Reviewed somewhat unsympathetically in the *Washington Post's Book World*, July 18, 1971, the critic, however, "ac-

cepts" the work as " . . . the most complete and detailed account I know of an African growing up, and it concerns a country which has produced very few African novels." Not only is the first assertion subject to strong rebuttal, but the second is palpably false. What is true and good about this book is its sincerity, its quiet tone of reasonableness about an unreasonable system, and its effect on the human spirit. The author has escaped hell, but there are millions more in it with no chance to get out. Getting to know personal freedom in London, learning how to be a true man for the first time, Mokgatle ends the work in this vein:

I was like a person who had been sick for a very long time, whose blood had been heavily poisoned by the sickness, and who could not get cured in his own country, so had gone to another country where doc-

245

tors began to work on him. My sickness was a very old one and my cure was long.

Writings: Autobiography: *The Autobiography of an Unknown South African*, Berkeley, The University of California Press, 1971; English edition, *Naboth Mokgatle of Phokeng: An Autobiography*, London, C. Hurst, 1970.

MOKONE, Nowen Godratius
b. November 25, 1900, Putfontein Location, Putfontein, Lichtenburg District, South Africa; d. July 25, 1960.
Tswana story teller, collector of folktales, teacher.

Son of the well-known Mangana Maake Mokone, N. G. Mokone started school in Putfontein and then attended Kilnerton Training Institute for four years, graduating in 1921. He went on to the Practising School of Kilnerton for advanced work, taking a certificate in Afrikaans in 1924. His teaching career included jobs as an assistant teacher in the Bethel Training School, 1924 to 1929; principal at Bethel, 1929; supervisor of Bantu education, 1930 to 1955, sub-inspector of Bantu education for the Potchefstroom Circuit, 1955 to 1960. He died four months short of his sixtieth birthday, and was buried on his farm in Putfontein.

Mokone's first published work was *Montsamaisa-bo-sigo* (He Who Leads Me from the Darkness), a series of six graded Tswana readers with much of the material being his versions of various folk literature of the Tswana speaking peoples. The title comes from the Tswana proverb: "When someone does you a favor in the darkness, be sure to say thank you in the light."

His second published work was a collection in German of talks and lectures he gave during a tour in Germany in 1957 to attend a church synod of the Free Church. The title is very literal: *Vater Mokone erzählt* (Father Mokone Says).

Writings: Language readers, six volumes: *Montsamaisa-bo-sigo*, Cape Town Juta, 1938; new series, 1941.

Lectures: *Vater Mokone erzählt*, details not known, probably 1957.

MOLEFE, Arthur Ignatius
b. March 30, 1908, Stoffelton, Bulwer District, Natal Province, South Africa.
Zulu novelist, poet, scholar, teacher.

Molefe's early schooling was at Stoffleton, Amanzimtoti (Adams) Training College (1924–27) which awarded him the Teacher's Certificate, and the Umpumulo Training School where he earned a University Education Diploma in 1928. He enrolled at Edendale Training School after a brief stint as a teacher at Umpumulo. It was 1944, however, before Molefe could complete his work at Edendale.

Appointed principal of the Caluza School at Edendale in 1947, he has remained to this day. By private study he earned the B.A. from the University of South Africa and in 1955 a Junior Certificate in Afrikaans. He was a sub-inspector of Bantu education for the Pietermaritzburg West Circuit from 1955 to 1966; the chairman of the Zulu sub-committee for Bantu education 1966–69; and has been vice president of the Bantu Advisory Board since 1969.

His first work was *USambulele*, (Umbrella-but here a boy's name), a juvenile novel published in 1933. His poem on Chaka won him the First Prize at the Transvaal Eisteddfod (Poetry Competition) and another from the International Institute of African Languages and Culture in London.

Molefe's scholarly works are a history, written with Titus Masondo, *Ezomdabu wezizwe zabantsundu nezokufika nokubusa kwabelungu* (The History of the Bantu Races and the Coming of the Whites), and Zulu readers in four volumes, *Indlela yolimi lwesiZulu* (The Method of the Zulu Language), 1966.

Writings: Novel: *USambulele*, Pietermaritzburg, Shuter and Shooter, 1933 (Jahn says 1935).

History: *Ezomdabu wezizwe zabantsundu nezokufika nokubusa kwabelungu*, with Titus Masondo, Shuter and Shooter, 1938.

Zulu readers: *Indlela yolimi lwesiZulu*, 4 volumes, Cape Town, Via Afrika, 1966.

MOLEMA, Moliri Silas

b. 1892, Mafeking, Botswana;
d. August 13, 1965, Mafeking.
Biographer, teacher, medical
doctor, scholar (wrote in English).

Molema, the son of the journalist, Silas Tseheho Molema (1856–1927), received his education in Healdtown in the Cape Province of South Africa. He graduated and then taught school at the Lyndhurst Road Public School in Kimberley for several years. About 1913 Molema left South Africa and went to Glasgow University to study medicine, graduating in 1919. He returned to South Africa, and spent most of the rest of his life in Mafeking. He was a lifelong Methodist, and supported the Botswana Government until his death. Though he was a member of the Barolong people, part of the Tswana-language group, Molema published only in English.

Molema's works are: *The Bantu, Past and Present* (1920); *Chief Moroka, His Life, His Times, His Country and His People; Montshiwa, Barolong Chief and Patriot (1815–1896)*, and an unpublished biography of Solomon Tshekisho Plaatje.

Writings: History: *The Bantu, Past and Present*, Edinburgh, W. Green and Son Ltd, 1920.

Biography: *Chief Moroka, His Life, His Times, His Country and His People*, Cape Town, Methodist Publishing House, 1952; *Montshiwa, Barolong Chief and Patriot (1815–1896)*, Cape Town, C. Struik, Ltd, 1966; unpublished biography of Solomon Plaatje.

MOLOTO, Davidson Pelman

b. August 6, 1910, Welgeval, Rustenburg District, Western Transvaal, South Africa.
Tswana novelist, educator.

First taught by his father, the Rev. S. D. Moloto of Witfontein, D. P. Moloto went on to Stofberg Memorial School to obtain his Teacher's Certificate. Appointed principal in 1930 of the Holfontein School, he continued private studies, taking both the Junior Certificate and the Afrikaans Certificate in 1935. He received his B.A. in 1939 from Fort Hare University College and while working on his degree completed his first novel, *Mokwena* (The Man of the Kwena [Crocodile] Clan), first published in 1942, about four years after he completed the work.

His teaching and educational posts

have been: Bethesda Practising School (1963–68); Emmarentia Geldenhuys Secondary School (1939–41); Wilberforce Training School (1942–44); principal at Bofokeng High School (1945–1956); supervisor in the Rustenburg Circuit (1957–65); and sub-inspector of schools (1965–present). His later degrees or diplomas are the B. Econ. (1944), and the University Teacher's Diploma (1956). While at Emmarentia, Moloto wrote the as-yet unpublished novel, "Motimedi" (The Drifter).

Moloto's series of six graded Tswana readers includes two of his novelettes, *Mogorosi I* and *Mogorosi II*, both about the kings.

Writings: Novels: *Mokwena,* Cape Town, Nasionale Pers Boekhandel, 1942; later printings, Cape Town, Via Afrika, 1961, 1966 (which was the tenth); *Mogorosi I; Mogorosi II,* 1940's?; "Motimedi," unpublished.

MOORE, Bai Tamia(h) Johnson
b. ca. 1916, Petajah, Liberia.
Autobiographer, poet, folklorist.

Moore attended elementary and secondary school in Richmond, Virginia after beginning to learn English in a mission school in Liberia. Born of Golah parents, he did not have the family background of the people of Monrovia and in mission school his name, Bai Tami'a, was changed to Johnson Moore after the pastor of the Richmond church that supported the mission. Planning to become a medical doctor in America and then to return home to help his people, he studied biology at Wayland College and Virginia Union University, taking the B.A. in 1938. On graduation, however, he began to write and never became a doctor.

Moore, on his return to Liberia, began to collect folk tales and poems which gradually found their way into his own poetry and stories. In 1937 his *Golah Boy in América* came out, and though written in Moore's still inadequate English it provides interesting contrasts between his life in Liberia and his attendance at the white mission school, with his experiences in America. The second half of the little book gives in some detail the customs and beliefs of his Golah people and provides Golah texts of verses from the Bible and various songs and poems.

His poetry was collected in the mimeographed volume, *Ebony Dust,* with an introduction by Rosina Robinson. In free and rhymed verse, the book is divided into three sections: African life, the American scene, and miscellaneous subjects, including a few poems on Moore's days in Europe and Asia. The title poem of the collection appeared in an 1958 Italian publication, *Liberia Today.* Another poem, "Jungle Melody," was included in a German anthology of West African literature (1954) and his story, "Murder in the Cassava Patch," appeared in *Liberian Writing,* and earlier was privately printed in Holland in 1968 but published in Monrovia. The author himself sold 2,000 copies of this work on streetcorners for 75 cents until the Liberian government took the remaining 3,000 copies for use as a school text. Based on an actual murder committed in 1956 which Moore had investigated as a journalist, the work first appeared as a serialized novelette in a Monrovian journal in 1956.

Though still not well known outside Liberia, Moore's poetry is receiving more attention and he has even received the not entirely happy accolade from Professor Roland Dempster of the University of Liberia as "one of West

Africa's outstanding jungle poets." Some of Moore's latest work, along with poetry of fellow Liberians, R. Tombekai Dempster and Harmon Carey Thomas, appeared in the collection, *Echoes from the valley,* and his collection of folksongs, *Categories of Traditional Liberian Songs,* appeared in 1969.

Writings: Autobiography: *Golah Boy in America,* Richmond, Quality Printing Company, 1937.

Poetry: *Ebony Dust,* Monrovia, Liberia, 1963.

Poem: "Ebony Dust" in *Liberia Today,* Italy, 1958; "Jungle Melody" in German anthology of West African literature, 1954; poems in *Echoes from the valley,* Cape Mount, Liberia, Douglas Muir Press, 1947.

Story: "Murder in the Cassava Patch" in *Liberian Writing: Liberia as seen by her own writers as well as by German authors;* Tübingen, Horst Erdman Verlag, 1970; earlier, Holland, Drukkerji Bosch, 1968, published Monrovia, 1968.

Folklore: *Categories of Traditional Liberian Songs,* Monrovia, printed for author, 1969.

MOORE, Richard (see RIVE, Richard)

MOPELI–PAULUS, Attwell Sidwell
b. January 15, 1913, Qoaqoa, Witzieshoek District, Orange Free State, South Africa, of Lesotho nationality.
Southern Sotho poet, novelist, playwright, story writer, translator (also writes in English).

A. S. Mopeli-Paulus, son of Chief Sidwell Mopeli and his wife Marie, attended Qoaqua and Stofberg Gedenk School for his primary education. About 1931 he entered Edendale College and finished in 1935. He became a student for a short period at the University of the Witwatersrand and after two years of private study won a B.A. in Bantu studies. He was in military service with the Cape Corps and served in Egypt and East Africa.

Mopeli, who added the Paulus to his last name as an adult, published his first work, a volume of poetry, *Ho tsamaea ke ho bona* (Travelling Helps One See) in 1945 and his second work, *Liretlo,* a study of ritual murder, in 1950. Peter Lanham three years later published in London a work based on *Liretlo,* entitled *Blanket Boy's Moon,* and in 1956, Mopeli-Paulus and Miriam Basner turned to the same work for a joint effort published as *Turn to the Dark.* The Lanham version appeared in the United States as *Blanket-Boy.* There are also Dutch, Danish, German, and Italian editions of one version or the other of *Liretlo.*

His only novel, or novelette, to date is the 23-page *Lilahloane oa batho* (The Unfortunate Lilahloane), 1950 and 1953. He has published Sesotho versions of Shakespeare's *MacBeth* and *Julius Caesar,* and an historical work on the founding chief of the Basotho people, *Moshweshwe moshwaila* (Moshoeshoe the Shearer), 1964. Various miscellaneous writings in Sotho have appeared in *Drum* and *Zonke,* leading Bantu journals in South Africa.

He has written three English language works: *The Prince,* a play first performed in 1967, "Lesotho, the Beloved," a story, and a long poem, "The Sinking of the Mendi" which dealt with the loss of hundreds of African soldiers during the Second World War when their ship, the *Mendi,* was torpedoed.

Awaiting publication is a second collection of his poetry, tentatively entitled "Ho tsamaea ke ho bona II" (Travelling Helps One See), and "At the Crossroads," genre unknown, the latter written in English.

Mopeli-Paulus at this date is considered one of South Africa's most important authors, though he is claimed as a fellow countryman by his Lesotho compatriots.

Writings: Poetry: *Ho tsamaea ke ho bona,* Morija, Morija Sesuto Book Depot, 1945; "Ho tsamaea ke ho bona II," unpublished; "At the Crossroads," unpublished; "The Sinking of the Mendi," publishing details not known.

Novels: *Lilahloane oa batho,* Bloemfontein, Nasionale Pers, 1953 (Jahn shows a 1950 edition by Via Afrika, Bloemfontein); *Blanket Boy's Moon,* with Peter Lanham, New York, Crowell, 1953; as *Blanket Boy,* London, Collins, 1953; and New York, Crowell, 1953; in Dutch as *Denken-Jongen,* Amsterdam, Nieuwe Wieken, 1953; as *Turn to the Dark,* with Miriam Basner, London, Cape, 1956.

Translations: Southern Sotho versions of Shakespeare's *MacBeth* and *Julius Caesar,* details not known.

Story: "Lesotho, the Beloved," unpublished.

Play: *The Prince,* performed in 1967.

History: *Moshweshwe moshwaila,* Johannesburg, Bona Press, 1964.

Study: *Liretlo,* Bloemfontein, Via Afrika, 1950.

Biographical/Critical Source: Albert S. Gérard, *Four African Literatures,* Berkeley, University of California Press, 1971.

MOREL, Marion
b. ca. 1935, South Africa.
Journalist.

Marion Morel wrote a regular column for *Drum,* the leading photogravure journal of Johannesburg devoted to local African writing. She is represented by "Girls About Town," a piece from her column, in Langston Hughes' *An African Treasury.*

Writings: Journalism: "Girls About Town," originally in *Drum;* in *An African Treasury,* New York, Pyramid, 1961.

MOROKE, Samson Alexander
b. 1912, Vereeniging, South Africa.
Tswana novelist, playwright, poet, minister.

After early schooling in and near his birthplace, Moroke went on to Kilnerton Training Institute where he earned a Teacher's Certificate. By private study he qualified for the Senior Certificate and was eventually ordained a Methodist minister. He presently has a church at Pietersburg. His first creative writing was the composition of brief dramatic sketches for his students.

His first published work was a play, *Puso yaga kgosi Farao* (The Administration of the King Pharaoh), 1957, followed by *Sephaphati* (The Coward), a novel written in the mid-1950's but published only in 1959. Other novels are *Lonaka lwa mahura mantsho* (The Horn of Black Grease), 1966, and *Bosa bo ganetsana le botsafe* (The Argument Between Youth and Age).

His two verse collections of verse are: *Matshotlho* (Bone Marrow), 1961, and *Tsa fa isong* (At the Hearth), 1968.

Two later plays were *Lobisa Radipitse* (Lobisa Radipitse, a person's name) and *Lehufa le lwa le thuto* (Polygamy vs. Teaching), both 1962.

Writings: Novels: *Sephaphati,* Bloemfontain, Via Afrika, 1959, 1963; *Lonaka lwa mahura mantŝho,* Cape Town, Via Afrika, 1960; Bloemfontein, Via Afrika, 1966; *Bosa bo ganetsana le botsafe,* Johannesburg, Bona Pers, 1968.

Poetry: *Matshotlho,* Johannesburg, Bona Press, 1961; *Tsa fa isong,* Pretoria, Better Books, 1968.

Plays: *Puŝô yaga kgôsi Farao,* Johannesburg, Afrikaanse, 1962; *Lobisa Radipitse,* Johannesburg, Bona Press, 1962; *Lehufa le lwa le thuto,* Cape Town, Via Afrika, 1962, 1970; Jahn terms *Lehufa* a novel rather than a play.

MOTSAMAI, Edward
b. May, 1870, Masite, Lesotho;
d. 1959.
Southern Sotho story writer,
biographer, minister.

Edward Motsamai attended the Morija Bible School, graduating with honors in 1886, and earned a teacher's certificate which enabled him to teach for the next three years at the Basutoland Training College and at Morija. In ill health, he left teaching for desultory study for the ministry and was finally ordained in 1900 after four years' of employment at the Morija Sesuto Book Depot which offered him time and encouragement to complete his studies. During most of his long life Motsamai was a preacher, his first post being at Litsunyane in the Maluti Mountains.

Motsamai's one work of creative literature was *Mehla ea malimo* (Cannibal Days), 1912, a collection of eighteen stories based on the memories of old men who kept alive the ancient pieties, not quite appreciated by Motsamai to judge by his title.

His religious works were: *Majoe a mahlano a molatsoana* (The Five Stream-

Pebbles), one of the earliest of Sotho works, and *Kereke* (The Church), a tract. The former work first appeared in the periodical, *Leselinaya* (The Little Light) in 1907, and was republished the same year at Morija in book form. According to the author, the five pebbles, or meditations, were designed to protect Christian youth from sin and paganism.

The last known work of Motsamai was the biography, *Morena Moshoeshoe mar'a Mokhachane* (Chief Moshoeshoe, Son of Mokhachane), published in 1942.

Writings: Stories: *Mehla ea malimo,* Morija, 1912.

Religious works: *Majoe a mahlano a molatsoana,* in periodical, *Leselinaya,*

Motsamai

1907; later in book form by Morija Sesuto Book Deposit, Morija, 1907; *Kereke,* Morija, 1925.

Biography: *Morena Moshoeshoe mar'a Mokhachane,* 1942.

MOTSISI, Moses Casey
b. 1931, Johannesburg, South Africa.
Short story writer.

Motsisi has contributed stories to *Drum,* the best of the journals open to black poets and fiction writers of South Africa. His story, "Riot," appears in Neville Denny's *Pan African Short Stories.* Motsisi contributed an article on Todd Matshikiza, South African writer and musician, to *The Classic* III, 1, 1968.

Writings: Story: "Riot" in *Pan African Short Stories,* London, Nelson, 1965; other stories in *Drum.*

Article: "Todd Matshikiza," in *The Classic,* III, 1, Johannesburg, 1968.

MOUMOUNI Abdou
b. ca. 1920, Niger.
Novelist, scientist, teacher, educator.

Locally educated at the lower level, he attended a lycée in Dakar and then went to Paris to study science at the Sorbonne. Moumouni has taught in Senegal, Guinea, his home country of Niger, and has traveled widely in Europe, Asia, and North America. After two years of research at the Academy of Sciences in Moscow, Moumouni returned to Africa to take a position as professor at the Ecole Normale Supérieure in Bamako, Mali, where he also works at the Laboratory of Solar Energy. He has contributed many articles on science and African

affairs to professional journals. His scholarly work, *Education in Africa,* appeared in English translation by Phillis Naults Ott, 1964.

Writings: Scholarly Study: *Education in Africa,* in English translation by Phyllis Naults Ott, London, The Trinity Press, 1964.

MPASHI, Stephen Andrea
b. ca. 1920, Zambia.
Bemba novelist, story writer, biographer, poet.

Mpashi has learned to combine some of the characteristics of oral Bemba stories with the subject matter of twentieth-century life in Northern Rhodesia (now Zambia). Two of his recent works, published in Bemba, are *Abapatili bafika ku Babemba,* 1962, and *Icibemba na mano yaciko,* 1963. In 1969, Longmans, Green published his biography, *Betty Kaunda,* in Lusaka. With his fellow Zambian, Joseph Musapu, he published a 33-page collection of Bemba poems, *Amalango,* 1962.

Mpashi's early work, stories or novelettes, were *Uwakwensho bushiku* (A Friend in Need is a Friend Indeed), 1951; *Uwauma nafyala* (One Might As Well Hang for a Sheep as a Lamb), 1955; *Pano calo* (Right Here on Earth), 1956, and *Pio akobekela Vera* (Pio Becomes Engaged to Vera), 1957. His first work was the novelette, *Cekesoni aingila ubosoja,* (Jackson Becomes a Soldier), 1950.

Writings: Stories: *Uwakwensho bushiku,* Cape Town, Oxford University Press, 1951, second edition 1955; *Uwauma nafyala,* Lusaka and Blantyre, The Publications Bureau, 1955; *Pano calo,* Cape Town, Oxford University Press, 1956;

Pio akobekela Vera, Cape Town, Oxford University Press, 1957.

Novels: *Abapatili bafika ku Babemba,* second edition, Cape Town, Oxford University Press, 1962; *Icibemba na mano yaciko,* second edition, Cape Town, Oxford University Press, 1963.

Biography: *Betty Kaunda,* Lusaka, Longmans Green, 1969.

Novelette: *Cekesoni aingila ubosoja,* Cape Town, Oxford University Press, 1950.

Poetry: *Amalango* (also contains poems by Joseph Musapu), Lusaka, Publications Bureau of Northern Rhodesia and Nyasaland, 1962.

MPHAHLELE, Ezekiel

b. December 17, 1919, Pretoria, South Africa.

Novelist, essayist, critic, short story writer, editor, teacher.

Mphahlele's father was a country man who worked as a messenger for a clothing shop; his mother did domestic work in the white homes of Pretoria. His first memories were of the black slums of the city, but from his fifth to twelfth years he lived the slow, traditional, life in the proverty-stricken countryside in and around Maupaneng, 75 miles from Pietersburg. He returned to Pretoria, this time to Marabastad, the teeming locale of his autobiography, *Down Second Avenue.* Then began the struggle for education, for manhood, and for understanding the prison that South Africa was becoming with every passing year.

Probably Black Africa's leading literary intellectual using the English language, Mphahlele obtained his education in local schools, at St. Peter's Secondary School, Johannesburg, and earned a Teacher's Certificate from

Adams' College in Natal in 1940. From 1941 to 1945 he worked as clerk-typist in an institute for the blind, then for the next seven years he taught English and Afrikaans in one of the largest high schools in Johannesburg. He was dismissed in 1952 because he had taken part in protests against the segregationist Bantu Education Act.

Prohibited from teaching, he tried journalism as literary editor of *Drum* in 1955, but soon quit and turned to a variety of other inconsequential jobs. During this discouraging period he helped organize the Syndicate of Artists to try to elevate cultural standards in Africa writing. At the same time he began to submit short stories to *Drum, Fighting Talk,* and *The World,* all journals open to black writing.

Mphahlele

In 1957 he succeeded in obtaining a passport and exit visa for himself, his wife and children and flew to exile in Nigeria. He taught there for four years, first in a grammar school in Lagos and then at the University of Ibadan, where he taught English language and literature. From 1960 to 1966 he was also editor of *Black Orpheus* magazine. He found the Nigerians strangely relaxed and complacent as compared to the tense, lost, and oppressed black South Africans.

He moved to Kenya, East Africa, in 1963, staying for three years to teach English at the University College, Nairobi, and to serve as Director of the ChemiChemi Cultural Center in Nairobi. In 1959 he spent almost five months in Britain, his first stay there, and his first trip out of Africa. In July, 1960, he attended the annual conference of the American Society of African Culture at Philadelphia where he was on a panel to discuss "Negritude and Culture." During the early 60's he also directed in Paris the African Program for the Congress for Cultural Freedom and worked for the leading black journal, *Présence Africaine*.

After two years in Paris, he moved to the University of Denver in Colorado as Visiting Professor in the Department of English (1966–68) where he completed the first draft of his novel, *The Wanderers* as his Ph.D. dissertation. Returning to Africa, he took up the post as Professor of Literature at the University of Zambia, but in 1970 he went back to the University of Denver where he presently is teaching. During the late 1960's Mphahlele also served as an editor of the *Journal of New African Literature and the Arts*, issued by the University of California at Los Angeles, a position he still holds.

His only novel won the first prize from *African Arts* magazine's literary competition. The first part of the work is based on the last sections of *Down Second Avenue,* looking back on his last years in South African from the vantage point of greater maturity, having experienced "the comedy and agony of exile," as he says in his foreword. *African Arts* gave the novel a thorough review in the Summer issue, 1971. The book is a continuation of the earlier autobiographical effort rather than a pure novel.

During the past ten years Mphahlele has become one of the most widely known anthologists and critics of new African writing, and is sought after by publishers to introduce new works or to review them. Most recent is his introduction to *Night of My Blood*, a collection of poems by the Ghanaian poet Kofi Awoonor. Typical of his sensitive discussion of poetry is this passage:

> The elegiac mood that pervades Kofi Awoonor's poetry reaches its high water mark in his 'Lament of the Silent Sister.' The cry for what Africa has lost in her traditional values with the accompanying exhortation for us to take a grip of ourselves, to ask our fathers to 'sew the old days' for us, finds in the 'Lament' a concrete and still elevating subject—that of Christopher Okigbo who died in the Nigerian war in 1967. I consider this elegy to be the finest in African writing, one of the finest in the English-speaking world. It is truly African, taking us on a wave that rises and falls to the deep tones of a funeral drum. And from deep down there the voice of the mourner rides on a diction that comes straight to the heart.

Mphahlele has published three collections of short stories: *Man Must Live and Other Stories, The Living and the Dead and Other Stories,* and *In Corner B.* In *Down Second Avenue,* his well received autobiography, Mphahlele writes:

> Now I don't have the impulse left to write

254

a short story anymore. The waves of something thrashing about inside me are too fierce and noisy to be contained by the short sharp precise statement that is the short story. I am now more confirmed than ever before in my belief that I wrote short fiction in South Africa because the distance between the ever-present stimulus and the anger was so short, the anger screamed for an outlet with such a burning urgency, that I had to find a prose medium that would get me to the focal point with only a few eloquent movements. The short story was such a medium. . . .

And he goes on to say, "Outside South Africa, in the bigger world of bigger ideas and in situations that demand a larger variety of emotional responses, one's reflexes take on a different quality, a greater complexity." Mphahlele now feels the need for the range of the novel and the long critical essay.

In 1959, Faber and Faber brought out *Down Second Avenue* which, though not quite literally autobiographical, has become possibly the most important statement of how it feels to grow up black in the slums of South Africa. The work has been translated into French, German, Serbo–Croatian, Bulgarian, Hungarian, Japanese, Swedish, and other languages. In closing his up-dated introduction to the work, Mphahlele, looking back over the eleven years since its publication, asked, "What does a book about my life mean in the South African context? Maybe nothing beyond the fact that it is the autobiography of most Africans in that chamber of horrors. It reminds me, for my own edification, [of] the fortitude of my people. It is so far, I think, the best thing I have ever written." (Faber and Faber, brought out an abbreviated and school reader version of this work in 1965.)

His most important critical work is *The African Image* which has become a classic

of sorts. The chapter titles give a clear idea of the scope of the work: The African Personality; What Price 'Negritude'?; Roots; Those Cheeky Kaffirs, Those Impertinent Natives; The Nationalist; Going My Way? and the very interesting last two sections: The White Man's Image of the Not-White in Fiction; and, The Black Man's Literary Image of Himself.

The chapter, "The Non-European Character in South African English Fiction," was in its earlier form submitted in 1956 for a senior paper for his B.A. This unpublished work dealt with Oliver Schriner, Sarah Gertrude Millin, Alan Paton, William Plomer, Laurens van der Post, Peter Abrahams, Thomas Pringle, Percy Fitzpatrick, William Charles Scully, Nadine Gordimer, Joseph Conrad, E.M. Forster, and the American, William Faulkner. The new version in *The African Image* contains much new matter on many of these writers and, additionally, discusses Doris Lessing, Elspeth Huxley, David Karp, Joyce Cary, Sylvester Stein, Uys Krige, Jack Cope, and Ethelreda Lewis.

Considering this book from the vantage point of eight years, Mphahlele writes of this work in 1970:

I say in The African Image *that I cannot think of a South without the white population, that their destiny and ours are interlocked. This can of course only be realized after a bloody revolution. The black man will have no mercy, and rightly so. White technicians will still be required by a black government. This way the whites have yet a chance of becoming cultured and civilized. . . . Anybody who sincerely wants to help the African must try to do what will, at some point along the line, promote guerilla activity in southern Africa.*

It has been a long path since exile.

Mphahlele

As Mphahlele puts it in his introduction to *Down Second Avenue:* "Thirteen years. Six major moves in that time: Nigeria (four years); France (two years); Kenya (three years); Denver (two years); Zambia (twenty-one months). Now back to Denver, as an immigrant. In between teaching sessions there have been conferences: on race politics and on literature; writers' and artists' workshops; arts festivals. And now I must call a halt to this—for myself."

One of the significant products of that exile was his editing of *African Writing Today* which he declared was intended "to give the intelligent reader a map of themes and styles of African writing in the metropolitan languages—English, French, and Portuguese. It is a young and still tender literature. Most of the authors represented here are between thirty and forty-five years of age." Mphahlele has tried to collect writing which shows Black Africa becoming aware of itself. Though most of the writers share a common history of colonialism, independence, and the trails of untried and often dangerous freedom, it is "the peculiarly African experience that is superimposed on that of the common denominator of world concerns." But "superimposed" seems too harsh, certainly almost an inaccurate term to apply to many of the works in this collection. They could only have been written by Black Africans. All of the selections carry some conviction and naturalness. All of them are worthy of attention in themselves, something not always true in other anthologies.

Possibly the most interesting item in the anthology is Mphahlele's own essay, "Remarks on Négritude" (originally delivered at the Conference on African Literature in French and the University Curriculum, Dakar, March 26–29, 1963). After ten years, his words still define the two sides of the African attitude to literature (neither of which accept Jean Paul Sartre's Marxist thesis that literature, particularly the work coming from the former colonial world, ought to serve revolution and is unimportant itself as a matter of individual or esthetic expression). The negritude position is of course that work by African writers should bespeak the particular qualities of being Black and African. Mphahlele states the opposing position, urging that writers should strive "to assert our *human* and not African dignity." He argues that too much of negritude writing, particularly the poetry, is a romanticising of Africa—making it "a symbol of innocence, purity and artless primitiveness."

European modes and experiences, he concludes, will have to be absorbed and exploited by the African writer, for they are, irremediably, part of the African's experience. Though many African intellectuals, particularly the francophone writers, find him too soft and westernized, Mphahlele's closing words in the address still ring in the mind: " . . . literature and art are too big for negritude, and it had better be left as a historical phase."

Perhaps the words that best describe Mphahlele's position are the lines of the Portuguese-language poet, J. Craveirinha, in his "Poem of the Future Citizen" collected in the anthology:

I came from somewhere
from a Nation which does not yet exist.
I came and I am here!

Most recently, Mphahlele has published *Voices in the Whirlwind and Other Essays,* six essays treating of the culture and literature of America and Africa.

Writings: Autobiographical novels: *The*

Wanderers, New York, Macmillan, 1971; *Down Second Avenue*, London, Faber and Faber, 1959, 1971; Berlin, Seven Seas Books, 1962; New York, Anchor, 1971; London, Faber, 1971; translations in French, German, Serbo-Croatian, Bulgarian, Hungarian, Japanese, Swedish.

Short Stories: *Man Must Live and Other Stories*, Cape Town, African Bookman, 1947; second edition, Ibadan, Ministry of Education, 1958; *The Living and the Dead, and Other Stories*, Ibadan, Black Orpheus, Ministry of Education, 1961; *In Corner B*, Nairobi, East African Publishing House, 1967.

Criticism: *The African Image*, London, Faber and Faber, 1962; New York, Praeger, 1962.

Anthologies: *African Writing Today*, London, Penguin, 1967; *Modern African Stories*, with Ellis Ayitey Komey, London, Faber, 1964, 1966.

Essays: *Voices in the Whirlwind and Other Essays*, New York, Hill and Wang, 1972.

Biographical/Critical Sources: Review of *Down Second Avenue* in *African Arts*, Summer, 1971; Gerald Moore, "Ezekiel Mphahlele: The Urban Outcast," *Seven African Writers*, London, Oxford University Press, 1962; *Palaver: Interviews with Five African Writers in Texas* (Achebe, J.P. Clark, Brutus, Mphahlele, and Kofi Awoonor), Austin, Texas, the University of Texas at Austin, 1972.

MQHABA, Alton A. M.
B. 1928, Matatiele, Cape Province, South Africa.
Xhosa short story writer.

The son of Christian parents who were members of the Moravian Church in Matatiele and Alton, and one of seven children, young Alton Mqhaba was an earnest student in the Mpharane Higher Primary School, the Langa Secondary School in Cape Town and the Eagle's Peak College in Lesotho. His parents lost what little funds they had, and Mqhaba left school in 1945 for a period to help the larger family. Fortunately, he had done so well at Eagle's Peak that the principal, learning of the family's difficulties, offered him a scholarship which enabled him to complete his Junior Certificate examination successfully in late 1946.

Though he had been converted to the Roman Catholic faith while at school, the efforts of the priests to have him enter a seminary and eventually the priesthood caused a strong reaction. He abandoned his studies, and sought a job in Durban and then in Johannesburg. Finally employed in Germiston in the Native Affairs Department, he remained for many years before he resigned in 1957. During this period he earned his General Certificate of Education (similar to the American high school diploma) from the University of London by correspondence courses.

Mqhaba's first major writing effort was during the late 1940's when he composed a novel in Southern Sotho (he was bi-lingual in both Sotho and his native tongue Xhosa) which the Morija Sesuto Book Depot refused for publication. Undaunted, he sat down to write a second novel, this time in Xhosa, and sent it to his former teacher, the Rev. James Jolobe. Jolobe was less than pleased with it, suggested a complete revision and offered observations concerning correct usages of Xhosa. (Scholars had gradually standardized Xhosa as a written language and had developed a more or less accepted grammar and orthography). Mqhaba, no language specialist, was severely discouraged. He lapsed into a four years' silence, broken finally by the publication of his short stories, *Hayi ke beth' iinto zomhlaba* (Oh my, how worldly are these things) in 1957. This volume of 200 pages remains his only published work.

Writings: Short stories: *Hayi ke beth' iinto zomhlaba,* Lovedale, Lovedale Press, 1957 (Jahn declares this volume to be a novel).

MQHAYI, Samuel Edward Krune Loliwe
b. December 1, 1875, Gqumahashe Mission Station, Chumie Valley, Cape Province, South Africa;
d. July 29, 1945.
Xhosa language novelist, biographer, poet, teacher, scholar.

This most famous of the Xhosa poets was born into an illustrious family. He was the son of Ziwani, scholar of all the Bantu languages of South Africa and teacher, and the great grandson of Mqhayi the chief of the Amacira clan of the Xhosa people. Born near the town of Alice in the Victoria East District of the Cape Province, Samuel was named after the Old Testament prophet, and given several Xhosa names, one ot them Loliwe (Railway), for the fact that the first trains began to run in the Chumie Valley in the year of his birth.

Samuweli, as he was often called, began school in Evergreen, six miles from his home in Allandale, staying there from 1882 to 1885. There he met Mpambani Jeremiah Mzimba and John Tengo Jabavu who were to become leading Xhosa personalities and writers. At the age of nine, the family moved to Centane in the Transkei because of famine and the young Samuel listened closely

to the old warriors' tales and to the arguments of the "Great Place," the meeting area where his great-uncle Chief Nzazana held court. This material later appeared in his great novel, *Ityala lamawela* (The Case of the Twins) published in 1914 but possibly written during the earliest years of the 20th century.

He studied at Lovedale off and on from 1891 to 1895, was confirmed in the Presbyterian Church, and took a teachers' training course. In 1897 Mqhayi taught at the West Bank Location in East London and his first small group of collected "praise-songs" were published in the *Izwi labantu* (The Voice of the People). He worked as a sub-editor for that journal from 1897 to 1900 and then moved on to teach at Centane from 1900 to 1906. His first publication in book form, *U-Samson,* told the biblical story of Samson in Xhosa. In this period he lost his first wife and, after a few years, was remarried to Amy Cukudu.

From 1905 to 1909 he was again sub-editor of *Izwilabantu,* leaving, at the demise of that journal, for Mcentsho to teach among the Mdlambe clan, a part of the Xhosa nation. After one year he went to Mpongo to teach, remaining until 1920. He was an editor of John Tengo Jabavu's *Imvo zabantsundu* from 1920 to 1922, and was invited to work as a proofreader of Bantu and English language scripts at Lovedale Press in 1922. Instead, he began standardizing Xhosa orthography and establishing grammatical and syntactical practices with William Govan Bennie, the inspector for Native Education. His novel, *Ityala lamawele,* later translated as *The Case of the Twins,* published in 1914 in Xhosa, quickly found a wide popular reception and he became famous, the work going through eight editions by 1930. An enlarged edition in 1931 also contains a play, Xhosa tales and praise-poems, a few of Mqhayi's own original and modern poems in Xhosa, and several sections on various Xhosa authors, including Jabavu, Rubusana, W. W. Gqoba, and Bokwe.

In 1929 Mqhayi published *U-Don Jade,* a Bantu utopian work looking toward an ideal world of social justice and the elimination of racism. Part III of this novel won the May Esther Bedford Prize in 1935.

His works of biography are: *U-bomi bom-Fundisi u J. K. Bokwe* (The Life of the Reverand J. K. Bokwe), 1925; *U-Sogqumahashe,* on Chief Cyril Mhalla (ca. 1850–1920); *Isikhumbuzo sika Ntsikana,* a short study of the prophet Ntsikana. His autobiography, *U-Mqhayi wase-Ntab'ozuko* (Mqhayi from the Mountain of Glory), was composed in the early 1930's but not published until 1939.

His considerable works in poetry were: *I-Bandla labantu* (The Church ot the People), 1923; *Imihobe nemi-Bongo* (Songs of Exaltation), 1927, which also contained works by other poets; *Yoko-fundwa ezikolweni* (Lullabies to be Studied in School. Other volumes were: *U Mhlekazi u-Hintsa: Um-bongo ewasiya izibongo zamadoda ngomnyaka we 1937,* a long epic work in eight cantos on Chief Hintsa; *I-nzuzo* (Reward), 1942, which contains some of Mqhayi's best work, including praise poems on Simon Petrus Sihlali, William Govan Bennie, Charlotte Maxeke, John Tengo Jabavu and John Knox Bokwe. An early work, about 1920, was *Ama-gora e-Mendi* (The Heroes of the Mendi) which he had set to the music of A. M. Jonas.

His translations into Xhosa were: *U-Aggrey um-Afrika,* 1935, from E. S. Smith's *Aggrey of Africa;* a translation of William George Dowsley's book *Farming for Schools,* called in Xhosa, *U-limo, lucazelwe izikolo zase-Afrika esezantsi;* and *U-Adonisi wase-ntlango* (Adonis of the Desert), a translation of the Afrikaans novel of G. C. and S. B. Hobson, *Mees van die Kalahari* (Mees of the Kalahari Desert).

Settling down in Ntab' ozuko, his house on Tilana's Hill in the Berlin district near King William's Town in 1925, he began a series of trips through the country of the Xhosa speaking peoples. Davidson Don Tengo Jabavu in 1920 had called him "Imbongi yesizwe jikelele" (The praise-poet of the entire Xhosa nation) and in effect he was accepted as the poet laureate of his people. Dressed in traditional garb he recited praise-poems for important African and European guests at celebrations of various sorts. Benedict Vilakazi called him "the father of Xhosa poetry."

He died on July 29, 1945 in his home

on the mountain. Mqhayi was remembered in songs and poems by the writers of the entire Xhosa nation. Herbert Isaac Ernest Dhlomo, the famous Zulu poet, eulogized Mqhayi as the last link between the old tribal bards who extemporized their verses and the modern Westernized African who writes. Mqhayi left miscellaneous manuscripts unpublished though a few historical essays and several poems appeared in the anthologies, *Imibengo* (Titbits), edited by William Govan Bennie, and Walter B. Rubusana's *Zemk' inkomo magwale ndini* (Away go the cattle, you cowards).

Writings: Novel: *Ityala lamawele*, East London, South Africa, 1914; the 1931 edition also contains a play, Xhosa tales, praise-poems, essays on Jabavu, Rubusana, W. W. Gqoba, and John Knox Bokwe; Jahn also declares this work was published in Lovedale, 1914; translation by August Collingwood as *The Case of the Twins*, in *New African*, Volume V, 1966; *U-Don Jade*, Lovedale, 1929.

Poetry: *Ama-gora e-Mendi*, Lovedale, 192?; *I-Bandla Labantu*, 1923; *Imihobe nemi-Bongo*, London, Sheldon Press, 1927; *U-Mhlekazi u-Hintza: um-bongo ewasiya izibongo zamadoda ngomnyaka we*, 1937, Lovedale, Lovedale Press, 1937; *I-nzuzo*, Johannesburg, University of Witwatersrand Press, 1942; also as Volume VII of Bantu Treasury Series; later in Bantu Treasury Series in new orthography and format, 1957. Poems and essays in *Zemk' inkomo magwale ndini*, W. B. Rubusana, editor, London, Butler and Tanner, 1906; *Imibengo*, W. G. Bennie, editor, Lovedale, 1939.

Biography: *U-bomi bom-Fundisi u J. K. Bokwe*, Lovedale, 1925; *U-Sogqumahashe; Isikhumbuzo sika Ntsikana*, Lovedale, date unknown.

Autobiography: *U-Mqhayi wase Ntab'-ozuko*, Lovedale, 1939; first published in German in Diedrich Westermann's *Afrikaner erzähler ihr Leben*, Essen, 1938.

Translations: *U-Aggrey um-Afrika*, abridged version of E. S. Smith's *Aggrey of Africa*, London, Sheldon Press, 1935; *U-Limo lucazelwe izikolo zase-Afrika esezantsi* (of Wm. G. Dowsley's *Farming for Schools*), Cape Town, Nasionale Pers, 1922; *U-Adonise wase-ntlango* (from the Afrikaans language novel of G. C. and S. B. Hobson, *Kees van die Kalahari*), Lovedale, 1945.

Biographical/Critical Sources: Diedrich Westermann, *Afrikaner erzähler ihr Leben*, Essen, 1938; French translation: *Autobiographies d'Africains*, Paris, 1943; A. C. Jordan, "Samuel Edward Krune Mqhayi," *South African Outlook*, LXXV, 1945; Albert S. Gérard, *Four African Literatures*, Berkeley, University of California Press, 1971.

MSELEKU, Malcolm Raymond Dunford
b. December 8, 1912, at Umzumbi South Africa; d. January, 1961. Zulu-language story teller, poet.

Mseleku's father was an evangelist of the American Board Mission in Natal. He attended mission school, then Adams' Training College, obtaining his Teacher's Certificate in 1936. In 1937, he went to teach at Nhlophenkulu School in Nongoma, staying there for two years before going on to Imkulukeko School for three years. From 1942 to 1946, Mseleku taught at several other country schools before being appointed the superintendent of school meals in Drefontein, a post he held from 1946 to 1949. In 1949 he became a superindendent of schools, remaining in that position until 1955 when he was made a sub-inspector of Bantu education. Ill health forced him to resign in mid–1960.

Mseleku is the author of "Uvum-indaba" (The One Who Pretends), published about 1935, a moralistic tale of a young boy. Another early work, "Unkosiyezeve," also appeared in an obscure printing in the 1930's. His poems, published in miscellaneous newspapers and Zulu-language journals, include "Ukwethwasa Kwehlobo" and "Ukuduma Kwezulu."

Writings: Story: "Uvumindaba," ca. 1935; "Unkosiyezeve," 193?

Poems: "Ukwethwasa Kwehlobo" and "Ukuduma Kwezulu": details not known.

MTHEMBU, Robert Hiram
b. December 13, 1907, at Adams Mission, Natal Province,
South Africa; d. December, 1959.
Zulu novelist, educator.

R. H. Mthembu's early schooling was in local schools and later at Amanzimtoti (Adams') College from which he received his Teacher's Certificate in 1927. He taught at various schools in Natal before becoming examiner for Bantu Schools in Northern Zululand from 1949 to 1955. That latter year he was appointed sub-inspector of Bantu education on the Northern Zululand Circuit.

His one literary work is the novel, *UMamazana*. He also served on a committee which produced Zulu readers at graded levels of difficulty, *The Africa Zulu Readers*.

Writings: Novel: *UMamazana*, Durban, T. W. Griggs, 1947; assisted in writing

The Africa Zulu Readers: details not known.

MUBITANA, Kafungulwa
b. ca. 1930, Zambia.
Poet, art historian, museum curator.

Mubitana was locally educated, but travelled to Uganda to take his university training at Makerere University, Kampala, where he received his B.A. in Fine Arts. After graduation he began work with the Livingston Museum in Dar es Salaam, where he became deputy director and keeper of art and ethnography. In the late 1960's, he began research and special studies on a doctorate at the University of Edinburgh.

His literary work is usually ethnographic in nature with passages or extracts from songs cited to illustrate his essays on the dance or other dramatic performances of the Zambian peoples. A recent article, "Wiko Masquerades," is an example of this approach to African art.

Writings: Article: "Wiko Masquerades" in *African Arts*, Spring, 1971.

MUHAMMAD wad Daif Allah
b. ca. 1750 in eastern Sudan;
d. 1809–10.
Arabic-language historian,
collector of legends.

This scholar of the Fundj kingdom is the author of the *Tabakat*, a collection of the centuries-old annals and legends of the area in the eastern Sudan.

Writings: Legends: *Tabakat*, in Arabic manuscript.

Muhammed

MUHAMMED, Said Abdulla (see ABDULLA, Muhammed Said)

MUKASA, Ham
b. ca. 1868, Mamba, Uganda; d. 1956.
Luganda-language scholar,
statesman, traveloguist.

Son of Sensalire, a minor chief of the Mamba clan whose totem was the lung-fish, Ham Mukasa early became a page to King Mutesa of Uganda. He converted to Christianity about 1887 when he was about 19 and was wounded in the knee in the first war between Christians and Mohammedans, remaining lame the rest of his life. After the war he became chief of Kiyoza, but was more interested in the teaching which he began in 1893 and his work as a lay-reader of the Uganda Anglican Church. He helped the Ugandan admiral,

Gabunga, administer the country's navy of canoes, dhows, etc. and owned the island of Lujabwa given him by King Mutesa. He was one of the first Ugandans to learn to speak, read, and write English.

In 1901 Ham Mukasa and Apolo Kagwa, the Katikiro (prime minister) to the boy-king Kabaki Daudi Chwa, traveled to England to attend the coronation of Edward VII in London. The voyage, a fabulous one for Africans of that day, took them to Mombasa on the coast, then up the Indian Ocean and through the Suez Canal to the Mediterranean, and on to Europe with visits to factories, churches, prisons, palaces, and many ports and great cities. When the two returned—Mukasa was appointed to capture the whole journey in Luganda from the point of view of his superior, the Katikiro. Apolo Kagwa, about 37 years old in 1901 was a tall, vigorous man, some six feet, three inches tall, a great fighter and Christian, and an intelligent commentator and mild satirist of things European. Though the resultant work, translated into English and published in London in 1904, is entitled *Katikiro in England,* Mukasa's experiences and personality is fully integrated into the Katikiro's report.

Mukasa also wrote and had published two other works, *Luganda Language,* and a *Commentary on the Gospel of St. Matthew,* both in Luganda, and the *Commentary* was said to have had a "good sale" by Ernest Millar, the translator of *Katikiro in England.*

Writings: Travel Report: *Katikiro in England,* London, 1904, translated from Luganda by Ernest Millar, and republished as *Uganda's Katikoro in England,* Freeport, New York, Books for Libraries Press, 1971.

Grammar and Glossary: *Luganda Language,* in Luganda, details not known.

Biblical Study: *Commentary on the Gospel of St. Matthew,* in Luganda, details not known.

MUKASA–BALIKUDDEMBRE, Joseph
b. ca. 1943, Uganda.
Playwright (in Luganda and Runyoro-Rutoro languages), actor, teacher (also writes in English).

Educated locally in his early years, Joseph Mukasa-Balikuddembre took his B.A. (with Honors) in English at the University of East Africa, Kampala. His plays, *The Famine* and *The Mirror* appear in Cook and Lee's *Short East African Plays in English.* The first is a translation-adaptation from Luganda and the second from Runyoro-Rutoro, made for the Ugandan Travelling Theatre. The author took a leading role in each one, ad-libbing to bring in local customs, gossip, names, etc., of the towns the troups happened to be playing, a practice similar to that of the Commedia dell' Arte in Italy during the renaissance.

Writings: Plays: *The Famine; The Mirror;* both in *Short East African Plays in English,* Cook and Lee, editors, Nairobi, London, Heinemann, 1968.

MUKASA–SSALI, Paul
b. 1946, Uganda.
Poet.

Paul Mukasa–Ssali attended Busoga College in Mwiri, Makerere College School, and Makerere University, in Kampala, taking the B.A. in English (with honors) in 1970. He began writing poems and essays in high school, winning both the Taylor Essay Prize and the Brooke Bond Tea Essay Prize in 1964. He was the editor of one issue of the Makerere student journal, *Penpoint,* in 1970, and won a new literary award, the Makerere University Exhibition Prize. Three of his poems, "Katebo Port," "The Sentinel," and "When you come," appear in *Poems from East Africa.* "Ketebo Port" is particularly attractive for its picture of the busy lake port and the boys firing their sling shots at circling birds. Even better is "The Sentinel" which in seven lines captures something of the ironic, taciturn qualities of one of T. S. Eliot's "Preludes."

Writings: Poems in *Poems from East Africa,* Cook and Rubadiri, editors, London, Heinemann, 1971.

MULAISHO, Dominic
b. 1933, Mkando, Zambia.
Novelist, economist, government official.

After local schooling, Mulaisho attended Chalimbana Teachers' College and then the University College of Rhodesia and Nyasaland, studying English, history, and economics. After service with various ministries, he was named permanent secretary in the office of the president. In 1971, he became chairman of the Mining Development Corporation, the new nationally owned company organized to control copper mining in Zambia previously in the hands of international interests. Mulaisho is married, with four children.

His only novel to date is *The Tongue of the Dumb,* 1971, a story of the struggles of Lubinda, royal councillor to Chief Mpona, to oust Mpona by having him execution by his subjects. Christianity, witchcraft, old beliefs, all clash and interact as the plot moves to Mpona's last-minute victory over the evil councillor and his henchman, the kamscape or witchdoctor. Although there are telling scenes of village life, the over-all point of view is very Western, or Westernized, and there is little of the feeling of intimate involvement with the people so richly evident in the novels of Chinua Achebe, a writer who exploits somewhat similar themes. What is important in the

Writings: Novel: *The Tongue of the Dumb,* London, Heinemann, 1971.

MULIKITA, Fwanyanga Matale
b. 1928, Sefula, Mongu, Barotse Province, Zambia.
Lozi and English short story writer, playwright, teacher, diplomat.

novel, however, is the picture of a very intelligent, but dishonest man, Lubinda, manipulating his fellow villagers with both African and European ideas and pressures. On the village level the plotting could be symbolic of the struggles by the new elites against the traditional power of the chiefs.

Receiving his primary education in Mongu, Mulikita began his secondary education in 1945 at Munali, Lusaka, passing the Cambridge School Certificate with distinction in English literature and in general science. After high school, he worked for two years as a clerk–interpreter for the local High

Court and then went on to his B.A. degree at Fort Hare University College in 1954 where he studied English and psychology.

Mulikita did his first teaching at Mongu Secondary School (1954–56) and then became a welfare officer for the municipality of Kitwa, and finally a teacher at Kitwe Teacher Training College (1947–48). In 1958 he took a certificate in freelance journalism, and travelling to the United States, completed a M.A. in psychology at Stanford in 1960 after two years of study. After a three-year period (1961–64) at home during which he opened the Chalimbana Secondary School where he served as headmaster, he returned to the United States, this time to study at Columbia University in the field of diplomacy and international relations. When Zambia became independent in 1964, he was named his country's ambassador to the United Nations. In 1966 he was permanent secretary in the Ministry of Agriculture and on March 1, 1968, he was named permanent secretary to the Ministy of Foreign Affairs.

Mulikita's collection of stories, *A Point of No Return*, was published in 1968. The charming, naive stories have such diverting titles as "Human caterpillars were eating away the leaves of his family," "Back to rural romance," and "A baby reforms a notorious thief " which is similar to an O. Henry story of the same general theme. His poetic drama, *Shaka Zulu*, focuses on the great Zulu king and soldier, first celebrated by Thomas Mofolo in his novel *Chaka* (1925).

His one collection of vernacular stories (in Lozi) is *Batili ki mwanaka* (No, This is My Child) appeared in 1958.

Writings: Stories: *A Point of No Return,* Lusaka, National Educational Company of Zambia Limited, 1968; *Batili ki*

mwanaka, Lusaka and Blantyre, The Publications Bureau, 1958.

Poetry: *Shaka Zulu,* Lusaka, Longmans of Zambia, 1967.

MUNONYE, John
b. 1929, Akokwa, Eastern Nigeria.
Novelist, educator.

Munonye studied at Christ the King College, Onitsha, from 1944 to 1948, took a B.A. in 1952 from Ibadan University where he majored in Latin, Greek and history, and did post-graduate work in education at London University. Returning to Nigeria, he became inspector of education in Eastern Nigeria.

Recently he has been serving as principal of the Advanced Teacher Training College at Owerri. He is married and has two children.

The author demonstrates sympathy and pathos in showing the clash of worlds and culture in his first novel, *The Only Son*, published in 1966. The 202-page work convincingly shows the pull the Western-run schools had for African children and how (though the children might in the long run have helped themselves and their people by their education) they often hurt their parents and caused strife in their villages by seeking out the new Western institution. Here, Nnanna, the only son of his widowed mother Chiaku, goes to school of his own free will, but against the wishes of most of his relatives. Eventually he becomes isolated from his mother and alienated from most of the people in his village and painfully must become a new kind of African.

Munonye's second novel, *Obi*, 1969, shows the difficulties a young couple have in readjusting to their village after years away in the city. His fine third work, *Oil Man of Obange*, 1970, is a close study of the new rural proletariat in Africa. Jeri, the protagonist, each day must carry into town his heavy load of palm oil on his old, rented bicycle to support his family. He has no other resources. Robbed of his bicycle and the receipts for the oil he was transporting for his employer, Jeri's mind cracks and he soon dies, a ruined man.

Writings: Novels: *The Only Son*, London, Heinemann, 1966; reprinted, 1967; *Obi*, London, Heinemann, 1969; *Oil Man of Obange*. London, Heinemann, 1970; *A Wreath for the Maidens*, London, 1973.

MUSA, Hajji Ismail Galaal (also MUSA GALAAL, and simply GALAAL)
b. 1919, outskirts of Mogadishu, Somalia.
Somali poet, story teller, collector of oral literature.

Rising from camel-herder to teacher, Musa was employed from 1951 to 1954 at the School of Oriental and African Studies, University of London. With the independence of Somalia in 1960, he became the chairman of the Linguistic Committee charged with the introduction and diffusion of a new orthography for the Somali language. Later he was appointed director of the Cultural Relations Division of the Ministry of Education in Mogadishu.

His one volume of poems and folk tales is *Kikmad Soomaali*, 1956. Some of the items were translated into English and published in *A Selection from African Prose, 1. Traditional Oral Texts*, 1964. Musa and B. W. Andrezejewski also translated many of the stories from the collection for *A Tree of Poverty, Somali Poetry and Prose*, 1954.

Writings: Poems and folktales: *Kikmad Soomaali*, 1956; stories in English in *A Selection from African Prose, 1. Traditional Oral Texts*, Oxford, Clarendon Press, 1964; *A Tree of Poverty, Somali Poetry and Prose*, Kampala, Nairobi, Dar es Salaam, The Eagle Press, 1954.

MUSOKWA, Jackson Willis Anyigwile (see WILLIS, Jackson)

MUTABARUKA, Jean Baptiste
b. 1937, Eastern Ruanda, now Rwanda.
Poet.

Educated among the highly traditionalist Tutsis, Mutabaruka was the son of a large cattle owner who was, however, a Christian. Mutabaruka received, consequently, a European education from the Catholic Fathers in the former Belgian Congo. Though a Christian and a product of the religious and social training of the Catholic School, he never rejected his people's ways, religious ideas or lost his interest in Tutsis rituals. He lived in exile in neighboring Burundi, but in 1972 was teaching in the Ecole Secondaire de Jemba, diocese of Goma, in Zaïre. He published his poetry in French.

Mutabaruka is represented in translation in Ezekiel Mphahlele's *African Writing Today*. His poem, "Song of the Drum," exploits the idea of the dance, or rather, the waiting for an African dance to begin, in a song of lament which ends:

> *A blow at the friendly fire*
> *A quick touch of father's weapons.*
> *Who will reawaken this long smothered*
> *flame*
> *To its burning?*

It is a negritude poem completely naturalized in its imagery of starting a fire in the chill morning. Africa, too, has cooled and must be kindled anew.

Writings: Poem: "Song of the Drum" in *African Writing Today*, Ezekiel Mphahlele, editor, London, Penguin, 1967.

MUTOMBO, Dieudonné
b. ca. 1928, Zaïre.
Novelist.

Mutombo's 1953 novel, *Victoire de L'amour*, though written in the colonial period, reflects a deep, underlying hostility to Belgian rule. This work, along with *N'gando* (The Crocodile) of Paul Lomami-Tshibamba, published in 1948,

and Timothy Malembe's *Le mystère de l'enfant disparu* (The Mystery of the Lost Child), 1962, appears in a Krause Reprint in a combined volume.

Writings: Novels: *Victoire de l'amour*, Léopoldville, Bibliothèque de l'Etoile, 1953; republished with *N'gando* by Paul Lomami-Tshibamba and *Le mystère de l'enfant disparu* by Timothy Malembe, Kraus Reprint, Nendeln, Liechtenstein, 1971.

MUYAKA (HAJI AL–
GHASSANIY and IBN HAJI)
b. 1776 in Mombasa area, now Kenya; d. 1840.
Swahili poet.

Muyaka is credited with the popularization of Swahili poetry, moving its themes and tones away from the religious and contemplative to more contemporary concerns with politics, recent events, intrigues, and human passions. The poet was a close friend of the Mazrui rulers of the Mombasa area on the coast. Little of his work is extant. Two of his poems, "The World is like a Dry Tree" and "Dialogue Poem, Concerning a Debtor to His Friend," appear in *African Poems and Love Songs*.

Biographical/Critical Source: Charlotte and Wolf Leslau *African Poems and Love Songs*, Mount Vernon, New York, Peter Pauper Press, 1970.

MVOMO, Rémy Gilbert Médou
(also MEDOU, Rémy Gilbert Mvomo)
b. ca. 1945, Cameroon.
Novelist, (publishes and writes in English and French).

Mvomo

Educated in southern Cameroon, Mvomo has published two novels, *Afrika Ba'a,* 1969, set in a South Cameroon village; *Mon amour en noir et blanc,* 1971, and a 48-page story in English, "Nancy in Blooming Youth," 1961.

Writings: Novels: *Afrika Ba'a,* Yaoundé, C.L.E., 1969; *Mon amour en noir et blanc,* Yaoundé, CLE, 1971.

Story: "Nancy in Blooming Youth," Port Harcourt, Nigeria, Eastern City Press, 1961.

MWALILINO, Katoki
b. ca. 1942, Malawi.
Poet.

Mwalilino was educated in local schools. His poetry, of the "old school" of ode writing of the English tradition, lacks the sophistication of such Nigerians as Gabriel Okara, John Pepper Clark or Christopher Okigbo, but it is an early example of the use of the English tongue to express African, or "nationalist" mood. His poem, "The Awakening Malawi on July 6th 1964," is in *New Sum of Poetry from the Negro World.*

Writings: Poem: "The Awakening Malawi on July 6th 1964" [sic], in *New Sum of Poetry from the Negro World,* Paris, Présence Africaine, Volume 57, 1966.

MWANA, Kupona
b. 1810, in area now Kenya; d. 1860.
Swahili poet.

Kupona Mwana was the wife of Bwana Mataka, sheikh of the Siu region in Kenya who carried on a running guerrila

battle for two decades against Zanzibar Island's Sultan Saiyid Said.

Kupona is best remembered for one poem, "Utendi wa Mwana Kupona" (The Conversation of Mwana Kupona).

Writings: Poem: "Utendi wa Mwana Kupona."

MYEZA, M. D. (see last paragraph NYEMBEZI)

MZAMANE, Godfrey Isaac Malunga
b. March 7, 1909, Fobane, Mount Fletcher, South Africa.
Xhosa novelist, teacher, scholar.

Son of a lay preacher of the Anglican Church, Godfrey Mzamane did his primary schooling at Umzimkhulu and the French-run mission school at Lupindo, completing the sixth form (equivalent to junior high school in the United States) in 1921. He returned to his parents to tend the family's cattle until 1926 when he was able to attend St. John's College and then Adams' Teacher Training College in Natal. With a scholarship he was enabled to attend Fort Hare for further university work, but adversity forced him out in 1934 and he began teaching. From 1936 to 1939 he was an instructor at Mariazell in Matatiele.

Mzamane began the study of museum-curatorial work in Cape Town in 1940 after finally winning his B.A. at Fort Hare by part-time study that year. In 1942 he was named assistant curator of the F. S. Malan Museum at Fort Hare and four years later he replaced Prof. A. C. Jordan as professor of Bantu languages when Jordan resigned.

He won a B.A. in Bantu language studies in 1947, an M.A. in 1948, and is presently completing a doctorate. He now serves as chairman of the Bantu Language Department at Fore Hare.

His didactic novel, *Izinto zodidi* (Things of Value), published in 1959, concerns the failure of the father, Deyi, to cope with modern life as compared to the splendid scientific achievements of his son, Manzodidi, who goes to Canada to study.

Writings: Novel: *Izinto zodidi*, Johannesburg, Afrikaanse Pers-Boekhandel, 1959.

Biographical/Critical Source: Albert S. Gérard, *Four African Literatures*, Berkeley, University of California Press, 1971.

N

NAGENDA, John
b. 1938, Gahini, Uganda.
Poet, story writer, playwright,
scholar.

Nagenda studied at local schools and
took his B.A. at Makerere University,
Kampala, Uganda. He has been a
member of Uganda's national cricket
team.

As a college student, Nagenda edited
the Makerere Journal, *Penpoint,* which
encouraged and published many young
African writers. Since graduation,
Nagenda's stories and poems have
appeared in *Transition* and other journals.

In a speech at the African-Scandi-
navian Writers' Conference in Stockholm, 1967), later published in *The
Writer in Modern Africa,* Nagenda said
that African writers should begin to
express themselves in language which
could be understood by the 80% of the
people who are workers and peasants.
This would imply, presumably, that writing should be done in African tongues
rather than in borrowed European languages, but his own practice is to publish
in English.

His essay, "Generations in Conflicts,"
concerns the Ghanaian writers, Ama Ata
Aidoo, J. C. de Graft and R. Sarif Easmon.

Writings: Story: "And This, At Last,"
originally in *Penpoint* and *Transition*
(Kampala); also in *Pan African Short
Stories,* Neville Denny, Editor, London,
Nelson, 1965; other stories and/or
poems in *Origin East Africa,* David Cook,
editor, London, Heinemann, 1965; *New
Voices from the Commonwealth,* Howard
Sergeant, editor, London, Evans, 1968.

Essays: "Generations in Conflict" in
Protest and Conflict in African Literature,
Pieterse and Munro, editors, New York,
1969; speech in *The Writer in Modern
Africa,* Per Wästberg, editor, Uppsala,
Sweden, The Scandinavian Institute of
African Studies, 1968.

NAIGIZIKI, J. V. Savério
b. 1915, Mwulire–Busanga,
Rwanda.
Novelist, playwright.

As a young man Naigiziki worked as an
assistant chauffeur, an import agent's
clerk, translator, printer and country
school teacher.

His first work was an autobiographical
journal, *Escapade ruandaise. Journal d'un*

Naigiziki

clerc en sa trentième année (Ruandan Escapade: Journal of an Intellectual in his Thirtieth Year), 210 pages, published in Brussels in 1950. He later reforged this work into a two-volume novel, the 483-page, mystical *Mes transes à trente ans* (My Trances at Thirty), 1955.

Naigiziki's one published play to date is *L'optimist*, a three-act drama reaching print in 1954.

Writings: Novel: *Mes transes à trente ans*, Astrida, Ruanda, Groupe Scolaire, 1955; Volume I is entitled *De mal en pis* (From Bad to Worse), and Volume II *De pis en mieux* (From Poor to Better); this work an expansion of the original *Escapade ruandaise; journal d'un clerc en sa trentième année*, autobiographical, Brussels, Deny, 1949.

Play: *L'optimist*, Astrida, Rwanda, Groupe Scolaire, 1954.

Extracts of his prose: in *Darkness and Light*, Peggy Rutherford, editor, Johannesburg, Drum Publications, 1958, and London, Faith Press, 1958.

NAKASA, Nathaniel Ndzivane
b. 1937, Johannesburg, South Africa; d. July 14, 1965.
Short story writer, editor, journalist.

"Nat" Nakasa was the first black South African to write a weekly column in a "white" newspaper, the *Rand Daily Mail*. He founded and edited *The Classic*, a journal devoted to giving black writers an outlet for their work in a racist society. Nakasa was contributing articles to the *New York Times* and other American journals when, in America on a Nieman Journalism Fellowship to Harvard, he died under rather mysterious circumstances on July 14, 1965. The official version is that he committed suicide by leap-ing from a window while visiting New York City, but some of his friends whisper that it was a political assassination.

Much of Nakasa's own creative work appeared in *The Classic* or other South African journals, but he is represented in *South African Writing Today*, 1967.

Writings: Stories and articles: in *The Classic*, and other South African journals; the article, "Johannesburg, Johannesburg," in *South African Writing Today*, Harmondsworth, England, Penguin, 1967.

NASSIR, Ahmad (also known as BHALO, Ahmad Nassir bin Juma)
b. ca. 1890, Kenya.
Swahili poet.

Nassir's poetry has been widely popular with his own people and in 1966 he had some of his works translated by L. Harries in *Poems from Kenya, Gnomic Verses in Swahili*, a bi-lingual edition.

Writings: Poetry: *Poems from Kenya, Gnomic Verses in Swahili*, L. Harries, translator and editor, Madison, Wisconsin, University of Wisconsin Press, 1966.

NDAO, Cheik A.
b. ca. 1940, Senegal.
Poet, playwright, professor; writes in French, English, and Wolof.

Son of a veterinarian, Cheik A. Ndao often followed his father from post to post in Senegal, coming into contact with the various peoples of the country and learning their cultures and oral litera-tures. After finishing lycée in Dakar, Ndao attended the universities of

Grenoble in France and Swansea in Great Britain. He is presently a professor of English at the Ecole Normale William Ponty in Dakar, his local alma mater.

Ndao's first published work was a collection of poems, *Kaïrée*, in English, French, and his native Wolof. The volume won the Senegalese Poets' Prize for Francophone Poets in 1962, the year of its publication in Grenoble.

His first play, *Le marabou* (The Religious Leader) was performed in 1961 but remains unpublished. *L'exil d'Albouri* (The Exile of Albouri), published in 1967, deals with events in the Senegalese or Djolof part of the ancient empire of Mali. Though the author depended on historical-scholarly studies of the period,

he freely recreated the times and actions to suit his dramatic and polemical purposes. Premiered at the Théâtre Daniel Sorano in Dakar in 1968, it has been frequently performed throughout Africa since, and won the first prize at the Pan African Cultural Festival, Algiers, 1969.

In the same 1967 volume with *L'exil d'Albouri* is Ndao's third play, *La décision*, devoted to an examination of the problems of preserving and enhancing African values and black identity in the white American Deep South.

Two new plays, *Le fils de L'Almany* (The Son of the Almany) and *La case de l'homme* (The Case of Man), are scheduled for publication in 1973 by P. J. Oswald, his regular publisher.

Writings: Poetry: *Kaïrée*, Grenoble, Impr. Eymond, 1962, published under name of Chéc Ndao; poems in *New Sum of Poetry from the Negro World*, Paris, Présence Africaine, Volume 57, 1966.

Plays: *L'exil d'Albouri* and *La décision*, preface by Bakary Traoré, Honfleur, P.-J. Oswald, 1967, 1972; in manuscript: *Le marabou* (produced in 1961); *Le fils de l'Almany* and *La case de l'homme*, both set for publication by Oswald in 1972 or 1973 in it "Théâtre Africain" series.

NDAWO, Henry Masila
(pseudonym for NDAWO,
Hendrick Masila)
b. March 29, 1883, Cape Province,
South Africa; d. May 4, 1949.
Xhosa novelist, poet, collector of
folktales, teacher.

A member of the Hlubi tribe, Henry Ndawo received his high school training in schools in the Herschel District, Northern Cape Province. He then qualified as a teacher and held posts at Matatiele and Maimkulu, teaching students from the Sotho and Hlubi peoples. He remained a teacher until his retirement in 1943 at the age of 60.

For many years Ndawo was a member of the General Council for the Transkei at Mtata and was a life-long Anglican. He died in 1949 in a fall from a jolted train platform, leaving his wife and eight children. His poetry won him the title "Imbongi yase Mahlutyeni ka Bungani" (The praise poet of the Bungani people).

Ndawo's novels were: *U-hambo luka Gqoboka* (The Voyage of Gqoboka the Christian), considered the first Xhosa novel and used in high schools in the 1920's in the Xhosa-language area of South Africa, 1909; *U-Nolishwa*, 1931; *U-Nomathamsanqa no Sigebenga* (Nomathamsanqa and the Hoodlum), 1938; and *U-Mwe*, 1951, published posthumously.

His two collections of folktales and other folk material were: *Inxenye yentsomi zasezweni* (Some Peoples' Folktales), the first book of Xhosa stories, 1920; and *Iziduko zama-Hlubi* (Ancestral, or Clan, Names of the Hlubi People), 1939, collected painstakingly over many years.

The one volume of poetry published by Ndawo was his collection of original praise-poems, *Izibongo zenkosi zama-Hlubi nezama-Baca* (Praises of the Hlubi and Bhaca Chiefs), 1928. His history "Ibali lamaHlubi" (The Story of the Hlubi People), remains unpublished.

Writings: Novels: *U-hambo luka Gqoboka*, Lovedale, Lovedale Press, 1909; *U-Nolishwa*, Lovedale, 1931; second edition, 1958 by Lovedale Press; *U-Nomathamsanqa no Sigebenga*, Lovedale, 1938; A. S. Gérard says 1937; *U-Mwe*, Lovedale, 1951.

Poetry: *Izibongo zenkosi zama-Hlubi nezama-Baca*, Mariannhill, Mariannhill Mission Press, 1928 (A. S. Gérard says 1925).

Folk stories: *Inxenye yentsomi zasezweni*, Mariannhill, 1920; *Iziduko zama-Hlubi*, Lovedale, 1939.

History: "Ibali lamaHlubi," unpublished.

Biographical/Critical Source: Albert S. Gérard, *Four African Literatures*, Berkeley, University of California Press, 1971.

N'DEBEKA, Maxime
b. 1944, Brazzaville, Congo.
Poet, playwright, army officer, government official.

After local schooling in Brazzaville, including the Collège Chaminade, N'Debeka took electrical engineering courses at military schools in France and the Soviet Union. On his return he served in the Congolese army for a period, but is now a civilian serving as Director General of Cultural Affairs for the Popular Republic of the Congo.

First well known in his country because of his satirical poem, "980,000," which quickly was learned by heart by thousands of the 980,000 literate and illiterate citizens of the Congo, N'Debeka has published one volume of verse, *Soleils neufs* (New Suns), 1969, and one play, *Le président*, 1970. "980,000" is a severe, sarcastic attack on the new politicians and bureaucrats of post-independence Africa. His play deals with the greed, inefficiency, and arrogance in ruling circles, but focuses on the sycophants surrounding the "President" and the arrival of a Brutus who will destroy the once good man now drugged by his servile, self-serving court.

Writings: Poetry: Satirical poem,

274

"980,000," publishing data unknown' *Soleils neufs (Poèmes),* Introduction by Henri Lopes, Yaoundé, CLE, 1969.

Play: *Le président. Drame satirique en trois actes.* Introduction by Henri Lopes, Honfleur, P.-J. Oswald, 1970, 92 pages.

NDEBELE, Nimrod Njabulo T.
b. October 12, 1913, Ladysmith, Natal Province, South Africa.
Zulu playwright, teacher.

Ndebele, the first Zulu playwright, had his early education at Ethembeni School, Harrismith; at St. Cyprian's in Sophiatown; St. Peter's High School, Resettenville, Johannesburg (1929–31), and was awarded the Junior Certificate in 1931. After miscellaneous jobs he attended Amanzimtoti (Adams') College (1933–34), receiving the Teacher's Certificate, and taught as an assistant teacher at Khaiso Secondary School (1935–1945). By private study he earned the A.B. in 1948 from the University of the Witwatersrand in the Zulu language and political science. He was an assistant teacher at Madibane High School, Johannesburg, (1945–1953), principal at Charterston High School, Nigel (1953–57), and since 1957 has been inspector of schools for the Middelburg Circuit.

His one play *UGubudele namazimuzimu* (Gubudele and the Cannibals), is considered the first drama written and published in Zulu, 1941. Composed in the mid-1930's, it won the 1937 Esther May Bedford prize and was published in 1959 as Volume VI of the Bantu Treasury series.

Writings: Play; *UGubudele namazimuzimu,* Johannesburg, University of the Witwatersrand Press, 1941, republished as Vol. VI of Bantu Treasury Series, 1959 in a new edition.

NDELA, B. Z. B. (see last paragraph NYEMBEZI)

NDHAMBI, Etienne Penyisi
b. 1914, Tlangolani, Sibasa District, Northern Transvaal, South Africa.
Tsonga-language poet, novelist, scholar, educator.

Etienne Ndhambi had his early schooling at Tlangolani Primary School, the Vladezia Primary School, and the Lemana Training Institute where he earned his Teacher's Certificate. He taught at Valdezia from 1938 to 1941 before being named principal at the Tlangolani School, staying till 1944. He moved on to be principal of the Mashamba Primary School (1944-46), Ribolla Primary School (1947-1958), and then became a supervisor of Bantu education on the Pietersburg East Circuit.

His earliest published volumes dating to the early 1940's were *Swiphato swa xitsonga* (Tsonga Praise Songs) (1949,), and *Mambuxo,* a novel. His little collection of original poetry for children, *Switlhokovetselo swa Vana,* is his most recent publication. A biblical story, *Ntsandza Vatima,* completes the list of his published works.

His volume *Xitsonga Xo Saseka* (Tsonga Made Easy) is a product of his private linguistic studies as are other works still in manuscript.

Writings: Poetry: *Swiphato swa Xitsonga,* Doornfontein, South Africa, Swiss Mission, 1949; *Switlhokovetselo swa Vana,* Pretoria, Van Schaik, 1966.

275

Novel: *Mambuxo*, Doornfontein, Swiss Mission; second edition, 1960.

Story: *Ntsandza Vatima*, Johannesburg, Afrikaanse Pers-Boekhandel, no date.

Linguistic study: *Xitsonga Xo Saseka*, unpublished.

N'DINTSOUNA, Francesco (see SENGAT-KUO, François)

N'DJOK, Kindengve
b. ca. 1925, Cameroon.
Novelist.

N'djok has published one work of fiction, a 263-page novel for the young reader: *Kel'lam, fils d'Afrique* (Kel'lam, Son of Africa).

Writings: Novel: *Kel'lam, fils d'Afrique*, Paris, Alsatia, 1958.

NDLOVU, Joshua
b. ca. 1946, Zimbabwe, Rhodesia.
Short story writer.

Educated in Rhodesian grammar schools, he went on to take his B.A. at Whitworth College, Spokane, Washington.

Ndlovu's story, "Not Enough," appears in *New African Literature and the Arts,*. The story dramatizes the return from the Second World War of a brave young African who, to save his family from punishment, must kneel and make no protest before a white policeman who has just arbitrarily shot his family's faithful old sleeping dog. Such are the seemingly insignificant but "important" facts of life in Rhodesia as Ndlovu presents them, for where oppression is everywhere, every minor harrassment

can lead to disaster if rage is not only controlled, but concealed.

Writings: Story: "Not Enough" in *New African Literature and the Arts*, Joseph Okpaku, editor, New York, Crowell, 1970.

NDU, Pol N.
b. November 14, 1940, Eastern Nigeria.
Poet, professor.

Pol Ndu studied at Nsukka University where he later became a professor, remaining in that post until 1967. *Black Orpheus* magazine in Ibadan first published his verse, and he is represented in Moore and Beier's *Modern Poetry from Africa* and other anthologies. His interesting poem, "Ritual Dance," appeared first in *The New African*, 1966.

Writings: Poem: "Ritual Dance" in *The New African*, September, 1966, London; poems in *Modern Poetry from Africa*, Moore and Beier, editors, revised edition, 1968; *Black Orpheus* magazine.

NENEKHALY–CAMARA, Condetto
b. September 10, 1930, Beyla, Guinea.
Poet, playwright, ethnologist, government official.

After local schooling in upper Guinea, and lycée in Dakar, Nénékhaly–Camara went on to France to earn two degrees: the "licence" in modern letters and English from the University of Paris, and a diploma from the Institute of Ethnology in Paris.

During the 1950's, he was a contributor to *Présence Africaine* (1955–1958) and to other professional journals, and served as an officer of the General

Union of West African Students and the Federation of Black Students in France. He also represented for many years the Student Union of Revolutionary Africa in many countries and was named to represent Guinea at the Havana Cultural Congress. After Guinea became an independent republic in 1958, Nénékhaly-Camara held a variety of posts in the "présidence" or staff of the president.

His first published work was *Lagunes*, 1956, a 23-page volume of verse. His two plays, *Continent-Afrique* and *Amazoulou* (The African Continent and The Amazulu) were published in a single volume in 1970. The first play concerns Antar, an Arab warrior of the sixth century (first century of the Moslem chronology), and son of a black African woman. The second play deals with the great Zulu king, Chaka, who ruled in the early 19th century in what is now Natal, South Africa. Both works seek to exploit the epic qualities of the heroes, yet, at the same time, the plays do not succumb to a facile mythologization. Greatness there was, but the achievements of Antar and Chaka must be models for new heroism in modern Africa, not superhuman efforts which can offer no models for emulation in the present.

Bakary Traoré points out in the introduction to Cheik A. Ndao's *L'exil d'Albouri*, a play devoted to a great Wolof king, that modern Africa needs to feel the past greatnesses of men such as Chaka and Albouri, for "Le théâtre africain sera épique ou ne sera pas." (African drama will be epical or it will fail to come into being). Such at any rate is the feeling of many of the francophone writers though such a felt necessity seems much milder in the area of former British control where dramatists are more concerned with cosmological and nature myths, dance ritual, and, conversely, with the modern scene in many cases.

Writings: Poetry: *Lagunes*, La Courneuve, Seine, France, Edition de l'Académie Populaire de Littérature et de Poésie, 1956, to be republished as *Poèmes pour la révolution* by P.-J. Oswald in 1972 or 1973.

Plays: *Continent-Afrique* and *Amazoulou*, in one volume, preface by Mário de Andrade, Honfleur, P.-J. Oswald, 1970

Political Essay: "Vocation de l'Afrique," manuscript being prepared for the press.

Articles: political and critical, in *Souffles* (Morocco), *Présence Africaine* and others.

NETO, António Agostinha
b. September, 1922, Catete, Icolo e Bengo, Angola.
Poet, physician.

Neto studied in local schools in Luanda, the capital of Angola, but had to interrupt his schooling and go to work. From 1944 to 1947 he was employed by the Department of Health in Angola. He helped in the organization of a local working men's group in late 1947 which supported his trip to Portugal where he took up medical studies at Coimba and later at Lisbon. The local labor group, or "cultural" society, increasingly became a nationalist or independence group for Black Angolans and was eventually attacked by the Portuguese authorities.

Neto's first poems were written and published during his student days in Portugal, some of them as early as 1948 in Luanda. He was quickly seen as a new voice of the African population of the colony, for his poems celebrated African men and women and expressed the sentiments of many Black Africans for freedom. While studying and writing, he was active in the circle of young Angolan intellectuals in Lisbon who began to consider means of publicizing their protests against the Salazar regime. Neto was arrested in 1952 when, going from door to door to drum up support for a petition protesting Salazar's colonial regime, he was stopped by a policeman whose home he had stopped to argue in. The prison sentence was short and he returned to his studies. Despite this experience, Neto accepted the leadership of the Angolan students in Portugal and went to Paris in December, 1953, to represent his countrymen at the annual congress of the Fédération des Etudiants d' Afrique Noire en France. There he criticized the conditions of the African people in all of the Portugese colonies and the invariably inadequate educational system available to the native Angolans.

Returning to Portugal, he was allowed to work and to study until 1955 when he was arrested again on charges of subversive activities, this time by the PIDE (Portugal's secret police, the feared Policia Internacional de Defesa do Estado). By now, European intellectuals knew of him and such artists as François Mauriac, Louis Aragon, Jean-Paul Sartre, and Simone de Beauvoir, of France; Diego Rivera of Mexico; André Kebros of Greece; and Nicolas Guillén of Cuba, rallied to his defense in the international press. The Portugese were unmoved and held him from December, 1955 until June, 1957.

Despite all this, however, he was permitted to continue his medical education, taking the M.D. degree in 1958. Returning to Angola in 1959, some twelve years after the Angolan workers had sent him off, he soon took up political work again. In 1960, he became president of the Movimento Popular de Libertação de Angola (the M.P.L.A.). On June 6 of that year, the director of PIDE came to arrest Neto personally at his office in Luanda. Hearing of his third arrest, the people of his natal town Icolo e Bengo tried to organize a peaceful protest but Portuguese troops moved in, firing, reportedly killing thirty and wounding 200 persons. The troops then burned the town.

Again various intellectuals ralled to support Neto, including C. Day Lewis and John Osborne of the United Kingdom. Because of Portugal's long connection with Britain, such protests may have been effective, for the government at first was relatively mild in its treatment of its distinguished prisoner. Neto and his wife and children were exiled to the Cape Verde Islands where he remained for more than three months under house arrest. Possibly judging that the world's attention had shifted to other matters, the authorities then arrested Neto formally on September 21, 1961, transporting him back to Lisbon where he was incarcerated in Aljube.

The poet, who, has published only one short collection of his work in Portuguese, *Colectânea de poemas*, 1961, still has best sung the message of the oppressed peoples in Africa:

My Desire
transformed into strength,
inspiring desperate consciences.

Poems from his unpublished Portuguese-language manuscript, "com os olhos secos," appear in Italian translation "Con occhi asciutti" (With Dry Eyes) by Joyce Lussu, 1963.

Writings: Poetry: *Colectânea de poemas*, Lisbon, Edição da Casa dos Estudantes do Império, 1961; translated into Russian and published with a title signifying "Sacred Hope, publishing date unknown; it also was published in Serbo-Croatian with the poem "com os olhos secoso" as *Ociju bez suza*, with an introduction by Costa Andrade, Belgrad, Kultura, 1968, illustrated; the poem "com os olhos secoso" in a translation into Italian by Joyce Lussu appeared as "Con occhi asciutti," Milan, *Il Saggiatore*, 1963. Other poems appeared in *Caderno*, Mario de Andrade, editor, Lisbon, 1953; *Antologia da poesia negra de expressão portuguêse*, de Andrade, editor, Lisbon, 1958; in English translation in *Modern Poetry from Africa*, Moore and Beier, editors revised edition, London, Penguin, 1968.

Story: "Náusea," *Mensagem*, Luanda, 1952; others in *Contistas angolanos*, Lisbon, Casa dos Estudantes do Império, 1960; "Friend Mussunda," in Mphahlele's *African Writing Today*. London, Penguin, 1967, in English translation.

Biographical/Critical Source: W. S. Merwin, article, "Agostinho Neto," in *Introduction to African Literature*, Ulli Beier, editor, Evanston, Northwestern University Press, 1967.

NGANDJON, Thomas (see NGANTHOJEFF, Job)

NGANGU, Jackson
b. ca. 1920, near Banza Manteka, Congo. (Zaïre).
Kikongo poet.

Trained in Protestant mission schools, Ngangu published in 1944 a collection of stories and verse entitled *Tangeno nsamu* (Let's Read the Stories). Though the stories are primarily adolescent reading matter, the verse is more mature and of greater intrinsic interest.

Writings: Tangeno nsamu, written with the collaboration of Mary Bonar, an American missionary, Léopoldville, Maison SIMS, 1944, and second edition, Léopoldville, Ed. LECO, 1955.

Biographical/Critical Source: Mbololo ya Mpiku, "Introduction à la littérature kikongo," *Research in African Literatures,* African and Afro-American Research Institute, The University of Texas, III, 2 (Fall 1972), 42 pages, with many extracts of poetry in Kikongo and accompanying French translations.

NGANI, Alfred Zwelinzima
b. ca. 1905, Ngwenya, Middledrift District, Cape Province, South Africa: d. January, 1950.
Xhosa poet, biographer, teacher.

Ngani's early schooling was at Ngwenya Primary School and the Lovedale Practicing School. While teaching at Queenstown in the 1920's he helped establish other primary schools in the area and in the 1930's was at Lovedale for a few years. In the mid-30's he became principal of the Falconer Higher Mission School at Ngewazi in the area of Chief Shadrock Fuba Zibi.

Having taken a course in agriculture and farming at the Fort Cox School run by the Department of Public Education of Cape Province, he was appointed a departmental visiting teacher in the 1940's.

Ngani's works include an historical study of the Gqunukhwebe people, *Ibali lama Gqunukhwebe* (The Story of the

Gqunukhwebe), 1937; a posthumously published volume of praise-poems, *Intlaba-mkhosi* (The Battle Cry); and a biography of Chief Kama of the Gqunukhwebe clan, *Ubom bukaKama* (The Life of Kama), the latter two both issued in 1952.

When King George VI visited Lovedale in 1947, Ngani, called "Imbongi" or praise poet, composed and recited a praise-poem in honor of the King, "Utyelelo leKumkani nokuKumkanikazi" (The Visit of the King and Queen to the South of Africa).

Ngani's son Marcus Ngani (b. 1932) also became a writer, with one play and two novels published thus far.

Writings: Poetry: *Intlaba-mkhosi*, Lovedale, Lovedale Press, 1952.

Poem: "Utyelelo leKumkani nokuKumkanikazi," 1947; also poems in *A Review of Zulu Literature*, C. L. S. Nyembezi, editor, Pietermaritzburg, University of Natal Press, 1961.

History: *Ibali lama Gqunukhwebe*, Lovedale, Lovedale Press, 1937.

Biography: *Ubom bukaKama*, Lovedale, 1952.

NGANI, Marcus Aurelius Pakamila
b. 1932, Ngewazi, South Africa.
Xhosa novelist, playwright.

Son of the teacher and praise-singer of the Gqunulhwebe clan of the Xhosa people, Marcus received local schooling in Ngewazi. He has published one play, *Umkhonto kaTshiwo* (Tshiwo's Spear) (1962), and two novels, the first, *Abantwana bethu* (Our Children) in 1959, and the second, *Umqol' uphandle* (You are Exposed), in 1967.

Writings: Novels: *Abantwana bethu,*

Johannesburg, Afrikaanse Pers-Boekhandel, 1959; *Umqol' uphandel,* Cape Town, Via Africa, 1967.

Play: *Umkhonte kaTshiwo,* Johannesburg, Afrikaanse, 1962.

NGANTHOJEFF, Job (also NGANDJON, Thomas)
b. 1940, Cameroon.
Poet.

Nganthojeff's first poems were collected in the volume, *Mélange* (Mixture), republished by Kraus Reprint, 1971.

Writings: Poetry: *Mélange,* Tours, Jeune Force Poétique Française, 1965; republished, Kraus Reprint, Nendeln, Liechtenstein, 1971.

NGCOBO, Moses John
b. 1928, Durban, South Africa.
Zulu novelist.

Ngcobo moved to Clermont in 1934 and attended local schools. He then went on to Cape Town where he enrolled in college, but passed his matriculation examination through private study. Moving to the United States for further education he began to write, projecting, in his youthful feelings of power, a corpus of 21 novels.

His first novel, *Inkungu maZulu* (Watch Out, Zulus!), won the first prize of 45 pounds sterling in the 1956 Afrikaanse Pers-Boekhandel literary competition. When published in 1957, it was awarded the S. E. K, Mqhayi prize. His succeeding novels are: *Wo he bantu* (Well, that's That), 1964; *Akusoka lungenasici* (No Young Man is Without Faults), 1964; and *Ukufika kosuku* (The Coming of the Day), 1969.

Writings: Novels: *Inkungu maZulu*, Johannesburg, Afrikaanse Pers-Boekhandel, 1957; *Wo he bantu*, Cape Town, Via Afrika, 1964; *Akusoka lungenasici*, Johannesburg, A. P. B. Bona Press, 1964; *Ukufika kosuku*, Cape Town, Via Africa, 1969.

NGENGI, Kamau wa (see KENYATTA, Jomo)

NGIBA, W. V. (see last paragraph NYEMBEZI)

NGIDI, Andreas Henry
b. May 1, 1882, Nchanga, South Africa; d. July 22, 1951, Nongoma, Natal Province.
Zulu poet, teacher, minister.

Ngidi was educated locally before going to Rome to seminary where he became a Catholic priest and where he later obtained doctorates in humanities, classics, theology and philosophy. His ordination was in 1907, and he taught for many years in church schools at Mariannhill and Lesotho. In 1926, he returned to Natal to teach at St. Francis' College, Mariannhill. He was a poet whose work appeared in the Zulu journals, *Umafrika* and *ILN*, and influenced Benedict Vilakazi's poetry. H. I. E. Dhlomo called Ngidi's poems "fluid," but also classical in style and "African" in sentiment or form. His poems, which appeared in various newspapers and journals, have never been collected. He died of diabetes.

Writings: Poems in *Umafrika* and *ILN*.

NGUBANE, Jordan Khush
b. November 15, 1917,
Ladysmith, Natal, South Africa.
Zulu novelist, short story writer, scholar, journalist, farmer (also writes in English).

Jordan Ngubane's early schooling was in Ladysmith and his college training at Adams'. For a period he was assistant editor of *Ilanga lase Natal* (The Natal Sun) in Durban, and of the *Bantu World* in Johannesburg, editor of *Inkundla ya Bantu* (Bantu Forum) in Verulam, and correspondent for *The Forum, Indian Opinion*, and the *London Observer*. He worked closely with Chief Lutuli during the latter's busiest period from 1940 on, and especially prior to Lutuli's confinement by the South African authorities to his farm in the late 1950's.

Ngubane

Ngubane's one novel, *Uvalo Lwezinhlonzi* (His Frowns Struck Terror), 1957, is written in his native Zulu. It was very popular when it appeared, but then the government prohibited a reprinting and any further circulation for five years from 1962 to 1967. Recently, strangely enough, and without the consent of or the profit to, the author, who was by then living in Swaziland, the South African regime has permitted the work to be republished and in fact to be used in the African schools. The novel deals with the Zulu world of 1905 to 1910 and though not particularly anti-colonial, it does express bitterness at the destruction of African culture and the loss of power and significance in Zulu-land (Natal).

Two of his non-fictional works are *An African Explains Apartheid* and "Conflict of Minds," an essay in *South Africa: Sociological Perspectives*.

Ngubane moved his family to Swaziland in 1962, and he came to the United States in 1969 on a Ford Foundation and Howard grant to teach at Howard University, Washington, D. C. and to lecture on apartheid throughout the country. He has been preparing a new book on South African apartheid and American race prejudice for the press.

Writings: Novel: *Uvalo Lwezinhlonzi*, Johannesburg, Afrikaanse Per-Boekhandel, 1957.

Stories: "The Answer He Wanted," *Drum* (December 1951), and "Man of Africa," *Drum* (August 1956).

Non fiction: *An African Explains Apartheid*, New York, Praeger, 1963; "Conflict of Minds," essay in *South Africa: Sociological Perspectives*, London, Oxford Press, 1971.

NGUBENE, M. (see last paragraph NYEMBEZI)

NGUGI, James Thiong'o (also WA THIONG'O, James)
b. 1938, Limuru, Kenya.
Novelist, playwright, short story writer, journalist, teacher.

Considered the major African writer from East Africa, James Ngugi began his education in a local school in 1946 at the encouragement of his mother. In 1947 he attended a Kikuyu School in Karinga for one year, then had to drop out until 1950, when he went back for another five years. He graduated from Alliance High School where he wrote his first play, a work loosely based on a novel by Edgar Wallace, the once popular American writer and author of *Ben Hur*.

(The juvenile work and its specific source are unknown.)

Ngugi took a B.A. at Makerere University in Kampala, Uganda, 1963, majoring in English, and a second B.A. in 1964 at the University of Leeds in Yorkshire, England. While at Makerere, Ngugi was editor of *Penpoint*, a student journal that encouraged many of the

young writers whose voices are now being heard in East Africa.

After his university years, he served as the first editor of *Zuka* (Swahili for "Emerge" or "Emergent"), an important English-language review published in Dar es Salaam, Tanzania. He also served a period as an editor of the *Sunday Nation*, published in Nairobi. In 1959, he published three stories in the *Kenya Weekly News* and a fourth story written that year, "The Fig Tree," appeared in

1964. He taught in various East African Schools from 1964 to 1970.

Ngugi continued as editor of *Zuka* with Jonathon Kariara until 1970 when he left Tanzania to go to America as a lecturer in African literature at Northwestern University in Evanston, Illinois.

Though considered the leading novelist of East Africa, Ngugi has also published the successfully performed play, *The Black Hermit*, about an educated young man who hates to give up his English girl friend and life in Nairobi to return to his mother, his brother's widow, and tribal responsibilities in his natal village. His unpublished play, *This Time Tomorrow*, about slum clearance in Nairobi and the tragedies resulting therefrom, is a 22 page B B C radio script. At present, Ngugi is working on a book of personal impressions about East Africa.

Ngugi's novels, all published in Heinemann's African Writers Series, are *Weep Not, Child* (1964) about the Mau-Mau rebellion and its impact on the lives of a young boy and his family; *The River Between* (1965) a beautiful, lyric treatment of the Kikuyu people just before the break in of the English into the highlands of Kenya; and *A Grain of Wheat* (1967) about the divisions in Kikuyu society brought on by the pressures from the guerrillas on one side and the British and white settlers on the other. These novels are now available in the United States in paperback Collier Books.

Ngugi's style is smooth, sinewy and intelligent. He has a lyrical grace and rhythmical way of handling the experiences of his characters which unobstrusively brings the reader inside the Kikuyu world. In *A Grain of Wheat*, Ngugi's plotting becomes extremely complex as attention moves backwards and forwards from the false hero to the non-hero to the true hero (dead early in the novel), to their women, to the British and their African allies, to the land, and back again. The contrasts are not only between different personalities but also between different roles—or rather—different conceptions held by the various characters of what can or should be achieved in the struggle against British rule. No one is pure hero, no one pure villain. But in the end, there is sadness and new corruption, this time by the new politicians who grab for power and profit now coming to Africans for the first time.

The play, *The Black Hermit,* partly in verse, is an interesting though not very compelling drama with rather ineffectual dialogue. It concerns an educated Kikuyu, Remi, vainly holding off efforts of his mother, the Christian minister, and the elders of his village, to "reclaim" him from his British girl friend and his other sophisticated friends in Nairobi.

His short stories have appeared in various journals. Two of the best, "Return," appeared in *Transition, 3,* and "*A Meeting in the Dark,*" in *Pan African Short Stories,* and in *Modern African Short Stories.*

Writings: Novels: *Weep Not, Child,* Heinemann, 1964; *The River Between,* 1965; *A Grain of Wheat,* 1967; all also in Collier Books, paperbacks, Macmillan, New York.

Plays: *The Black Hermit,* London, Heinemann, 1968; *This Time Tomorrow,* unpublished.

Stories: "Return" in *Transition,* No. 3, Kampala; "Limits," in *Africa in Prose,* Dathorne and Fenser, editors, London, Baltimore, Penguin, 1969; "A Meeting in the Dark" in *Pan African Short Stories,* Neville Denny, editor, London, Nelson, 1965, 1967; "The Fig Tree," in *A Selection of African Prose,* II, W. H. Whiteley,

editor, Oxford, Oxford University Press, 1964; also stories in *Modern African Short Stories,* Koomey and Mphahlele, editors, London, Faber and Faber, 1964, and *The Kenya Weekly News.*

Biographical/Critical Sources: Anne Tibble, *African/English Literature,* London, Peter Owen, 1965; Charles R. Larson, *The Emergence of African Fiction,* Bloomington, Indiana, Indiana University Press, 1972.

NIANE, Djibril Tamsir
b. ca. 1920, Mali or Northern Guinea.
Story teller, collector of folk and legendary stories, playwright.

Born of griot (professional story teller) ancestors, Niane has collected and retold the old legends of ancient Mali in his *Soundjata ou l'épopée Mandingue* (Sundiata: An Epic of Old Mali), 1960, translated and published in English in 1965. The work is based on the oral legends of the hero Soundjata, which were recited in Malinké. The French publisher, Pierre Jean Oswald has recently issued Niane's two plays, *Sikasso* and *Chaka* (1971?).

Niane obtained the major part of the legend of *Soundjata* from Djeli Mamoudou Kouyaté, an "obscure griot, from the village of Djeliba Koro," near Sequiri, Guinea. As Niane puts it, the traditional griots in northern Guinea and Mali still flourish, although their numbers are declining and most so-called griots are now only strolling singers and guitarists. Towns such as Ka-ba (or Kangaba), and Krina have griot families "which conserve traditional stories and teach them to the next generations"—and Niane mentions some names: the griot Fadama for the province of Hamana (in Kouroussa,

Guinea); Djééa (for Droma, Siguiri, Guinea); and Keyla in southern Mali. The epic begins:

I am a griot. It is I, Djeli Mamoudou Kouyaté, son of Bintou Koyuaté and Djeli Kedian Kouyaté, master in the art of eloquence. Since time immemorial the Kouyatés have been in the service of the Keita princes of Mali; we are vessels of speech, we are the repositories which harbour secrets many centuries old. The art of eloquence has no secrets for us; without us the names of kings would vanish into oblivion, we are the memory of mankind; by the spoken word we bring to life the deeds and exploits of kings for younger generations.

Soundjata recounts the marvelous story of a crippled, scorned boy who rose to be leader of the Malinké or Mandingo people, and the emperor of the great Mali empire of the second quarter of the 13th century and the successor states.

With the French historian, Jean Suret-Canale, Niane published a richly illustrated history of West Africa, the *Histoire de l'Afrique occidentale.*

Writings: Epic: *Soundjata ou l'épopée Mandingue,* Paris, Présence Africaine, 1960; *Sundiata,* English translation by G. D. Pickett, London, Longmans, 1965; Czech edition, Prague, 1964; Russian edition, Moscow, Leningrad, 1963.

History: *Histoire de l'Afrique occidentale,* Paris, Présence Africaine, 224 pages, 170 photos, with Jean Suret-Canale.

Plays: *Sikasso,* and *Chaka,* Honfleur, France, P. J. Oswald, 1971?

NIANI, Djibril Tamsir (see NIANE, D. T.)

NICOL, Abioseh (pseudonym for NICOL, Davidson
b. 1924, Freetown, Sierra Leone. Poet, short story writer, biochemist, physician, administrator.

Nicol attended primary schools in Nigeria and the Government Model School and Prince of Wales School in Freetown, Sierra Leone. He then won a competitive colonial scholarship which enabled him to study medicine in England, at the University of London, 1943, and at Cambridge University (Christ's College) where he took at B. A. in natural science with first class honors in 1947. He has served as a physician at London Hospital and at other hospitals in Lagos, Kaduna and Port Harcourt in Nigeria and in the medical service of Sierra Leone. Much of his professional life has been in research or in advanced training in medicine, combined with work at various hospitals in England.

From 1952 to 1954, Nicol lectured at University College, Ibadan. Since 1957 he has been a fellow at his college at Cambridge, the first African to be so elected at either Oxford or Cambridge. In 1961 he was appointed principal of the University College of Sierra Leone at Fourah Bay, and in 1964 he completed his study as a research fellow in biochemistry at Cambridge. He had an important role in the discovery of the structure of human insulin, and has served as a delegate to the UNESCO General Conference in Boston for his country. He has served as vice-chancellor of the University of Sierra Leone, and in 1968 was named ambassador to the United States. Other positions have been as a senior pathologist in Sierra Leone, member of the Public Service Commission, and a director of the National Bank of Sierra Leone. He is married to the former Marion Bieber.

Nicol's poems and stories have been broadcast by the BBC, in Nigeria and elsewhere in West Africa, and published in various English and American magazines, including *Encounter, Blackwood's Magazine* and *Twentieth Century.*

Nicol's best known work, *Africa: A Subjective View*, 1965, contains the 1963 Aggrey-Fraser-Guggisberg Lectures delivered at the University of Ghana in Legon. The chapters are: "Our Politicians," "Our Critics and Lovers," "Our Universities," and "Our Writers and Our Public Servants." Nkosi has also written widely on African matters and on literature for such journals as the *Economist, The London Times, The Guardian,* and *Encounter.*

His work, including his poetry, is broad and open, universal in theme, occasionally astringent. He has won the Margaret Wrong Prize and Medal for Literature in Africa, 1952. His work is found in such anthologies as *Poems from Black Africa, An African Treasury,* and Donatus Ibe Nwoga's *West African Verse.*

His volume, *The Truly Married Woman,* 1965, contains the following stories: "The Truly Married Woman," "The Devil at Yolahun Bridge," "The Judge's Son," "Love's Own Tears," "As the Night, the Day," "The Leopard Hunt, and "Life is Sweet at Kumansenu." "The Leopard Hunt" which dramatizes the death of an African civil servant by a leopard is particularly well done, for it has fully developed English and African characters and resolves bitterness through understanding at tale's end. Also published in 1965 was his *Two African Tales.*

In introducing his stories, Nicol writes: "Others have written better than I shall ever do about Africa. However, I started writing because I found that most of those who wrote about us seldom gave any nobility to their African characters unless they were savages or servants or facing impending destruction. I knew differently."

With his deep understanding of the modest Westernized clerks and other representatives of the middle class, Nicol has written well of the minor heroism of civil servants, white-collar breadwinners, and their wives and families.

In 1970 he published in England and America a collection of papers written by the 19th century African scholar, Africanus Horton.

Writings: Essays: *Africa; A Subjective View,* London, Longmans, 1965. Editor of *Africanus Horton: the dawn of nationalism in modern Africa,* London, 1970; called *Black Nationalism in Africa 1867,* New York, 1970.

Stories: *The Truly Married Woman,* London, Oxford University Press, 1965;

Two African Tales, London, Cambridge University Press, 1965; poems or stories in *Poems from Black Africa*, Bloomington, Indiana University Press, 1963; *An African Treasury*, New York, Pyramid, 1961; *West African Verse*, London, Longmans, Green, 1967.

NICOL, Davidson (see NICOL, Abioseh)

NJAU, Rebecca
b. 1932, Kanyariri, Kenya.
Playwright, novelist, teacher.

Rebecca Njau attended the Alliance School for Girls and Kabete Intermediate School in her early years, then went on to receive her diploma in education from Makerere University College. She has taught at Alliance Girls' School (1958–59) and at Makerere College School from 1960 to 1962. She has since been headmistress at the Nairobi Girls' School, beginning in 1964. Miss Njau also was the Kenyan representative to the University College Council from 1965 to 1966.

She is the author of several short plays, two of which, *The Scar* and *The Round Chain* were first published in *Transition*, March 1963. She also was awarded the East African Writing Committee Prize for her first novel, *Alone with the Fig Tree* (unpublished).

Writings: Plays: *The Scar* and *The Round Chain* in *Transition*, No. 8, March 1963; *The Scar*, Moshi, Tanzania, Kibo Art Gallery, 1965.
Novel: *Alone with the Fig Tree*, unpublished.

NJOROGE, James Kingangi
b. 1933, Kiambu, Kenya.
Short story writer, folk tale collector, teacher.

Njoroge graduated from Alliance High School in 1952 and in 1958 received diplomas in education and public administration from Makerere University College. He has been permanent secretary of education in Kenya since 1964. Among his many other civil service positions held at one time or another are: general secretary and treasurer, Kenya National Union of Teachers; assistant secretary of the Kenyan Government in 1961; member of the Ministry of State for Constitutional Affairs and Administration, 1962; under secretary, and later of the Ministry of Commerce and Industry of which he became permanent secretary in 1963. He also served as Permanent Secretary of Education since 1964.

Njoroge's works are: *Tit for Tat and Other Stories*, 1966, 1969, folktales of human beings and animals; *The Proud Ostrich and Other Stories*, 1967, six folktales; *The Greedy Host*, 1968, animal stories; and *Pestle and Mortar*, 1969.

Writings: Stories: *Tit for Tat*, Nairobi, East African Publishing House, 1966; *The Proud Ostrich and Other Stories*, 1967; *The Greedy Host*, 1968; *Pestle and Mortar*, 1969, all by East African Publishing House.

NKABINDE, Abram Charles
b. ca. 1925, South Africa.
Zulu journalist, translator.

Nkabinde graduated in 1950 with distinction in Zulu language studies. He trained as a teacher and taught at the Emmarentia Geldenhuis High School

Nkabinde

and the Kwa-Phakama Secondary School in Springs. In 1960, he was appointed editor of the Government-sponsored journal, *Inthuthuko*. In 1961 he earned an American B.A. He has translated Waldemar Bonsels' *Die Kleine Maya* (The Little Bee) into Zulu.

Writings: Translation: *Die Kleine Maya*, by Waldemar Bonsel, into Zulu, unpublished.

NKETIA, John Hanson Kwabena
b. 1921, Ashanti Mampong, Ghana. Assante-Twi novelist, playwright, collector of folk-tales, scholar, musicologist.

Nketia worked for awhile as a musicologist in the sociology department at the University of Ghana and is now with the University's Institute of African Studies.

After early schooling in Mampong, he attended Akropong Teacher Training College, taking degrees in music, English and history. In 1944 he went to London to teach the Twi language at the School of Oriental and African Studies, remaining until 1949 when he returned to Ghana to teach at the Akropong Teachers College. In 1952 he joined the staff of the University of Ghana at Legon and was appointed to the staff of the Institute of African Studies. In 1962 he was appointed director of the School of Music and Drama at the Institute of African Studies in Legon.

Nketia has published 12 works on the Twi language of Ghana and many studies of African music, including *Folk Songs of Ghana* which provides vernacular and English texts with musical notation.

One fictional work, *Kwabena Amoa*, written in Twi, appeared in 1953 and

the well-known *Funeral Dirges of the Akan People* appeared in 1955. His essay, "Akan Poetry," appears in Ulli Beier's *An Introduction to African Literature* and a shorter essay on the same subject is included in Langston Hughes' *An African Treasury* and *Black Orpheus* magazine.

Professor Nketia has travelled throughout West Africa to record folk music and has built up a fine collection of tapes at the University of Ghana at Legon. His efforts are reflected in *African Music in Ghana* and *Drumming in the Akan Communities of Ghana*. He has also published various works in Asante-Twi since *Kwabena Amoa*. In a variety of genres they are: *Semodi* (An Agreeable Bit of News), a collection of stories; *Ananwoma*, a play; and two volumes of poetry: *Anwonsem 1944–1949* (Poems, 1944–1949), and *Akwansosem bi* (Some Travel Tales).

Writings: Novel: *Kwabena Amoa*, London, Oxford University Press, 1953.

Play: *Ananwoma*, London, Oxford University Press, 1951; five subsequent printings by 1963.

Poetry: *Anwonsem 1944–1949*, Cape Coast, Methodist Book Depot, 1952; *Akwansosem bi*, Legon, Ghana, Institute of African Studies, University of Ghana, 1967.

Stories: *Semodi*, Kumasi, Ghana, Boul Mission Book Depot, 1936; London, Macmillan, 1936.

Musicology: *African Music in Ghana; Drumming in the Akan Communities of Ghana; Funeral Dirges of the Akan People*, Achimota, Ghana, 1955, 1958; *Folk Songs of Ghana*, Legon, London, 1963.

Criticism: "Akan Poetry" in *Introduction to African Literature*, Ulli Beier, editor, London, Longmans, 1967; and Evanston, Ill., Northwestern University Press, 1967; shorter essay in *An African*

Treasury, Langston Hughes, editor; *Black Orpheus* magazine; *Ethnomusicology in Ghana,* Accra, 1970, a 23-page essay.

NKOMBA, Lester L.
b. ca. 1926, Nyanja area, Malawi.
Nyanja-language novelist.

Nkomba published one novel, *Ukawamba* (Resentment), in 1953, a work of 134 pages.

Writings: Novel: *Ukawamba,* Guy Atkins, ed., Annotated African Texts II, Cewa (London, Oxford University Press, 1953).

NKOSI, Lewis
b. 1935, Natal, South Africa.
Playwright, critic, editor,
short story writer.

Nkosi attended local schools in Zululand areas and studied for one year at the M. L. Sultan Technical College in Durban. In 1955 he went to work for the Zulu-English weekly paper, *Ilanga lase Natal* (The Natal Sun). The next year he joined the staff of *Drum* magazine, a publication open to Black writers, and at the same time he worked as chief reporter for the *Golden City Post,* a Sunday paper in Johannesburg.

In 1961–62, Nkosi was awarded a Nieman Fellowship in journalism for one year's study at Harvard University, Cambridge, Massachusetts, and as a result he has been barred from returning to his homeland by the South African authorities. Now a resident of London he has been the literary editor of *The New African,* (published in London) and has published in such journals as *West Africa, The Guardian, The Spectator, The New Statesman, The Observer, The New Yorker,* and *Black Orpheus.* During one period in the middle 1960's he was an editor of a journal in Dar es Salaam.

Nkosi's collection of essays, *Home and Exile* (1965), has become a standard source for serious students of African literature, and was recognized by an award at the first World Festival of Negro Arts in Dakar in 1966. For several years he was the interviewer of leading African writers in a film series produced by NET, the US National Educational Television organization.

The Rhythm of Violence, his only play, is collected in Fredric N. Litto's *Plays from Black Africa.* It deals with a group of young Boer, English and African students who, in the early 1960's, try to ignore the racial prejudice around them and the oppressive atmosphere of the apartheid policies of their government. The students plan to bomb the Johannesburg City Hall and actually plant a large device in the building on the night a large rally of whites is to be held. Love blooms between Tula, the younger brother of Gama, the leader of the African and white liberal youths, and Sarie, a South African white girl. Tula rushes off to warn the whites because Sarie's father is in the group. Tula arrives too late, the hall is completely destroyed and he is killed in front of the building. Sarie finds Tula's body, weeps over it, is slapped and threatened by two policemen who discover her connection with Tula and through him, with Gama, the leader of the black student opposition to apartheid. At play's end, Sarie has in effect pointed the way to the arrest of the plotters and is herself led away in handcuffs. Her father and sweetheart are dead, the plot is about to be discovered, her friends are arrested, and she herself is doomed to prison. But at least an actual and symbolic blow for freedom has been struck.

The play is strident, staccato, and at time catches the anger and feeling of helpless rebellion of the blacks and their white allies, but the dialogue seems contrived and unconvincing. In the characters of the two Boer policemen, Jan and Piet, however, Nkosi shows his audience the distorted views of the white racists who are not, however, depicted as totally without humanity, but as persons trapped in a racist world.

In his essays, Nkosi offers balanced, if deeply felt, views on the plight of the captive millions in South Africa, depicts the jars and blur and size of America, and explores the meaning of American black poetry and creative work of every origin.

In his short story, "The Prisoner," published in *African Writing Today*, Nkosi imagines the turning of tables by his black protagonist on his hated white master. Working with Zaza, the black maid, the hero entraps George, the boss, by photographing him unequivocally in the embraces of Zaza. Blackmailed and driven to shame and idiocy, the once superior white becomes the prisoner of his former servant, losing also his wife to that same former servant. The tale is told in a rather precious prose, similar to that of Edgar Allen Poe in his story, "The Cask of Amontillado." The icy irony is, however, to a degree appropriate here to express the brooding bitterness of sufferers from apartheid and the hypocrisy of the prohibitions against inter-racial sex.

Writings: Play: *The Rhythm of Violence,* London, Oxford University Press, 1964; also in *Plays From Black Africa,* Fredric M. Litto, editor, New York, Hill and Wang, 1968.

Story: "The Prisoner," in *African Writing Today,* Ezekiel Mphahlele, editor, London, Penguin, 1967.

Essays: *Home and Exile,* London, Longmans, Green, 1965.

NKRUMAH, Francis Nwia Kofie Kwame
September 21, 1909, Nkroful, Western Province, old Gold Coast, (Ghana); d. Romania, April 27, 1972. Autobiographer, statesman.

Nkrumah was born a member of the Nzima group of the Akan people near the Gold Coast's frontier with the Ivory Coast. His father was a goldsmith in Half Assini, and Nkrumah lived there for a considerable period after his third year. A German Roman Catholic priest, George Fischer, helped his primary schooling and Nkrumah was baptized in the Church. On completion of the eight-year grammar course he became a student-teacher for one year at Half Assini and in 1926 began his studies at Accra's Government Training College (now Achimota College). Finishing in 1930 he took a series of teaching jobs and in 1935 with the help of his uncle and his own scanty savings went to America.

Graduating from Lincoln University in 1939 after concentrating in economics and sociology, he remained to study theology and eventually philosophy and education at the University of Pennsylvania, taking advanced degrees in both subjects. While at Lincoln, where he was a lecturer in political science, he was elected president of the African Students Organization of America and Canada. It was during this period that he became familiar with the works of the Jamaican black nationalist, Marcus Garvey, who argued for the total independence of Africa as early as the 1920's.

In May 1945, he sailed from New York for London, and took up the study of law and completed his doctoral dissertation in philosophy. In England he rapidly became an important figure in student politics and in 1947 he was called back to the Gold Coast to become general secretary of the United Gold Coast Convention. The next ten years brought Nkrumah to power and in April 1956 the Gold Coast along with the former British Togoland became independent Ghana, a name Nkrumah had chosen from the most ancient of the three great African empires of the Sudanic region. These matters and the ensuing fourteen years are properly the subjects of a political biography rather than of a literary one and can be studied in such works as Ronald Segal's *African Profiles*.

Nkrumah's own story, *Ghana: the Autobiography of Kwame Nkrumah* was followed by such political works as *I Speak of Freedom; Towards-Colonial Freedom; Africa in the Struggle Against World Imperialism; Africa Must Unite; Neo-Colonialism: The Last Stage of Imperialism: Challenge of the Congo;* and *Handbook of Revolutionary Warfare: A Guide to the Armed Phase of the African Struggle* (1968). His philosophical work, *Consciencism: Philosophy and Ideology for De-Colonization and Development with particular reference to the African Revolution,* is an obscure work composed in sociological jargon which employs mathematical formulae to demonstrate the historical necessity of socialism in Africa. Nkrumah, after providing a long list of symbols representing various aspects of socialism and colonialism, writes (p. 8): ... *Southern Rhodesia is such a colony. In either type of colony, however, negative action is essentially greater than positive action. Hence the symbolic representation of a territory g which is a colony is (i) col. g (na) pa)g.*

Ever more complex equations are provided for the next eight pages. The work ends with: *In the case of Africa, by means of the foregoing set theoretic methods the necessity of a union of independent African states is established, a union integrated by socialism, without which our hard-won independence may yet be perverted and negated by a new colonialism.*

As he grew more powerful and more threatened by assassination, Nkrumah took his country further to the left and in 1966, while he was on a state visit to Peking, a revolt led by the Ghanaian Army quickly took over the government and charged him and his ministers with treason and corruption. Nkrumah was unable to rally forces in his support and was forced to take up residence in nearby Guinea as a guest of President Sekou Touré. The latter at the time of

Nkrumah

Nkrumah's arrival announced to his surprised but complacent people that Nkrumah henceforth was the "Co-President" of Guinea.

From exile in Guinea he wrote several works defending his regime and attacking his enemies in Ghana and elsewhere. One such publication is *Dark Days in Ghana* wherein he expressed his bitterness at his overthrow, his criticisms of his opponents in Accra, and his prediction that the military junta which had ousted him would never turn the government back to civilian leaders, something now proved false by events, though the military has ousted a civilian government recently. Another work was *Axioms of Kwame Nkrumah* which declares in lucid terms his principles on which he believes the African Revolution is, or has been based.

Seriously ill with cancer, Nkrumah sought medical help in Romania in 1971 but died after months of unavailing treatment, April 27, 1972 in Bucharest. Knowing his condition to be terminal, he requested permission of the Accra regime to return home for his last days, but the matter was still under discussion when he died. His death was first announced to the world by President Sekou Touré from Conakry, Guinea.

Writings: Autobiography: *Ghana: The Autobiography of Kwame Nkrumah*, New York, Edinburgh, Nelson, 1957; 1965 in paperback.

Political: *I Speak of Freedom*, London, Heinemann, 1961; New York, Praeger, 1961; *Towards Colonial Freedom;* London, Heinemann, 1962, 1967; *Africa in the Struggle Against World Imperialism*, London, Heinemann, 1962; *Africa Must Unite*, London, Heinemann, 1963; London, Mercury paperback, 1965; New York, Praeger, 1963; *Neo-Colonialism:*
The Last Stage of Imperialism, London, Nelson, 1965; New York, International Publishers, 1966, 1969; London, Heinemann, 1968; *Challenge of the Congo*, New York, International Publishers, 1967, 1969; London, Nelson, 1967; *Handbook of Revolutionary Warfare: A Guide to the Armed Phase of the African Struggle*, London, Panaf Books, 1968; New York, International Publishers, 1969; *Dark Days in Ghana*, London, Lawrence and Wishart, 1968; New York, International Publishers, 1969; *Axioms of Kwame Nkrumah*, New York, Humanities Press, 1967; London, Nelson, 1967.

Philosophy: *Consciencism: Philosophy and Ideology for De-Colonization and Development with Particular Reference to the African Revolution*, London, Heinemann, 1964.

Biographical/Critical Sources: Ronald Segal, *African Profiles*, London, Penguin, 1963; *The New Africans*, Sidney Taylor, editor, New York, G. P. Putnam's Sons, 1967; Timothy Bankole, *Kwame Nkrumah-His Rise to Power*, London, Allen and Unwin, 1955; Francis Botchway, *Political Development and Social Change in Ghana: Ghana Under Nkrumah*, Buffalo, New York, Black Academy Press, 1972; Bob Fitch and Mary Oppenheimer, *Ghana: End of Illusion*, New York and London, Monthly Review Press, 1966.

NOGAR, Rui (pseudonym for BARRETO, Rui Moniz)
b. 1933, Lourenço Marques, Mozambique.
Poet.

Nogar has worked on various literary Mozambique journals, including *Notícias de Bloqueiro*. His work is found in several international poetry collections and the work, "Poem of the Conscripted Soldier," appears in *African Writing Today*.

The Portuguese police arrested Nogar on December 22, 1964, with many other young Mozambique poets and intellectuals. He is still in prison.

Writings: Poetry: works in various journals, including *Notícias de Bloqueiro* and collections including *New Sum of Poetry from the Negro World*, Paris, Présence Africaine, Volume 57, 1966, and *African Writing Today*, Ezekiel Mphahlele, editor, London, Penguin, 1967.

NOKAN, Charles
b. December 28, 1936, Yamoussokra, Ivory Coast.
Novelist, poet, playwright, sociologist.

Nokan's early schooling was in Yamoussokra and Toumodi. After study in a lycée in Paris, he continued at the University of Poitiers and then in Paris, taking two degrees in sociology: the "licence" and the doctorate.

He published in 1962 a long, poetic novel, *Le soleil noir point* (The Sun a Black Dot), which received good reviews. His work has also appeared in various collections, including *Modern Poetry from Africa*. In 1970 he published *La voix grave d'Ophomoi. Poème*.

Violent était le vent (Wild Blew the Wind), completed in 1962 at Yamoussokra, was his first novel, published in 1966. The author in his preface said his work sought to conform to the esthetic of his own Baoule people where the dance "satisfies at one and the same time the ear and the eye, thanks to its use of masks, chants. . ." He has, therefore, mixed poems with prose passages in

musical order so as "to recapture the quality of the tom-toms which cradled (his) infancy." In the novel, the character Kôtiboh represents the past which resists change—in Nokan's words, with "an infernal force," and the young Kossia is characterized in contrast as "the torch of the present."

Nokan has three plays, two published and one being prepared for the press. *Les malheurs de Tchakô* (The Miseries of Chaka), 1968, is a melancholic treatment of the African soul. Tchakô is a Hamlet here, rather than a warrior. All he has is regrets. The second play, *Abraha Pokou ou une grande africaine* and *La voix grave d'Ophomoi. Poème* (Abraha Pokou, or A Great African, followed by the poem,

Nokan

The Grave Voice of Ophomoi), came out in a combined volume in 1970. His third dramatic work, due for publication by P. -J. Oswald, is *La traversée de la nuit noire ou Les exploités dressent le poing* (Getting Through the Dark Night or The Exploited Shake Their Fists).

Also in manuscript being prepared for publication is a sociological study and a second novel, "Les petites rivières ou Les prolétaires Africains," due out in 1972.

Writings: Poetry: *Le soleil noir point,* Paris, Présence Africaine, 1962; *La voix grave d'Ophomoi. Poème,* published with the play *Abraha Pokou,* Honfleur, France, Oswald, 1970; poems in *Modern Poetry from Africa,* Moore and Beier, editors, revised edition, London, Baltimore, Penguin, 1968; *New Sum of Poetry from the Negro World,* Présence Africaine, Volume 57, 1966.

Novels: *Violent était le vent,* Paris, Présence Africaine, 1966; in manuscript: "Les petites rivieres ou Les prolétaires Africains;" *Le soleil* also has prose.

Plays: *Les malheurs de Tchakô,* Paris, Honfleur, Oswald, 1968; *Abraha Pokou ou une grande africaine,* Honfleur, Oswald, 1970; in manuscript being prepared for print: *La traversée de la nuit noire ou Les exploités dressent le poing.*

Sociological Study: *Totétisme Baoulé et le Mindilésisme,* in manuscript, being prepared for the press, for Présence Africaine.

NORONHA, Rui de (see de NORONHA, Rui)

NORTJE, Kenneth Arthur
b. December, 1942, Port Elizabeth, Cape Province, South Africa; d. England, 1970.
Poet, teacher.

Called by Dennis Brutus "perhaps the best South African poet of our time," K. Arthur Nortje died alone and apparently in despair in England of an overdose of sleeping tablets. Nortje had taught from 1964 to 1965 at South End High School, Port Elizabeth, took a B.A. at Belleville "Coloured" College, and then, with a scholarship, went to Jesus College in Oxford to earn a B.A. in English in 1967. Earlier he had studied at two schools reserved for "coloureds,"— St. Marks Mission School and Paterson High School in Schauder Township, Port Elizabeth. During this period he often called himself "Kan" and began to ignore his first given name. At this time he also began to write poetry under the inspiration of his eighth grade teacher, Dennis Brutus, who remained his friend the rest of his life. Nortje was a good athlete, playing cricket and rugby well.

He had taken a special interest in the poetry of Gerard Manley Hopkings. Winning a scholarship from high school he was able to attend Belleville "Coloured" College (Western Cape), where he took his first B.A. At the time of his death he was working on a B. Phil degree at Oxford after a short period in Canada where he had taught for a time in Hope, British Columbia, and in Toronto.

Nortje won an Mbari Poetry Prize in 1962 (Ibadan University, Nigeria), sponsored by the Congress for Cultural Freedom, and his early work was published in Mbari's *Black Orpheus* magazine in 1961 when he was only 19. He is represented in Moore and Beier's *Modern Poets from Black Africa* and has nineteen poems under the general title, "Hollows for Travelling Music," in Pieterse's *Seven South African Poets.* Other poems have appeared in the American review, *African Arts/Arts d'Afrique*, in the Oxford student magazine, *Strumpet*, and in *Sechaba*, the "Official Organ of the African National Congress South Africa," published in London.

Heinemann is preparing for the press 95 of Nortje's poems, mostly from manuscript, for its African Writers Series. To be entitled, "Dead Roots;" the scheduled publication date is 1973.

Nortje's first poem in the Pieterse collection, "Midnight," closes with:

Night after night I lie and wait
for sleep's return, but she, but she
is gripped in spastic fists of fear,
trembling at noises made by me.

A companion poem, "Transition,"

ends in a nostalgic mood, with a surge of passion mingled with despair:

For your success, black residue,
I bear desire still, night thing!
Remain in the smoky summer long
Though I be gone from green-
/flamed spring.

The last poem in the Pieterse collection is "Immigrant," a long, free-verse poem of three pages which closes:

Maybe she is like you, maybe most
/women
deeply resemble you, all of them are
all things to all poets: the cigarette
/girl
in velvet with mink nipples, fishnet
/thighs.
whose womb is full of tobacco.
Have a B.C. apple in the A.D. city
/of the saviour,
and sing the centennial song.

In his black-bordered essay, "In Memoriam," published in Texas' *Research in African Literatures*, Spring, 1971, Brutus wrote of Nortje's power: " . . . He could be lyrical colloquial dramatic and complexly augmentative by turns. . ." and "He refers surprisingly often to death: throws up images of and sidelights on it which show he had looked closely at it. . ." Of compelling interest, therefore, is the poem, "Autopsy," in the Pieterse collection which begins:

My teachers are dead men. I was
/too young
to grasp their anxieties, . . .

and goes on to picture the "hygienic blasts of justice," "the harsh sunlight of arc-lamps," and the "sterile quarantine of dungeons."

Part II of the three-page poem is a mini-biography of Dennis Brutus which includes the fine lines:

He glided down escarpements like
/the wind, until

pursued by banshee sirens
he made their wails the kernel of
/his eloquence,
turning for a time to irrigate
the stretches of our virgin minds.

The poem tells us Brutus not only was shot when he tried to flee his captors, but that later, his "warder kicked the stitches open." The poem ends on the plangent note that Brutus (and the older poets), tired now, are "grave and patient—the years have stilled him." Fortunately, this is not the case—though it may once have seemed so to the younger Nortje.

Writings: Poems in *Black Orpheus*, Mbari Press, 1961, Ibadan, Nigeria; *Modern Poets from Black Africa*, revised editions, London, Penguin, 1968; *Seven South African Poets*, Cosmo Pieterse, editor, London, Heinemann, 1971; *African Arts/Arts d'Afrique*, Palo Alto, California, Stanford University; *Strumpet*, Oxford, England; *Sechaba*, London, African National Congress of South Africa.

Biographical/Critical Sources: Protest and Conflict in African Literature, Cosmo Pieterse, editor, London, Heinemann, 1969; *Literary Review*, Fall, 1971, Fairleigh Dickinson University; *Poetry II*, Jill Potter, editor, London, 1971; *Research in African Literatures*, II, 1, Spring, 1971, University of Texas, Austin, Texas.

NSIMBA, Samuel A.
b. ca. 1910, near Banza Manteke, Congo (Zaïre); d. 1948.
Kikongo poet and hymn writer, minister, teacher.

Educated at Kimpese mission school and its Cours de Théologie during the 1930's and early 1940's, Nsimba became a Protestant minister. His first post was at Matadi where he began writing the articles which appeared in the first Kikongo-language journal, the *Minsamu Miayenge* (The Message of Peace), established at Mukimbungu in 1892. En route to Brussels to attend the 70th aniversary celebration of the founding of protestant missions in the Congo, Nsimba's plane crashed and he died in the area of Libenga, near Kinshasa (then Léopoldville).

Nsimba wrote many hymns, eleven of which appear in the collection *Minkunga mia Kintwadi*. His work has been found very original and imaginative and he is considered one of the finest of the writers developed in and around Kimpese mission.

Writings: Poetry: in *Minsamu Miayenge,* printed at Manianga-Matade, the Swedish Mission (S.M.F.), in 1940's, and eleven works in *Minkunga mia Kintwadi,* Léopoldville, LECO, 1956.

Biographical/Critical Source: Mbololo ya Mpiku, "Introduction à la littérature kikongo," *Research in African Literatures,* African and Afro-American Research Institute, the University of Texas, III, 2 (Fall 1972). The text of one of his hymns in Kikongo, with accompanying French translation appears in this detailed article.

NTANTALA, Phyllis P.
b. January, 1920, South Africa.
Short story writer, editor, journalist, teacher.

Phyllis Ntantala graduated with a B.A. from the University of South Africa, in 1946, and took a diploma in comparative African government and law at the

University of Cape Town, 1957–58. Earlier, she had taken the Teachers' Diploma, Fort Hare College, 1938, and taught at various schools: Kroonstad High School (Orange Free State) 1939–1944; Lovedale High School (Cape Province) 1945; Langa High School (Cape Province) 1948–1951). She has worked as a researcher and editor and has published numerous articles including "The Abyss of Bantu Education" in *Africa South,* and "Five Years of Bantu Education" in *Fighting Talk.*

Her essay, "The Widows of the Reserves," is a beautifully restrained but searing and tragic picture of African women, whose husbands must work under long labor contracts in distant mines and factories, and who are, in effect, apartheid's widows. The lonely women live out their lives in the back country with the children who know no fathers. The essay originally appeared in *Africa South.* Other work has been published in various African journals.

Widow of the noted writer, Dr. A. C. Jordan, she has lived for the past decade in Madison, Wisconsin, doing research and writing in the field of South African vernacular and English language works.

Writings: Articles: "Abyss of Bantu Education," *Africa South;* "Five Years of Bantu Education," *Fighting Talk,* Volume 15, No. 3; "The Widows of the Reserve," *Africa South.*

NTARA, Samuel Yosia
b. 1905, Nyasaland, now Malawi.
Cewa-Nyanja novelist, scholar,
teacher, biographer.

Ntara won a prize for biography given by the International Institute of African Languages and Cultures for his 1934 work, *Man of Africa.* He gives an authentic personal view of the life of an African village, silhouetted by contemporary events. Though biographic, the work has some invented scenes to dramatize daily life.

His autobiographical novel, *Headman's Enterprise,* appeared in 1949, one of the earliest creative works ever to be written and published in Cewa. He then translated the work into English for publication.

Writings: Biographical novels: *Man of Africa,* London, Religious Tract Society, 1934; *Headman's Enterprise,* London, Lutterworth Press, 1949

NTLOKO, President Mthetho
b. August 11, 1914, Nqabara Location at Mahlungulu, Willowvale District, Cape Province, South Africa.
Zulu poet, playwright, collector of folk material, educator.

Second son of Japheth Ntloko, President Ntloko attended local schools before taking his junior certificate and teacher's certificate in 1935 after five years at Clarkebury Training School. His early teaching positions were at the Clarkebury school and Nqabara Higher Primary School. In 1941, the Tonic Solfa College of Music awarded him his music certificate whereupon he became principal of Nkanga Primary School in Libode. Subsequently, he served as principal of Ngoma School, and in 1944, as principal of the Manxeba Higher Primary School. Later positions were superintendant of schools for the Kokstad Circuit (1950–57) and sub-inspector of Bantu education for the Matatiele Circuit (1957–present).

Ntloko

Ntloko has poems in many journals and has published three volumes: *Iqhashu* (Roasted Corn Patties), 1954; *Isitha* (Shock of Corn), 1961, and his third, *Zonwabise* (Keep Them Happy), 1965. His two plays in Zulu are *UNgodongwana* (Dingiswayo), 1961, and *Kukh' u Thixo kule nto* (God Is in This Thing), 1965. His songs were very popular, too, including the well-known "Intambanane" (In the Afternoon). Several collections of his prose and verse await publication.

Writings: Poetry: *Iqhashu,* London, Cape Town, Oxford University Press, 1954; *Isitha,* London, Cape Town, Oxford University Press, 1961; *Zonwabise,* London, Cape Town, Oxford University Press, 1965 (Jahn gives Cape Town, Oxford University Press, 1962).
Plays: *UNgodongwana,* Cape Town, Via Afrika, 1961 (Jahn has Cape Town, Oxford University Press, 1961). *Kukh' u Thixo kule nto,* Cape Town, Via Afrika, 1965.
Song: "Intambanane," details unknown.

NTSANE, Kemuele Edward
b. April 4, 1920, Kholojane Village, Leribe District, Lesotho.
Southern Sotho novelist, poet, teacher.

The son of Edward Chaka and Evelina Ntsane, of the Kwena people, Kemuele studied from 1928 to 1932 at the 'Muela Primary School, the Cana High School (1933–34), the Basutoland Training School, Morija (1935–39), where he earned his junior certificate. After 1940, he taught at Mlotse Government Intermediate School, Roma, Maseru High School, and at several other schools in the area and spent a few months in the Rand gold fields. He married Julia 'Machaka, a school teacher in July, 1945 and they now have four children.

A student at the Institute of Education of the University of London (1947–48), he specialized in the teaching of English to foreigners. While in London he and his wife met the scholar Gladstone Llewellyn Letele (1913–1950) and his wife, a daughter of Thomas Mokopu Mofolo, the greatest of South African novelists. During this fruitful year he worked with Letele in the Sotho section of the London University School of Oriental and African Studies, and earned his teacher's certificate. Returning to South Africa to teach, he began his writing career while working for the still elusive B.A. from the University of South Africa.

Ntsane's volumes of poetry are: *'Musa-pelo* (the Heart Invigorator), published in 1946, and *'Musa-pelo, II,* 1961. His novels are: *Masoabi, ngoan'a Mosotho'a kajeno* (Masoabi, Today's Sotho Child), 1947; *Bana ba Roma* (Children of Roma), 1954; *Boa batho* (These People), 1968; and the novelette, *Makumane* (Titbits or Small Crumbs), 1961. One of his rare poems, unpublished, is "Beat Heart, Beat!"

Ntsane has translated Shakespeare's *Merchant of Venice* as *Mohwebi wa Venisi,* 1961, as well as two works aimed at the popular market, *Nna Sajene Kokobela, C.I.D,,* (That's Me, Sergeant Kokobela of the C.I.D.), 1963; and a murder-mystery, *Manganga* (Stubborn). Another work is *Moqoqo oa Abiela le Johannese* (The Conversation between Abiele and Johannese).

Writings: Poetry: *'Musa-pelo,* Morija, Morija Sesuto Book Depot, 1946, revised, 1962; *'Musa-pelo, II,* Morija, 1961.

Poem: "Beat Heart, Beat!" unpublished.

Novels: *Masoabi, ngoan'a Mosotho'a kejeno,* Morija, 1947, 1958; *Bana ba Roma,* Morija, 1954; *Makumane,* Johannesburg, 1961; *Bao Batho,* Johannesburg, Bona Press, 1968.

Translations: *Merchant of Venice* as *Mohwebi wa Venisi,* Johannesburg, Afrikaanse Pers-Boekhandel, 1961; *Manganga,* date and place unknown; *Nna Sajene Kokobela, C.I.D.,* Johannesburg, Bona Press.

Other: Conversations: *Moqoqo oa Abiela le Johannese,* date and place unknown.

NTSANWISI, Hudson William Edison
b. July 11, 1920, Shiluvane, Letaba District, Northern Transvaal, South Africa.
Tsonga novelist, biographer, scholar, teacher.

Hudson Ntsanwisi attended schools at Shiluvane, Douglas Laing Smit High School, where he passed the Standard VI in 1936, and the Lemana Training School which gave him his teacher's certificate in 1939 and the University Education Diploma in 1940. By private study he gained the matriculation certificate in 1942 and the B.A. from Fort Hare in 1946.

He was a teacher at Shiluvane (1941–43), the Emmarentia Geldenhuys High School, Warmbad (1943–49), principal of the Bokgaka Secondary School, Letaba District (1949–1956), and sub-inspector of Bantu education for the Pietersburg East Circuit (1957–1959). Since then he has been a teacher at the University College of the North, and since 1966 a professor of the Department of Bantu Languages. After many years he earned a B.A. (Honors) from the University of South Africa in 1962, and the M.A. from the same university in 1965. With his wife, Beatrice, he visited England and Western Europe. Since 1971 he has been Chief Minister of Gazankulu (the Tsonga homeland).

Ntsanwisi's first novel, *Masungi, m'fana ka Maxele* (Masungi, Child of Maxele), was awarded Afrikaanse Pers-Boekhandel's first prize in the literary competition of 1954 in the Tsonga language area and probably published in 1957. *Mahlasela–hundza* (The Warriors), 1960, was his second novel. The Swiss Mission Press in 1958 published his biography of Chief Muhlaba, *Muhlaba hosi ya va ka Nkuna Nkanyi wa le Ndzelakaneni,* written with P. M. Shilubana.

Beginning in 1957, his eight graded readers for the study of Tsonga, *Makomba-ndlela* (This Is The Way), containing Tsonga stories, were published. His most recent scholarly work is *Tsonga Idioms,* 1968, a descriptive language study.

Writings: Novels: *Masungi, m'fana ka Maxele,* Johannesburg, Afrikaanse Pers-Boekhandel, 1957; *Mahlasela–hundza,* Johannesburg, Afrikaanse, 1960.

Biography: *Muhlaba hosi ya va ka Nkuna Nkanyi wa le Ndzelakaneni,* with P. M. Shilubana, Edendale, Swiss Mission, 1968.

Language Studies: *Makomba-ndlela,* Johannesburg, Voortrekkers Pers, 1957, 1961; Johannesburg, Bantu-Publikasies, 1964; *Tsonga Idioms,* Johannesburg, Swiss Mission Press, 1968.

NTSIKANA
b. ca. 1783, Transkei, South Africa;
d. 1820, near Gwali (later Old Lovedale), South Africa.
Xhosa poet, religious leader.

Ntsikana

Ntsikana's hymns were not only sung frequently and fervently by his followers, they were also memorized. First influenced by Dr. Johannes Theodosius

van der Kemp (1747–1811) of the London Missionary Society and the Reverend Joseph Williams of the same society, Ntsikana slowly accepted the Christian faith. Son of Gabo and Gabo's second wife, members of the Ngqika part of the Xhosa people, Ntsikana lived for the first 13 years of his life in exile with his mother's family, followers of Chief

Ndlambe. His mother returned to her husband about 1796 and at this time the future poet came to hear the teachings of van der Kemp.

Various visions turned Ntsikana increasingly toward Christianity and in 1818 he had established his own "mission" at Makanzara. There he composed songs for his followers, and encouraged them to leave off their "heathen ways." He also exposed them to writing and other Western arts. The first Xhosa work ever written down was a hymn by Ntsikana. It began with the words: "He the great God, high in Heaven." Not until 1828, however, was a song version recorded by Dr. John Phillip of the mission of the Church of Scotland.

Writings: Oral hymns, mostly unrecorded, except that written down in 1828 by Dr. John Philip: "He the great God, high in Heaven."

Biographical/Critical Sources: R.H. Shepherd, *Bantu Literature and Life,* Lovedale, 1955; Shepherd and B. G. Paver, *African Contrasts,* Cape Town, 1947; A. C. Jordan, "Towards an African Literature: (V) The Early Writers," *Africa South,* II, 4, 1958; John Philip, *Researches in South Africa,* London, 1928; John Knox Bokwe, *Ibali lika Ntsikana* (in Xhosa: a biography of Ntsikana), Lovedale Press, 1904, augmented second edition, 1914; Albert S. Gérard, *Four African Literatures,* Berkeley, University of California Press, 1971.

NTSIKO, Jonas A.
b. ca. 1860, Xhosa area, South Africa; d. ca. 1915.
Xhosa poet, hymn writer, teacher, preacher.

Little is known of Ntsiko other than that he was once a preacher and teacher at St. John's Mission Station at Mtata (Umbata), and born about 1860. Probably the most popular of the poets contributing poetry to the literary columns of *Isigidimi sama-Xosa* (The Xhosa Courier), the pioneering Xhosa-language newspaper, Ntsiko signed his work, "UHadi wase-luhlangeni," or the "Harp of the Nation."

Always honest and outspoken, the poet's comments in the paper became very influential. His attacks on the hypocrisy of the church and the white government were particularly strong. John Tengo Jabavu, the editor, rejected one of his articles in 1884 whereupon the paper lost many readers and much of the power and allegiance it once had commanded as the independent voice of Black South Africans. Most of "Hudi's" pieces could not be published in his day because of their independent opinions and the majority remain in manuscript at the Umbata Library.

Nineteen of his hymns appeared in *Xhosa Hymn Book,* 1881, his only published verse in book form.

Writings: Hymns: nineteen in the collection, *Xhosa Hymn Book,* Grahamstown, South Africa, 1881.

Journalism: Many articles, occasional verse, etc. in *Isigidimi sama-Xosa,* published under the name, "UHadi waseluhlangeni."

Biographical/Critical Source: A. C. Jordan, "Towards an African Literature: (XI) The Harp of the Nation," *Africa South,* IV, 2 (1960).

NTUYAHAGA, Monseigneur, Lord Bishop of Usumbura (now Bujumbura, capital of Burundi)
b. ca. 1910, Rwanda.
Rwanda-language storyteller.

Mgr. Ntuyahaga "composed" an *imigani,* a spoken traditional story about the past which is often full of monsters, strange heroes and their adventures, or animal stories, all with proverbs and old folk saws. In writing down such an *imigani* in Rundi or Rwanda, Ntuyahaga has helped begin a new literature, for there was before him no written record of the old stories modified by the demands of the written page, except for the histories of Abbé Alexis Kagame written in Rwanda. His work, "The Departure and Return of the Cattle in Burundi," has been translated by Joan Nicholson of the Usumburo Church Missionary Society and appears in W. H. Whiteley's second volume of *A Selection of African Prose* along with Miss Nicholson's useful essay on Rundi folk literature.

Writings: Story: The Departure and Return of the Cattle in Burundi," translated by Joan Nicholson, in *A Selection of African Prose,* W. H. Whiteley, editor, Oxford, Clarendon Press, 1964, with comments by Miss Nicholson.

NUNES, António
b. 1917, Santiago, Cape Verde Islands; d. Portugal, 1951.
Poet.

An active participant in the neo-realistic movement in Portugal, Nunes published two volumes of poetry: *Devaneios* (Dreams), in 1938, and *Poemas de longe* (Poems from Far-Away), in 1945. He is also represented in Mário de Andrade's *Literatura africana de expressão portugêse.*

Writings: Poetry: Devaneios, Praia, Cape, Verde, 1938; Poemas de longe, Lisbon, 1945; poems in Literatura africana de expressão portuguêse, Volume I, Poesia, Algiers, 1967.

NWANKWO, Nkem
b. 1936, Nawlia-Awka, Onitsha, Nigeria.
Novelist, playwright.

Educated locally, Nwanko finished his education at the University of Ibadan. He became a teacher at the Ibadan Grammar School after graduation. During the Biafran war he wrote, with Samuel X. Ufejika, Biafra: The Making of a Nation.

Nwanko's first novel, Danda, published in 1963, has been made into a musical that has been widely performed in Nigeria and at the first Festival of Negro Arts in Dakar, 1966. The hero of the novel is Danda, who, like Okonkwo's flute-playing father, Unoka, in Things Fall Apart by Chinua Achebe, ignores the traditional Ibo virtures of hard work, ambition, thrift, and respect for the village elders. Though he is the son of a chief, Danda prefers to work at play, to go about in his ringing cloak of small bells, to gossip, dance, drink palm wine and to make love to the young wives of the tired old men of the village. Danda, (his name means "rain"), patters through the lives of his people, inpudent, charming, irresponsible. A chapter from the novel, entitled "Rain," is published in Frances Ademola's Reflections: Nigerian Prose and Verse.

When Danda is finally pushed into marriage he appears to settle down for awhile and in due time there is a little Danda to carry on the tradition of laughter. But even as chief at the novel's close,

he is gay and free. Essentially anti-heroic, Danda never takes life as overwhelming or serious business. He is not prepared to suffer or to make others suffer except through his insouciance. In her fine discussion of this work, Margaret Lawrence rightly praises Nwanko's bouncy prose and quotes this excellent passage in illustration:

The scorch season was dying. The happiest time of the year, the season for feasts, when men and women laughed with all their teeth and little boys, their mouths oily, oily, ran about the lanes blowing the crops of chicken to make balloons.

In 1963, Nwankwo published Tales Out of School, printed in Hungary, a volume of naive stories concerning a young African boy as he goes off to school to get westernized. But more than school is treated, for Nwankwo is far-ranging, and brings in even the old slaver days. More Tales Out of School followed in 1965.

His work is zesty and dynamic, full of Ibo words and terms. Few if any European values are reflected and those that are are usually embodied in the aggressive, puritanical Christianized villagers. His style hews to the line of Ibo oral story-telling, though the mind behind such prose is mocking and not at all naive or rustic.

An early play of his is Eroya (1963).

Writings: Novel: Danda, Lagos, African Universities Press, 1963; London, André Deutsch, 1964; later made into a musical; a chapter, "Rain," in Reflections: Nigerian Prose and Verse, Lagos, African University Press, 1962.

Play: Eroya, Ibadan, University College, 1963, mimeographed.

Stories: *Tales Out of School,* Lagos, African Universities Press, Ltd., 1963; *More Tales Out of School,* Lagos, A.U.P., 1965.

Biographical/Critical Sources: Margaret Laurence, *Long Drums and Cannons,* London, Macmillan, 1968.

NWANODI, Glory Okugbule (see WONODI, Okugbule)

NWAPA, Flora
b. 1931, Oguta, Eastern Nigeria.
Novelist.

The eldest of six children, Flora Nwapa attended Archdeacon Crowther's Memorial Girls' School and CMS Girls' School in Lagos before going on to the University College of Ibadan where she received her arts degree in 1957. In 1958, she was awarded a diploma in education from Edinburgh University.

Upon completion of her studies Flora Nwapa was appointed a Woman Education Officer in Calabar and the following year was transferred to Queen's School, Enugu, where she taught English and geography. In 1962 she moved to the post of assistant registrar (Public Relations) at the University of Lagos. She is married and has one son.

Her novel, *Efuru,* published in 1966, gives an interesting insight into the woman's world in Africa. The work revolves around a distinguished African woman and her trials as she loses two husbands and a child. Failing in her efforts to fit into the simple village life, she cannot understand how she can lose so much and still retain great respect.

The same folk story of the woman, spouse of the sea-god, is told by Elechi Amadi in his *The Concubine,* published in 1966, the same year as Flora Nwapa's work appeared.

Her second novel, *Idu,* 1970, tells the tale of the love of Idu for her dead husband, Adiewere. So strong is her grief that she seeks him out in the land of ghosts. In 1971 her most recent work was issued, a collection of short stories, *This Is Lagos and Other Stories.*

Writings: Novels: *Efuru,* London, Heinemann, 1966; *Idu,* London, Heinemann, 1970.

Stories: *This Is Lagos and Other Stories,* Enugu, Nwankwo, Ifejika, 1971.

Biographical/Critical Source: Maryse Conde, "Three Female Writers in

303

Modern Africa: Flora Nwapa, Ama Ata Aidoo, and Grace Ogot," in *Présence Africaine,* second trimester, 1972.

NXUMALO, Henry
b. 1917, South Africa; d. 1956.
Short story writer, journalist.

Nxumalo was an important early contributor to the *Drum,* the most important of the journals open to creative writing by black South Africans.

A prominent journalist noted for his exposés, Nxumalo was killed, it is thought, in 1956 by South African government agents.

NXUMALO, James Alfred Walter
b. January 16, 1908, Natal Province, South Africa.
Zulu novelist, scholar, teacher.

Nxumalo's early schooling was at St. Chad's College, Ladysmith (1926–28), and Amanzimtoti (Adams') College (1931–35) which granted him the Teacher's Certificate. He then became principal of the Ethaleni Training College. By private study he earned the B.A. from the University of South Africa in the mid-1940's and became supervisor of schools in 1950 for the Dundee Circuit, remaining till 1955 when he became the inspector for Bantu education for all of Natal.

He married Natalie Victoria Nxaba (b. 1908) in 1936 who that same year published her successful novel, *Ubude abuphangwa* (It's Not So Easy to Get to the Top) (Maritzburg, Shuter and Shooter) and composed a second work still in manuscript. Violet Dube (b. ca. 1910)

was one year earlier as a published woman author in Zulu with her folktale collection, *Wozanazo izindaba zika Phushozwayo* (Tell Us the Stories of Phoshozwayo) (London, Oxford University Press, 1935). James Nxumalo retired in 1970.

His first book, the novel *UZwelonke* (The Entire Nation), appeared in 1950. The Zulu grammar, *Umtapo wolwazi lwesiZulu* (The Source for the Understanding of the Zulu language) came out in 1951. Other readers were: *Isangoma somcwebo wolimi lwesiZulu* (The Key to the Book of the Whey, or Heart, of the Zulu Language), 1951, and *Igugu likaZulu* (Zulu's Precious Stone), 1953, along with his handbook on the language, *Umthombo wegugu likaZulu* (A Sourcebook of Zulu's Precious Stone).

Writings: Novel: *UZwelonka,* Pietermaritzburg, Shuter and Shooter, 1950.

Zulu language studies: *Umtapo wolwazi lwesiZulu,* Shuter and Shooter, 1951; *Isangoma somcwebo wolimi lwesiZulu,* Shuter and Shooter, 1951, *Igugu likaZulu,* 1953; *Umthombo wegugu likaZulu,* Shuter and Shooter, 1953.

NXUMALO, Natalie Victoria (née Nxaba)
b. 1908, Natal, South Africa.
Zulu novelist.

Married to James A. W. Nxumalo, Natalie Nxumalo published the first novel and the second creative work by a woman Zulu writer, *Ubude abuphangwa* (It's Not So Easy To Get to the Top) in 1936. Violet Dube's collection of stories, *Wozanazo izindaba zika Phoshozwayo* (Tell Us the Stories of Phoshozwayo), 1935, was the first published book by a female Zulu artist.

Writings: Novel: *Ubude Abuphangwa,* Pietermaritzburg, Shuter and Shooter, 1936. By Violet Dube: *Wozanazo izindaba zika Phoshozwayo,* London, Oxford University Press, 1935.

NXUMALO, Otty Ezrom Howard Mandlakayise
b. 1938, Natal Province, South Africa.
Zulu poet, novelist, collector of folklore.

A nephew of James Alfred Nxumalo, Otty Ezrom received his education in local schools and published his first volume of verse as *Ikhwezi* (The Morning Star) in 1965. With Cyril Lincoln Sibusiso Nyembezi, he wrote an account of Zulu customs, *Inqolobane yesizwe* (Customs of the Nation), published in 1966.

With Simeon Thandindawo Zeblon Khwela, Otty Nxumalo published original stories in *Emhlabeni, nezinye izindaba* (On Earth, and Other Stories), 1963, and in *Amanqampunqampu* (The Harvesters), 1966. He had also published, 1969, a work of unknown genre, *Ngisinga empumalanga* (I Am Travelling Eastwards), and the earlier work, the 124-page novel, *Ikusasa alaziwa* (Tomorrow We Can Not Know), 1961.

Writings: Poetry: *Ikhwezi,* Pietermaritzburg, Shuter and Shooter, 1965; Jahn states work was published Cape Town, Oxford University Press, 1965.
Novel: *Ikusasa alaziwa,* Johannesburg, Bona Press, 1961.
Stories: *Emhlabeni, nezinye izindaba,* with Simeon Thandindawo Zeblon, Pietermaritzburg, Shuter and Shooter, 1963; *Amanqampunqampu,* Pietermaritzburg, Shuter and Shooter, 1966.
Folklore: *Inqolobane yesizwe,* with C. L.

S. Nyembezi, Pietermaritzburg, Shuter and Shooter, 1966.
Other: *Ngisinga empumalanga,* Pietermaritzburg, Shuter and Shooter, 1969.

NYABONGO, Prince Akiki K.
b. 1904, Uganda.
Autobiographer, storywriter.

A member of the royal family of the Baganda, Prince Nyabongo studied in local schools, then went on to Yale University and Oxford for advanced training in philosophy and psychology. His first work, an autobiography, *The Story of an African Chief,* was published in 1935. The English edition was entitled *Africa Answers Back,* 1936. His second work, *Bisoro Stories I and II, Winds and Lights,* and *African Fairy Tales,* was published in 1939.

These works were among the first by an African to receive a fairly wide audience in Europe and America. Their exploitation of African culture and customs was an important early vehicle to show African life from the inside. The autobiography, a delightful work, is a collection of general essays, personal comments, and history and begins with the arrival of Stanley in the Kingdom of the Buganda.

Nyabongo's collection in Swahili, *Hadithi za wabisoro,* came out in an abbreviated two volume edition in 1937. A complete two volume edition of the collection was published in 1961, as *Hadithi za wanyama.*

Writings: Autobiography: *The Story of an African Chief,* New York, Scribner and Sons, 1935; entitled: *Africa Answers Back,* London, Routledge, 1936.

Stories: *Bisoro Stories I and II, Winds and Lights,* and *African Fairy Tales,* New York, Voice of Ethiopia, 1939; in Swahili as *Hadithi za wabisoro,* Oxford, B. Blackwell, 1937; *Hadithi za wanyama,* London, Sheldon, 1961.

Technical report: *A Report on Town Planning,* Kampala, 1964.

NYEMBEZI, Cyril Lincoln Sibusiso
b. December 6, 1919, Babanango, Natal Province, South Africa.
Zulu novelist, poet, scholar, teacher, editor.

The second of four brothers, Cyril Nyembezi attended local primary schools, then went to Mariannhill for high school. He received a B. A. from the University of South Africa in 1946, and his second B. A., with Honors, in 1947, from the University of the Witwatersrand in Johannesburg. From 1948 to 1953, Nyembezi was a lecturer in the Department of Bantu Studies, Witwatersrand, teaching Zulu and Xhosa. He took the M. A. at that university in 1954 and the next year was appointed to teach at the University College of Fort Hare, remaining until 1959 when he resigned in a protest against restrictive new policies being enforced at Fort Hare by the Government. Others who resigned were Ambrose Phahle, Ethan Mayisele, and Selbourne Ngcobo. Out of work for a period, he took an editorial job with the publishers Shuter and Shooter in Pietermaritzburg, where he is today.

Nyembezi's three novels are *Mntanami! Mntanami!* (My Child! My Child!), published in 1950; *Ubododa abukhulelwa* (A Man Must Control His Strength), 1953; and *Inkinsela yaseMgungundlovu* (The V.I.P. from Pietermaritzburg), 1961. His Zulu version of Alan Paton's Cry, *The Beloved Country* is entitled *Lafa elihle kakhulu* (literally, That Which is Beautiful Perishes), published in 1958.

His poetry was published in three anthologies he edited: *Imisebe yelanga* (Sunbeams), issued in 1960; *Imikhemezelo* (Drizzle), 1963; and *Amahlangu aluhlaza* (Green Leaves), 1963. He brought out *Zulu Proverbs* in English translation in 1954. With Otty Ezrom Nxumalo he collected and edited two volumes of Zulu folklore: *Inqolobane yesizwe* (The Treasury of the Nation), 1966, and the earlier *Izibongo zamakhose* (Praises of the Kings), 1958.

He collaborated with D. M. Lupuwana on a series of eight Zulu graded readers, *Ulutya* (Thongs) in 1965 and more recently a new series of eight, entitled

Igoda (Friendship), late 1960's. His Zulu grammar, *Uhlelo lwesiZulu*, 1956; his manual, *Learn Zulu*, 1958, and his *Compact Zulu Dictionary*, date unknown, are a few of his scholarly works.

African Studies published his essay, "The historical background of the Izibongo of the Zulu military age," in two parts, June and December, 1948. He has also had articles in other journals such as the *Bantu Education Journal* and his *Review of Zulu Literature*, according to Albert S. Gérard, is "one of the most valuable sources of information on the subject."

Of particular interest is his very useful anthology of young Zulu poets, *Izimpophoma zomphefumulo* (The Waterfalls of the Soul), issued in 1963. It contains the verse of such men as Daniel Nkumbalume Gulube (b. 1938), Michael Jubulani Mphelakwakhe Khumalo (b. 1938), Abner Azariah Sinanka Kunene (b. 1917), Criswell Sipho Mkhize (b. 1931), Elliot Elphas Nsizwane kaTimothy Mkhize (b. 1931), Michael Deda Myeza (b. 1927), Bethuel Zintaba Blose Ndela (b. 1927), William Velaphi Ngiba (b. 1925), Michael Mpandeni Ngubeni (b. 1934), Anthony Madodanenzani Nzimande (b. 1917), and Abel Bernard Phakathi (b. 1931).

Writings: Novels: *Mntanami! Mntanami!*, Pietermaritzburg, Lincroft Books, 1950; later entitled *Ushicilelo lwesithathu* in third printing, 1965; *Inkinsela yaseMgungundlovu*, Pietermaritzburg, Shuter and Shooter, 1961; *Ubododa abukhulelwa*, Pietermaritzburg, Shuter and Shooter, 1953, 1966.

Poetry: *Imisebe yelanga*, Johannesburg, Afrikaanse Pers Boekhandel, 1959–61, in three volumes; *Imikhemezelo*, 1963; *Amahlunga aluhlaza*, 1963, the last two in Pietermaritzburg, Shuter and Shooter.

Folklore: *Zulu Proverbs*, Johannesburg, University of Witwatersrand, 1954, revised, 1963; *Inqolobane yesiziwe*, with Otty Ezrom Nxumalo, Pietermaritzburg, Shuter and Shooter, 1966; *Izibongo zamakhose*, Pietermaritzburg, Shuter and Shooter, 1958.

Translation: *Cry, The Beloved Country*, by Alan Paton, into Zulu as *Lafa elihle kakhulu*, Pietermaritzburg, Shuter and Shooter, 1958.

Zulu language studies: *Ulutya*, 1965; *Igoda*, no date; *Uhlelo lwesiZulu*, 1956, new, enlarged edition, Pietermaritzburg, Shuter and Shooter, 1970; *Learn Zulu*, 1958, all by Shuter and Shooter, *Compact Zulu Dictionary*, London, Dent.

Essay: "The Historical Background of the Izibongo of the Zulu Military Age," in *African Studies*, June and December, 1948.

Anthology: *Izimpophoma zomphefumulo*, Pietermaritzburg, Shuter and Shooter, 1963 (of young Zulu poets).

Linguistic-Literary Study: *A Review of Zulu Literature*, Durban, 1961.

Some works of young authors referred to in *Izimpophoma zomphefumulo: E. E. Mkize:* Novelette: *Inhliziyo ingugo Wami* (I Believe My Heart), Cape Town, Via Afrika, 1969; and verse in *Izimpophoma . . .*, 1963, and in *Imbongi YakwaZulu* (The Poet of the Zulus), Pietermaritzburg, Shuter and Shooter, 196?

B. B. Ndelu: Play: *Mageba lazihlonza* (I Swear By Mageba), Pietermaritzburg, Shuter and Shooter, 1962; and verse in *Izimpophoma . . .*, 1963.

NYERERE, Julius Kambarage
b. March, 1922, Butiama, near the eastern shore of Lake Victoria, Northern Province, Tanganyika, now Tanzania.

Essayist, statesman, translator (English into Swahili), political writer.

Nyerere's father was a chief of the small Zanaki tribe, and his mother the eighteenth wife of Chief Nyerere Burito. Thought to be clever because of his skill in playing a complicated game called *soro*, the young Julius was sent at the age of twelve to Tabora Government School and then to a Roman Catholic school at Musoma where he became a Christian, a faith he adheres to today. He went on to Makerere University in Uganda from 1943 to 1945 where he earned a teacher's diploma. He then taught at St. Mary's Mission School in Tabora. In 1949, as the first student from Tanganyika to attend a British university, he took a degree in arts in Edinburgh and returned home in 1952 to teach. By this time, however, he was already deeply interested in forming a group to win increased freedom for his people, and he helped to form the African National Union.

He was elected to the Legislative Council in 1958 and became Chief Minister in 1960. He subsequently led his country to complete independence in 1961 and became Tanzania's first president in 1962. Since then he has weathered several grave political crises and has become a major leader of the new Africa.

His writings are mostly collected essays from his experience in African politics. He is noted for favoring interracial cooperation, universal franchise, limitation of tribal controls, and a federation of East African states. He was instrumental in the drafting and signing of a treaty of cooperation by East African leaders in June, 1967. To form a moderate socialist state he developed a unique one-party democracy, led by his party,

TANU ((Tanganyika, now Tanzania African National Union).

Nyerere's translation of Shakespeare's *Julius Caesar* into Swahili is his major work in literature. Among his numerous political or polemical works are: *Freedom and Socialism*, 1968, and *Democracy and the Party System*, 1965.

Writings: Translation: Shakespeare's *Julius Caesar*, rendered into Swahili as *Juliuz Caesar*, London, Oxford University Press, 1963, *Mabepari wa Venisi* (Shakespeare's *Merchant of Venice*) in Swahili, Dar es Salaam, Oxford University Press, 1969.

Polemics: *Uhuru na Ujamaa: Freedom and Socialism*, London, New York, Nairobi, Oxford University Press, 1968; *Democracy and the Party System*, London, Oxford University Press, 1965, *Education for Self-Reliance*, Dar es Salaam, Government Printer, 1967 (?); *Freedom and Development*, Dar es Salaam, Government Printer, 196(?).

Biographical/Critical Sources: Ronald Segal, *African Profiles*, London, Penguin, 1962; *The New Africans*, Sidney Taylor, editor, New York, G. P. Putnam's Sons, 1967; William Edgett Smith, *We Must Run While They Walk: A Portrait of Africa's Julius Nyerere*, New York, Random House, 1972.

NYUNAI, Jean-Paul
b. July 26, 1932, Yaoundé,
Cameroon.
Poet.

Nyunaï's two earliest works, written in French, are entitled: *La nuit de ma vie* (The Darkness of My Life), 1961 and *Piments sang: Poèmes 1953* (Blood-red Peppers: Poems 1953), published in

1963. The first collection comprises about forty short poems which are predominantly Western in their themes and subjects. The second volume is more general. A third volume with his later work is *Chansons pour Ngo-lima* (Songs for Ngo-lima), dealing with African concerns. Three of his poems appear in *New Sum of Poetry from the Negro World* and his first volume has been republished by Kraus Reprint.

Writings: Poetry: *La nuit de ma vie*, Paris, Nouvelles Editions Debresse, 1961; Nendeln, Liechtenstein, Kraus Reprint, 1971; *Piments sang: Poèmes 1953*, Paris, Debresse, 1963; *Chansons pour Ngo-lima*, Monte Carlo, Eds. Regain, 1964; poems in *New Sum of Poetry from the Negro World*, Paris, Présence Africaine, Vol. 57, 1966.

NZEKWU, Onuora
b. 1928, Kafanchan, northern Nigeria. Novelist.

Nzekwu was a teacher before he joined the staff of *Nigeria Magazine,* a publication of which he now is editor-in-chief. He has published three novels: *Wand of Noble Wood,* 1961, *Blade Among the Boys,* 1962, and *Highlife for Lizards,* 1965, which deals with Ibo life and folklore.

The widely acclaimed *Blade Among the Boys* dealt with the contrast and conflict between Christianity and traditional African rites. The hero of Nzekwu's novel decides to join the Roman Catholic priesthood. Unable to imagine a life of celibacy and one without the familial and tribal rites, the hero's family is shocked at the decision. Troubles ensue.

Wand of Noble Wood presents a Lagos journalist who, although engaged in a very demanding and "modern" job,

strongly feels the tug of ancestral pieties and family loyalties.

Nzekwu's technique of concentrating on the central character offers strength but the reader at times wishes for other personalities to deal with and a greater variety in tone and psychological texture. Ibo customs and problems, however, are skillfully interwoven into the action of the novels.

Nzekwu has also published one children's book of stories, with Michael Crowder, *Eze Goes to School,* 1963.

Writings: Novels: *Wand of Noble Wood,* London, Hutchinson, 1961; U. S. paperback, New York, Signet, 1963, 1966; London, Heinemann, 1970; *Blade Among the Boys,* London, Hutchinson, 1962; London, Arrow Books, 1964; London, Heinemann, 1970; *Highlife for Lizards,* London, Hutchinson, 1965.

Children's Stories: *Eze Goes to School,* with Michael Crowder, Lagos, African University Press, 1963.

NZIMANDE (see NYEMBEZI)

NZOUANKEU, Jacques Mariel
b. ca. 1940, Cameroon. Playwright, novelist.

Nzouankeu has published one play, *L'agent spécial. Pièce en 5 actes* (Special Agent. A Play in 5 Acts), 1964, and one novelette, *La souffle des ancêtres* (The Breath of the Ancestors), 1965.

Writings: Play: *L'agent spécial. Pièce en 5 actes, Abbia* magazine, No. 5, March 1964 and No. 7, October, 1964, in Yaoundé.

Novelette: *La souffle des ancêtres,* Yaoundé, Abbia, and CLE, 1965; Jahnheinz Jahn terms this volume a collection of stories.

O

Obeng, R. E.
b. ca. 1918, Ghana.
Novelist.

Obeng has published one work, a novel, *Eighteenpence*, in 1943 and a second edition in 1950.

Writings: Novel: *Eighteenpence*, Ilfracombe, Devon, England, Stockwell, 1943; Birkenhead, England, Willmer Brothers, 1950.

OBENGA, Théophile-Joseph
b. February 2, 1936, Brazzaville, Congo.
Poet.

Obenga is well represented with three poems, "Je tiens seul le secret," "Tu parleras," and "Hommage à David Diop," in *New Sum of Poetry from the Negro World.*

Writings: Poems: "Je tiens seul le secret," "Tu parleras," and "Hommage à David Diop," in *New Sum of Poetry from the Negro World,* Paris, Présence Africaine, Volume 57, 1966.

OBIANIM, Sam J.
b. ca. 1920, Ewe country, Eastern Ghana.
Ewe-language novelist.

Obianim's two works in his native Ewe are the novels, *Amegbetoa alo Agbezuge she n(g)utinya* (Humanity, or the Struggles of Agbezuge), 1949, and *De menye de* (Had I Known), 1954.

Writings: Novels: *Amegbetoa alo Agbezuge she n(g)utinya,* London, Macmillan, 1949; *De menye de,* London, Macmillan, 1954.

OBIECHINA, Emmanuel Nwannonye
b. September 20, 1933, Nkpor, Nigeria.
Poet, story writer critic, scholar.

After local schooling, Emmanuel Obiechina attended Ibadan University in Nigeria, taking the B.A. in English (Honors) in 1961, and then went to Cambridge University for graduate work in English. He took the Ph.D. at Cambridge in 1966. He is now professor of English at Nsukka University. Though primarily a scholar he has published occasional verse, including "Song of a Madman—a poem" which appears in *Okike, A Nigerian Journal of New Writing.* He is also a member of the editorial committee of *Okike* which is edited by Chinua Achebe. He is married and the father of three children.

His most important work thus far is *Literature for the Masses: An Analytical Study of Popular Pamphleteering in Nigeria*, with a forward by Achebe. Obiechina's introduction provides a useful citation and discussion of much of the scholarship on the subject of the Onitsha chapbooks. This work serves as the critical core of his up-coming book for Heinemann, London, *A Selection of Onitsha Market Literature*, to be published in 1972 or shortly thereafter.

Obiechina's first critical book was *Commentary, Notes and Exercise To James Baldwin's Go Tell It On the Mountain*, published in 1966.

Short stories, essays, and book reviews have appeared in *Présence Africaine, African Forum, The Voice, The Conch*, and *African Literature Today*.

Writings: General Scholarship: *Literature for the Masses*, Enugu, Nigeria, Nwankwo-Ifejike, 1971; "Commentary, Notes and Exercises To James Baldwin's *Go Tell It On the Mountain*, "London, Longmans, 1966; "Cultural Nationalism in Modern African Creative Literature," *"African Literature Today,"* I, 1, London, 1968; "Transition from Oral to Literary Tradition," *Présence Africaine*, No. 63, Paris, 1967; "Growth of Written Literature in English Speaking West Africa," *Présence Africaine*, No. 66, Paris, 1968.

Poem "Song of a Madman," in *Okike*, I, 1, April, 1971, Enugu, Nigeria.

Unpublished Ph.D. dissertation: "Cultural Change and The Novel in English in West Africa," Cambridge University, Cambridge, 1966.

OCULI, Okello
b. 1942, Dokolo County, Lang'o, Northern Uganda.
Poet, novelist, journalist.

Oculi was educated locally at Soroti College, St. Peter's College (Tororo), at St. Mary's College (Kisubi), and at Makerere University in Kampala, Uganda where he received a B.A. in political science. He has worked as a journalist and columnist for *The People* (Uganda) and has served as news editor for *The Makererean*. He travelled to England in the mid-1960's and wrote his second book, *Prostitute*, while in Essex.

Oculi's first volume, *Orphan*, 1968, has an episodic movement following the early experiences of Okello the orphan through his encounter with his various relatives to the closing scenes with his father. The volume is attractively illustrated with black and white wood-block type cuts by E. Christensson. The Prologue starts:

You are going to watch a village opera performed. You will see each character walking along a path. All paths criss-cross at a junction. An orphan boy is seated cross-legged at the junction, writing pictures of animals in the sand. He is pensive. Today the people who talk in these pages all pass through this junction. Each of them notices the orphan boy. In the village the problem of unnoticing is still minimal. Each person performs a drama for the orphan boy, and all of them with the orphan boy perform for you and me.

The story is told in a loose, lively, free verse. The characters are alive and often acerbic. There is a sprightly insouciance in this work that is demanding increasing attention.

Published the same year as *Orphan* was *Prostitute*, though written earlier. This work, written in prose, is more a study (sometimes tender, sometimes harsh) of village life as it swirls around a young woman of the village returned from the city to revisit her elderly parents. Her reputation is tarnished and she, like the villagers, must make certain adjustments.

Writings: Tale or novel written in free verse: *Orphan*, Nairobi, East African Publishing House, 1968.
   Novel: *Prostitute*, Nairobi, East African Publishing House, 1968.

ODEKU, Emmanuel Latunde
b. ca. 1937, Nigeria.
Poet.

Odeku's two volumes of verse are: *Twilight Out of the Night*, 1964, and *Whispers from the Night*, 1969.

Writings: Poetry: *Twilight Out of the Night*, Ibadan, 1964; *Whispers from the Night*, Ibadan, 1969.

ODINGA, Ajuma Oginga
b. 1912, Luo-country, Kenya.
Autobiographer, politician.

Educated at Makerere University, Kampala, Uganda, Odinga taught for several years, then entered politics and became a businessman.
   Odinga's autobiography, *Not Yet Uhuru*, published in 1967, with an introduction by Kwame Nkrumah, puts him clearly in opposition to Jomo Kenyatta and the ruling politicians of Kenya. Organizer of his fellow Luos in the Kenyatta-led K. A. U. (The Kenya African Union), Odinga became one of the leaders in the days before independence. He moved increasingly to the left, becoming eventually the leading opponent of the new Government and was imprisoned for a time. He has been out of politics since 1967.

Writings: Autobiography: *Not Yet Uhuru*, London, Heinemann, 1967; New York, Hill and Wang, 1967.

Biographical/Critical Source: The New Africans, New York, G. P. Putnam's Sons, 1967.

ODOI, Nicholas Akrong
b. ca. 1925, Ghana.
Ga-language story writer, playwright (also publishes in English).

Odoi has published two books of stories: *Gbomo ke wala* (Man and Life), 1953, and *The Adventures of Esi Kakraba*, published in English in 1964. The former volume contains one play, title unknown.
   He has published one non-fictional work, *Facts To Remember*, 1961.

Writings: Stories: in Ga: *Gbomo ke wala*, Accra Scottish Mission Book Depot, 1953; London, Longmans, Green, 1953; in English: *The Adventures of Esi Kakraba*, Accra, Waterville Publishing House, 1964.
   Non-fiction: *Facts To Remember*, Accra, Presbyterian Book Depot, 1961.

OFORI, Henry
b. 1925, Ghana.
Playwright, short story writer, journalist.

Ofori was educated locally and received

his B.A. from Achimota College in upper Ghana in 1949. After school he lived for awhile in a rural area which gave him the setting, characters and incidents for his mildly satirical play, *The Literary Society*, which pricks the pomposities, ignorances, and provincialisms of a half-Westernized rural intelligentsia who form a group to discuss literature. Two recent works are *Tales from Dodora Forest* and *Life Gets Tedious*. According to the American critic, Fredric M. Litto, Ofori has published more than two thousand separate articles, stories, and plays in miscellaneous journals.

Ofori was a teacher of physics at the Takoradi Government Secondary Technical School from 1951 to 1955. Since 1958 he has been an editor, journalist and twice-weekly columnist for the *Ghanaian Times* of Accra. He is presently also working in the Ghana Information Service in the capital. Having recently completed a visit to Europe, the Caribbean, North and South America, Asia, and Africa, he is writing up his experiences for publication as *One Short Boy*.

Writings: Play: *The Literary Society* in *Plays from Black Africa*, F. M. Litto, editor, New York, Hill and Wang, 1968.

Stories: *Tales from Dodora Forest*, Accra, Waterville Publishing House, date unknown; *Life Gets Tedious*, Accra, date unknown.

Travel: "One Short Boy," manuscript being prepared for the press.

OGALI, Ogali Agu
b. Oct. 27, 1935, Item, Bende Division, East Central State, Nigeria.
Novelist, playwright, journalist.

Ogali received his diploma in journalism from the Ghana School of Journalism.

He worked for a time at the United Africa Company, Ltd. and then for the Nigerian Railway Corporation.

His novelettes include: *Eddy, the Coalcity Boy*, 1959; and *Okeke the Magician*, 1958; *Long, Long Ago*, 1957; and *Smile Awhile*, 1957. His plays are: *Patrice Lumumba*, 1961; *Veronica, My Daughter*, 1956; *Adelabu*, 1958; *Mr. Rabbit Is Dead*, 1958; and *The Ghost of Lumumba*, 1961.

Variant editions of his work with slightly changed titles were issued by little presses in and around Onitsha or under different imprints. At least seventeen separate works ranging from historical fiction, through novels dealing with contemporary problems, to plays, are known to carry his name.

Writings: Plays or playlets: *Veronica, My Daughter*, Enugu, Printed by Zik Enterprises Ltd., 1956; Onitsha, Appolos Brothers Press, no date; Onitsha, Tabansi Printing Press, no date; *Adelabu*, Uzuakoli, 1958; *Mr. Rabbit Is Dead*, Ovim, 1958; Onitsha, Appolos Brothers, no date; *Patrice Lumumba*, Enugu, 1961; Onitsha, Tabansi Printing Press, no date; *The Ghost of Lumumba*, 1961.

Stories or novelettes: *Long, Long Ago*, Enugu, Printed by Omaliko and Sons, 1957; *Smile Awhile*, Enugu, Printed by Zik Enterprises Ltd., 1957; *Okeke the Magician*, Uzuakoli, 1958; *Eddy, the Coalcity Boy*, Uzuakoli, 1959; *Caroline the One Guinea Girl*, Enugu, 1960; Port Harcourt, Goodwill Press and Bookshop, 1965, and many others.

OGBALU, Fred Chidozie
b. ca. 1920, Nigeria.
Igbo story teller, collector of folktales, scholar, teacher.

Ogbalu received his B.S. degree in

economics from the University of London and later taught at the Dennis Memorial Grammar School. He is the editor of *Amanala Igbo* (The Book of Igbo Customs), issued in 1960, and *The Book of Igbo Proverbs*, 1961. Writing in both Igbo and English, he deals mainly with folklore and customs but he has adapted some of the traditional stories for his *Niger Tales*, probably published in the early 1960's.

Ogbalu also edited the collection of stories, published in Igbo, *Dimkpa taa aku, ahu ichere ya* (A Man Digesting the Richness Which Is Presented To Him), which were selected from entries submitted to an Igbo competition held by the Society for Promoting Igbo Language and Culture.

Writings: Folklore: *Amanala Igbo*, Onitsha, Nigeria, Varsity Press, 1960; *The Book of Igbo Proverbs*, Onitsha, Nigeria, Varsity Press, 1961; *Niger Tales*, Onitsha, United Brothers Press, no date but probably early 1960's.

Short Stories: editor of contemporary stories written in Igbo: *Dimkpa taa aku, ahu ichere ya*, Onitsha, African Literature Bureau, 1960; second edition, Onitsha, University Publishing Co., no date, but believed to be 1966.

Other: *Selected Speeches*, Onitsha, University Publishing Co., 1964.

OGOT, Grace Akinye
b. 1930, Butere, Central Nyanza District, Kenya.
Novelist, short story writer.

Educated in Butere High School and Ng'iya Girls' School, Grace Ogot trained as a nurse and midwife in Uganda and in England.

She worked as a script writer and announcer for the British Broadcasting Company in London from 1955 to 1958, and as Community Development Officer in Kisumu. She has served as a nursing sister and midwifery tutor at Maseno Hospital, Nyanza. She has also worked as a public relations officer for Air India in Nairobi. In 1959 she married the historian, Dr. Bethwell Allan Ogot, who is now chairman of the history department at University College, Nairobi, and went with him to England, 1959–1961. They now have three children.

Ogot's first novel, *The Promised Land*, 1966, describes the social atmosphere of rural life in western Kenya.

She has also written short stories and childrens' tales. Her "The Year of the Sacrifice" published in *Black Orpheus* magazine tells of a virgin who almost sacrifices herself for her drought-stricken land, but is rescued by her daring lover. Another of her stories, "The Dead Spirit Cat," has been translated into German as "Die Getötete Zauberkatz" and relates the story of a magical cat-ghost which drives a brutal farmer mad after he has killed the harmless animal. Her story, "The Rain Came," appeared in Neville Denny's *Pan African Short Stories*.

Her one collection is *Land Without Thunder. Short Stories*, 1968.

Writings: Novel: *The Promised Land*, Nairobi, East African Publishing House, 1966.

Stories: *Land Without Thunder. Short Stories*, Nairobi, East African Publishing House, 1968; stories in *Pan African Short Stories*, London, Nelson, 1965, *Black Orpheus*, magazine.

Biographical/Critical Source: Maryse Conde, "Three Female Writers in Modern Africa: Flora Nwapa, Ama Ata Aidoo, and Grace Ogot" in *Présence Africaine*, second trimester, 1972.

OGUNDE, Hubert
b. 1916, Yoruba-land, Nigeria.
Yoruba-language playwright,
theatre manager, musician.

The son of a Baptist clergyman and church organist of the Church of the Lord in Lagos, Hubert Ogunde, in addition to his involvement with Christianity, has also sought to return to Yoruba cultural roots. He was initiated into the Osùgbó and Egúgún cults and later into the Sango cult. In the early 1940's he organized the African Music and Dance Research Party. In 1944, his dramatization of the Adam and Eve story was presented as a devotional service for the Lagos Church of the Lord. This production, featuring as off-altar orchestra and simple action, may be considered the first Yoruba popular opera. The following year he organized a professional troupe, the Ogunde Concert Party, and went on tour in West Africa. In 1968–69, he and his present troupe toured Great Britain.

Ogunde writes for and manages a troupe which speaks and sings in Yoruba for both city and rural audiences. He has been a policeman, teacher, and in the late 40's exclusively a professional theatre manager and playwright. His plays have been performed all over Nigeria and West Africa. In 1962 he founded the Mbari Mbayo Club in Oshogbo as a theatre and theatre workshop.

Some fifteen operatic plays have come from his hands along with many skits and shorter theatrical pieces. His technique is to sketch out the basic situations and actions and then to allow the actors to improvise as audience and inspiration move them. His works often exploit the old Biblical plays first developed by the breakaway Christian churches of Nigeria which dramatized stories from the Old and New Testament in extremely free fashion. In contrast, he also often uses the traditional Yoruba dance-dramas in modified form in his work with his professional troupe. All of his plays employ some elements of dance, masks, song, set recitations of chorus, improvisation, and musical accompaniment.

Three of his Yoruba-language plays are: *O tito koro* (Truth Is Bitter), performed in Glover Memorial Hall, Lagos, 1965; *Aropin n't'enia* (Men Don't Wish Each Other Well), performed 1967; and *Ologbo dudu* (The Black Cat), also performed in 1967.

Ulli Beier in his very useful chapter, "Yoruba Theatre," in *Introduction to African Literature,* discusses in some detail Ogunde's contribution to the modern African drama. Excellent, if brief studies of Ogunde and the origins of popular Yoruba drama are Oyekan Owomoyela's "Folk-lore and Yoruba Theater," in *Research in African Literatures,* and J. A. Adedeji's "Oral Tradition and the Contemporary Theater in Nigeria," in the same issue of *Research in African Literatures.*

One might summarize Ogunde's importance by saying that he has been able to merge both traditional folk and Christian elements with a jazzy, village-mentality, marked by a personal artistic freedom and gusto. The result is a genuinely "popular" drama which has exposed an increasingly wider audience to staged plays. Additionally, his works, with their choreographic and scenaric freedoms "keep up" with the currents of political and social controversy, scandal, and news, so that his satirical efforts provide a folk newspaper or sounding board for criticism of foibles and corruption in Nigeria and elsewhere.

Ogunde was particularly successful with his political play, *Yorùbá Ronú* (Yorubas, You Must Think), published in 1964 but performed earlier. This work hit hard at political abuses of the period just before the outbreak of violence all over Nigeria which led to the Ibo-seccession and Biafran War. For a period his plays were banned in the Western (Yoruba) region.

Yorùbá Ronú shows the leadership quarreling and divided. An actor early declares:

Yorubas undo themselves because of money.
Yorubas conspire against each other
because of jobs,
They turn the guilty to the innocent
And the innocent to the guilty.

and he goes on to attack the complacent people:

Those who were once the masters
Are now people to be pushed around.
Yo! Yo! Yo!

Yorubas have turned themselves into a football
They kick you up,
They kick you down.
. . .

Lazily you squat on your haunches,
Patient like goats led to the slaughter.
Yo! Yo! Yo!
Yorubas think.

Ogunde in his more idealistic days tried to write "serious" plays, but he quickly found that the "jeun-jeun," or bread and butter plays of burlesque, light music, maskers, etc. were commercially much more attractive. He and his troupe put on his *Black Forest*, (still unpublished), a "literary" play, in the

Ivory Coast and Ghana but he returned with debts and his actors unpaid. Today, his performances often begin with a jazzy number where scantily-clad girls dance wildly to saxophone music, some of it provided by Ogunde who taught himself to play the instrument. The little plays or skits which follow are lively, semi-impromptu, and full of sexual innuendo and broad humor. Having established himself with these works, he now is turning slowly to more complex efforts, hoping both to make a good living for himself and his company as well as to help develop a more mature and intellectual body of works for more experienced or educated audiences.

His actors and actresses are trained by him and are relatively experienced. According to Beier, Ogunde has married all of his actresses so as not to lose them to husbands who might pull them out of the company. On occasion he has even put on plays with women taking both male and female roles, reversing the common Elizabethan English practice of employing all-male troupes.

E. Kolawole Ogunmola, a former colleague of Ogunde's, has gone on to capitalize on the latter's work with folkloric and popular themes, as has Duro Ladipo. The three men have accordingly "fertilized" the ground with vernacular plays which apparently will provide sustenance for succeeding generations of playwrights and audiences for years to come.

Writings: Plays: In Yoruba: *Yorùbá Ronú*, Yaba-Lagos, Pacific Printers, 1964; *O tito koro*, performed in Glover Memorial Hall, Lagos, 1965; *Aropin n't'enia*, Lagos, West African Book Publishers, 1967, in three volumes; *Ologbo dudu*, Lagos, West African Book Publishers, 1967; In English: *Black Forest,* produced in late 1960's, unpublished.

Biographical/Critical Sources: Ulli Beier, "Yoruba Theater" in *Introduction to African Literature,* Evanston, Northwestern University Press, 1967; Oyekan Owomoyela, "Folk-lore and Yoruba Theater," *Research in African Literature* II, 2, Fall, 1971, Austin, Texas, University of Texas; J. A. Adedeji, "Oral Tradition and the Contemporary Theater in Nigeria," *Research in African Literatures,* II, 2, Fall, 1971, Austin, Texas, University of Texas; J. A. Adedeji, "The Alárìnjó Theatre: The Study of a Yoruba Theatrical Art from its Earliest Beginnings to the Present Times," unpublished Ph.D. dissertation, University of Ibadan, 1969.

OGUNMOLA, Elijah Kolawole
b. 1925, Yoruba-land, Western Nigeria.
Yoruba playwright, actor, producer.

Kola Ogunmola was educated in local schools and studied formally for six months at Ibadan University on a Rockefeller grant. Though he has been a primary school teacher, his main career has been in the vernacular Yoruba theatre for which he writes and directs.

His Ogunmola Traveling Theatre has introduced to a wide audience some of the old Yoruba classics in adapted form as well as new plays written in some degree in the old modes. He and his group participated at the Festival of Negro Arts at Algiers.

Stimulated and influenced by Ogunde, his gifted Yoruba fellow playwright and director, Ogunmola avoids the more rustic and buffoonish aspects of the Ogunde plays. Ogunmola uses

bongo drums in a simple but energetic, even electric rhythm that underscores the dramatic and sung roles of his plays, thereby providing a unity of tone and impression rare in modern theatre anywhere.

Ogunmola is a gifted actor and a splendid mime and at times can get his company to give memorable performances. As a writer he is less versatile, less imaginative, than Ogunde or Ladipo. As a playwright he often falls back on the older Biblical plays of the *Seraphim, Cherubim,* and other of the Apostolic break-away churches of Nigeria. As is the case with Ogunde, he is at his best in satires. Possibly his most interesting, certainly most commercially successful play, *Ife owo* (Love of Money), first produced in 1954, shows only too clearly the agonies of a man who is so anxious to please his second wife that his life becomes a hell with the first, who is still in the compound. It saw print in 1965 (Oshogbo, Mbari Mbayo).

Ogunmola's first plays were *Morakinyo,* which was very popular in the late 1950's, and his still unpublished *Agbaraj'agbara* (The Reign of the Mighty) concerning power, produced with acclaim by the Ibadan Arts Theatre of Ibadan University in 1962. An even greater favorite was his Yoruba adaptation for the village stage of Amos Tutuola's pioneering novel, *The Palm-Wine Drinkard,* which has seen performance throughout Nigeria and West Africa. The printed version of the Yoruba text of Tutuola's play, *Omuti Apa kini,* was published in 1967 and 1968 and translated and transcribed into English by R. G. Armstrong, Robert L. Awujoola and Val Olayemi, in 1968.

Two other plays of Ogunmola's are the *They Were Enemies,* produced in the early 1950's, and a recent satire, *Con-*

science, which uses dance and music in a more organic way and appears to show a definite advance over his previous work. Both he and Duro Ladipo, a strong new figure, are breaking new ground in Nigerian theatre.

Ogunmola's more than a dozen plays are adaptations, with modern themes or treatment, of the classic Yoruba "folk-operas," many of which are highly complex and often lasting three days in complete performance in a cycle of related dramas. Though his original works are much shorter and to some degree influenced by Western standards (greater time unity, less repetition, a plot that explains as it goes on, and more dramatic highlighting of psychological conflicts), they are deeply "African" and have been widely accepted by Nigerian audiences. Ulli Beier offers these comments in his chapter, "Yoruba Theatre" *(Introduction To African Literature):*

> *Ogunmola's capacity for mime, his eye for detail, his intimate knowledge of the Yoruba people–all these add to the delights of the performance. Ogunmola does not seem like a writer who is at the beginning of a tradition. He has no axes to grind, he does not attempt to change the world. . . . In European theatre nothing comes closer to him than the degenerate fin de siecle Viennese comedies by Nestroy and Raymund. There is the same sophisticated feeling of resignation in both.*

Writings: Plays: *Ife owo,* Oshogbo, Mbari Mbayo, 1965 *Morakinyo; Agbaraj'agbara,* unpublished, staged by Ibadan Arts Theater, Ibadan University, 1962; *Omuti Apa kini,* (Ogunmola's Yoruba adaptation of Tutuola's *The Palm-Wine Drinkard)* Heinemann, London, 1968; Lagos, West African Book Publishers, 1967; translated and transcribed into English by R. G. Armstrong, Robert L. Awujoola,

Val Olayemi, Occasional Publication No. 12, Ibadan, Institute of African Studies, Universtiy of Ibadan, 1968; *They Were Enemies,* produced in 1950's, but not published; *Conscience,* produced in late 1960's, but not published.

Biographical/Critical Sources: Ulli Beier, "Yoruba Theatre," *Introduction To African Literature,* Evanston, Northwestern University Press, 1967; Bruce King, *Introduction to Nigerian Literature,* New York, Africana Publishing Co., 1972.

OGUNYEMI, Wale
b. ca. 1932, Yoruba country,
Western Nigeria.
Yoruba language playwright,
scholar (also published in English).

Ogunyemi is considered one of the most important Yoruba playwrights. His play, *Born With Fire on His Head,* has appeared in the 1967 volume edited by Ulli Beier, *Three Nigerian Plays.* In 1970, Ogunyemi's play, *Ijaye War. A Historic drama,* offered the dramatization of the bitter battle between Kununmi, the Aare (or king) of Ijaye and the Alaafin of Oyo (now Ibadan) for control of the Yoruba peoples. Drawing on the research of J. F. Ade Ajayi and Robert S. Smith in their *Yoruba Warfare in the Nineteenth Century,* and the *History of the Yorubas* and the *Iwe Iroyin* of the Reverend Samuel Johnson, Ogunyemi has produced a lively and historical chronicle.

His play, *Eshu Elegbara,* celebrates the Yoruba creation myth of gods and goddesses coming down to earth led by Obatala, the chief deity. Another play based on myths is *Be Mighty, Be Mine* (1968), dealing with the cosmic battle for prestige between the gods of rain and

319

lightning, Shango and Ogun, the gods of iron and war, respectively.

Ogunyemi adapted Shakespeare's Macbeth for a student production in Yoruba at the University of Ibadan as *Aare Akogun,* published in 1969. His most recent work, *The Vow,* a film script, won a top prize for new work awarded by *African Arts* magazine, 1971.

Writings: Plays: *Born With Fire on His Head,* in *Three Nigerian Plays,* London, Longmans, 1967; *Ijaye War. A Historic drama,* Ibadan, Orison Acting Editions, 1970; *Eshu Elegbara,* Ibadan, Orison Acting Editions, 1970; *Be Mighty, Be Mine, Nigeria Magazine,* No. 97, Lagos, June, 1968; *Aare Akogun,* adaptation of *Macbeth, Nigeria Magazine,* No. 100, Lagos, April, 1969.

Film Script: *The Vow,* unpublished, but awarded prize in 1971 by *African Arts* magazine, The University of California, Los Angeles.

OJIKE, Mazi Mbonu
b. 1914 or 1915; d. 1956 or 1957, Nigeria.
Autobiographer, teacher, pamphleteer.

Ojike graduated from elementary school in 1925, went on to Normal College on a scholarship in 1929, and then taught elementary subjects for three years. In 1938 he completed his work at the University of London in education and in 1939 he travelled to the United States for further education. Since returning to Nigeria he has taught and has written several works: *My Africa,* 1946, essays and autobiography, and *The Road to Freedom,* 1948. His earliest work was *Portrait of a Boy in Africa,* 1945.

Writings: Autobiography: *Portrait of a Boy in Africa,* New York, East and West Association, 1945; *My Africa,* New York, The John Day Co., 1946; London, Blandford Press, 1955; *I Have Two Countries,* New York, The John Day Company, 1947.

Pamphlets: *The Road to Freedom,* Aba, Nigeria, D. D. Onyemelukwe Printing Works, 1948; *Guide to Federal Elections,* Kano, Nigeria, National Council of Nigeria and Cameroons, 1954.

OKAFOR–OMALI, Dilim
b. ca. 1940, Ibo–country, Eastern Nigeria.
Biographer, sociologist.

In his *A Nigerian Villager in Two Worlds,* 1965, Okafor–Omali describes the customs, tribal authority, and general tenor of daily life in his father's village in Iboland. Important also are the discussions of the changes brought by colonial domination, including the impact, for both good and bad, of Christian missionaries. The work is not polemical but it is serious and hard-hitting.

Writings: Biography: *A Nigerian Villager in Two Worlds,* London, Faber and Faber, 1965.

OKARA, Gabriel Imomotimi Gbaingbain
b. April 21, 1921, Bumodi (or Bumdi), Ijaw District, Delta Region, Western Nigeria.
Poet, novelist, scriptwriter, short story writer, civil servant.

Gabriel Okara, one of the leading African poets writing in English, was born into the noble house of Prince Sampson

G. Okara of the Ijaw people. He was educated locally at the lower-school level and later at Government College, Umuahia. In 1959, he completed his studies in journalism at Northwestern University in Evanston, Illinois. He worked in the Ministry of Information as Principal Information Officer in the Eastern Nigerian Government Service before joining the Biafran (Ibo) cause as an Information Officer in the 1967–69 Nigerian Civil War and traveled to the United States with Chinua Achebe in 1969 to seek help for Biafra. Starting modestly as a book-binder in his youth he is now well-respected at home and abroad. He now works in Port Harcourt for the Rivers State Ministry of Information.

He published his first poetry in the germinal pages of *Black Orpheus* magazine at Ibadan University in 1957 and his works, in translation, have been published in Sweden, West Germany and Italy as well as in the original English in anthologies in Africa, America and England. Okara is also well known through frequent appearances at writers' conferences in Africa and elsewhere.

Okara has attempted with some success to work from Ijaw directly into English, preserving some of the power and style of the original. Though his tone is often elegiac and his theme that of the loss of the pure African past, he is not a bitter writer, nor are his poems pure nostalgia as so many of the Negritudist francophone poets are. Possibly his most popular poem is "Piano and Drums" which contrasts the " . . . jungle drums telegraphing/the mystic rhythm, urgent, raw/like bleeding flesh" to "a wailing piano/solo speaking of complex ways/in tear-furrowed concerto" to end with "wandering in the mystic rhythm/of jungle drums and the concerto" in a kind of cultural resolution.

Okara's poem "The Call of the River Nun" won the Nigerian Festival of Arts award in 1953 and is one of the earliest of "modern" poems written by an African. It begins:

I hear your call!
I hear it far away;
I hear it break the circle
of these crouching hills.

and goes on with:

I want to view your face
again and feel your cold
embrace; or at your brim
to set myself and
inhale your breath; or
like the trees, to watch
my mirrored self unfold
and span my days with
songs from the lips of dawn.

His novel, *The Voice,* (1964), meant to reflect the rhythms and characteristics of his native Ijaw, appears in the African Writers Series of Heinemann with an excellent 21-page introduction by Arthur Ravenscroft, professor of African literature at Leeds University, Yorkshire, England. Ravenscroft in his closing paragraph writes:

> Readers of this introduction may well think that it reads far more into Okara's 'simple' story than is justifiable. But a parable is a kind of extended poem, and the poetic method works by both precise statement and suggestion; by, as it were, the setting up of echoes of meaning, which derive from the actual words used and cannot exist independently of those words in their context.

Earlier, Ravenscroft offered this comment:

> Okolo's name means 'the voice', and Okara never allows us to forget his character's interest in language, in the precision of thought and feeling which a careful use of language produces. Okolo usually makes up his mind about people by examining what their ways of using language tell him about their inner lives.

Okara has done some film scripts for the Nigerian government's Information Service and his short stories, not nearly so well known as his poems, have appeared in various journals. He also has written plays produced on Nigerian radio, and has done features for radio. An article, "The Ijaw creation myth," appeared in *Black Orpheus*, No. 2, January 1958.

Writings: Novel: *The Voice*, London, André Deutsch, 1964; London, Heinemann African Writers Series, 1970, introduction by Arthur Ravenscroft.

Poetry: in various journals as early as 1953; and in *Black Orpheus*, 1957 and later.

Story: "Okolo," in *Black Orpheus* magazine, No. 10, Ibadan, Mbari Press.

Article: "The Ijaw Creation Myth," in *Black Orpheus*, No. 2, January, 1958, Ibadan, Mbari Press.

Biographical/Critical Sources: Margaret Lawrence, *Long Drums and Cannons*, London, Macmillan, 1968.

OKEKE, Uche
b. 1935, Ibo–land, Nigeria.
Poet, story teller, painter, teacher.

Locally educated in the lower years, Okeke studied art at Zaria University and at Munich and has exhibited his paintings and drawings on all continents except Australia. For a period in the late 1960's, he lived in West Germany. He is presently a teacher of art in the Department of Fine Arts, Nsukka University, Nigeria.

Three of Okeke's poems, "The Home of Images," "Moon Dance," and "Mamiwata" appeared in *Okike,* April, 1971.

Ibo Folktales, written and illustrated by Okeke, saw publication in 1971. Didactic as are so many folktales of Africa, Okeke's are, in addition, humorous and robust. The central figures are pruned of their excesses during the adventures they undergo and emerge wiser, if sadder, than when they started out.

Okeke's recent film script, *Ekeama,* won a prize in the 1971 *African Arts* magazine competition for new work. It is an "ogbanje drama," dealing with the spirit or ogbanje which may be reborn seven times in its spiritual cycle.

Writings: Poems: "The Home of Images," "Moon Dance," and "Mamiwata" in *Okike,* Chinua Achebe, editor, Enugu, Nigeria, I, 1, April, 1971.

Folklore: *Ibo Folktales,* New York, Doubleday, New York, 1971.

Filmscript: *Ekeama,* unpublished, but awarded a prize in 1971 by *African Arts* magazine, University of California at Los Angeles.

OKIGBO, Christopher
b. 1932, Ojoto, near Onitsha, Eastern Nigeria; d. late August, 1967.
Poet, teacher.

Okigbo, considered the finest and most complex of all the Nigerian poets, was educated in his home area, went to high school at Government College, Umuahia, and took his B.A. in classics in 1956 from University College in Ibadan. Later he worked for a period as the private secretary to the Federal Minister of Research and Information

(1955–56), and from 1956 to 1958 as a member of the library staff at the University of Nigeria at Nsukka. He then taught at Fiditi near Ibadan, and served as West African representative for the Cambridge University Press in the 1960's, and later was one of the editors of *Transition* magazine (Kampala, Uganda) and of Mbari Press at Ibadan. In 1967, with Chinua Achebe, he founded a small publishing company in Enugu, but in August of that year, he was killed in action near Nsukka, the provisional capital of Biafra at that time. He left a wife and one daughter.

Okigbo has been very widely anthologized and analyzed in scores of studies of African literature. Published in his lifetime were the volumes: *Heavensgate* (1962), and *Limits* (1964), and *Silences* 1965. The Dakar Festival of African Arts in 1966 awarded him its first prize, but he refused it, arguing there was no specifically African writing, just good and bad writing. A posthumous collection, *Labyrinths with Paths of Thunder,* was published in 1971. Heinemann had earlier published *Labyrinths* as No. 62 of its African Writers Series. He is memorialized in Ali Mazrui's philosophical novel *The Trial of Christopher Okigbo.* Also promised for the near future is a larger-scale study of Okigbo's work by Sunday Anozie to be published by Evans of London.

Okigbo's introduction to *Silences,* dated October, 1965, provides insights into the poet's intentions, experiences, and the influences of older writers on his work, including Gerard Manley Hopkins, Herman Melville, Malcolm Cowley, Mallarmé, Tagore, and Lorca.

Though Okigbo cannot fail to be seen as an "African" poet because of his use of local terms, themes, and impressions common to a writer with an African culture, he knew and loved the European and especially English classics, including Ezra Pound and T.S. Eliot.

He employs the images of his native forests, sacred streams and shrines to create a rare, distinctive, often difficult verse in large architectonic clusters. Apparently complex, but clear on a careful reading, is his "The Stars Have Departed" where the poet sees the large, late moon ("the sky in monocle") and wonders whether he can "tune in" to what is coming (an echo of Ezra Pound's famous phrase that poets are the "antennae of the race"). As dawn faints into day, so the poet's African world, too, is departing, to become—what? The poet's task is to catch the first whispers of what is to come and to give "flesh/words" to the "not-yet." Once enunciated, his words will in fact become the "nowness" that first the sensitive few, and then, most people, will accept as the truth of

their lives. The significance of the happenings in those lives and the collective experience of a race and of a land will be signaled by the poet's words.

More imagic and less comprehensible, even after several readings, are the poems from *Limits* (1964). Part I of "Siren Limits" reads:

SUDDENLY becoming talkative
like weaverbird
Summoned at offside of
dream remembered

Between sleep and waking.

I hang up my egg-shells
To you of palm grove,
Upon whose bamboo towers hang
Dripping with yesterupwine

A tiger mask and nude spear . . .
and he ends this part with:
Queen of the damp half light,

I have had my cleansing,
Emigrant with air-borne nose,
The he-goat-on-heat.

More and more is this difficult, acerbic spirit and rare poet mourned—and the lost poetry, now never to be written, to be regretted.

Writings: Poetry: *Heavensgate,* Ibadan, Mbari Press, 1962; *Limits,* Ibadan, Mbari Press, 1964; *Labyrinths with Paths of Thunder,* posthumous, London, Heinemann; New York, Africana Publishing Company, 1971; Heinemann, Number 62, African Writers Series: this volume contains *Labyrinths, Heavensgate, Limits, Silences* (all these somewhat changed from the original Mbari Press editions), *Distances,* and *Paths of Thunder: Poems Prophesying War* (this last contains the individual poems: "Thunder can break"); the group, "Silences," first published in *Transition Magazine,* No. 8, Kampala, 1963; "Distances," in *Transition,* No. 16, Kampala, 1964; "Path of Thunder, *Black Orpheus,* Volume 2, No. 1, 1968.

Biographical/Critical Sources: Marjory Whitelaw, "Interview with Christopher Okigbo, 1965," *The Journal of Commonwealth Literature,* No. 9, London, July, 1970; Paul Theroux, "Christopher Okigbo," in *Introduction to Nigerian Literature,* Bruce King, editor, New York, Africana Publishing Co., 1972; S. D. Anozie, *Christopher Okigbo,* New York, Africana, 1972?; S. D. Anozie, "A Structural Approach to Okigbo's 'Distances,'", *The Conch,* I, 1, Paris, March, 1969; and mythological subject of Ali Mazrui's novel, *The Trial of Christopher Okigbo,* London, Heinemann, 1971.

OKOT, p'Bitek (see p'BITEK, J.P. Okot)

OKPAKU, Joseph Ohiomogben
b. ca. 1935, Nigeria.
Playwright, novelist, critic, editor, engineer.

Locally educated at the lower level, he took his B.A. at Northwestern University in Evanston, Illinois in civil engineering, his M.S. at Stanford in California in structural engineering, and his doctoral work also at Stanford, 1968, in theatre history. Okpaku is president and publisher of the Third Press in New York City, the first major black-owned trade book publishing firm in the United States, and associate professor at Sarah Lawrence College. He is also presently editor of the *Journal of the New African Literature and the Arts* (UCLA) whose first two volumes were published by Crowell in 1970 and covered work published in the period 1966–68.

His three-act play, *Born Astride the Grave* was a BBC prize-winning play. A volume, *New African Literature and the Arts,* which he edited, reprinted the play in 1970. Okpaku's play, *The Virtues of Adultery,* a one-act play, was published in 1969 with introductory notes by Arthur Miller and Martin Esslin. This play also won a BBC first prize.

Two of his plays remain unpublished: *The King's Son, or, After the Victory was lost; An African Play in Three Acts,* mimeographed in the fall of 1966 (but no imprimatur or publisher known), and *The Silhouette of God,* performed in Berkeley, California, May 17, 1969.

Okpaku's short novel, *Under the Iroko Tree,* appeared in the summer 1968 *Literary Review,* republished in *Africa Writing Today,* 1969.

More topical were his publications, *Four Months and Fifteen Days—The Chicago Trial,* with co-author Verna Sadock, and his *Verdict: The Exclusive Pic-*

ture *Story of the Trial of the Chicago Eight,*
both published by Third Press. Similar
journalistic work was his *Nigeria-Biafra:
Dilemma of Nationhood-An African Analysis
of the Biafran Conflict.*

Writings: Plays: *Born Astride the Grave,* in
Journal of the New African Literature, I,
Spring 1966; Stanford University , Palo
Alto, California; also in *New African Lit-
erature and the Arts,* Joseph Okpaku,
editor, New York, Crowell, 1970; *The
Virtues of Adultery,* Palo Alto, Stanford
University Press; *The King's Son, or, After
the Victory Was Lost; An African Play in
Three Acts,* unpublished, but mimeo-
graphed in 1966, details not known; *The
Silhouette of God,* performed in Berkeley,
California, May 17, 1969.

Novel: *Under the Iroko Tree,* in *Literary
Review,* XI, 4, Rutherford, New Jersey,
Summer, 1968, and in *African Writing
Today,* New York, Maryland Books,
1969.

Journalism: *Four Months and Fifteen
Days-The Chicago Trial,* with Verna
Sadock; *Verdict: The Exclusive Picture Story
of the Chicago Eight;* both by Third Press;
Nigeria/Biafra-Dilemma of Nationhood-An

African Analysis of the Biafran Conflict,
Westport, Connecticut, Greenwood
Publishing Corp., 1971.

OKPEWHO, Isadore
b. ca. 1942, Abraka, Urhobo
Division, mid-western Nigeria.
Novelist.

Okpewho grew up in Asaba where he
attended St. Patrick's College. He went
on to graduate with first class honors in
classics at the University of Ibadan in
1964 where he won the classics departmental prize and the College Scholarship. He also won the Sir James Robert-
son Prize for best classics student and
the faculty of arts prize for over-all excellence. The University's journal *Phron-
tisterion* published his long juvenile satire
in its original Latin.

Presently Okpewho is a publishing
executive in Nigeria. He has completed

one novel, *The Victims* (1970) and has a second almost finished. The published work deals with the institution of polygamy in a society which no longer provides a sufficient economic or psychological support for it. In the end there is tension, suffering, and loss by the husband, his wives, and the children. All lose.

Writings: Novel: *The Victims*, London, Longmans, 1970.

OLAGOKE, David Olu
b. ca. 1935, Yoruba country,
Western Nigeria.
Playwright, teacher.

Educated locally, Olagoke is presently principal of the Lisabi Grammar School in Abeokuta, Western Nigeria.

His plays appear to be patterned on those of Ene Henshaw, the popular Nigerian writer of one-acters. Olagoke's works are *The Incorruptible Judge* (1962, 1966), *The Iroko-man and the Wood-carver.*

Writings: Plays: *The Incorruptible Judge,* London, Evans Brothers, 1962, 1966; *The Iroko-man and the Wood-carver,* London, Evans Brothers, 1963, 1966.

OLISAH, Sunday Okenwa
(pseudonym: Strong Man of the Pen)
b. 1936, Ibo-country, Eastern Nigeria;
d. 1964.
Novelist.

Not much is known about most writers of the so-called Onitsha market novels, or "chapbooks," which were popular in the late 1950's and the early 1960's, mostly printed in and around Onitsha.

Olisah's *Elizabeth My Lover,* undated, but probably early 1960's, is one of these novelettes designed for a wide, semi-literate audience in English who were hungry for inexpensive books. The novel has been republished, along with eleven other chapbooks, by Kraus Reprint.

Olisah's *The Life story and the death of Mr. Lumumba* (Onitsha, 1964) is a 55-page biography in the vivid style common to this class of writing. It deals with the rise to power and assassination of the Congolese hero, Patrice Lumumba, who became a folk hero all over Africa through rumour, government propaganda in some cases, and through popular literature of the sort produced at Onitsha.

Writings: Novels: *Elizabeth My Lover,* early 1960's; Reprinted, Kraus Reprint, Nendeln, Liechtenstein; *Money Hard To Get But Easy To Spend,* J. O. Nnadozie, undated; *My Wife; No Condition is Permanent,* N. Njoku, undated; *Money Palaver,* 1960; *The World is Hard,* 1957; *Life turns man up and down, money and girls turn man up and down,* Onitsha, 1963(?); *The Life of the Prison Yard,* 1966; *The Story About Mammy-Water, Dangerous Man Vagabond versus Princess,* 1960; *Half-educated Messenger,* 1960.

Play: *My Seven Daughters Are After Young Boys,* no date.

Biography: *The Life Story and the Death of Mr. Lumumba,* Onitsha, 1964; *Mr. Lumumba and President Kasavubu in Congo Politics.*

OLIVEIRA, Mário António
Fernandes de (see ANTONIO,
Mário, pseud. for OLIVEIRA)

OLOGOUDOU, Emile (also
Hologoudou)
b. 1935, Ouidah, Dahomey.
Poet.

Ologoudou studied sociology and law at
Dakar University, 1957–60, and economics and sociology at the University of
Cologne, West Germany, 1960–66. He
is represented in various anthologies,
including Moore and Beier's *Modern
poetry from Africa.*

He is also represented by five poems,
"Sexte," "Laude," "Vêpres," "La legende
et le Mythe," and "Liberté," in *New Sum
of Poetry from the Negro World* (Paris).

Writings: Poems: "Sexte," "Laude," "Vé-
pres," "La Legende et le Mythe," and
"Liberté" in *New Sum of Poetry from the
Negro World,* Paris, Présence Africaine,
Vol. 57; represented in *Modern Poetry
from Africa,* Moore and Beier, editors,
revised edition, London, Penguin, 1968.

OLUWA, I. I.
b. ca. 1920, Calabar, Eastern
Nigeria.
Short story writer in Yoruba and
English.

Of Yoruba stock, Oluwa was educated
in local schools, graduated from Sapele
High School, King's College, Lagos, and
the School of Agriculture in Ibadan. He
served in the civil service in agricultural
economics and is an expert on birds, a
subject on which he has written several
prize essays. He reads French and speaks
Hausa, but normally does his work and
writing in his native Yoruba or in English. The story, "His Own Medicine,"
appeared in *African New Writing* in 1947,
and other tales have been published in
various other journals and collections.

Writings: Story: "His Own Medicine," in
African New Writing, London, Lutterworth Press, 1947.

OMARA, Tom
b. 1946, Uganda.
Playwright.

Educated at Lira, Uganda and King's
College, Budo, Omara was skilled at
debate. He began writing plays while still
in school and took part in several college
productions. A fine athlete, he also won
several awards in boxing.

His play, *The Exodus,* appears in *Short
East African Plays in English* and was produced with great popular success before
many audiences by the Makerere Travelling Theatre of Kampala, Uganda during 1965. Generally, however, Western
audiences have not appreciated the play
and, as Cook and Lee explain in their
introduction to *Short East African Plays,*
this coldness is due possibly to the fact
that "it is difficult to grasp the full depths
of specifically epic material if one is
totally unfamiliar with the social values
from which it springs. Another difficulty
may be that the verse form employed
creates different, irrelevant expectations
in the Westerner. People close to oral
tradition may unselfconsciously adopt
verse form when rhythmic tensions... are
felt very strongly."

Writings: Play: *The Exodus,* a play based
on a Luo myth, in *Short East African Plays
in English,* David Cook and Miles Lee,
editors, London, Nairobi, Heinemann,
1968.

OMBEDE, Philippe-Louis (see
PHILOMBE, René)

ONIORORO, Niyi
b. ca. 1942, Nigeria.
Story writer.

Oniororo's most important works are the story collections, *Lagos Is a Wicked Place* (1967), *Persevere Dear Brother*, and *No More a Minister*. The first and third works were published by the Ayo-olu Finery Press which has issued the works of younger writers who are not yet well known.

Writings: Stories: *Lagos Is a Wicked Place*, Ibadan, Ayo-olu Finery Press, 1967, 1968; *Persevere Dear Brother*, first edition unknown, second edition, Ibadan, 1969; *No More a Minister*, Ibadan, Ayo-olu Finery Press, 196?.

OPARA, Ralph C.
b. 1933, Ibo-land, Eastern Nigeria.
Poet, playwright, journalist,
television personality.

Educated in Nigerian secondary schools, Opara later studied at Government College (a high school) at Umuahia, and at University College, Ibadan, taking his B. A. there in English. Opara has written some poetry and several satirical plays, most unpublished, but his major efforts were devoted to his television talk show, "The Ralph Opara Show," a very popular program before the interruption of the Nigerian Civil War. During the mid-1960's he also was Head of Talks of the Nigerian Broadcasting Corporation.

Opara's article entitled "Lagos Interlude," is a biting sketch of the new urban culture of Lagos which appears in *Reflections*, an anthology published in 1962.

Writings: Article: "Lagos Interlude" in *Reflections*, Frances Ademola, editor, Lagos, African Universities Press, 1962.

OSADEBAY, Dennis Chukude
b. 1911, Asaba, west Nigeria.
Poet.

Like most Africans, Osadebay began his life in extremely modest circumstances and worked and fought his way to an education. He saved for a long time before being able to travel to Britain for his advanced schooling in law. He has been a clerk in the Nigerian civil service, a journalist, a lawyer, a member of parliament, a president of the Senate, and a Nigerian delegate to many international congresses in Europe.

In 1944 he was one of the founders of the NCNC party (the National Council of Nigeria and the Cameroons) and later served (1963) as Premier of the Mid West Region of Nigeria until political changes and coups pushed him out of government and politics.

Osadebay began to write poetry while studying in England and has published in West African, English and Indian journals and has had his poems read on the BBC.

His poetry, written in English, mostly appeared in the period from 1930 to 1950 and was probably the first original poetry in English to be published in Nigeria. Much of this work has been collected in the volume, *Africa Sings*. The poems are representative of the style and the preoccupations of the generation of African writers who still had not found their own voice. His work is, consequently, didactic and derivative of English models, but as it springs from the poet's own deepest feelings, it has some power and urgency. His "Young

329

Africa's Plea" as given in Nwoga's *West African Verse* is a strong call for a new Africa:

Don't preserve my customs
As some fine curios
To suit some white historian's tastes.

Writings: Poetry: *Africa Sings,* Ilfracombe, Devon, England, Stockwell, 1952; Liechtenstein, Kraus Reprint, 1970; poem "Young Africa's Pleas" in *West African Verse,* Donatus I. Nwoga, editor, London, Longmans, 1967.

OSADEBY (see OSADEBAY, Dennis Chukude)

OSOGO, John
b. ca. 1930, Kenya.
Story writer, collector of folktales.

Osogo's most important volume is *The Bride Who Wanted a Special Present: and Other Tales from Western Kenya,* 1966. There are 13 tales in the little volume, beginning with "The Beautiful Bride and Her Hunchback Sister," and ending with archetypal "How the People Fetched Fire." The E.S.A. Bookshop in Nairobi published his works for children: *An Old Man and His Children* and *Let's Make a Play.*

Writings: Stories: *The Bride Who Wanted a Special Present; and Other Tales from Western Kenya,* Kampala, Nairobi, Dar es Salaam, East African Literature Bureau, 1966.
Children's Books: *An Old Man and His Children; Let's Make a Play,* both by E.S.A. Bookshop, Nairobi, 196?

OSORIO, Ernesto Cochat
b. ca. 1930, Angola.
Poet, story writer, physician.

Osório received his medical training in Portugal and today he practices medicine in Angola. In 1957 he published his first collection of stories, *Capim verde; contos* (Green Grass: Stories), and in 1962 he published a 34-page novelette, *O homen do chapéu. Contos* (The Hatted Ones--with stories), the main story giving its name to the volume.

Primarily a poet, Osório has published verse in three volumes: *Calema: poemas* (Calema: Poems), 1956, a collection of 162 pages; *Cidade* (Fortress, 78 pages, 1960; and *Biografia da noite; poemas* (Night's Biography: Poems), 216 pages, 1966.

Writings: Poetry: *Calema; poemas,* Luanda, Livraria Lello, 1956; *Cidade,* Luanda, Edição de Rotary Club de Luanda, 1960; *Biografia da noite; poemas,* Luanda, Ed. Lello, 1966.
Stories: *Capim verde; contos,* Luanda, Lello, 1957; *O homen do chapéu. Contos,* Sà da Bandeira, Angola, Publicações Imbondeiro, 1962.

OUOLOGUEM, Yambo (also pseudonym, RODOLPH, Utto)
b. 1940, Dogon country, Eastern Mali.
Poet, novelist.

A member of the strongly conservative and highly organized Dogon peoples, Ouologuem was the only son of a school inspector. He began his education in local schools and then went on to the classical lycée in Bamako, Mali's capital. He began his advanced studies in Paris in 1962 in philosophy, literature, and sociology, taking the "licence" in those subjects and a "Diplôme d'Etude supérieure d'anglais" (English Language certificate). He is completing his doctorate in sociology in Paris.

Though Ouologuem has written interesting poetry, his present fame rests on a controversial novel, *Le devoir de violence,* published in Paris in 1968 by Seuil. The work won the Prix Renaudot, and in its English translation as *The Wages of Violence,* published in 1971, it was widely acclaimed as a true African novel of great power and originality. The reviewer for the prestigious Parisian journal, *Le Monde,* asserted, apparently sincerely, that the novel showed its author as the first African writer of international standing since Senghor. However, the novel's very force and bizarre qualities to a great extent are evidently due more to the influence of André Schwarz-Bart's pseudo-historical novel, *Le dernier des Justes* (The Last of the Just) which was published in Paris in 1959 by Seuil, the same firm as Ouologuem's, than they are to the originality of the African author.

According to Dr. Eric Sellin in his essay, "Ouologuem's Blueprint for *Le Devoir de Violence,*" the publisher himself had informed Mohamed-Salah Dembri, a friend of Sellin's, that Seuil had "commissioned" Ouologuem to write an African version of *Le dernier des Justes.* Sellin compares paragraphs, phrases, images, the general flow and structure of the novel, characters etc. in the two works and is convincing in his argument that *The Wages of Violence* is a highly derivative work. Even the dust jacket note on Ouologuem's novel closely reflects the jacket squib on Schwarz-Bart's novel which, though it won the Prix Goncourt, has been attacked as a spurious history,

specially commissioned for its sensationalist aspects.

Sellin further points out that Ouologuem has ironically, or puckishly, played on the nature of his free adaptation of facts and historical events and that it is not "just" an African novel, as he declared in an interview with Mel Watkins, *New York Times Book Review* (March 7, 1971). His other interviews with various American reviewers on the novel become even more interesting, when read in the light of Sellin's revelations.

The Times Literary Supplement in May 1972 also showed some six or seven pages to be either identical or very close to passages from Graham Greene's novel *It's a Battlefield.* The *TLS* questioned whether Ouologuem was carrying on a one-man revenge for "the much chronicled sins of territorial imperialists."

Ouologuem appeared as a flamboyant writer with a rococo version of the style of Flaubert in *Salammbô,* and his attacks on the arrogant past and the vileness of the present colonial era made *Le Devoir* read as a true revelation. Eight centuries of vicious history had reduced the "Black Man" to a *négraille* ("nigger rabble" in its Englished version of Ouologuem's coined phrase). In his article, "Brotherhood of Victims," in *Time Magazine,* March 15, 1971, Melvin Maddocks emphasized the novel's parade, for over seven centuries, of slavery, wars, tortures, and other barbarisms:

> *"After such knowledge, what forgiveness?" cried T. S. Eliot. At the conclusion of his bloody chronicle Ouologuem does not presume to forgive either blacks or whites. But in the remarkable final chapter—having turned from historian to novelist—he turns from novelist to mystic. "Politics," he writes accusingly, "does not know the*

goal but forces a pretext of a goal." Negritude or colonialism, black power or white
power—on these terms, history makes victims, if not slaves of us all. With a skepti-
cism nearly as pure as faith, Ouologuem
concludes: one ought to despair of men's
ancient compulsion to rationalize tyranny
and "believe one is right to despair. Love
is nothing else." That is the way a victim
can triumph, even as victim. It is the way
Ouologuem at last turns his back on his
past—without for a single moment turning
his back on life.

Commonweal (June 11, 1971) offers an
excellent interview with Ouologuem by
Linda Kuehl. Many points are covered
in the long discussion but there is one
particularly interesting response to a
question concerning technical
difficulties:

> The technical difficulties came from not
> wanting to write a mere story. I wanted
> to convey the rhythm of Africa, the rhythm
> of the blues when I was singing despair,
> sometimes the rhythm of jazz. And, of
> course, it's horrible to try to translate the
> beat of music and the idea of pure sound
> into phrases and sentences, though not
> because I was writing in French per se,
> but because French was for me a foreign
> language. I had to be somewhat half black
> and half white because I was dealing with
> a foreign civilization.

Ouologuem also published a 338-page
novel in 1969 with the intriguing title,
Utto Rodolph. Les milles et une bibles du sexe
(Utto Rodolph. The Thousand and One
Bibles of Sex).

His strong and original poetry has
been anthologized and particularly original poems in the original French are
to be found in New Sum of Poetry from
the African World. His "A Mon Mari" is
a mocking bitter-sweet monologue of an
African wife to her husband, who,
increasingly Westernized, begins to for-

bid her the usual diet and the usual eating arrangements. The poem starts:

> Tu t'appelais Bimbircokak
> Et tu était bien ainsi
> Mais tu devins Victor-Emile-Louis-Henri-
> Joseph
> Et achetas un service de table

> Your name was Bimbircokak
> And you were OK that way
> But you became Victor-Emile-Louis-
> Henry-Joseph
> And bought a dinner service
> (trans. D.H.)

and ends with the line that after being
"underdeveloped" she has ended up as
"underfed"

In his Letter à la France Nègre, published in 1968, Ouologuem offers a long
collection of acerbic letters addressed to
the President of France, to Negro-
Lovers, to Professional Non-Racists, etc.
He attacks knee-jerk liberals whose
unthinking approval of everything black
is worse than racism. The volume of 194
pages carries the sub-titles: "Love letter
to all the victims of Anti-Racism" (trans.
D. H.). This work, too, according to
Professor Sellin, reflects to some degree
Schwarz-Bart's Le dernier des Justes.

Writings: Novels: Le devoir de violence,
Paris, Seuil, 1968; in English as The
Wages of Violence, London, Secker and
Warburg, 1968; also as Bound to Violence,
translation by Ralph Manheim, New
York, Harcourt, Brace, Jovanovich,
1971; London, Heinemann, 1971; pub-
lished under the pseudonym of Utto
Rodolph: Les milles et une bibles du sexe,
Paris, Eds. du Dauphin, 1969.

Poetry: poems in New Sum of Poetry
from the Negro World, Paris, Présence
Africaine, No., 57, 1966.

Essays: *Lettre à la France Nègre*, Paris, Ed. Edmond Nalis, 1968.

Biographical/Critical Sources: Eric Sellin, "Ouologuem's Blueprint for *Le devoir de violence*," *Research in African Literatures*, II, 2, Fall, 1971, Austin, Texas; review in *Le Monde;* interviews in *New York Times Book Review*, March 7, 1971; *Commonweal*, No. 13, June 11, 1971; Melvin Maddocks, "Brotherhood of Victims," *Times Magazine*, March 15, 1971. Work by André Schwarz-Bart: *Le dernier des Justes*, Paris, Seuil, 1959.

OUSMANE, Sembène (see SEMBENE, Ousmane)

OWOMOYELA, Oyekan
b. ca. 1935, Nigeria.
Playwright.

After studying in local schools, Oyekan Owomoyela took his B.A. at Ibadan and travelled to the United States to take an M.A. in fine arts in film work at the University of California at Los Angeles. He is currently working on a Ph.D. in Yoruba theatre history and Yoruba folklore there. He taught speech and drama for one year at Lake Erie College in Ohio. An excerpt from a film script, "Candles and Incense", appears in *New African Literature and the Arts*, 1970.

Writings: Film script: "Candles and Incense," in *New African Literature and the Arts*, Joseph Opaku, New York, Crowell, 1970.

OWONO, Joseph
b. ca. 1932, Cameroon.
Novelist.

Owono published one of the earlier works in Cameroonian fiction when he brought out *Tante Bella* (Aunt Bella) in 1959.

Writings: Novel: *Tante Bella*, Yaoundé, Librarie "Au Messager," 1959.

OWOYELE, David
b. ca. 1935, Yoruba-land, western Nigeria.
Short story writer

Owoyele has been an officer in the Information Service of the Northern Region. His short story, "The Will of Allah," first appeared in *Reflections: Nigerian Prose and Verse*, 1962. He has contributed a number of short stories and articles to various African journals.

Writings: Short story: "The Will of Allah" in *Reflections: Nigerian Prose and Verse*, Frances Ademola, editor, Lagos, African University Press, 1962, reprinted 1965; also in *Modern African Stories*, London, Faber and Faber, 1964.

OWUOR, Henry
b. ca. 1938, Kenya.
Luo song collector.

Owuor received his first schooling in local institutions in Kenya and has taught at Friend's School in Kamusinga. He began studying for his B.A. in English literature at Cambridge in the mid-1960's. During his teaching days at Kamusinga, Owuor compiled traditional Luo songs. His essay, "Luo Songs, " appears in Ulli Beier's *An Introduction to African Literature*, 1967.

Writings: Luo Folk Songs: unpublished; essay on his material: "Luo Songs" in

An Introduction to African Literature, Ulli Beier, editor. Evanston, Illinois, 1967.

OYELESE, J. O.
b. ca. 1915, Western Nigeria
Collector of Yoruba proverbs.

One of the earliest African scholars to publish his work on folk literature, Oyelese issued his useful collection, *Alo o apa kini alo apamo* (Yoruba Proverbs) in 1948.

Writings: Folklore: *Alo o apa kini alo apamo,* London, Oxford University Press, 1948.

OYONO, Ferdinand Léopold
b. September 14, 1929, N'goul'emakong, near Ebolowa, Cameroon.
Novelist, short story writer, lawyer, diplomat.

Oyono did his early schooling near his home, took the lycée courses at Ebolowa and at the lycée in Provins, and received the French "Bachot" in 1950. He was aided in his university work at Paris by his father, an important chief and an official in his home city, who began to help his son only after a neighbor's son had begun a similar course, however.

Oyono earned the "licence" in law at the University Law School, Paris. His struggle for an education was accompanied by tension in his family between his devout Catholic mother and his polygamous, traditionalist father. The mother, who left home and took her children with her when Ferdinand was very young, supported her family by working as a seamstress. Oyono, to help out, served as a choirboy, studied classical literature for some years as a priest's "boy" or personal servant, and lived

through the hardships which later went into his first and very bitter novel, *Une vie de boy,* 1956.

Oyono acted the title role of Louis Sapin's *Papa bon dieu* at the Théâtre d'Aujourd'hui in Paris in 1959. He has served as a member of the executive committee of the National Committee of French Writers, has worked in his country's foreign service in Paris and Rome, and has been Minister Plenipotentiary to the Common Marker and later ambassador to Liberia. After his bar exams in Paris, taken after completion of his French studies, Oyono returned home to assume the directorship of the Bureau d'Etudes at Yaoundé, the capital, and has since, combined his professional work with the life of the novelist. Recently, he was the Cameroonian permanent delegate to the United Nations in New York and presently he is Consul General in Brussels.

Oyono's satirical novels have been widely appreciated. *Le vieux négre et la médaille* (The Old Man and the Medal in its English translation), 1956, was based on an incident in his father's life. *Chemin d'Europe* (The Road from Europe), 1960, less known, and the very popular *Un vie de boy*, 1956, have seen translations into German, Czech, Dutch, Norwegian, and English, and American editions. His most recent fiction, the novel, *Le pandémonium* (The Big Confusion), was published by Julliard in 1971.

One of his best-known short stories, "Un lépreux sur un tombe" (A leper on the tombstone), first appeared in the 1958 collection *Hommes sans épaules* (Men Without Shoulders).

Writings: Novels: *Une vie de boy*, Paris, Julliard, 1956; in English translation by John Reed as *Houseboy*, London, Heinemann, 1966; as *Boy!* New York, Collier, Macmillan, 1970; *Le vieux nègre et la médaille*, Paris, Julliard, 1956; in John Reed's translation, *The Old Man and the Medal*, London, Heinemann, 1967; *Chemin d'Europe*, Paris, Julliard, 1960; *Le pandémonium*, Paris, Julliard, 1971.

Story: "Un lépreux sur un tombe," in *Hommes sans épaules*, Paris, 1958.

Biographical/Critical Sources: A. C. Brench, *Writing in French from Senegal to Cameroon*, London, Oxford University Press, 1967; *Ferdinand Oyono, écrivain camerounais*, Roger Mercier, Monique and Simon Battestini, editors, Paris, F. Nathan, 1964.

OYONO-MBIA, Guillaume
b. 1939, Mvoutessi, near Sangmélima, Cameroon.
Playwright, teacher (publishes in French and English).

After attending schools near his home, including the Collège Evangélique de Libamba, Oyônô–Mbia studied for his B.A. at the University of Keele, Staffordshire, England from 1964 to 1968, taking the degree in 1969. A native speaker of Bulu, he has taught French, English, and German at the Collège Evangélique. He is currently assistant department chairman of English at the Federal University of the Cameroon, Yaoundé.

Onônô-Mbia has published two plays, *Three Suitors: One Husband,* and *Until*

Further Notice in the paperback Methuen Playscripts, 1968. The former play was originally published in French as *Trois prétendants: un mari*, 1964, revised and expanded in a 1969 edition. The second play was originally published in English by Big O Press Ltd. of London.

Another play, *His Excellency's Special Train. A radio play in one act*, appeared in *Ozila; forum littéraire camerounais--cameroon literary workshop*, 1970, in mimeographed form.

Three Suitors, originally composed in French in 1960, was the first modern play written by a Cameroonian to be staged in Yaoundé when it was produced in the capital in 1961. Later, the Jeune Théâtre Africain staged it in France.

Until *Further Notice*, written for radio in 1966, has been broadcast by the BBC and received its premiere in England in 1967. Later it was published in French as *Jusqu'à nouvel avis*, 1970. The BBC African Service awarded the work its first prize in 1967 and in its French form it won the newly instituted El Hadj Ahmadou Ahidjo literary prize, named after Cameroon's president.

Writings: Plays: *Three Suitors: One Husband*, first performed in Yaoundé, 1961; published London, Methuen and Company, Ltd., 1968; originally in French as *Trois prétendants: un mari*, Editions CLE, Yaoundé, Cameroon, 1964; second edition, revised and enlarged, 1969; *Until Further Notice*, London, Big O Press Ltd., 1967; in French as *Jusqu'à nouvel avis*, Yaoundé, Ed. CLE, 1970; second English edition, London, Methuen, 1968; *His Excellency's Special Train*, in *Ozila; forum littéraire camerounais—cameroon literary workshop*. Supplement to No. 3, Yaoundé, April, 1970, mimeographed.

P

PALANGYO, Peter K.
b. 1939, Tanzania.
Novelist, teacher, biologist.

Beginning his schooling at Nkoaranga in Tanzania, he was successful, along with three others of 150 fellow students, in qualifying for entrance to Old Moshi Secondary School. He took the B.A. in biology and chemistry at St. Olaf College (Minnesota) in 1962 and did graduate work in genetics at the University of Minnesota. While in the United States, Palangyo decided his major interest lay in literature in the late 1960's and he attended the Writers' Workshop at the University of Iowa, after having spent some years at Makerere University earning a teacher's certificate and serving as a principal of two schools, the Lyamungu Secondary School and the H. H. The Aga Khan Boys' Secondary School, Dar es Salaam.

Palangyo's first novel, *Dying in the Sun*, published in 1968, deals with Ntaya, who, alienated from his father and the villagers of Kachawanga, tries to piece together a new life during and after his father's last illness and death. Set in post-independence Tanzania, the novel not only captures some of the new tensions of life in contemporary Africa but is a documentary of the world of family, love and death, pain and ecstasy suffered by all men regardless of empires, states, or politics. The novel was the first Tanzanian work of fiction to appear in the well-known Heinemann African Writers Series.

Palangyo's second novel will shortly be issued by Heinemann.

Writings: Novel: *Dying in the Sun,* London, Heinemann, 1968; in Heinemann African Writers Series, 1969.

PARIS, Prince Modupe (born, MODUPE, Paris)
b. 1901, Dubreka, Guinea.
Autobiographer, novelist.

Locally educated at the lower level, Paris was that rare African who went to the United States instead of the Metropolitan country, or ruling colonial state, France, for university work. He studied at Hampton Institute, Hampton, Virginia and became a professional lecturer on African subjects in the United States after leaving college. He lived during the fifties and sixties in Los Angeles.

Modupe's best work is his ironically titled autobiography, *I Was a Savage,*

337

published in 1957 with an introduction by Peter B. Hammond, professor of anthropology at the University of Pittsburg, and published in London in 1958, with a foreward by the white Kenyan writer, Elspeth Huxley. The work is divided into three parts: the first concerns Modupe's childhood in his Soussou village located in an area along the coast of Guinea which includes the present capital, Conakry; the second section deals with the Western and American influences which led to his voyage to the United States; and the third covers his trip to America and his experiences there. Written with nostalgia and in a mood of one who has irretrievably lost a beautiful world, it presents accurate descriptions of village life and other manners and customs of his people who are not at all "savages."

Written after 36 years in the United States, the book is not a graphic rendering of African patterns of life as is Camara Laye's *The African Child*. As Ulli Beier's wrote in reviewing the work in *Black Orpheus* magazine, November, 1959, "... nothing in this book seems to be told from personal experience, everything is based on a knowledge of facts.... He was away too long to be able to conjure up the vision of his home." However, Beier quotes one passage with approval:

> *Why was every good act held to be exclusively Christian even when it had a counterpart in tribal life? All tribal things were denounced as bad—"the bad old ways." Confusion sat on me. If the teacher had said, "A Christian treats all men, everywhere, as though they were members of his own tribe," that would have made clear sense. I would have gained some concept of the Christian ideal.*

Writings: Autobiography: *I Was A Savage,*

New York, Harcourt, Brace, 1957; London, Museum Press, Ltd., 1958; New York, Washington, F.A. Praeger, 1969.

Biographical/Critical Source: Review, Ulli Beier, *Black Orpheus* magazine, No. 6, November, 1959.

PARKES, Frank Kobina (also PARKES, Francis Ernest Kobina)
b. 1932, Korle Bu, Ghana.
Poet, journalist.

Son of a Sierra Leonean father, he grew up in Sierra Leone and the old Gold Coast, and attended Adisadel School (Ghana) before going on to England to high school, where he graduated in 1949. Since then he has been a clerk, reporter, editor, and radio program producer. He has served as president of the Ghana Society of Writers and has had many of his poems read over Ghana and Nigerian radio. Much of his verse appears in anthologies. He lived in London during the mid-1960's, but is now in Accra employed by the Ministry of Information.

Parkes is represented by three long poems, "Blind Steersman," "The Spectre and the Talking Drum," and Apocalypse," in *New Sum of Poetry from the Negro World*. He also has eight poems in the 1971 collection of Ghanaian poets, *Messages*.

Parkes' volume, *Songs from the Wilderness* tells us that the wilderness is all about us, that it is the modern world entire. Though strongly pro-Africa, Parkes' belief is in all mankind. He particularly directs his attention to young persons of college age, for he asserts the need for and the possibility of creative leadership arising from the present younger generation.

In his poem "African Heaven" published in Austin J. Shelton's *The African Assertion,* Parkes addresses these very Negritudist lines to God (the poem continues for another three pages):

Give me black souls,
Let them be black
Or chocolate brown
Or make them the
Color of dust—
Dustlike,
Browner than sand,
But if you can
Please keep them black,
Black
Give me some drums;
Let them be three
Or maybe four
And make them black—
Dirty and black:
Of wood,
And dried sheepskin,
But if you will
Just make them peal
Peal

Writings: Poetry: *Songs from the Wilderness,* London, University of London Press, 1965; "Blind Steersman," "The Spectre and the Talking Drum," and "Apocalypse" in *New Sum of Poetry from the Negro World,* Paris, Présence Africaine, Volume 57, 1966; other poems in *The African Assertion,* Austin J. Shelton, editor, New York, The Odyssey Press 1968; and *Messages,* London, Heinemann, 1971.

p'BITEK, J. P. Okot (also OKOT, p'Bitek)
b. 1931, Gulu, Northern Uganda.

Luo or Acoli language novelist, English-language poet, anthropologist, essayist, song collector.

This pioneering Ugandan writer received his early education at local primary schools, attended Gulu High School and went on to King's College in Budo, Uganda for his university training. While at college he wrote and produced a student opera.

p'Bitek completed a novel in his mother tongue, Lwo (sometimes called Luo or Acole), entitled *Lak tar miyo kinyero we lobo* (Are Your Teeth White: If So, Laugh). It was published in 1953, while the author playing professional football for a living. During the mid-and later 1950's, he earned a Certificate in Education from Bristol University in England and attended law school at the University of Wales at Aberystwyth for his LL. B. degree. He then studied social anthropology at Oxford where he earned his B. Litt with a thesis in 1963 on the traditional songs of the Acole and Lango peoples.

During the middle 1960's, p'Bitek served as director of the Uganda National Theatre and as a professor at Makerere University, Uganda. After a period at the Writers' Workshop at the Universty of Iowa, he took a position in Kisumu, Kenya to organize the Art Festival of 1968, returning to the United States in 1971 to be a writer-in-residence at the University of Iowa.

p'Bitek's first narrative "poetic-novel," *Song of Lawino. A Lament,* a widely popular work, was published in 1966 after being rendered into English from its original Lwo by the author. Well received in England and America, it not only is a telling study of the effects of Westernization on African family life, but is a warm and at times sarcastic study of the characters of Lawino's world, particularly that of her husband who seeks to become a white man. Lawino, entrenched in her African-ness, becomes a telling spokesman for the old African verities and common sense in a fast changing world.

In 1970, the East African Publishing House issued his prose-poem, *Song of Ocol.* The same firm also has recently issued two more of Ocot p'Bitek's prose-poems, *The Song of the Prisoner,* and *The Revelations of a Prostitute.* The former work also has recently appeared under the Third Press imprint. p'Bitek's two-page poem, "Order of the Black Cross," lamenting the losses of the Biafran War, with an accompanying letter, appeared in the Winter-Spring 1971 issue of the *Journal of the New African Literature and the Arts.*

Writings: Poetic-novels: *Song of Lawino. A Lament.* Nairobi, London, East African Publishing House, 1966; Cleveland, Ohio, World-Meridian Books, 1969, illustrated by Frank Horley; *Song of Ocol,* Nairobi, East African Publishing House, 1970; *The Song of the Prisoner,* Nairobi, East African Publishing House, 1970; New York, Third Press, 1971; *The Revelations of a Prostitute,* Nairobi, East African Publishing House; original Luo or Acoli version of *Song of Lawino,* published as *Wer pa lawino,* Nairobi, East African Publishing House, 1971. *Song of Lawino* and *Song of Ocol,* republished in one volume, Narobi, East African Publishing House, 1972, as a revised, school edition, with introduction by G. A. Heron of Thogoto College, Kenya. The long poem, *The Song of the Prisoner,* was republished with a new work, *The Song of Malaya,* a poetic farce attacking the new politicians of Africa, in a double volume, *Two Songs,* Nairobi, East African Publishing House, 1971.

Novel, in Luo: *Lak tar miyo kinyero wi lobo,* Kampala, Uganda, The Eagle Press, 1953.

Poem: "Order of the Black Cross" in *Journal of the New African Literature and the Arts.* New York, Winter-Spring, 1971.

Scholarship: *African Religion in Western Scholarship,* Nairobi, East African Literature Bureau, 1970.

Essay: in *East Africa Past and Present,* B. A. Ogot, editor, Paris, Présence Africaine, 1971.

PEDEREK, Simon
b. ca. 1930, Ghana.
Poet.

Locally educated, Simon Pederek early turned to the writing of poetry and his work has appeared in several journals. A short poem, "Vultures," is found in Langston Hughes' *An African Treasure.* First published in the *Ghanaian,* the poem contrasts unfavorably the humans' attitude to vultures with the vultures' superior vision of human beings, for the vultures can rise above the streets and burning plains to soar close to the moon, thereby having higher and, ironically, nobler, thoughts than mankind.

Writings: Poem: "Vultures," in *Ghanaian;* also in *An African Treasury,* New York, Pyramid, 1961.

PEREIRA, José de Fontes
b. May, 1823, near Luanda, Angola;
d. May 2, 1891.
Journalist, lawyer, amateur historian.

An Angolan mestiço of part African and

part Portuguese heritage, Pereira became a lawyer, a leading journalist and civil servant, earning a reputation as the *enfant terrible* of the liberal press from the not entirely repressive Angola of his day. Probably the son of João de Fontes and an African mother, he was enrolled at the local primary school and later read law, obtaining his licence to practice sometime in the 1850's. His first job was as a clerk in Luanda. A faithful Catholic who attended mass at the Luanda Cathedral, he married Izabel Josephina de Fontes Pereira by whom he had several children.

Beginning his journalistic writings in the late 1860's, Pereira was deeply engaged for the next two decades in praising good government and in protesting the corrupt and grossly inefficient rule of Portugal in the colony. Increasingly, he called for more and better schools, the abolition of forced labor and the slavery or quasi-slavery imposed upon black Angolans in nearby São Tomé. He read and was influenced by muckraking pieces in the liberal press from France, Brazil, and Portugal. The journal, *O Cruzeiro do Sul* (The Southern Cross), was his major organ for dissent in his first free-swinging days as a reformer. For his courage and passion he suffered arrest, two dismissals from his job in 1875 and 1890 and had his life threatened. Supported, however, in Luanda by a small, cosmopolitan group of Brazilians, liberal Portuguese, and a handful of educated mestiços, including the pioneering Angolan writer, J. D. Cordeiro da Matta (1857–94), he continued to strike out in all directions.

His articles harshly criticizing the government, published in *O Arauto Africano* (The African Herald) of January 6, 20, and 29, 1890, finally resulted in his being

silenced. His death from pneumonia 15 months later ended his 20-year protest against racial prejudice and injustice. Angolans of all ranks and political points of view attended the funeral and burial in the main cemetery of Luanda.

Writings: Articles in newspaper, *O Arauto Africano*, Luanda, Angola, January 6, 20, 29, 1890.

Biographical/Critical Source: Douglas L. Wheeler, "An Early Angolan Protest: The Radical Journalism of José de Fontes Pereira (1823–1891)" in *Protest and Power in Black Africa*, Rotberg and Mazrui, editors, New York, Oxford University Press, 1970.

PETERS, Lenrie
b. 1932, Bathurst, The Gambia.
Poet, novelist, physician.

Lenrie Peters' early education was in Bathurst primary schools until 1949, when he attended high school in Freetown, Sierra Leone at the Prince of Wales School and the Cambridge Technical College. He travelled to England to study medicine at Trinity College, Cambridge and the University College Hospital, London, taking his M.D. in 1959. In 1967 he completed an advanced course in surgery at Guildford, England. He is also a student of music and is reputed to be an excellent singer.

Peters served as president of the African Student Union in his younger days, acted and sang in various amateur musicals and has broadcast on BBC's "African Forum" for which he served for awhile as chairman of the program, "Calling

West Africa." He now practices medicine in The Gambia.

Lenrie Peters is considered one of the leading West African poets and has appeared in *Black Orpheus,* and in many other anthologies and journals. His first volume of verse was *Poems* (1964). Peters states that writing is a trial to him but that he must express himself and thus his creative work is a necessary release from the tense routine of his medical practice. His dual career brings to mind the great American poet, William Carlos Williams, who during a long life practiced medicine in Rutherford, New Jersey, while writing his poems. Peters' verse is mostly in the European-English

tradition with African motifs important but never dominant. His usual concerns are those of modern man anywhere in an urbanized milieu.

Peters' poem "After They Put Down Their Overalls," appears in Ezekiel Mphalele's *African Writing Today*. It pictures the black workers turning to drink in their rage at oppression.

In 1965, Heinemann published his novel, *The Second Round,* set in Freetown, and in 1967 his second volume of verse, *Satellites,* which contains the entire 21 poems from the out-of-print Mbari Press volume, *Poems,* plus 34 new ones, and a new verse volume, *Ketchikali,* 1971.

Writings: Poetry: *Poems,* Ibadan, Mbari Press, 1964; *Satellites,* London, Heinemann, 1967; *Ketchikali,* 1971.

Poem: "After They Put Down Their

Overalls" in *African Writing Today*, London, Penguin, 1967.
Novel: *The Second Round*, London, Heinemann, 1965.

PHAKATHI, A. B. (see last paragraph of NYEMBEZI)

PHATUDI, Cedric Namedi Makepeace
b. May 27, 1912, Molsgat, Petersburg District, Transvaal, South Africa.
Northern Sotho novelist, playwright, translator, educator.

Son of Chief Mmutle Phatudi Mphahlele, Cedric M. M. Phatudi began his education in the Mmutle Central Primary School, completed his work at the Kilnerton Training Institute (1929–1932), took his B.A. from Fort Hare in 1947, and his University Education Diploma in 1950. In 1963 he earned the B.Ed. degree from Witwatersrand University.

His career in education included posts as an assistant teacher at the Berger Dutch Reformed Mission School, Sekhukhuneland (1932–35); principal, Marishane Community School in the same community as the Mission School (1935–1942); supervisor of schools for the East Rand and Eastern Transvaal (1943–1946); supervisor of schools for the West Rand (1946–1955); sub-inspector of Bantu education for the Krugersdorp Circuit of the Southern Transvaal region (1955–1963); and sub-inspector, Johannesburg East Circuit (1963–present). He was appointed chairman of the North Sotho sub-committee of the Bantu Education Advisory Board in 1965 by the South African Minister

Phatudi has published one novel to date, *Tladi wa dikgati* (The Footstep of the Lightning) and one play, *Kgôši Mmutle III*, a historical treatment of king Mmutle. His two translations into the Sepede or Northern Sotho language are his rendering of Defoe's *Robinson Crusoe* (1958), and Shakespeare's *Julius Caesar* as *Julease Sisare* (1966).

Writings: Novel: *Tladi wa dikgati*, Johannesburg, Voortrekkers Pers Beperk, 1958.
Play: *Kgôši Mmutle III*, Pretoria, Union Books, 1966.
Translations: *Robinson Crusoe*, Johannesburg, Voortrekkers, 1958; Shakespeare's *Julius Caesar* as *Julease Sisare*, Johannesburg, Voortrekkers, 1966.

PHILOMBE, René (also OMBEDE, Philippe-Louis)
b. ca. 1934, Beti tribal area, south of Yaoundé, Cameroon.
Novelist, ethnographer, autobiographer.

Philombe's first published work was the ethnographic pamphlet, *La passerelle divine* (The Divine Foot-bridge), which appeared in 1959. There followed his autobiographic journal, *Lettres de ma cambuse* (Letters from My Storeroom), written while he was ill in an obscure Cameroonian village, published in 1964. *Lettres de ma cambuse* won the French Academy's Mottart Prize.

His two creative works are the novels: *Sola, ma chérie* (Sola, My Darling), 1966, and *Un sorcier blanc à Zangali* (The White Sorcerer at Zangali), 1969. The latter tells the tale of a white missionary who arrives to work "wonders" among the Beti people.

Philombe

Writings: Folklore: *La passerelle divine,* Yaoundé, Association des Poètes et Ecrivains Camerounais, 1959.

Autobiography: *Lettres de ma cambuse,* Yaoundé, Eds. Abbia; CLE, 1964.

Novels: *Sola, ma chérie,* Yaoundé, CLE, 1966; *Un sorcier blanc à Zangali,* Yaoundé, CLE, 1969.

Genre unknown; *Histoire queue de chat,* Yaoundé, CLE, 1972.

PIETERSE, Cosmo George Leipoldt
b. 1930, Windhoek, South West Africa.
Poet, teacher, anthologist, playwright, actor.

Locally educated in lower schools, Cosmo Pieterse went to South Africa for his university work, taking a B.A. from the University of Cape Town. He taught for ten years in South Africa before moving to London, and he now teaches there while collecting the works for his important anthologies. In 1971–72 he was a visiting lecturer in English at Ohio State University in Athens, Ohio. Heinemann, has published his anthologies: *Ten One Act Plays* (1968), *Eleven Short African Plays* (1970), and *Seven South African Poets* (1971). He writes scripts, poems, and reviews, and has acted in and produced plays for the stage and radio. His most recent anthology offers extensive selections from the works of Dollar Brand, Dennis Brutus, I. Choonara, C. J. Driver, Timothy Holmes, Keorapetse Kgositsile, and K. Arthur Nortje. All of these poets are highly politically conscious and the poems are of a very fine quality. At the end of his useful preface Pieterse writes:

> This collection brings to mind many questions—does South African poetry become shrill, hysterical, thinly disguised political propaganda? Is it bad for the poetic product if this element is an important ingredient? Does exile affect the poet's vision, style, range and diction? How do these South Africans compare with the poets of Angola and Mozambique? How does exile affect a poet?

and he waves aside the opportunity to answer by saying:

> It is certainly not the intention of this volume to answer these questions. But it is hoped that the reader who is interested by such questions will be stimulated and helped by this collection."

The themes of Pieterse's collected dramas in *Ten One Act Plays* range from the personal and domestic to the social and political and deal with war, bribery, deceit, marriage, prison life, ignorance, and brutality. The plays were prepared from manuscripts taken from stage, radio, and television scripts. Three authors are from West Africa, three from East Africa, and three from South Africa, and all write in English.

With Donald Munro he has edited *Protest and Conflict in African Literature.* In 1970 Pieterse edited *Poems of Conflict.*

His long poem, or verse-play, "Ballad of the Cells: A Physiology in Twenty-Seven Pulses and a Choral Elegy," appeared in *New African Literature and the Arts* 2.

Writings: Anthologies: *Ten One Act Plays,* London, Heinemann, 1968; *Eleven Short African Plays,* London, Heinemann, 1970; *Seven South African Poets,* London, Heinemann, 1971; *Protest and Conflict in African Literature,* edited with Donald Munroe, New York, Africana Publishing Corporation, 1969; London, Heinemann, 1969; *Poems of Conflict,* London, Heinemann, 1970. (He served as collector and editor to these collections.)

Poem: "Ballad of the Cells: A

Physiology in Twenty-Seven Pulses and a Choral Elegy" in *New African Literature and the Arts,* 2, Joseph Okpaku, editor, New York, Thomas Y. Crowell Co., 1968, 1970.

PINTO DE ANDRADE, Mário
(see de ANDRADE, Mário Coelho Pinto)

PLAATJE, Solomon Tshekiŝo
(sometimes PLAATJIE, Tshekisho)
b. 1878, Boskop Farm, Boshof District. Orange Free State, South Africa; d. June 19, 1932, Johannesburg, South Africa.
Tswana novelist, scholar, statesman (also wrote in English).

Born the fourteenth child of Christian parents, Kushumene Johannes Mogodi (of the Morolong or Moto clan) and Kethanecwe Botsingwe (of the Seleka or Tshipi clan), Plaatje attended the Pniel Missionary School, Barkly West (1884–1890), where he passed his Standard IV examination, his highest formal education in western schools. Despite his limited schooling he eventually became proficient in English, Afrikaans, High Dutch, German, and French, as well as the related languages to his own native Tswana: Sotho, Zulu, and Xhosa. While still in school he decided to accept his father's nickname, "Plaatje," as his "family name," and Afrikaans word which signified a short, stocky body.

From 1894, Plaatje's progress was determined and energetic. After seven months of private study in Kimberley he passed the Cape Civil Service Certificate Examination while working full time as a postman. He was an interpreter and clerk in the Mafeteng Magistrate's Office

about 1895 and then was interpreter for the Court of Summary Jurisdiction under Lord Cecil. When the Boer War broke out, Plaatje served as an interpreter and signal man for the British Army, seeing duty at the seige of Mafeking, October 16, 1899 to May 17, 1900. During this period he became a war correspondent and learned the then rare skill of typing.

Having married Lilith, the sister of the writer Isaiah Budlwana Mbelle, Plaatje settled down in Mafeking to edit a Setswana weekly journal, *Koranta ea becoana* (The Tswana Gazette), from 1901 to 1908. The financial support for the paper came from Chief Silas Molema of Mafeking, father of Silas Modiri Molema (1892–1965), destined to become a celebrated physician. Moving to Kimberley in 1912, Plaatje began to edit and publish a new paper, the *Tsala ea batho* (The Friend of the People). That same year, he was elected the first secretary general of the South African Native National Congress (later, the African National Congress).

Plaatje contributed many articles to his own journal and to others, but his work for the Congress, including help in drafting a constitution, was his major activity at this time and he was even forced to suspend his new journal in 1914. In later years he published articles in the English-language journal, *Diamond Fields Advertiser*. In 1913, he traveled about the Orange Free State gathering data to be presented in England the next year by a delegation protesting the racist policies of the government. Joining Plaatje in the trip to England were John L. Dube, Walter B. Rubusana, Thomas Mtobi Mapikela, and Saul Msane. The group's efforts fell on deaf ears in London, but Plaatje stayed on after the delegation's departure to address what groups he could, supporting himself by writing articles for various British journals.

Remaining in England until close to the end of the war, Plaatje wrote and published three works: *Native Life in South Africa; Sechuana Phonetic Reader,* with Professor Daniel Jones, Linguistics Department of the University of London; and *Sechuana Proverbs with Literal Translations and their European Equivalents-Diane tsa Secoana le maele a sekgoca a a dumalanang naco.* The third work contained 732 proverbs in Setswana with equivalent renderings in German, Dutch, French and English.

Returning to South Africa, Plaatje helped organize a deputation which sought recognition from the delegates to the Versailles Peace Conference. Composed of the Rev. Henry Reed Ngcayiya (1863–1928), Joseph Tshangana Gumade, Richard Vletor Selope Thema (1886–1955), Levi Thomas Mvabaza (1875–1955), and Plaatje, the group was ignored by everyone from U.S. President Woodrow Wilson on down. Their only satisfaction was that the unofficial delegation of Boers, led by General Hertzog and Doctor D. F. Malan, also was ignored. Only General Louis Botha and Jan Christiaan Smuts of the official delegation was received. Minority opinions were not considered by the conferees and the former German West Africa was awarded to South Africa as a mandate.

Once again the African delegation returned home with Plaatje remaining behind—this time to attend the first Pan-African Congress (Paris) organized by W.E.B. DuBois. Meeting many blacks from other parts of Africa and North America for the first time was an enriching experience for Plaatje, and he found further opportunities to travel and lecture in France, Canada and the United States. His little pamphlet, *The Mote and the Beam,* (1920), written to help defray his travel costs, dealt with personal and, particularly, sexual relations between the races in South Africa.

By 1920 he was home in Kimberley, working on temperance matters and trying to improve the lot of his fellow Africans. The next year he founded the Brotherhood Society in Kimberley, dedicated to improving race relations, and he became a member of Dr. Abdurahman's African Peoples' Organization. In 1927 he visited the then Belgian Congo to study the working conditions of the native Africans there and discovered that his fellow Africans in South Africa, though terribly discriminated against, were in better circumstances than the Congolese. His report was studied with attention by the South African Government and resulted in more jobs for Black Africans on the nation's railways. In appreciation of his efforts, his fellow townsmen of Kimberley purchased a freehold piece of land, and presented it to him on his fiftieth birthday in 1928. In December, 1930, Plaatje made one final attack on the country's racist laws, condemning especially the pass law which strictly regulated the movement of African citizens.

His excellent novel, *Mhudi*, Plaatje's only work in the genre, was completed by 1919 but not published until 1930 by Lovedale Press. The full title is *Mhudi, an epic of South African Native Life a hundred years ago*, and is the first novel written and published in English by a Bantu African author. (R. R. R. Dhlomo's novel, *An African Tragedy*, published in 1928, was written that same year.) Plaatje's story concerns the defeat of the Zulus by the Boers after the death of Chaka. The most impressive characters are Mhudi, a refugee from Zulu King Mzilikazi's attack on the Baralong city of Kunana, and Nandi, Mzilikazi's chief wife. Their efforts to find their respective husbands, separated from them by war, and the eventual defeat of Mzilikazi and his retreat over the Drakensberg Mountains gives the novel both personal and historical dimensions. Plaatje inserts songs and other African folkloric material into his story in an organic fashion with great originality.

In 1930, Plaatje's translation of Shakespeare's *The Comedy of Errors* appeared as *Diphóshó-phoshó*. Left in manuscript at his death in Johannesburg

while on a visit, are other translations of Shakespeare's plays: *Maswabi-swabi* (The Merchant of Venice), *Matsapa-tsapa a lêfela* (Much Ado about Nothing), and *Otelo* (Othello).

Also left in manuscript were many proverbs intended to supplement his 1916 collection, many equivalent terms for a Tswana-English dictionary and a work entitled *Monkey Voodoo*. Posthumous publications have included his collection in Tswana, *Mabolela a ga Tshikinya-Chaka* (Sayings from Shakespeare), and in 1937, *Dintshontsho tsa bo-Juliuse Kesara*, rendered from Shakespeare's *Julius Caesar*. Oxford University Press plans publication of his diaries, *The Journals of Solomon T. Plaatje*.

Writings: Novel: *Mhudi*, Lovedale, Lovedale Press, 1930, 1957; reprint, New York, Negro University Press, 1970 (published only in English).

Scholarship: *Native Life in South Africa*, London, P. S. King, 1916; second edition, Kimberley, Tsala ea batho Office, 1918; *Sechuana Proverbs with Literal Translations and Their European Equivalents*, London, Kegan Paul, Trench, Trubner and Company, 1916; *Sechuana Phonetic Reader*, London, University of London Press, 1916.

Pamphlet: *The Mote and the Beam*, New York, Young's Book Exchange, 1920.

Translations: *Diphóshó-phoshó* (Shakespeare's *The Comedy of Errors*), Morija, Morija Sesuto Book Depot, 1930; *Dintshontsho tsa bo-Juliuse Kesara* (Shakespeare's *Julius Caesar*), Johannesburg, University of the Witwatersrand Press, 1937; *Mašwabi-šwabi* (Shakespeare's *The Merchant of Venice); Matsapa-tsapa a lêfela* (Shakespeare's *Much Ado About Nothing); Otelo* (Shakespeare's *Othello*); the last three in manuscript; Extracts from Shakespeare, *Mabolela a ga Tshikinya-*

Chaka (Sayings from Shakespeare), Morija, Morija Sesuto Book Depot, 1935. Category Unknown: "Monkey Voodoo," in manuscript. Journal: "The Journals of Solomon T. Plaatje," in manuscript but planned for publication by Oxford University Press.

Biographical/Critical Source: Ezekiel Mphahlele, *The African Image*, New York, Praeger, 1962 and London, Faber and Faber, 1962.

PLIYA, Jean
b. ca. 1935, Dahomey.
Novelist, short story writer, teacher.

Pliya received his primary schooling in local schools. He has been a teacher and, in the late 1960's, an elected member of the Dahomeyan parliament. In 1966, his three-act play appeared in print in Porto Novo as *Kondo le requin* (Kondo the Shark).

His interesting story, "The Fetish Tree, in a translation by Robert Baldick, is found in Mphahlele's *African Writing Today* (1967). It dramatizes the fate which befalls Dousson, a woodsman, who cut down the sacred Iroko tree, and was crushed by it as it fell. His corpse was thrown on the rubbish heap for the jackals, for his crime was deicide and death itself was not severe enough punishment. Pliya collected some of his tales in *L'arbre fétiche* (The Fetiche Tree) in 1971.

Writings: Play: *Kondo le requin*, Porto Novo, Librarie Nationale, 1966.

Stories: *L'arbre fétiche*, Yaoundé, CLE, 1971; story: "The Fetish Tree" in *African Writing Today*, Ezekiel Mphahlele, editor, *African Writing Today*, London, Penguin, 1967, and in *L'arbre fétiche*.

Q

QAMAAN, Bulhan
b. mid-19th century, Somalia-Ethiopia border region; d. ca. 1915.
Somali oral poet.

Qamaan lived most of his life in Somali areas of Eastern Ethiopia. As is the case with other Somali poets, his works are known today because passages from a few of his poems have become part of the oral, proverbial traditions of his people and others. They appear in a few written collections, in the original, and in translation into several European languages.

Qamaan's poems often were polemical, arguing the cause of his tribe in regional disputes. Others were philosophical or personal ruminations. Heavy alliteration was an oft-used classical poetic device in his poetry.

QUAYE, Cofie
b. ca. 1947, near Apan in Fanti-country, Ghana.
Novelist, story writer.

Self-educated after he left school in the ninth grade, Cofie Quaye read a wide range of books in his private struggle for an education and eventually passed the "Cambridge" examinations required for entrance into British universities. However, he did not attend the university and instead did a variety of jobs leading to his present minor position as a clerk in the Registrar General's Office in Accra which deals with permits and licences. His first story appeared in the monthly journal *When and Where* in 1969, and a few others have appeared in the popular little magazine since.

In 1970, Quaye published the first of his detective stories in the "Moxon Paperbacks Crime Series," the 62-page *Sammy Slams the Gang*. Billed as "A Sammy Hayford Story," the little novel in the words of the back-cover, "presents an amazingly fast moving story" in which the young hero "cracks open wide a devilish plot" to flood Ghana with counterfeit five cedi notes (worth about $5.00 before the 1972 devaluation). Patterned casually on the gun-sagas of cheap paperbacks from the U.S., the one non-American aspect of the naive story is the absence of any "femme fatale" whatsoever, or of any girl, good or bad. This first title and the following two of a promised longer series has a bright orange and white cover with strong typeface to resemble the well-known cover of the Heinemann African Writers Series in fiction.

Murder in Kumasi, dealing with smugglers, and *The Takoradi Kidjackers*, both 1971, complete the trio of these pioneering detective stories in a Ghanaian setting.

Writings: Novels: *Sammy Slams the Gang*, Accra, Moxon Paperbacks Ltd, 1970; *Murder in Kumasi*, Accra, Moxon Paperbacks Ltd, 1970; *The Takoradi Kidjackers*, Accra, Moxon Paperbacks Ltd, 1970.

Stories: in *When and Where* Magazine, Accra, Moxon, 1969–1972.

QUENUM, Maximilien Possey Berry
b. 1911, Dahomey.
Anthropologist, collector of legends.

Quénum has written about a wide range of subjects within the general area of his interest in the cultural heritage of African peoples. He has a forceful and vivid style. Locally educated at the lower level, he did university work in France, winning the "License" (akin to the American M.A.). His nephew is the well-known writer Bhêly–Quénum.

His three works are: *L'Afrique noire: rencontre avec l'occident* (Black Africa: Encounter with the West); *Au pays des Fons. Us et coutumes de Dahomey* (In the Country of the Fon: Usages and Customs of Dahomey); and *Trois légendes Africaines* (Three African Legends). Quénum's *Au pays des Fons* received the distinction of being chosen by the French Academy as a notable work in the year of its publication.

Writings: Anthropology: *Au pays des Fons. Us et coutumes de Dahomey*, Paris, Larose, 1938; *Trois légendes africaines*, Rochefort-Sur-Mer, Imprimerie A. Thoyon-These, 1946; *L'Afrique noire: rencontre avec l'occident*, Paris, 1958; an extract from *Trois légendes africains* appears in *Anthologie de la littérature négro-africaine: romanciers et conteurs négro-africains*, Volume II, Léonard Sainville, editor, Paris, Présence Africaines, 1963, 1968, extract also in *Anthologie africaine des écrivains noirs d'expression française*, Paris, Institut Pedagogiques Africaine, 1962.

R

RAAGE, Ugaas
b. probably 18th century, Somali area.
Somali oral poet.

Son of a Sultan, a member of the Ogaden clan and a fervent believer in Islam, Raage's thoughtful and sweetly flowing poetry was widely popular in his day and is preserved in private collections in modern Somalia. He is considered a master in using the widest possible range of the Somalia language which he employed in the most "classical" or traditional manner. Two of his poems, "The Respect Due to Power," and "Poet's Lament on the Death of his Wife," have so far found their way into print in *Somali Poetry*.

Writings: Poems: "The Respect Due to Power," and "Poet's Lament on the Death of his Wife" in *Somali Poetry*, Andrzejewski and Lewis, editors, Oxford, Clarendon Press, 1964.

RABEARIVELO, Jean-Joseph
(originally, Joseph-Casimir)
b. March 4, 1901, Antananarivo, Malagasy; d. June 22, 1937.
Poet.

Born in a poor but noble famiy, Rabéarivelo is the founder of modern poetry in Madagascar. An only son, he spent only eight years in school (the Ecole des Frères des Ecoles Chrétiennes d'Andohalo and the Collège Saint-Michel at Amparibe) and a few months of schooling at Flacourt, Farovohitra, Malagasy, from 1906 to 1915. He quit school to work as a publisher's clerk and moved from one poorly paid job to another, always hoping to be able to get to France which he idealized, but never getting the chance. Despite his family's extreme poverty, he was encouraged to write by his devoted mother, Rabozivelo, and did get some advanced schooling for a short period from the Collège Saint-Michel in Amparibe. Writing when he could, burdened by an early marriage and five children (one died in infancy), the poet struggled in illness and despair, succumbing to the temptation of drugs to which he became addicted. In loneliness, apparent artistic defeat, and great sickness, he took his own life in 1937 at the age of 34 by swallowing potassium cyanide.

Rabéarivelo, with Gabriel Razafintsambaina, founded a literary review, *Capricorne* (1930–31), and led the way in the creation of a native strain of Madagascan writing, all in French. Loving France with a mystical passion that had nothing of subservience in it, he dreamed and brooded in his adopted tongue. Combining French with local forms and rhythms, particularly the popular *hainteny*, a ballad-type verse form, he wrote hundreds of poems and many volumes in his short life. His first poems were published in 1923 in the Tananarive journal, *18° latitude Sud,* when he was just 20 years old.

Rabéarivelo's verse collections were: *La coupe de cendres* (A Cup of Ashes) of 1924; *Presque-songes* (Half-Dreams), 1924, 1934; *Sylves: Nobles dédain, Fleurs melées, Destinée, Dixains, Sonnets et poèmes d'Iarive,* 1927; *Volumes: Vers le bonheur, La guirlande à l'amitié, Interlude rythmique,* *Sept quatrains, Arbres, Au soleil estival, Coeur et ciel d'Iarive,* (Volumes: Toward Happiness), 1928; *Enfants d'Orphée* (Children of Orpheus), 1931; and *Imaitsoanala, fille d'oiseau—Cantate* (Imaitsoanala, Daughter of a Bird—Cantata), 1935, all published in Tananarive except *Enfants d'Orphée.* Published in Tunis in 1935 was *Traduit de la nuit* (Night Translations), and in 1937 *Chants pour Abéone* (Songs for Abéone) appeared, the last before his death. Posthumous editions of his verse were *Vieilles chansons des pays d'Imerina* (Old Songs of the Imerina Country), 1939, edited by Robert Boudry who also provided a biography; *Lova,* edited by F. Rajaofera, 1957; and *Des stances oubliées* (Some Forgotten Positions), 1959. *Presque-songes, Traduit de la nuit,* and the previously unpublished group of poems, *Saiky-Nofy,* came out in Malgache and French language texts in 1960, with an introduction by Jacques Rebemananjara.

Mbari Press at the University of Ibadan, Nigeria, published translations by Gerald Moore of Rabéarivelo's verse in *24 Poems.* Some of his work has also appeared in Spanish in the volume *Vientos de la Mañana* (Winds of Tomorrow, Rio de Janeiro).

Today, Rabéarivelo is increasingly regarded as a writer of the very highest level of francophone poetry from Africa. He strives for an illusory effect and though his work is highly personal it is created in a long and flowing, almost abstract line. His earliest poetry, influenced by the French symbolists, was from the beginning extremely rich in its imagery and ardent in its emotions, but, as noted, he employed the local *hainteny* ballad form for its colloquial and fresh flavor and its song-like quality. His influence on later poets in his homeland is clear in the works of Rebémananjara and Ranaivo.

The early style of the poet may be seen in his poem, "Désert" from *Volumes* (1928):

Joie unie et chaude du désert!
Nulle part, l'azur n'est aussi bleu
que sur ces monts de sable et de feu
sillonnés de vol puissant et clair.

What a joy, the grasp and sear of the
/desert!
Nowhere is the blue so blue
As it is on the dunes of sand and fire
Furrowed by the potent and brilliant
/wind.
(trans. D. H.)

One of the poet's last lyrics was "Vieilles Chansons des Pays D'Imerina" (Old Songs from the Imerina Country) from the 1939 volume of the same name. It offers an example of his most mature and complex verse:

La, si près, au nord, il y avait deux
/oranges jumelles: l'une*
était mûre, et l'autre belle à rendre
/heureux. J'ai donné la*
mûre à la Chère, et la belle à rendre
/heureux à l'Aimée. Mais*
j'ai beau chérir l'une et vraiment
/aimer l'autre, si elles me*
voulaient trop violemment dompter,
/je n'en saurais que faire.*

There, so close, to the north, there
/were two twin oranges:
one of them was richly ripe, the other
/most pleasingly beautiful.
I gave the ripe one to my dear one,
/and the beautiful one to my loved one.
But, I have cherished the one and
/truly love the other—
If these girls too strongly tame me,

I won't know how to feel.
(trans. D. H.)

Still awaiting publication is Rabéarivelo's unpublished diary," Calepins Bleus" (Blue Notebooks), some 1800 pages in loose manuscript, which certainly should contribute very much not only to his biography but to the history of poetry in Madagascar and the francophone world. The last few pages, edited by Robert Boudry, appeared in *Mercure de France* in 1939.

Writings: La coupe de cendres, Pitot de la Beaujardière, 1924; *Presque-songes,* translated from Hova, a language of Malagasy, Henri Vidalie, 1924, Imprimerie de l'Imerina, 1934; republished in one volume in 1960 (see below); *Sylves,* Imprimerie de l'Imerina, 1927; *Volumes,* Imp. de l'Imerina, 1928; *Enfants d'Orphée,* Ile Maurice, The General Printing and Stationery Ltd., 1931; *Imaitsoanale,* Imprimerie Officielle Edit., 1935; *Traduit de la nuit,* translated into French from Hova, (Malagasy) Tunis, Editions des Mirages, 1935; *Chants pour Abéone,* Imp. Henri Vidalie, 1936 or 1937; *Vieilles chansons des pays d'Imerina,* Imprimerie Officielle, 1939; *Lova,* Imprimerie Volamihitsy, 1957; *Des stances oubliées,* published by Mme. Veuve (Widow) Rabako–Rabéarivelo, 1959; combined volume of *Presque-songes, Traduit de la nuit,* and *Saiky–Nofy,* in dual texts, French and Malagasy, Gabriel Razafintsambaina and others, editors, introduction by Jacques Rabémananjara, Nouvelle Ed. Tananarive, Comité "Les Amis de Rabéarivelo," 1960: this was a second edition: date of first edition unknown; early individual poems in many journals including *Capricorne* (1930–31), and *18° Latitude Sud,* both of which he helped to edit; translations into

Rabéarivelo

English: *24 Poems*, by Gerald Moore and Ulli Beier, Ibadan, Nigeria, Mbari Press, 1962. All above editions published in Tananarive unless otherwise stated. (N.B. *Enfants d'Orphée*, termed poetry by many sources, is termed a critical essay and stated to have been published in Port-Louis, Ile Maurice, by Ed. Esclapon, 1931, by P. Valete in *J. J. Rabéarivelo*, Paris, F. Nathan, 1967.)

Diary: "Calepins Bleus," in manuscript, except for last pages published in *Mercure de France*, September 15, 1938, edited by Robert Boudry, under the title, "La mort tragique d'un poète."

Biographical/Critical Sources: Robert Boudry, *Jean-Joseph Rabéarivelo et la Mort*, preface by Jean Amrouche, Paris, Présence Africaine, 1958; A. Guibert, *Notre frère Rabéarivelo*, Algiers, Charlot, 1941. *J. J. Rabéarivelo*, in series "Littérature Malgache," Paris, F. Nathan, 1967; biographical sketch by Robert Boudry in *Vieilles chansons des pays d'Imerina*, for which see above; possibly the best essay in English is Ulli Beier's "Rabearivelo" in *Introduction to African Literature*, Evanston, Illinois, Northwestern University Press, 1967.

RABEMANANJARA, Jean-Jacques
b. June 23, 1913, Maroantsetra, Tamatave Province, Malagasy.
Poet, playwright, journalist, statesman, government official.

Rabemananjara was born into a Betsimisaraka family and educated locally through the lycée at the Grand Séminaire de Tananarive, a Jesuit College in Tananarive. His family was not able to get him into the university. While at school he helped found the student literary magazine, the *Revue des Jeunes* (The Review of Youth).

After "college," he entered the French colonial administration in 1939 and served in Paris at the Ministry of Colonies after a course at the Ministry. Caught in the French capital during the war he was able to study, surprisingly, for an arts degree which he achieved with high honors. With the defeat of Germany he returned home, and in 1946 was elected deputy to the Paris parliament representing his home district. He joined the Malagasy revolutionaries who rose in 1947 to oppose French colonialism. When the French broke the back of the revolt an estimated 2,000 people were killed and the poet was captured, tortured, and exiled. Originally sentenced to life imprisonment at hard labor and incarcerated at such prisons as Antanimore in Tananarive, Nosy-Lava, and Baumettes in Marseilles, he was later given less severe punishment in Paris, remaining there from 1956 to 1960. He then returned home to take a seat from Tamatave in the newly constituted national assembly of his independent country, having been elected in absentia.

The patriots whom he had joined in 1947 had previously organized the MDRM (Democratic Movement for Malagasy Revival), electing Rabemananjara its first secretary-general and the old patriot, Joseph Ravoahangy Andriana-Valona (b.1893) the president. The poet from the very beginning had fought for independence and was rewarded with cabinet posts: Minister of Economic Affairs in the early 1960's; from August, 1965, Minister for Agriculture, Land and Food; and, most recently, Minister of Foreign Affairs. Until the outbreak of violence and student strikes in 1972 which forced the army to take over the Government, Rabemananjara was Vice President for Cultural Affairs. It is believed he has been arrested and he has been stripped of his office. He is married and the father of three children.

During his earlier years in Paris, Rabemananjara came to know important French poets, as earlier he had come to know his countryman, Rabéarivelo, who had encouraged him. His work is rich, full of patriotism and the glory of the songs and scenery of his own land. It is not complex, but its lines swing with the grand style of the older French poets. Individual works often recall his days of torture and humiliation and his half decade of poverty-striken exile in

France. He began by writing verse influenced by the French romantics and the Parnassians, but later began using the *hainteny,* the popular ballad form so creatively manipulated by Rabéarivelo earlier. As he grew more confident, his poems of the middle 1950's reflected a more personal, grandoise, often even florid style.

His poetic volumes are: *L'éventail du rêves* (The Fan-tail of Dreams); *Aux confins de la nuit (At the Borders of the Night)* and *Sur les marches du soir* (On the Marches of the Night), *Rites millénaires* (Millenniel Rites); and *Antidote; poèmes.* *Présence Africaine* magazine published two of his poems, "Lamba," and "Antsa" in 1956, both written in prison. The magazine *Presence Africaine* issued a second edition of "Antsa" with an introduction by Aimé Césaire in 1961.

The following stanza, the next to last from his poem, "Pâques 48" (Easter, 1948), from the volume *Antidote,* is of particular beauty:

Un sanglot monte des entrailles de la terre.
La nuit entr'ouvre ses paupières
/sur le sein nu de la douleur.
Un morceau d'espace et de brise,
/serait-ce une âme qui palpite
dans la serre des barreaux?

A sob issues from the entrails of the earth
The night flutters its eye-lids
Over the bare breasts of sorrow.
A touch of space and of the breeze,
Would this be a soul which shudders in
/the grip of prison irons.
(trans. D. H.)

In this verse one can hear the poet and see him, looking out of his narrow cell window, searching for a hint of the silver moonlight, stirred by the momentary kiss of a soft breeze. His sigh moans out into the night from the grim building. But of course this is merely a concretization of a much more abstract universe of suffering.

Rabémananjara has published several plays: *Les dieux malgaches* (The Malagasy Gods) a five-act drama in verse, originally issued in 1942, and re-issued in 1945, and 1947; *Les boutriers de l'aurore* (The Boutriers from the East), three acts and six scenes, on the arrival of the original Malayan settlers from the east according to the old myths; and *Agapes des dieux ou Tritriva,* (The Feast of the Gods: or Tritriva), a prose tragedy in six scenes with a Malagasy theme, premiered in 1963 at the Théâtre Universitaire de Tananarive.

Writings: Poetry: *L'éventail du rêves*, Paris, 1939, 1942; *Aux confins de la nuit* and *Sur les marches du soir,* both Gap, France, Ed. Ophrys, 1940; *Rites millénaires;* Paris, Seghers, 1955, Présence Africaine, 1961; *Antidote; poèmes,* Paris, Présence Africaine, 1961.

Poems: "Lamba", "Antsa" in *Présence Africaine* magazine, 1956; second edition of "Antsa," introduction by Aimé Césaire , Paris, Présence Africaine, 1961.

Plays: *Les dieux malgaches,* Paris, Ed. Ophrys, 1942, 1947; Gap, 1945, 1947; Paris, Hachette, 1964; *Les boutriers de l'aurore,* Paris, Présence Africaine, 1957; *Agapes des dieux ou Tritriva,* Paris, Présence Africaine, 1962.

Critical and scholarly works of Rabémananjara's are: *Témoignage malgache et nationalisme* (Madagascan Testament and Colonialisme), a long essay, Paris, Présence Africaine, 1956; *Nationalisme et problèmes Malgaches,* Paris, Présence Africaine, 1958. Also, *Madagascar sous la rénovation malgache,* Paris, 1953; and a brief history of Madagascar published in Paris by Gentilly in 1952.

Biographical/Critical Sources: For details on his career and works and a few selections from his major works see *J. Rabémananjara* in the series, "Littérature Malgache" by the firm, Fernand Nathan, Paris, 1970. A much more extensive collection of his poetry and an analytical essay is in Eliane Boucquey de Schutter's *Jacques Rabémananjara,* which includes photos, portraits, facsimiles of holograph pages, and a 188-page bibliography, Paris, Seghers, 1964.

RABU, Wad Hasad
b. ca. 1920, Sudan.
Shukria (Butane-Arabic) oral poet.

Relatively untouched by new Western ways, Rabu herds his own cattle and sings the four-line *dobeit* around camp-fires of the nomadic Shukria people. Some of his Shukria poems, sung unaccompanied to a male audience of camel drivers in Butana in 1963, were taped and later rendered into more classical Arabic by Sheikh Akmed Khalid and then translated into English by Ali Sayed Lufti. Two of his "dobeit" appear in Anne Tibble's *African/English Literature.*
The more interesting verses are:
my love is a cream, Hisseiniya she-camel,
/a virgin whose neck's a silk garland;
She makes me sleepless as the thorn-eyed
/sugda-bird.
The longing to touch her gazelle-like,
/smooth body
Is a fire that will never go out in my heart.

My heart is the target of her best-of-all
/eye;
I will not keep my love secret
/though custom demand it.
Her beauty spills over, a full bowl of
/"durra," unequalled by any;

*Her large black eye needs no "kohl;" her
/cheek lights the dark.*

Writings: poems in Anne Tibble, *Afri-
can/English Literature*, London, Peter
Owen, 1965.

RADITLADI, Lettle Disang
b. July, 1910, Serowe, Botswana;
d. June, 1971.
Tswana playwright, poet.

Born in Serowe, the ancient capital of
the Bamangwato clan of the Tswana
nation, Raditladi first attended school at
the Tigerkloof Institute, and then at the
Lovedale School about 1926. By the
early 1930's he was a student at University College at Fort Hare but a severe
illness forced him to abandon his university career and turn to writing and other
work for a livelihood. Banished from
Botswana in 1939, along with his father
in a dispute with Chief Tshekedi Khama
(1905–1959), he found a job as a clerk
in the Bechuanaland Administration,
and soon became the tribal secretary of
Chieftainess Elizabeth Pulani Moremi of
the Batawana of Ngamiland, staying
until 1953. Permitted to return to the
Bamangwato tribal area in 1957, he
opened a small grinding mill for locally
grown grain and took the job of secretary
to the Bamangwato Tribal Council, a
subordinate African authority in the
Mahalye District, keeping that position
till the late 1960's.

In 1959 he helped found the Bechuanaland Protectorate Federal Party,
was elected to the Legislative Council of
Botswana in 1961, serving for several
years with a close colleague, Dr. Silas
Modiri Molema (1892–1965). In
December, 1969, Raditladi became ill

and underwent a period of intense care
until his death in 1971.

Raditladi published three plays: *Motŝwasele II*, chosen as Volume IX in the
Bantu Treasury Series and winner of the
May Esther Bedford Competition; *Dintŝhontsho tsa loratê* (Love Stories), published by Afrikaanse Pers-Boekhandel;
and his second historical drama, *Sekgoma
I*. His one volume of verse is *Sefalana
sa menate* (A Granary of Joy), issued by
Afrikaanse in 1960. Submitted many
years prior to their publication, both his
second play and the verse volume won
first prize in their respective genres in
the Afrikaanse Literary Competition of
1954.

Writings: Plays: *Motŝwasele II*, Johannesburg, Witwatersrand University
Press, 1945; reprint, Bantu Treasury,
Vol IX, 1961; *Dintŝhontsho tsa loratô*,
Johannesburg, Afrikaanse Pers-Boekhandel, 1956, 1962; *Sekgoma I*, Johannesburg, Bona Press, 1967.

Poetry: *Sefalana sa menate*, Johannesburg, Afrikaanse, 1961; Johannesburg,
Bona Press, 1964.

RAJEMISA-RAOLISON, Régis
b. May 8, 1913, East Antsirane
(Diégo-Suarez), Malagasy.
Poet, novelist (in Malgache),
journalist, scholar, statesman, teacher.

Régis Rajémisa-Roalison did his primary
studies at l'Ecole Officielle d'Ambinanin-
drano and then at the Frères Maristes
at Betafo and at Antsirabe (1921–1922),
and finally at the Frères des Ecoles Chrétiennes à Andohalo (1923–24). He continued his secondary schooling at the
Séminaire d'Ambohipo Tananarive
(1924–31).

He taught for 33 years, from 1932 to 1965, 25 of them at the Collège Saint-Michel. He was the founder of the *Revue des Jeunes de Madagascar, (Anivon'ny Riaka-L'île Australe)* and was editor-in-chief of *Feu Malagasy—La Voix Malgache.* In 1958, he became president of the Committee of Defense and the leading proponent of traditional culture in the island.

At one time he served as the chief assistant to the Minister of Health and Population in the independent Malagasy and was, from July 1959, a consultant to the Center of Studies and Information in the Language and Civilization of Malagasy. He is a member of the Malagasy Academy.

His one volume of verse, which appeared in 1948, is *Les fleurs de l'île rouge* [The Flowers of the Red Island], in French. His novels in the Malagache language are *Kilalaon' afo* [Sparks from a Thatched Roof] and *Mpitantana,* 1967.

His other works are a school manual of ethics, *MBA Olom-Banona* (1951); *Vokoka* (1948), a dictionary of Malagasy proverbs, translated into French; his *Grammaire de la langue malgache* (1959); and his *Dictionnaire historique et geographique de madagascar.*

Writings: Poetry: *Les fleurs de l'île rouge,* Tananarive, Les Presses de l'Imprimerie Tananarivienne, 1948.

Novels: *Kilalaon' afo,* Tananarive, Volamahitsy, 1948; *Mpitantana,* Tananarivo, Librairie Mixte, 1967. (J. Jahn shows both works to be the same.)

Grammatical and Linguistic Studies: *Dictionnaire historique et geographique de madagascar,* Fianarantsoa, Librairie Ambozontany, 1966; *Grammaire de la langue Malgache,* 1959; *Vakoka,* 1948, a dictionary of proverbs.

School manual: *MBA Olom-Banona,* 1951.

RAKOMA, Joseph Ramathea Debele
b. June 15, 1915, Damara, Tzaneen, South Africa.
Northern Sotho novelist, scholar, educator.

Rakoma's early schooling was at Mabeleke Lutheran School, Mamaklola Reserve and Botshebelo Training Institute (1936–1940). In the mid 1940's he passed the Matriculation Examination. His educational positions were: assistant teacher for six months at Botshabele Institute (1940); Motshabela Secondary School (1940–48); principal of the Matholo School, Pietersburg District (1949–1956), supervisor of Bantu schools, Pietersburg West Circuit (1956–present).

His first published book was a collection of common phrases and idioms in Sepedi (Northern Sotho) in *Marema-ka-dika: tsa Sesotho sa Transvaal* [Those Who Cut Figuratively: Sesotho of the Transvaal], published in 1949. His two novels are *Mathakgoleng ga bo Hlogokgolo* [Mathakgoleng of the Hlogokgolo Clan], and *Motlhotlhomi morwa Mapudi* [Motlhotlhomi, Son of Mapudi], published in 1968.

In 1952, Van Schaik published Rakoma's Sepedi language manual, *A o ka hlatha* [Do You Understand?].

Writings: Novels: *Mathakgoleng ga bo Hlogokgolo,* Pretoria, Van Schaik, 1955; *Motlhotlhomi morwa Mapudi,* Bloemfontein, Via Afrika, 1968.

Language Manuals: *Marema-ka-dika: tsa Sesotho sa Transvaal,* Pretoria, 1949; *A o ka hlatha,* Pretoria, Van Schaik, 1952.

RAMAILA, Epafras Mogagabise
b. January 30, 1897, Botshabelo Mission Station, near Middleburg, Transvaal, South Africa; d. August 28, 1962. Northern Sotho short story writer, novelist, poet, biographer, educator, scholar.

Epafras M. Ramaila, considered the father of Sepedi (or Northern Sotho) literature, received his first schooling at Botshabelo Mission Station and the Mission's Training School (1912–15), graduating as a teacher and evangelist. For the next five years he was an assistant teacher at the Lydenburg Mission School and then from 1920 to 1929 served as principal of the Saron Lutheran School, Phokeng, Rustenburg District. Later assignments were Botshabelo Training School as assistant teacher (1929–1933) where he also studied music and singing; principal of Lydenburg Mission School (1933–35); principal at Sabre Luther School and evangelist at Lutheran Congregational Church (1935–36); and teacher-preacher at Thabeng Community School (1936–1962). He was ordained February 27, 1944 at the Marshall Street Lutheran Church in Johannesburg.

Ramaila became an early popular contributor to *Abantu-Batho* (1917–1929), and for many years was editor of *Mogwara wa babaso,* the newspaper of the Berlin Mission. His first book was a biography of the Rev. Abraham Serote (1865–1930), published in 1935 in the Transvaal as *Tsa bophelo bya Moruti Abraham Serote.*

Even earlier he had privately published a pamphlet on Pedi history, *Ditaba tsa South Africa* (The Affairs of South Africa). A second historical publication was: *Setloxo sa batau* (The History of the Tau Clan), issued by the Literature Depot of the Berlin Mission. It was entitled *Setlogo sa batau* in a new edition in 1946.

Ramaila published several collections of short stories: *Molomatsebe* (The Story Teller), and *Taukobong* (Out of the Lion-Skin Cape), in 1953. His two volumes of poetry were: *Direto* (Praise Songs) in 1950 and *Seriti sa Thabantsho* (The Grass of Mount Thaba Nchu), which won first place in Afrikaanse's literary competition in 1960.

The only novel of Ramaila's was *Tsakata,* portraying the wandering adventures of a young man on the Rand.

When he died at Brakpan, Ramaila left his wife and a son, Henry Segome Habakkuk Ramaila (b. 1924), the author of a book of verse, *Peolane etela masakeng a diphoofola* (A Swallow Visits the Zoo). Epafras Ramaila also left several works in manuscript.

Writings: Stories: *Molomatsebe,* Pretoria, van Schaik, 1951; second edition, 1954, third edition, 1960; *Taukobong,* van Schaik, 1953, 1961.

Poetry: *Direto,* van Schaik, 1956; *Seriti sa Thabantsho,* Johannesburg, Afrikaanse Pers-Boekhandel, ca. 1960.

Novel: *Tsakata,* Cape Town, Juta, 1953, 1962.

Biography: *Tsa bophelo bya Moruti Abraham Serote (1865–1930),* Transvaal, Literature Commission of the Berlin Mission, 1935.

History: *Ditaba tsa South Africa;* privately printed, date unknown; *Setloxo sa batau,* Edendale, Literature Depot of the Berlin Mission, 1938; republished as *Setlogo sa batuau,* in new edition, 1946.

RAMANANATO
b. ca. 1780, Isevatera, near Ifiva,

in the realm of Isandra, Malagasy;
d. 1840(?).
Malagasy oral poet (Betsileo dialect).

Born of a family native to the Isandra
region, he is reputed to have been so
brilliant that he frightened his neighbors
and finally even the ruling prince, and
his parents were instructed to leave the
area or suffer the consequences.
Another tradition has it that the poet's
mother was of such a loose disposition
that she and her second husband were
asked to depart. What seems evident
from the poetry which has come down
through the oral tradition is that
Ramanato hated his mother with a very
Hamlet-like mixture of contempt, anger,
and thwarted love. Whatever the actual
state of affairs in the poet's family, he
grew up in the north of the island in
the territory of Prince Ianakalaza of
Manandriana, in or near the present
town of Nandihizana.

Ramananato's brilliance continued
but his new prince was not in awe of
his verbal powers and asked the poet to
serve as his councillor in certain matters,
and eventually as his chief councillor.
The latter post was refused by the poet
who had constant difficulties with the
courtiers and preferred the quiet and
honesty of his cattle herd to his rivals
around the prince. Extremely conscious
of personal slights, he was keenly aware
of general social injustices and made
arrogance and social cruelty the theme
of many of his works. Working in what
might be termed the troubadour or
bardic tradition, Ramananato accompanied himself on the *romy*, a type of
bowl-shaped drum played on with the
fingers or hand only, and often improvised poems to celebrate a special event
or to praise a generous act or brave deed.
It is said he composed his more serious

works by tapping out rhythmical ideas
on his *romy* as he worked out his favorite
kind of poem, the *dombolana,* at that time
a chanted, solemn ode-like form. Some
12 poems and some fragments are extant
of his works, published in scholarly
Malagasy and French texts.

Writings: Poetry: 12 poems and fragments in scholarly publications; extracts
and French translations of all of his
work, with detailed discussion of his life,
in "Recherches sur la littérature
traditionnelles malgache" by Lucien X.
Michel Andrianarahinjaka, Paris, *Présence Africaine,* third trimester, 1965.

RAMATHE, A. C. J.
b. February 20, 1907, Palmyra Location,
Ladybrand District, Orange Free State,
South Africa; d. December 21, 1958.
Southern Sotho novelist, teacher,
educator.

A member of the Taung clan of the
Sotho-speaking people, A.C.J. Ramathe
did his early schooling at Boshof and
later studied at Edenville United School,
where he took the Standard VI in 1922.
Stofberg Memorial School awarded him
the Teacher's Certificate in 1925 and
Adams' College the Junior Certificate in
1927. Beginning in 1929, he taught at
various schools in the Orange Free State,
Botswana and as far north as Zambia
(then Northern Rhodesia). He passed
the matriculation examination in 1931
at Fort Hare University and took the
B.A. in 1953 through private study at
Fort Hare.

Ramathe was named supervisor of
Bantu Schools in 1953 and sub-inspector
of Bantu education for the Bloemfontein North Circuit in 1955, holding that
position till his death in 1958.

A late starter as a writer, Ramathe's one published work, *Tšepo*, (Hope) won first prize in the Afrikaanse Pers-Boekhandel Literary competition for novels in 1956, and was published the next year.

Writings: Novels: *Tšepo* (or *Tshepo*), Johannesburg, Afrikaanse Pers-Boekhandel, 1957; 102 pages; new edition, King William's Town, Johannesburg, Umtata, no date, 127 pages.

RAMMALA, Joseph Lesibe
b. 1915, Mamabolo Location, near Pietersburg, South Africa.
Northern Sotho translator.

Rammala obtained his teacher's certificate at the Grace Dieu Training School in Warmbad. He obtained his B.A. degree from the University of South Africa in 1944, and for the next sixteen years taught at various schools. He is today a free-lance writer and a member of the North-South Language Committee.

He translated *Pilgrim's Progress* (I) into Northern Sotho with the title *Leeto la Mokriste*.

Writings: Translation: *Leeto la Mokriste* (John Bunyan's *Pilgrim's Progress*, I), Pretoria, Unie-Boekhandel, 1966.

RAMOKGOPA, Herbert Daniel
b. ca. 1920, Northern Sotho language area, South Africa.
Northern Sotho story writer, educator, journalist.

Ramokgopa entered Lemana Training School where he obtained his teacher's certificate. He taught at the Salvation Army School in Orlando, then at Orlando High School which is now Nakene High School. In 1954 he was appointed secretary of the Orlando School Board, a position he held until 1960 when he was made the editor of the Northern Sotho edition of *Tswelopele* (Progress), the Government's publication. He now lives in Johannesburg.

At Lemana Training School, Ramokgopa assisted H. J. van Zeyl in compiling *Thika-polelo*, a collection of folk stories. He has contributed stories to *Bona* magazine and has published the volume *Ditaba tša dipoko-le tše dingwe* (Ghost Stories and others), 1962.

Writings: Stories: *Thika-polelo*, with H. J. van Zeyl, details not known; *Ditaba tša dipoko-le tše dingwe*, Johannesburg, Afrikaanse Pers-Boekhandel, 1962; stories in *Bona* magazine, Johannesburg, Bona-Afrikaanse.

RANAIVO, Jacques Flavien
b. May 13, 1914, Arivonimamo,
the Imerina District, Malagasy.
Poet, playwright, essayist, historian,
(in French and Malgache) film-maker,
teacher, journalist, government official.

Ranaivo was the sixth son of the governor of Arivonimamo, a member of a noble family. His father was a musician and writer and the poet grew up in substantial prosperity and received better than ordinary schooling, though he lost his father while in his third year. A bright child, he learned to read western musical notation before he learned French which he began only in his fourteenth year. Since childhood, his poetic temperament has led him to take long, solitary walks about the capital, Ananariva. He did his university work at the prestigious French military school, Saint-Cyr, and then returned home to become a professor of English and mathematics at a private college in Tananarive and to an early marriage.

From 1950 to 1952 Ranaivo served as the first Madagascan minister in the French cabinet. He was called home to serve as chief of the press section of the Malagasy Information Service from 1952 to 55, an indication of his growing stature. He then served as director of the National Tourist Office in the early 1960's and is presently director of information. During the past years he has also been the director of the weekly newspaper, *Vaovao Frantsay-Malagasy*, which is published in Malagasy, served as the director of the daily, *Information de Madagascar*, and worked as editor-in-chief of the *Revue de Madagascar*. He

managed to do one year of study in the social sciences at the University of Paris (1955–56), was head of Madagascan student affairs for the French Government (1956–59), and for several years served as a member of the French National Commission for UNESCO.

Senghor's inclusion of selections of Ranaivo's poetry in his important collection, *Anthologie de la nouvelle poésie nègre et malgache* insured a wide audience for his work. His volumes of verse are *L'ombre et le vent* (Shadow and Wind), with a preface by O. Mannoni; *Mes chansons de toujours* (My Songs of Always), preface by Senghor, which won the Grand Prize for Literature of Madagascar for that year; and *Le retour au bercail* (Return to the Fold) which also won the island's Grand Prize. These three collections have appeared in Kraus Reprint Series in one volume in 1970.

Ranaivo's poetry, although conceived and published in French, is lyrical and very sensitive, rooted in his country's folklore and full of Madagascan symbols and proverbs. He uses the popular *hainteny*, the ballad form, as do most other poets from Madagascar. Use of such love songs and nativist elements makes his poetry much more "regional" or Madagascan than, for instance the poetry of Rabéarivelo.

Two of his poems, "Song of a Young Girl," and "Song of a Common Lover," appear in Moore and Beier's *Modern Poetry from Africa*. The latter poem ends:

Love me like a beautiful dream,
your life in the night,
my hope in the day;
like a piece of money,
ever with me on earth,
and for the great journey
a faithful comrade;
like a calabash,
intact, for drawing water;

in pieces, bridges for my guitar.
(trans. G. Moore and U. Beier)
Raniavo has also published works in anthropology, linguistics, and history. Important prose works have been: "La jalousie ne paie pas: contes malgaches" (Jealousy Doesn't Pay: Malagache Stories), published in the *Revue de Madagascar,* fourth quarter, 1952; "Les Hain-Teny" (The Hain-Teny [local verse form]) which appeared in the *Revue de Madagascar,* fourth quarter, 1949, republished in "Madagascan Literature" by *Présence Africaine,* 1956; and "Le grande dictionnaire de madagascar" (The Great Dictionary of Madagascar) scheduled for the early 1970's, written with Jean Valette. His historical essay, "Un testament de Rasoherina" (A Testament of Rasoherina) appeared in the April, 1950 issue of the *Bulletin de Madagascar.*

At the present time, Ranaivo, besides his editorial work, is engaged in film making and he has won the Diplôme d'Honneur of the ninth Festival of Tour Films (1967).

Writings: Poetry: *L'ombre et le vent,* Tananarive, Les Presses de l'Imprimerie Officielle à Tananarive, 1947, 1967; *Mes chansons de toujours,* Paris, 1955; *Le retour au bercail,* Tananarive, Impr. Nationale, 1962; these three collections in one volume, Kraus Reprint Series, Nendeln, Liechtenstein, 1970.
Poems: in *Anthologie de la nouvelle poésie nègre et malgache,* Paris, 1948; "Song of a Young Girl" and "Song of a Common Lover," in *Modern Poetry from Africa,* Moore and Beier, editors, revised edition, Baltimore, Penguin, 1968.
Linguistics, criticism: "La jalousie ne paie pas: contes malgaches" in *Revue de Madagascar,* fourth quarter, 1952; "Les Hain-Teny" in *Revue de Madagascar,*

fourth quarter, 1949; republished in "Madagascan Literature," *Présence Africaine,* 1956; "Le grande dictionnaire de madagascar," with Jean Valette, awaiting publication.
History: "Un testament de Rasoherina" in *Bulletin de Madagascar,* April, 1950.

Biographical/Critical Source: Flavien Ranaivo, a biography in the series "Littérature malgache," Paris, Fernand Nathan, 1968.

RANDRIANARISOA, Pierre
b. ca. 1920, Betsileo, Malagasy.
Poet, novelist, playwright, in French and Malagasy film-scenario writer, diplomat, scholar.

Locally educated through high school, he took the French *agregé* (doctorate) in history at the University of Montpellier. At the present time he is on the Faculty of Law and Economics at that institution.

Randrianarisoa has published three volumes of poetry: *Premiers visages* (First Appearances), *Terre rouge* (Red Earth), and *Vetson my Lavi-Kavana,* published in the Malagasy language in the 1960's.

His novels and scenarios are *Abus de méfiance* (Abuse of Mistrust); *Les nègres blancs* (White Negroes); *Rien ne va plus* (Nothing's Worth Anything Anymore); and *Notes et réflexion d'un étudiant* (Notes and Reflections of a Student). He also published in Paris in 1964, *L'évolution de la poésie africaine et malgache* (The Evolution of African and Malgache Poetry).

His other works are *Rapport de stage sur les services consulaires et diplomatique français* (Report on Training in the Consular and Diplomatic Services of France); *Les institutions et l'économie de Madagascar dans la deuxième partie de XIXe siècle* (The Madagascan Institutions and Economy in the Second Half of the 19th Century); *La diplomatie malgache (Madagascan Diplomacy);* his 1966 doctoral dissertation for the University of Rennes in France; and *Madagascar et les croyances et coutumes malgaches* (Madagascar and the Malagasy Beliefs and Customs), published in 1967.

Writings: Poetry: *Premiers Visages,* Vire, Calvados, France, Ed. Le Cornec, 1961; *Terre rouge,* date unknown; *Vetson my Lavi-Kavana,* in Malagasy 196?.

Novels, scenarios: *Abus de méfiance; Les nègres blancs; Rien ne va plus; Notes et reflexion d'un étudiant,* dates unknown.

Literary history: *L'évolution de la poésie africaine et malgache,* Paris, 1964.

Scholarship: *Rapport de stage sur les services consulaires et diplomatique français,* Paris, 1963; *Les institutions et l'économie de madagascar dans la deuxième partie de XIXe siècle,* Rennes, 1965; *La diplomatie malgache,* Rennes, 1966; *Madagascar et les croyances et coutumes malgaches,* Caen, Imprimerie Caron, 1967.

RANSOME-KUTI, Rev. Canon Josiah Jesse
b. June 1, 1855, Igbein, Nigeria;
d. September 4, 1930.
Yoruba poet, collector of folk songs.

Born of a royal Yoruba family, Ransome-kuti graduated from the Christian Mission Society Training Institute in Lagos in 1875. He became a teacher-catechist, an accomplished musician, a fine singer, and was known for his inclusion of African instruments in church services. *The Singing Minister of Nigeria* by Issac O. Delano, 1942, celebrates his success at bringing Africans into the Christian faith through his use

of folk songs and original African church music. His poetry which is strongly akin to Yoruba traditional verse is one of the earliest efforts by an African to set his peoples' own art into English.

Biographical/Critical Source: Isaac O. Delano, *The Singing Minister of Nigeria,* London, United Society for Christian Literature, 1942.

RAOLISON, Régis Rajemisa
(see RAJEMISA-RAOLISON, Régis)

REINDORF, Reverend Carl Christian
b. May 31, 1834, Prampram, Gold Coast, now Ghana; d. July 1, 1917.
Historian, educator, collector of traditional tales.

Reindorf graduated from a high school for the training of catechists (African lay priests) in missionary work in 1855. He became in time Full Minister of the Church of the Evangelical Mission Society and served as pastor of the Basel Mission, Christianborg, Gold Coast, from 1872 to 1910. He helped in revising the translation of the Bible in Ga, the language native to his area. He is best remembered for his *The History of the Gold Coast and Asante,* first published in 1889. The work is based on the traditional stories and legends of the Asante people handed down from 1500 to 1860. It contains detailed maps, accurate for the time, charts, useful appendices, and valuable genealogies of the royal lines of the Asante.

The product of over 30 years of collecting material, the history is the first Ghanaian one in the European manner. An excerpt entitled, "Events of the years, 1782–4," appears in *A Selection of African*

Prose. Proud of his mixed Danish and Ga descent, Reindorf often extolled Ga virtues, going so far as to compare his peoples' social and religious institutions to the ancient Hebrews', thereby implying that the Ga had a lead on neighboring peoples in the progress towards "civilization."

His son, Dr. Charles Elias Reindorf (b. 1877), became an important scholar in the Gold Coast in his turn.

Writings: History: *The History of the Gold Coast and Asante,* first edition, London, 1889; second edition edited by his son, Dr. Charles Reindorf, contains a biography of the author, Basel, 1895, reprinted 1951, and in 1966 by Ghana University Press, Accra; excerpt in *A Selection of African Prose: 2. Written Prose,* Oxford, Clarendon Press, 1964.

Biographical/Critical Sources: second edition of *The History of the Gold Coast and Asante,* cited above; Robert W. July, *The Origins of Modern African Thought,* New York, Praeger, 1967.

RIBAS, Oscar Bento

b. 1909, Luanda, Angola; d. 1961.
Novelist, story writer, playwright, poet, anthologist, ethnologist.

Born of mixed European and African parentage, Ribas attended local schools, including the College Salvador Correia where he was a brilliant student. At the age of 21 his eyesight began to fail and he gradually became totally blind. Despite this handicap, he became a noted student of the Kimbundu- (or Quinbundo) speaking people of the Luanda area. His scholarly and creative works, produced with the aid of friends and a secretary, won him the reputation of being the major intellectual and artist of Portuguese Africa. He visited Portugal twice: in 1923–24, and again in 1962. He served as an official in the local government of Angola.

Ribas' work deals mainly with the Kimbundu people. Some 18 years of research went into his study of their religion and culture, *Ilundo: divindades e ritos angolanos* (Ilundo: Angolan Divinations and Rites), which won its author the Prémio de Etnografia awarded by the Instituto de Angola in 1958.

His two earlist volumes of original stories were *Sunguilando* (Long Evening Chats), 1941, and revised in 1967, and *Flôres e espinhos* (Blossoms and Thorns), published in 1948. Ribas' first novel, *Uanga,* completed before 1934, but not published until 1951, exploits Angolan folklore. Corrected and amplified, and entitled *Uaanga—Feitico: Romance* (Uaanga—Witchcraft: A Romance), in 1969, the work carries a foreward in which the author repudiates the apparently unauthorized 1967 republication of his story collection, *Sunguilando,* because of unauthorized spelling, punctuation and other changes he did not nor could not accept. Kraus Reprint brought out in 1970 an edition of *Uaanga* in 1970 and a new reprint edition of *Flôres e espinhos.* An obscure work on which publishing data is lacking, is the historical romance, *Rainha Jinga* (Queen Jinga).

Ribas's first published work, *Nuvens que passam* (Passing Clouds), a long folk tale or novella, appeared in 1927. Two years later he published *O resgate de uma falta* (Expiation of an Error). His later stories were collected in the 187-page *Ecos da minha terra. Dramas angolanos. Contos* (Echoes of My Land, Angolan Dramas: Stories), 1952. One of the stories in that volume, "A Praga," (In

Prague), won the Margaret Wrong Medal and Prize in 1952. Another story, *"A Medalha,"* appears in *A Selection of African Prose,* as "The Medaillon," and the story, "A quianda," was published in the review, *Imbondeiro Gigante,* Volume I, 1963. Ribas has also helped edit the anthology, *Christ Ercheint Am Kongo* (Christ Shines Out in the Congo), a German translation of songs and chants composed in Portuguese, 1958.

His linguistic work, *Missossa: Literatura tradicional angolana* (Missossa: Traditional Angolan Literature), 1961–64, offers Portuguese versions of Angolan folktales and contains a detailed dictionary of regional terms and vernacular expressions. It includes 26 tales *(missossa)* and 500 proverbs *(jissabu),* along with recipes, challenges, songs, puzzles, prayers, cries, and children's games.

Writings: Novels and novelettes: *Uanga,* Luanda, Lello, 1951; revised, *Uaanga— Feitico: Romance,* Luanda, Tip. Angolana, 1969; reprint, Nendeln, Liechtenstein, Kraus Reprint, 1970; *Rainha Jinga,* no data; *Nuvens que passam,* Luanda, 1927; *O resgate de uma falta,* Luanda, no date shown but believed to be 1929; *Sunguilando,* Lisbon, 1941, republished as *Sunguilando. Contos tradicionais angolanos,* Lisbon, Agência-Geral do Ultramar, 1967; *Flôres e espinhos,* Luanda, 1948; Nendeln, Liechtenstein, Kraus Reprint, 1970; *Ecos da minha terra,* Luanda, Lello, 1952. Stories: "A Medalha," in *Contos d'Africa,* Sà da Bandeira, Luanda, 1961; and in W. H. Whiteley's *A Selection of African Prose,* Oxford, Oxford University Press, 1964; "A Quianda," in *Imbondeiro Gigante,* Volume I, 1963.

Linguistics and Folklore: *Ilundo: divindades e ritos angolanos,* Luanda, Museu de Angola, 1958; *Missossa: Literatura tradicional angolana,* Luanda, Tipografia Angolana, Volume I, 1961, Volume II, 1962, Volume III, 1964.

Anthology: *Christ Erscheint am Kongo. Afrikanische Erzählungen und gedichte,* Peter Sulzer, Heilbronn, Salzer, 1958 (contributor and co-editor).

RIVE, Richard (pseudonym Richard Moore)
b. 1931, District VI; Cape Town, South Africa.
Novelist, short story writer, poet, teacher.

Rive attended local schools and then went on to the University of Cape Town, taking an B.A. His father was an Afro-American from the United States and his mother a "colored" South African. He began writing as a student and his work quickly began to appear in South African journals and then in European and American magazines. He won the Farfield Foundation Fellowship in 1964. During the 1960's he taught English and Latin in a high school in Cape Town and thanks to the Farfield Fellowship he was able to tour Africa and Europe to study contemporary literature.

African Songs (1963) was his first collection of short stories, followed by his first novel, *Emergency.*

The anthology, *Quartet,* edited by Rive, offers stories by Rive, Alex La Guma, James Matthews and Alf Wannenburgh. The stories are divided by theme: Without Justice, The Dispossessed, The Possessed, and The Outsider.

Rive has also edited *Modern African Prose,* an anthology of short stories or excepts from novels by 19 African authors.

Other stories have appeared in *Transition* (Uganda) and one poem appears in

Langston Hughes' *Poems from Black Africa*. He is also represented by the story, "Rain," in Neville Denny's *Pan African Short Stories*.

Emergency, Rive's one novel, takes the events leading to the Sharpeville massacre of March 28, and then focuses on the following three days in the life of his protagonist Andrew Dreyer which end in the proclamation of a state of emergency throughout South Africa. The culminating moment of the novel is the riot on March 30 with the burning of an armed personnel carrier and the freeing of the wounded hero from the police by an African crowd no longer able to contain its fury.

Rive's work, though impassioned and full of the rancors and hostilities of exacerbated relations between Black, White, and Colored, still maintains a humorous balance to celebrate victories over physical weaknesses.

Writings: Novel: *Emergency,* London, Faber and Faber, 1964; paperback, by Collier-Macmillan, 1970.

Stories: *African Songs,* Berlin, Seven Seas, 1963; Various works in *Transition,* Uganda; "Rain" in *Pan African Short Stories,* Neville Denny, editor, London, Nelson, 1965; *Quartet,* London, Oxford University Press, Crown, 1963; Heinemann, 1965.

Poetry: in *Poems from Black Africa,* Langston Hughes, editor, Bloomington, Indiana, Indiana University Press, 1963.

Editorial work: *Modern African Prose,* London, Heinemann, 1964; 1965, 1967.

ROBERT, Shaaban
b. January 1909, near Tanga, Tanzania;

Robert

d. June 20, 1962, Dar es Salaam.
Swahili poet, novelist, essayist,
biographer.

Robert is considered the most distinguished of all the East African writers.
He was honored with the K.B.E. (Knight
of the British Empire) and he won the
Margaret Wrong Medal and Prize.
Educated in Dar es Salaam, Shaaban
Robert spent all of his life on or near
the coast, much of it in British governmental service. He introduced the essay
(insha) into Swahili literature. He served
as chairman of the Swahili Committee
in Dar es Salaam.

Robert's first works were *Pambo la
lugha* (The Embellishment of Language)
and his "self-portrait" *Maisha yangu . . .*
(My Life . . .). Considered possibly his
finest work is *Kusadikika, nchi iliyo angani*
(Faith for the Country of the Sun), a
Swiftean satire on contemporary events
as seen by a Tanzanian. The year 1952
saw two of his works being published,
his translation into Swahili of Omar
Khayyam's *Rubaiyat,* entitled *Khayyam
kwa Kiswahili,* a novelty in Swahili literature, and the novelette, *Adili na nduguze*
(Adili and His Brothers).

Others of his varied writings are:
Kielezo cha insha (Essays); *Masomo yenye
adili* (Readings in Behavior); *Almasi za
Africa* (African Diamonds), poems; *Insha
na mashairi* (Essays and Poems); *Marudi
mema* (Good Advice), poems; and the
biography, *Wasifu wa Siti Binti Saad* (The
Narrative of the Life of Siti Binti Saad).
W. H. Whiteley has translated the story,
"Difficulties of life in the city and how
they were overcome," which appears in
A Selection of African Prose, Volume II.
1964.

Left in manuscript after his death in
1962 was a long epic, *Utenzi wa Vita vya
uhuru* (The War for Freedom). It is still
unpublished although Witwatersrand
University announced plans some time
ago to bring it out.

A fervent Moslem and an African patriot, Robert's work protests subjugation
to European colonialism, and though
moralistic, his writing reveals a deep and
gifted mind and passionate soul.

In regretting his death, the *East African Committee Journal* commented in
1962:

> *Sheikh Shaaban was the undisputed
> Poet Laureate of the Swahili language,
> and a pioneer in the development of this
> language. He opened up new ways of
> expression, new modes of thought. He will
> for ever be known as a turning point in
> the evolution of the Swahili language. His
> work will remain a link between the Classi-
> cal literature of the past and the modern
> Swahili of the future.*

The same journal also published
Robert's last public address, given in
Kampala, Uganda, in November 1961,
and announced the plan to publish a
Memorial Volume in his honor which
would include his last completed work,
Siku ya Watenzi Wote (The Day of Every
Worker). Seven years later it did see
print.

Writings: Novels: *Kusadikika, nchi iliyo
angani,* London, Nelson, 1951, 1960,
1964; *Siku ya watenzi wote,* 1968.

Novelettes: *Adili na nduguze,* London,
Macmillan, 1952; *Utoboro mkulima*
(Utoboro, the Farmer), 1968; the vol-
ume includes the work, genre unknown,
Siku ya Watenzi Wote (The Day of Every
Worker).

Poetry: *Pambo la lugha,* Johannesburg,
Witwatersrand University, 1948, as
Volume XI of the Bantu Treasury
Series; reprint 1960, Lusaka, Addis

Ababa, Oxford University Press, 1966, 1968; *Marudi mema* (Good Advice), London, Macmillan, 1952; *Almasi za Africa*, Tanga, Art and Literature, 1960; *Ashiki kitabu hiki* (Love this Book), 1968; *Masomo yenye adili* (The Lesson of Justice), 1967, 1968; *Koja la lugha* (The Base of the Language, Nairobi, Lusaka, Addis Ababa, Oxford University Press, 1969; *Utenzi wa Vita vya uhuru*, epic scheduled for publication by Witwatersrand University; *Mashairi ya Shaaban Robert*, 1968; translation into English by Robert and Gerald Moore of Robert's poem, "Our Frame," in Anne Tibble's *African/English Literature*, London, Peter Owen, 1965.

Essays: *Pambo la lugha*, Johannesburg, Witwatersrand University, 1947, 1960; *Kielezo cha fasili* (Models for the Children), Johannesburg, Witwatersrand University Press, 1954, 1961, 1968; *Insha na mashairi*, Dar es Salaam, The Eagle Press, 1960, and Tanga, Art and Literature, 1959, 1961, 1967; *Masomo yenye adili*, Tanga, 1959.

Translations: *Khayyam kwa Kiswahili* (Omar Khayyam), into Swahili, 1952.

Biography: *Wasifu wa Siti Binti Saad, mwimbaji wa Ugoja*, Tanga, Art and Literature, 1955, 1960, 1967, 1969; somewhat different version as *Maisha ya Siti binti Saad, mwimbaji wa Unguja*, Arusha, Tanganyika, 1958, as published in *Supplement to the East African Swahili Committee Journal*, 28/1, January, 1958.

Autobiography: *Maisha yangu na Baada ya miaka hamsini*, London, Nelson, 1949, 1962, 1964 (in mixed poetry and prose).

Stories: *Adili na nduguze* (Adili and His Brothers), London, Macmillian, 1952, 1961; "Difficulties of life in the city and how they were overcome," translation into English by W. H. Whiteley, *A Selec-*tion of African Prose, No. 2, Oxford, Oxford University Press, 1964.

Being prepared for the press: Complete edition of Roberts' works.

ROBINARY, Michel François
b. ca. 1896, Tananarive, Malagasy.
Novelist, poet, in French and Malagasy.

Educated in local schools, Robinary absorbed the French culture and his work, though nostalgic for the precolonial world, is French in diction and style with little influence evident from his own peoples' traditions. He was a member of the National Association of Writers of the Sea and Overseas (L'Association Nationale des Ecrivains de la Mer et de L'outre Mer).

His novels are: *Sous le signe de Razaizay* (Under the Sign of Razaizay), published in 1957 and winner of the Grand Prix Littéraire de Madagascar, given in Paris in 1967, and the 316-page work, *Au seuil de la terre promise* (At the Threshold of the Promised Land, 1965.) (Jahnheinz Jahn in his *Bibliography of Creative African Writing* terms this work a collection of poetry.)

Other works were: a collection of poems, *Les fleurs défuntes* (Dead Flowers), 1927, 1958; historical essays, *Deux villes saintes (Tananarive et Ambouimangue)* (Two Holy Cities: Tananarive and Ambouimangue); *La raçon de la vie*, essays and memoires; and *Initiation philosophique* (Philosophical Initiation), written in the Malagasy language and serialized from August 10, 1951 to January, 1952, in the Malagasy journal, *Vaovao-Frantsay-Malagasy*.

Writings: Novels: *Sous le signe de Razaizay*,

369

Robinary

1957; *Au seuil de la terre promise,* Tananarive, Voahirana, 1965.
Poetry: *Les fleurs défuntes,* Tananarive, Impr. Pitot, 1927, 1958.

Scholarly Essays: *La raçon de la vie; Deux villes saintes; Initiation philosophique,* in *Vaovao-Frantsay- Malagasy,* August 10, 1951–January, 1952.

RODOLPH, Utto (see OUOLOGUEM, Yambo)

ROMANO, Luís Madeiro de Melo
b. ca. 1935, Santo Antão,
Cape Verde Islands.
Novelist, poet, folk-lorist, engineer.

Trained as an engineer, Luís Romano went into exile in Brazil and there wrote and published in 1962 a 337-page proletarian novel *Famintos. Romance de um povo* [The Famished, The Tale of a people], and a long collection of poems (307 pages), *Clima* [Climate], in 1963. His scholarly work, listed below, deals with the Portuguese-influenced literature and culture of the Cape Verdes. He published in 1967 one collection of stories and poems based on folk-lore: *Renascença de uma civilização no Atlântico médio,* [Renaissance of a Civilization in the Middle of the Atlantic].

Writings: Novel: *Famintos. Romance de um povo.* Rio de Janeiro, Editôra Leitura, 1962, with prefaces by Luís da Câmara Cascudo and Edgar Barbosa.
Poems and Stories: *Renascença de uma civilização no Atlântico médio.* Lisbon, Ocidente, 1967. *Clima.* Recife, Brazil, 1963.
Critical Essay: *Evocação de Portugal e presença do Brasil na literatura cabover-deana* [Evocations of Portugal and the Brazilian Presence in Cabo-Verdean Literature]. Mossoró, Brazil, Prefeitura Municipal, 1966.

ROTIMI, Olawale
b. ca. 1940, Yoruba-land, Western Nigeria.
Playwright, play director, teacher, scholar.

Ola Rotimi is one of the most vigorous of the new Nigerian playwrights, for he employs Yoruba motifs and the oral tradition possibly better than any of the older generation of Yoruba dramatists in his country. His B.A. is from Boston University and he did graduate work at Yale's School of Drama in New Haven, Connecticut. Active as a director, Rotimi has produced Aimé Césaire's *La Tragedie d'Henri Chrostophe,* the one-act play, *Gbe-*

370

Ku-de, by the young Yoruba dramatist, Adegoke Durojaiye, and his own very avante-garde "sketches": *The Prodigal* and *Holding Talks.* Durojaiye's play as performed by Rotimi's Olukun Players won the Oxford University Press play prize in 1969.

Rotimi's first play, *To Stir the God of Iron,* is set in a Nigerian village during a time of war. It was performed by the Boston University Drama School, May, 1963. *Kurunmi,* considered one of his best works, and *The Prodigal,* saw performance at the second Ife Festival of the Arts, Ile-Ife, 1969.

The Gods Are Not to Blame was premiered at the Ori Olukan Theatre, December, 1968, and has seen partial publication in *African Arts,* 1970, and in complete form by Oxford University Press in 1971. The blank verse is broken and imagic. This passage shows the power and verve of his lines:

When Ogun the god of Iron
Was returning from Ire
His loin cloth was
A hoop of
Fire.
Blood . . . the deep red stain
Of victim's blood
His cloak.

An early play, *Our Husband is Gone Mad Again,* premiered at Yale in 1966 under the direction of the late Jack Landau, and *Ovonramwen Nogbaisi,* first performed at the fourth Ife Festival of the Arts in 1971, complete the list of his dramatic works. In the latter play, Rotimi seeks to correct the distorted image of the maligned Oba (chief or king) Ovonramwen who was blamed for the crushing defeat by the British invading troops who destroyed the Benin Empire in 1897.

Writings: Plays: *To Stir the God of Iron,*

performed Boston University Drama School, May, 1963; *Our Husband is Gone Mad Again,* performed Yale Drama School, 1966; *The Gods Are Not to Blame,* premiered at Ori Olokun Cultural Centre, an arm of the Institute of African Studies, University of Ife, December, 1968; to be published by Oxford University Press, Nigeria, in 1973; the "sketches": *Kurunmi* and *The Prodigal,* performed at second Ife Festival of the Arts, Ile-Ife, 1969; *Ovonramwen Nogbaisi,* produced in 1971 at fourth Ife Festival, to be published by Oxford, Nigeria in 1972, in collaboration with Ethiope Publishing. Only *The Gods Are Not to Blame* has been published: first in part in *African Arts,* III, 2, Los Angeles, Winter, 1970, then in complete text, London and New York, Oxford University Press, 1971.

Critical article: "Traditional Nigerian Drama," in *Introduction to Nigerian Literature,* cited below.

Biographical/Critical Sources: Samuel Omo Asein, "Ola Rotimi and the New Dramatic Movement at Ife, " *Bulletin of Black Theatre,* I, 2, Winter, 1972, American Theatre Association, Washington, D. C.; J. A. Adedeji, "Oral Tradition and the Contemporary Theatre in Nigeria," *Research in African Literatures,* II, 2, Austin, Texas; "Traditional Nigerian Drama," by Ola Rotimi, in *Introduction to Nigerian Literature,* Bruce King, editor, New York, Africana Publishing Corporation, 1972.

RUBADIRI, James David
b. July 19, 1930, Tanganyika (of Malawi parents), modern Tanzania.
Novelist, poet, anthologist, teacher, diplomat.

Rubadiri grew up in old Nyasaland, now Malawi, though he was born on the Tanzanian side of Lake Victoria during a brief visit by by his parents. He studied in Nyasaland until he entered Makerere University in Kampala, Uganda (King's College, Budo). Arrested in 1959, and imprisoned in Southern Rhodesia during the political emergency, he was able to get to England to study at Kings College, Cambridge where he successfully took the *tripos* (triple major examination) for the British B.A., worked for BBC for a period, and began creative writing.

He served for a few years as lecturer at Makerere University in English, as principal of Soche Hill College in Limbe, Malawi, and is presently teaching English at Makerere. In 1963 he was named his country's first ambassador to the United States and to the United Nations, remaining in these posts until 1965. He is married and has six children.

He was elected president of the Association for Commonwealth Literature and Language Studies for a three-year term during the Jamaica meeting, January 4–8, 1971. His home university, Makerere, will host the Association's 1974 meeting.

With David Cook, Rubadiri has collected and edited *Poems from East Africa,* 1971. Fifty poets, most of them young or relatively unknown, have work in this volume. Of those who have become frequently published are Taban Lo Liyong, Joseph S. Mbiti, Okello Oculi, Okot p'Bitek and Rubadiri himself.

Rubadiri's 1967 novel, *No Bride Price,* concerns the tensions experienced by Lombe, the protagonist, in his job in a corrupt government bureau and as the lover of the village belle, Miria. A coup finally topples the government and Miria, once despised by Lombe as too countrified, dies giving birth to her child by Lombe, alone in prison. The shattered hero must start life over with less scorn for the old values represented by the lost lover. His life is symbolic of the mixed-up values of modern Africa, and the author seems to be saying that more realistic and humane expectations about the future might provide a better world.

His poetry is deeply concerned with being an African in a world just emerging from foreign domination. His poem, "The Tide that from the West Washes Africa To the Bone," ends with these bitter lines:

The tide that from the west
Washes the soul of Africa
And tears the mooring of its spirit,
Till bloodred the tide becomes

And heartsick the womb—
The tide that from the west
With blood washes Africa
Once washed a wooden cross

It is interesting to compare this later version with the same basic lines from the original poem, written while he was in college:

The tide that from the West
Washes Africa to the bones
Gargles through my ribs
Gather the bones clustering
Rough and polished
To fling them back destitute
To the river bank
The tide that from the West
Washes the soul of Africa,
Washes the bouys of its spirits
Tears the mornings apart
Till blood red the tide becomes
And heartsick the wounds.
The tide that from the West
Washes Africa
Once, washed a wooden cross.

The more mature version expresses the bitterness in shorter compass, but it is also more graphic, cutting, and passionate.

If the poem above looked to the past; the following, "Black Child," croons to the future in six simple, if somewhat prosaic lines:

Black Child
I see your wings
Sprout and grow,
I see the dull eyes
Catch fire and glow
And then you must fly.

Some fourteen of his poems appear in *Pergamon-2,* including the popular "Stanley Meets Mutesa," often anthologized, and presented in *Modern Poetry from Africa.*

Writings: Novel: *No Bride Price,* Nairobi, East African Publishing House, 1967; in manuscript, a second novel scheduled for publication, 1973.

Poetry: "Stanley Meets Mutesa" and others in *Pergamon Poets 2,* Oxford, Pergamon Press Ltd., 1968; "Stanley..." in *Modern Poetry from Africa,* Moore and Beier, editors, London, Penguin, revised edition, 1966.

Poem: "The Tide that from the West Washes Africa to the Bone," from *Pergamon 2;* earlier, "college" version from *New African Literature and the Arts,* Vol. II, New York, Crowell, 1970; *"East African Poets,"* with David Cook, to be published in 1973 by Heinemann.

Anthology: *Poems from East Africa,* editor with David Cook, London, Heinemann, 1971.

Biographical/Cricial Source: Interview with Lewis Nkosi in series, "African Writers of Today," in *The Classic,* I, 4, Johannesburg, 1965.

RUBUSANA, Walter Benson

b. February 21, 1858, Nnandi, near Somerset East, South Africa;
d. April 19, 1936.
Xhosa story-teller, collector of folk material, teacher, preacher, politician.

The son of Rubusana Mbonjana, Walter Rubusana was adopted as a child by the Rev. R. Birt of the London Missionary Society. He grew up in Peelton where he began study in 1874, going on to Lovedale in 1876. Taking the elementary teacher's certificate in 1878, he returned the following year to Peelton to work with Birt. In 1882 he graduated from the three-year course in theology at Lovedale and then was sent to the Peelton Mission School from 1882 to 1886. During his last year he was ordained as a minister of the Congregational Church of the London Missionary Society. He married Deena Eudora Nzanzana, daughter of Nzanzana Mquyi, July 3, 1883, in Adelaide.

Rubusana's first writings were religious tracts and Xhosa articles for the Labantu newspaper, *Izwi labantu*. He aided in revising an earlier translation of the Bible into Xhosa in 1905. The following year he published *Zemk' inkomo magwala ndini* (Away Go the Cattle, You Cowards), a volume of 570 pages on the history of the Xhosa people, their proverbs, customs, and praise songs, many of which had been collected by William Wellington Gqoba. For this work he was given an honorary doctorate by McKinley Memorial University in America.

In 1909, Rubusana journeyed to London with W. P. Schreiner and John Tengo Jabavu in an effort to stimulate opposition in the British parliament against the color bar being written into the new constitution for the Union of South Africa then being drafted. Unfortunately, only thirty Labour and Liberal Party members agreed with this position and South Africa, with the sanction of its new constitution, was on its way to *apartheid*. In the next five years Rubusana was active in public affairs, having been elected in 1910 to the Cape Provincial Council as Representative for Tembuland, the first African to take such a position in the Council. He presided at the opening session of the South African Native Congress. In 1914, in an election contest against John Tengo Jabavu and a white, the black vote was split and Rubusana's seat, until then held by an African, was lost to the white candidate, never to be recaptured. That same year he went with the Rev. John L. Dube, Solomon T. Plaatje and other leading Africans to London to protest the Land Act of 1913 that had (alienated) large territories from the Africans to the whites. The House of Parliament virtually ignored their presence and their protest. Still the loyal citizen, however, Rubusana offered in a letter to the Minister of Native Affairs in 1915 to seek to enlist 5,000 African volunteers and to lead them against the Germans in South West Africa. The Minister thanked him for his loyalty but informed him the matter was between whites and that the government was anxious "to avoid the employment of its Native citizens in a warfare against whites."

Frustrated, Rubusana retired from public life, and devoted himself to church work in his remaining twenty-one years. Called "Umcir emkhuln" or, "The Great Man of the Cira clan," he was buried with honors before crowds of thousands in the East London area of the Cape of Good Hope where he had lived for many years.

Writings: History and Folklore: *Zemk' inkomo magwala ndini,* London, Butler and Tanner, 1906.

Articles: *Izwi labantu,* newspaper.

Translations: *Amanyatelo okuya ku Kristu,* a translation of E. G. White's *Steps to Christ,* 1898; Revised translation of Bible into Xhosa, 1905.

Religious Works: *U Yesu uyeza* (Jesus is Coming); *Inkonzo zehlelo lase Rabe* (The Presbyterian Service Book), dates unknown.

Ruhumbika

RUHUMBIKA, Gabriel
b. 1938, Tanzania.
Novelist.

Locally educated, Ruhumbika took his B.A. at Makerere University College in Kampala, Uganda. In 1964 he went to France to start work on a doctorate at the Sorbonne on African theatre.

His only published work to date is a novel, *Village in Uhuru* (1969), which dramatizes the events leading to independence for Tanganyika, now Tanzania. An isolated village, conservative, and suspicious of change, gradually moves into the new world of African freedom and nationalism.

Writings: Novel: *Village in Uhuru,* London, Longmans, 1969.

RUKN AL-DIN BAIBARS
al-Bunduqdari
(Sultan al-Malik al-Muzaffar)
b. ca. 1268, place unknown; d. ca. 1310.
Arabic-language poet, story-teller,
Sultan of Egypt and Syria.

Rukn al-Din Baibars is believed the first author of the collection, *Sirat Baibars* (The Romance of Baibars), which celebrates the exploits of Baibars I (or Al-Malik al-Zahir Rukn al-Din al Salihi), fourth Sultan of the Bahri Mamluks. Baibars I is believed to have been born in Kipcak, 620 after the Hegira (AD 1223), and sold into slavery at Damascus. Eventually he enlisted as a slave soldier of the Mamluks of Egypt, and rose to become Sultan and one of the greatest

375

political and military leaders of Islam in his period.

The poet, son of a black African woman, himself rose to the Sultancy from service with the Bahri Mamluks, or the "Barracks Soldiers," purchased in the hundreds by Aiyubid Sultan Salih Aiyub. Supported by the Burdji Mamluks, another group of slave soldiers, Rukn came to share power with Sultan Sallar whose eventual overthrow and flight from Cairo left Rukn to be chosen Sultan in sole control of Egypt.

The Romance mixes historical fact, pseudo-historical reconstructions, fantasy, and picaresque adventures and has been a rival to the *Sirat Antarah* (The Romance of Antar) for popularity in North Africa. The authorship and dating of the *Sirat Baibars,* composed over many centuries in its extant versions, is obscure and the earliest manuscript dates mostly to the 18th century.

Writings: Poetic legends: *Sirat Baibars,* manuscript in Arabic from 18th century, published in Arabic in Cairo, 1908–1909.

Biographical/Critical Sources: Encyclopaedia of Islam, London, 1934, Carl Brockelmann, *Geschichte der arabishen Literature,* Volume I, second edition, Leiden, 1943.

RWAKYAKA, Proscovia
b. ca. 1945, Fort Portal, Uganda.
Poet, teacher.

Proscovia Rwakyaka attended Kyebambe Girls School and Gayaza High School and received her B.A. in 1967 in English from Makerere University in Kampala, Uganda. She began to teach English at Tororo Girls' school the following autumn, remaining there until she went to Columbia University's Teachers College in New York City, 1969–70, for work on an M.A. in education. She is now back with her classes at Tororo.

Two of her poems, "The Beard," and "The Inmates," appear in *Poems from East Africa.* The first satirizes the intellectual-emotional distance between a preacher who thinks he has moved his congregation on the theme of sin and the girl who tells him she has sobbed in church only because the preacher's beard had made her remember her dead goat. The second poem, less effective, laments childhood's lost wonders.

Writings: In *Poems from East Africa,* Cook and Rubadiri, editors, London, Heinemann, 1971; *New Voices of the Commonwealth,* Howard Sergeant, editor, London, Evans, 1968; *Africa Writing Today,* Angoff and Povey, editors, New York, Maryland Books, 1969.

S

SADI, Abdulrahman as-
(or Abd al-Rahman as-Sadi, or
Abd al-Rahman b. 'Abd Allah
B. Imran B. Amir)
b. 1596, Timbuktu (modern Mali);
d. March 14, 1656.
Collector of legends and tales in Arabic;
scholar, diplomat, historian.

As a very young child he experienced
the Moroccan invasion of Timbuktu
which effectively ended that city's great
reputation as an intellectual center. Born
into an old family of learned men, Sadi's
greatest teacher was Ahmad Baba (d.
1627). But, what might have been a tranquil life of study at home was shattered
when Sadi refused to accept a role as
apologist for the Mauridic conquerors
of his homeland and he began his itiner-
ant life as scholar in residence in various
cities in and along the Niger River. He
lived for awhile in Djenne but by 1626
was named Imam (Holy Man) of the San-
kore Mosque. Later he traveled to the
Fulbe Kingdom of Masina on the left
bank of the Niger in 1630 for a brief
period and a second time in 1633. From
1646 till his death ten years later, he
served as secretary of state for the Pasha
of Timbuktu.

Never forgetting the shock and horror
of the Mauridic capture of Timbuktu in
1591 and saddened by signs of decay
and despair throughout the once proud
empire of Songhai, Sadi sought to capture the countless stories and legends of
the area's past. Gone were most of the
libraries and bookshops, gone the meetings of scholars and the tranquility
needed to sustain a culture. Only the
past, if it could be recaptured, offered
glory and pride. In his efforts, Sadi came
upon legends reaching back to the days
of Ghana (800–1240) and Mali (1240–
1550), so that his *Ta'rikh al-Sudan* is an
immensely valuable compendium of
almost a thousand years of African history and culture. This work also covers
the Taureg and town histories of Djenne
and Timbuktu. He ceased writing on
October 28, 1653 for a period but started
up again and continued till March 14,
1656.

A continuation of Sadi's work was
called *Tadhkirat al-Nasyan*, written in
1751 by a grandson, name now unknown, of the Emir Muhammed b.
Suwu.

Writings: Legends and Tales: *Tarikh al-
Sudan*, written in Arabic, completed ca.
1656; translated into French by O. Hon-
das and Edmund Benoist, Paris, 1898,

377

1900; Heinrich Barth published extracts of the Arabic text in 1853–54 in German.

Biographical/Critical Source: Encyclopaedia of Islam, Volume IV, London, 1934.

SADJI, Abdoulaye
b. 1910; d. December 25, 1961, Rufisque, Senegal.
Novelist, short story writer, polemicist, educator.

Abdoulaye Sadji, who was a close friend of Léopold Senghor, attended Koranic primary schools. At the age of 11, he transferred to French-run grammar schools and later studied at a teachers' training college, graduating in 1929 with a diploma. In 1932 he took his French bachelor's degree. Sadji worked as the director of a school in his natal city, as an inspector for the primary grades, and as director of the State Schools in Rufisque. He contributed to productions for Senegal Radio and has taught in the Senegalese school system.

Sadji collaborated with Senghor in the writing of a school reader, *La belle histoire de Leuk-le Lièvre* (The Splendid History of Leuk-the Hare), published in 1953, which offered stories with African subjects. The goal was to provide an alternative to the French school texts which had nothing African in them and which still dominate much of francophone elementary education in Africa.

The story, "Maimouna, petite fille noire" (Maimouna, Little Black Girl), was the original study for Sadji's full-length novel, *Maïmouna: la petite fille noire,* Dakar, 1953 and Paris, 1958. Sadji has received little critical recognition for that work or his succeeding novelette, *Nini, mulâtresse du Sénégal* (Nini,

Mulatress of Senegal), published in *Trois écrivains noirs* by Présence Africaine in 1954, after that review first serialized it in 1947–48.

A volume of short stories of death and disaster, *Tounka, nouvelle africaine* (Tounka, African Stories), first serialized in 1946, later came out in book form in 1965. An earlier form of the title story for that volume earlier had been published as *Tounka. Une légende de la mer* (Tounka, A Legend of the Sea) in Dakar in 1952.

Sadji's works are devoted to the world of the hybrid society of Dakar and the old port city of Saint-Louis. His tone is warm and he seeks to create characters, mostly women, who dominate their societies. He is fascinated by the new cities of Africa, and often contrasts the country people and their simple values with the more complex inhabitants of Dakar and other large cities. He dramatizes well the terrible strains the rural man and woman must endure as they try to earn a toe-hold in the metropolis. According to A. C. Brench, Sadji "believed ardently in the Africans' struggle for independence yet he was never able to free himself from the colonialist mentality."

Sadji's books reflect the viewpoints of both the Frenchman (or the Gallicized African) and that of the Muslim-African. The cosmologies of the two cultures are different and the psychologies often in sharp conflict. The result is a lack of focus, even of confusion. Nevertheless, Sadji was a gifted storyteller, especially when he concentrated on a narrow theme. Important stories of this sort are "Tragique hyménée" (Tragic Wedding), "Beau et Tiat" (Handsome and Tiat [the name of the characters]), "Un rappel de solde" (A Call for Pay), and "Moudou-Fatim" (a name).

Writings: Novel: *Maïmouna: la petite fille noire,* Dakar, 1953; and Paris, Présence Africaine, 1958.

Novelette: *Nini, mulâtresse du Sénégal,* Paris, Serie Spéciale, No 16, *Présence Africaine,* issue entitled *Trois écrivains noirs,* 1954, second edition, 1965.

Stories: Collection: *Tounka, nouvelle africaine, Paris-Dakar Journal,* September 3–October 12, 1946; May 5–12, 1946; reprinted by Présence Africaine, 1965, in Paris; first version of the story "Tounka," was published as *Tounka, Une légende de la mer,* Dakar, Impr. Abdoulaye Diop, 1952; "Tragique hyménée," *Afrique-matin,* January 16–31, 1948; "Maïmouna, petite fille noire," Dakar, *Les Lecture Faciles,* 1953; "Beau et Tiat," Dakar, *Paris-Dakar Journal,* March 26, 1955; "Un rappel de solde," Dakar, *Bingo* magazine, No. 57, 1957; "Moudou-Fatim," Dakar, *Paris-Dakar Journal,* November 25–December 5, 1957.

Criticism: "Littérature et colonialisme," Paris, *Présence Africaine,* No. 6, 1948; "La logique du romancier, à propos de Moudou Fatim," Dakar, *Paris-Dakar Journal,* January 3, 1958.

Reader: *La belle histoire de Leuk-le Lièvre,* with Léopold Sédar Senghor, Paris, Classique Hachette, 1953.

Biographical/Critical Sources: L. Diakhaté, "Abdoulaye Sadji et le roman de nègre nouveau," *Condition humaine,* March 11, 1955; "Abdoulaye Sadji est mort," *Présence Africaine,* XXXIX, December, 1961; A. C. Brench, *Writing in French from Senegal to Cameroon,* London, Oxford University Press-Three Crowns Book, 1967.

SAGAYE, Gabre Medhin (see TSEGAYE, Gabre–Medhin)

SAHLE (see SELLASIE, Sahle, B. M.)

SAI, B. Akiga (see AKIGA, BENJAMIN)

SAIYID, Abdallah b. Ali b. Nasir
b. ca. 1720 in area now Tanzania;
d. ca. 1810.
Swahili oral poet.

Saiyid prided himself on his shared lineage with other famous Swahili poets from Shaikh Abu Bakr b. Salim of Tarim in the Hadramawt (b. 1584). Only a few of his works are known to modern scholarship. One, a long narrative poem entitled "Takhmis ya Liyongo" (Poem of Liyongo), exists in manuscript form in the British Museum. The subject of a second work is a contemplative poem of Liyongo. The manuscript has been published in the original Swahili and in English translation by William Hichens as *al–Inkinshafi,* 1939. The long dramatic monologue recites the loss of the old Arab fortified towns along the East African coastline and reflects the traditional Swahili resignation toward death and the decay of man's hopes on earth.

Writings: Poetry: "Takhmis ya Liyongo," in manuscript in British Museum; an extract of "Liyongo" appears in A. J. Shelton's anthology, *The African Assertion,* New York, Odyssey Press, 1968; *al–Inkishafi,* or *The Soul's Awakening* in English translation by William Hichens, London, Sheldon Press, 1939; and in *Swahili Poetry,* Lyndon Harries, Oxford, The Clarendon Press, 1962. The original manuscript used by Hichens and Harries is reproduced in a series of plates in Harries' volume.

SAIYID, ABU BAKR (or bin Abd al-Rahman Saiyid Mansab)
b. 1828, Lamu, present-day Kenya; d. 1922.
Swahili oral poet.

Saiyid Abu Bakr studied the required subjects, Islamic law and theology, at Mecca and later served as a judge or Kadhi at Zanzibar during the reign of Sultan Saiyid Majid. He composed a shorter version of "Maulid al–Barzanju," the long oral poem celebrating the birth of Muhammed. An original work of his was the long, didactic poem on religious duties, "Utendi wa Akida tu 'l–Awami."

Writings: Homiletic poem: "Utendi wa Akida tu 'l–Awami," in manuscript.
  Translation: Swahili version, shortened of the "Maulid al Barzanju," original Arabic-language author unknown, in manuscript.

SAIYID MANSAB (see SAIYID ABU BAKR)

SAIYID UMAR (born Amin ben Nasir al–Ahdal)
b. 1800, near Mombasa, Kenya; d. 1870.
Swahili poet.

Saiyid Umar was a Kadhi or judge at Siu in the northern region above Mombasa, Kenya. His greatest renown came from poems on Islamic religious themes written as acrostics. Still remembered are his poems, "Wajiwaji," and "Dura Mandhuma" (The Necklace of Pearls).

Writings: Poems: "Wajiwaji," "Dura Mandhuma."

SAKUBITA, M. M.
b. ca. 1930, Zambia.
Lozi–language story writer.

One of the few writers in Lozi, Sakubita has published a 72-page story, *Liswanelo za luna li lu siile* in 1954. This was later corrected and republished as *Liswanelo za luna kwa lifolofolo* (How Not to Handle Animals), 1958, 1961.

Writings: Prose: *Liswanelo za luna li lu siile*, London, Macmillan, 1954; corrected version. *Liswanelo za luna kwa lifolofolo*. London, Macmillan, 1958, 1961.

SALAAN, 'Arrabey
b. ca. 1850, Somali-land; d. ca. 1940.
Somali oral poet.

An inveterate traveller like his clansmen of the Habar, Tolja 'lo, Salaan visited Aden, parts of East Africa, and got to know many Europeans during the course of his long life. He became conversant with Arabic, Hindustani, Swahili, and English, and was successful as an interpreter and merchant. The range of his interests and experiences produced a highly individual poetry, full of foreign borrowings, new themes, and numerous innovations in style. His skill was such that he was reputed to have been able to start or to quell feuds between the quarreling Somali clans by reciting an appropriate poem. Many of his poems, now extant in the private manuscript collection of Musa H. I. Galaal, reflect conflicts among the Somali. One of these is the important "Mayn" (Landmine) which celebrates a clash between clans in Burao Town.

His poems, "The Unpaid Bride-wealth," "Ingratitude," and "O Clansmen, Stop the War," in their English versions, appear in *Somali Poetry*.

Writings: Poems: "The Unpaid Bridewealth," "Ingratitude," "O Clansmen, Stop the War" in *Somali Poetry*, Andrzejewski and Lewis, editors, Oxford, Clarendon, 1964; "Mayn," in manuscript.

SALIH, Tayeb
b. 1929, Northern Province, Sudan. Arabic-language novelist, short story writer, radio broadcaster.

Born into a family of modest farmers whose sons became religious scholars, Salih planned to be an expert in agriculture, but his career, except for a brief period as a teacher, has instead been in broadcasting. Currently he is Head of Drama for the BBC's Arabic services. He began his education in local schools, took his B.A. at Khartoum University, and did further work at several universities in London.

Salih's stories appeared in the 1969 volume, *The Wedding of Zein and Other Stories*. His other works include *Season of Migration to the North*, a novel, published in 1969 by Heinemann and translated by Johnson–Davies. This work is a bizarre tale of a sexually talented African scholar, abroad in a violent London full of women who lust for exotic sensations. Both at home and abroad, the protagonist, Mustafa Sa'eed, moves about in a dreamlike trance. The book is bitter and poetic. Every woman who wants Mustafa dies. In the end he is emotionally destroyed by the maddest of them all, a certain Jean Morris whom he labels "the shore of destruction." Despite the sensational sexual aspects of the novel, it is sharply etched and extremely well written.

Writings: Novel: *Season of Migration to the North*, translation by Denys Johnson–Davies, Heinemann, 1969.

Stories: *The Wedding of Zein and Other Stories*, English translation by Denys Johnson–Davies, London, Heinemann, 1969.

SAM, Gilbert A.
b. ca. 1930, Ghana. Short story writer.

Writer of short, popular tales, Sam has published five works of fiction: *A Drunkard's Positive Action; A Christmastide Tragedy; Who Killed Inspector Kwasi Minta?; Love in the Grave;* and *A Tragedy in*

Kumasi, all published in Accra by the Gilisam Publishing Syndicate, his own company.

Writings: Novelettes: *A Drunkard's Positive Action,* 1955; *A Christmastide Tragedy,* 1956 (?); *Who Killed Inspector Kwasi Minta?,* 1956; *Love in the Grave,* 1959; all Accra, Gilisam.

SAMKANGE, Stanlake J. T.
b. 1922, Mariga, Chipata, Zwimba Tribal Area, Rhodesia.
Novelist, teacher, politician.

Son of a Methodist minister, a member of the Muzezuru group of the Mushona nation, Samkange spent his early years in Bulawayo, the ancient capital of Lobengula, the last of the Matabele kings. (Lobengula's hopeless struggle against the plots and power plays of Cecil Rhodes is the subject of Samkange's one published novel, *On Trial for My Country,* 1966.)

Samkange attended the Waddilove Institution for primary schooling, Adams' College for high school, both in Rhodesia, before going on to Fort Hare University College in South Africa for an Honors degree in history, won in 1947, and a second B.A. (also Honors) earned at the University of South Africa in 1950.

Returning home to be a teacher, he began an intense decade of political and organizational work with the African National Congress for which he served as secretary general for many years. In 1961 Nyatsime College opened its doors after eleven years of planning by Samkange and his associates. The new college offered technical-commercial courses as well as basic academic subjects and was the first of its kind in the area.

Samkange worked on his M.S. in education in 1957–58 at Indiana University in Bloomington and then, after a period as a journalist, he became the publisher of a business paper, and owner and director of his own public relations and advertising firm in Bulawayo and Gwelo, Rhodesia. He returned to the United States to complete a doctorate in history at Indiana, 1965 to 1968. He then taught at Tennessee State University, 1967–68, was Associate Professor at Fisk University, 1968–69, and Professor at Fisk, 1969–71. Presently he is Lecturer in the Afro-American Studies Department of Harvard University. His wife, Tommie Marie (an American), holds a Ph.D. in psychology. They have two sons.

On Trial for My Country, written during June–October, 1965, describes the dramatic confrontation of King Lobengula with his father Mzilikazi and the elders of the Matabele who accuse him, during a long ghost-trial, of failing to stop the loss of their land to the English. Cecil John Rhodes and his allies and agents likewise stand trial in a church at Bishop's Stortford, England, with Cecil's father, the Reverend Francis William Rhodes, rector of the church, as the prosecutor. The narrator is an old Matabele, Gobinsimbi, son of Dabulamanzi of the house of Khumalo, who meets the young Samkange one mysterious night at the mouth of a cave "somewhere on the Matopo Hills." Gobinsimbi is a spectator at both "trials" and as he relates first what happened at Bishop's Stortford in England, and then at the tribal council near Bulawayo called by Mzilikazi, the reader begins to understand the history of the conquest and the nature of the African defeat in 1893.

Though the rather formal rhetoric and action of the "trials" is slow going at first, the reader gradually enters into the period and becomes familiar with the African, Boer, and English personalities involved. By the close of the book, one has a clear picture of British motives —commerical, religious, and racial— for the invasion. He also appreciates the cautious but unavailing efforts of the intelligent Lobengula to save his land and his people from Rhodes, a man absolutely bent on the destruction of Matabele power in the area.

Essentially, the novel relates events similar to those which took place in America between the whites and the indians: treaty after treaty was written and then broken by the whites or manipulated so that the original inhabitants were either pushed off their ancestral lands or made serfs or dependents. The

dust jacket reproduces a rare photograph of Lobengula and a striking one of Cecil J. Rhodes.

Samkange has published various other works outside of creative literature and has a novel and a collection of folktales in manuscript awaiting publication. He is living in voluntary exile in the United States and hopes to return to Rhodesia some day.

Writings: Novel: *On Trial for My Country,* London, Heinemann, 1966; "The Mourned One," in manuscript.

History: *Origins of Rhodesia,* London, Heinemann, 1968; New York, Praeger, 1969; *African Saga; Introduction to African History,* Nashville, New York, Abingdon Press, 1971.

Folklore: "Some African Fireside Tales," in manuscript.

Category Unknown: *Chief's Daughter Who Would Not Laugh,* Cape Town, Longmans, Green, 1964.

SANCHO, Ignatius ("Africanus")
b. 1729, on a slave ship bound for South America; d. 1780, England.
Letter-writer, poet, playwright.

Sancho's mother died soon after his birth and his father committed suicide. Baptized Ignatius in Cartagena, Columbia, he was sent to England in 1731 as a gift to two English sisters.

Sancho entered the domestic service of the enlightened Duke of Montagu (1718–1792) and became the family butler for twenty years. Educated, witty, and sophisticated by his duties with the aristocracy, he eventually retired to a grocery shop, raised a large family with his West Indian wife, and wrote many letters, including some to Lawrence Sterne and the Duchess of Kent. They

Sancho

are collected in *Letters of the Late Ignatius Sancho, An African* (London, 1782), reprinted 1968 (London, Dawsons). One of his six children edited the fifth edition in 1803.

Sancho was a friend of Garrick's and other writers and actors of the period including Lawrence Sterne. His letters show him concerned with the fate of his fellow Africans. He wrote poetry and music and two pieces for the theatre.

Writings: Letters: *Letters of the Late Ignatius Sancho,* London, J. Nichols, 1782; second edition, 1783, fifth edition 1803; reprinted, London, Dawsons, 1968 in the Colonial History Series, introduction by Paul Edwards; Extracts of *Letters* appear in *Modern African Narrative,* Paul Edwards, editor, London, Nelson, 1966.
Poetry: Verse in 1803 in London.
Plays: Two pieces, details unknown.

Biographical/Critical Sources: O. R. Dathorne, "African Writers of the Eighteenth Century," in *Black Orpheus* magazine, No. 18 (October 1965); Sancho is caricatured in the anonymous *Memoir and Opinions of Mr. Blenfield,* London 1790; K. Little, *Negroes in Britain,* London, 1948; and *Dictionary of National Biography.*

SANKAWULO, Wilton
b. ca. 1945, Liberia.
Story writer, novelist.

Sankawulo's work, just now appearing in print, exploits the folk tales of the Kpelle people in Liberia. His story, "The Evil Forest," which he first heard from a Kpelle "professional" story-teller, shows concern with the traditional way of doing things and the dangers of doing anything more than the usual. The new

is feared, and *known* to be dangerous if not deadly.

Writings: Story: "The Evil Forest," *African Arts,* Summer, 1971.

SANTO, Alda de Espírito (see ESPIRITO-SANTO, Alda de)

SANTOS, Marcelino (see dos SANTOS, Marcelino)

SAOLI, Jacob Russell
b. September 1, 1914, Thabachicha Location, Mount Fletcher District, Cape Province, South Africa.
Sotho song-writer, poet, teacher.

Saoli attended local schools in his early years, earning his Teacher's Certificate in 1933 after four years at the Mvenyane Institution. He took the Matriculation Certificate in 1939 after private study. He taught at the Stegi Nazarene Higher Mission School (1935–36) in Swaziland, at St. Patrick's Higher Mission School, Bloemfontein (1937–38). From 1938 to 1942 he was a teacher and principal at the Arthurseat Nazarene Mission School which he founded. From 1942 to 1947 Saoli was an instructor in science at Pholela High School, the Bulwer District, Natal; and from 1948 to 1956 he was back at the Arthurseat Mission School as principal. Since 1956 he has been principal of the Arthurseat Practising School.

A remarkable linguist in English, Afrikaans, Northern and Southern Sotho, Tswana, Tsonga, Zulu and Xhosa, he has contributed many scholarly and religious articles, poems and translations to journals and is assistant editor of *Montsosa-bosigo* (Valuable Counsel), the publication of the Nazarene Church of South Africa.

His one published collection of songs appeared in 1951, *Meloli ea tumelo* (Songs of Faith). Unpublished are his "Melitiesane" (Wardrobe), some of his verses, and "Ntlose lenyora" Please Quench My Thirst, a volume of nursery rhymes.

Writings: Songs: *Meloli ea tumelo,* Morija, Morija Sesuto Book Depot, 1951;

Poetry: "Melitiesane," unpublished.

Nursery rhymes: "Ntlose lenyora," unpublished.

SARBAH, John Mensah

b. June 3, 1864, Gold Coast; d. 1910, Cape Coast, Gold Coast (now Ghana).

Journalist, educator.

Sarbah completed his secondary schooling at Wesleyan High School and went on to undergraduate studies at Wesleyan College. He then attended Lincoln's Inn, London, where he studied law. He was appointed to the bar in 1887 at the age of 23 in West Africa, the First Gold Coaster ever to be given this honor.

Sarbah founded the newspaper *The Gold Coast People* which was published from 1891 to 1898. He also worked on the journals, *Gold Coast Aborigines* and the *Gold Coast Weekly.* He was a member of the Gold Coast Aborigines' Protection Society and fought against the various Land Bills proposed by the British which would authorize control of the Africans' farm land. He became a member of the Legislative Council in 1901 and was awarded the Order of the C.M.G. in 1910.

Sarbah was a leading defender of Afri-
can rights, and his historical and sociological works attempted to preserve the time-honored customs of the African people from destruction. His *Fanti Customary Law* underwent three printings, the most recent in 1968. Another of his works, *Fanti National Constitution,* was published in 1906.

Writings: History of Law: *Fanti Customary Law,* London, Frank Cass and Company, Ltd., 1897; *Fanti National Constitution,* London, Frank Cass and Company Ltd., 1906. An extract of *Fanti National Constitution,* entitled, "Coup," is in *African in Prose,* Dathorne and Feuser, editors, Baltimore, Penguin, 1969, with a brief introduction.

SAYYID, Mahammed 'Abdile Hasan (see MAHAMMED, Sheikh 'Abdille Hasan)

SEBONI, Michael Ontepetse Martinus

b. July 9, 1912, Molepolele, old Bechuanaland Protectorate, now Botswana.

Tswana novelist, scholar, educator, poet, translator.

Seboni, primarily a novelist, studied at Molepolele Primary School, St. Matthew's College Practising School, and the South African Native College. Later he went to University College, Fort Hare (1934–36), taking the B.A. in education and the University Education Diploma. He won a D.Ed. degree in 1956 with the dissertation "The South African Native College, Fort Hare, (1903–1954)," and a Ph.D. (1958) from the University of South Africa.

His positions, mostly in education,

have been as a teacher at several schools near his home town. He also served as principal (ca. 1940 to 1951) of the Nigel United Christian School, Transvaal, which, with Cedric Phatudi, he improved into the Charterston Secondary School. He has also been Senior Lecturer and Department Head of Fort Hare's Bantu Languages Department (1951–53); named Senior Lecturer, Department of Education (1953); Councillor to the Paramount Chief of the Bechuanaland Protectorate, Chief Ngari Sechele II. Presently, he is Professor of Empirical Education at the University College, Fort Hare, and a member of Fort Hare's Advisory Council and Senate.

Beginning to write in his mid-30's, his first work was a children's novel, *Rammona wa Kgalagadi* (Rammone of the Khalahari Desert). His two later novels are *Kgosi Isang Pilane* (Chief Isang Pilane), and *Koketsa-kitso ya lefatshe*. He has published one volume of praise poems, *Maboko maloba le maabane* (Praise Poems, Old and New), and a collection of Tswana idioms, riddles, tales, proverbs and idiomatic phrases, *Diane le maele a Setswana* (Tswana proverbs and maxims).

His translations of Shakespeare are *Morekisi wa Venisi* (The Merchant of Venice) and *Kgosi Henry wa bone* (King Henry IV), published about 1959 or 1960.

Writings: Novels: *Kgosi Isang Pilane,* Johannesburg, Afrikaanse Pers-Boekhandel, 1958, 1961; *Koketsa-kitso ya lefatshe,* Afrikaanse Pers-Boekhandel 1965(?).

Children's novel: *Rammona wa Kgalagadi,* Bloemfontein, Nasionale Pers, 1947, second revised edition,

Bloemfontein, Cape Town, Via Afrika, 1958.

Poetry: *Maboko maloba le maabane,* Johannesburg, Nasional Pers, 1949; Cape Town, Bloemfontein, Johannesburg, Via Afrika, second edition, 1962, 1968.

Folklore: *Diane le maele a Setswana,* Johannesburg, Afrikaanse, 1964.

Translations from Shakespeare: *Morekisi wa Venisi* (The Merchant of Venice); *Kgosi Henry wa bone* (King Henry IV), 1959 or 1960.

SEGOETE, Everitt Lechesa

b. 1858, Morife (Mohale's Hoek), Lesotho; d. February 7, 1923.
Southern Sotho novelist, journalist, educator.

The second son of Mencah Segoete, Everitt Segoete attended school at Maphutseng under the Reverend D. F. Ellenberger who, when he was transfered to Masitise School encouraged Everitt to join him there. Later, Segoete, with the aid of a scholarship, earned a Teacher's Certificate at the Basuto-land Training College at Morija. His African name "Lechesa" signified "fire," in memory of the Boer invasion and the subsequent burning of villages in his parents' area.

After work at the Morija Book Depot and a period on the staff of a newspaper in Aliwal North (where he met his future wife), he served as principal and head teacher at Qomoqomong where his prize student was Thomas Mofolo, destined to become one of the most famous of all South African writers. Mofolo modeled the central figure in his third novel, *Pitseng,* 1910, on Segoete.

Segoete's experiences on a long, wandering trip through the Cape Colony later furnished material for his 221-page autobiographical novel, *Monono ke moholi mouoane* (Wealth Is But Mist, But Steam), published in 1910. *Monono*, later re-issued as a 107-page work in 1962, is a three-part story which shows the progress and problems of a village youth, Khitsane, who goes to town for education and adventure. He becomes a petty criminal, but, finally reformed by his old Christian friend, now a preacher, he begins to lead an exemplary life. His death comes on Good Friday, and Segoete adds to the religious echo by furnishing a symbolic resurrection for the redeemed Khitsane in the miraculous escape from a cave of a man formerly led to Christ by the hero—all this on Easter Sunday.

Segoete, as pious as his hero, was ordained a minister after study at the Morija Ministry Seminar and long served his church at the Lesotho mission Station at Hermone, at Koeneng, and finally again at Hermone.

His four non-literary works were: *Mefiboshethe kapa pheelo ea molimo he moetsalibe* (The Patience of God With the Sinner), 1910; *Raphepheng ba Basotho ba khale* (Old Man Scorpion), about the days before colonialism, issued in 1913; *Moea oa balisa* (The Spirit of the Shepherd), 1915, a religious tract; and *Mohlala oa Jesu Kreste* (The Footsteps of Jesus Christ), issued in 1924. At the time of his death he was working on another religious tract, *Mofa le mehi*.

The novel *Monono* and the study of Africa before colonialism, *Raphepheng*, reflect Segoete's mixed cultural heritage. Though he was a convinced Christian he nevertheless regretted the passing of much of the old life and the rise of a new generation only partially Christian and only vaguely concerned with the old tribal values. *Raphepheng* particularly was warmly nostalgic over the lost culture and only the author's status as a sincere minister of the faith protected his work from attack as a work extolling pagan ways.

Writings: Novel: *Monono ke moholi mouoane*, Morija Sesuto Book Depot, 1910, 1962.

Religious Works: *Moea oa balisa*, Morija, 1913, 1915; *Mohlala oa Jesu Kreste*, Morija, 1924; Mofa le mehi, in manuscript; *Mefiboshethe kapa pheelo ea molimo ho moetsalibe*, Morija, Morija Press, 1910; earlier reprinted serially in the journal *Leselinyana*, 1910.

History: *Raphepheng bophelo ba Basotho ba khale*, Morija, Morija Press, 1913.

Biographical/Critical Source: A. S. Gérard,

Four African Literatures, Berkeley, University of California Press, 1971.

SEGUN, Mabel Joloaso (née Imoukhuede)
b. ca. 1938, Nigeria.
Poet, journalist, story writer.

Mrs. Segun was educated in Lagos at the C. M. S. Grammar School and did her university work at Ibadan. She has taught and worked as an editor of the *Hansard* (the daily report) of the West Nigerian Parliament. Recently she has done overseas publicity for the Information Services of Western Nigeria. Presently she is a free-lance broadcaster and journalist, and has been publishing poems in *Black Orpheus* and *Odu,* both published in Ibadan, and in Swiss and German journals for the most part. One of her articles, "The Unfinished House," appears in *Reflections: Nigerian Prose and Verse.*

Her one separate volume to date is *My Father's Daughter,* 1965, an 80-page novelette for juveniles.

Writings: Poems in *Black Orpheus, Odu,* in Ibadan, in Swiss and German journals.
Article: "The Unfinished House," in *Reflections: Nigerian Prose and Verse,* Frances Ademola, editor, Lagos, African Universities Press, 1962, 1965.
Novelette: *My Father's Daughter,* Lagos, African Universities Press, 1965.

SEID, Joseph Brahim
b. 1927, Fort–Lamy, Chad.
Short story writer, lawyer, statesman.

After local grammar school, Seid attended high school in Egypt and com-

pleted his professional studies at the Faculté de Droit (Law) at Lyons, France and at the University of Paris. Presently he is Chad's Minister of Justice.

Seid's first work, *Au Tchad sous les étoiles* (Chad Under the Stars), appeared in 1962 in an attractive volume with a yellow buff cover and a design by the African artist Kotoko.

In the preface, Seid discusses his country which takes its name from "the great lake of blue waters, lightly salted, and covered with papyrus." He charmingly writes: "Those countless children of the Chad, by means of one of them (the author), invite you to come and to sit down among them, under a blue sky, sprinkled over with stars, to listen to these stories and legends which contain more of the marvelous than of the natural. Only one thing do they beg of you: that is to join them with an open heart in the joy of their candour and of their innocence." (trans. D. H.)

Three of the tales, "Gamar et Guimerie," "Nidjema L'Orpheline," and "Le Vagabond," are offered in *New Sum of Poetry from the Negro World.*

Seid's most recent work is an autobiographical story of 112 pages, *Un enfant du Tchad* (A Child of Chad), published in 1967.

Writings: Stories: *Au Tchad sous les étoiles,* Paris, Présence Africaine, 1962; *Un enfant du Tchad,* Paris, Sagerep, 1967; "Gamar et Guimerie," "Nidjema l'Orpheline," and "Le Vagabond" in *New Sum of Poetry from the Negro World,* Paris, Présence Africaine, 1966.

SEKESE, Azariele M.
b. 1849, Tsereoane, Berea District, Lesotho; d. 1930.
Southern Sotho story writer,

collector of tales and proverbs, scholar, teacher.

Sekese was one of the first pupils to enroll at the Reverend A. Mabille's new school, Sekolo sa thabeng (The Basotholand Training College) at Morija in 1866, remaining there for three years. In 1872 he worked in Tlapaneng as a teacher and lay preacher. By 1881 he was the personal secretary to Chief Jonathane, but he left for a seven-year period beginning in 1884 to teach at Hlotse and then to clerk for a trading company. He returned to Chief Jonathane as secretary in 1891 and became in addition the Chief's envoy to the British assistant commissioner in the area, Sir Charles Bell.

He began collecting Sesotho proverbs and making notes on folkways in the early 1870's, but it was not until the 1880's that his work began to appear in articles in *Leselinyana* (The Little Light), the Sotho-language journal. In 1893 his collection was published in the volume, *Buka ea pokello ea mekhoa ea Basotho le maele le litsome* (A Collection of Basotho, or Sesotho, Proverbs and Tales. This work was reissued in a shorter version as *Mekhoa le maele a Bosotho* (Basotho Proverbs and Customs) ten years later, and in an expanded edition in 1907. As late as 1953, Morija Sesuto Book Depot put out a large section of his work specifically dealing with Basotho customs in the volume, *Mekhoa ea Basotho*.

Sekese's very popular satirical tale of his thinly disguised experiences at Chief Jonathane's court, "Pitso ea linonyana" (The Meeting of the Birds), was dramatized by many groups of students from the 1880's onwards. Probably written in collaboration with Job Moteane, it was finally published in 1930, two years before his death, as *Bukana ea tsomo tsa*

pitso ea linonyana le tseko ea sefofu le seritsa (The Little Book That Tells of the Meeting of the Birds and the Quarrel Between a Blind Man and a Lame).

Writings: Folk Stories and Proverbs: *Buka ea pokello ea mekhoa ea Basotho le maele le litsome*, 1893; as *Mekhoa le maela a Basotho*, 1903; expanded edition, 1907; special edition devoted to customs, *Mekhoa ea Basotho*, 1953.

Satirical Story: *Bukana ea tsomo tsa pitso ea linonyana le tseko ea sefofu le seritsa*, 1928; sixth printing, 1955; dramatized from 1880's on, but no play manuscript apparently extant or published. (All publications by Morija Sesuto Book Depot, Morija.)

Biographical/Critical Source: Albert S. Gérard, *Four African Literatures*, Berkeley, University of California Press, 1971.

SELLASSIE, Sahle Berhane Mariam (also SAHLE, Sellassie Barhane Mariam)
b. 1936, Wardéna, Ethiopia.
Amharic and English language novelist, short story writer, journalist, government official.

Sellassie studied at the University College in Addis Ababa, at the University of Aix–Marseilles in France, and at the University of California at Los Angeles. At present, he is a staff training officer for his government in Addis Ababa.

He has contributed articles and short stories in English and Amharic to journals in Ethiopia and has three published novels. The first was *Shinega's Village*, 1964, translated from the original Chaha, an Amharic dialect previously not employed in written literature. The work recaptures the decades of the

1940's and 1950's in post-war Ethiopia. His second novel, *Wotat Yifredew*, was published in Amharic in Addis Ababa, date unknown and remains untranslated. Published in English without an earlier Ethiopian edition was the third novel, *The Afersata*, 1969. This work shows the folk "moot-court" or *afersata* in action as it seeks, through slow, half-magical, half common-sense procedures, to discover who supposedly has burned down one of the villager's houses and stolen the owner's buried money.

All of the novels are short and dramatize the daily lives of Ethiopian villagers. To some extent they seek to explain characteristic folkways and predicaments of a people as they adjust to changes in their lives brought on by new governmental, social, and educational developments throughout the country.

Writings: Novels: *Shinega's Village, Scenes of Ethiopian Life,* translated from the original Chaha-Amharic version (for which publishing data is unavailable) by Wolf Leslau, Berkeley, University of California Press, 1964; *Wotat Yifredew* (in Amharic), Addis Ababa, date unknown; *The Afersata: An Ethiopian Novel,* London, Heinemann, 1969.

SELORMEY, Francis
b. 1927, near Keta, coast of Ghana.
Novelist, teacher, sports executive, film script writer.

Educated in Roman Catholic schools and at St. Augustine's College, Cape Coast, Selormey went on to study physical education at the University of Ghana and in Germany. Returning to Ghana, he was for seven years chief physical education instructor at St. Francis Teacher Training College, Hohoe, before becoming senior regional sports organizer for his country's Central Organization of Sport.

During this time Selormey turned to writing, first as an avocation and finally as a career. He is now a feature and script writer for the Ghana Film Corporation. His recent scripts for films are: *Toward a United Africa* and *The Great Lake.*

His only novel is *The Narrow Path* (1966), which recounts the story of the boy, Kofi, son of a severe and often cruelly punitive father. Partially protected by his gentle mother from his over zealous father's too ready whippings to spur his son's scholarship, the boy gradually nears manhood, learning his Christian father meant well, though his methods still seemed too harsh to ensure his boy became a good scholar. Kofi, at the story's end, settled in the bus to begin his journey to college two hundred miles away. He turned his head to bid his father goodbye, and "saw the hardest thing in all that desolated parting. There were tears in my father's eyes."

Writings: Novel: *The Narrow Path*, London, Heinemann, 1966; New York, Praeger, 1966, Heinemann Educational Books, 1967.

Film scripts: *Toward a United Africa; The Great Lake.*

SEMBENE, Ousmane
b. January 8, 1923, Ziguinchor-Casamance, Senegal.
Novelist, short story writer, director, film-maker.

Born to a family of Wolof fishermen, Sembène struggled for his education. After three years at a technical school in nearby Marsassoum, he worked at manual tasks in Dakar (plumber, fisherman, brick-layer, mechanic's helper) before serving in the French colonial army in Italy and Germany during World War II. His unit took part in the invasion of Italy and he was a military port worker or stevedore in Marseilles at that stage of the war. He finished his military duty in Baden-Baden on the Rhine.

He returned to Dakar and worked as a fisherman, but soon returned to France as a dock-worker, eventually becoming the trade union leader of the African dockers. During the past fifteen years he has travelled widely in Europe, Africa, Cuba, China and the U.S.S.R. Despite the difficulties he encountered, he read whenever possible and began to write in Marseilles. His first work, *Le docker noir* (The Black Docker) came from these efforts and experiences. Falling ill and severely affected in his spine, he was forced to give up physical labor, his only genuine monetary resource, to seek a living solely from literature.

His second novel, *O pays, mon beau peuple!* (O My Country,–My Beautiful People) was well-received in France and translated into Dutch, Albanian, Japanese, German, Hungarian, Slovak, Rumanian and Bulgarian. The story is that of a young Senegalese, who after eight years away from home, returns with his white wife to his village and there meets defeat in his misguided effort to change the old folks and their ways.

The third novel, *Les bouts de bois de Dieu* (*God's Bits of Wood* in the Doubleday American edition of 1962) was published in Paris in 1960 by Amiot-Dumont. The work describes the long, bitter strike of African workers on the Dakar-Niger railroad to obtain decent wages and working conditions from October, 1947 to March 1948. It was one of the earliest African efforts to break free of the bondage of the worst aspects of colonialism. Widely translated, including an English version in the U. S., it appeared in Italian, Dutch, Japanese, Lithuanian, Uzbek, Ukrainian, and Hungarian as well. The author's note to the novel in the American edition is of particular importance:

> The men and women who, from the tenth of October, 1947, to the nineteenth of March, 1948, took part in this struggle for a better way of life owe nothing to anyone: neither to any "civilizing mission" nor to any parliament or parliamentarian. Their example was not in vain. Since then, Africa has made progress.

The novel ends:

> As the crowd scattered into the shadows of the rapidly descending night, Lahbib heard someone singing. It was the Legend of Goumba, the old song of Maimouna, the blind woman.
>
> From one sun to another,
> The combat lasted,
> And fighting together, blood-covered.
> They transfixed their enemies.
> But happy is the man who does battle
> /without hatred.

Sembene's fourth work was *Voltaïque*, 1962, and his fifth, *L'harmattan* (The Storm), the first of a trilogy. The first volume carried the title *Référendum* and appeared in the review, *Présence Africaine*, 1964. During the early 1960's he was also working on a collection of short stories which was published in 1965 as *Véhi Ciosane ou Blanche-genèse*, published with *Mandat* (Véhi Ciosane or the Origin of Whiteness, followed by The Money Order). The volume won the literature

prize at the first Festival of Negro Arts, Dakar, '966.

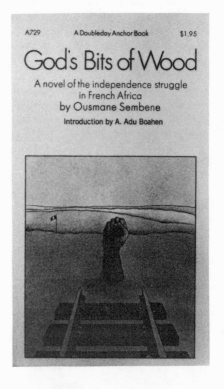

A729   A Doubleday Anchor Book $1.95

God's Bits of Wood

A novel of the independence struggle
in French Africa
by Ousmane Sembene

Introduction by A. Adu Boahen

A. C. Brench's *Writing in French from Senegal to Cameroon* includes an excerpt in French from *Les bouts de bois de Dieu*, along with a useful criticism of the work and an extensive bibliography. In his discussion of Sembène's novel, Brench quotes from the first paragraph of *L'harmattan*:

> I do not theorize about the African novel. I recall just the same that once in this Africa that may be called "classique" (or traditional), the griot professional singer was not only the dynamic element in his tribe, clan, village, but also the obvious testimony or "witness" of every event. It was he who captured, and laid out before everyone

under the tree of talk the deeds and mannerisms of each. The conception of my work will spin out in that manner: to remain as close as possible to the reality and to the people, . . ."

As Brench points out, such a *modus operandi* is true for his other works as well, and he goes on to say that Sembène's *God's Bits of Wood* was a "serious attempt to synthesize a traditional African narrative form with an alien medium of expression and to use this synthesis to portray the evolution of modern Africa with its mixtures of indigenous and Western technological elements." Sembène remains, then, central to any thorough-going consideration of the African novel, particularly to francophone ones.

Works of his are now appearing in film as he has turned to that medium in order to reach an African popular audience, few of whom know French or have access to books in any language. Mostly self-taught, except for his film work in Russia, warm, and socially courageous, his films ask deep questions about poverty, ignorance, and the general human condition.

Two are well-known in the United States: *Barom-Saret* (1963), a semidocumentary treatment of one disastrous day in the life of a Dakar donkey-cart driver and *Le noire de . . .* (Black Girl), a short film which won a major prize at the 1967 Cannes Film Festival, showing the humiliations of a servant girl at the hands of her French master and his wife. The film earlier had been shown at the first World Festival of Negro Arts, in Dakar in 1966. The short story from which it was created appeared in the journal, *Présence Africaine*, 1961, and in English as "Black Girl" in a translation by Ellen Conroy Kennedy in *African Short Stories*.

Trained for a year in film-making at the Gorki Film Studios in Moscow, Sembène is improving with each work. He often sits in the medina or market of Dakar, working as a scribe for the illiterate peasants and workers. A product of this deep involvement with the people of the new Africa has been his most famous picture, *Mandabi*, first shown at the Venice Film Festival in 1968, and later at the New York Film Festival, in 1969, the International Film Festival in San Francisco and the London Film Festival, all also in 1969. The work was chosen as the Best Foreign Film at the 1970 Atlanta Film Festival. Léopold Senghor's story, "Mandabi" (The Money Order, or "Le Mandat" in its French title), served as the original source of the scenario. The complex tale concerns Ibrahim Dieng, a devout Moslem with two loving wives, who receives a large money order from his nephew in Paris. The money is not all for him and he has instructions on how to use it. But, illiterate and inexperienced in such matters, he is tricked and finally ruined in his efforts to cash the order. Everyone seeks to cheat him, or, conversely, encourages him to spend on credit because he is now a rich man.

In an interview with Guy Flatley (*New York Times*, November 9, 1969), Sembène spoke of his feeling about American civilization and his own purposes in making films:

One cannot say, of course, that New York is America. But all over America there is a certain amount of corruption. That is why black people in America want things that come from Africa to be superior. Africa is their identity. They have a nostalgic, idealistic version of Africa. That's the reason the middle class blacks in New York feel badly about my movie Mandabi—it

393

doesn't present a beautiful, glowing picture of Africa.

Sembène went on to explain his purposes:

The thing I was trying to do in it was to show Africans some of the deplorable conditions under which they themselves live. When one creates, one doesn't think of the world; one thinks of his own country. It is, after all, the Africans who will ultimately bring about change in Africa—not the Americans or the French or the Russians or the Chinese.

Writings: Novels: *Le docker noir,* Paris, Nouvelles Editions Debresse, 1956; *O pays, mon beau peuple!* Paris, Amiot-Dumont, 1957; *Les bouts de bois de Dieu,* Paris, Amiot-Dumont, 1960; translated by Francis Price as *God's Bits of Wood,* New York, Doubleday, 1962, New York,

Doubleday-Anchor, 1970; and London, Heinemann, 1970; *L'harmattan,* Volume I: *Réferundum,* Paris, Présence Africaine, 1964, the first of a projected trilogy.

Novelettes: *Voltaïque: nouvelles,* Paris, Présence Africaine, 1962; *Véhi Ciosane ou Blanche-genése,* and *Mandat,* combined volume, Paris, Présence Africaine, 1965; reissued as *Mandat et Véhi Ciosane,* Paris, Présence Africaine, 1969; English translation of both plays, London, Heinemann, 1972.

Stories: "Le noire de..." in *Présence Africaine,* Paris, 1961; and translated as "Black Girl" by Ellen Conroy Kennedy, in *African Short Stories,* Charles R. Larson, editor, New York, Macmillan, 1970.

Films: *Barom-Saret,* 1963; *Le noire de...,*" 1967; *Mandabi,* 1968.

Biographical/Critical Sources: A. C. Brench, *Writing in French from Senegal to Cameron,* London, Oxford University, 1967; interview by Guy Flatley, *New York Times,* November 9, 1969.

SENGAT–KUO, François (also N'DINTSOUNA, Francesco)
b. August 4, 1931, Douala, Cameroon.
Poet, essayist, teacher, diplomat.

François Sengat-Kuo presently serves as secretary general to Cameroon's President Ahmadou Ahidjo and is a professor of public administration at the Ecole Nationale d'Administration et de Magistrature in Yaoundé. His education began at the Akwa Regional Primary School outside Douala, continued at the Lycée Leclerc in Yaoundé and the Lycée Pierre d'Ailly, in Compiègne, France. He took the Licence en Droit at the University of Paris and the Diplôme d'Etudes

Supérieure in economics at the same school.

President of the Union of Cameroonian students from 1953 to 1959 in Paris, he also began his writing career as a contributor and editor of *Présence Africaine*, and served as director of the review, *Kaso*.

Returning home in 1960, Sengat-Kuo took on a variety of governmental posts in the Ministry of Foreign Affairs (Director of the Cabinet, Technical Advisor, Director of Economic and Technical Affairs, in 1960); he was Secretary-General of the Conférence des Chefs d'Etat Africaine (the Conference of the Chiefs-of-State) of the Monrovia-Western-oriented African States in 1961; was Permanent Secretary of the African and Malagasy Union at the United Nations from 1961 to 1965; and from 1965 to 1967 he headed the Cameroonian Delegation at the 8th Session of the Economic Commission of the UN.

His three collections of verse in French are: *Fleurs de latérite* (Laterite Flowers), a 29-page volume; *Heures rouges, poèmes* (Red Hours, Poems), produced in a special edition of the *Revue Camerounaise*, 1957; and *Collier de cauris (poèmes), suivi d'Une étude de Thomas Melone* (Necklace of Cowrie Shells [poems], followed by a study by Thomas Melone) a 61-page work published in 1970. The first two volumes are extremely vigorous and negritudist in their attacks on colonialism and race prejudice, while the recent collection is more tranquil and seeks a wider world to contemplate. *Jonala, the Journal of the New African Literature and the Arts,* presented seven poems in the French text from *Colliers de cauris* (Winter-Spring issue, 1971). His two-page poem, "Préjugée (Prejudiced), appears in *New Sum of Poetry from the Negro World*. The poem shows the influence of the great French Guianese poet, Léon Gontran Damas, with its repetitive cadences and phrases.

Writings: Poetry: *Fleurs de latérite,* Monte Carlo, Eds. Regain, 1954; *Heures rouges, poèmes,* in special edition, *Revue Camerounaise,* 1957; *Collier de cauris (poèmes), suivi d'une ètude de Thomas Melone,* Paris, Présence Africaine, 1970.

Poems: "Préjugée" in *New Sum of Poetry from the Negro World*, Paris, Présence Africaine, Vol. 66, 1966; seven poems in *Jonala, the Journal of the New African Literature and the Arts,* Winter-Spring, 1971, and P. J. Trout article on author.

SENGHOR, Léopold Sédar
b. October 9, 1906, Joal, Senegal.
Poet, essayist, teacher, statesman.

Born into a prosperous Serer family of Catholic religious beliefs, in the small town of Joal, 75 miles south of Dakar, Senghor grew up in a predominantly Moslem community. His father, Basile Diogoye, was a very successful merchant of ground-nuts, able to give his gifted son an excellent education. The young Léopold attended a Catholic mission school run by the Catholic Fathers of the Holy Spirit at N'Gasobil, then went on to Libermann College, a classical lycée, in Dakar. A brilliant student, he was enrolled in the prestigious Lycée Louis-le-Grand in Paris where he took the French bachelor's degree in 1928. In 1933 Senghor became the first Black African to earn the "aggregation" (somewhat like the American master's degree) from the Sorbonne.

In 1934 he was awarded the Diplôme d'Etudes Supérieures, akin to the American doctorate, after writing the thesis,

"Exoticism in Baudelaire" (English translation). The following year Senghor earned the Licence-ès-Lettres from the Sorbonne, a prerequisite for teaching in the French lycée. During the middle 1930's he also studied African languages at the Ecole des Hautes Etudes, Paris, and fulfilled his military service.

Senghor joined the faculty of the Lycée Descartes in Tours to teach the Greek and Latin classics there from 1935 to 1938, then went on to the Lycée Marcellin Berthelot from 1938 to 1940, in St. Maur-des-Fossés, a suburb of Paris. During the latter part of this period he did not actually teach, though he was on the faculty, for he had been called into active military service at the outbreak of the Second World War in September, 1939, serving as an officer in the French Army at the front.

He was captured June 29, 1940, with many of his unit in the French rout of that spring. He was wooed by the Germans to desert the French cause, but though an African nationalist, he was also loyal to his dual cultural inheritance. He refused and sought to organize resistance in the prison camp to German pressures, particularly those directed at his fellow African prisoners. Released in 1944, along with many others before the war's end, he returned to Paris to teach African languages at the Ecole Nationale de la France d'Outre-mer, in Paris and St. Maur on whose faculty he again served.

During his student days in Paris, Senghor, along with Aimé Césaire of Martinique and Léon Gontran Damas of French Guiana, started the movement called Negritude, a neologism coined by Césaire. Arguing for African pride and a recognition by Africans of their humanity and long cultural inheritance, Senghor and his friends began their life-long effort to redeem the past and to elevate African art, ideas, and history into genuine matters of pride for black Africans and of intellectual concern to all others. Many young black writers, African Caribbean, and North and South American, were encouraged and stimulated to seek out their own ethnic and regional values and beliefs by this movement and the literature and discussions it helped generate. In France particularly, Negritude inspired many African writers and students. Developing a truly African idiom in their work, though usually expressed in French, these newer writers joined Senghor to produce a strong new African literature, particularly during the heady days of the

1950's when independence became more and more a possibility for the African colonies of France.

Senghor was also busy tilling the political vineyards in those days. Because of the important role Africa had played during the war, and particularly because of the leadership exerted by Félix Eboué, the black governor of Chad who had rallied to the cause of De Gaulle's Free French, the post-war government of France invited representatives from Africa to establish a new relationship with France at a Constituent Assembly in Paris, 1945. Senghor, with Lamine Guèye, a senior statesman from Senegal, quickly helped organize the Bloc Africain, a socialist-oriented group which allied itself with the S.F.I.O., the French Socialist Party.

Senghor and Guèye were elected deputies to the meeting and for a year and a half worked with the S.F.I.O., but the French socialists' slowness in helping advance genuine African liberty and social progress led Senghor to break with Guèye who stayed close to the S.F.I.O. Senghor founded the journal, *Condition Humaine,* and organized a mass party of Senegalese, the majority of whom were not yet citizens of France but merely subjects with no political rights of any importance. In October, 1948, his Bloc Démocratique Sénégalais (B.D.S.) was born, affiliating itself only with a group of black Africans who refused an alliance with any of the metropolitan political parties of France.

During this period, Senghor founded with Alioune Diop in 1947, the vigorous black cultural journal, *Présence Africaine,* which with its publishing house of the same name, has put many works by black writers from all parts of the world into print and become a major stimulus to creative writing for the entire continent.

Senghor's newly organized party, the I.O.M., by 1951 had come to dominate Senegalese politics and he defeated Guèye in a show-down battle for supremacy by taking one of the two seats in the French national parliament reserved for Senegal and taking with him in victory the other seat for a member of his party. From this point on, Senghor in a series of political maneuvers, with and against Lamine Gué led Senegal to republic status in 1959 within the French Community. In 1959, he became the first president of the new state of Mali, a union of Senegal and the former French Soudan, but when the strains became too much for the partners in the new state, Senegal broke away as an independent entity with the Soudan going its way with the new name. (Mali as a term, of course, recalls the medieval sub-Saharan kingdom in West Africa.)

Elected president of Senegal in 1960, he led his country into the newly formed group of moderate African states, called first the "Brazzaville" and later the "Monrovia" group, which balanced the more radical Guinea, Ghana, Mali, Algeria, Morocco, Egypt and Algeria in the so-called "Casablanca" group.

Domestically, Senghor broke with Mamadou Dia, his Premier. In a tense, brief confrontation with Dia who was backed by units of the army, Senghor, supported by the paratroops, took over complete control of the country on December 17, 1962. On the 18th, the Senegalese National Assembly unanimously authorized Senghor to work for a new constitution or a major reform of the old one, and to submit the proposed document to the people in a nationwide referendum. The following

January, the deposed Mamadou Dia and four of his allies from the former Cabinet were charged by the Assembly with treason and moved to a trial before the High Court. Unlike the pattern in some African states, the sentences in April resulted in exile for five years and severe house arrest in the hinterland for the men found guilty, rather than death.

During the 1950's, Senghor twice represented France at General Conferences of UNESCO; from March, 1955 to February, 1956, he was the Secretary of State of the Presidency of the Council (the French Prime Minister's Office) during the government of Edgar Faure. He was also one of the chief negotiators in the discussions leading to Tunisia's independence from France. From July 1959 to July 1960, he served as Minister-Counsellor of the French Ministry of Cultural Affairs, Education, and Justice.

As a Christian from the small subnation of the Serer people, Senghor has been able to hold together the strong rival factions in Senegal, balancing the majority Moslem peoples (themselves divided between the Mouride and the Tidjani sects) and the powerful groups of Wolofs, Peuls, Malinkés, Toucouleurs, and others, pagan, Christian and Moslem. He has been successful because his political base did not threaten any of the larger groupings. Ironically, it was the generally better educated and more Westernized Christian youths who supported Prime Minister Dia's efforts to align Senegal with the more radical states of the Casablanca group and to pursue a more Marxist policy at home. In 1973 Senghor was still President and though the country was suffering the usual strains of all new nations, it apparently is continuing a reasonably quiet progress.

Through all his varied political activity, Senghor has continued to live the life of an intellectual, and to write as a polemicist, poet, critic, anthologist, student of language, and grammarian. Of world-wide importance was his sponsorship in Senegal of the first World Festival of Negro Arts in Dakar, in 1966, organized by Senghor's old friend and publisher of *Présence Africaine*, Alioune Diop. In April, 1971, a select group of artists, scholars and critics gathered in Dakar to discuss Negritude: its past, present, and future. Papers were prepared and many read at the gathering, with a publication in the offing from *Présence Africaine* covering the conference.

In 1962, rumor had it that Senghor was seriously being considered for the Nobel Prize in literature, but he failed to win, if indeed he was nominated. He remains possibly Africa's leading claimant to such an award—and no Black African has yet been so honored. Senghor has been elected into the extremely exclusive French academic society, the Agrégés de Grammaire, the highest organization of intellectuals in France.

From his earliest student days in Paris, Senghor wrote poetry and today the list of his works is an extensive one. Spanning 20 years, they are: *Chants d'ombre* (Songs of the Shade) 1945; *Hostie noires* (Black Victims), 1948; *Chants pour Naëtt* (Songs for Naëtt), 1949; *Ethiopiques*, 1956; and *Nocturnes* (1961), the latter including *Chants, Pour Naëtt*, and previously unpublished poems. In 1956, Seuil, his major publisher, reissued *Chants d'ombre et Hosties noires* which combined those collections, and in 1964 republished all of the original volumes except *Pour Naëtt* in a large, 253-page edition called *Poèmes*.

Senghor edited the pioneering anthology, *Anthologie de la nouvelle poésie nègre et malgache*, preceded by the now famous, if controversial preface "Orphée noir," by Jean-Paul Sartre. (1948). It was this collection that pushed many black African writers, into the limelight and made evident how much good work had already been done in French by African artists. More recently, in 1967, he published *Nègritude, Arabisme et Francité* (Negritude, Arabism and French-ness), sub-titled *Réflexions sur le problème de la culture.*

Wishing to provide an elementary text for African children which could serve as an alternative of the standard and exclusively French-oriented school books, Senghor and Abdoulaye Sadji wrote and had published in 1953 *La belle histoire de Leuk-le-Lièvre* (The Clever Story of Leuk-the-Hare). Senghor also created in the prose tale, "Mandabi" (The Money Order), a memorable tale of old and new ways in Dakar which was exploited in a film of that name by Ousmane Sembène.

Senghor's poems have been widely anthologized and his work in English translation appears in several good British collections. Possibly the most comprehensive is *Senghor: Prose and Poetry,* edited and translated by John Reed and Clive Wake (1965), and Reed and Wake's *Selected Poems* (1964). Many dissertations on Senghor have recently been completed in European, British and North American universities and scores of articles continue to come out on various aspects of his poetry or career. An early but still useful biographical and critical study is in Gerald Moore's *Seven African Writers.* The Paris firm, Fernand Nathan, published in 1964 *Léopold Sédar Senghor* in its "Littérature Africaine" series which provides biographical, critical, and bibliographical information plus some extracts of his poetry. Of particular value in the original French is *Léopold Sédar Senghor,* the collection of prose and

poetry in the Segher's volume edited by Armand Guibert which also offers a good biography and bibliography plus photos. A useful study of one aspect of his work is Lamine Diakhaté's "Le mythe dans la poésie populaire au Sénégal et sa présence dans l'oeuvre de L.-S. Senghor et Birago Diop," published in *Présence Africaine,* 39 (1961).

Two of Senghor's own studies of poetry are "Langage et poésie négro-africaine," published in *Poésie et language;* "L'apport de la poésie nègre," in *Témoignage sur le poésie du demisiècle* (1953).

Senghor has published four technical works on Wolof grammer and in 1961 Présence Africaine published his important political work, *Nation et voie Africaine du Socialisme* (The African Way to Statehood and Socialism), called *African Socialism* in its American edition by the American Society of African Culture.

For the literary world, of course, Senghor is primarily the poet. His youthful writings before 1939 were full of wistful memories of home and impregnated by the negritudist need to recall a vanished and beautiful Africa. He had sought to make his poetic work a bridge of unity between all African peoples and an expression of their cultural tragedy and their worth. As a prisoner of war he was inspired to write some of his most powerful works on being black and being African, and though he has gradually embraced other ideas he remains more purely than any other African poet, the singer of nostalgia and African warmth. Yet, in many ways, Senghor is the most thoughtful and forebearing critic of colonialism.

His poems have been published in many journals: *Chantiers; Les Cahiers du Sud; Poésie, 1947–49; Les Lettres Françaises, Les Temps Modernes; Le Temps de la*

Senghor

Poésie; La Revue Socialiste, Présence Africaine, Prévue, and others.

Essentially the lyric poet, Senghor has essayed a quasi-dramatic poem, "Elégie à Aynina Fall. Poème dramatique a plusieurs voix" (Elegy for Aynina Fall: Dramatic Poem with or For Many Voices), which has been successfully staged several times. First published in Présence Africaine, 1956–57, it was republished in Nocturnes, 1961, and in Poèmes, 1964.

Senghor frequently employs the African woman as symbol for the total African past and spiritual present. In his early poem, " Femme Noire," from Chants d'ombre, 1945, he begins:

Femme nue, femme noire
Vêtue de ta couleur qui est vie, de ta forme
/qui est beauté!
J'ai grandi à ton ombre; la douceur de
/tes mains bandait mes yeux.
Et voilà qu'au coeur de l'Eté et deMidi,
/je te découvre Terre
promise, du haut d'un haut col calciné
Et ta beauté me foudroie en plein coeur,
/comme l'éclair d'un aigle.

Translation into English of Senghor's work often weaken's emphases highly significant in the original text. For example, in the first three lines translated into English, by having the adjective first, there is an unintended displacement of the frontal importance of "femme":

Naked woman, black woman
Clothed in your color which is life, with
/your shape that is beauty!
I grew in your shadow; the softness of your
/hands swathed my eyes.
(trans. Reed and Wake)

Attention now goes to the words, naked, and black, which, though important in the French text, are only secondary to the focus on the woman as mother, and ultimately, as Mother Africa.

Though Senghor is a master of French, is married to a French woman, has a vacation retreat in Normandy, and has kept up good relations with France, he still could write such powerful lines as these from "Prayer for Peace: II: For Grand Organ":

Lord God, forgive white Europe.
It is true, Lord, that for four enlightened
/centuries, she
has scattered the baying
and slaver of her mastiffs
over my lands
And the Christians, forsaking thy light and
/the gentleness of the heart
Have lit their camp fires with my parch-
/ments, tortured
my disciples, deported
my doctors and masters of science.
. . .
Lord, forgive them who turned the Askia into
/maquisards, my princes into sergeant-
/majors
My household servants into 'boys', my peas-
/ants into wage-earners,
my people into a working class.

He finishes with:

Lord, the glasses of my eyes grow dim
And lo, the serpent of hatred raises its head
/in my heart,
that serpent that I believed was dead.
(trans.: Reed and Wake)

Senghor also does not forget the Africans carried off to the plantations of the Americas although he admits he has been slow to regard them as brothers. In the poem "To the American Negro Troops" he writes:

Formerly, I did not recognize you in the pri-
/son of your tight drab uniform.
I did not recognize you under your
/gourd of a plumeless helmet.
. . .
Behind your strong face, I did not recognize
/you.
Yet I had only to touch the warmth of
/your dark hand—my name is Africa!

and he ends the 26-line poem with the lines:

400

Oh, black brothers, warriors whose mouths
/are singing flowers—
Delight of living when winter is over—
You I salute as messengers of peace!

(trans.: Reed and Wake)

Here not only does he see the American blacks in uniform as partners of the end of the war but also as harbingers of a time when Africa will be free again, at peace with itself and others, and, more wistfully, no doubt, of a time when blacks in the New World, will feel their own dignity and not have to beg or fight for it.

The product of the finest education France and possibly the West can offer, and a true Cosmopolite, Senghor, can turn, quite naturally, in his poem, "Priére aux Masques" (Prayer to the Masks) to the still relevant though almost forgotten faces of the ancient African gods and earth-spirits:

Masks! O Masks!
Black mask red mask, you black and white
/masks,
Masks with the four points from which the
/Spirit blows:
I greet you in the silence!

(trans. D. H.)

After seeing his own face as a black mask above the white paper, he concludes:

Fix your immutable eyes upon your children
/who are commanded
Who give their lives like the poor man his
/last garment.
May we answer "Present" at the rebirth
/of the World.

Thus, Senghor, the man; Senegal, the nation; and Africa, the lost, now found-again continent, sings to the world.

Writings: Poetry: *Chants d'ombre*, Paris, Seuil, 1945; *Hosties noires*, Paris, Seuil, 1948; *Chants pour Naëtt*, Paris, Seghers, 1948; *Ethiopiques*, Paris, Seuil, 1956; *Noc-*

turnes, Paris, Seuil, 1961, includes *Chants pour Naëtt*, and unpublished poems; *Chants d'ombre* and *Hosties noires*, Paris, Seuil, 1956; *Poèmes*, Paris, Seuil, 1964, which includes *Chants d'ombre*, *Hosties noires*, *Ethiopique*, *Nocturnes*, and *Poèmes divers*. Also: the collection by Armand Guibert, *Léopold Sédar Senghor*, Paris, Seghers, 1962, 215 pages, which includes a biographic-critical introduction, texts of prose and poems, bibliography, portraits, and facsimiles of a few holograph pages; and special edition: *Elégie des alizés*, with an original lithograph of Marc Chagall, Paris, Seuil, 1969, 25 pages.

Poems in English: *Selected Poems*, Reed and Wake, editors, London, Oxford University Press, 1964; New York, Atheneum, 1964; *Prose and Poetry*, Reed and Wake, editors and translators, London, Oxford University Press, 1965; *Nocturnes: love poems*, Reed and Wake, London, Heinemann, 1970.

401

Anthology: *Anthologie de la nouvelle poésie nègre et malgache, précédée de Orphée noir,* par Jean-Paul Sarte, Paris, Presses Universitaires de France, 1948, 1969.

Dramatic Poem: "Elégie à Aynina Fall. Poème dramatique à plusieurs voix," in *Présence Africaine,* No. 11, December 1956–January 1957; also in *Nocturnes,* Paris, Seuil, 1961, and in *Poèmes,* 1964.

Criticism: "Language et poésie négro-africaine," in *Poésie et Language,* Brussels, 1954; "L'apport de la poésie nègre," in *Témoignage sur la poésie du demisiècle;* Paris.

Phonograph Recording: *Poèmes de Léopold Sédar Senghor,* read by Georges Aminel, 33 rpm, in series "Poésie de Demain," by Vega-Seghers, Paris.

Linguistic Studies: "Les classes nominales en Wolof et les substantifs a l'initiale nasale," *Journal de la Société des Africanistes,* XIII, 1944; "L'harmonie vocalique en sérère, dialecte du dyéguème," Ibid, XVII, 1947; "La dialectique du nom-verbe en wolof," Ibid, date unknown. These articles were written under the pseudonyms, Silmang Diamano or Patrice Maguilene Kaymor.

Sociology and Culture: *Négritude, Arabisme et Francité,* preface by Jean Rous, Beirut, Lebanon, Editions Dar Al-Kitab Allubnani, 1967 republished as *Les fondements de l'Africanité ou Négritude et Arabité,* Paris, 1967; "Elements constructifs d'une civilization d'inspiration négro-africaine," in *Présence Africaine,* February-May, 1959; "Défense de l'Afrique noire," in *L'esprit,* July, 1945; "L'esprit de la civilization ou les lois de la culture négro-africaine," in *Présence Africaine,* June-November, 1956; *Liberté I: Négritude et humanisme,* Paris, 1964, "Pourquoi une ideologie négro africaine" in *Présence Africaine,* second trimester, 1972.

School text: *La belle histoire de Leukle-Lièvre,* Paris, Hachette, 1953.

Politics: *Nation et voie africaine du socialisme,* Paris, Présence Africaine, 1961; translated by Mercer Cook as *Nationhood and the African Road to Socialism,* New York, Praeger, 1965; London, Pall Mall Press, 1965; as *African Socialism,* in English text by Présence Africaine, Paris, 1962; *La communauté imperiale française,* with R. Lemaigne and Prince Sissowath Youtevong, Paris, Ed. Alsatia, 1945; *Pierre Teilhard de Chardin et la politique africaine,* Paris, Ed. du Seuil, 1962.

Biographical/Critical Sources: Herbert de Leusse, *Léopold Sédar Senghor, l'Africain,* Paris, Hatier, 1967; Armand Guibert, "Léopold S. Senghor," *Encounter,* London, February, 1961; A. Guibert, "Avec Léopold Sédar Senghor, chef d'état africain et poète français, *"Le Figaro littéraire,"* April 15, 1961; A. Guibert, *Léopold Sédar Senghor, l'homme et l'oeuvre,* Paris, Présence Africaine, 1962; *Léopold Sédar Senghor,* R. Mercier, M. and S. Battestini, editors, Paris, Fernand Nathan, 1964; Irving Leonard Markovitz, *Léopold Sédar Senghor and the Politics of Negritude,* New York, Atheneum, 1969; Gerald Moore, in *Seven African Writers,* London, Oxford University Press, 1962; Sebastian Okechukwu Mezu, *Léopold Sédar Senghor et le défense et illustration de la civilisation noire,* Paris, Didier, 1968; René Piquion, *Les 'Trois Grands' de la négritude,* Port-au-Prince, Haiti, Impr. H. Deschamps, 1961; Marcien Towa, *Léopold Sédar Senghor, négritude ou servitude,* Yaoundé, CLE, 1971; and Jean Rous, *Léopold Sédar Senghor* Paris, J. Didier, 1968.

SENTSO, Dyke (or Sentsho)
b. 1924, Kroonstad, Orange Free

State, South Africa, of Lesotho parents.
Southern Sotho poet, short story writer.

Dyke Sentšo's father was a pastor of the Dutch Reformed Church for Africans at Kroonstad at the time of his birth. He attended local schools and then trained as a teacher at the London Missionary Institution of Tigerkloof in the Cape Province. After graduation he began to teach at a middle school in Bredefort in the Orange Free State. He has written one book in Sotho and has published many short stories, some of which have been translated into European languages and published abroad. His one volume of verse is *Matlakala* (1948).

Writings: Poetry: *Matlakala,* Morija, Basutoland, Morija Sesuto Book Depot, 1948; poems in *Darkness and Light: an Anthology of African Writing,* Peggy Rutherford, editor, Johannesburg, Drum Publications, 1958; London, Faith Press, 1958; published as *African Voices,* New York, Grosset, 1959, 1970.

SENYATSI, Charles Phuti
b. October 16, 1921, Sekuruwe, Pietersburg District, South Africa, Northern Sotho novelist, journalist, teacher.

C. P. Senyatsi entered school in Bethesda, South Africa, where he completed his primary education, moving on to the Grace Dieu School in Warmbad. He then became a teacher at the Emmarentia Geldenhuis School from 1943 until 1950. In 1948, he obtained his B.A. from the University College of Fort Hare, and in 1962 was made a member of London's

College of Preceptors. He is the editor of the newspaper *Motswalle wa Bana* and is a member of the Southern Sotho Sub-Committee of the Bantu Education Advisory Council.

He has published two novels in the Northern Sotho (or Pedi) language: *Maroba,* 1961, and *Thariyatshepe* (Springbuck-skin-for-carrying-a-baby or, Good Child Rearing), 1962.

Writings: Novels: *Maroba,* Bloemfontein, Via Afrika, 1953, fourth printing, 1965; *Thariyatshepe,* Bloemfontein, Via Afrika, 1962, third printing, 1966.

SENYI, Kobina
b. ca. 1890, Nigeria.
Playwright.

Kobina Senyi's play, *The Blinkards,* was performed in Lagos in 1917, but has not been published. This pioneering play expressed a nostalgic pride in the "older ways" and decried a too easy acceptance of the European. The closing speech catches the point of the play:

If only we were national we should be more rational and infinitely more respectable. Our ways and our things suit our climate. For one thing, our drinks have not the same maddening effect on our people that European drinks have. The people of the old days were wise indeed; if only we would follow the customs they left us a little more and adopt the ways of other races a little less we should at least be as healthy as they were.

For a discussion of early plays from Africa see "A Play by a Fanti Author, *West Africa,* April 28, 1917 which cites Senyi's work, and the essay "J. B. Danquah: Evolué Playwright," by Anthony Graham-White in *New African Literature and the Arts.*

Writings: Play: *The Blinkards,* performed in Lagos, 1917, unpublished.

Biographical/Critical Sources: "A Play by a *Fanti Author," West Africa,* April 28, 1917; Anthony Graham-White, "J. B. Danquah: Evolué Playwright," *New African Literature and the Arts: I,* Joseph Okpaku, editor, New York, Crowell, 1970.

SERUMA, Eneriko (pseudonym for KIMBUGWE, Henry Seruma) b. ca. 1940, Uganda. Novelist, story writer.

Seruma has published two works: *The Experience,* 1970, an "expressionistic" rendering of Africa today, declares the author, and *The Heart Seller,* a collection of short stories, two of which have won international prizes.

Writings: Novel: *The Experience,* Nairobi, East African Publishing House, 1970; being prepared for publication, "The King's Hunt."

Stories: *The Heart Seller,* Nairobi, East Africa Publishing House, 197? All of the stories previously had appeared in journals.

SERUMAGA, Robert b. 1939, Uganda. Novelist, playwright, theater director, economist.

Robert Serumaga attended Makerere University in Kampala, Uganda and Trinity College, Dublin, taking the M.A. there in 1965. Though he is an economist by profession, he has acted in stage, radio, and television plays, and has published stories in *Transition,* the important journal published in Kampala until the late 1960's. His first interest is the drama and for some years he produced the BBC program, "Africa Abroad."

He has founded a recording studio and theater company in the capital, Theatre Limited, which has performed his most recent play, *Elephants,* in Kampala in 1969 and Nairobi in 1970, and *Majangwa,* considered by some critics to be the best play premiered in Africa in 1971. Serumaga acted in and directed his own play and has performed in England and Uganda in Soyinka's *The Trials of Brother Jero* and Edward Albee's *Who's Afraid of Virginia Woolf?* His one-act drama, *A Play,* was first performed at the National Theatre, Kampala, October, 1967, and was published that year. In 1970, while in the United States negotiating the performance of that work, he successfully sought funds that will enable Theatre Limited to tour the United States in the fall of 1972.

Serumaga's first novel, *Return to the Shadows,* 1969, dramatizes the plight of the mildly idealistic Joe Musizi in the brutal new world of political roughhouse in independent Africa.

Writings: Plays: *A Play,* Kampala, Uganda Publishing House, 1968; *Elephants,* unpublished, but performed in 1969 and 1970; *Majangwa,* performed in 1971, published Nairobi, East African Publishing House, 1972.

Novel: *Return to the Shadows,* London, Heinemann, 1969; New York, Atheneum, 1970.

SEY, Kofi
b. ca. 1925, Ghana.
Poet, teacher.

Kofi Sey is presently a professor of English at the University of Ghana, Legon. He has published only occasionally, but he is represented by five poems in *Messages: Poems from Ghana:* "We Sat Down There," "The Vampire," (two of that name), "How Dare You," and "Suicide."

In addition, Sey has privately published a very limited edition of some of his poems set to music by his friend, Ebenezer Laing, but title and other information is unavailable.

Writings: Poems in *Messages: Poems from Ghana,* London, Heinemann, 1971; limited edition of poems, details unavailable, except that verses were set to music by Ebenezer Laing.

SHAIKH, Muhyi 'l-Din al-Waili
b. 1778, East Africa (present Tanzania); d. 1869.
Swahili oral poet.

Shaikh Muhyi served as Kadhi or chief judge of the island of Zanzibar in his later years. He composed many poems, including "Kitab al-Sulwa" (now extant in manuscript at the British Museum, London), and "Dua ya Kuombea Mvua" (Prayer for Rain).

Writings: Poems: "Kitab al-Sulwa," in manuscript, British Museum; "Dua ya Kuombea Mvua."

SHEMBE, Isaiah
b. late 1860's, Zululand, Natal, South Africa; d. May 2, 1935.
Zulu poet, hymn-writer, preacher, religious leader.

Believed to have been the son of a farm laborer, Isaiah Shembe had no schooling nor little experience with European culture in his youth. However, he was influenced by members of a Baptist Mission sometime in the late 1890's or early 20th century, and in 1906 was baptized by the Reverend Leshaga, a minister in the African Native Baptist Church.

According to one student of Shembe's career, Gerharus C. Oosthuizen, Shembe had originally found that church most acceptable because of its literal belief in the Bible's teachings, the strong symbolism of Christian baptism, and the over-all nativist aspects of this denomination. Such fundamentalist Christianity blended with traditional Zulu beliefs and practices made the Baptist Church a transmission belt of certain Western ideas to the largely unlettered Zulu people. Shembe, ordained a minister immediately after his baptism, and already something of a seer and prophet, went out by foot or oxcart to drive out devils, to produce rain to break droughts, and to heal and purify with holy water. He preached at poolside, in kraals, in the open, and rarely used Western forms of transportation.

In 1911, five years after his ordination, Shembe broke away from the Baptists, by then felt to be alien, to form his own syncretic church, the "iBandla lamaNazeretha" (The Church of the Nazarites). In 1913, he went to the mountain Nhlangakazi which became his sacred peak. In 1914 (or 1916 according to some authorities) he founded the holy city of the new Nazareth, called

Ekuphakameni, some 18 miles from Durban near the school in Ohlange established by the Zulu scholar John L. Dube. On Shembe's death in 1935, he was succeeded in the church leadership by his son, Johannes Galilee Shembe (b. 1904), who had trained at Fort Hare University College. Shembe is today considered the greatest of the religious leaders of South Africa who have sought to meld the old and new faiths of Africa and Europe.

A Trinitarian, Shembe during his religious progress increasingly came to see himself and was so accepted by his followers as Jesus Christ come again, joining God the Father and the Holy Ghost as a new triune God for the Zulus. Shembe restored the once outlawed Zulu dances into his church's religious worship, accepted polygamy which he had earlier preached against, taught the respect due the chiefs, and otherwise sought to integrate the Zulu culture's own traditions and beliefs with the alien Christian concepts and teachings.

Shembe's poetic talents found their outlet in his syncretist Zulu-Christian hymns, first published in 1940 along with some of his son's work in the collection *Izihlabelelo zaNazarethe* (Nazarite Hymns). Possibly the oldest hymn of Shembe's was one that he had taught to children of his followers who sang it as they accompanied him to Natal in 1910 and it may have been the first Zulu poem or song reflecting Western influences. A second famous hymn car.,e to him as he climbed Nhlangakazi Mountain.

From 1920 on Shembe wrote many more hymns and prayers for his services. Some 219 hymns of the 1940 edition of Nazarite Hymns are believed to be his, including a few believed by his most fervent followers to have been composed *after* Shembe's "resurrection" in May, 1939, a central fact in the religion which he founded.

Writings: Hymnal: *Izihlabelelo zaNazarethe*, 1940.

Biographical/Critical Sources: Albert S. Gérard, *Four African Literatures*, Berkeley, University of California Press, 1971. Gerharus C. Oosthuizen, *The Theology of a South African Messiah: An Analysis of the Hymnal of the Church of the Nazarites*, Leiden, 1967; Bengt G. M. Sundkler, *Bantu Prophets in South Africa*, London, 1948, 1961; John L. Dube, *uShembe*, a biography, Pietermartizburg, 1936; Absalom Vilakazi, " 'Isonto Lamanazaretha,' The Church of the Nazarites," unpublished Ph. D. dissertation, Hartford Seminary Foundation, 1954.

SIDAHOME, Joseph E.
b. 1917, Owaha, Iokan Division of Benin Province, Nigeria; d. July 1963.
Collector of folktales, lawyer.

Locally educated in primary and high schools, Sidahome attended King's College, Onitsha, where he took the Senior School Certificate which earned him an exemption from the London Matriculation examination, for he went on to study law at King's College, London. He has practiced law since taking his legal degree.

Sidahome became interested in the folk tales which preserved the history of the Benin Empire which flourished from 1400 to 1800, and he set about collecting the stories in the work published as *Stories of the Benin Empire*, the year after his death.

Writings: Folktales: *Stories of the Benin*

Empire, London, Oxford University Press, 1964.

SILVA, Terêncio Casimiro Anahory
(see ANAHORY, Terêncio)

SILVEIRA, Onésimo (see da SILVERIA, Onésimo)

SINDA, Martial
b. ca. 1930, near Brazzaville, Congo (now République Populaire du Congo).
Poet.

One of the earliest Congolese poets to be published, Sinda has one volume of verse in print, *Premier chant du départ,* 1955, and is represented in Clive Wake's *An Anthology of African and Malagasy Poetry in French.*

Writings: Poetry: *Premier chant du départ,* Paris, Segher, 1955; poems in *An Anthology of African and Malagasy Poetry in French,* Oxford, Three Crowns Press, 1965; *A Book of African Verse,* Reed and Wake, editors, London Heinemann, 1964.

SINXO, Guybon Budlwana
b. October 8, 1902, Fort Beaufort District, Cape Province, South Africa; d. June 14, 1962.
Xhosa novelist, poet, biographer, playwright, translator, teacher.

Born a member of the Zangwa clan, Sinxo had local schooling and attended St. Matthew's from 1916 to 1919, leaving with a Teacher's Certificate to instruct at Richmond school in the Karree area,

his first assignment as an educator. Married to Samuel Mqhayi's eldest daughter, Beula Nohle in 1924, and a friend of James Jolobe and Enoch Stephen, both St. Matthew's graduates and later famous Xhosa writers, Sinxo himself early turned to literature. His first novel, *U-Nomsa,* appeared in 1922; his second *Umfundisi wase-Mtuqwasi* (The Preacher from Mtuqwasi), 1927, dedicated to his wife; and his third, *Umzali wolahlêko* (The Prodigal Parent), in 1933.

His one play, *Imfene ka Debeza* (Debeza's Baboon), was issued by Lovedale Press in 1925. His many short stories appeared in the collections, *Isakhono somfazi namanye amabalana* (A Woman's Skill and other short stories); *Imbadu* (Tramping Along), Johannesburg; and a 1960 edition of the first play collection with a few stories added, *Imfene ka Debeza neminye imidlalwana* (Debeza's Baboon and other tales). Three collections of stories came out as *U-Nojayiti wam* (Vols. 1, 1961, and II, 1965, translated as *My Wife Nojayiti),* and *Isitiya* (The Corn Field). His one collection of poems was *Thoba sikutyele; amabali emibongo angama-76* (Rush, That We Might Tell You; 76 Praise Poems).

Sinxo's translations were: *Umbanjwa wase Zenda,* from Anthony Hope's *The Prisoner of Zenda;* and *Uzibaningashekazi;* a Xhosa version of *She* by Rider Haggard, the Victorian writer whose 19th century novels on South Africa are still in print and read throughout the world and whose *King Solomon's Mines (Imigodi kakumklani USolomon)* was translated by James Jolobe in 1958; and *U-Robinson Crusoe,* a 1961 translation of Defoe's novel. Posthumously (1965), Afrikaanse Pers-Boekhandel brought out his Xhosa version of *Jock of the Bushveld* by Fitzpatrick, entitled *UJock wasezindle.* The same publisher also issued Sinxo's trans-

Sinxo

lation of a biography of Abraham Lincoln, *Ubomi buka Abraham Lincoln*, 1959.

Sinxo lived in Port Elizabeth from the early 1950's, teaching, contributing poems and occasional articles to *Drum, Our Africa*, and other journals. He was awarded the Vilakazi Memorial Award in 1954 for his writings. He left a wife, his second, Elizabeth Lena Tutu Sinxo, and two children, when he died at the age of 60 in 1962.

Writings: Novels: *U-Nomsa*, Lovedale, Lovedale Press, 1922; *Umfundisi wase-Mtuqwasi* (or *Mthuqwasi*), Lovedale, Lovedale Press, 1927; *Umzali Wolahlêko*, Lovedale Press, 1933.

Plays: *Imfene ka Debeza*, Lovedale, Lovedale Press, 1925; *Imfene ka Debeza neminye imidlalwana*, Cape Town, Oxford University Press, 1960, which contains new stories as well as a reprint of *Imfene ka Debeza.*

Short Stories: *Isakhono somfazi namanye amabalana*, Johannesburg, Afrikaanse Pers-Boekhandel, 1956; 3rd printing, 1958; *Imbadu*, Johannesburg, Bantoe-Publikasies, 1960; *U-Nojayiti wam*, Lovedale, Lovedale Press, Volume 1, 1961; Volume II, 1965; *Isitiya*, Lovedale, Lovedale Press, 1964.

Poetry: *Thoba sikutyele; amabali emibongo angama-76*, Lovedale, 1959.

Translations: Biography: *Ubomi buka Abraham Lincoln* (from Mary A. Hamilton's *The Life of Abraham Lincoln*), Johannesburg, Afrikaanse Pers-Boekhandel, 1959; from novels: *Umbanjwa wase Zenda* (Anthony Hope's *The Prisoner of Zenda*), Johannesburg, Afrikaanse, 1958; *Uzibaningashekazi*, Rider Haggard's *She*, Johannesburg, Afrikaanse, 1958; *U-Robinson Crusoe*, Cape Town, Maskew Miller, 1961 (Defoe's *Crusoe*); *Ujock wasezindle*, from Fitzpatrick's *Jock of the Bushveld*, Johannesburg, Afrikaanse, 1965.

408

Biographical/Critical Sources: Four African Literatures, Albert S. Gérard, Berkeley, University of California, 1971; C. M. Doke, "A Preliminary Investigation into the State of the Native Languages of South Africa with Suggestions as to Research and the Development of Literature," *Bantu Studies*, VII, 1933; B. W. Vilakazi, "Oral and Written Literature in Nguni," unpublished doctoral dissertation, Johannesburg, University of the Witwatersrand, 1945.

SIRIMAN, Cissoko (also CISSOKO, Siriman)
b. ca. 1940, Mali.
Poet.

Though he considers himself a Malian, Siriman has long been a resident of Senegal and lives in Dakar. His poetry has appeared in several anthologies and various journals. *New Sum of Poetry from the Negro World* offers two of his poems, "Coupeur de bois" (Wood-Cutter), and "O Terre," (O, Mother Earth). The latter poem begins with the beautiful lines:
Je les ai couchés
mes morts
dans la douceur de tes seins aimés
là où les cataractes lavent les pieds
des falaises.

I laid down my dead
in the sweetness of your loved breasts
there, where the cataracts wash the feet
of the cliffs.

(trans. D. H.)
Siriman's one volume thus far is *Ressac de nous-mêmes* (The Undertow of Ourselves), 1967, with a useful introduction and brief biography by André Terrisse.

Writings: Poetry: *Ressac de nous-mêmes*, Paris, Présence Africaine, 1967; poems in *New Sum of Poetry from the Negro*

World, Paris, Présence Africaine, Volume 57, 1966.

SISSOKO, Fily-Dabo
b. 1900, Mali; d. 1964.
Poet, story writer, novelist.

Sissoko's first three volumes of poetry were: *Crayons et portraits* (Sketches and Portraits), 1955, *Harmakhis; poèmes du terroir africain* (Harmakhis: Poems of the African Land), 1955, and *La savane rouge* (Red Savannah), 1962. The third volume commemorates the revolt of the Tauregs against the French during the first World War. Sissoko has many of his poems in the volume, *Poèmes de l'Afrique noire* (Poems from Black Africa) which also has works by U Tam'si. His one novel was *La passion de Djimé*, 1956, and the year before, he published a collection of folktales, *Sagesse noire* (Black Wisdom). In 1970 he published a new collection of poems, *Les jeux du destin* (The Play of Destiny).

Writings: Poetry: *Crayons et portraits*, Mulhouse, France, Impr. Union, 1953; *Harmakhis; poèmes du terroir africain*, Paris, Eds. de la Tour du Guet, 1955; *La savane rouge*, Avignon, Presses Universelles, 1962; *Harmakhis*, republished in collection *Poèmes de l'Afrique noire*, Paris, Debresse, 1963; and *Les jeux du destin*, Paris, 1970.

Novel: *La passion de Djimé*, Paris, Eds. de la Tour du Guet, 1956.

Folktales: *Sagesse noire, sentences et proverbes malinkés*, Paris, Eds. de la Tour du Guet, 1955.

Genre unknown: *Au dessous des nuage (de Madagascar au Kenya)*, (Under the Clouds [from Madagascar to Kenya]), Paris, 1970.

SOCÉ, Ousmane Diop (or, DIOP, Ousmane Socé)

b. 1911, Rufisque (some sources give Saint-Louis), Senegal.
Novelist, poet.

Socé studied in local schools and afterwards trained to be a veterinary surgeon, a profession he has followed while writing his poetry and fiction. He was appointed Senegalese ambassador to the USA and to the United Nations in the late 1960's.

Socé's first, pioneering novel was *Karim; roman sénégalais* (1935), later published Paris, 1948, as *Karim; roman sénégalais;* followed by *Contes et légendes d'Afrique noire* (Karim, Senegalese Novel, followed by Stories and Legends of Black Africa).

The work tells the sad tale of the humiliations suffered by the leading character (and by all Africans symbolically) at the hands of the Europeans. Young Karim, the protagonist, and his companions resemble their ancestors in their efforts to be heroic, but they meet defeat in an Africa no longer theirs just as completely as their own fathers had gone down to disaster in their time. A six-page excerpt from the novel is in Mphahlele's *African Writing Today* in an English text.

Socé's second novel, *Mirage de Paris*, 1937, concerns the tribulations of the educated African in France in the pre-independence world of the 1930's when the black African struggled to realize his own identity and cultural pride.

His remaining volumes are a collection of verse; *Les rythmes du khalam* (The Rhythms of the Khalam), 1956, 1963; and *Contes et légendes d'Afrique noire* (Stories and Legends from Black Africa), a very attractive work, 1962, and earlier published with *Karim*, 1949–50.

Writings: Novels: *Karim; roman sénégalais,* Paris, Impr. Puyfourçat, 1935; as *Karim; roman sénégalais;* followed by *Contes et légendes d'Afrique noire,* Paris, Nouvelles Editions Latines, 1949–50; Casablanca, Morocco, Eds. France-Afrique, 1949; *Mirage de Paris,* Paris Nouvelles Eds. Latines, 1937, 1964; *Mirage de Paris,* followed by *Les rythmes du khalam,* Paris, Nouvelles Eds. Latine, 1956; an extract from *Karim* is in *African Writing Today,* Ezekiel Mphahlele, editor, London, Penguin, 1967.

Stories: *Contes et légendes d'Afrique noire,* Paris, Nouvelles Eds. Latines, 1962; earlier published with *Karim,* 1949–50.

Poetry: *Les rythmes du khalam* Paris, Nouvelles, Eds. Latines, 1963; earlier published with *Mirage de Paris,* 1956.

SOGA, John Henderson
b. February 10, 1860, Peelton, South Africa; d. March 11, 1941.

Xhosa hymn-writer, poet, minister, translator.

Second son of the famous Tiyo Soga (1829–1871), young John Henderson's career paralleled his father's. Though crippled from birth, he studied hard, and went to Scotland in 1870 to study at Glasgow High School. Graduating in 1873, he went on to Dollar Academy for university work from 1873 to 1877, and to Edinburgh University from 1886 to 1890. He was ordained by the United Presbyterian Church of Scotland in 1893 after training at the United Presbyterian Divinity Hall from 1890 to 1893. Like his father, John Soga also married a Scotswoman, returning with Isabella Brown to work in the home missions. His first major act in Africa was to found the Mbonde Mission in the Mountfrere district in the area of the Bhaca peoples.

Soga's main literary works were translations of English tracts and sermons into Xhosa, and hymns. Important works for the time were his translations: *The Traveller's Guide from Death to Life* as *Inkokeli yomkombi osuka ekufeni esiya ebomini*, 1924; Mrs. J. Penn-Lewis' *The Holy Ghost*, as *Umsebenzi womoya oyingcwele*, 1929; and his most influential, Book II of Bunyan's *Pilgrim's Progress* as *U-hambo lom-hambi*, 1926, a completion of the task begun by his father sixty years earlier with the publication of Book I in 1868. A useful effort though less typical of his religious orientation was his translation of Dr. Elsie Chubb's *Our Bodies and how they work* as *Imizimba yetu nokusebenza kwayo*, 1929.

Some of Soga's hymns are in the basic Xhosa hymnal, *Amaculo ase-Rabe*, 1885, including "Iziyolo zelilizwe" (The Pleasures of This Land), and "Yesu, tob' amehlo Ako" (Jesus, Lower Your Eyes). He translated into English his scholarly study of the Bantu, "Abe-Nguni, Ama-Mbo, Ama-Lala," unpublished in Xhosa but printed in 1930 as *The South-Eastern Bantu*. In 1931 he wrote and published in English *Ama-Xhosa: Life and Customs*.

His last book was *Indonzo sama-bandla ka-Krestu* (How to Conduct a Religious Service), 1934.

Retiring in 1936, he took his family to England for his remaining years. He was killed in his home, March 11, 1941, with his wife and one son in a German bombardment of Southampton.

Writings: Poetry: Hymns: "Iziyolo zelilizwe" and "Yesu, tob' amehlo Ako" in *Amaculo ase Rabe* (Lovedale Hymns), Lovedale, 1885, containing also hymns and music by John Knox Bokwe.

Scholarship and Folklore: *The South-Eastern Bantu*, Johannesburg, Witwatersrand University, 1930 (entitled in Xhosa: "Abe-Nguni, Ama-Mbo, Ama-Lala," but unpublished); *Ama-Xhosa: Life and Customs*, Johannesburg, Witwatersrand University Press, 1931.

Translations: *The Traveller's Guide from Death to Life*, author unknown, as *Yomkombi osuka ekufeni esiya ebomini*, Lovedale, Lovedale Press, 1924; Elsie Chubb's *Our Bodies and how they work* as *Imizimba yetu nokusebenza kwayo*, London, Sheldon Press, 1929; Bunyan's *Pilgrim's Progress* as *U-hambo lom-hambi*, II, London, Sheldon Press, 1926; J. Penn-Lewis' *The Holy Ghost* as *Umsebenzi womoya oyingcwele*, Lovedale, Lovedale Press, 1929.

Religious Service Manual: *Indonzo zama-bandla ka-Krestu*, Lovedale, Lovedale Press, 1934; in manuscript: translation of some of Aesop's fables.

Biographical/Critical Source: Albert S. Gérard, *Four African Literatures*, Berkeley, University of California Press, 1971.

SOGA, Tiyo (pen name, "N.W." or "UNonjiba waseluhlangeni")
b. 1829, Gwali mission station, Cape Province, South Africa;
d. August 12, 1871.
Xhosa religious poet, translator, minister.

Tiyo Soga was the seventh child of 29 children born to Jotela Soga and Nosuthu, the first of Jotela's eight wives. The father was a leading councillor, as had been his father, to Chief Ngqika, an important clanleader of the Xhosa. Though progressive in some matters (Jotela Soga was the first African in his area to use a plow and to irrigate his land by cutting water ditches through his fields), he resisted conversion to Christianity. Nosuthu, a strong Christian, consequently left her polygamous husband to make a new home for a period near the Lovedale Mission and later at the Glasgow Missionary Society's Gwali Mission on the Mgwali River, a tributary stream to the Tyume River in the Chumie Valley, Victoria East District. Born at Gwali Mission, Tiyo Soga received his early schooling in his father's village under his eldest brother Festire Soga, but later attended the mission school at Gwali with the Reverend William Chalmers of the United Presbyterian Church of Scotland. An excellent student, he was able to enter the Theological Seminary of the Free Church of Scotland at Lovedale in 1844.

When the war of 1846-47 closed Lovedale, the principal, the Reverend William Govan, retired to Scotland, taking Tiyo with him and assuring him a Scottish education. Tiyo studied first at a school in Inchinnan (1846–47) and then at the Glasgow Free Church Normal Seminary in Glasgow (1847–48). Adopted by Dr. William Anderson of Glasgow, and baptized in May, 1848 by him, Tiyo Soga prepared to return home as a Presbyterian missionary. He traveled to South Africa with the Reverend George Brown for whom he served as an interpreter for a time at Chumie and later he served as a catechist (local preacher) at Keiskamahoek and as an evangelist at the Umondale Mission Station with the Reverend Niven.

When a new war broke out in 1850 which pitted some of the Xhosa clans against the British, Soga and Niven returned to Scotland. In June 1851, Soga graduated in theology from Glasgow University, and in 1852 he transferred to the Theological Hall of the United Presbyterian Church in Edinburgh. On December 23, 1856, Tiyo Soga received ordination, becoming the first black African to be ordained in Great Britain. On February 27, 1857, he married Janet Burnside, a Scotswoman, and in March left for South Africa with his bride to take up a mission of his own.

From 1857 to 1861 he lived first at Peelton on the Mgwali River, working with the remnants of old Chief Ngqika's group, scattered after the cattle war of 1857. Then, with the Reverend Robert Johnston he went to the Chumie Valley to re-establish the abandoned Gwali Mission Station, which by 1861 had 4,000 persons settled near it. In 1860 he was honored by an invitation to meet Prince Alfred, the Duke of Edinburgh, then visiting Cape Town and Governor Sir George Grey.

In 1862 he established *Indaba* (The News) at Lovedale, the first issue appearing in August of that year, and for two years contributed a column, "Ezivela kubabalelani" (Readers' View) under the pen name, "UNonjiba waseluhlangeni" (The Dove of the Nation), or, often, simply as "N.W." Though most of his work was close to the sermon form and all of it was evangelistic in intention, there was sometimes an informal, humorous, quality.

In 1866 he resigned his missionary work because of poor health but continued his literary interests. In November 1866 he completed a translation of John Bunyan's *Pilgrim's Progress,* Part I, under the Xhosa title of *U-hambo lom-hambi,* a project begun ten years earlier at Glasgow University. Published in 1866, it had later editions in 1868, 1875, 1889, and 1902. He composed many hymns during this period, 26 of which appear today in the hymnal, *Amaculo ase-Rabe* (Presbyterian Hymns), 1885. Three of his most remembered hymns are "Lizalis ' indinga lakho" (Fulfill thy promise), "Khangelani nizibane izibele ezingaka" (Open your eyes and behold how great the blessings are) and "Sinesipho esikhulu esisiphiweyo thina" (We have a great gift which was given to us). His Xhosa translation of the Four Gospels and his uncompleted translation of the Acts of the Apostles remain in manuscript.

Indaba, his newspaper, occasionally published excerpts from his collection of fables, proverbs, and genealogical lists of important Africans, but the greater portion of his large mass of material remains unpublished.

In early 1871, though ill from a chronic throat infection, he volunteered to serve in Chief Sarili's area along the Kei and Bashee Rivers, and came to settle in Tutura (today's Somerville) in the Transkei. On August 12, 1871, after having been caught in a downpour, he died of acute congestion of the lungs. He left his wife, four sons, and three daughters, most of whom became leading writers and leaders of the Xhosa.

His nephew, Tiyo Burnside Soga (1866-1938), inspired by his uncle's example, published in 1916 the important *Intlalo ka Xosa,* concerned with Xhosa customs, at the Tutora Mission.

Despite many racial slights received from his Christian colleagues in the local pastorates, Soga strove for calm. John A. Chalmer, his biographer, wrote: "He was a black man. He knew it, and like Othello, never forgot that he was black. Despite his colour there never lived a more polished gentleman." Today, the word "despite" rings harshly and patronizingly, but the truth remains that Tiyo Soga was a great social and intellectual pioneer, sophisticated, poised, and motivated to understand and to express the best of two cultures. He endured the grim psychological hardships of living on a frontier between two worlds, and remained a calm leader and a source of encouragement to men of good will everywhere.

Writings: Translation: *U-hambo lom-hambi* (Bunyan's *Pilgrim's Progress,* Book I), Lovedale, Lovedale Press, 1868, 1875, 1889, 1902.

Hymns: in *Amaculo ase-Rabe* (or *ase-Lovedale*), Lovedale, 1885; Four Gospels, and partial Xhosa text of Acts of the Apostles, in manuscript.

Journalism: in *Indaba,* Lovedale, 1862 (fables, proverbs, genealogical lists of important Africans), mostly uncollected: most items published in the column "Ezivela kubabalelani" (Readers' View), under pen name of "UNonjiba waseluhlangeni" (The Dove of the Nation), or simply as "N.W." Writings by Tiyo Burnside Soga (1866–1938), Tiyo Soga's nephew: *Inlalo ka Xosa*, Tutora Mission, South Africa, Butterworth, 1916; Lovedale, Lovedale Press, 1917; revised, enlarged edition, Lovedale, 1927.

Biographical/Critical Sources: John A. Chalmers, *Tiyo Soga*, Edinburgh, 1877; Albert S. Gérard, *Four African Literatures*, Berkeley, University of California Press, 1971.

SOGA, Tiyo Burnside (see item for T. B. Soga's uncle, Tiyo SOGA)

SONTONGA, Mankayi Enoch
b. ca. 1860, South Africa;
d. Johannesburg, 1904.
Xhosa songwriter, poet.

Sontonga's parents were members of the Thembu people of the Northern Transkei region. Sontonga is remembered today for his song, "Nkosi sikelel' i-Africa" (God Bless Africa), the national anthem of the Transkei which was adopted in 1925 as the anthem of the African National Congress. It was first sung in 1899 though written two years earlier, but its success at the first meeting of the South African Native National Congress, Bloemfontein, January 8, 1912, spread it through out the country.·

The song remains today the most famous in South Africa and the tune has been picked up in many of the new African states and set to local words.

Little is known of Sontonga other than that he was a teacher in a minor mission school near Johannesburg at the turn of the century and that he wrote many hymns for his pupils. He usually employed the simple solfa tonal system introduced by the missionaries as being closer to Xhosa and other African peoples' music. His famous hymn, however, according to J. F. A. Swartz, "unlike most written in the 19th century by South Africans, was in the regular European staff notation; in fact, it was the very first to be so composed and published."

Apparently Sontonga had gathered a collection of his work for publication, but his death ended these efforts and the works have disappeared completely. Only "Nkosi sikelel' i-Africa" remains. The first verse in translation is given below, but of course it is the music that made the song so compelling.

Nkosi Sikelel' I-Afrika
Maluphakanyisw' Uphondo Lwayo
Yiva Nemithandazo Yethu
Nkosi Sikelela
Nkosi Sikelela
Yiza Moya
Yiza Moya
Oyingcwele
Nkosi Sikelela Thina
Lusapho Lwakho

God bless Africa
God bless Africa
Let its horn be raised
Listen also to our pleas
God bless
God bless
Come spirit
Come Holy spirit
God bless us
Us, thy children.

Writings: Hymns: mostly unpublished and the majority no longer extant. Only "Nkosi sikelel' i-Africa," sung as early as 1899, exists in various versions, but early publication data unavailable.

Biographical/Critical Sources: J. F. A. Swartz, "A Hobbyist Looks at Zulu and Xhosa Songs," *African Music*, I, 3 (1956);

Four African Literatures, Albert S. Gérard, Berkeley, University of California Press, 1971. English and Xhosa version of "Nkosi Sikelel' I-Africa" from Mary Benson's *South Afrika: The Struggle for a Birthright,* Harmondsworth, England, Penguin, 1966.

SOW, Alpha (also SOW, Alfâ Ibrâhîm and Ibrahima)
b. ca. 1935, Guinea.
Poet, folklorist.

In 1968, Sow published *Chroniques et récits du Fouta-Djalon* (Chronicles and Tales of the Fouta-Djalon Mountains), a work reflecting his great interest in the songs, epics, poems and history of his area of upper Guinea and lower Mali in the Peul or Foulah region. He is also represented in various journals and collections, including *New Sum of Poetry from the Negro World* with "Où sont-ils donc allés" (Wherever Have they Gone?), and "Chimères" (Mirages).

After calling up the beauties of his lost Kalé, a vision of the vanished Africa, Sow completes "Chimères" with the lines:
Elle était belle dans sa fierté sauvage.
Par ces temps de détresse, je ne pus la
/*chanter.*
Je le portai au coeur, souvenir incurable
A l'abri des tourments! Trésor de légendes,
D'expériences éphémères, de projets pré-
/*coces, de Chimères!*

She was beautiful in her savage pride.
But for her time of anguish, I can not
/*even try to sing.*
I wear her in my heart, an incurable mem-
/*ory*
Sheltering under torture! The golden spoils
/*of legend,*
Of wraithlike experiences, of youthful
/*plans, of Illusions.*
(trans. D. H.)

Jahnheinz Jahn in his recent bibliography cites the work, *C'est simple* (It's Easy) as a work of verse of an Ibrahima Sow, believed by him to be from Mali. It is possible that that work is by Alpha Sow. The grammar, *Janngen fulfulde,* also must be added to this writer's list of writings, along with an anthology of folk stories and poetry: *La Femme.*

Writings: Poetry: *C'est simple (poèmes ou paroles),* Dakar, 1964; *Chroniques et récites du Fouta-Djalon,* Paris, Librairie Klincksieck, 1968; poems in *New Sum of Poetry from the Negro World,* Paris, Présence Africaine, Volume 57, 1966.

Critical Scholarship: "Notes sur les precédés poetiques dans la littérature des Peuls du Fouta Djallon," in *Présence Africaine,* second trimester, Paris, 1972.

Grammar: *Janngen fulfulde,* Paris; Présence Africaine, 196(?).

Stories: *Le Femme la Vache la Foi,* Paris, Julliard, 1966.

Bibliographical/Critical Source: Jahn and Dressler, *Bibliography of Creative African Writing,* Nendeln, Liechtenstein, Kraus-Thomson, 1971.

SOYINKA, Kayode
b. ca. 1938, Yoruba-land, Nigeria.
Playwright, actor, teacher.

Younger brother of 'Wole Soyinka, Kayode studied in local schools and at the Drama School at Ibadan University. He has been an actor, dancer and playwright at home and in 1969 made a trip to the U.S. He has been on tour in his brother's plays in France and England during the 1960's. In 1969 he completed a two-hour play of his own employing Oshugbo and Igbale masquerade dances which saw performance in France. Several of his plays have since appeared on Nigerian television.

SOYINKA, Oluwole (but usually Wole, less often 'Wole; sometimes Akinwande Oluwole)
b. July 13, 1934, Isara, Ijebu Remo, near Abeokuta, Yoruba country, Western Nigeria.
Playwright, poet, novelist, play director, actor, teacher.

'Wole Soyinka, Black Africa's most famous playwright, began his education in local schools in Abeokuta, then in 1952 went on to Government College at Ibadan, some 45 miles away. In 1954 he went to Leeds University in Yorkshire, England, which was establishing the first Department of English dedicated to studying the writing of all literatures produced in English, earning a B.A. in literature (English, honors), in 1957. An extremely important influence on him in these early years in London was George Wilson Knight, drama critic and Shakespearean actor. Soyinka married an English girl during his days at Leeds and his first son was born.

He went down to London in the summer of 1957 as a play-reader and began to teach, write, act, and finally to direct for the Royal Court Theatre which produced his first play, *The Invention*, November 1, 1959. That same year the group also performed his now well-known comedy, *The Lion and the Jewel* which also was performed in Lagos that year. *The Lion* was subsequently published by Oxford Press, 1963, along with four of his later plays, in the volume, *Five Plays*, 1964, which included: *A Dance of the Forests, The Trials of Brother Jero, The Strong Breed*, and *The Swamp Dwellers*.

The Trials of Brother Jero and *The Swamp Dweller* were produced in London in the late 1950's, the latter at Student Movement House in September 1958, and entered in a competition at the University of London Drama Festival, but it did did not win an award. The author played the role of Igwezu, the troubled son returned to the swamp from Lagos. On February 20-21, 1959, at the Arts Theatre, Ibadan, *The Swamp Dwellers* and *The Lion and the Jewel* were performed in a twin-feature. *The Trials of Brother Jero* was first performed at the same theatre by a student group from Ibadan University in the late spring of 1960. In 1966, the Injinle Theatre Company of Nigeria performed *The Lion* at the Royal Court Theatre, London, bringing a Nigerian company back to the theatre where Soyinka had had his start.

In 1966, Farris-Belgrave Productions, with Afolabi Ajayi as director, put on *The Trial of Brother Jero* and *The Strong Breed* at the Greenwich Mews Theatre in New York. The role of Brother Jero was played by James Spruille, and Eman, the protagonist of *The Strong Breed*, was played by Vernon Washington. The latter play had received its first stage production in 1966 in a student performance by players from Ibadan University and St. Anne's Girls School, Ibadan. The same year it was also produced on Nigerian television and, in an adapted version by Soyinka, it was filmed for an Esso-sponsored documentary about Nigeria, "Culture in Transition." In April, 1967, directed by Betty Okotie, a leading Nigerian actress, *The Strong Breed* was presented to the Nancy (France) World Festival of University Drama and in May of that year was staged at the Ibadan Arts Theatre by Ibadan players. The play won only third prize in Nancy, but it has been since considered one of Soyinka's most important works and has been widely performed in America and elsewhere.

The early one-act play, *The Invention*, was first performed in an informal setting after the poet-dramatist himself had read some of his poetry, including the now widely anthologized piece, "Telephone Conservation." The play's simple spring of action is the accidental landing and explosion of a powerful American rocket in South Africa in 1976 which turns everyone white who was not white to begin with. Robbed of the usual heady atmosphere of fear, superiority, and social distinction, the surviving scientists (they are known to be truly white) are quickly put to work devising a fool-proof method of detecting true whites from new whites.

Other lesser plays of Soyinka's are: *The Detainee; Camwood on the Leaves,* the latter performed on Nigerian radio in 1960; and *Before the Blackout,* performed by the Orisun Theatre Company at the Arts Theatre in Ibadan, March 11, 1965. *Blackout* was published in Ibadan in the

Orisun Acting Editions (n.d., but probably 1965) with a two-page preface by Soyinka. The volume of 73 pages comprises 13 sketches or skits, many of which had important parts for mimes and allowed for improvisation on the part of the cast. All of them are satirical attacks on the political and social climate in Nigeria of the early 1960's. These sketches, called *Simply Blackout* in performance, were staged March 11 and April 22–24, 1965 at the Arts Theatre, Ibadan and on April 10, 1965 at the J. K. Randle Memorial Hall in Lagos.

In 1960, Soyinka returned to Nigeria, and, aided by a Rockefeller grant, traveled widely after an absence of five years, getting reacquainted with the various cultures of his country, now close to independence. Commissioned to write a play for the Independence Day Celebrations on Oct. 1, 1960, he created the most complex of all his works, *The Dance of the Forests.* Since its premier performance in Lagos, the play has received serious and favorable scholarly attention, but has evoked possibly more puzzlement from its audiences and readers than any of his other plays. It did win the *Encounter Magazine's* award in 1960, however, and is widely believed to be the writer's most important work to date. Except for the October 1 performance at Yaba Technical College and one given the following year at the Arts Theatre at Ibadan University, the play has not been performed.

During this busy first year at home, Soyinka began to do research in African drama at his old university, Ibadan; and he quickly organized a repertory company, the 1960 Masks, in Lagos. In 1961 he helped establish the Mbari Writers and Artists Club in Ibadan which became a germinal center for new work in theatre, prose and poetry, ceramics and painting. Also in 1961 he produced his own play *Brother Jero* in September, as well as *Dear Parent and Ogre* by Sarif Easmon, a dramatist from Sierra Leone, in a premier performance. Soyinka took the lead role of the politician, Dauda Touray, and directed the play as well. In 1962 he produced John Pepper Clark's *Song of a Goat,* in which a live goat was slaughtered at the first performances, giving rise to a loud peal of nervous laughter from the surprised audience. Also in 1962 he accepted an appointment to the new University of Ife, but because of political developments surrounding the arrest, trial and conviction of Chief Awolowo on a charge of treason, Soyinka, with others, resigned. He was married a second time in 1963, to Olayide Idowu, a fellow teacher and began to write polemical works attacking corruption and political drift.

The first series of linked sketches he produced in these efforts to influence men and events were called *The Republican.* He directed and acted in the skits along with some of the leading actors of the newly organized Orisun Theatre troupe, March 21, 1964 at the Arts Theatre in Ibadan. The month before, a somewhat simpler performance of these brief works had been given by his original group, the 1960 Masks, before most of the same politicians and bureaucrats who were the butts of the skits. This topical work, with the revue *Blackout,* made Soyinka an important name in the new Nigeria.

The 1960 Masks did the first stage production of Clark's *The Raft* on April 9, 1964, on the occasion of the visit of President Léopold Senghor of Senegal. That year also saw Soyinka's major efforts to move drama to center stage in the cultural life of the country. In August, taking over the largest hall in Ibadan, he offered five different plays by three separate companies in 12 nights of performance at Obisesan Hall. At the same time the Mbari Club in its own quarters offered *Brother Jero* thrice weekly during the month. The Obisesan Hall plays were then put on in Lagos for six straight nights at Glover Memorial Hall. Both English and Yoruba dramas were seen during this rich program: Soyinka's *The Lion and the Jewel,* in English, the Yoruba-language plays of Ogunmola: *Love of Money* and his musical dramatization of Amos Tutuola's *The Palm-Wine Drinkard,* and Ladipo's *Oba Ko So* and *Oba W'aja.* Both Ogunmola and Ladipo had their own vernacular theatre groups and their joining Soyinka's efforts showed the compatibility and the vigor of the old and new traditions in Nigerian dramaturgy.

The 1960 Masks and the Orisun Theatre troupes performed Soyinka's new play, *Kongi's Harvest,* before an excited audience on August 12 and 13, 1965 at the Federal Palace Hotel in Lagos. Soyinka then went to London to direct a mixed cast of West Indians and South Africans in his play, *The Road,* at the Theatre Royal in London's East End. An entry in the Commonwealth Arts Festival, the play gave Soyinka a needed breather, because the political crisis at home deepened and on his return he rapidly became involved in political activities which eventually led to his detention from 1966 to 1969. Before this happened, however, he was able to mount a production of *Kongi* at the first Festival of Negro Arts, Dakar, April 1, 1966, in the Daniel Sorano Theatre before an enthusiastic audience. The play had an earlier trial run in performances in March at the Arts Theatre in Ibadan. During this busy period, his novel, *The Interpreters,* meanwhile, had appeared in 1965; and he had spent a short period in prison; his first book of poetry, *Idanre,* came out in London (1967); and he had accepted the chairmanship of Ibadan's Drama Department and Arts Theatre (1967).

Soyinka's Orisun Theatre primarily was intended to perform works in Yoruba, in the country-side of Western Nigeria. It acquired a simple, portable stage, mounted on a short truck-body and villagers were enabled to see plays, some heavily influenced by Western drama, and others, closely akin to the long cycle dramas of the classical Yoruba dance-plays of pre-European times. (For information concerning some of these travelling companies and the plays performed, see the essays in this volume on Hubert Ogunde, E. Kolawole Ogunmola, Wale Ogunyemi, Obotunde Ijimere, Duro Ladipo and John Pepper Clark.)

In the early 1960's Soyinka also taught English at the University of Ibadan and at Ife and continued to write plays. A product of this immensely fertile period was the bizarre play, *The Road,* produced as noted, at the Commonwealth Arts Festival, London, 1965, and later published in London. The work reflects his horror of death by auto and lorry (truck) on the often maniacally-driven roads of Nigeria. His play, *Kongi's Harvest,* 1967, a study of a modern, post-independence dictator in Africa, is widely believed to have been influenced by the career of Kwame Nkrumah of Ghana. *The Road* was awarded the prize for published drama at the African Arts Festival in Dakar, 1966, and *Kongi* has been widely produced in Africa and in the West.

The first dramatic work of Soyinka's to be published was *The Lion and the Jewel,* printed in the fifth number of *Black Orpheus* magazine (1959) of which he

served as co-editor, 1961–63, with Ulli Beier and Ezekiel Mphahlele, and with Mphahlele only, 1963–64. Of his remaining plays, *The Detainee* exists only as a 19-page mimeograph script prepared for BBC Soyinka's latest full-length play, *Madmen and Scientists,* concerns a politician visiting the former head of the "opposition" now jailed in a detention camp. This work saw performance on August 2, 1970 at the Eugene O'Neill Memorial Theatre Center in Watertown, Connecticut, directed by the author and performed by the Ibadan Theatre Arts Company. The second act of "The House of Banigeji," not otherwise published, appeared as "The Exiles," in Frances Ademola's anthology, *Reflections* (1962).

After the outbreak of the Nigerian Civil War, The Federal Government took the poet-dramatist into custody on August 17, 1966, because of his outspoken disgust with the corruption and violence of Nigerian politics and his supposed sympathy with the Ibo (Biafran) cause. In fact, he is believed to have offered to go to Biafra to seek reconciliation between the Central Government at Lagos and the Biafrans. While he was under house arrest from 1966 to 1969 in the north of Nigeria, rumors of his death, or execution, were common and even reached print in Western newspapers several times. There was genuine concern about his safety, for there was a great deal of bitterness on both sides in the war. The rather murky details of Soyinka's having taken over a radio station at gun-point in Lagos to force the broadcast of a taped speech denouncing the country's leadership offer a strong reason why the Federal Government was so hostile to him. During his incarceration Soyinka apparently was able to write, and he reportedly even taught English in a little school he set up in his quarters. During this period he was awarded a British Arts Council prize, the John Whiting Award, for his work as a playwright. Two of his poems written during this period, "Burial," and "Flowers for my land," reached print in a slim collection entitled *Poems from Prison,* published as a loose sheaf of pages. (These poems also appeared as *A Shuttle in the Crypt* in a Hill and Wang edition, 1972.)

Since his release in October, 1969 at the termination of the Biafran War, he has traveled to various conferences and otherwise sought to reestablish the rhythms of his interrupted career. He has begun work again in the English and drama departments of the University of Ibadan and in other Nigerian universities. Most recently he played the central role in the dramatic film, *African Themes and Perspectives,* under the American black director, Ossie Davis, and published the collection, *Plays from the Third World. An Anthology,* 1972.

In addition to his creative work, Soyinka has proved himself a trenchant commentator on literary developments in Africa. Soyinka's most famous remark, often referred to in studies of modern African literature, was made in protest against a too facile and often over-nostalgic Négritude at a writers' conference in Kampala, Uganda, in 1962. He said then that a tiger does not go around protesting its "tigritude," but instead just acts like a tiger by pouncing, and that is enough. His point was that if an African writer truly had something to say, and said it well enough, his message and his African-ness would be evident. Though francophone writers from Africa at the conference protested, many anglophone writers present applauded, for they have generally avoided an over-

idealization of the past, preferring the tiger's relaxed and self-confident role. Today, of course, such philosophical-esthetic conflicts have largely diminished, but the different approaches to creating a new African awareness and literature once reflected the significantly different experiences of the peoples living in French and British colonies.

Plastic in his use of English, Soyinka is able to write the purest of English lines, and then to follow it with one or several expressive of an African nuance of feeling, often employing either Yoruba or pidgin-English terms or expressions. Though he deals with universals—hope, hatred, defeat, sacrifice—he still weaves into all of his plays the daily texture of common African life. Humorous, satirical, mythopoeic, he never falls into preachment nor rises to an undeserved apotheosis of bravura or sentiment.

The Lion and the Jewel, Soyinka's second produced play, serves up three stock characters in what is in part a very broad farce: Lakunle, the foppish, half-Westernized school-teacher in love with the giddy Sidi, the village belle called the "Jewel of Iluninle," and the wily old Baroke, a village chief who is not so lacking in virility as he pretends. All the characters act out their predestined roles on both the naturalistic and symbolic levels; and masks, dances, ritualistic movements turn the play at times away from European stage craft conventions to those prevailing in Yoruba village theatre.

The chief, impressed by the girl's photograph appearing on the cover of a news magazine issued in Lagos decides to win the contemptuous beauty. She is eventually trapped into a close duel with him which begins with her taunting him for his supposed impotence and ends with the girl in his muscular arms. She seems soon not to care. It is the school teacher who is most deeply outwitted, but even in defeat he has a certain foolish dignity and is obviously a harbinger of a new wave of men who will wrest prestige and power from less clever chiefs.

The Trials of Brother Jero is another farcical play which pits a religious charlatan, Brother Jeroboam, against the credulity of his followers and the craft of his leading disciple's termagant wife. Though Jero is unmasked at play's end in hilarious fashion to his follower's pleasure and the audience's delight, one man still believes him, an up-and-coming politician who desperately needs the encouragement of Jero's predictions that he will become a leading stateman of Nigeria. Soyinka's amused contempt for the syncretist new religions of Africa, part Christian, part local African, and sometimes part fraud and fantasy, provides the cutting edge to make the play a witty and vivid vehicle that, despite its bitterness, avoids polemicism or snobbishness.

In *The Strong Breed*, Soyinka offers another study of African and Western values in conflict, again in a religious context. This time, however, his central character, Eman, is an earnest, intelligent man, Western-trained in medicine though he is no doctor, who has repudiated his sacramental priest-like role, inherited from his father. Fleeing to English schooling, and taking an assignment in a village distant to his own, Eman inexorably becomes the man he was born to be, a scapegoat. Though he has gained a broader view than that held by the villagers, he gratuitously insists on intervening in a ceremony he does not understand. He dies, a victim of a cleansing ritual which has no room for altruism.

Time and again, Eman's sweetheart, the daughter of the village chief, warns him in veiled terms to leave the village for a period, for during the year's end purification rites, a stranger must be hunted by masked men (gods) and killed to expiate the sins of the villagers committed over the past year. Eman ignores these pleas, and, horrified to learn that an idiot boy who had wandered into the village is the intended scapegoat that year, he takes the boy's role in the hunt-ceremony, not realizing until too late that it is not a ceremonial or symbolic ritual only, but literally a human sacrifice. Death must be the fate of the scapegoat, be he loved or not as a person, and useful or not to the village as a whole.

At play's end, the two villagers, Oroge and Jaguna, on their way home after the killing of Eman, comment on the blood shed that night:

Jaguna: I am sick to the heart of the cowardice I have seen tonight.
Oroge: That is the nature of men.
Jaguna: Then it is a sorry world to live in. We did it for them. It was all for their own common good. What did it benefit me whether the man lived or died? But did you see them? One and all they looked up at the man and words died in their throats.
Oroge: It was no common sight.
Jaguna: Women could not have behaved so shamefully. One by one they crept off like sick dogs. Not one could raise a curse.

And then in the most powerful line in the play, Oroge answers: "*It was not only him they fled. Do you see how unattended we are?*" Here we learn that the villagers are not only terrified at the sight of the sacrificed Eman, but that they are repulsed by the sight of the very men in the village who (till this night) were encharged ceremonially with the cleansing task of sacrifice. This time something has happened which will not permit the village to continue as it has for generations. The victim has left the realm of the impersonal or the easily repudiated; he is human, valuable, sympathetic to the village's own interests. To kill such a person seems no longer holy, but, obscene.

It is a revelation of shared humanity between victim and victimizer which renders cruel and horrible not only the villagers' belief but the actions of their most venerable men. What they have been cleansed of is not the past year's transgressions but of their acceptance of a process of cleansing *in itself*. But, bereft of such an age-old belief they are alone and they must build from the ruins of the past some new, more generous life and governing ritual.

The third of what might be termed Soyinka's religious trilogy, *The Swamp Dwellers,* concerns Alu, an old woman; Makuri, her husband; their son, Igwezu; a beggar come from the distant dry lands of the north; Kadiye, a corrupt priest; and a few villagers. Igwezu, defeated and cheated and cuckolded in the distant city of Lagos by his conniving twin brother, returns to his home in the Niger River delta country to reap his crop planted earlier along the river. All the crops have been ruined, however, by high water, though the villagers had paid to Kadiye, priest of the Python-god of the river, many gifts to prevent such a flood. Igwezu, deeply embittered, and no longer in awe of the priest, bluntly accuses the fat Kadiye of consuming the gifts and exploiting his people. The horrified parents protest and the priest storms off to raise a punishing force against the young man. The same evening a mysterious blind beggar has arrived and found protection in Makuri's home. In rather puzzling fashion he begins to obtain a spiritual ascendance over the family and offers his strength to the despairing Igwezu, even offering to return to Lagos with him. Forced to flee that very night, Igwezu hesitates a moment before leaving, and then says, "Only the children and the old stay here, bondsman. Only the innocent and the dotards."

The blind man, refused in his offer to accompany Igwezu to Lagos, and not given a clear answer to his question about Igwezu's possible return to his parents' house, closes the play in poetic and enigmatic words:

The swallows find their nest again when the cold is over.
Even the bats desert dark holes in the trees and flap wet leaves with wings of leather. There were wings everywhere as I wiped my feet against your threshold. I heard the cricket scratch himself beneath the armpit as the old man said to me...

As Igwezu silently departs his father's house, the beggar sighs, imparts a blessing with a gesture, and cries out: "I shall be here to give account."

There are several strands in the play in the final scene which are not easily explicated. What is evident to some degree is Soyinka's intention to exploit the contrasts between the younger and older generations, and to dramatize the pull and terrible dangers of Lagos and other large, Europeanized settlements in the new Africa, the diminution of the role of the priesthood, and the failure of the old tribal-village faiths and leadership to provide either spiritual or physical security for the younger generation.

The stranger-beggar remains, but he is blind, almost helpless in a poor, marshy land. But, as he has said, he had walked from the arid world of the North as far south as he could go, till there was dry land no longer. Here, in the Delta, he must wait out his destiny. Is Soyinka asking whether Africa, starved out increasingly from its own older, religious world, but often twisted and brutalized in the new city culture, must no longer seek to change or flee further? Might he be saying that Africa must settle down with what it has, both good and bad, to work out, with what folk-wisdom and human values it has preserved, the future in an enigmatic world? The past, though not very beautiful, is all man has; the future is only the past, not yet realized.

These three "religious" plays are, despite their deep involvement with the African scene, more "Western" in structure and action than the earlier, at times incoherent, but always fascinating *A Dance of the Forests*. Owing a debt to D. O. Fagunwa's stories and to Yoruba plays and folklore in general, the play is an intense effort to marry Western to Yoruba traditions and dance-drama. Drums, masks, and dance are as important elements in this work as are the actors and their words.

The audience of *A Dance of the Forests* must keep in mind a cast of characters who play two roles, one in a contemporary setting in which ancestors are being called back for a religious ceremony, and the other in which the modern African is living his life over again as his own ancestor in a dream-like scene.

The two worlds merge like smoke in a summer's night, in a new reality with cruelty and generosity, hate and love, being enacted in past and present though in different times in a vine-like embrace of universal human weakness and integrity. Gods and men, monsters and drummers, poets and historians, whores and faithful wives merge their beings and natures in a timeless dance. It is an Ovidian-like metamorphosis in a deeper, more solemn African investiture.

And if African purists object to classi-cal allusions, Soyinka himself has one character, known simply as historian, state quite explicity:

. . . I have here the whole history of Troy. If you were not the swillage of pigs and could read the writings of wiser men, I would show you the magnificence of the destruction of a beautiful city. I would reveal to you the attainments of men which lifted mankind to the ranks of gods and demi-gods. And who was the inspiration of this divine carnage? Helen of Troy, a woman whose honour became as rare a conception as her beauty. Would Troy, if it were standing today, lay claim to preservation in the annals of history if a thousand valiant Greeks had not been slaughtered before its gates, and a hundred thousand Trojans within her walls?

The Historian is speaking to a brave Captain who has refused further conquests and rebelled. Punished by the bitch-queen Rola-Madame Tortoise, along with his faithful wife dead with a child within her, the soldier and his spouse rise from the mouldy graves of the past to reproach the present. The Historian's words have the ring of bitter truth, for the message is that the bloody hero is better remembered than the generous soldier who has refused battle in an unjust and unprovoked war, and that Helen of Troy is more honored in legend than are most women who remained faithful at home, and that the courtier becomes more famous than the humble farmer, scholar, or worker.

The inclusion of the Homeric story in the confines of this very African play may strike one as unfortunate, but the play is an intended alloy of many metals, some scrap, and the play is not only "just" African; it is a drama for all seasons and for all cultures.

Soyinka's sole novel to date, *The Interpreters* (1967), eschews the journalistic "style" of Cyprian Ekwensi, and shows a group of intelligent young men and women in Lagos attempting to come to grips not only with their own natures but with a fast-changing world that both fascinates and frightens them. The language is sometimes dreamlike, sometimes staccato and hard. There is cruelty and warmth; love is sought but, if found at all, it is productive of pain and full of surprises. In short, the figures wander in a modern labyrinth which seems at times to have no center and no exit.

In this book, too, is a strand of Soyinka's obsession with death by automobile. Chapter II opens with the death, one stormy night, of Sekoni, a member of the novel's intellectual circle:

. . . The Dome cracked above Sekoni's short-sighted head one messy night. Too late he saw the insanity of a lorry parked right in his path, a swerve turned into a skid and cruel arabesque of tyres. A futile heap of metal, and Sekoni's body lay surprised across the open door, showers of laminated glass around him, his beard one fastness of blood and wet earth.

John Povey, in his essay "Changing Themes in the Nigerian Novel," published in *New African Literature and the Arts,* (1970) compares Soyinka's novel to James Joyce's experimental autobiography, *Portrait of an Artist.* "Memory," Povey says of the novel, "is intertwined with activity in a way that opens up a whole new potential world to the African writer."

Soyinka's Englishing of *The Forest of a Thousand Daemons* with D. O. Fagunwa is an effort in another direction—that of the past kept accurately before our gaze though dressed in a foreign idiom. The English is free, vivid, and obviously reflects the style and expressive imagery of the original Yoruba folk tale manner:

My friends all, like the sonorous proverb do we drum the agidigbo; it is the wise who dance to it, and the learned who understand its language . . .

The 133-page story ends:

. . . I have a feeling that we shall meet again before long; let me therefore utter a short prayer and then raise three cheers –the world shall become you, your nation will wax in wisdom and in strength, and we black people will never again be left behind in the world. Muso! Muso! Muso! I trust you have enjoyed this tale.

The highly personalized poetic idiom of Soyinka is naturally found most concentrated in his relatively small amount of verse. One of his earliest poems, "The Other Immigrant," was written during his days at Leeds University, and ap-

424

peared in *Black Orpheus* magazine, No. 5 (May 1959). His poems are most easily accessible in Moore and Beier's *Modern Poetry from Africa* and in this first volume of verse, *Idanre and Other Poems,* 1967.

The poems in *Idanre* are presented in seven groups: "of the road," lone figure," "of birth and death," "for women," grey seasons," "october '66," and the major work and title poem, "Idanre," which contains a preface and notes.

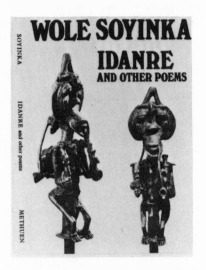

Chief Fagunwa, Soyinka's close friend, died in an automobile accident in 1963 as had many other friends of the poet. The poem, "Death in the Dawn," in the first set "of the road" once more shows the horror the author has of the deadly roads of Nigeria. The poem's last four lines are:

But such another Wraith! Brother,
Silenced in the startled hug of
Your invention - is this mocked grimace
This closed contortion - I?

A few poems later "In Memory of Segun Awolowo" speaks tersely of another accident:

For him who was
Lifted on tar sprays
And gravel rains

In metallic timbres
Harder than milestone heart

For him who was.

The road, the aged road
Retched on this fresh plunder
Of my youth

The 18-page poem, "Idanre," written in one day after an all-night walk to the top of Mt. Idanre in the midst of a violent electric storm, suffered only minor changes of words or phrases over the next two years. Soyinka writes in his preface to the work: *"Idanre lost its mystification early enough. As events gathered pace and unreason around me I recognized it as part of a pattern of awareness which began when I wrote A Dance of the Forests."* The poem celebrates the awesome power of the God of Iron, Ogun. Soyinka, looking back to the events before and after the outbreak of rebellion, massacre and civil war in Nigeria, writes: "And since then, the bloody origin of Ogun's pilgrimage has been, in true cyclic manner most bloodily re-enacted. Still awaited is that postscript image of dawn, contained even in the beginning, the brief sun-led promise of earth's forgiveness."

The personal, cosmological poem has seven parts: "deluge," ". . . and after," "pilgrimage," "the beginning," "the battle," "recessional," and "harvest." The first part sets the scene with the great storm overhead. Part II offers the metamorphosis of the wine girl into lover and fertility goddess:

At pilgrims' rest beneath Idanre Hill
The wine-girl, dazed from divine dallying
Felt wine-skeins race in fire-patterns within
/her

Her eyes queried, what then are you? At
/such hour
Why seek what on the hills?
A few stanzas further the image is of
a girl crushed on the road:
The sky cracked halfways, a greying skull
On blooded highways. I turned, vapours
/rose
From sodden bitumen and snaked within
Her wrap of indigo, her navel misted over
A sloe bared from the fruit
Here there are two allusions. One, from
an ancient cosmological story concerned
with the breaking of the head of the
"first" diety by the rebellious Atoóda or
Atunda. Each bit of the god rose up to
be one of the many gods of the present
Yoruba pantheon. The second allusion
is of course to the present dangers of
the bitumen road of modern Nigeria.
A history of a culture flows through
the long free-verse lines. The beginning
and the end of the universe and man's
progress in it are told in often brittle,
sometimes supple stanzas. Ogun's storm
dances sheets of flame on modern man's
electric pylons and cables strung across
the gulfs of Idanre. All things, African
and non-African, substantial and
spiritual, the void and pure energy, all
come together in the last stanza as they
have been interweaving thoughout the
poem:
And they move towards resorption in His
/alloy essence
Primed to a fusion, primed to the sun's
/dispersion
Containment and communion, seed-time
/and harvest, palm
And pylon, Ogun's road a 'Mobius' orbit,
/kernel
And electrons, wine to alchemy.
Soyinka, possibly more than any other
of the new African writers, seeks to break
down his experiences into shards and
then to reassemble them into new wholes

neither African nor European, but universal. It makes for whorls of seemingly
inchoate passages at times but also for
an expressiveness and reach rare in any
literature.

Writings: Plays: *The House of Banigeji.* Act
II: "The Exiles," in *Reflections,* Lagos,
African Universities Press, 1962; *The
Lion and the Jewel,* in *Black Orpheus*
magazine, No. 5, Ibadan, 1959; also in
separate paperback edition by Oxford
University Press, London, Ibadan,
Three Crowns Book, 1963; *Three Plays:
The Swamp Dwellers, The Trials of Brother
Jero,* and *The Strong Breed,* Ibadan, Mbari
Publications, 1963; the same three plays
in *Three Short Plays,* London and New
York, Oxford's Three Crowns Books,
1969; *The Trials of Brother Jero,* and *The
Strong Breed: two plays,* New York,
Dramatists' Play, 1969, illustrated (a spe-
cial acting edition with production
notes); *A Dance of the Forests,* London and
Ibadan, Oxford University Press, 1963;
*Five Plays: The Lion and the Jewel, The
Swamp Dwellers, The Trials of Brother Jero,
The Strong Breed,* and *A Dance of the For-
ests,* London and Ibadan, Oxford
University Press, 1965; *The Road,* Lon-
don and Ibadan, Oxford University
Press, 1965; *Kongi's Harvest,* London and
Ibadan, Oxford University Press, 1967;
Blackout (published version of the skits,
"Before the Blackout") Ibadan, Orisun
Acting Editions, n.d., but probably 1965;
Madmen and Scientists (produced 1965,
as "Madman and Specialists," The
University of Ibadan Theatre Arts Com-
pany, and again with Wole Soyinka,
director at the Eugene O'Neill Memorial
Theatre Center, Watertown, Conn.,
August 2, 1970), London, Methuen,
1971 and New York, Hill and Wang,
1972; Unpublished: *The Invention,* pro-
duced at the Royal Court Theatre, Lon-

don, 1955; *Camwood on the leaves,* radio play aired on Nigerian Broadcasting Corporation, possibly 1960; *The Detainee,* given in German on Cologne program aired on West German radio and prepared in mimeographed form, 1968.

Novels: *The Interpreters,* London, André Deutsch, 1965, New York, Collier Books, 1970; *The Forest of a Thousand Daemons* (with Chief Fagunwa), London, Nelson, 1968.

Poetry: *Idanre and Other Poems,* London, Methune, 1967; New York, Hill and Wang, 1968; *Poems from Prison,* London, Rex Collings, 1969, republished as *A Shuttle in the Crypt,* New York, Hill and Wang, 1972; in many anthologies, including *Modern Poetry from Africa,* revised edition, Moore and Beier, editors, London, Penguin, 1966.

Anthology: Collected and edited by Soyinka: *Plays from the Third World. An Anthology.* New York, Doubleday, 1971.

Criticism: "Towards a True African Theatre," *Transition 8,* Kampala, Uganda, March 1963; "And After the Narcissist?" *African Forum,* New York, I, 4 (Spring, 1966); "The Writer in An African State," *The Writer in Modern Africa,* New York, Scandinavian Institute of African Studies and African Publishing Corporation, 1969; but first published in *Transition 31,* Kampala, June, 1967; "The Fourth Stage," Chapter 5 of *The Morality of Art,* essays published in a memorial volume for George Wilson Knight, edited by D. W. Jefferson, London, Routledge and Kegan Paul, 1969.

Biographical/Critical Sources: Eldred Jones, "Progress and Civilization in the Work of Wole Soyinka," unpublished paper, read at Ife University, December, 1968; Gerald Moore, *Wole Soyinka,* illustrated, with bibliography, New York, Africana Publishing Company, 1971,

and London, Evans Brothers Ltd, 1971; Anne Tibble, *African/English Literature,* London, Peter Owen, 1965; "Changing Themes in the Nigerian Novel," *New African Literature and the Arts,* I, New York, Crowell, 1970; Margaret Laurence, *Long Drums and Cannons,* London, Macmillan, 1968; Alain Ricard, *Théâtre et nationalisme: Wole Soyinka et Leroi Jones,* Paris, Présense Africaine, 1972; Adrian A. Roscoe, *Mother is Gold: A Study in West African Literature,* Cambridge, Cambridge University Press, 1971; *Introduction to Nigerian Literature,* Bruce King, editor, New York, Africana Publishing Corporation, 1972; Charles R. Larson *The Emergence of African Fiction,* Bloomington, Indiana, Indiana University Press, 1972; T. Murphy, "The English Writings of Chinua Achebe and Wole Soyinka with Special Reference to the Theme as Illustrated in their Writings of the Impact of Western Civilization upon the Ibo and Yoruba Cultures of S. Nigeria from the Late 19th Century Onwards," unpublished Ph. D. dissertation, University of Newcastle-upon-Tyne, 1966; "Our Authors and Performing Artists," *Nigeria Magazine,* No. 88, March, 1966, pp. 57–64, and No. 89, January, 1966, pp. 133–40.

STEPHEN, Felix N. (also possibly CHINAKA, B. A.)
b. 1925, eastern Nigeria.
Novelette writer in popular English.

One of the most prolific of the Onitsha "chap-book" writers, Stephen has published his many "popular" works under a variety of titles. There are possibly as many as 14 individual works and conceivably many more. A partial list includes: *How to play love,* 1963, a 48-page work; *The trials and death of*

Lumumba, 1965, 44 pages; *The life story of boys and girls*, 1962; *The temple of love*, 1964; and *Lack of money is not lack of sense*, 1966. Though all but *The temple of love* are called plays in the above list, this seems only because they are cast in dialogue form for staccato vivacity, rather than being conceived as stage vehicles.

Stephen's *How to play love* has been found by Bernth Lindfors to be identical with B. A. Chinaka's *How to speak and write to girls for friendship* except for the quite literal instructions in love making in the "Chinaka" work substituted for Stephen's final scene.

"The Sweetness of Love," Stephen's short story written exclusively in dialogue, appears in the volume, *The Work of Love* by Cyril Nwakuma Ariruguzo, published in 1963.

Writings: Novelettes: *How to play love*, Onitsha, Njokuandsons, 1963; *The trials and death of Lumumba*, Onitsha, M. Allan Ohaejesi, 1963; *The life story of boys and girls*, Onitsha, Chinyelu Printing Press, 1962; *The temple of love*, Onitsha, B. C. Okara and Sons, 1964; *Lack of money is not lack of sense*, Onitsha, Chinyelu, 1966. *How to speak and write to girls for friendship*, Onitsha, Njoko and Sons, no date, by "B. A. Chinaka," is similar to *How to play love*.

Story: "The Sweetness of Love," in *The Work of Love* by Cyril Nwakuma Ariruguzo, Onitsha, Ariruguzo and Sons, 1963.

Biographical/Critical Source: Emmanuel Obiechina, *Literature for the Masses: An Analytical Study of Popular Pamphleteering in Nigeria*, foreword by Chinua Achebe, Enugu, Nigeria, Nwankwo-Ifejika and Co., 1971.

SUMAILI, Gabriel
b. ca. 1935, Zaïre.
Poet.

Sumaili's one verse volume, *Aux flancs de l'équateur* (At the Edge of the Equator), published in 1966, is one of the rare works of poetry published in French in Zaïre.

Writings: Poetry: *Aux flancs de l'équateur*, Kinshasa, Les Belles Lettres, 1966.

SUTHERLAND, Efua Theodora
(née Morgue)
b. 1924, Cape Coast, Ghana.
Playwright, poet, essayist, teacher.

Efua Sutherland, Black Africa's most famous woman writer, studied at Saint Monica's School, and then took a B.A. at Teacher Training College, Homerton College, Cambridge University. She also studied at the School of Oriental and African Studies at the University of London. On returning to the Gold Coast in 1951, she taught for three years before marrying William Sutherland, an American, in 1954. She helped found the Writer's Workshop at the Institute of African Studies at the University of Ghana in Legon, and taught African literature and drama in 1963. Earlier, in 1958, she had helped found the Ghana Drama Studio, mostly devoted to childrens' theater, and the Ghana Society of Writers.

With her husband she has also established a school in the Trans-Volta region of upper Ghana, and has founded an experimental theater for village productions in Ghana's Central Region. Much of her work has recently been with Legon University's School of Drama and the Kusum Agoromba, a childrens' theater group performing plays throughout Ghana. She is the mother of three children.

For the Ghana radio she has written and helped produce many plays, including: *You Swore an Oath: Anansegora; Odasani* (A Ghanaian "Everyman"), Foriwa (a three-act play), *The Marriage of Anansewaa* (one act,), *The Pineapple Child* (a fantasy), *Nyamekye* (music, dance, song mixture), *Ananse and the Dwarf Brigade* (a children's play), and *Two Rhythm Plays* (for children). Most of these were produced for the popular radio program, "The Singing Net." In the late 1950's Sutherland directed many adaptations of traditional plays concerned with the rogue-spider-man, Ananse.

The radio play, *Anansegora*, saw publication in *Présence Africaine* magazine, in 1964, and *Foriwa* was published in a separate volume by the State Publishing Corporation, Accra, in 1967, though it had been produced as early as 1962 by the Ghana Dance Studio in Accra. Her most recent dramatic work in print is *Vulture! Vulture! Two rhythm plays,* 1968, which contains, along with the title play, the one-acter, *Tahinta.*

The "story-telling" play, *The Marriage of Anansewaa,* originally presented on radio, saw a stage production in September, 1971 in Accra, but has not yet been published. Very slow moving and purposefully "undramatic" in Western terms, this play seeks to combine the deliberate pace of the story teller's art with set scenes of dramatized or "visualized" action.

Mrs. Sutherland also has produced two works of photo-journalism, *The Roadmakers,* 1961, and *Playtime in Africa,* 1960. Before her marriage, as Efua Morgue, she published three childrens' stories, "Mumunde my Mumunde,"

"Little Wild Flowers," and " It Happened."

In 1964, her play, *Edufa,* appeared in a production of the Writers' Workshop in Accra. It was later published by Longmans, Green in 1967 with photographs of the premiere production on the cover and accompanying the text.

The basic story is that of Edufa, a clever, too-wealthy, educated merchant who gradually moves closer and closer to the secret horror in his life. Having learned from a sorceror that death was coming for him, Edufa pleads for some magic which will save him. Only if he can find someone who will trade his life for Edufa's, he is told, will he escape. Edufa's own father on being asked, jeeringly refuses to sacrifice himself for his aggressive, selfish son; but the lovely Ampona, Edufa's wife, volunteers to her husband's genuine consternation. Fate marches through the play and there is nothing Efufa can do to prevent Ampona's mysterious decline (only too obvious to the horrified husband) and final death, for her offer seals Edufa's selfish promise to the sorceror to find a substitute. Though the play has its awkward moments and Edufa really seems a better sort than many of the characters in the play give him credit for being, it is a compelling study of the conflicts between the "superstitious" world of old Africa and the jaundiced, often shallowly cynical world of the new rich and quasi-Westernized elites.

The play has a chorus, a choragos or chorus leader, and a certain solemn tone which obviously reflect the classical Greek drama. Sutherland, however, also employs African dance-drama and contemporary stage conventions which make of *Edufa* an original amalgam. Staged originally in some scenes in European-style evening clothes for the

Accra premiere, the play is strangely good and quite bad at the same time. The text of the play is probably most readily available in *Plays from Black Africa*, edited by F. M. Litto, 1968.

Eight of Sutherland's poems appear in the recent collection of Ghanaian poets, *Messages:* "The Redeemed," "Once Upon a Time," "The Dedication," "Song of the Fishing Ghosts," "While Mother and Father Drowned," "A Professional Beggar's Lullaby," "Our Songs are About It," and "Observation on a Cockerel About to Crow, for a Young Man." The first poem, "Redeemed," is a tense picture of a venomous snake lying in wait for a beautiful woman on her way to market with a towering load of the banana-like plaintain on her head. The first five stanzas imply the snake will be successful, as it lies in her path:

Love I the shine of your skin
Yet must I dull it
With venom from my sting–

but the last stanzas show the woman discovering the lurking killer:

She paused in her pace, and
turned on me
A soul that speared my reptile frame
Until I writhed in a helpless coil

The lines are Miltonic in phrasing; "reptile frame" or "venom from my sting" seem quaint and heavy, but the picture is African.

More original is "Song of the Fishing Ghosts" which ends:

Phantoms black
Phantoms red
Phantoms white
For nets their heads
And the dark, dark, dark river flows.

Writings: Plays: *Edufa*, London, Longmans, Green, 1967 and 1969; first published in *Okyeame*, 1966; *Edufa* also appears in *Plays from Black Africa*, Fredric M. Litto, editor, New York, Hill and Wang, 1968.

Short plays: *Anansegora*, Paris, *Présence Africaine*, English language edition, No. 22, Summer, 1964; *Foriwa*, Accra, State Publishing Corp. 1967, first published in *Okyeame*, 1964; *Vulture! Vulture! Two Rhythm Plays*, Accra, Ghana Publishing House, 1968 (contains the play *Tahina* and the title play); unpublished: *Odasani; The Marriage of Anansewaa; The Pineapple Child; Nyamekye; Ananse and the Dwarf Brigade;* and *Two Rhythm Plays.*

Photo-journalism: *Playtime in Africa*, with photographs by the American photographer, Willis E. Bell, Accra, 1960 and New York, Atheneum, 1962; *The Roadmakers*, Accra, 1961; both by Ghana Information Service.

Stories: "Mumunde my Mumunde," "Little Wild Flowers," "It Happened," in *Pan African Short Stories*, Neville Denny, editor, London, Nelson, 1966; other stories in *Modern African Prose*, Richard Rive, editor, London, Heinemann, 1964; and many other anthologies.

Poetry: in *Messages*, Awoonor and Adali-Mortty, editors, London, Heinemann, 1971; and many other collections.

Biographical/Critical Source: A Reader's Guide to African Literature, Zell and Silver, editors, New York, Africana Publishing Corp., 1971.

SWAARTBOOI, Victoria Nombulelo Mermaid (sometimes SWAARTBOI)
b. September 27, 1907, Emgewe, Nqamakwe District, South Africa;
d. September 23, 1937.
Xhosa novelist, teacher.

Daughter of Christian parents, Victoria Swaartbooi attended the Methodist School at Emgewe where her father was principal. Finishing the sixth form she entered Emgwali Training School in January, 1924, and in 1926 entered Healdtown School for two years of study leading to her Junior Teacher's Certificate. Joining the staff of the Emgwali Girls' Practising School in January 1929, she took charge of the older girls, taught domestic science and sought to inculcate ambition in her pupils. She also was active in church affairs and was a leader of the Wayfarer-Guides, a Scout movement open to Blacks. (In South Africa regular scouting was open to whites only.) A few months before her intended marriage she suffered an extreme attack of tuberculosis and died September 23, 1937, a few days short of her 30th birthday.

Swaartbooi's only novel *U-Mandisa*, autobiographical and moralistic in tone, recounts the experiences of a young Christian girl whose name means "Bringer of Joy." Though her book is of no particular artistic significance, it did mark an advance for women, for creative works by women authors have remained very rare in black South Africa. Only the novel, *U-Tandive wakwa Gcaleka* (Tandive of the Gcaleka Clan), by Lota G. (or Lillith) Kakaza (Mrs. V. Kwatsha, ca. 1885–1950), published 1914, antedates *U-Mandisa*. After her in the pre-World War II era of Xhosa writing there has only been *U-Jujuju* (1938), and *Mhla ngenqaba*, 1960 by Zora Z. T. Futshane (Mrs. Lechele, ca. 1915–1951).

Writings: Novel: *U-Mandisa*, Lovedale, Lovedale Press, 1933, 57 pages. Other early novels by women writers: *U-Tandive wakwa Gcaleka*, by Lota G. (or Lillith) Kakaze (Mrs. V. Kwatsha), Cape Town, Methodist Book Room, 1914; *U-Jujuju* (Magic) by Zora Z. T. Futshane (Mrs. Lechele), Lovedale, Lovedale Press, 1938, 1962; *Mhla ngenqaba* (Mhla in Trouble), Lovedale, Lovedale Press, 1960.

Biographical/Critical Source: J. Mac Gregor, "The Late Miss Victoria Swartbooi," *South African Outlook*, LXVII (1937), 267.

SYAD, William Joseph Farah
b. 1930, Djibouti, French Somalia (Territory of Afars and Issas).
Poet (writes and publishes in both French and English).

Syad now lives in Mogadishu, the Somali Democratic Republic's capital. He has published a poetic journal, *Khamsine*, 1959, with an introduction by Léopold Sédar Senghor. His poems in French and English texts have appeared in various collections including the eclectic anthology of Présence Africaine, *New Sum of Poetry from the Negro World*.

Writings: Poetry: *Khamsine*, Paris, Présence Africaine, 1959; poems: "L'ange aux ailes brisées" (The Angel with the Shattered Wings), "Hier" (Yesterday), and "La femme et le chien" (The Woman and the Dog), in *New Sum of Poetry from the Negro World*, Paris, Présence Africaine, Volume 57, 1966.

T

TAIWO, Oladele
b. ca. 1935, Nigeria.
Anthologist, story writer, folklorist.

Locally educated through the university level, Taiwo took an M.A. in education at Durham University in England. During 1962–63 he did research and studied the teaching of English as a foreign language under a UNESCO fellowship. He presently is head of the department of English, in the College of Education, University of Lagos, Yaba, Nigeria.

Taiwo has published the useful anthology, *An Introduction to West African Literature,* and two collections of stories for juvenile readers: *The King's Heir,* 1965, which contains proverbs, riddles, tales and other folkloric materials; and *The Hunter and the Hen,* also 1965, which offers 24 tales. The anthology has three sections: the first devoted to the oral-folk traditions of African literature; the second concerned with the Western genres of the novel, poem and play as they have been employed by new African writers; and the third focused on Camara Laye's *The African Child,* Cyprian Ekwensi's *People of the City,* Chinua Achebe's *No Longer at Ease,* and Wole Soyinka's *The Lion and the Jewel.*

Writings: Juvenile novelettes, stories, folklore: *The King's Heir,* London, Nelson, 1965; *The Hunter and the Hen,* Lagos, African Universities Press, 1965.

Anthology: *An Introduction to West African Literature,* London, Nelson, 1967.

TAKLA, Hawaryat
b. ca. 1881, Kassat (Tagulat), Shoa, Ethiopia.
Amharic playwright, government official.

Takla Hawaryat studied the old, religious language Ge'ez, in Dabra Berhan and then became a member of the entourage of Ras Makonnen, an ally of Emperor Menelik II in the Harar region. He visited Russia in 1896 where he moved in liberal circles led by Princess Volkonsky, granddaughter of the Decembrist leader, Prince S. G. Volkonsky, and by V. P. Kochubei the chief of the Ukrainian nationalist group. Attending the Mikhailovskaia Military School in Moscow and the St. Petersburg Military School, he graduated and was quickly appointed a colonel in the Russian army.

After only a few months at home in 1909, he left to study agriculture in France and England for three years. From 1912 on, he took part in many international and domestic chores including the work of negotiating the English-held Sudanese border with Ethiopia and service as comptroller of the railway line from Addis Ababa to Jibuti on the coast. He was a governor of the provinces of Jijiga, Ogaden, and Chercher from 1917 to 1931, founded the town of Asba Tafari and served as Minister of Finance from 1931 to 1933. He introduced the country's new constitution, modeled on Japan's of 1889, to the new Parliament. Takla was named Envoy Extraordinary to various European States in 1933; he headed Ethiopia's delegation to the League of Nations at Geneva; and at the outbreak of war with Ethiopia he was recalled to head the defense of the Awash Valley. He begged Emperor Haile Selassie not to leave the country, arguing the matter personally with him; but he himself went into exile without a fight when the Emperor went to England. He lived in Madagascar until 1955, and only then, at the age of 74, returned to a model farm at Hirna in the province of Chercher where he lives today.

Takla's one contribution to Ethiopian creative literature was a play believed to have been written and produced in 1912 or shortly thereafter. The text and title have disappeared, but it is known to have been based on some of La Fontaine's animal fables and to have exploited local customs and motifs in a satirical attack on court officials, their corruptions and inefficiencies. Eventually banned, it joined other plays in limbo until Haile Selassie I took power in 1930.

TATI, Jean–Baptist (also TATI–LOUT and TATTI–LOUTARD)
b. 1938, Pointe Noire, Congo,

Brazzaville.
Poet, teacher.

Tati was educated in his natal city, later in Brazzaville, and finally at the University of Bordeaux where he took the Licence ès Lettres in modern literature, a second "licence" in Italian, and a "Diplôme d'études." His thesis in Italian was on the Italian philosopher, Benedetto Croce. Presently, he is completing a doctorate on French African poetry and is teaching in Brazzaville at the Ecole Normal Supérieure.

Both of Tati's books of poetry were published in 1968: *Poèmes de la mer* (Poems of the Sea), and *Les racines congolaises* (Congolese Roots). He is represented in English translation in Moore and Beier's *Modern Poetry from Africa.*

Writings: Poetry: *Poèmes de la mer,* Yaoundé, CLE, 1968; *Les racines congolaises,* Honfleur, Paris, P. J. Oswald, 1968; poems: in English translation, "News of my mother" and "Liberty" in *Modern Poetry from Africa,* revised edition, Moore and Beier, editors, London, Baltimore, Penguin, 1968.

TATI–LOUT (see TATI, Jean–Baptiste)

TATTI–LOUTARD (see TATI, Jean–Baptiste)

TAVARES, Eugénio (de Paulo)
b. 1867, Brava, Cape Verde Islands:
d. Brava, 1930.
Poet, public official.

Born on the island of Brava in the Cape Verde group, Tavares struggled for an education, lived for a short while in New England in the United States, and, discouraged, returned to Cape Verde to live out his life as a minor civil servant.

This pioneering poet published three volumes of verse in his native Creole-Portuguese: *Mornas: Cantigas crioulas* (Listless Airs: Creole Songs), published in 1932 after his death by his friend, José Osório de Oliveiro; and two early works in 1916: *Amor que salva* (The Love That Saves), and *Mal de amor: coroa de espinhos* (Love's Sickness: The Crown of Thorns).

The earlier volumes were inspired by the folkloric poems of João de Deus, a once popular Portuguese poet of the 19th century. Encouraged by high governmental officials, including Governor Guedes Vaz, himself a poet, Tavares often composed his own verses in Creole to be accompanied by guitars for the local dance, the morna. It was the first serious poetry to be written in the island patois. The power of true love, or *cretcheu*, the sadness of old sweet memories or the *sodade* (from the Portuguese *saudade*, "home-sickness"), and the *hora di bai*, or the grief of separation, are his main themes. His writing in classical Portuguese also appeared in the pioneering Cape Verdean journal, *Almanach Luso-Africano*, established in 1894. His important poem, "Amor que salva," appeared in that journal in 1916.

Writings: Poetry: *Amor que salva*, Praia, Cape Verde, Santificação do beijo, 1916; *Mal de amor: Coroa de espinhos*, Praia, Cape Verde, 1916; *Mornas: Cantigas crioulas*, epilogue by José Osório de Oliveiro, Lisbon, J. Rodrigues and Co., 1932; poem, "Amor que salva," in *Almanach Luso-Africano*, Cape Verde, 1916.

Essay: "A morna e o povo de Cabo Verde," in his volume of verse, *Mornas*, Lisbon, 1932.

TAVORA, Orlando (see JACINTO, António)

TAYLOR, W. H.
b. 1940, Freetown, Sierra Leone.
Poet.

Educated locally in Sierra Leone until he began his wanderings in 1956, Taylor eventually arrived in the United Kingdom. He has published two little volumes of poetry, *A Poet's Palatte*, 1969. and *Till We See Again*, 1971.

Writings: Poems: *A Poet's Palette*, London, Regency Press Ltd., 1969; *Till We See Again*, Walton-on-Thames, Surrey, England, 1971.

TCHIBAMBA (see LOMAMI-TSHIBAMBA)

TCHICAYA, Gérard-Félix (see U TAM'SI, Tchicaya, Gérard Félix)

TENREIRO, Francisco José de Vasques
b. 1921, São Tomé;
d. Lisbon, Portugal, 1963.
Poet, story writer, anthologist, geographer.

A graduate of the Superior School of Colonial Administration, Tenreiro

435

worked as a distinguished scientist at the Center of Geographic Studies under Professor Orlando Ribeiro in Lisbon. He did graduate work and research at the London School of Economics and was named assistant professor of human geography in the Arts Faculty of the University of Lisbon. A product of this period was a study of the geography of Sao Tomé, published in Lisbon in 1962.

Though primarily a scholar, and resident for most of his short life in Portugal, Tenreiro's heart was in his poetry and the general study of African literature. He was a collaborator with Mário de Andrade and António Domingues in the pioneering work, *Caderno de poesia negra de expressão portuguesa* (Notebook of Negro Poetry in Portuguese), published in a modest 18 pages in Lisbon, 1953.

This work has seen many versions since, including the important *Antologia da poesia negra de expressão portuguesa, precedida de "Cultura negro-africana e assimilação,"* (Anthology of Negro Poetry in Portuguese, preceded by the essay, "Negro-African and Creole Culture), published in France, 1958, which had grown to 106 pages, and *Literatura africana de expressão portuguêsa,* two volumes, 1967–68, in 326 pages. His interests also spread to American writing and in 1945 he published the study, *Panorama of North American Literature* (English translation) in Lisbon.

Published in his lifetime were the volumes of his own verse *Ilha de nome santo* (The Island of the Holy Name), a work of 53 pages, 1942: and *Acêrca do diálogo entre a Europa e a Africa negra.* (Something of a Dialogue Between Europe and Black Africa), issued in 1959, an essay of 20 pages. His neo-realist poems are considered the first major work of négritude by an African writing in Portuguese, and they had great influence on other African writers in the Portuguese empire. *Ilha de nome santo,* the long poem which gives its name to the volume, attacks social injustice on Saint Thomas and insists that "being black" is a positive attribute, something never before so strongly stated. Further, white superiority is denied. Published four years after his death, *Obra poética* (Poetic Works) contained much of his earlier poetry, including the previously unpublished collection, "Coração em Africa" (Courage in Africa).

Four of his poems are found in Volume I of the 1967 *Literatura africana,* and his puzzled, angry poem, "Canção do Mestiço" (Song of the Métis or Mixed-Blood), appears in *Poetas e contistas africanos de expressão portuguêsa,* 1963. His

Romance de seu Silva Costa (The Ballad of one, Silva Costa) is a pseudo "biography" of a typical white settler on São Tomé which bitterly contrasts the life style of the Portuguese settler with the native Africans and the only slightly more fortunate Creoles of mixed blood. As the immigrant whites enrich themselves on the sweated labor of the native creoles, the reader feels both sorrow and anger.

Despite these early initiatives, however, Alfred Margarido in his article, "The Social and Economic Background of Portuguese Negro Poetry," finds Tenreiro still too isolated from the genuine concerns of the African, for he had lived most of his life in Lisbon and only vaguely could identify himself with the peasants of his home island. To some extent true, this charge must be tempered when one recalls his early work with Mário de Andrade and his own strong enunciation of nativist sentiments before most of his fellow writers.

Writings: Poetry: *Ilha de nome santo,* Coimbra, Portugal, 1942; *Obra poética,* Braga, Lisbon, 1967 (contains *Ilha de nome santo* and *Coração,* first published in 1964); poems in *Poetas e contistas africanos de expressão portuguêsa,* São Paulo, Editôra Brasiliense, 1963; translation of Portuguese poetry into English: "Coração em Africa" and "O Mar" in G. M. Moser, *Essays in Portuguese-African Literature,* Penn State Studies, 26, University Park, Pennsylavania, The Pennsylvania State University, 1969.

Stories: "Romance de seu Silva Costa," in *Diogenes,* XXXVII, 1962, No. 37, "Nós voltaremos juntos," in *Modernos authores portuguêses,* Volume II, 1942.

Essays: "Acêrca da literature negra," in *Estrada Larga,* Volume III, Porto, Portugal, 1962; *Acêrca do diálogo entre a Europa e a Africa negra, Dados para a sua compreensão,* Coimbra, Portugal, 1959; *Panorama of North American Literature.*

Anthologies: (Edited and contributed to): *Caderno de poesia negra de expressão portuguêsa,* Lisbon, Libraria Escolar Editôra, 1953; *Antologia da poesia negra de expressão portuguêsa,* Honfleur, J. P. Oswald, 1958; *Literatura africana de expressão portuguêsa,* Algiers, 1967.

Biographical/Critical Source: G. M. Moser, *Essays in Portuguese-African Literature,* Penn State Studies, 26.

THAGE, Johannes Ralakiti
b. 1950, Sophiatown, Johannesburg, South Africa.
Story writer.

Locally educated through high school, Thage now lives in Diepkloof in the ore country of the Witwatersrand. One of his published stories "It Came like a Waterfall," appeared in *African Arts,* Spring, 1971. The tale is episodic, dealing in a casual, often cruel, sometimes humorous way, with the daily lives of the poor in the black slums of South Africa.

Writings: Story: "It Came Like a Waterfall," in *African Arts,* Spring, 1971.

THEMBA, Daniel Canadoise Dorsay
b. 1924, Pretoria, South Africa;
d. 1969, Manzini, Swaziland.
Short story writer, journalist.

Locally educated at Pretoria and Pietersburg schools, Themba earned a B.A. with distinction at Fort Hare University

College where he studied on a Mendi Scholarship. He taught English for several years in Western Native Township, Johannesburg. Themba worked on the well-known journal *Drum* as a reporter and then as an assistant editor after service with a now defunct magazine in Johannesburg. He also worked as an editor of the weekly *The Golden City Post.* During the 1960's, he taught high school in Manzini, Swaziland where he died in 1969.

Themba's vigorous if somewhat hackneyed stories are generally ones of protest. In 1953 he won *Drum* magazine's short story competition with his "Mob Passion," describing a feud between two factions of an African tribal nation. His two published sketches are "The Bottom of the Bottle," nostalgic stories of the vanished Sophiatown, and "Requiem for Sophiatown," an even stronger lament for the old, loved, if violent and raw life of South Africa in the days before Prime Minister Verwoerd moved to absolute apartheid. He is cynical in his work but obviously is restraining his anger at the well-nigh hopeless situation of the black population.

Writings: Stories: "Mob Passion," "The Bottom of the Bottle," "Requiem for Sophiatown," in various South African journals.

Anthologies: in *Modern African Stories,* Komey and Mphahlele, editors, London, Faber, 1964, 1966; *African Writing Today,* E. Mphahlele, editor, Harmondsworth, England, Baltimore, Penguin, 1967; *South African Writing Today,* Nadine Gordimer and Lionel Abrahams, editors, Harmondsworth, England, Penguin, 1967.

TIACOH, Gabriel Kouadio (see KOUADIO-TIACOH)

TIENDREBEOGO, Yamba Larhallé-Naba
b. 1907, Ouagadougou, Upper Volta.
Poet, anthologist, collector of folklore.

Tiendrébéogo, educated in Africa, served as vice president of the traditional Chiefs' Syndicate in French-controlled West Africa from 1947 until the coming of independence to the area's former colonies. He collected sayings and proverbs of Volta, publishing them in *Chez le Larhallé* (At Home with the Larhalle People).

Since independence he has served in an official capacity as his country's historian of traditional literature and folkways. He has also been active as a reciter of tales on the Upper Voltaic radio (Radio-Diffusion de Haute Volta), and has been a leading member of the Cercle d'Activités Littéraires et Artistique de Haute Volta.

Writings: Collection of Folklore: *Chez le Larhallé,* Ouagadougou, Naba, 1964.

Anthology (compiler): *Contes du Larhallé,* details unknown.

History: *Histoires des Mossi de Ouagadougou,* details unknown.

TORRES, Farinha (pseudonym for MILHEIROS, Mário)

TOURE, Sadan-Moussa
b. ca. 1932, Guinea.
Poet.

Touré has published one volume of verse, *Les premières guinéades. Contes, Légendes de chez nous* (The First Guineades: Legends of Our Home), 1961, a work of 80 pages. He is also represented with the patriotic poems: "Pour la liberté" (For Liberty) and "Notre liberté" (Our Freedom) in *New Sum of Poetry from the Negro World.*

Writings: Poems: *Les premières guinéades. Contes, légendes de chez nous. Poésies,* Conakry, Sily-Edition, 1961; poems in *New Sum of Poetry from the Negro World,* Paris, Présence Africaine, Vol. 57, 1966.

TRAORE, Mamadou
(pseudonym: AUTRA, Ray)
b. 1916, Guinea.
Poet, writer on political subjects.

Traoré's one known work of literature was produced during the early heady days of independence in Guinea, the first of the francophone states to break with Paris. *Vers la liberté*, like Sadan-Moussa Touré's *Les premières guinéades*, celebrates his country's political independence, but as felt while he was a student in China. His other works include a tourist guide and a study of the French law governing relations with the African colonies.

Writings: Poems: *Vers la liberté*, Peking, Librarie du Nouveau Monde, 1961.
Journalism: *Connaissance de la République de Guinée*, Conakry, Ministère de l'Information et du Tourisme de la République de Guinée, 1960; *Considérations sur la Loi-Cadre dans les territoires d'outre mer*, Porto Novo, 196?

TRAVELE, Moussa
b. late 1800's, Mali.
Novelist, poet, collector of folklore, ethnologist, scholar.

Travele worked for a period as the principal interpreter for the French in the colony of the French Soudan, now Mali, and has been honored by being named Chevalier de la Légion d'Honneur. His collection of folklore was *Proverbes et contes bambara* (1913), believed to be the first such book from Soudanese sources. His other works are: *Petit manuel français-bambara* (1910); *Le chatechisme des noires;* and *Petit dictionnaire français-bambara, bambara-français* (1913).

Travele was well known in his time in France and in the Soudan for his interest in Soudanese customs and languages. His chief distinction is his 1913 dictionary. His creative works rarely saw print.

Writings: Folktales: *Proverbes et contes bambara*, Paris, 1913.
Linguistic studies: *Petit manuel français-bambara*, 1910; *Le chatechisme des noires*, date unknown; *Petit dictionnaire français-bambara*, 1913.

TSEGAYE, Gabre-Medhin (also
MEDHIN, Tsegaye Gabre,
SAGAYE Gabra Madhen, and
GABRE-MEDHIN, Tsegaye)
b. August 17, 1935, Ambo, Ethiopia.
Amharic and English language
playwright, poet, novelist.

Tsegaye is generally considered the finest writer in the new group of Ethiopian writers in the English language, and is also an excellent Amharic author. After local schooling, he attended the Blackstone School of Law in Chicago, Illinois, taking the degree of LL.B. in June, 1960. Interested also in drama, he trained at Windsor's Theatre Royal, London's Royal Court Theatre in England and at the French National Theatre and the Rome Opera. On his return home, he wrote several plays, translated others, and by 1966 was acting director of the Haile Selassie I Theatre in Addis Ababa.

Tsegaye's Amharic plays, *Blood Harvest,* which concerns the Italian

439

invasion of Ethiopia, and *Listro or Shoe Shine Boy,* were produced at the Addis Ababa Commerical School but have not been published. *Tewodros,* his first play in English, was performed May 5, 1963, at the Creative Arts Centre at Haile Selassie I University, with the Emperor attending.

The central figure of Tewodros, or Theodore, is seen from a more favorable, and in a more complex, light than he was in Makonnen Endalkacaw's novel, *Taytu Betul,* published six years earlier. Employing the fruits of his own studies of the records on this emperor, Tsegaye's reading of Theodore's personality, motives, and the significance of his actions are similar to the conclusions reached by Sven Rubensson in his *King of Kings: Tewodros of Ethiopia* (1966), according to A. S. Gérard. Tsegaye's play was published in the *Ethiopian Observer* in 1966 and his second play, *Azmari* (The Minstrels) appeared in the same issue. The latter play reflects a wide-ranging knowledge of Western dramatic craft and the influence of Chekhov, Shaw and symbolist drama.

His English-language novel, *Oda Oak Oracle* is possibly the best fiction in English to come from Ethiopia. The novel pits the collective wisdom and fears of the tribe of Shanka, the protagonist, against the love of Ukutee for Shanka who is urged by his newly Christianized friend, Goaa, to ignore the baleful prophecy that Ukutee's first born must be sacrificed. Ukutee wishes to ignore the oracle; Goaa says it's all superstitious nonsense, but Shanka refuses to consumate his marriage. Eventually Goaa seduces the yearning Ukutee, and in due time their child is born, only to die. Shanka kills Goaa in a ceremonially enjoined duel but is himself exiled. Though the hero obeyed the oracle, he represents a turning away from the crueler aspects of ancestral belief. He is personally untouched by alien influences except the shallow Christian beliefs of Goaa.

Tsegaye has also directed Amharic and foreign language plays, including Molière's *Le médecin malgré lui* and *Tartuffe,* and Shakespeare's *Othello, Hamlet,* and *Macbeth.* He has also contributed an article "Literature and the African Public" to the *Ethiopian Observer.*

His verse first appeared in "Poems," in the *Ethiopia Observer* in 1965 in English. He is well represented with five poems in the original English in *New Sum of Poetry from the Negro World* and with three poems in Shelton's *The African Assertion.* "Home-Coming Son," the third poem in the Shelton volume begins very beautifully, with its warning to the returned son, a "stranger" now because of his sojourn in Europe:

Look where you walk, unholy stranger—
This is the land of the eighth harmony
in the rainbow: Black.
It is the dark side of the moon
brought to light:
this is the canvas of God's master stroke.

Writings: Plays: *Tewodros, Ethiopian Observer,* X, 3, 1966; *Azmari,* in *Ethiopian Observer,* X, 3, 1966; unpublished plays: *Blood Harvest; Listro or Shoe Shine Boy.*

Novels: *Oda Oak Oracle,* London, Three Crowns-Oxford, 1965.

Poetry: in *Ethiopian Observer,* XI, 1, 1965; *New Sum of Poetry from the Negro World,* Paris, *Présence Africaine,* Vol. 57, 1966; *The African Assertion,* Austin J. Shelton, editor, New York, The Odyssey Press, 1968.

Articles: "Literature and the African Public," *Ethiopian Observer,* XI, 1, 1967.

Biographical/Critical Sources: "Introduction to Modern Ethiopian Literature," by Menghistu Lemma, mimeographed; Stockholm, 1967; A. S. Gérard, *Four African Literatures*, Berkeley, University of California Press. 1971.

TSHAKATUMBA, Matala Mukadi
b. ca. 1940, South Kasai, Zaïre.
Poet.

A member of the Mulubu people, Tshakatumba attended local schools through high school in Boma in the Lower Congo. He began to write in school, and continued while working on his university degree in political science at the University of Liege, Belgium, from 1965 on. He is still a resident of Belgium.

Tshakatumba's only published volume to date is *Réveil dans un nid de flammes (la foudre et le feu)*, 1969 (Waking Up in a Burning Nest [The Thunderbolt and the Fire]). He is represented by two poems (both in the original French and the English translation), "Prayer Without Echo" and "Message to Mputu Antoinette, Girl of the Bush, Friend of My Childhood," in Austin J. Shelton's *The African Assertion*. The latter poem begins:

African sister black sister
you who do not know Damas or Mackay
you who must learn Césaire and Senghor
you who are ignorant of the boundaries
/of your continent
and in the half-light go to draw water
like an ancient goddess
wearing an Edenic smile
and the first stanza ends:
Sister of the sapodilla tree loving sister
Africa will be the fruit of our accord.
As the woman (symbol of mother Africa to Léopold Sédar Senghor and to many other negritude poets) is com-

pared in that stanza to the sapodilla tropical evergreen, so in the second and concluding stanza we meet the locumé tree, both signifying constant growth:
O loving friend in the giant locumé:
Africa will be what together we make it.
Five of Tshakatumba's poems were published in the 1965 issue of *Afrique:* "Message," "Baobob," "Deception," "A Kanika" (To Kanika), and "Prière sans echo" (Prayer Without an Echo).

Writings: Poetry: *Réveil dans un nid de flammes*, Paris, 1969; poems in *The African Assertion*, Austin J. Shelton, editor, New York, The Odyssey Press, 1968; *Afrique*, Paris, 1965; *Black African Voices*, Glenview, Illinois, Scott, Foresman, 1970.

TSHIBAMBA, Paul Lomami (see LOMAMI-TSHIBAMBA, Paul)

TULYA-MUHIKA, Sam
b. ca. 1940, Kabale, Uganda.
Playwright.

Educated locally, Tulya-Muhika took his B.A. in mathematics at Makerere University College, graduating with honors, and recently went to the United Kingdom for advanced study in that subject. He began writing while in school, has had several radio plays performed, and has one play, *Born to Die*, in Cook & Lee's *Short East African Plays in English.*

Writings: Plays: *Born to Die*, in *Short East African Plays in English*, Cook and Lee, editors, Nairobi and London, Heinemann, 1968.

TUTUOLA, Amos
b. 1920, Abeokuta, Yoruba-country,

441

Tutuola

Western Nigeria.
Novelist, short story writer.

Amos Tutuola, son of Charles Tutuola, a cocoa farmer, in 1932 at the age of 12, took his first schooling in a Salvation Army School in his natal village. He completed only a few years because his family was poor and he was needed to work on the farm. His first formal employment was as a houseboy or domestic servant for F. O. Moru, a civil servant of the colonial government and an Ibo. Upon Moru's transfer to Lagos in 1934, he was interested enough in the young boy to take him along and there Amos was able to pick up the thread of his education, and eventually entered Lagos High School. Unfortunately, he was badly treated by the wife of Moru's friend with whom he and Moru were living and for whom he was working in Lagos, and he felt it necessary to return to Abeokuta in 1936 where he began classes again at his original school. He also did some study in 1938 at the Anglican Central School, Ipose Ake, Abeokuta, before finally leaving school for good upon the death of his father in 1939.

Burned out by a drought and failing in his effort to earn his way as a farmer, he returned to Lagos in 1940 to live with a brother and to learn the trade of a blacksmith which included his actual metier, that of coopersmith. In 1942 he joined the Royal Air Force in Lagos as a blacksmith. Serving until the end of the war, he was "demobbed" (discharged) in 1945 with the rank of grade-two blacksmith. He then tried and failed to establish a blacksmith shop. After a discouraging year of unemployment he caught on as a messenger in the Department of Labor in Lagos and there with some minimum security and

peace of mind began and completed his great first romance, *The Palm-Wine Drinkard*, considered by most critics to be the first "modern" African novel in English.

Tutuola wrote the first draft in two days, inspired by the thought that an ad he saw of a local religious society's book offerings was a solicitation for manuscripts. When the United Society for Christian Literature received the version, completed after another three months of feverish work, a wise and generous member of the firm sent it on to Faber and Faber in London. The rest is publishing history, though it took Faber seven years finally to publish this highly original work. The young author was sanguine enough, however, despite not being published immediately, to marry Victoria Alake in 1947. Years of menial labor remained but he was beginning his remarkable career as a story teller.

Continuing his modest work as a messenger for the next ten years, he completed and had published *My Life in the Bush of Ghosts,* 1954, and *Simbi and the Satyr of the Dark Jungle,* 1955.

In 1957, Tutuola moved to the Ibadan office of the Nigerian Broadcasting Corporation, to work as a storekeeper or stock clerk. Working with Professor Collis of the University of Ibadan, he produced in 1958 a version for the stage of *The Palm-Wine Drinkard* which was later also rendered into Tutuola's mother-tongue, Yoruba. The English version was produced in 1962 by the Arts Theatre of the University of Ibadan, at many places in Nigeria, and at the University of Ghana in Accra. In its Yoruba version it was put on by E. Kolawole Ogunmola and his folk opera actors and by the University of Ibadan's Travelling Theatre.

Dramatic versions of the novel, in both English and Yoruba, saw formal publication in 1967 and 1968, though typescript or mimeographed texts of the manuscript were furnished groups in Europe and America which staged adaptations, including ballet versions. Though some critics believe the Collis-Tutuola text departs from the better aspects of the novel and is somewhat cheapened, it apparently is successful with audiences everywhere.

In 1958 Tutuola's fourth novel, *The Brave African Huntress* appeared, and in 1962, his fifth, *Feather Woman of the Jungle,* was published.

Tutuola's work began receiving increasing attention in the West in the late 1950's and in 1962, Gerald Moore's *Seven African Writers* provided an important survey of his career to date and some analysis of his work. A much later and much more complete biographical study of Tutuola is Harold R. Collins' *Amos Tutuola.* Finally, in 1967, his most recent novel, *Ajaiyi and His Inherited Poverty,* appeared. A short story, "Ajaiyi and the Witch-Doctor," something of a sketch for the later novel on Ajaiyi, was published in *The Atlantic Monthly* of April, 1959.

Though enlisted as a member of the leading writers' group in Nigeria, the Mbari Club at the University of Ibadan, Tutuola gently evades interviews and avoids, when possible, involvement in the usual activities of the *literati.* Though now one of Africa's most famous authors he has kept the genuine "naiveté" of his first days as a writer. It is said he believes in the tales he writes as a "report" from a truer world than the daily one known to less imaginative men. He lives quietly with his wife and two children.

Both African and Western readers have quickly become aware of the extraordinary powers of imagination this shy and self-effacing author demonstrates in his bizarre and often mythopoeic romances. Western critics and readers in Europe and America have also reacted warmly to the freshness and charm of a "new" English which exploits powers of the language often passed over or forgotten in contemporary usage, and to an attractive simplicity which quickens interest in his tales. For the Western reader, Tutuola's work combines in a fascinating medley: African motifs, names, British or European terms, lists and catalogues, a bookkeeper's obsession with pounds and pence, and rare inventions of beast and monster. The result is a creative mélange which seems half-dream, or surrealist film fantasy. But this mixture, and the "imperfect" English gave severe embarrassment, at least in the early days, to African critics who were shamed by the qualities they felt to be "primitive," "naif," or half-educated in the Western sense.

Characteristic of the early African response to *The Drinkard* and *Bush of Ghosts* was Adeagbo Akinjogbin's letter to the editor of the Nigerian journal *West Africa* (June 5, 1954): "... most Englishmen, as perhaps Frenchmen, are pleased to believe all sorts of fantastic tales about Africa, a continent about which they know they are profoundly ignorant." He went on to write that Tutuola's books catered to such misconceptions and scornful opinions, and,

even worse, that they contain "some of the unbelievable things in our folklores." He finishes by strongly insinuating that Westerners like such novels primarily because they do, in effect, put the African down.

Even stronger is the attack launched by Babasola Johnson in an earlier letter published in *West Africa* (April 10, 1954) which argues that any narrative which employs the traditions of West African story telling, even in good, academic, English, is bad. But, he argues, to find works exploiting, even flaunting, the repetitive, naive, and fabulous characteristics of Yoruba myths and folktales, in early school-leavers' English, is inexcusable. Johnson finishes by virtually charging the culprit with filching his work, from D. O. Fagunwa's story, "Ogbuju Ode."

The irony in all this is that today Africans have come to accept the creativeness of Tutuola's work and are no longer so nervous about his English, while Western critics have tired of the very naif qualities of language and expression once found so entrancing and have dismissed his later work with condescension, allowing only the first novel to stand as a great work of inexplicable quality, but almost as a flash-in-the-pan. *The Times Literary Supplement*, reviewing *Feather Woman of the Jungle*, complained that "it is pointless to look for any exact symbolism" in the "mixture of sophistication, superstition, and primitivism" of the book. Besides, "the early interest in Tutuola was due to a search for novelty," and the work offered raw material to propagandists "for the coloured races, and rooters for the Avant Garde." The importance of this shifting debate, and the gradual reversal of positions on the value of Tutuola's work by African and Western critics and concerned readers, is not merely historical, nor, even critical. The issue is larger, for what is important is the example Tutuola's work can offer other African writers, highly educated or not in Western terms, of employing the English or any other European language, in an organic, truly African way, creating an unembarrassed merger of African and Western modes, forms, concerns, genre, and organizational structures.

Wole Soyinka in his plays, particularly in his *Dance of the Forests* and *The Road*, and Gabriel Okara in the Ijaw-slanted English in his novel, *The Voice*, for instance, seek to exploit the possibilities of English insofar as they can be made to express the African sensibility and inner reality. But they break the English and give it a new swing, a new range of meanings, even a new vocabulary when necessary, to say what the authors must say. The issue Tutuola and other artists are confronting goes beyond language *per se*. Rather, the new writers are dealing with modes of thought, the acceptance of African truths, ranges of belief, and whole strata of traditional ways of seeing and feeling. In the creative work of a handful of contemporary African artists, all of the African and the borrowed European elements are melded in an effort to make this newest literature more than a colonial, and consequently, a short-lived, phenomenon. Rather, they are slowly forging new uses for their borrowed tongues—and new forms for their traditional ones.

Faced with a plethora of languages and dialects, many of which have not yet found print, hampered by small audiences at home, and endangered by cosmopolitanism or the felt need to please an alien, non-African readership, African literature seems to need expression in a European tongue for wide diffusion both at home and abroad. But Tutuola and others are saying that this new literature should be free to work out its own destiny and to re-cut the coat of the European language appropriated, even to un-twist the yarn and fibers and to reweave its stuff into forms and textures natural and fitting to the African experience. In this effort, Tutuola's blend of tradition and personal inventiveness, naiveté and genuine artistic skills, with his courage to use English in his own way, is valuable and instructive.

The Palm-Wine Drinkard appeared in an American edition in 1953 and went through nine printings in the United States by 1970, including a new American paperback issue that year by Greenwood Press. The work has been translated into Czech, Danish, Dutch, Finnish, French, Italian, Magyar, Serbian, and Swedish. The novel opens with the now well-known paragraph:

I was a palm-wine drinkard since I was a boy of ten years of age. I had no other work more that to drink palm-wine in my life. In those days we did not know other money, except COWRIES, so that everything was very cheap, and my father was the richest man in town.

One of the most striking of all of Tutuola's creations is his "very complete gentleman" whom a "lady" followed to her dismay and, as a prisoner of skulls, nearly to her death. But the Drinkard "could not blame the lady" for following this gorgeous apparition,

Because if I were a lady, no doubt I would follow him to wherever he would go, and still as I was a man I would jealous him more than that, because if this gentleman went to the battle field, surely, enemy would not kill him or capture him and if bombers saw him in a town which was to be bombed, they would not throw bombs on his presence, and if they did throw it, the bomb itself would not explode until this gentleman would leave that town, because of his beauty.

The Drinkard, who begins his archetypal journey to the land of the Deads (sic) in search of his tapster who had fallen from a high palm tree while going after the sap which becomes palm-wine, faces many adventures, undergoes many punishments and imprisonments, and finally, returned to his home village, offers abundance to all from his magical egg. As in most tales, however, mankind becomes greedy and the egg is broken by the quarrelsome crowd. Magically transformed into many whips which scourge the mob from the hero's house, the egg, first, great gift, then punishment, returns to its beneficent form once again when quiet is restored but then quickly disappears for good, leaving the ungrateful villagers to face a famine. The story ends with the sacrifice of a slave who is thereby "sent" to Heaven as a messenger asking for rain and forgiveness. A great downpour comes and abundance finally returns with three months of rain.

In the second novel, *My Life in the Bush of Ghosts,* 1954, the hero enters the Bush by dropping down a hole in a large mound, probably a giant termite cone, to undergo extremely bizarre transformations. Though a slave most of the time, the hero has some good luck, is married for four months to a "ghostess," and later has a child by his more permanent wife, the Super Lady, who bears a son, half human, half immortal. (Ghosts in Yoruba tradition are of two sorts; the first are the spirits of the departed as in the West; the second are what might be termed, Ghost-ghosts, true ghosts in and of themselves, beings who inhabit their own realms but who are in constant touch with mankind's world and often operate in it.) After 24 years in the Bush of Ghosts, an amazing Ghostess, equipped with multiple television sets in her finger-tips, gives the hero the chance to return to his own world. Like a risen Lazarus he knows all, and can say in the novel's last words, thinking of his experiences, "This is what hatred did."

The third novel, *Simbi and the Satyr of the Dark Jungle* (1955), concerns the sought after experiences of poverty and suffering of the heroine, who, at book's beginning "was not working at all, except to eat and after that to bathe and then to wear several kinds of the costliest garments." Simbi was, moreover, "a wonderful singer whose beautiful voice could wake deads and she was only the most beautiful girl in the village." After the kidnapping of her friends, Rali and Sala, the heroine decides to repudiate "my mother's wealths. I can no longer bear to remain in the happiness... It was like that Simbi thought within herself, because she had never experienced neither the difficulties of the poverty nor had experienced the difficulties of the punishments since when she was born."

Simbi goes out to find her lost companions and through the usual complicated trials wins her way home again, but only after Rali and Sala have perished in the ordeal of life in the jungle. Simbi's greatest enemy has been the Satyr who is monster and magician, and in what quite possibly is Tutuola's greatest stroke of imagination, the Satyr, knowing Simbi's great love of singing, seeks to imprison her in a vast cage of singing birds. Everywhere she looks she see the feathered bars and is entranced by the song. She is literally swallowed in pure music.

This work shows growing facility in the use of dialogue and the scenes shift more expectedly, but all in all it is considered by many critics a less interesting work than *The Drinkard.*

The Brave African Huntress (1958) offers the spectacle of a feminine super-hunter who is able to liberate her four captured brothers. Much more European influence appears in this work, much of it trivial, with Nordic monsters and beings, elves, genii, goblins, demons, imps, and gnomes, all of whom are specifically named at the novel's opening. The short, enormously broad dwarfs offer a diverting spectacle, however, and there are other typically diverting examples of the author's imagination to carry the reader through.

Feather Woman of the Jungle (1962) is fairly tightly organized for a Tutuola novel, though the tales or chapters are each concerned with the separate journies of the narrator, a newly installed chief. The tales are told on successive moonlit nights during the dry season. Though most of the stories or "entertainments" are related in theme, three seem quite separate, and there is also an introductory chapter which offers the reader information on the Egba Yorubas of the author's home town of Abeokuta which has little to do with the remainder of the book. The theme of the pursuit of wealth, and the narration of all the tales by the chief does offer some unity. Fairly useful transitions between the tales and a certain amount of repetition also help.

The last novel, *Ajaiyi and His Inherited Poverty* (1967) uses the by now familiar device of the quest, as the hero and his faithful younger sister set out to win deliverance from their poverty. The second paragraph of the opening chapter offers this amazing statement:

This story happened about two hundred years ago when I first came to this world
through another father and mother. By that time I was a boy and not a girl, by that time I was the poorest farmer and not as a storyteller, ...

Though the work begins with a harsh picture of rural poverty as the old parents of Ajaiyi and his sister die in their termite-eaten hut, and with a confusing flashback to an ancient time, the book wends its way through many adventures to end on a pious, missionary note. It closes with acts of Christian faith and miracles which result in the building of churches in the towns of the various benefactors of the hero. The people, seeing that good works were being accomplished in these churches, including cures of all sorts, throw off their old idols. Even the Witch Doctor

threw away all his gods and he joined us and it was not long when he became one of the leaders.

Better yet, the people decide to lend money to Ajaiyi so

within a few months I had plenty of money. Out of the money, I paid all of my debts and then I was free from my inherited poverty. . . . but in a clean way.

Thus ends the most recent romance of this son of Christian parents, a man full of Sunday school tracts, biblical stories, shopkeepers' lists of goods, catalogues of machines and parts of machines, the lingo of the capital, the droning wisdom of the village sages, and the scary bed-time tales of the old women around the campfire. All of this, plus Tutuola's own unrivaled imagination, purity, and rambling, intuitive mind, make these books a prized part of the new African expression in English.

Writings: Novels: *The Palm-Wine Drinkard,* London, Faber and Faber, 1952; New York, Grove Press, 1953 (nine printings); Westport, Conn., Greenwood Press, 1970; *My Life in the Bush of Ghosts,* London, Faber and Faber, 1954; New York, Grove Press, 1954, Evergreen edition, 1970; Japanese edition, Tokyo, Shinchosha, 1962; *Simbi and the Satyr of the Dark Jungle,* London, Faber and Faber, 1955; *The Brave African Huntress,* London, Faber and Faber, 1958, New York, Evergreen-Grove Press, 1970; *Feather Woman of the Jungle,* London, Faber and Faber, 1962; *Ajaiyi and His Inherited Poverty,* London, Faber and Faber, 1967.

Plays: *The Palm-Wine Drinkard,* adapted from novel by the author with Professor Collis of the University of Ibadan, 1958; English version produced at University of Ibadan and elsewhere, 1962; produced in Yoruba version by E. Kolawole Ogunmola at University of Ibadan's Travelling Theatre, published Lagos, West African Book Publishers Ltd., 1967, 32 p. illustrated; as opera, in version by Kola Ogunmola, transcribed and translated by R. G. Armstrong, R. L. Owujoola and Val Olayemi, Ibadan, Institute of African Studies, *Occasional Paper, 12,* University of Ibadan, 1968.

Short story: "Ajaiyi and the Witch-Doctor," in *Atlantic Monthly,* April, 1959, improved version in *Black Orpheus,* No. 19, March, 1966, Ibadan, Mbari Press, University of Ibadan.

Biographical/Critical Sources: Amos Tutuola, Harold R. Collins, New York, Twayne Publishers, 1969; *African-English Literature,* Anne Tibble, editor, New York, October House, 1965 and London, Peter Owen, 1965; *Long Drums and Cannons,* Margaret Laurence, editor, London, Macmillan, 1968; "Amos Tutuola and D. O. Fagunwa," *The Journal of Commonwealth Literature,* No. 9, London, July, 1970; E. N. Obiechina, "Transition from oral to literary tradition," in *Présence Africaine.* No. 63, Paris, 3rd trimestre. 1967; O. R. Dathorne, "The Nightmare of the Tribe," in *Introduction to Nigerian Literature,* Bruce King, editor, New York, Africana Corp., 1972; Gerald Moore's *Seven African Writers,* London, Oxford University Press, 1962; Adrian A. Roscoe in *Mother is Gold: A Study in West African Literature.* Cambridge, Cambridge University Press, 1971.

U

UKOLI, Neville Mene
b. 1940, Warri, Nigeria.
Novelist.

After attending local schools, N. M. Ukoli went to Government College, Ughelli, a high school, and graduated with a B.A. in 1965 from the University of Nsukka. While at the university he was the first editor of the school weekly, *The Record.* His training led to a position with the Nigerian Broadcasting Corporation's "Schools' unit," where he had responsibility for the magazine *Notes for teachers.*

Longmans of Nigeria published his children's reader, *The twins of the rain forest* in 1968 from sheets printed and bound in Great Britain. Though written for high school level students, this novelette deals realistically with the bravery of a boy Oshare and his mother Omote when they succeed in saving the lives of twins born to Omote. The father, Okoro, is shocked and at first angered when he hears about the birth, for in many of Nigeria's cultures, twins or triplets were considered monsters who must be left in the forest to die or to be eaten. At the story's end, however, Okoro decides to flee his village with his family and to seek a new home with strangers who will tolerate the healthy twins, and,
of course, the victorious Oshare and his mother.

Writings: Children's Novel: *The Twins of the Rain Forest,* Ibadan, Ikeja, Longmans of Nigeria, 1966.

ULASI, Adaora Lily
b. ca. 1945, Nigeria.
Novelist.

Lily Ulasi published one prose work set in West Africa in 1935, *Many Thing You No Understand,* a novel of 189 pages. The work contrasts the experience of the Old African hand, District Officer Mason, wise in the ways of Africa, and his young Scot assistant, who naively tries to unravel a mysterious event in the district. Though urged to let matters rest, the assistant goes on prying into the affairs of the nearby village until all parties are embarrassed.

Writings: Novel: *Many Thing You No Understand,* London, Michael Joseph 1970.

UMEASIEGBU, Rems Nna
b. October 1, 1943, Amessi, Aguata, Nigeria.
Folklorist.

Rems Umeasiegbu received his education both in Africa and Europe, including a year (1969–70) in Prague. He has published articles on the countries he has visited: the United States, Australia, England, Czechoslavakia, and Poland.

His first book, *The Way We Lived* (1969), attempts to recapture the fast disappearing usages and attitudes of the Ibo people. The work is divided into a section of customs and another on folklore. The latter offers a rich storehouse of information in idiomatic English which recreates old folk stories rather than literally translating them from Ibo. In the first section such matters as "breaking a Kola nut," "circumcision," "divorce," "naming a new-born baby," "teething," "the birth of twins," and "farm-work" are dealt with. In 1970, Heinemann published his *Ibo Legacy*, a more formal study of Ibo customs and traditional stories.

Writings: Stories: *The Way We Live,* London, Heinemann, 1969.

Folktales and Customs: *Ibo Legacy,* London, Heinemann, 1970.

U TAM'SI, Tchicaya Gérard-Félix
(pseudonym of TCHICAYA, Félix)
b. August 25, 1931, M'pili,
Congo (Brazzaville).
Poet.

Tchicaya U Tam'si accompanied his father, a deputy in the French National Assembly for the "Moyen Congo" as the present Congo, Brazzaville was then called, to Paris in 1946. He has remained in Paris and has completed his education there after study at a lycée in Orleans and at the Lycée Janson de Sailly in Paris.

Though preoccupied by African themes and cultural loss, U Tam'si is not in close personal touch with the world of his ancestors. From 1957 to 1960 he adapted over a hundred African folk tales for French radio. He has contributed to various journals including *Vie Africaine* and in 1960 he became editor of *Congo*, a daily journal which comes out in Zaïre. At present he is an official with UNESCO. Though his earlier poetry shows the influence of Aimé Césaire of Martinique, his work is increasingly original, passionate, and avant-garde in its "random" images which, upon scrutiny, relate both to general themes and other images in a coherent manner.

U Tam'si's six volumes are: *Le mauvais sang* (Bad Blood); *Feu de brousse* (Brush Fire); *A triche-coeur* (The Tricky Heart); *Epitomé* (Tunis, SNED-Oswald, 1962); and *Le ventre* (The Belly); his most recent volume is *L'arc musical*. *Epitomé* won the grand Prize for Poetry at the Festival of African Arts, Dakar, 1966, and *Brush Fire*, made available in English by Mbari Press, 1964, in a translation by Sangodare Akanji, has been a rich source of poems for anthologies of African poetry in both French and English. Heinemann has published a volume of his poems, *Selected Poems* with translations by Gerald Moore taken from the last four volumes only.

In 1968, U Tam'si published a collection of stories, *Légendes africaines*, with a preface by Dr. Mercer Cook, which offers selections from fourteen tales from a wide range of authors. The first is a "collection" myth from the Ivory Coast; another is a section of Thomas Mofolo's famous novel *Chaka;* others come from Niane's epic *Sundiata;* a story

collected by the German ethnologist Leo Frobenius; and there is even a selection from the pioneering anthology of Blaise Cendrars published in Paris fifty years ago. U Tam'si provided an introduction to the work, explaining his plan, justifying his selections and giving a brief "introduction" to each of the fourteen legends.

His poetry has been translated into Polish, Czech and Hungarian and *The Atlantic Monthly* published some of his verse recently. He is considered to be, with Senghor, Bernard Dadié, and Birago Diop, one of the major poets from francophone Africa.

A few quotations, even in English, may suggest his talent. This selection is from the Mbari Press translation by S. Akanji of *Brush Fire:*

still he is left with the gentle act of
/laughter
and the giant tree with its living cleft
what was the country where he lived
/like a beast
behind the beasts before behind the
/beasts
his stream was the safest of cups
because it was of living bronze
because it was his living flesh
(from "A Mat to Weave")
and:
the fire the river that's to say
the sea to drink following the sand
the feet the hands
within the heart to love
this river that lives in me repeoples me
only to you I said around the fire
my race
it flows here and there a river
. . .
my race
remembers
the taste of bronze drunk hot.
(from the title poem "Brush Fire")
And from the very lovely "Presence":

451

U Tam'si

treacherous christ
here is my flesh of bronze
and my blood closed
by the numberless I—copper and zinc
by the two stones of my brain
eternal through my slow death
which ends:
perfume of verbena and hind
torments me and I hear voices
born late in the day
day passes zenith
with a learned retinue of crickets
if I indulged myself this were the
                    /moment to take leave
but I still have no task

Tchicaya U Tam'si still awaits a detailed critical study but increasingly he is the subject of scholarly papers and theses. Mercer Cook's impression of him is: "Tchicaya est un Bantou: petit, mais solide, timide et tetu, sauvage dans la brousse de sa moustache, mais tendre; pour tout dire, homme de rêve et de passion." (Tchicaya is a Bantu, small but husky, shy but stubborn, savage in the brush of his moustache, but tender; in short, a man of dreams and passion.) These lines from his poem, "March," in *Brush Fire* might express part of his attitude and value:

child take this hand
I was among those who pounded the
                              /red blood
among the adders

Writings: Poetry: *Le mauvais sang,* Paris, Caractères, 1955; *Feu de brousse. Poèsie visions,* Caractères, 1957; *A triche-couer,* Paris, Hautefeuille, 1958; Honfleur, Pierre-Jean Oswald, 1960; *Epitomé. Les mots de têtes pour le sommaire d'une passion',* Tunis, SNED-Oswald, 1962; Paris, Oswald, 1970; *Le ventre,* Paris, Présence Africaine, 1964; *L'arc musical, précédé de Epitomé,* Paris, Oswald, 1969 and Honfleur.

English translations: of *Feu de brousse* as *Brush Fire,* by Sangodare Akanji, Ibadan, Mbari Press, 1964; *Selected Poems,* translations by Gerald Moore (from last four of U Tam'si's volumes), London, Ibadan, Nairobi, Heinemann, 1970; reissued in one volume: *Le mauvais sang, Feu de brousse,* and *A triche-coeur,* Honfleur, Oswald, 1970; individual poems in many journals and anthologies including *Atlantic Monthly, Poems from Black Africa,* L. Hughes, editor, 1966; *Anthologie négro-africaine,* Verviers, Belgium, 1967; *African Writing Today,* Mphahlele, editor, Harmondsworth, England, Penguin, 1967; *An Anthology of African and Malagasy Poetry in French,* Clive Wake, editor, London, Oxford University Press, 1965; *Black Orpheus* magazine, No. 13, Ibadan; *Transition,* No. 9, Kampala.

Legends: Editor of *Légendes africaines,* Paris, Segher, 1968.

Biographical/Critical Sources: A Reader's Guide to African Literature, Hans Zell and Helene Silver, editors, New York, Africana Publishing Corp., 1971; "Surrealism on the River Congo," *African Literature and the Universities,* Gerald Moore, editor, Ibadan, Ibadan University Press, 1965.

UZODINMA, Edmund Chukuemeka Chieke
b. 1936, Eastern Nigeria.
Novelist, short story writer.

E. C. Uzodinma received his education in Eastern and Northern Nigeria and then attended Ibadan University and the University of London where he received his B.A. He has served as the first principal of Aguata Community Grammar

School and he has also taught at Our Lady's High School in Onitsha, the great market town on the Niger.

work has been recommended for use in Nigerian grammer schools.

His two works of interest are *Brink of Dawn, Stories of Nigeria,* 1966, and the novel, *Our Dead Speak,* 1967, a murder mystery set in Eastern Nigeria, but basically a story of the old Nigeria. The latter

Writings: Stories: *Brink of Dawn. Stories of Nigeria,* Ikeja, Ibadan, Enugu, Longmans of Nigeria, 1966.

Novel: *Our Dead Speak,* London, Longmans, 1967.

V

VALENTE, Malangantana Gowenha
b. June 6, 1936, Magaia (Marracuene),
Mozambique.
Poet, painter.

Basically self-educated, with his father
often away in the mines of South Africa
and his mother mad, Valente struggled
to emerge from the depths of ignorance
and poverty. He attended high school
while working as a servant in the
Lourenco Marques club and began
painting in his few free hours. Discovered by the architect, Amancio Guedes,
who took the young Valente into his
studio group, Valente developed into a
fine decorative artist and a painter of
distinction. His paintings hang in the
Museum of African Art in Salisbury,
Rhodesia, and in private collections.

He has contributed poems to *Black
Orpheus* magazine in Ibadan; other verse
is to be found in *Poems from Black Africa*.
He also appears in *New Sum of Poetry
from the Negro World* and Moore and
Beier's *Modern Poetry from Africa*. His subtly worked poems proclaim the life-
giving power of the artist as a source
of intellectual inspiration and woman,
of physical. *Black Orpheus* magazine has
also reproduced some of his paintings.

His autobiography remains unpublished.

Accused of being a member of the outlawed political group, FRELIMO, he was
arrested by the Portuguese authorities
in December, 1964, but was released in
March, 1966.

Writings: Poetry: in *Black Orpheus*
magazine, *Poems from Black Africa*, L.
Hughes, editor, Bloomington, Indiana
University Press, 1966; *New Sum of Poetry
from the Negro World*, Paris, Présence
Africaine, Vol 57, 1966; *Modern Poetry
from Africa*, revised edition, London,
Penguin, 1963, 1966, 1968; *Présence
Africaine*, Paris, 1966.

Autobiography: in manuscript.

**VASA, Olauday Gustavus
the African,** or EQUIANO, Olauda(h)
b. 1745 or 1746, Essaka, in the
Benin area, present Nigeria;
d. ca. 1802.
Autobiographer, merchant.

Carried off by slavers in his eleventh year
and sold to the captain of a slaving vessel,
Vassa was transported to America and
put in bondage in Virginia. Freed by a

generous master, he entered marine service, finally making his way to England where he settled down as a ship's chandler, general merchant, and militant worker in the cause of abolition of the slave trade. In 1790 he presented a petition to the British Parliament to abolish slavery. He married an Englishwoman and had children. After a busy life he died in England about his 56th year.

His autobiographical work is *The Interesting Narrative of the Life of Olaudah Equiano, or Gustavus Vassa, the African, Written by Himself*. This work, published in 1789, is one of the first literary efforts by an African to deal with the inhumanity of slavery and to recount his own experiences. Vassa traveled widely in his early career as a seaman, became a highly articulate and sophisticated spokesman for his people and was well regarded in his own time. The London firm of Dawsons issued a reprint of Vassa's original, two volume edition, in its Colonial History Series in 1969, under the title *The Life of Olauda Equiano: Or, Gustavus Vassa, the African*. Heinemann in London, in 1967, issued a paperback edition of an abbreviated edition as did Praeger in the United States in 1966. There were also early editions in Gottingen, Germany, 1792, Rotterdam, 1790; and in Stockholm, a recent edition, 1964.

Writings: Autobiography: *The Interesting Narrative of the Life of Olaudah Equiano, or Gustavus Vassa, the African, Written by Himself*, London, printed for and sold by the author, 1789; 2 volumes; enlarged 3rd edition, 1790, enlarged Dublin edition, 1791; 5th edition, 1792; there were further early British editions in 1793, 1794, 1809, 1813, 1814, 1815, 1819, 1829. Reprint of original 1789 edition was *The Life of Olaudah Equiano: Or, Gus-*

tavus Vassa, The African, London, Dawsons, 1969; abbreviated editions, modernized spellings, etc., London, Heineman, 1967; New York, Praeger, 1967. The first American edition of the London work was: New York, W. Durrell, 1791. The second American printing was Boston, J. Knapp, 1837, in one volume.

Biographical/Critical Sources: Robert W. July, *The Origins of Modern African Thought*, London, Faber and Faber, 1968; Ulli Beier, ed., *Introduction to African Literature*, Evanston, Illinois, Northwestern University Press, 1967; O. R. Dathorne, "African Writers of the Eighteenth Century," in *Black Orpheus* magazine, No. 18 (October 1965).

VAUGHAN, J. Koyinda
b. 1927, Lagos, Nigeria.
Journalist, film critic, lawyer.

Koyinda Vaughan studied locally and prepared for legal work which he pursued along with free lance writing. He is particularly known for his articles on films, and is represented with "Africa and the Cinema" in Langston Hughes' *An African Treasury*.

VERA, Cruz (see BARBOSA, Jorge)

VIANA de ALMEIDA (see de ALMEIDA, José Maria)

VIDEROT, "Mensah," Toussaint (see MENSAH, Toussaint Viderot)

VIEIRA, Luandino (pseudonym for da GRACA, José Vieira Mateus)
b. 1935, Braga, Angola.
Poet, story writer, journalist
(sometimes writes in Kimbundu).

A leading Angolan writer, Luandino Vieira had a Portuguese father and African mother and he grew up in a *musseque,* or Angolan-African market quarter of the city of Braga. His fiction employs the rich Creole mixture of Portuguese and the local Kimbundu. For a period he was employed in various offices and worked and studied to be a painter. Vieira worked on the Angolan review *Imbondeiro* and on the short-lived but courageous journal of Luanda, *Cultura,* which sought in 1957 to establish a voice for the new African writers. He has also published in various other Portuguese-language journals. His poetry is often written in the proletariat patois or pequeno-português, spoken by illiterate Africans and his scenes are often drawn from the life of the *musseques.*

His volumes of stories are *A cidade e a infância; contos* (The City and Childhood; Stories), published in 1960; *Duas histórias de pequenos burgueses* (Two Stories of the Petty Bourgeoisie); and *Luuanda* (sic) which was issued in 1963 in Angola. *Luuanda* won the "Grande Premio da Novela" for 1965 which raised a tempest of protest in Portuguese governmental circles. Many members of the jury awarding the prize were subsequently arrested by the Portuguese authorities and the awarding group, the Portuguese Society of Writers in Lisbon, was dissolved. Vieira, subsequently arrested for Angolan independence sentiments, was sent to prison on Santiago Island in the Cape Verde Islands in 1961 along with the young poets António Jacinto, Viriato da Cruz and António Cardoso.

He was then sentenced to 14 years in the prison at Tarrafal, Cape Verde Islands.

Writings: Stories: *A cicade e a infância; contos,* Lisbon, Edição da Casa dos Estudantes do Império, 1960; *Duas histórias de pequenos burgueses,* Sá da Bandeira, Publicações Imbondeiro, 1961; *Luuanda,* Luanda, Edição ABC, 1963; Belo Horizonte, Brazil, Editôra e Distribuidora "Eros," Ltda., 1965; *Vidas Novas,* Portugal, Editions Anti-Colonial, reprinted in France, dates of both editions unknown, but probably early 1960's, for one long story, translated as "Le complet de Mateus" (The Business Suit of Mateus), appeared in the Algerian review, *Novembre,* No. 4, 1965, and again in the Paris bi-weekly, *France Nouvelles,* date unknown. That story, originally entitled "O Fato completo de Lucas Matesso," and the story *A Vida Verdadeira de Domingos Xavier,* not published in Portuguese, appeared together in French translation in the volume, *La vraie vie de Domingos Xavier* with *Le complet de Mateus,* preface by Mário de Andrade, translation into French by Andrade and Chantal Tiberghien, Paris, Présence Africaine, 1971. These two stories in Portuguese manuscript received the João Dias Prize of the Casa dos Estudantes do Ultramar, Lisbon, November, 1962 according to Gerald M. Moser in *A Tentative Portuguese-African Bibliography,* Bibliographical Series, No. 3. The Pennsylvania State University Libraries, University Park, Pa., 1970; "Os miúdos do Capitão Bento Albano," in *Novos contos d'Africa,* 1962; "Primeira canção do mar," in *Colecção Imbondeiro,* 14, Sá da Bandeira, Imbondeiro, 1961.

Poetry: in various journals including *New Sum of Poetry from the Negro World,* Paris, Présence Africaine, Vol. 57, 1966.

Film Essay: "Africa and the Cinema," in *An African Treasury*, L. Hughes, editor, New York, Pyramid, 1961.

VILAKAZI, Benedict Wallet Bambatha
b. January 6, 1906, Groutville
Mission Station, Groutville, Natal
Province, South Africa; d. Ocotber 26, 1947.
Zulu poet, novelist, scholar, teacher.

The fifth child of six born to Mshini kaMakhwatha and Leah Hlengwane kaMnyazi, both Christian converts, Benedict Vilakasi grew up near Stanger, the place where the great Zulu king, Chaka, had his homestead or kraal. Called Bambatha kaMshini as a child, the young Benedict herded cattle, and attended school sporadically. His parents did make efforts to get him in Groutville school as early as age six and, despite enforced absences, he finished Standard IV. He then studied at St. Francis College, Mariannhill, the Roman Catholic monastery just outside Durban, and, in 1917, came under the special tutelage of Father Bernard Huss. At his mother's insistence he took on the family name of Vilakazi at the time he was baptized with the names Benedict Wallet.

Achieving the Teacher's Certificate in 1923, Vilakazi taught first at Mariannhill College and then at the Catholic Seminary at Ixopo from 1924 to 1930. For a period he was at St. Francis College again but finding he did not have the vocation for the Catholic priesthood, he left, moving in 1933 to the Ohlange Institute where he worked with the founder, John L. Dube. Studying on his own, he passed various lower certificate

examinations, and finally earned the B.A. with distinction from the University of South Africa in 1934 with special work on the Zulu language.

In the early 1930's, Vilikazi began to publish his poetry in various journals, including *Ilanga lase Natal* (The Natal Sun), *UmAfrika* (The African), *The Bantu World*, and *The Star;* and scholarly articles in Zulu and English in such reviews as *African Studies, Bantu Studies, The Native Teachers' Journal* and *the Forum.*

Published as Volume I of the Bantu Treasure series was his collection of early poetry *Inkondlo kaZulu* (Zulu Songs), 1935, the first collection of western influenced poetry in Zulu to be published. Vilakazi's next collection of verse, published as *Amal' eZulu* (Zulu Horizons), later appeared as Vol. VIII of the Bantu Treasury series.

Three novels of his appeared in the 1930's: *Nje nempela* (Really and Truly), 1933, and *Noma nini* (Forever and Ever), 1935, and *U-Dingiswayo ka Jobe* (Dingiswayo, Son of Jobe), issued in 1939. *Noma nini,* written in 1932 or earlier, won a prize in 1933 in the third competition of the International African Institute. It is considered the first work of fiction written in Zulu to handle modern subject matter, if Herbert I. E. Dhlomo's morality story, *An African Tragedy* (1928), is excepted. With Professor Doke, his mentor, as senior scholar, he helped in the compilation of the *Zulu-English Dictionary.*

Vilakazi became as assistant to Professor Doke in 1935 in the Bantu Studies Department as a teacher of Zulu. At Witwatersrand he earned a second B.A. (Honors) in 1936 with special work in Bantu languages. Two years later he won the M.A. with a thesis "The conception and development of poetry in Zulu." The D. Litt, the first doctorate won by an African, was awarded to him on March 16, 1946. His dissertation was "The Oral and Written Literature in Nguni." He became a Senior Lecturer in the Department of Bantu Studies, farmed, and at the time of his death, was a member of the Pius XII University College at Roma, Lesotho, where he served as president of the Catholic African Teachers' Federation and editor of the *Catholic African Teachers' Review.*

He lectured to African troops during the Second World War, and, though he avoided politics, began in early 1947 to rally support for an African Authors Conference in Bloemfontein, scheduled for December. Invited were Herbert I. E.

Dhlomo, Jordan Khush Ngubane (1917–), Davidson Don Tengo Jabavu, Richard Victor Selope Thema (1886–1955), Jacob Mfaniselwa Mhlapho (1940–1957), and Jacob Robert Malie (1912–1960). Struck down by meningitis, Vilakazi died on the afternoon of October 26, 1947, at the Coronation Hospital, Johannesburg. He left his second wife, Emily Nomsa Phoofolo Vilakazi (his first died in 1942), and five children by his two marriages.

Writings: Poetry: in *Llanga lase Natal, Umafrika, The Bantu World, The Star;* Volumes: *Inkondlo kaZulu,* Vol. 1 of Bantu Treasury Series, Johannesburg, Witwatersrand University Press, 1935; in new orthography, 1965; *Amal' eZulu,* Vol. VIII of Bantu Treasury Series, 1945, in new orthography, 1962; English translation of *Amal' eZulu* as *Zulu Horizons. The Vilakazi Poems Rendered into English,* by D. Mck Malcolm and Florence Louie Friedman, Cape Town, H. Timmins, 1962, 190 pages, illustrated.

Novels: *Nje nempela,* Mariannhill, Mariannhill Mission Press, 1933, 1955, 1963; *Noma nini,* Mariannhill, 1935, 4th printing, 1962; *U-Dingiswayo ka Jobe,* London, Sheldon Press, 1939.

Journalism: articles in *African Studies, Bantu Studies, The Native Teachers' Journal, The Forum.*

Critical/Scholarly Articles and Others: "The Conception and Development of Poetry in Zulu," *Bantu Studies,* XII, No. 2, Johannesburg; "African Drama and Poetry," *South African Outlook,* LXXIX, 1939; "Some Aspects of Zulu Literature," *African Studies,* I, Johannesburg; 1942; "The Oral and Written Literature in Nguni," unpublished doctoral dissertation, The University of Witwatersrand, Johannesburg, 1945.

Language study: *Zulu-English Dictionary,* Johannesburg, Witwatersrand University Press, 1953.

Biographical/Critical Sources: Raymond Kunene, "An Analytical Survey of Zulu Poetry Both Traditional and Modern," Kunene's unpublished doctoral dissertation for Durban University, 1961; Albert S. Gérard, *Four African Literatures,* Berkeley, University of California Press, 1971.

VIMBE, John Muir
b. 1811, South Africa;
d. October 17, 1898, near Kokstad, South Africa.
Xhosa collector of folktales, journalist, preacher.

One of the first four Africans who were pupils at the Lovedale Institution in 1849, Vimbe was an evangelist trained by the Rev. John Brownlee and sent to assist the Rev. William Shaw in the Transkii. He later preached in all of the Wesleyan Mission Stations throughout Natal and the Eastern Cape Provinces. In 1878, he and his wife settled in Griqualand East, where he died. He was a frequent contributor from 1871 on to *Isigidimi sama Xhose,* a leading journal, and wrote several reminiscences of Ntsikana, a religious leader of the Zulus, which later appeared in John Knox Bokwe's *Ibali lika Ntsikana* (The Story of Ntsikana). His work also appeared in Walter Benson Rubusana's *Zemk' inkomo magwala ndini* (Away Go the Cattle, You Cowards), a collection of Xhosa folklore, and in W. G. Bennie's collection *Imibengo* (Titbits).

Writings: Folktales: in *Isigidimi sama*
Xhose; in *Demk' inkomo magwale, ndini,* W. B. Rubusana, editor, London, Butler and Tanner, 1906; and in *Imibengo,* W. G. Bennie, editor, Lovedale, Lovedale Press, 1935.
Historical Sketch: in *Ibali lika Ntsikana,* J. K. Bokwe, editor, Lovedale, Lovedale Press, 1914.

VINGADIO, Timotéo
b. ca. 1890, near Banza (Mbanza) Manteke, Congo (modern Zaïre).
Kikongo story writer, poet, translator.

One of the first Bakongo pupils at the newly established American Protestant mission school at Mbanza Manteke in 1899, some 50 miles inland from Matadi, Vingadio published, with the aid of the American missionary, Catherine L. Mabie, the first book of stories and poems in Kikongo, *Nsweswe Ansusu Ampembe ye ngana zankaka* (Nsweswe Ansusu Ampembe and other stories), Kimpese, 1928. The title story of the collection was "Nsweswe Ansusu Ampembe," literally, "The White Pullet," but here the name of the hero. The most popular of the stories in the collection was "Ndwalu Ntumani," the name of the hero who is entrusted with important tasks but always makes a fool of himself and fails in trying to accomplish them. The poems, in several genre, which appear in the collection, were closely based on folk traditions, including the "malenge" form which employed the question and answer technique (the *kinkonzi,* the craft of making an intelligent conversation).

Vingadio and Mabie also had published in 1928 their adaptation and translation of *Robinson Crusoe, Nsamu wa Nsau Kuluso.*

Writings: Stories: *Nsweswe Ansusu Ampembe ye ngana zankaka,* Kimpese, Kimpese Mission Station, 1928, second edition, Bolenge, 1932, third edition, Léopoldville, Ed. LECO, 1950. (This work also contains many poems.)

Translation: *Nsamu wa Nsau Kuluso* (Kikongo adaptation of *Robinson Crusoe*), Matadi, Imprimerie de S.M.F., 1928.

Biographical/Critical Source: Mbololo ya Mpiku, "Introduction à la littérature kikongo," *Research in African Literatures,* African and Afro-American Research Institute, The University of Texas, III, 2 (Fall 1972), 42 pages, with many extracts of poetry in Kikongo and accompanying French translations.

VITOR, Geraldo Bessa (see BESSA-VICTOR)

W

WACHIRA, Godwin
b. ca. 1938, Kikuyu-land,
Kenya.
Novelist, trade unionist, journalist.

Wachira was active in Kenyan Trade
Union activities, engaged in politics, and
was a professional journalist, working
for a leading Nairobi weekly journal.
More recently, he has joined the local
staff of the *Nation* group of newspapers.

His first novel, *Ordeal in the Forest*
(1968), concerns the bitter experiences
of five African youths, Kato, Choti,
Mefru, Nundu and Iru, during the Mau-
mau rebellion against British colonial
rule. Other youths join in the action of
the story which ends in the sleepy
monologue of *Mefru*, "Yes, how confused [we] are.... a generation ... of
confusion..."

Writings: Novel: *Ordeal in the Forest,*
Nairobi, East African Publishing House,
1968.

WADE, Amadou Mustapha
b. ca. 1940, Senegal.
Poet.

This young poet's one collection to date
is *Présence. Poèmes* (Present: Poems),
1966. His patriotic poems celebrating
independence for Senegal and Guinea

are collected in *New Sum of Poetry from the Negro World.*

Writings: Poetry: *Présence. Poèmes,* Paris, Présence Africaine, 1966; poems in *New Sum of Poetry from the Negro World,* Paris, Présence Africaine, Vol. 57, 1966.

WALDA, Giyorgis Walda Yohannes
b. 1896–97, Bulga, Waged District of Shoa, Ethiopia.
Amharic poet, novelist, journalist, statesman.

Born into the working class, son of a saddle-maker and leather-tanner, Walda attended various schools in Gojam, Wadela, and Gondar provinces from 1907 to 1921, became a scholar of Ge'ez and Amharic, and developed a special interest in the old philosophical poetic exercises, the *Qené.* With some training also in French and English he began work as an interpreter in the Menelik II hospital in Addis Ababa, then became assistant editor of the journal, *Berhanenna Sälam* (Light and Peace), established in 1924. He remained in that post until 1935–36 when he became a confident of Emperor Haile Selassie and followed him into exile. Returning with Haile Selassie in 1941 he was named editor of the new daily paper, *Addis Zä-män* (New Times), and the weekly journal appearing in English and Amharic, *Sändäg Alamacin* (Our Flag).

He then became Minister of the Pen, a post equivalent to the head of the Emperor's personal correspondence, but his work of modernization stirred up anger and resentment and he was overthrown in 1955. Semi-exiled as Governor of Arusi, he bided his time and returned in 1961–62 as head of the government press with the rank of vice minister.

His major creative works are five volumes of poetry: *The Glory of Kings* (1939–40 and 1946–47); *Gift of Love and Peace* (1939–40, 1946–47); *Gift to Celebrate H. M. Emperor Haile Selassie's 58th Birthday* (1942–43, 1949–50); *The Gift of Kingship* (1948–49, 1955–56); all celebrating the Emperor and his leadership, and *Dialogue of Husband and Wife* (1945–46, 1952–53), poems on love and family life. All went into print in Addis Ababa.

Walda's one novel is *Ag'azi* (I Went Abroad), issued in 1955, a historical and psychological study of a young man who must brave the conservative influence of his family to obtain a foreign education.

He also published in the creative period from 1946 to 1953 five works in the fields of history, moral theology, and agriculture.

Writings: Poetry: *The Glory of Kings,* 1939–40; *Gift of Love and Peace,* 1939–40; *Gift to Celebrate H. M. Emperor Haile Sellassie's 58th Birthday,* 1942–43, 1949–50; *The Gift of Kingship,* 1948–49, 1955–56; *Dialogue of Husband and Wife,* 1945–46; 1952–53; all in Addis Ababa by the Government Information Service. There is also some poetry in his volume *Through Agriculture,* Addis Ababa, 1948–49.

Novel: *Ag'azi,* Addis Ababa, 1955–56.
History: *He Who Made History Does Not Lie,* 1946–47.
Moral Fables: *The Way of the World,* 1947–48.
Religious Tract: *Proper Conduct,* 1950–51.
Riddles: *After Work,* 1950–51.
Essay: *The New Ethiopia,* 1952–53.
   Agriculture: *Through Agriculture,* 1948–49.

Biographical/Critical Source: Albert S. Gérard, *Four African Literatures,* Berkeley, University of California Press, 1971.

WEAKLY, John Marangwanda
(also MARANGWANDA, John
Weakly)
b. 1923, in the Reserve of Chiweshe,
District of Inimazoi, Rhodesa.
Shona novelist, teacher.

John Marangwanda Weakly first began
school at Howard Mission in the District
of Mazoi in 1947 when he was 24 years
old. In 1950, he had reached high school
in Goromonzi, but the following year he
left to serve as a teacher at Howard Mission, remaining there for three years.
In 1954 he took a position in private
industry in Queque.

His only novel, one of the earliest by
a Rhodesian, is *Kumazivandadzoka,* (The
School of Experience). Saraoga, the protagonist, wanders away from his village
and comes to live a criminal, meaningless
life. Though partly reformed at novel's
end, he repudiates his mother—and his
own people—to live a frustrated life with
no personal or national identity. An
extract of the work, called "Saraoga
vient a la ville" (Saraoga Comes to
Town), is given in Léonard Sainville's
Romanciers et conteurs négro-africains,
Volume II.

Writings: Novel: *Kumazivandadzoka,* London, Longmans, 1959, 1965; extract
entitled "Saraoga vient a la ville," in
Romanciers et conteurs négro-africains, Vol.
II, Présence africaine, 1968.

*Biographical/Critical Source: African Litera-
ture in Rhodesia,* E. W. Krog, editor,
Gwelo, Rhodesia, Mambo Press, 1966.

WHEATLEY, Phillis (Mrs. Phillis
Peters)
b. ca. 1753, Senegal;
d. United States, 1784.
Poet.

Captured as a child on the banks of the
Senegal River, Phillis Wheatley whose
African name has been lost, was trans-
ported to the slave markets of the United
States. At the age of seven she fell into
the kindly hands of John Wheatley, a
Boston tailor who helped her obtain
schooling. She learned English in sixteen
months and quickly began to read the
Bible.

Her first poem was published in 1770,
an elegy on the famous preacher George
Whitefield. She accompanied John
Wheatley's son on a trip to England
where plans to present her at the court
of King George III were thwarted by
an illness which forced her return to
America. It was during her stay in London in 1773, however, that her slim volume of verse was published, *Poems on
Various Subjects,* believed until recently
by scholars to have been the earliest creative work to be published by an African
in America. Other miscellaneous poems
were published during her last years and
posthumously.

Other Africans who wrote in the 18th
century in North America were Briton
Hammon (ca. 1725–?), John Marrant
(1755–?), Prince Hall (1748–1807), Jupi-
ter Hammon (ca. 1725–?), and Lucy
Terry who wrote, as far as is known, at
least one poem about 1745. Two early
African poets, much more favored by
fortune, were the Afro-Brazilians,
Manoel Ignacio da Silva Alvarenga
(1749–?) and Domingos Caldas Barbosa
(ca. 1739–1800).

Wheatley's fortunes changed at the
death of her benefactor. Though she was
given her freedom, she received little
further help from Wheatley's family and
she married, apparently hoping to find
a modicum of security, but was disappointed. She had three children, labored
hard as a maid of all work in a country
inn, and died at the age of 31.

Her style was, as might be imagined, reflective of the classical English works popular at the time, particularly those of Alexander Pope. Though her work is extremely important historically, it seldom demonstrates any African tones or memories though, in a few cases, it speaks out for understanding for black Africans. Jefferson vouched for the authenticity of her work when it was challenged in England, but he stated rather bluntly that it was beneath the dignity of criticism.

Writings: Poetry: *An Elegiac poem, . . . on) George Whitefield . . .* , Boston, Ezekial Russell and John Boyles, 1770; *Poems on Various Subjects, Religious and Moral,* printed for A. Bell in London, for sale in Boston, 1773; other editions in 1786, 1789, 1793, 1802, 1813, 1814, 1819, 1887; reprint of original 1773 edition by Kraus, Nendeln, Liechtenstein, 1970, 124 pages; *An Elegy* (for) *Dr. Samuel Cooper . . .* , Boston, E. Russell, 1784; *Liberty and Peace, a poem,* Boston, Warden and Russell, 1784; *Poems on Comic, Serious, and Moral Subjects,* second edition, London, 1787; *A Beautiful Poem on Providence,* Halifax, E. Gay, 1805; *Memoir and Poems of Phillis Wheatley, a Native African and a Slave. Dedicated to the Friends of the Africans,* Boston, George Light, 1834, 1835, 1838, 1969 (the last by Mnemosyne Publishing Co., Miami, Florida); *The Poems of Phillis Wheatley,* Julian D. Mason, Jr., editor, Chapel Hill, N. C., The University of North Carolina Press, 1966.
Letters: *Letters of Phillis Wheatley, the Negro Slave Poet of Boston,* Boston, 1864, 19 pages.

Biographical/Critical Sources: Jahnheinz Jahn, *Neo-African Literature,* New York, Grove Press, 1969, London, Faber and Faber, 1968; Jahn and Dressler, *Bibliography of Creative African Writing,* Nendeln, Liechtenstein, Kraus-Thomson, 1971; on early Afro-American writers: Jahnheinz Jahn, *Neo-African Literature,* New York, Grove Press, 1969; William H. Robinson, Jr., *Early Black American Poets: Selections with Biographical and Critical Introductions,* Dubuque, Iowa, W. C. Brown Co., 1969.

WILLIS, Jackson Anyigwile Musokwa (also MUSOKWA, Jackson Willis Anyigwile)
b. February 16, 1939, near Mbeya, Tanzania.
Story writer, forester.

Able to attend school for only a few years, Jackson Willis struggled to teach himself the rudiments of story writing while he studied by correspondence courses for his high school diploma. His long story, translated as "Les Rivaux" (The Rivals), appears in its French translation in Sainville's *Romanciers et conteurs négro-africains* in an extract entitled "Je ne suis pas un homme libre" (I Am Not a Free Man).

Writings: Novelette: *Les Rivaux,* extract in *Romanciers et conteurs négro-africains,* Léonard Sainville, Vol. II, Paris, Présence Africaine, 1968.

Biographical/Critical Source: Sainville, *op. cit.*

WINFUL, E. A.
b. ca. 1920, Ghana.
Poet, civil servant.

Winful is presently principal secretary of the Ghanaian Civil Service. He has published in various journals, including *Okyeame,* Ghana's literary review, and is represented by five poems, "Increase and Multiply," "A Civil Servant's Dirge," "At the Night Club," "Voices or Aphraisa," and "The Toy" in *Messages: Poems from Ghana.*

Writings: Poetry: in *Messages: Poems from Ghana,* Kofi Awoonor and G. Adali-Mortty, editors, London, Heinemann, 1971.

WONODI, Okogbule (also known as NWANODI, Glory Okugbule) b. 1936, Diobu, Ibo-land, near Port Harcourt, eastern Nigeria. Poet, teacher.

Wonodi is partly self-educated, for on the death of his father he left school to work as a day laborer. With great perseverance he trained as a teacher and finally was admitted to Nsukka University, graduating in June, 1965 with honors in English. Later, he went to the United States where he took an M.A. at the University of Iowa and worked as resident poet in Paul Engle's Writers' Workshop.

He published his first volume of poetry, *Icheke and other poems,* with Mbari Press in 1964 under the name of Glory Okugbule Nwanodi, a pseudonym he has since abandoned. He is represented in Moore and Beier's *Modern African Poets* and Donatus Ibe Nwoga's *West African Verse.*

His poem, "Icheke: IV," from the volume *Icheke,* opens with the imagistic lines:

We fell into the river,
splashing the water
on the riverweeds;
we heard the rushing of water,
smelt the offshore farmtime songs.
We moved with the currents
showing Kola-free teeth.

Writings: Poetry: *Icheke and other poems,* Ibadan, Mbari Press, 1964 (published under name of Glory Okugbule Nwanodi); poems in *Modern Poetry from Africa,* revised edition, Moore and Beier, editors, London and Baltimore, Penguin, 1968; *West African Verse,* Donatus Ibe Nwoga, editor, London, Longmans, 1967.

Y

YAMBO, Ouloguem
(see OUOLOGUEM, Yambo)

YILMA, Darasa
b. 1907, Galla-country, Ethiopia.
Amharic anthologist, critic, government official.

Born into the royal Galla house of Wallega, Yilma Darasa had his early education in Addis Ababa, attended Victoria College in Alexandria, Egypt, and studied at the London School of Economics where he took the B.A. in 1933, and completed his European training by studying international law at Geneva. He joined a resistance movement to the Italians in the mid and late 1930's, was captured and narrowly missed execution in the massacre of young intellectuals ordered by the Italian Marshal Graziani. He eventually escaped to the British-held Sudan in early 1941 and returned with Emperor Haile Selassie and the victorious British army in May, 1941. He served subsequently in high-level finance posts, becoming Finance Minister in 1961, and, in partial political decline, was moved to the Ministry of Commerce, Industry, and Tourism in February, 1969.

Yilma's importance in Amharic literature comes from his having edited and provided a preface to the pioneering anthology of poetry, *In Praise of Independence: Hymns of the New Era by Young Ethiopian Writers* (1941–42). Though in the traditional form of praise-poems, the new work was a sign of Haile Sellasie's hopes for revivifying the contemporary Amharic literature after the years of efforts by the Italians to destroy it. Yilma in the preface also urged young writers to employ the novel and short story as modes of expression and particularly praised the drama as a popular vehicle for new ideas and education.

Writings: Anthology: Editor of *In Praise of Independence: Hymns of the New Era by Young Ethiopian Writers,* Addis Ababa, Marha Tebab Press, 1941–42.

YOFTAHE, Neguse
b. ca. 1900, Gojam, Ethiopia;
d. 1948 or 1949.
Amharic playwright, poet, teacher.

Yoftahe received all of his education from an Ethiopian church school, served as headmaster at St. George's School, and was a fine public speaker. His

469

allegorical play, *Vain Entertainment,* (1923), dramatizes the marriage of Faith and Fortune commanded by King Solomon. This, his first play, was published, but two subsequent dramatic works were not though they saw performance in the Imperial Palace in 1931–32. The drama, *The Punishment of Belly-Worshipper,* captures in transparent fashion the events surrounding the revolt of Ras (Prince) Haylu of Gojam in 1932 and his defeat and trial. It was popular when performed at the royal court.

During the brief war against Italy, Yoftahe published a thin volume of nationalistic poetry, believed to be one of the last published by Goha Sebah, the national press. Two of his moralistic works were published: *We Saw a Brave Man,* and *You Destroyed Me.*

Writings: Plays: *Vain Entertainment,* Addis Ababa, 1923; unpublished: *The Punishment of Belly-Worshipper,* performed at the Imperial Palace, 1931–32.

Moral Essays: *We Saw a Brave Man,* Addis Ababa, 1928; *You Destroyed Me,* Addis Ababa, 1958.

Poetry: one volume of nationalistic verse, title unknown. Addis Ababa, Goha Sehah Press, ca. 1935.

Biographical/Critical Source: Albert S. Gérard, *Four African Literatures,* Berkeley, University of California Press, 1971.

Z

ZIRYAB (or ABU 'L-HASAN
Ibn 'Ali Ibn Nafi)
b. ca. 785, possibly in or near Baghdad;
d. 852, Spain.
Arabic-language poet, musician.

Ziryab was called the "Black Night-
ingale" for his African origin and his
remarkable poetry and skill in singing.
Son of an African slave-woman, he
learned music surreptitiously from
Ishak al-Mawsili, his master, and
became so famous that he was called to
the court of the famous Harun al
Raschid to perform. He did so well that
Ishak began a persecution that forced
the young singer to flee Baghdad. After
many misadventures he arrived in
Kairawan, Morocco, to sing and write
at the court of Ziyadat Allah I (816–837)
in the year 821, but again incurred
jealousy and had to flee once more, this
time to the court of Caliph 'Abd ar (or
al) Rahman II at Córdoba where he
found a home for the rest of his life.
His arrival in 822 touched off the
popularity of the Eastern poetry and
musical modes he was a master of, and
gave a stamp to Andalusian music it still
carries a thousand years later. Ziryab is
even given credit for introducing the eating of asparagus to Spain and thence
to Christian Europe, of fringed hair for

men, and the use of cut-glass tableware.
More important, he is credited with the
addition of a fifth string to the lute and
the use of a wood plectrum which
replaced a hawk's talon.

The poet's poems were brief and witty,
and says A. R. Nykl, "It would require
a whole volume to describe Ziryab's
enormous contribution to the evolution
of Andalusian music and the art of singing."

All of Ziryab's ten children became
fine musicians and several of them continued their father's famous singing
school in Córdoba. Carried across the
Pyrennees during the Islamic invasion
of France, his music and the spirit and
genius of Arabic poetry, most notably
that of Antar, provided much of the
stimulus for the development of the
Provençal literature and the courtly
tradition in Western Europe.

Biographical/Critical Works: A. R. Nykl,
*Hispano-Arabic Poetry and Its Relations with
the Old Provencal Troubadours,* Baltimore,
1946; *Encyclopaedia of Islam,* London,
1934, the Supplement, pp. 266– 267 contains an extensive bibliography; H.
Morland, *Arabic-Andalusian Casidas,* London, 1949; J. Jahn, *Neo-African Literature: A History of Black Writing,* New York,
Grove Press, 1968.

APPENDICES

Contents of Appendices

PART II
Authors By Category
509

APPENDIX E
Authors, by Chronological Period
511

APPENDIX F
Authors, by Genre
531

APPENDIX G
Authors, by Country of Origin
551

APPENDIX H
Authors, by African Languages
557

APPENDIX I
Authors, by European Languages
561

APPENDIX J
Authors, Female
595

PART III
Publishers, Journals, Bookshops
567

APPENDIX K
Major Publishers of African Literature
569

PART I
CRITICAL ESSAYS

Appendix A

The Development of Contemporary African Literature

Abiola Irele
University of Ibadan, Nigeria

Although the current interest in African literature is a recent development, writing by Africans in the European languages dates back to the very beginning of active contact between Africans and Europeans. From this contact, as it has progressed and increased over the centuries, the European languages and the civilisation which lay behind them have come to assume such a significance on this continent as to have created a new literary culture, alongside the oral tradition within which literary expression had been largely confined in Africa from time immemorial.

The fact that this contact between Europeans and Africans has also taken place within a specific historical and sociological context has determined to a considerable extent the very orientation of modern African literature and the themes and preoccupations of the African writer. Through most of its development, African literature has reflected the conditions which have shaped Africa's historical relationship with the European world. Repercussions from the colonial period still influence our present existence as a people.

Most of the earliest examples of African writing in the European languages were inspired by the reaction to slavery. Those Africans who, by the 17th and 18th centuries, had acquired the use of the European tongues to a significant level contributed to the propaganda writing of the abolitionist movement which began in France and in Britain. But in such eighteenth century works as Equiano's *Travels,* they also went beyond the straightforward discussion of the moral problem posed by slavery and expressed in imaginative terms their responses to the peculiar pressures of European civilisation and the special sentiment for Africa as the image of their fundamental identity. In so doing, they had begun to establish the dominant psychological and moral background of African expression in modern times.

The nature and implications of the African encounter with Europe assumed a new significance with the active penetration, from the middle years of the 19th century onwards, of the Continent by the European powers and the subsequent imposition of colonial rule over the overwhelming majority of our people. This historical development also implied the rising importance of European culture as a social force in Africa. If a significant number of Africans welcomed European education and embraced Western values, especially as it was expressed through the Christian religion, the very strain and stresses of the conversion within the

481

context of the colonial situation, underscored by the rise of racialist ideologies in Europe, provoked in many a strong emotional conflict and even a reaction which led them to a re-assessment of their African background. It was out of this mood that the ideology of "African personality" was derived, and given formulation, particularly in the writings of the great African scholar of the 19th century, Edward Wilmot Blyden. Although Blyden was not a creative writer, his work exercised a considerable influence on the intelligentsia of his day, and has also strongly influenced the intellectual climate within which African literature has developed in the 20th Century. Many of his ideas are leading themes in African literature in our own time.

The colonial situation can be said to have created a new order in Africa, not only because it implanted Western Civilisation among us Africans, but also because it favoured the emergence of an African bourgeoisie. But although it tended to establish European culture as a reference culture for this new elite, it also created within African societies whole areas of conflict which embraced the political, social, and cultural levels of African experience. This explains the close association of creative writing with political activity, a feature of African literature which first came to the fore in the work of the Gold Coast statesman Joseph Casely-Hayford in his *Ethiopia Unbound* (1911). Not to be forgotten is the wealth of published writing, verse and prose fiction, by South African, Lesotho and Botswana writers and Amharic writers, beginning in the early part of the 20th century. And elsewhere, Somalia and the old French Sudan (Mali), writers are known from the 16th century.

Other influences were at work in the early years of this century which were to contribute to the development of a mature literary expression in the European languages by Africans. The influence of the European literary tradition created an incentive for imaginative writing which at first took the form of sterile imitation. Later, the dominance of social themes in 20th European writing as a result of the trauma of the two world wars, as well as the innovations introduced by contemporary European writers which reflected a significant shift in sensibility, created a modern idiom which had a direct relevance to the preoccupations of the new African writer.

Even more immediate was the influence of Black American writers, especially those of the Harlem Renaissance dominated by the personality of the poet Langston Hughes, who began in the years between the two world wars to explore racial themes, and in the process, began to employ the image of Africa as a symbol of racial consciousness. They furnished an important precedent to their racial brothers in Africa, who were not long to follow their lead. It is important in this respect to take the example of René Maran, an Afro-Caribbean by birth, but with a direct experience of Africa, whose series of African novels, beginning with *Batouala* (1921) was determinant in the development of francophone African writing.

The intimate connection between the literature of the Harlem Renaissance and the racial awakening among black people in the United States, spearheaded by W.E.B. Du Bois and Marcus Garvey strengthened the association of literature with politics in the reaction against colonial rule.

The example of the black intellectuals and writers in the United States inspired a parallel movement in Haiti under the influence of Jean Price-Mars, which was to culminate in the emergence in Paris in the 1930's of what has come to be known as the Négritude Movement among black writers from the French Colonies. The leading ideas and attitudes of this movement were given expression as much in literature as in ideological writings, notably in the work of Léon Damas, Aimé Césaire, Léopold Sédar Senghor and Alioune Diop, the founder of the review *Présence Africaine*. The main themes of this group of writers center upon a revaluation of Africa and an assertion of the African personality and of the collective identity of Black men the world over.

These are also the motivating factors in the strongly nationalist writing which grew up in the years after the Second World War, especially among French speaking writers such as the poet David Diop, and the novelists Ferdinand Oyono and Mongo Beti. In addition to the overt nationalist strain, the new awareness of the African heritage also inspired a return to the oral tradition, exemplified in the tales of Birago Diop, and a new feeling for the quality of life within the ancestral culture, as in the novels of Camara Laye. The poetry of Senghor in particular brings together all these elements and weaves them into a comprehensive vision of the African world as a living and intense universe of moral and spiritual values.

The appearance in 1952 of Amos Tutuola's *The Palm-wine Drinkard* marked the entry of English speaking Africans upon the scene, but this entry did not become decisive until the publication in 1958 of Chinua Achebe's *Things Fall Apart*. Achebe's first novel, taken together with the rest of his work which followed, gave to African literature a new direction which consisted in the more sober exploration and more reflective appraisal than hitherto of the tragic conflicts created within African society by the intrusion of the white man and his values. (Earlier novels in English had appeared, however, such as Varfelli Karlee's *Love in Ebony* (London, 1932) and Samuel Ntara's *Man of Africa* (London, 1934). Often because of the encouragement of missionaries there also developed in such places as the Congo, Angola, Uganda and Malawi, creative writing in African languages beside the very extensive works in Xhosa, Sesotho, Zulu, from southern Africa. Some poetry in English, French, and Portuguese had also appeared in the early part of the twentieth century.)

Even more significant, perhaps, has been the orientation introduced by Wole Soyinka with plays, especially *A Dance of the Forests*, first performed in 1960, the "year of African independence." His work has tended to direct the concerns of the African writer towards a more attentive consideration of African society which are inherent in its very nature as a human creation. A similar attitude can be discerned in the poetry of Tchikaya U' Tamsi on the French-speaking side which contrasts with the romantic attachment to the African past in the work of his colleagues.

It is from this critical awareness expressed by Soyinka and Tchikaya that much African writing since 1960 has received its impulse and derived its themes. These center upon an examination of the contemporary tensions within our societies and involves a candid realism in dealing with the modern dilemma facing Africa. Although the trend has taken in older writers such as Achebe *(A Man of the People)*, Camara Laye *(A Dream of Africa)* and Sembene Ousmane *(Le Mandat)*, the new realism in African literature is best represented by the work of the generation of writers who are rising into prominence at the present moment—the novelists

African Authors

Ayi Kwei Armah and Yambo Ouologuem, and the poet Jean Baptiste Tati-Loutard.

Thus, when the development of African literature in English and French is considered in its full range, it can be seen that the modern African writer, working within the context of a new social order brought about by the impact of European culture on traditional life, has tended to focus his attention on the special problems involved in the African encounter with Europe and in the transformations taking place in our society and in our minds as a result of this historical phenomenon. This is also true of the unjustly neglected writers in Portuguese-held Africa whose work reaches further back than francophone or anglophone writing and who have created important works in all European genres as well as in some African languages and forms. In short, contemporary African literature has been concerned in the main with our modern experience in Africa.

Apart from its concern in its themes with the modern African experience, contemporary African literature also has a social significance in that it has developed, as a movement and as a body of writing, out of the same socio-economic conditions which have attended the rise of the Western educated elite in African societies. In the 19th century in particular, the West African intelligentsia developed a tradition of serious journalism which set standards that have since been rarely equalled. In our time, the elites' concern for expression has been channelled through creative writing.

The importance of Western education in this development can hardly be exaggerated. In this respect, the role of educational institutions in Africa, such as the Ecole Normale William Ponty in Senegal and University of Ibadan in Nigeria has been crucial in producing writers as well as in creating a public for them. More lately, educational centers, by introducing African literature courses into their curricula, are also training critics. The special contribution of the institutions of higher learning, both in Europe and abroad, has been to present models in European literature and to create an intellectual disposition towards written expression. The local African universities have also served specifically as centers of cultural awareness, and it is significant that many African writers began their career by contributing to student journals, such as *The Horn* in Ibadan.

Outside the universities, contemporary African literature has developed largely through the efforts of individuals. If the activities of men like Ulli Beier cannot be said to have created literature, it can be said that they generated widespread interest in the work of African writers and serious consideration of their writings. Cultural centers such as Mbari in Ibadan, and Chemi-Chemi in Nairobi, Kenya also served as meeting points for artists. International conferences such as those organised by *Présence Africaine* in 1956 and 1959 in Paris and Rome respectively, and the one held for English-speaking writers in Makerere College, Kampala, in 1962, helped to stimulate general awareness of African writing. Thus, alongside the literature, there has developed critical writing which was at first channelled through journals and reviews, such as *Présence Africaine,* the dean of African publications, *Black Orpheus, Transition,* and *Abbia.* In the past five years there have also grown up academic journals as a result of the introduction of African literature courses into the universities—examples are *African Literature Today* and *Research in African Literatures.* These journals and reviews were closely related to the rising interest since the second world war in African Affairs and African Studies, of which creative writing by Africans formed an essential part.*

The most important development at the present moment with regard to African literature has been the growth of critical writing devoted to it. This secondary literature, which began with the occasional article in a European journal, has been growing steadily over the years, through the publication of anthologies and general reviews, into a sizeable body of criticism which is today becoming more varied and more refined in its approaches. The fact, too, that African scholars are beginning to devote their attention to the literature of the continent seems destined to give a new dimension to the criticism of modern African literature.**

It is not likely that the present interest in African writing which we are witnessing could have assumed such proportions without the basic infra-structure provided by the publishing houses. European publishers brought out many early books by African authors; in the years immediately after the second world war, Présence Africaine based in Paris had begun to develop a special interest in this field. The importance of this area of publishing activity is perhaps best demonstrated by the collection initiated by Heinemann Educational Books, the "African Writers Series." It is also interesting to note that, following the lead provided by Mbari Publications, indigenous publishing houses are turning more and more to the publication of works by African writers. The East African Publishing House in Nairobi, Kenya, and Editions CLE, in Yaoundé, indeed began their operations in this way, and they have been joined in Nigeria by Nwankwo-Ifejika, publishers based in Enugu.

Thus, a new literary culture has struck roots in Africa, with all its ramifications for the social and economic transition through which our society is passing. The important position of Nigeria in this development is borne out by the fact that writers such as Achebe and Soyinka have become important international figures, and the late Christopher Okigbo is recognised as a major modern poet. At the same time, it is important to recognise the fact that important developments are also taking place in other places, especially in East Africa which is witnessing a literary renaissance at the moment, with the work of writers such as James Ngugi and Okot p' Bitek, and critics such as Taban Lo Liyong. Only in South Africa is a once flourishing and growing literature facing difficulties and a decline because of Apartheid.*** African writing of course is very dynamic in French and despite their hardships African authors using Portuguese continue to publish important works.

The ultimate significance of all this is that, if much of the modern literature of Africa is being written in the European languages, it is nonetheless a reflection of an authentic African world as it is being lived. The best of this literature is African not only in its content and references, but also in its feeling. Efforts have been made of late to relate the English speaking writers to Commonwealth literature,

*For a more detailed listing see Appendix L.

**See Appendix O.

***See Appendix C for a discussion of South African writing.

and the French speaking writers to the idea of "Francophonie." The criterion of language which commands these efforts appears to be tenuous, however, when considered against the real affinities which exist in the works of African writers despite language barriers. Thus Achebe's novels are more closely related to Oyono's than to those of an English or Commonwealth writer; similarly, the closest parallel to the poetry of Senghor, who writes in French, is that provided by the poetry of Okigbo, whose language was English. Even more significant is the connection of literature in the European languages with the traditional literature, which is best demonstrated by the line of inspiration which links the Yoruba oral tradition with the writings of D.O. Fagunwa, and also connects them with the work of Amos Tutuola and Wole Soyinka. Here we have proof of the same imaginative tradition, an irrestible expression of continuity.

So we might say that although much of modern African literature is related to the literatures of the former colonial masters, through language and other factors, it should begin to be seen, not as forming regional schools to the metropolitan tradition, but, as an independent literary area. African traditional literatures obviously long ante-dated written work and are still strongly influencing new published work. It seems inevitable, nevertheless, that future African writing, whether in European or African languages, will reflect the new poly-valued world called into being by the intrusion of Europeans into the African continent.

Appendix B

The Black Writer
and the
African Revolution[1]

Lilyan Kesteloot

More and more importance is now being given to the study of the sociological conditioning of literary works, and it is generally accepted that the writer's product not only takes form and develops in the midst of an ensemble of social facts, but also reflects those facts. But the opposite phenomenon, which is also true, has been neglected: literary works born out of a concrete social context react against reality and exercise an influence that can accelerate the development of social and political crises. This generalization is particularly relevant in the case of Black African literature.

Above all we must ask ourselves: was the African revolution a sudden and improvised event? And we must answer, after examining the intellectual history that preceded it, that it certainly was not. For decades before the era African nations began to regain their historic independence, Black writers and intellectuals had been prophetically preparing the way for these events. Of special importance, then, is the examination of how the Black intellectual came to play the role of spiritual guide to a political revolution of major global significance—the African revolution.

II

It has become a cliché that the year 1960 is remembered as the "year of Africa." Some observers undoubtedly saw the sudden eruptions that led to the independence of African country after African country as the product of a kind of "chain reaction." According to this view, no African country wanted to be left behind, and was induced, often without sufficient preparation, to demand the independence its neighbors had just gained. Only one country had to start, and the others had to follow! Thus, the African peoples are seen as being reluctantly carried away by a sort of collective hysteria.

What is generally overlooked is that the demand for independence was being prepared on the intellectual plane at least as early as the 1920's, and that the African revolutions of the 1960's erupted only after a slow evolution. It was in

---

[1]This appendix is adapted from Lilyan Kesteloot's study *Intellectual Origins of the African Revolution* (Washington, D.C.: Black Orpheus Press, 1972).

African Authors

1921 that René Maran, a Black West Indian, received the *Prix Goncourt* for his pioneering novel, *Batouala: A True Black Novel.*[2]

Maran's book strongly challenged the conventional wisdom of the "civilizing and colonizing mission of the West," and began the awakening of the conscience of the Western public. He denounced the errors of the colonizers and the serious misdeeds for which they were responsible. After the publication of *Batouala,* the writers of what came to be called the "négritude" school began to ask many of the same questions as Maran, but they put more and more emphasis on the wrongs of colonization. In turn insinuating, reasoning, and threatening, they were the only ones who, at the height of colonialism and Western power, stood up and dared to face it, saying no to the subjugation others sought to impose.

Black writers were prophesying revolt, but the West did not want to listen at all. In fact, during this same period, the West was deeply involved in questioning its own values. Since the beginning of the twentieth century, new currents in philosophy, art, and literature had shaken the cultural foundations of European society in general and French society in particular. Measure, reason, progress, absolute truth—all the pillars the preceding centuries had been built upon—lost their status, besieged by a prodigious wave which freed the mind and the emotions from all shackles. First came surrealism and philosophies of action; philosophies of the absurd soon followed. The democratic ideas of the middle class which had nourished the 19th century became obsolete. And because of the economic crisis of the interwar years, Marxism was a major international force and Fascism was triumphant in Germany, Italy, and Spain.

This intellectual, political, and economic collapse and its implicit contradictions hardly could have been ignored by the nonwhite peoples of the world. Indeed, were they supposed to wait patiently for Europe to solve its family affairs, without learning lessons from the sad spectacle presented them? How could they fail to question the supposed omnipotence of the West? And can anyone wonder that this period saw the awakening of the African nationalisms? The myth of the exemplary and all-powerful western civilization taught in the colonies began to crumble as soon as Africans reached Europe.

It was in this atmosphere that some Black writers began to criticize the West, unmasking its hypocrisy and denouncing its errors. This time they started to use stronger and harsher language. Aided by the works of European scholars such as Frobenius, Delafosse, Mauss, and Leiris, they started to demand the right finally to be themselves. Levi-Strauss wrote: "There is no people without culture." They then responded that it is wrong to contend that the Black man is an "uncivilized" creature who must "come out of his savagery" and be dominated in order to be educated! There is a Black civilization and the task of the intellectual will be to rediscover and glorify it. Cultural Revolution! Literature of Combat! First symptoms of decolonization on the march!

We must, then, consider the appearance and development of Black African literature as an important phenomenon, political as well as cultural. If contact with the West, in retrospect, can be seen as inevitable for Africa, which had been so

---

[2]Originally published by Albin Michel, Paris, 1921; definitive edition, Paris, 1937, the latter translated as *Batouala: A True Black Novel* (Washington, D.C.: Black Orpheus Press, 1972).

long isolated from the rest of the world, no one today questions the fact that this contact materialized in the worst possible manner. Aside from some positive material results, colonization has shamelessly and unnecessarily deprived the Black African of his customs and traditional framework. It embittered him even as it exploited him, thus preparing the way for his revolt.

But Black writers did not want to push their peoples toward an unplanned insurrection. The mission of those Aimé Césaire calls the "men of culture"—and he classifies writers among them—was to "prepare a good decolonization and not just any kind of decolonization!" "We are propagators of souls at the cutting edge of history, indeed, creators of a new consciousness," he proudly proclaimed.

III

From the first moment, colonization provoked an acculturation: men who had previously lived in the milieu of stable social and moral structures found themselves in a brutal confrontation with other men who were stronger than they were, who professed nothing but contempt for their ancient traditions, and who planned to substitute a new political and societal structure.

As a result either of their powerlessness or passivity, the colonized at first submitted to the orders of their new masters without understanding them, or seduced by the prestige of the invaders, attempted in a clumsy way to imitate them.

In these cases, we saw appear a class of "highly civilized" or *"évolués"* individuals whose assimilation was encouraged by the colonizer. It is this class which would come to stand apart from the great mass of the people.

But this situation deteriorated quickly. For numerous reasons—fundamental contempt for the so-called inferior races, fear of seeing the emergent new elite take over the more important functions—the colonizer maintained the colonized in an inferior status and rarely allowed assimilation to reach its ultimate state, i.e., perfect equality. Neither the masses nor the highly educated were satisfied. The former felt colonial exploitation deeply; the latter lived in a continual tension of heart and mind, pulled between traditional practices which embarrassed them and the foreign civilization which many of them were wholeheartedly trying to acquire.

At a certain level, however, the Black intellectual who had managed to get a deep knowledge of European culture—and to acquire its essentially critical mind—became aware of the failures of this imported culture and, contrarily, regained a respect for the values of the African tradition it tended to suppress. The Black intellectual saw his people becoming lost morally, debasing itself slowly and acting out of ignorance; he saw the half-educated, either out of snobbery or self-interest, complacently admiring the new values proposed to them by people who did not even respect them.

The intellectual then felt the need to give back to his people freedom of choice and a critical sense. He wanted to prove to them that the past, the path traced by their ancestors, has not been a gigantic error the West had "luckily" freed them from. He also wanted to prove that the traditions remained capable of providing the elements which would solve new problems, whether cultural or social. "With respect to art," wrote Léopold Senghor, "we do not need to receive any advice from anyone." The intellectual believed that while modern science and technique might be indispensable for Africa, one had to be extremely cautious, even reserved, with respect to Western ideologies, social forms, or even material goods.

Criticism of the West and a re-evaluation of African cultures increased together, and as they did, the colonized intellectuals and the African peoples in general regained their *dignity*. This was really the intended goal. They learned that they did not have to imitate the colonizers: they were the *equals* of the colonizers and yet were also *different*. For them, the time to deny their race, to be ashamed of their color, of their body, of their fundamental and particular passions, was all over. And having become conscious of their own alienation, they felt more vividly that of their people, and especially came to resent the docile domestication of many of the educated elite.

The Black intellectuals then set out to assume their own responsibilities. They made it their duty to lead the way on a new path, to restore order to the chaos of acculturation, and to bring their downcast people back to life. They analyzed this new vision of the world—the reality of the relationships between the colonized and his masters—in literary works which allowed the Black man to regain his pride. From slaves and servants, they set out to become real men who would be educators and "propagators of souls."

The publication of poems, novels, and political essays in the colonies was the symptom of an imminent rebirth, the sign that the African could now seize the historical initiative which had eluded him. Acting as a catalyst for the unconscious aspirations of the people, the writers helped them to fathom their nationalism, their place in history, and briefly, "to become a people which had faith in its own destiny," as the Black writer Claude McKay wrote. And here we have the essence of how Black writers prepared and defined the intellectual horizons of the African revolution, and, since the 1960's, have explored the new world of post-independence.

490

Appendix C

Vernacular Writing in Southern Africa
A Brief Introduction

Gideon Lebakeng Mangoaela
Howard University

Any discussion of vernacular writing in the south of Africa must begin with the unwritten traditional literature. It is a literature rich and vast, embodying the thought and life of the major linguistic groups of the South Eastern Bantu. This oral tradition is still alive today despite the prevalence of a comparatively strong and growing written literature. Myths, legends, folktales, animal tales, songs, lyrics and heroic poetry still are recited, and in fact, created, throughout the entire continent; this oral tradition still strongly influences the better writing of the new poets and novelists who seek to maintain their African qualities as they produce works for the printed page. With the emergence of free African states, there has been a resurgence and reawakening of traditional value which also find expression in the drama schools and new forms of theatre suited to the African environment. What is more, it is slowly finding its way into standard schoolbooks and in general becoming part of the active self-consciousness of the new generations.

In Lesotho, Swaziland, Botswana, and South Africa, there are four major language groups, all of which fall within the South-Eastern Bantu languages category. These languages possess a long, oral tradition and an extensive written literature.

The major groups and the languages that they use are the Nguni group consisting of Xhosa, Ndebele, Swazi, and Zulu; the Sotho group consisting of Southern Sotho (or Sesotho), Northern Sotho (or Sepedi) and Tswana; the Venda group; and the Tsonga group. The first two groups contain what are called "clicks," represented in roman letters by "c," "q," and "x"—sounds not ordinarily heard in English words.

The written vernacular literatures of South Africa by its indigenous peoples began shortly after the arrival of the early missionaries. In the process of conversion, Africans were taught to read and write the Western languages. Among the earliest missionaries was Johannes Theodorus van der Kemp who was sent to South Africa in 1799 by the London Missionary Society. He and other missionaries established mission stations and schools throughout southern Africa, culminating in the opening of the celebrated Lovedale Institution in 1841. Missionaries encouraged the writing down of oral literatures of the various peoples and the efforts of African writers to express their thoughts and cultures in writing in their own languages.

The first Xhosa poet known to have his work written down and printed was Ntsikana, the "First Christian Bard." His hymns, composed in the early decades

491

of the 19th century, were first written down in 1828 by Dr. John Philip, a missionary of the Church of Scotland. As Dr. A. C. Jordan, one of the most eminent of modern Xhosa writers has noted, Ntsikana's hymns were a bridge between the traditional oral poetry and European verse, for his poems showed that "the idioms, style and technique of the traditional lyric" were "easily adaptable to new conceptions." By the 1860's Tiyo Soga was publishing folktales in the Xhosa journal *Indaba* and within two decades other Xhosa writers were publishing verse and stories in newly established Xhosa-language journals.

In neighboring Lesotho, then called Basutoland, the first missionaries arrived from the Paris Evangelical Mission Society in 1833 to found their mission and school at Morija (see map), and by the 1860's, the literature of Lesotho—written primarily in Southern Sotho—was underway. The first press was set up at Beersheba in 1841, but the first work published in Sotho was a catechism printed on a press in Cape Town in 1837. The Morija Press began in 1861; and in 1864, the first Sotho journal, the monthly *Leselinyana la Lesotho (The Little Light of Lesotho)*, made its appearance. The first work by an African published in Morija was Azariele Sekese's collection of folktales and customs, *Buka ea pokello ea mekhoa ea Ba-Sotho* (1893), but a decade earlier many of his stories had appeared in the journal *Leselinyana*. The first long work of fiction by an African in Sotho was Thomas Mofolo's novel, *Moeti oa Bochabela* (1906).

In Natal, the successors to the famous Zulu king, Chaka, or Shaka, managed to resist complete European domination until 1906. As a result, missionary and therefore Western literary influence was several generations later in being felt than had been the case with the Xhosa and Sotho peoples. The first publications in Zulu were partial translations of the Bible made by Newton Adams of the American Board of Missions in Natal, printed in 1846 and 1847. Anglican Bishop John Colenso's *Elementary Grammar of the Zulu Kafir Language* and Perrin's *Kafir-English Dictionary of the Zulu Kafir Language as Spoken by the Tribes of the Colony of Natal*, both published in 1855, were important reference books for the development of a written literature.

Nevertheless, these works were designed to aid the white missionaries in their proseletyzing the Christian faith and it was not till the prophet Shembe began to compose his hymns in the years before the World War I that a syncretic Christian-Zulu and Zulu-British type poetry came about. However, one must not forget that probably as early as 1870 Magema ka Magwaza Fuze had composed in Zulu a collection of folk stories and comments on customs and Zulu history in his *Abantu abanmyama lapha bavela ngakhona (Black People: Where They Come From)*. Just as Ntsikana's Xhosa hymns had linked the vernacular poetry with the new English hymn style of music and verse, so Shembe's oral poems—which were sung by his followers—began the new period of writing and publishing in Zulu. The earlier Zulu bards, however, were, and are, well remembered; they include Magolwane (ka Mkhathini), Chaka's praise singer, his successor, Mshongweni, and Maphumzana, who died in 1933.

The arrival of Christian mission societies during the late 18th and early 19th centuries was followed by a period of strife and turmoil when white colonial settlers from various parts of Europe invaded African soil. The physical clash of the Western

492

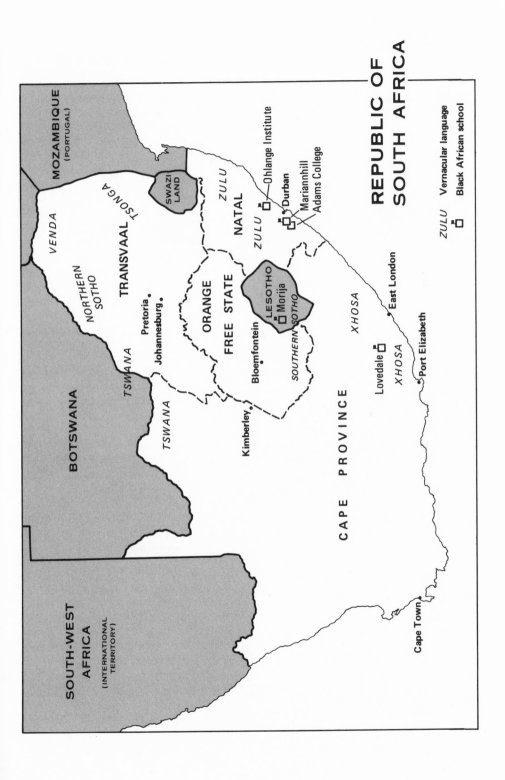

REPUBLIC OF
SOUTH AFRICA

ZULU   Vernacular language

☐   Black African school

world with Black Africans provoked conflicts in every sphere of human activity and altered drastically conditions on the continent. With his back to the wall, the African was called upon to defend not only his land, but his whole philosophy of life as reflected in his cultural institutions and value systems.

After conquest, the strong bond of communality and continuity of traditions, as portrayed in his verbalized literature, were loosened by both missionaries and colonial officials. The African's heritage, once removed, made the culturally naked African a mere tool in the hands of his colonial masters. He sometimes was taught to read and write, but almost always from the books of his masters, not his own cultures' literature. When he developed European skills, he was reminded of his obligations towards his pagan brothers and told to go out to the rural areas as a primary teacher or as a catechist. The new convert to Christianity and Western knowledge had to tread gingerly between two worlds, one of which he knew but was taught to despise, and the other which he only partially apprehended and often misunderstood. The African was cast for the worthy but non-intellectual role of teacher of his children and savior of Black souls. He was never encouraged to dream of taking a major role in the new society being erected around him by achieving distinction in writing.

Because of such bitter experiences, two early African writers, S. E. Mqhayi (Nguni-Xhosa) and T.M. Mofolo (Sotho), were forced to sullen retirement at the peak of their careers when their artistic literary development had gone beyond the straight jacket prescribed for them.

However, the new occupation and close contact with missionaries and other European educators opened new horizons for some. The African gained proficiency in various of the European languages and discovered an entire new world of literature. He intellectually encountered artists of other cultures whose thought and expression were reminiscent of the independence once enjoyed in his own lost traditions. Such experiences opened a new phase in African literature as the new African's subject matter inevitably broadened. He also emerged often as a translator of classics of European literature which found favor with the mission press. Tiyo Soga, a Xhosa writer trained and ordained for the ministry in Scotland, translated John Bunyan's *Pilgrim's Progress* into Xhosa and subsequently Bunyan's book was translated into all the more important languages of South Africa.

On the basis of this experience other African writers of this middle period took a new direction in producing works of a more imaginative character, such as Thomas Mofolo's *Moeti oa Bochabela (Traveler to the East)*, an allegorical novelette in a beautiful and lyrical Sesotho in the traditional narrative style. The Paris Evangelistic mission in Lesotho was highly flattered by this Christian Mosotho writer and regarded the work as a just reward for its tireless Christian educational endeavors among the Basotho of this region.* But *Chaka*, Mofolo's maturer work, offered a more independent view of the African past; it was a work which has since received world acclaim as a classic in vernacular literature, but at the time it was a scandal to the mission society which not only delayed its publication for more than a decade, but also expurgated substantial portions.

---

*"Mosotho" is singular; "Basotho" is plural.

The works of William Shakespeare, especially *Julius Caesar,* seem to have had a strong appeal for African writers of this middle period—not only in South Africa but in other parts of the continent. The leading figure of this group was Solomon Plaatjie of Botswana origin who lived in the then Union of South Africa and who had travelled extensively in Europe. He was a self-educated African and linguist of no mean order who included Dutch, German, French, and a working knowledge of other European languages in his repertoire of foreign languages. Two of his translations of Shakespearean plays, *Diphoshophosho (Comedy of Errors), Dintshontsho tsa bo-Kesara (Julius Caesar),* were published and are very popular. Others have so far remained in manuscript form. He also published a now popular novel in English with an African setting, *Mhudi.*

Though published in 1930 this work was composed in 1919 or even earlier and is consequently the earliest novel to be written—and subsequently published—in English by any African.

The late 19th and early 20th centuries saw the birth of African writers who were literally straining at the leash for independence and a clean break with concepts of moralistic, doctrinaire literature of missionary orientation. But this independence would never find acceptance by the press of the missionary world which dominated the field of education for Black South Africans. The plight of African writers since the institution of so-called Bantu Education by the present regime in South Africa is even worse since its chief object is to gear the development of the African to the restrictive policies of Apartheid.

Despite the hardships and frustration of vernacular writers a new class of modern artists has emerged since the 1930's and has produced a growing body of mature literature. The works of these new writers reflect the angry and more self-confident mood and tendencies of modern African society as well as a realistic view of their African heritage of which they are increasingly proud. Of the Nguni group who write either prose or poetry (or both), a few of the many important writers should be mentioned: R. R. R. Dhlomo; B. W. Vilakazi; J. K. Ngubane, S. L. Nyembezi; A. C. Jordan, and Mazisi Kunene. A representative few of the Sotho group are D. C. T. Bereng; S. Makwala; B. M. Khaketla, O. K. Matsepe; and L. D. Raditladi.

In conclusion, it must be stated that the African vernacular writer had to contend with a unique problem of producing a literature without a readership. As a teacher he had to create the required readership and small market for his creative works. His market was in fact limited to the church and school room. The bulk of the black population, even today, remains illiterate and, in the absence of compulsory education, the slow and tortuous progress to literacy will continue to delay progress in this respect. The Western educated African who belongs to the elite middle class has cultivated a taste for more complex and progressive forms of European literature than his fathers knew in the early colonial periods, and correspondingly, he has the ambition of expressing himself in European genres and employing a European language and thus gaining a wider audience.

It is to be regretted that the Christian mission societies that undertook the difficult task of educating and "civilizing" the African approached the problem with preconceived ideas about the superiority of Western culture. To uproot all elements of the heritage of a people and replace them with an alien culture creates an atmosphere of suspicion and distrust and perpetuates an unstable relationship between the races for all time. In retrospect it seems strange that people who professed themselves to believe in Western ideals could not see the profound values inherent in traditional African literature.

This point is made again in a somewhat different way by Mazisi Kunene in his *Zulu Poems* (1970): "Zulu literature, like most African literatures, is communal. This has fundamental stylistic and philosophical implications. . . . It is a communal organization which has evolved its own ethic, its own philosophical system, its own forms of projecting and interpreting its realities and experiences."

Cut off from his culture by his Christian/European education and by his experiences in a harsh colonial regime, the African writer only with the greatest effort could create meaningful work in his own tongue. Perforce, he was often forced into expression in an alien language which only gradually could be remolded to his needs and impregnated with his own sensibility. H. I. Dhlomo's *The Valley of a Thousand Hills* and B. Leshoia's story of the folk character Senkatana, combining European fairy tale traditions with those of Africa, are examples of the melding of two literary cultures. Later, there is the fine poetry of Dennis Brutus and of A. K. Nortje, and the prose of Can Themba, Louis Nkosi and Ezekiel Mphahlele in supple and sensitive English, to name just a few artists. This work shows the new African mind knowledgable of the outer world, but still suffused with African feeling and respect for the old traditions. Everywhere there is suffering, but everywhere, too, there is courage and a hope for a better world.

Appendix D

Three Key Afro-Caribbean Writers
Aimé Césaire, Léon Damas, René Maran

Donald E. Herdeck
Georgetown University

For centuries men and women of African descent had struggled to maintain their own culture in the Caribbean. Against incredible odds, many individuals resisted total absorption in the alien and European-oriented culture of the white and creole elites. It was only in the 1920's, however, that creative writers such as René Maran, Aimé Césaire and Léon Damas, administrators like Félix Eboué, and scholars such as Franz Fanon began to break free of racial stereotypes and the built-in restraints of colonialism to speak unequivocally of African and/or Pan-African concerns and needs.

The original work of these men and the new currents of independence summed up in the new rallying cry of *négritude* in the 1930's stimulated both Afro-Caribbean and African writers to publish in a variety of genre in a growing African oriented press. Though some important writing in English had been published by the 1930's in the Caribbean, it was primarily writers from Martinique, Haiti, and French Guiana who set the tone and direction of the exciting new African literature. Accordingly, it seems useful to offer below brief biobibliographic essays on the three major Afro-Caribbean writers working in French—Maran, Césaire, and Damas—who had the greatest impact on the genesis and subsequent development of contemporary African literature.

CESAIRE, Aimé (Fernand)
b. June 25, 1913, Basse Pointe, Martinique.
Poet, critic, statesman, teacher.

Son of a poor French civil servant and of a hard working mother who contributed to the family budget by sewing, Aimé Césaire got his start when he received a scholarship to the Lycée Schoelcher at the capital of Martinique, Fort-de-France. He was soon to be joined by Léon Damas from Cayenne, French Guiana, who became a close friend and eventually a co-fighter for *négritude*. Césaire won a further scholarship which permitted him to study at the prestigious Lycée Louis-le-Grand in Paris and at the Ecole Normale Supérieure, a prestigious teacher training school. He earned his *Licence ès lettres* and *Diplôme d'étude supérieure.* He married. Suzanne Roussi, a fellow teacher from Martinique.

During his lycée days, Césaire was influenced by Professors Le Senne and Louis Lavelle, both Marxist philosophers. He steeped himself in Marxism, joined the Communist party, and also studied Freud deeply. He soon joined Damas and Léopold Sédar Senghor of Senegal, all friends in Paris, in the work of renewing black pride. The early journal *Légitime défence* (Legitimate Defense), published by a small group of West Indians in Paris in 1932, had blown the first call for a new liberty in its single issue, but the term *négritude,* coined by Césaire and first proclaimed in *L'Etudiant Noir* (Black Student) in 1934, gave the struggle its slogan and definition. Senghor, Damas, Birago Diop, Ousmane Socé, and others, now well-known in francophone literature, had begun something with this journal, also short-lived, that could not be stopped—the growing self-consciousness of a race and the militancy of its artists.*

The discussions leading to the invention of the term and the intellectual currents of negritude stimulated Senghor and Damas to begin their poetry and led Césaire to destroy his earlier efforts which he saw as merely imitations of classical French verse. Birago Diop began to collect and copy down the folktales of Ahmadou Koumba, a griot, or folk poet, Damas to write his stories reflecting Guyanese dances and songs whose rhythms had already contributed to his very original poetry.

In 1939, Césaire returned to Martinique to teach at his alma mater, the Lycée Schoelcher; he later became a professor there. While teaching from 1940 to 1945, he changed the sleepy students to emotionally charged, hyper-alert critics of Virgil and Sophocles, of surrealism and many other subjects. For the first time in the school's history, there were no failures in his section in the state finals of that spring in Latin and Greek. Students from other classes began to study the notebooks of his students to prepare themselves "à la Césaire."

Despite this record of superior achievement as a teacher, Césaire soon entered politics, primarily to work for the betterment of his race. He served on two constitutional assemblies, 1945 and 1946, and was elected a member of the French National Assembly in 1946, 1951, 1956, 1958, 1962, 1967, and 1968. In 1945 he joined the Communist bloc in the French parliament but broke with it in 1956 after

*For a more detailed treatment see Appendix B: *Black Writers and the African Revolution*

the Hungarian uprising against the USSR. At this time he addressed his protests to the head of the French Communist Party in his *Lettre à Maurice Thorez*. He then became a member of the *Parti du Regroupement Africain et des Fédéralistes* from 1958–59 but has since been an independent in the National Assembly and member of no bloc. He was a founder and has been the president of the *Parti Progressiste Martiniquais* since 1959 and has served as mayor of Fort-de-France since that same year. From 1956 to 1970 he served as Conseiller Général of the Fourth Canton of Fort-de-France.

Fragments of his most famous work, *Cahier d'un rétour au pays natal* (Notebook of the Return to My Native Country) first saw print in *Volonté*, a Paris review, in 1939. The famous French surrealist poet André Breton saw them there and first proclaimed their importance. Later, Breton himself sought refuge from the Germans in Martinique and came to know Césaire well. During the war, Césaire published and edited the journal *Tropiques* (1941–45) with René Menil and Aristide Maugée in Fort-de-France.

Since the war the poet has published many volumes of poetry, three plays (including a French adaptation of Shakespeare's *The Tempest*), and several polemical and/or political works. As noted, the *Cahier*, his first work, appeared in part in Paris before the war, but only in 1945, with a preface by André Breton, was the full poem published. Though surrealist in appearance and to some extent reflecting Bretagne's esthetic and Marxist view of history, the work is seen by its admirers to be more reflective of the volcanic, tense world of Martinique and of Césaire's personal and antillean characteristics than of surrealism as such.

In short, though exploiting some of the linguistic devices and highly subjective associations permitted in surrealism, Césaire's poem is a highly personal and insular product. All of his poetry is difficult, demanding a careful study of the key images and some familiarity with the temperament of the artist and his very individualistic style. He is today considered by far the outstanding poet of the Caribbean world, French or English. The first prize for literature "Viareggio-Versilia" was awarded him in 1968 for the entire body of his work, and Cameroon issued a stamp in his honor in 1969.

Mme. Césaire, from whom he was estranged in her later years, died in 1964. The poet and his six children live in Martinique; he seldom leaves except for duty in the National Assembly in Paris or for participation at writers' conferences.

Writings: Poetry: *Cahier d'un rétour au pays natal*, in part in *Volonté*, a Paris review, 1939; first complete edition, with preface by André Breton, Paris, Bordas, 1945, 1946, 1947; second edition, Paris, Présence Africaine, 1956, 1971, with preface by Peter Gubérina; first English-language edition as *Memorandum on My Martinique*, New York, Brentano's, 1947, translation by Lionel Abel and Ivan Goll, also translation into English by Emil Snyders, Paris, Présence Africaine, 1968, and by John Berger and Anna Bostock, introduction by Mazisi Kunene, Baltimore, Penguin, 1969; *Les armes miraculeuses*, Paris, Gallimard, 1946, 1970; *Et les chiens se taisaient (Version théâtrale)*, in fragments in various journals, 1946, complete edition: Paris, Présence Africaine, 1956; *Soleil cou coupé*, Paris, Edition K, 1948; *Corps perdu* (illustrated by Picasso), Paris, Edition Fragrance, 1949; *Cadastre (Soleil cou coupé* renamed) and the *Corps perdu* in a combined volume, Paris, Seuil, 1961, *Cadastre* in Viking paperback in English, New York, 1973; *Ferrements*, Paris, Seuil, 1959. Poems in English in Ellen Conroy Kennedy's *The Negritude Poets: An Anthology of Black Poetry Translated from the French*, New York, Richard Seaver-Viking, 1974.

Plays: *La tragédie du roi Christophe*, Paris, Présence Africaine, 1963, translation into English by Ralph Manheim, New York, Grove Press, 1970, first performed in its original four-hour version at the Festival of Salzburg, 1964, then at Festival of Berlin at the Hebbel Theatre, September 21, 1964. Cut to two hours, the play was given with great success at the Théâtre Daniel Sorano in Dakar, April, 1966 during the first Festival of Negro Art. *Une saison au Congo*, Paris, Seuil, 1966; *Une tempête* (adaptation of Shakespeare's *The Tempest*), Paris, Seuil, 1969.

Essays: *Discours sur le colonialisme*, Paris, Réclame, 1950, Paris, Présence Africaine, 1955; "Réponse à Depestre, Poète Haitien," in *Présence Africaine*, April-July, 1955; "Sur la poésie nationale," in *Présence Africaine*, October-November, 1955; *Lettre à Maurice Thorez*, Présence Africaine, 1956; "Culture et colonisation," in *Présence Africaine*, June-November, 1956; "L'homme de culture et ses responsibilitiés," discourse delivered at second Congress of Black Writers and Artists, Rome, 1959, published in *Présence Africaine*, February-May, 1959; *Toussaint Louverture (La Révolution française et le problème colonial)*, in Collection "Portraits de l'histoire," Paris, Club Français du Livre, 1960, reprinted in *Présence Africaine*, 1963.

Biographical/Critical Sources: Lilyan Kesteloot, *Aimé Césaire* (in series "Poètes d'aujourdhui 85"), Paris, Seghers, 1962; H. Trouillot, L'Itineraire d'Aimé *Césaire*, Port-au-Prince, Impr. des Antilles, 1968; Hubert Juin, *Aimé Césaire, poète noir*, Paris, Présence Africaine, 1956; M. and S. Battestini, *Aimé Césaire*, in series "Littérature africaine," Paris, Fernand Nathan, 1967; Lilyan Kesteloot, *Les écrivains noirs de langue française*, Brussels, Free University of Brussels, Institut Solvay, 1963, English translation by Ellen Conroy Kennedy as *Negritude is Born*, Philadelphia, Temple University Press, 1973. A fine discussion in English of Césaire's career and the poem *Cahier* is in Mazisi Kunene's introduction to Penguin edition of *Cahier* (for which see above).

DAMAS, Léon Gontran
b. March 28, 1912, Cayenne, French Guiana.
Poet, story writer, critic, anthologist, teacher, statesman, scholar.

Born into a proud, middle-class and Catholic family, Damas studied in Cayenne, the capital of French Guiana, until his entrance into the Lycée Schoelcher in Martinique where he met Aimé Césaire. He moved on to study at the Ecole Normale Supérieure in Paris. With Césaire, Senghor, and others, he organized the magazine *L'Étudiant noir* in 1934 which made the first call for *négritude* and he was, with them, to become one of the leaders of the movement of pride in African culture which was to revolutionize black writing and thinking everywhere.

In 1934 he carried out ethnographic research in the Antilles and the three Guianas in South Africa for Professor Paul Rivet of the Museum of Natural History (now the Musée de l'homme), Paris. He also worked as a journalist in the 1930's and served in the French Army during the war. After being demobilized in 1942, he worked in the resistance and in 1945 was awarded the Commemorative Medal for the Liberation. After the war he was asked to serve on various commissions, including that sent to the Ivory Coast in 1949 to investigate the bloody riots of that year. His *Les incidents de Côtes d'Ivoire* (1951), gives his comments on the matter. That trip was his first to Africa but in succeeding years he made many others to lecture and in his responsibilities as an advisor to French overseas radio, the Radiodiffusion d'Outre-Mer, for whom he had been working since 1945.

During the early 1960's, Damas served as editor of the Overseas Department of *Éditions Fasquelles* and in the mid-1960's he travelled widely in the Caribbean and Brazil doing research on African culture, supported by grants from UNESCO and various foundations. Since 1966 he has been the representative of the Société Africaine de Culture (SAC) at UNESCO where he is also consultant on African and South African cultural matters. Among his awards and honors are: Officer of the National Order, *Honneur et Merite,* of the Republic of Haiti; membership in the Société des Africanistes; the Executive Council of SAC; of the Syndicat National des Ecrivains de France; of the Société des Gens de Lettres; and of PEN Club International.

Damas served for a brief period in the French National Assembly in the 1950's, representing Guiana. A life-long socialist, Damas is a militant anti-colonialist and has struggled for Guyanese independence. Though he maintained the family's house in Cayenne until its recent destruction by fire in 1971, he lived most of his life after the thirties in Paris. In the summer of 1970 he came to Georgetown University in Washington, D. C., to lecture on Caribbean and African literature and then received an appointment as professor of literature at Federal City College in Washington. He also is presently a Visiting Lecturer on African literature and negritude at Howard University's Institute of African Studies.

Of the negritude group, Damas is considered to be the most original in his use of African motifs from both the Antilles and Africa itself. His verse employs the repetitive, circular pattern of much African dance and song; it often is staccato and acerbic, and is neither nostalgic or free-associational and surrealistic as is Senghor's on the one hand or Césaire's on the other. In *Pigments* (1937), and *Graffiti* (1952), he uses duplications and repetitions of sound which are not aimed at developing a concept, but, rather, at advancing a feeling of motion and emotion. (The closest thing to his verse technique for readers of English would be the writings of Gertrude Stein.) Damas' early interest in African music bore fruit in his *Poèmes nègres sur des airs africains* (Negro Poems Written to African Airs), published in 1947.

Damas in his *Black-Label* (1956), an 84-page poem in four parts, sought for more complex expression. Employing his basic technique of staccato lines and overlapping, repetitive phrases and lines, he produced a complex intellectual structure through the device of "leitmotives" and recurring images which "key" his poetic ideas or themes from one part of the poem to the other. The harmonic interrelationships are evocative of the polyphonic textures of traditional African works played on the talking drum and accompanied by dance and chorus and of course also widely prevalent in the West Indies.

Névralgies (Neuralgies), issued in 1966, reflects Damas' growing pessimism and deepening mood of hurt and sorrow. He is planning a new volume of poems, many of them written in America, tentatively entitled *Mine de riens* (Mine of Nothing).

Stories collected and adapted for French appear in *Veillées Noires* Black Vigils), published in 1944. An autobiographical work is *Retour de Guyane* (Return from Guyane), published before the war in 1938.

During the past several years in the United States, Damas has lectured and spoken at many schools and conferences. He attended the Conference on Negritude in Dakar in 1971. Personal friend of Langston Hughes and other great contemporaries in Afro-American poetry, Damas has been active in helping young poets and has "sat for his portrait" to many graduate students in America for their studies of negritude and of black writing. He is represented in many anthologies and has edited several important ones in both French and English.

Writings: Poetry: *Pigments*, Paris, Guy Levi Mano, 1937; *Poèmes nègres sur des airs africains*, Paris, Guy Levi Mano, 1948; *Graffiti*, Paris, Seghers, 1952; *Black-Label*, Paris, Gallimard, 1956; definitive edition of *Pigments*, Paris, 1962; *Névralgies*, Paris, Présence Africaine, 1966; definitive edition, Présence Africaine, 1972.

Editor and compiler: with others, of *Nouvelle somme de poésie du monde noir*, Paris. Présence Africaine, 1966: editor of *Poètes d'expression française d'Afrique noire, Madagascar, Réunion, Guadeloupe, Martinique, Indochine, Guyane*, Paris, Seuil, 1947; and compiler of *African Songs of Love, War, Grief, and Abuse*, translated into English by Miriam Koshland and Ulli Beier, Ibadan, Mbari Press, 1961. In English translation by Ellen Conroy Kennedy, his poems appear in *The Negritude Poets*, E. C. Kennedy (comp.), New York, Richard Seaver-Viking, 1974.

Stories: *Veillées noires*, Paris, Stock, 1944.

Autobiography: *Retour de Guyane*, Paris, Librairie José Corti, 198.

Criticism and biography: *Hommage à Jean Price Mars*, Paris, Présence Africaine, 1969.

Journalism: *Les incidents de Côte d'Ivoire*, Paris, 1951.

Recordings (the poet reading his poems): Folkways, Album No. FL 9924.

Works in progress: *La moisson des trois domaines* (Guyanese folktales); *Langston Hughes* (A biographical study; and *Mine de riens* (new poems).

Biographical/Critical Sources: Lilyan Kesteloot, *Les écrivans noirs de langue française: naissance d'une littérature,* third revised edition, Brussels, Université Libre de Bruxelles, Institut Solvay, 1965; and English translation by Ellen Kennedy as *Negritude is Born,* Philadelphia, Temple University Press, 1973.

MARAN, René

b. November 5, 1887, Fort-de-France, Martinique; d. May 9, 1960, in Paris. Novelist, poet, biographer, critic, government official.

Son of Léon-Hermenégilde, an official of the French colonial service of Guyanese origin, René Maran lived his first years in Martinique. In 1890 his father was assigned to Gabon, and at age 3 the young Maran first arrived in Africa. After four years he was sent to school in Bordeaux because he was having difficulty adjusting to the Gabonese climate. He stayed on in Bordeaux schools until 1909, lonely and discriminated against, but learning to write and becoming saturated with French culture which he never repudiated though he became a severe critic of colonialism and assumed racial superiority of whites. He graduated from the Lycée de Talence in Bordeaux in 1909 and that same year published his first work, a collection of poems now out of print, *La maison du bonheur.* In his much later novel, *Le coeur serré* (The Oppressed Heart), published in 1931, Maran retells the lonely days in Bordeaux with his family in Africa and recalls the generally cool indifference of the French.

With few personal resources, Maran joined the French Colonial Service in 1909 and was posted to Equatorial Africa where his father had spent most of his career. Remaining until 1923 in the Service, all of it in Africa, Maran felt himself a Frenchman but always also a man of African origin. In his collection of stories, *Le petit roi de chimérie* (1924), Maran probably revealed his own attitude: "For now, with my French heart I yet feel I stand on the soil of my ancestors, ancestors whom I disapprove because of their primitive minds and ways—but, they are ancestors nonetheless." This sentiment reflects the young Maran, new in Africa, and as the years passed in his duty there his feelings of superiority decreased and his identification with the lives and culture of Africans intensified.

African Authors

During the six years Maran worked on the manuscript of his most famous work, his novel *Batouala* (1921), he saw the peoples of the Oubangi Chari (now the Central African Republic) suffer famines so severe that one sub-nation dropped in population from 10,000 to 1,080 between 1910 and 1918 by official French count. He saw that the heavy taxes either turned the populations into enslaved drudges for whatever employers they could find or drove them into the inhospitable bush to escape. The novel itself was descriptive; but the emotional preface provoked a violent reaction because it "simply pointed out what was so" about the horrors of colonialism.

Batouala is a series of set scenes, each offering in brief compass the predicaments or daily routines of the *mokoudji* (chief) Batouala as he moves from sleep to wakefulness of a chilly morning to a death resulting from the claws of a leopard. Fundamentally a work conceived in the veritist or naturalist tradition of the Zola novel, Maran's style also consciously employs an extremly rich vocabulary, delights in African terms, and is to some degree exotic, callous, reflecting the African natural world and the cruelty of man and beast in an imperfect world. Ernest Hemingway, covering the story of Maran's winning the coveted Prix Goncourt in 1921 for the work for the *Toronto Star,* wrote:

> You smell the smells of the village, you eat its food, you see the white man as the black man sees him, and after you have lived in the village you die there. That is all there is to the story, but when you have read it, you have been Batouala, and that means that it is a great novel.

Winning the Prix Goncourt made Maran the center of world interest, for he was the first and so far the only author of African blood ever to be so distinguished. The award also brought the attention of French chauvinists and racists and provoked a debate in the French National Assembly. This led to the despatch of a commission to Africa which chose, however, not to examine Maran's charges and "allowed" itself to be side-tracked into matters which would not force it to discover the evils of the colonial system. Maran, who was on station in Africa during most of the furor, found the hostility aroused by his book was so strong, that he shortly took advantage of a minor medical problem to "retire" from the Colonial Service. Thereafter, he became a professional writer, though he was almost always in economic straits. Though *Batouala* became a best seller in France, Russia, and Japan and proved successful in other countries, the author realized only modest royalties.

Despite these relative misfortunes, black artists everywhere recognized the work, and the award, as a break-through. Félix Eboué, fellow Antillan and member of the Colonial Service, and later to be world-famous as the only Governor in the French Colonial World to recognize De Gaulle's Free French movement, was the first to write Maran from Paris with news of the novel's success with the Prix Goncourt committee. He himself had provided much information concerning the Banda language and customs Maran had used in the novel, and it was he who encouraged the author to leave the Service to devote himself fully to a life as a writer.

During his writing career, Maran produced numerous works over the next thirty years. *Journal sans date* (1927), originally entitled *Roman d'un noir* (Novel of a Black Man), tells the painful story of the young manhood of Jean Veneuse and his thought-to-be-hopeless love for Andrée, a Parisienne who, despite Veneuse's bitter self-doubts about his race, agrees to marry him. Only veiled autobiography, Maran later expanded this short book into the novel, *Un homme pareil aux autres* (1947) which is quoted extensively in Frantz Fanon's popular study of black psychology, *Black Skin, White Masks.*

Djouma, chien de brousse (Djouma, Dog of the Bush) appeared in 1927, and celebrated the life and trials of Batouala's much abused dog. Stoned as a bad omen after his master's death, Djouma seeks refuge with a new white master. Here he is wonderfully treated, grows fat, and his meals are even brought to him in contrast to the abuse and starvation he suffered at Batouala's heels. He waxes as the Africans he had deserted grow sicker and weaker.

Bêtes de la brousse (Animals of the Bush), published in 1942, and the earlier *Le livre de la brousse* (The Book of the Bush), published in 1934, also have African settings. *Le livre de la brousse,* considered by its author to be his best, dramatizes the love triangle of Kossi and Tougoumali for Yassi. The work ends in violence and tragedy. Throughout, the laws of the jungle are seen as no better—and no worse—than the strictly enforced laws of man. *Bêtes* employs the age-old device of using animals as actors in a moral or, in this case, an a-moral world drama. The stories of the rhinoceros (Bessaragba), the buzzard (Doppelé), the python (Bokorro), the dog (Boum), and the buffalo (Dog) spell violence—and all are dead at book's end by virtue of the lightning-stick of the whiteman, except for Bokorro and he knows his days are numbered.

In all of his fiction Maran employs songs: work, hunting, funeral, lullabies and love songs. There are also dances, proverbs, and other typically African modes of expression. Combined with his graphic descriptions and the naturalist's desire to get all of reality down, these "African" works are among the most documentary and vivid ever written about people from the continent.

Maran's middle years were fulfilling, for he published more novels, several collections of verse, a biography of Livingston, and other special studies of Africa. Though restrained in his fiction, Maran actively sought the betterment of blacks everywhere through his journalism and was in close touch with American blacks in the arts and scholarship. In 1942 the French Academy awarded Maran the Grand Prix Broguette-Gonin, an especially significant award, particularly in the light of the Nazi occupation of Paris. Other awards were: Grand Prix de la Société des Gen de Lettres (1949), Prix de la Mer et de l'Outre-Mer (1950), and Prix de Poésie de l'Académie française (1959).

Although Maran did some travelling outside France after his resignation from the Colonial Service, he lived most of the time in Paris until his death in May 1960. His widow lives near their former apartment, actively concerned with his works and reputation.

Maran's work has generated new interest in the 1970's with the publication of the first English translation of the definitive 1938 edition of *Batouala* in 1972 (see Writings for details). This new translation by Barbara Beck and Alexandre Mboukou has been called "beautifully rendered" by Ezekiel Mphahlele. It was adopted as a Book-of-the-Month Club Alternate in early 1973, and was published by Heinemann in paperback in the distinguished African Writers Series.

Writings: Poetry: *La maison du Bonheur*, Paris, 1909; *La vie intérieure*, Paris, 1912; *Le visage calme*, Paris, 1922; *Les belles images*, Paris, Delmas, 1935; *Le livre du souvenir; Poèmes (1909–1957)*, Paris, Présence Africaine, 1958.

Novels: *Batouala*, Paris, Albin Michel, 1921; illustrated with designs by Iacovleff, Paris, Editions Mornay, 1928; definitive French edition, Paris, Albin Michel, 1938; in "Collection des Prix Goncourt," Monaco, Edition de l'Imprimerie Nationale, 1946, 1948; *Batouala* ("Edition définitive"), Paris, Albin Michel, 1938; English language translations of the 1921 edition: *Batouala* by Adele Szold Seltzer, New York, Thomas Seltzer, 1922; *Batouala; a Negro Novel from the French*, London, Jonathan Cape, 1922; *Batouala; a novel*, translated by Alvah C. Bessie, illustrated by Miguel Covarrubias, New York, The Limited Editions Club, 1932; and of the 1938 definitive edition: *Batouala: A True Black Novel*, Washington D.C., Black Orpheus Press, 1972, translated by Barbara Beck and Alexandre Mboukou; the same translation is also available in paperback in Heinemann's African Writers Series; there were also translations into Russian, Japanese, German, Dutch, Polish, Hungarian, Portuguese, Romanian, Swedish, and Arabic; *Djouma, chien de brousse*, Paris Albin Michel, 1927; *Journal sans date*, Paris, Artheme Fayard et Cie., 1927 (published in *Les Oeuvres Libres*, 1927, No. 73); *La coeur serré*, Paris, Albin Michel, 1931; *Le livre de la brousse*, Paris, A. Michel, 1934; *Youmba* (novelette), published with definitve edition of *Batouala*, Paris, Albin Michel, 1938; *Bêtes de la brousse*, Paris, Albin Michel, 1942; *Mbala, l'eléphant*, Paris, Ed. Arc-en-ciel, 1942; *Un homme pareil aux autres*, Paris, Editions Arc-en-ciel, 1947, 1962; *Bacouya, le cynocéphale*, Paris, A. Michel, 1953.

Stories: *Le petit roi de chimérie; contes*, Paris, A. Michel, 1924; *Peines de coeur*, Paris, 1944.

Biographies: *Livingston et l'exploration de l'Afrique*, Paris, Gallimard, 1938; *Les pionniers de l'empire*, Paris, Albin Michel, 1943, 1946, 1955; *Savorgnan de Brazza*, Paris, Gallimard, 1941, and definitive edition, Paris, Editions du Dauphin, 1951; *Félix Eboué: grand commis et loyal serviteur 1885–1944*, Paris, Editions du Dauphin, 1951, and Paris, Editions Parisiennes, 1957; *Bertrand du Guesclin; l'épée du roi*, Paris, Editions Albin Michel, 1961.

Articles: "French Colonization," in *Opportunity*, Volume 14 (February 1936); *Asepsie noire!* Paris, Les Laboratoires Martinet, 1931; "Gandhi," in *Opportunity*, Volume 3 (February 1925); "The Harriet Beacher Stowe of France," in *Opportunity*, Volume 3 (August 1925); "Negro Humanism in French Letters," in *Crisis*, Volume 56 (May 1949).

Essays: *Le Tchad de sable et d'or*, Paris, Librairie de la Révue Française, 1931.

Biographical/Critical Sources: Mercer Cook, *Five French Authors*, Washington D. C., The Associated Publishers Inc., 1943; Lilyan Kesteloot, *Les écrivains noirs de la langue française*, Brussels, 1963, and in English translation by Ellen Conroy Kennedy as *Negritude is Born*, Philadelphia, Temple University Press, 1973; Léon G. Damas, "Pour saluer René Maran," in *Les Lettres Françaises*, No. 825 (May 1960); for a recapitualation of the reactions to *Batouala* and its being awarded the Prix Goncourt see René Gillouin, *Le destin de l'occident,* Paris 1929, pp. 69–84, and D. Herdeck's introduction to the English translation for Black Orpheus Press of the 1938 edition of *Batouala* cited above in "Writings" section; for memorial essays, see *Hommage a René Maran,* Paris, Presence Africaine, 1965; also see Brian Weinstein's *Eboué,* New York, Oxford University Press, 1972, for useful and previously unknown material concerning Eboué's aiding of Maran and the life-long friendship of the two men. For as yet unpublished correspondence of Maran's, much of it bearing on *Batouala,* see his 18 letters addressed to the black American scholar Alain Leroi Locke, in holograph in the Moorland-Spingarn Collection, Howard University, Washington, D. C.

PART II
AUTHORS BY CATEGORY

Appendix E

Authors By Chronological Period

The dates cited for works are for first significant publication, play performance, literary prize, etc. which marked each author's entrance into mature creative writing and/or scholarship. Generally, when no clear date or period can be determined, an estimated date is assigned arbitrarily 30 years from the time of the author's birth, though in some cases the estimated date is based on general information available concerning the author's activities. All such dates are marked by an asterisk.

Author	Country	Work	Date	Genre	Language(s)
Pre-18th Century:					
Antar	Arabia	*Mo'allaqâ* (Ode) and *Sirat Antar*	580*	Verse	Arabic
ca. 550–615					
Abu Dulama Ibn al-Djaun	Iraq (?)	poem on death of Abu Muslim	754	Verse	Arabic
ca. 720–777					
Ziryab	Iraq	oral poetry and music	815*	Verse	Arabic
ca. 785–852					
Ishak	Ethiopia	*Kebra Nagast*	13th C.	Story	Amharic
13th century					
Rukn Al-Din	Egypt	*Sirat Baibars*	1298*	Legends	Arabic
ca. 1268-ca. 1310					
Kati, Mahmud	Mali	*Tarikh al-Fattash*	1519	Legends	Arabic
ca. 1468–ca. 1570					
Latino, Juan	Guinea	*Austrias*	1573	Verse	Latin
ca. 1516–1606	and Spain				
Baba, Ahmad	Mali	*Dhail al-Dibadj*	1586*	Legends	Arabic
1556–1627					
Sadi, Abdulrahman as-	Mali	*Tarikh al-Sudan*	1655	Legends	Arabic
1596–1656					
1700–1799:					
Raage, Ugaas	Somali	oral poetry	1730*	Verse	Somali
18th century					
Amo, Antonius	Gold Coast	*Dissertatio inauguralis*	1734	Schol.	Latin
1703–1750(?)	(Ghana)	*philosophica . . .*			
Capitein, Jacobus	Unknown	*Dissertatio politico-theologica. . . .*	1742	Schol.	Latin
1717–1747	birthplace,				
	lived in Holland				
Saiyid, Abdallah	Tanzania	"Takhmis ya Liyonga"	1750*	Verse	Swahili
ca. 1720–ca. 1810					
Wheatley, Phillis	Senegal and	*An Elegiac poem on George*	1770	Verse	English
ca. 1753–1784	America	*Whitefield*			
Barbosa, Domingos Caldas	Brazil	*Collecção de poesias feitas*	1775	Verse	Portuguese
ca. 1738–1800					

511

African Authors

Author	Country	Work	Date	Genre	Language(s)
Sancho, Ignatius	Unknown birthplace, lived in England	*Letters of the Late Ignatius Sancho*	1782	Letters	English
Cugoana, Ottobah ca. 1745–ca. 1790	Gold Coast and England	*Thoughts and Sentiments on the Evil and Wicked Traffic and Commerce of the Human Species*	1787	Tract	English
Vassa, Olaudah 1745 or 1746–ca. 1802	Nigeria and England	*The Interesting Narrative of the Life of Olaudah Equiano, or Gustavus Vassa, the African*	1789	Autobio.	English
Muhammad wad Daif Allah	Sudan	*Tabakat*	1790*	Legends	Arabic
Muyaka 1776–1840	Kenya	oral poetry	1796*	Verse	Swahili

1800—1899:

Author	Country	Work	Date	Genre	Language(s)
Ramanato ca. 1780–1840(?)	Malagasy	oral poetry	1800*	Verse	Malagasy
Shaikh, Muhyi 'l-Din al-Waili 1778–1869	Tanzania	"Kitab al-Sulwa"	1808*	Verse	Swahili
Ntsikana ca. 1783–1820	S. Africa	"He the great God, high in Heaven"	1813*	Verse	Xhosa
Saiyid, Umar 1800–1870	Kenya	"Wajiwaji," and "Dura Mandhuma"	1830*	Verse	Swahili
Mwana, Kupona 1810–1860	Kenya	"Utendi wa Mwana Kupona"	1840*	Verse	Swahili
Ferreira, José da Silva Maia ca. 1825–ca. 1850	Angola	*Espontaneidades da minha alma*	1855	Verse	Portuguese
Saiyid, Abu Bakr 1828–1922	Kenya	"Utendi wa Akida tu 'l'Awami"	1858	Verse	Swahili
Soga, Tiyo 1829–1871	S. Africa	folktales in *Indaba* (journal)	1862	Folklore	Xhosa
Horton, James 1832–1883	Sierra Leone	*West African Countries and Peoples, British and Native*	1868	Polemics	English
Vimbe, John 1811–1898	S. Africa	folktales in *Isigidimi sama Xhosa*	1871 (publ. 1922)	Folklore	Xhosa
Fuze, Magema ca. 1845–?	S. Africa	*Abantu abamnyama lapha bavela ngakhona*	1875?	Folklore	Zulu
Duuh, Ali ca. 1850–ca. 1910	Somalia	oral poetry	1880*	Verse	Somali
Faarah, Nuur ca. 1850–?	Somalia	oral poetry	1880*	Verse	Somali
Gqoba, William W. 1840–1888	S. Africa	poems in *Isigidimi sama-Xhosa*	1880*	Verse	Xhosa
Qamaan, Bulhan ca. 1850–ca. 1915	Somali and Ethiopia	oral poems	1880*	Verse	Somali
Pereira, José de Fontes 1823–1891	Angola	articles, etc. in *O Arauto Africano*	1880*	Journalism	Portuguese
Salaan, 'Arrabey ca. 1850–ca. 1940	Somalia	"The Unpaid Bridewealth"	1880*	Verse	Somali
Sekese, Azariele U. 1849–1930	Lesotho	folklore in *Leselinyana*	1880*	Folklore	So. Sotho
Ntsiko, Jonas A. ca. 1860–ca. 1915	S. Africa	hymns in *Xhosa Hymn Book*	1881	Verse	Xhosa
Alegre, Caetano da Costa 1864–1890	São Tomé	poems written between 1882–89 (publ. 1916)	1882	Verse	Portuguese
Jabavu, John 1859–1921	S. Africa	articles, etc. in *Imvo zabantsundu*	1884	Journalism	Xhosa/ English
Bokwe, John Knox 1855–1922	S. Africa	hymns in *Amaculo ase-Rabe*	1885	Verse	Xhosa
Citashe, I. W. W. ca. 1850–ca. 1930	S. Africa	"Weapon" in *Isigidimi Sama Xhosa*	1885*	Verse	Xhosa

Author	Country	Work	Date	Genre	Language(s)
Soga, John Henderson 1860–1941	S. Africa	"Iziyolo zelilizwe" and other poems and hymns	1885	Verse	Xhosa
da Matta, Joaquim 1857–1894	Angola	*Delirios: Versos 1875–1887*	1887	Verse	Portuguese
Reindorf, Rev. Carl 1834–1917	Ghana	*The History of the Gold Coast and Asante*	1889	Schol.	English
El Hardallo ca. 1860–1919	Sudan	poems in *ms.* extant	1890*	Verse	Shukria-Arabic
Gabra, Egzi'abeher ca. 1860–1914	Ethiopia	poems in ms. extant	1890*	Verse	Amharic
Ransome-Kuti, Rev. Cannon 1855–1930	Nigeria	folksongs	1890*	Folklore	Yoruba
Machado, Pedro ca.1865–ca. 1940	Angola	*Scenas d'Africa*	1892	Romance	Portuguese
Mahammed, Sheikh 'Abdille 1864–1920	Somalia	oral poetry in *ms.*	1894	Verse	Somali
Sarbah, John Mensah 1864–1910	Ghana	*Fanti Customary Law*	1897	Schol.	English
Rubusana, Walter Benson 1858–1936	S. Africa	*Amanyatelo okuya ku Kristu*	1898	Trans.	Xhosa
Sontonga, Mankayi ca. 1860–1904	S. Africa	"Nkosi sikelel' i-Africa" and other hymns	1899	Verse	Xhosa

1900—1919:

Author	Country	Work	Date	Genre	Language(s)
Afawark, Gabra 1868–1947	Ethiopia	*Psalms*	1902	Verse	Amharic
Mbelle, Isaiah B. 1870–1947	S. Africa	*Kafir Scholar's Companion*	1903	Schol.	English
Mukasa, Ham 1860–1956	Uganda	*Katikiro in England*	1904	Travel	Luganda/English
Aggrey, James 1875–1927	Ghana	his various writings in *Aggrey of Africa* by E. W. Smith and *Aggrey of Achimota* by N. Musson, etc.	1905*	Schol. and Polemics	English
Mofolo, Thomas 1875–1948	Lesotho	*Moeti oa bochabela*	1906	Novel	So. Sotho
Mqhayi, Samuel 1875–1945	S. Africa	poems in *Zemk' inkomo magwale ndini*	1906	Verse	Xhosa
Dube, John 1871–1946	S. Africa	*The Zulu's appeal for light and England's duty*	1909	Polemics	English and Zulu
Ndawo, Henry Masila 1883–1949	S. Africa	*U-hambo luka Gqoboka*	1909	Novel	Xhosa
Abdillaahi, Muuse 1880–?	Somalia	"An Elder's reproof to his wife" (publ. 1964)	1910*	Verse	Somali
Segoete, Everitt L. 1858–1923	Lesotho	*Monono ke moholi mouoane*	1910	Novel	So. Sotho
Shembe, Isaiah late 1860's–1935	S. Africa	*Izihlabelelo zaNazarethe* (hymns)	1910*	Verse	Zulu
Casely-Hayford, Joseph 1866–1930	Ghana	*Ethiopia Unbound*	1911	Novel	English
Mangoaela, Zakea 1883–1963	Lesotho	*Har'a libatana le Linyamatsane*	1912	Folklore	So. Sotho
Motsamai, Edward 1870–1959	Lesotho	*Mehla ea malimo*	1912	Stories	So. Sotho
Ngidi, Andreas 1882–1951	S. Africa	poems in *Umafrika* and *ILN* journals	1912*	Verse	Zulu
Takla, Hawaryat ca. 1881–?	Ethiopia	play, title unknown	1912	Play	Amharic
Kakaza, Lillith ca. 1885–1950	S. Africa	*Intyatyambo yomzi*	1913	Novelette	Xhosa
Travele, Moussa ca. late 1880's–?	Mali	*Proverbes et contes bambara*	1913	Folktales	French

African Authors

Author	Country	Work	Date	Genre	Language(s)
Mira, Ismaa'iil 1884–ca. 1950	Somalia	oral poetry	1914*	Verse	Somali
Cardoso, Pedro ca. 1890–1942	Cape Verde	Caboverdeanas	1915	Verse	Portuguese
Heruy, Walda S. 1878–1938	Ethiopia	My Friend, My Heart	1915	Parables	Amharic
Lopes, José da Silva 1872–1962	Cape Verde	Jardim das Hespérides	1916	Verse	Portuguese
Plaatje, Solomon T. 1878–1932	S. Africa	Sechuana Proverbs	1916	Folklore	English/ Tswana
Soga, Tiyo B. 1866–1938	S. Africa	Inlalo ka Xosa	1916	Folklore	Xhosa
Tavares, Eugénio 1867–1930	Cape Verde	Amor que salve	1916	Verse	Portuguese
Senyi, Kobina ca. 1890–	Nigeria	The Blinkards (performed in 1917)	1917	Play	English
Albasini, João ca. 1890–1925	Mozambique	articles in O Brado Africano	1918*	Journalism	Portuguese/ Xironga
Guma, Enoch S. ca. 1901–1918	S. Africa	U-Nomalizo okanye izinto	1918	Novel	Xhosa
Diagné, Ahmadou Hampaté ca. 1890–	Senegal	Un pays de pilleurs d'épaves	1919	Novelette	French

1920—1939:

Author	Country	Work	Date	Genre	Language(s)
Karim, Ahmed Awad ca. 1890–	Sudan	oral poems	1920*	Verse	Shukria- Arabic
Molema, Moliri S. 1892–1965	Botswana	The Bantu, Past and Present	1920	Schol.	English
Caluza, R. T. 1900–1965	S. Africa	Ixegwana	1921	Verse and music	Zulu
Jabavu, Davidson 1885–1959	S. Africa	The Black Problem	1921	Schol.	English/ Xhosa
Sinxo, Guybon 1902–1962	S. Africa	U-Nomsa	1922	Novel	Xhosa
Yoftahe, Neguse ca. 1900–1948	Ethiopia	Vain Entertainment	1923	Play	Amharic
Mohapeloa, John	Lesotho	Mating a pheheang	1924	Novelette	So. Sotho
Rabéarivelo, J. J. 1903–1937	Malagasy	La coupe de cendres	1924	Verse	French
Diop, Massyla ca. 1886–1932	Senegal	Le réprouvé—roman d'une Sénégalaise	1925	Novel	French
Diallo, Bakary 1892–	Senegal	Force-Bonté	1926	Novel	French
Ribas, Óscar Bento 1909–1961	Angola	Nuvens que passam	1927	Novella	Portuguese
Robinary, Michael ca. 1896–	Malagasy	Les fleurs défuntes	1927	Verse	French/ Malagasy
Dhlomo, Rolfus 1901–	S. Africa	An African Tragedy	1928	Novel	Zulu
Lopes, Manuel 1907–	Cape Verde	"Visão da madrugada"	1928	Story	Portuguese
Maile, Mallane 1895–	Lesotho	Ramasoabi le Potso	1928	Novel	So. Sotho
Vingadio, Timotéo	Zaïre	Nsweswe Ansusu Ampembe ye zankaka	1928	Stories	Kikongo
Acquah, Gaddiel 1884–1954	Ghana	Mbofraba asorye ndwom (hymns for children)	1929	Verse	Fante
Couchoro, Félix ca. 1905–	Togo	L'esclave	1929	Novel	French
Casely-Hayford, Gladys 1904–1950	Ghana	poetry in various journals	1930*	Verse	English

514

Author	Country	Work	Date	Genre	Language(s)
Diop, Birago 1906–	Senegal	stories and poems in various journals	1930*	Verse and stories	French
Ilmi, Bownderi ca. 1903–ca. 1938	Somalia	oral poetry	1930*	Verse	Somali
Osadebay, Dennis 1911–	Nigeria	poems in various journals	1930*	Verse	English
Karlee, Varfelli ca. 1900–	Liberia	*Love in Ebony: A West African Romance*	1932	Novel	English
Kabbada, Mika'el 1915–	Ethiopia	*The Light of Intelligence*	1933	Verse	Amharic
Molefe, A. I. 1908–	S. Africa	*USambulele*	1933	Novel	Zulu
Swaartbooi, Victoria 1907–1937	S. Africa	*U-Mandisa*	1933	Novel	Xhosa
Vilakazi, Benedict 1906–1947	S. Africa	*Nje nempela*	1933	Novel	Zulu
Assis Júnior, António de 1934–	Angola	*O segredo da morta*	1934	Novel	Portuguese
Duarte, Fausto 1903–	Cape Verde	*Auá (novela negra)*	1934	Novelette	Portuguese
Ntara, Samuel 1905–	Malawi	*Man of Africa*	1934	Biograph-ical Novel	English
Mal'aku, Baggosaw ca. 1900–1940	Ethiopia	*The Great Judge*	1934	Play	Amharic
Mockerie, Parmenas ca. 1910–	Kenya	*An African Speaks for his People*	1934	Schol.	English
Azikiwe, Benjamin 1904–	Nigeria	*Liberia in World Affairs*	1935*	Schol.	English
Barbosa, Jorge 1902–	Cape Verde	*Arquipélago*	1935	Verse	Portuguese
Dhlomo, Herbert 1903–1956	S. Africa	The Girl Who Killed to Save (Nongquase)	1935	Play	English/ Zulu
Dube, Violet ca. 1905	S. Africa	*Wozanazo izindaba Phoshozwayo*	1935	Stories	Zulu
Moikangoa, Cornelius 1877–1949	Lesotho	"Sebogoli"	1935	Story	So. Sotho
Mseleku, Malcolm 1912–1961	S. Africa	"Uvumindaba"	1935	Story	Zulu
Nyabongo, Prince 1904–	Uganda	*The Story of an African Chief*	1935	Autobio.	English/ Swahili
Ramaila, Epafras 1897–1962	S. Africa	*Tsa bophelo bya Moruti Abraham Serote (1865–1935)*	1935	Biog.	No. Sotho
Socé, Ousmane Diop 1911–	Senegal	*Karim; roman sénégalais*	1935	Novel	French
Alcantara, Osvaldo 1904–	Cape Verde	poems in *Claridade*	1936	Verse	Portuguese
Dadié, Bernard 1916–	Ivory Coast	*Assémien Déhylé, roi du sanwi*	1936	Play	French
Hinawy, Sheikh Mbarak 1896–	Kenya	articles in journals	1936*	Schol.	Swahili
Kenyatta, Jomo ca. 1893–	Kenya	*Facing Mount Kenya*	1936	Schol.	English
Nketia, John 1921–	Ghana	*Semodi*	1936	Stories	Assanti-Twi
Nxumalo, Natalie 1908–	S. Africa	*Ubude abuphangwa*	1936	Novel	Zulu
Azevedo, Pedro 1905–1942	Cape Verde	poems in *Claridade* magazine	1937	Verse	Portuguese
Bessa Victor, Geraldo 1917–	Angola	*A poesia e a política*	1937	Critical-polemical	Portuguese
de Almeida, José Maria 1903–	São Tomé	*Maiá Poçon*	1937	Stories	Portuguese

515

African Authors

Author	Country	Work	Date	Genre	Language(s)
Jolobe, James 1902–	S. Africa	*U-Mthuthula*	1937	Verse	Xhosa
Moore, Bai T. 1916–	Liberia	*Golah Boy in America*	1937	Autobio.	English
Ngani, Thomas	S. Africa	*Ibali lama Gqunukhwebe*	1937	Schol.	Xhosa
Fagunwa, Chief D. O. 1910–1963	Nigeria	*Ogboju ode ninu igbo Irunmale*	1938	Novelette	Yoruba
Hazoumé, Paul 1890–	Dahomey	*Doguicimi*	1938	Novel	French
Made, E. ca. 1905–	S. Africa	*Amaqhawe omlando*	1938	Biog.	Zulu
Mokone, N. G. 1900–1960	S. Africa	*Montsamaisa-bo-sigo*	1938	Schol.	Tswana
Nunes, António 1917–1951	Cape Verde	*Devaneios*	1938	Verse	Portuguese
Quénum, M. P. B. 1911–	Dahomey	*Au pays des Fons*	1938	Folklore schol.	French
Akiga, B. 1898–	Nigeria	*Akiga's Story*	1939	Autobiog. novel	English/ Tiv
Bengani, R. R. ca. 1899–	S. Africa	*Uphethani*	1939	Novel	Zulu
Masondo, Titus A. ca. 1907–	S. Africa	*UVulindlebe*	1939	Novel	Zulu
Rabémananjara, J. J. 1913–	Malagasy	*L' éventail du rêves*	1939	Verse	French
Walda, Giyorgis 1896–	Ethiopia	*The Glory of Kings*	1939	Verse	Amharic
1940—1959:					
Blay, J. B. ca. 1900–	Ghana	*Immortal Deeds*	1940	Verse	English
Jordan, A. C. 1906–1968	S. Africa	*Inggoumbo yeminyanya*	1940	Novel	Xhosa
Makonnen, Endalkacaw 1892–	Ethiopia	*The Inconstant World*	1940	Novel	Amharic
Mohapeloa, Joshua P. ca. 1910–	Lesotho	poems in *Meloli le litha Tsa Africa*	1940	Verse	So. Sotho
Nsimba, Samuel A. ca. 1910–1948	Zaïre	poems (hymns) in *Minsamu Miayenge*	1940*	Verse	Kikongo
Abrahams, Peter 1919–	S. Africa	"A Blackman Speaks of Freedom"	1941	Verse	English
Danquah, Joseph 1895–1965	Ghana	*Nyankonsem*	1941	Play	Twi/ English
Germacaw, Takla H. 1915–	Ethiopia	*Ar' aya*	1941	Novel	Amharic
Ndebele, Nimrod 1913–	S. Africa	*UGubudele namazimuzimu*	1941	Play	Zulu
Yilma, Darasa 1907–	Ethiopia	editor of important early Ethiopian journals or collections	1941	Schol.	Amharic
Madiba, Moses 1909–	S. Africa	*Tsiri*	1942	Novel	No. Sotho
Mahtama, Sellase 1905–	Ethiopia	*Memories*	1942	Schol.	Amharic
Moloto, D. P. 1910–	S. Africa	*Mokwena*	1942	Novel	Tswana
Tenreiro, F. J. 1921–1963	São Tomé	*Ilha de nome santo*	1942	Verse	Portuguese
de Noronha, Rui 1909–1943	Mozambique	*Sonetos*	1943	Verse	Portuguese
Disengomoko, A. E. 1915–1965	Zaïre	*Kwenkwenda*	1943	Novel	Kikongo
Kagame, Abbé 1912–	Rwanda	*Inganji Karinga*	1943	Schol.	Rwanda

516

Author	Country	Work	Date	Genre	Language(s)
Mopeli-Paulus 1913–	Lesotho	*Ho tsamaea ke ho bona*	1943	Verse	So. Sotho
Obeng, R. E. ca. 1918–	Ghana	*Eighteenpence*	1943	Novel	English
Bolomba, G. unknown	Zaïre?	*Kavwanga* (probably a forgery)	1944?	Novel	French
Ngangu, Jackson ca. 1920–	Zaïre	*Tangeno nsamu*	1944	Stories and Verse	Kikongo
Ogunde, H. 1916–	Nigeria	*Adam and Eve*, performed 1944 for church service	1944	Play	Yoruba
Awolowo, O. 1909–	Nigeria	*Path to Nigerian Freedom*	1945*	Polemics and Schol.	English
Fonseca, A. 1922–	Cape Verde	*Linha do horizonte*	1945	Verse	Portuguese
Kitereza, Aniceti ca. 1900–	Tanzania	*Bwana Myombekere na Bibi* *Bugonoka na Ntulanalwo*	1945	Novel	Kikerebe (and version in Swahili)
Malutama, Rémy ca. 1915–1956	Zaïre	poems in various journals	1945*	Verse	Kikongo
Ojike, Mazi 1914–1956?	Nigeria	*Portrait of a Boy*	1945	Autobio.	English
Raditladi, Leetile 1910–1971	Botswana	*Motswasele II*	1945	Play	Tswana
Senghor, L. S. 1906–	Senegal	*Chants d'ombre*	1945	Verse	French
Dei-Anang, M. F.	Ghana	*Wayward Lines from Africa*	1946	Verse	English
Ntsane, Kemuele 1920–	S. Africa	*'Musa-pelo*	1946	Verse	So. Sotho
Sadji, Abdoulaye 1910–1961	Senegal	*Tounka, nouvelle africaine*	1946	Novelette and stories	French
Adoki, G. ca. 1910–	Nigeria	"Emergency"	1947	Story	English
Bolamba, A. R. 1913–	Zaïre	*Premiers essais*	1947	Verse	French
Danquah, Mabel ca. 1910–	Ghana	stories in *African New Writing*	1947	Stories	English
Dempster, Roland 1910–1965	Liberia	*Echoes from a Valley*	1947	Verse	English
Ekwensi, Cyprian 1921–	Nigeria	*When Love Whispers*	1947	Novelette	English
Itayemi, Phebean 1928–	Nigeria	"Nothing So Sweet"	1947	Story	English
Khaketla, B. M. 1913–	Lesotho	*Moshoeshoe le baruti*	1947	Play	So. Sotho
Mphahlele, Ezekiel 1919–	S. Africa	*Man Must Live and Other Stories*	1947	Stories	English
Mthembu, Robert 1907–1959	S. Africa	*UMamazana*	1947	Novel	Zulu
Oluwa, I. I. ca. 1920–	Nigeria	"His Own Medicine"	1947	Story	English/ Yoruba
Ranaivo, Jacques 1914–	Malagasy	*L'ombre et le vent*	1947	Verse	French/ Malagasy
Robert, Shaaban 1909–1962	Tanzania	*Pambo la lugha*	1947	Verse	Swahili
Seboni, M. O. 1912–	Botswana	*Rammona wa Kgalagadi*	1947	Novel	Tswana
Bahelele, Jacques N. 1911–	Zaïre	*Kinzonzi ye ntekolo andi* *Makundu*	1948	Novel	Kikongo
Lomami-Tshibamba, Paul 1914–	Congo, Braz.	*N'gando*	1948	Novel	French
Nyembezi, Cyril 1919–	S. Africa	essay in *African Studies*	1948	Essays	Zulu

African Authors

Author	Country	Work	Date	Genre	Language(s)
Oyelese, J. O. ca. 1915–	Nigeria	*Alo o apa kini alo' apamo*	1948	Folklore	Yoruba
Rajemisa-Raolison, Régis 1913–	Malagasy	*Les fleurs de l'île rouge* and *Kilalaon' afo*	1948 1948	Verse Novel	French Malgache
Sentso, Dyke 1924–	S. Africa	*Matlakala*	1948	Verse	So. Sotho
Naigiziki, J. V. 1915–	Rwanda	*Escapade ruandaise*	1949	Autobio.	French
Ndhambi, Etienne 1914–	S. Africa	*Swiphato swa Xitsonga*	1949	Verse	Tsonga
Obianim, Sam 1920–	Ghana	*Amegbetoa alo Agbezuge*	1949	Novel	Ewe
Armattoe, R. 1913–1953	Ghana	*Between the Forest and the Sea*	1950	Verse	English
Chafulumira, E. W. ca. 1930–	Malawi	*Kazitape*	1950	Stories	Nyanja
De Sousa, Noémia 1927–	Mozambique	poetry in various journals	1950*	Verse	Portuguese
Egharevba, Chief Jacob ca. 1920–	Nigeria	1) *Ihun-an-Edo* 2) *Some Stories of Ancient Benin*	1950 1950	Verse Folklore	Edo English
Keita, Fodeba 1921–	Guinea	*Poèmes africains*	1950	Verse	French
Mohapeloa, Moeketsa Daniel 1912–	Lesotho	poems in, and editor of, *Letlole la lithoko tsa Sesotho*	1950	Verse	So. Sotho
Mpashi, S. A. ca. 1920–	Zambia	*Cekesoni aingila ubosoja*	1950	Novelette	Bemba
Ntantala, Phyllis P. 1920–	S. Africa	articles and stories	1950*	Stories	English
Nxumalo, James 1908–	S. Africa	*UZwelonka*	1950	Novel	Zulu
Ogunmola, Elijah 1925–	Nigeria	*They Were Enemies*	1950*	Play	English/ Yoruba
Bankole, Timothy ca. 1920–	Sierra Leone	stories and poems in various journals	1951	Stories, verse	English
Busia, Kofi A. ca. 1913–	Ghana	*The Position of the Chief in the Modern System of the Ashanti*	1951	Schol.	English
Desewo, P. M. ca. 1925–	Ghana	*The Three Brothers and Other Ewe Stories*	1951	Stories	Ewe
Kagara, Malam M. B. ca. 1905–	Nigeria	*The Life of the Emir of Katsina*	1951	Biography	Hausa
Lemos, Virgilio de 1929–	Mozambique	poems in *Antologia de poesia de Moçambique*	1951	Verse	Portuguese
Mncwango, L. 1926–	S. Africa	*Manhla iyokwendele egodini*	1951	Play	Zulu.
Saoli, J. R. 1914–	S. Africa	*Meloli ea tumelo*	1951	Verse	So. Sotho
Abubakar, Imam ca. 1920–	Nigeria	*Tafiya mabudin ilmi*	1952	Travel tales	Hausa
Dias, João 1926–1949	Mozambique	*Godido e outros contos*	1952	Stories	Portuguese
Mofokeng, Sophonia 1923–1957	S. Africa	*Senkatana*	1952	Play	So. Sotho
Neto, António 1922–	Angola	"Náusea"	1952	Story	Portuguese
Tutuola, Amos 1920–	Nigeria	*The Palm-Wine Drinkard*	1952	Novel	English
Bonne, Nii Kwabena III 1888–ca. 1960	Ghana	*Milestones in the History of the Gold Coast*	1953	Autobio.	English
Cardoso, António 1936–	Angola	*Poemas de circunstância*	1953	Verse	Portuguese
Laye, Camara 1928–	Guinea	*L'enfant noir*	1953	Novel	French

Author	Country	Work	Date	Genre	Language(s)
Mutombo, Dieudonné ca. 1928–	Zaïre	*Victoire de l'amour*	1953	Novel	French
Nkoumba, Lester ca. 1926–	Malawi	*Ukawamba*	1953	Novel	Nyanja
Odoi, N. A. ca. 1925–	Ghana	*Gbomo ke wala*	1953	Stories	Ga
p'Bitek, J. P. Okot 1931–	Uganda	*Lak tar miyo kinyero wi lobo*	1953	Novel	Luo/English
Senyatsi, C. P. 1921–	S. Africa	*Maroba*	1953	Novel	No. Sotho
Sissoko, Fily-Dabo 1900–1964	Mali	*Crayons et portraits*	1953	Verse	French
Themba, Daniel 1924–1969	S. Africa	"Mob Passion"	1953	Story	English
Abedi, Sheikh 1924–1964	Tanzania	*Sheria za Kutunga Mashairi, na Diwani ya Amri*	1954	Verse	Swahili
Akar, J. J. 1927–	Sierra Leone	*Valley Without Echo*	1954	Play	English
Beti, Mongo 1932–	Cameroon	*Ville Cruelle*	1954	Novel	French
Diakhaté, Lamine 1928–	Sengegal	*Le joie d'un continent*	1954	Verse	French
Fula, Arthur 1908–1966	S. Africa	*Johannie giet die beeld*	1954	Novel	Afrikaans
Joachim, Paulin 1931–	Dahomey	*Un nègre raconte*	1954	Verse	French
Malonga, Jean 1907–	Congo, Braz.	*La légende de M'Pfoumou Ma Mazono*	1954	Novel	French
Mama, Goodwill 1925–	S. Africa	*Indyebo kaXhosa*	1954	Verse	Xhosa
Maunick, Edouard J. 1931–	Mauritius	*Les oiseaux du sang*	1954	Verse	Poetry
Mbiti, J. S. 1931–	Kenya	*Matunga and His Story*	1954	Autobio.	English/ Kikamba
Mesatywa, Ezra 1909–1960	S. Africa	*Izaci namaqhalo esiXhosa*	1954	Folklore	Xhosa
Mohapeloa, Josias M. 1914–	Lesotho	*Mosikong oa thabana ea Borata*	1954	Verse	So. Sotho
Ntloko, President Mthetho 1914–	S. Africa	*Ighashu*	1954	Verse	Zulu
Sakubita, M. M. ca. 1930–	Zambia	*Liswanelo Za luna li lu siile*	1954	Story	Lozi
Sengat-Kuo, François 1931–	Cameroon	*Fleurs de latérite*	1954	Verse	French
Abubakar, Alhaji Sir Tafewa 1912–1966	Nigeria	*Shaihu Umar*	1955	Novel	Hausa
Ananou, David ca. 1930–	Togo	*Le fils du fétiche*	1955	Novel	French
Codjoe, Thomas ca. 1925	Ghana	stories and poetry in *Voice of Kushara*	1955*	Verse and stories	English
Coulibaly, A. S. 1933–	Upper Volta	*Les rives du Tontombili*	1955	Novel	French
de Andrade, Mário 1928–	Angola	poetry in various collections, etc.	1955*	Verse	Kimbundu/ Portuguese
Mariano, Gabriel 1928–	Cape Verde	stories and poems in *Claridade*	1955*	Verse and stories	Portuguese
Mathieu, Jean ca. 1930–	Zaïre	*La consultation de midi*	1955	Novel	French
Mohapi, Michael 1926–	Lesotho	*Sebobolane*	1955	Verse	So. Sotho
Nkabinde, Abram ca. 1925–	S. Africa	*Die Biene Maya* (Afrikaans title)	1955	Trans.	Zulu

African Authors

Author	Country	Work	Date	Genre	Language(s)
Rakoma, Joseph 1915–	S. Africa	Mathakgoleng ga bo Hlogokgolo	1955	Novel	No. Sotho
Sam, Gilbert ca. 1930–	Ghana	A Drunkard's Positive Action	1955	Novelettes	English
Sinda, Martial ca. 1930–	Congo Braz.	Premier chant du départ	1955	Verse	French
Soyinka, Oluwole 1934–	Nigeria	The Invention	1955	Play	English
U Tam'si, Tchicaya 1931–	Congo, Braz.	Le mauvais sang	1955	Verse	French
António, Mário 1934–	Angola	Poesias	1956	Verse	Portuguese
Bomela, Bertrand 1928–	S. Africa	Umntu akanambulelo	1956	Novel	Xhosa
Dazana, S. 1905–	S. Africa	Ukufika kukaMadodano (prize 1956, published 1957)	1956	Novel	Xhosa
Diop, David 1927–1960	Senegal	Coups de pilon	1956	Verse	French
Gonçalves, António A. ca. 1920	Cape Verde	Pródiga	1956	Novelette	Portuguese
Henshaw, James E. 1924–	Nigeria	A Man of Character	1956	Play	English
Khaketla, Caroline ca. 1918–	Lesotho	Mosali eo u 'neileng eena	1956	Play	So. Sotho
Kunene, Mazisi 1930–	S. Africa	poems in various journals	1956	Verse	Zulu/ English
Maboko, F. M. ca. 1920–	S. Africa	Aggrey wa Afrika	1956	Trans.	Tsonga
Matip, Benjamin 1932–	Cameroon	Afrique nous t'ignorons	1956	Novel	French
Musa, Hajji Ismail 1919–	Somalia	Kikmad soomaali	1956	Verse and tales	Somali
Nénékhaly-Camara, Condetto 1930–	Guinea	Lagunes	1956	Verse	French
Ogali, Ogali Agu 1931–	Nigeria	Veronica, My Daughter	1956	Play	English
Osório, Ernesto F. ca. 1930–	Angola	Calema	1956	Verse	Portuguese
Oyono, Ferdinand 1929–	Cameroon	Une vie de boy	1956	Novel	French
Sembène, Ousmane 1923–	Senegal	Le docker noir	1956	Novel	French
Akinsemoyin, Kunle ca. 1930–	Nigeria	poems in Anthology of West African Verse and journals	1957	Verse	English
Badian, Seydou 1928–	Mali	Sous l'orage	1957	Novel	French
Kayper-Mensah, A. W. 1923–	Ghana	poems in various collections	1957*	Verse	English
Margarido, Maria Manuela 1926–	São Tomé	Alto como o silêncio	1957	Verse	Portuguese
Mensah, Toussaint ca. 1935–	Togo	Courages	1957	Verse	French
Milheiros, Mário 1916–	Angola	Entre negrose corsarios	1957	Romance	Portuguese
Mqhaba, Alton 1928–	S. Africa	Hayi ke beth' iinto zomhlaba	1957	Stories	Xhosa
Ngcobo, M. J. 1928–	S. Africa	Inkungu maZulu	1957	Novel	Zulu
Ngubane, Jordan 1917–	S. Africa	Uvalo Lwezinhlonzi	1957	Novel	Zulu
Nkrumah, Francis Kwame 1909–1972	Ghana	Ghana: The Autobiography of Kwame Nkrumah	1957	Autobio.	English

Author By Category

Author	Country	Work	Date	Genre	Language(s)
Ntsanwisi, Hudson 1920–	S. Africa	*Masungi, m'fana ka Maxele*	1957	Novel	Tsonga
Okara, Gabriel 1921–	Nigeria	poems in *Black Orpheus* magazine	1957	Verse	English
Olisah, Sunday 1936–1964	Nigeria	*The World Is Hard*	1957	Novelette	English
Paris, Prince Modupe 1901–	Guinea	*I Was a Savage*	1957	Autobio.	English
Ramathe, A. C. J. 1907–1958	S. Africa	*Tsepo*	1957	Novel	So. Sotho
Achebe, Chinua 1930–	Nigeria	*Things Fall Apart*	1958	Novel	English
Adali-Mortty, G. ca. 1920–	Ghana	poems in *Voices of Ghana*	1958	Verse	English
Babalola, Soloman ca. 1930–	Nigeria	*Pàsán sìnà*	1958	Play	Yoruba
Brew, Kwesi 1928–	Ghana	poems in *Voices of Ghana*	1958	Verse	English
Chidyausiku, Paul ca. 1935–	Rhodesia	*Nhoroondo dzukuwanana*	1958	Stories	Shona
Chitepo, H. W. T. 1923–	Rhodesia	*Soko Risina Musoro*	1958	Verse	Shona
Cissé, Emile ca. 1930–	Guinea	*Faralako*	1958	Novel	French
Gicaru, Mugo 1920–	Kenya	*Land of Sunshine*	1958	Novel	English
Mulikita, Fwanyanga 1928–	Zambia	*Batili ki mwanaka*	1958	Stories	Lozi/English
N'djok, Kindengue ca. 1925–	Cameroon	*Kel'lam, fils d'Afrique*	1958	Novel	French
Phatudi, Cedric 1912–	S. Africa	*Tladi wa dikgati*	1958	Novel	No. Sotho
Aluko, Timothy 1918–	Nigeria	*One Man, One Wife*	1959	Novel	English
Bâ, Mallam A. H. ca. 1920–	Mali	Bambara tales in *Black Orpheus* magazine	1959	Folktales	French
Casely-Hayford, Adelaide 1868–1959	Sierra Leone	Autobiography	1959	Autobio.	English
Dos Santos, Marcellino 1929–	Mozambique	poetry published in Soviet Union in Russian	1959	Verse	Portuguese
Lesoro, Ephraim A. 1929–	S. Africa	*Raneketso tsa bana*	1959	Verse	So. Sotho
Maimo, A. O. ca. 1940–	Cameroon	*I Am Vindicated*	1959	Play	English
Makiwane, T. X. 1930–	S. Africa	*They Call Us Jim*	1959*	Story	English
Massaki, André ca. 1915–	Angola	*Nsamu a Nsiamiudele*	1959	Novel	Kikongo
Morel, Marion ca. 1935–	S. Africa	"Girls About Town"	1959*	Story-journalism	English
Mzamane, Godfrey 1909–	S. Africa	*Izinto zodidi*	1959	Novel	Xhosa
Ngani, Marcus 1932–	S. Africa	*Abantwana bethu*	1959	Novel	Xhosa
Owono, Joseph ca. 1932–	Cameroon	*Tante Belle*	1959	Novel	French
Philombe, René ca. 1934–	Cameroon	*La passerelle divine*	1959	Folklore	French
Syad, William 1930	Somalia	*Khamsine*	1959	Verse	French/English
Weakly, John M. 1923–	Rhodesia	*Kumazivandadzoka*	1959	Novel	Shona

521

African Authors

Author	Country	Work	Date	Genre	Language(s)
1960—1972:					
Abdulla, Muhammed ca. 1940–	Kenya	*Mzimu wa Watu we Kale*	1960	Novel	Swahili
Andrade, Costa 1936–	Angola	"Um conto igual a muitos"	1960	Story	Portuguese
Bamboté, Pierre 1932–	Central African Republic	*La poésie est dans l'histoire*	1960	Verse	French
Bhêly-Quénum, Olympe 1928–	Dahomey	*Un piège sans fin*	1960	Novel	French
Cole, R. W. 1907–	Sierre Leone	*Kossoh Town Boy*	1960	Autobio.	English
Conton, W. F. 1925–	The Gambia	*The African*	1960	Novel	English
da Silveira, Onésimo 1935–	Cape Verde	*Toda a gente fala: Sim, senhor.*	1960	Verse	Portuguese
Dembele, Sidiki ca. 1930	Mali	*Les inutiles*	1960	Novel	French
Domingues, Mário 1899–	São Tomé	*Menino entre gigantes*	1960	Novel	Portuguese
Epanya-yondo, Elolongué 1930–	Cameroon	*Kamerun! Kamerun!*	1960	Verse	French
Freire, Albuquerque 1935–	Mozambique	*O livro dos sonetos*	1960	Verse	Portuguese
Guma, Samson M. ca. 1923–	S. Africa	*Morena Mohlomi, mor'a Monyane*	1960	Novel	So. Sotho
Hutchinson, Alfred 1924–	S. Africa	*Road to Ghana*	1960	Autobio.	English
Jabavu, Noni Helen 1919–	S. Africa	*Drawn in Colour*	1960	Novel	English
Kumalo, Peter E. 1929–	S. Africa	stories in various journals	1960*	Stories	English
Loba, Aké 1927–	Ivory Coast	*Kocoumbo, l'étudiant noir*	1960	Novel	French
Maimane, J. Arthur 1932–	S. Africa	"Just a Tsotsi"	1960	Story	English
Makouta-Mboukou, J. P. 1929–	Congo, Braz.	"Les initiés"	1960*	Story	French
Markwei, Matei ca. 1925–	Ghana	"Life in our Village" in *An African Treasury*	1960	Verse	English
Miranda, Nuno de ca. 1930–	Cape Verde	*Cais de ver partir*	1960	Verse	Portuguese
Niane, Djibril Tasmir ca. 1920	Mali	*Soundjata ou l'épopée Mandingue*	1960	Legend	French
Ogbalu, Fred ca. 1920	Nigeria	*Amanala Igbo*	1960	Folklore	Igbo
Vieira, Luandino 1937–	Angola	*A cicade e a infância*	1960	Stories	Portuguese
Burns-Ncamashe, Sipo 1920–	S. Africa	*Masibaliselane*	1961	Verse	Xhosa
Clark, John P. 1935–	Nigeria	*Song of a Goat*	1961	Play	English
da Cruz, Viriato 1928–	Angola	*Colectânea de poemas*	1961	Verse	Portuguese
Dáskalos, Alexandre 1924–1961	Angola	*Poesias*	1961	Verse	Portuguese
Fafunwa, Babs ca. 1940	Ghana	articles in various journals	1961*	Journalism	English
Gbadamosi, Bakare 1930–	Nigeria	*Oriki*	1961	Verse	Yoruba
Jacinto, António 1924–	Angola	*Poemas*	1961	Verse	Portuguese

Author	Country	Work	Date	Genre	Language(s)
Jeboda, Joshua ca. 1930–	Nigeria	*Olowolaiyemo*	1961	Novel	Yoruba
Kane, Sheikh Hamidou 1928–	Senegal	*L'aventure ambiguë*	1961	Novel	French
Koffi, R. A. ca. 1935–	Ivory Coast	*Les dernières paroles de Koime*	1961	Novel	French
Koné, Maurice 1932–	Ivory Coast	*La guirlande des verbes*	1961	Verse	French
Lara Filho, Ernesto 1932–	Angola	*Picada de Marimbondo*	1961	Verse	Portuguese
Lima, Manuel 1935–	Angola	*Kissange: poemas*	1961	Verse	Portuguese
Makumi, Joel ca. 1945–	Kenya	*The Children of the Forest*	1961	Novel	English
Matshikiza, Todd 1922–1968	S. Africa	*Chocolates for My Wife*	1961	Autobio.	English
Mvomo, Rémy Gilbert ca. 1945–	Cameroon	*Nancy in Blooming Youth*	1961	Story	English/ French
Nortje, Kenneth Arthur 1942–1970	S. Africa	poems in *Black Orpheus* magazine	1961	Verse	English
Nxumalo, Otty E. 1938–	S. Africa	*Ikusasa alaziwa*	1961	Novel	Zulu
Nyunaï, Jean-Paul 1932–	Cameroon	*La nuit de ma vie*	1961	Verse	French
Nzekwu, Onuora 1928–	Nigeria	*Wand of Noble Wood*	1961	Novel	English
Oyônô-mbia, Guillaume 1939–	Cameroon	*Three Suitors* (first performed in French version in 1961)	1961	Play	French/ English
Pederek, Simon ca. 1930–	Ghana	"Vulture" in *An African Treasury*	1961	Verse	English
Randrianarisoa, Pierre ca. 1920–	Malagasy	*Premiers visages*	1961	Verse	French/ Malagasy
Touré, Sadan-Moussa ca. 1932–	Guinea	*Les premières guinéades. Contes, légendes de chez nous*	1961	Verse	French
Traoré, Mamadou 1916–	Guinea	*Vers la liberté*	1961	Verse	French
Uzodinma, Edmund 1936–	Nigeria	*Brink of Dawn: Stories of Nigeria*	1961	Stories	English
Ademola, Frances ca. 1930–	Ghana	*Reflections: Nigerian Prose and Verse*	1962	Anthology	English
Anahory, Terêncio 1934–	Cape Verde	*Caminho longe*	1962	Verse	Portuguese
Bã, Oumar 1900–	Mauritania	"Dix-huit poemes peuls moderns"	1962	Verse	French/Peul
Bognini, Joseph 1936–	Ivory Coast	*Ce dur appel de l'espoir*	1962	Verse	French
Boni, Nazi 1910–1969	Upper Volta	*Crépuscule des temps anciens*	1962	Novel	French
Chum, Haji ca. 1920–	Kenya	*Utenzi wa vita vya Uhud*	1962	Epic-tale	Swahili
de Graft, Joe ca. 1932–	Ghana	*Visitors from the Past*	1962	Play	English
Ekwere, John ca. 1930–	Nigeria	"Rejoinder"	1962	Verse	English
Ladipo, Duro ca. 1930–	Nigeria	*Oba Moro*	1962	Play	Yoruba
La Guma, Alex 1925–	S. Africa	*A Walk in the Night*	1962	Novel	English
Lutuli, Chief Albert 1898–1967	S. Africa	*Let My People Go*	1962	Autobio.	English
Machaka, Samson 1932–	S. Africa	*Mehlodi ya polelo*	1962	Verse	Tswana

African Authors

Author	Country	Work	Date	Genre	Language(s)
Makwala, Silpha ca. 1930–	S. Africa	*Kgasane* and *Tselakgopo*	1962	Novel	No. Sotho
Malembe, Timothée ca. 1935–	Zaïre	*Le mystère de l'enfant*	1962	Novel	French
Martins, Ovídio de Sousa 1928–	Cape Verde	*Caminhada*	1962	Verse	Portuguese
Matsepe, Oliver Kgadine 1962–	S. Africa	*Sebata-kgome*	1962	Novel	Tswana
Matthews, James 1929–	S. Africa	*Azikwelwa* (published in Swedish)	1962	Stories	English/ Swedish
Moroke, Samson 1912–	S. Africa	*Pusô yaga kgosi Farao*	1962	Play	Tswana
Ndao, Cheik A. ca. 1940–	Senegal	*Kaïrée*	1962	Verse	French/ Wolof/ English
Ndelu, Bethuel B. 1927–	S. Africa	*Mageba lazihlonza*	1962	Play	Zulu
Nokan, Charles 1937–	Ivory Coast	*Le soleil noir point*	1962	Verse	French
Okigbo, Christopher 1932–1967	Nigeria	*Heavensgate*	1962	Verse	English
Olagoke, David ca. 1935–	Nigeria	*The Incorruptible Judge*	1962	Play	English
Opara, Ralph C. 1933–	Nigeria	"Lagos Interlude"	1962	Essay	English
Owoyele, David ca. 1935–	Nigeria	"The Will of Allah"	1962	Story	English
Ramokgopa, Herbert ca. 1920	S. Africa	*Ditaba tsa dipoko-le tse dingwe*	1962	Stories	No. Sotho
Romano, Luís ca. 1935–	Cape Verde	*Famintos. Romance de um povo*	1962	Novel	Portuguese
Segun, Mabel ca. 1938–	Nigeria	"The Unfinished House"	1962	Journalism	Portuguese
Seid, Joseph 1927–	Chad	*Au Tchad sous les étoiles*	1962	Stories	French
Stephen, Felix N. 1925–	Nigeria	*The Life Story of Boys and Girls*	1962	Novelette	English
Ali, Andullah ca. 1940–	Somalia	"To Arms"	1963	Verse	Somali
Brutus, Dennis 1924–	S. Africa	*Sirens, Knuckles, Boots*	1963	Verse	English
Dogbeh-David, Richard ca. 1935–	Dahomey	*Les eaux du Mono*	1963	Verse	French
Edyang, Ernest ca. 1936–	Nigeria	*Emotan of Benin*	1963	Play	English
Ferreira, António B. ca. 1938–	Guinea, Bissau	"Infância"	1963	Verse	Portuguese
Horatio-Jones, E. B. B. 1930–	Nigeria	short stories in various journals	1963	Stories	English and publishes in German
Ikelle-Matiba, Jean 1936–	Cameroon	*Cette Afrique-là*	1963	Novel	French
Mathivha, Matshaya Edward	S. Africa	*Tsha ri vhone*	1963	Novel	Venda
Medeiros, António 1931–	São Tomé	"Meu canto Europa"	1963	Verse	Portuguese
Mkize, E. E. N. 1931–	S. Africa	poetry in *Izimpophoma zomphefumulo*	1963	Verse	Zulu
Modisane, "Bloke" 1923–	S. Africa	*Blame Me on History*	1963	Novel	English
Moiloa, James J. 1916–	S. Africa	*Dipale le metlae*	1963	Stories	So. Sotho

Author	Country	Work	Date	Genre	Language(s)
Njau, Rebecca 1932–	Kenya	*The Scar* and *In The Round Chain*	1963	Plays	English
Nwankwo, Nkem 1936–	Nigeria	*Panda*	1963	Novel	English
Nyerere, Julius 1922–	Tanzania	*Juliuz Caesar*	1963	Trans.	Swahili
Rabu, Wad Hasad ca. 1920–	Sudan	oral poetry	1963	Verse	Arabic
Rive, Richard 1931–	S. Africa	*African Songs*	1963	Stories	English
Rotimi, Olawale ca. 1940–	Nigeria	*To Stir the God of Iron*	1963	Play	English
Tsegaye, Gabre-Medhin 1935–	Ethiopia	*Tewodros*	1963	Play	Amharic
Aig-Imoukhuede, Frank 1935–	Nigeria	*Ikeke*	1964	Play	English
Awoonor, Kofi 1935–	Ghana	*Rediscovery and Other Poems*	1964	Verse	English
Bart-Williams, Gaston 1938–	Sierra Leone	*Poems*	1964	Verse	English
Bemba, Sylvain ca. 1930–	Congo, Braz.	"La Chambre Noire"	1964	Story	French
Craveirinha, José 1922–	Mozambique	*Chigubo*	1964	Verse	Portuguese
Easmon, Raymond ca. 1930–	Sierra Leone	*Dear Parent and Ogre*	1964	Play	English
Gatheru, Reuel 1925–	Kenya	*Child of Two Worlds*	1964	Autobio.	English
Honwana, Luís 1942–	Mozambique	*Nos matámos o cão-tinhosa*	1964	Stories	Portuguese
Iroaganachi, J. O. ca. 1940–	Nigeria	"I'm Afraid of the Night"	1964	Story	English
Kariuki, Joseph 1931–	Kenya	*Ode to Mzee*	1964	Verse	English
Egbuna, Obi ca. 1942–	Nigeria	*Wind Versus Polygamy*	1964	Novel	English
Konadu, Samuel Asare 1932–	Ghana	*Wizard of Asamang*	1964	Novelette	English
Ngugi, James 1938–	Kenya	*Weep Not, Child*	1964	Novel	English
Nkosi, Lewis 1935–	S. Africa	*The Rhythm of Violence*	1964	Play	English
Ntuyahaga, Mgr. Lord Bishop ca. 1910–	Rwanda	"The Departure and Return of the Cattle in Burundi"	1964	Story	Rwanda
Nzouankeu, Jacques ca. 1940–	Cameroon	*L'agent spécial*	1964	Play	French
Makgaleng, Mamagase ca. 1930–	S. Africa	*Tswala e a ja*	1964	Play	No. Sotho
Mazrui, Ali Al'Amin 1933–	Kenya	"The United Nations and Some African Political Attitudes"	1964	Schol.	English
Moumouni, Abdou ca. 1920–	Niger	*Education in Africa* (originally in French)	1964	Schol.	French
Odeku, E. L. ca. 1937–	Nigeria	*Twilight Out of the Night*	1964	Verse	English
Peters, Lenrie 1932–	The Gambia	*Poems*	1964	Verse	English
Sellassie, Sahle 1936–	Ethiopia	*Shinega's Village, Scenes of Ethiopian Life*	1964	Novel	Amharic
Sidahome, Joseph 1917–1963	Nigeria	*Stories of the Benin Empire*	1964	Folklore	English

African Authors

Author	Country	Work	Date	Genre	Language(s)
Sow, Alpha ca. 1935	Guinea	C'est simple (poèmes ou paroles	1964	Verse	French
Sutherland, Efua 1924–	Ghana	Edufa	1964	Play	English
Tiendrébéogo, Yamba 1907–	Upper Volta	Chez le Larhalle	1964	Folklore	French
Wonodi, Okogbule 1936–	Nigeria	Icheke and Other Poems	1964	Verse	English
Abruquah, Joseph ca. 1940–	Ghana	The Catechist	1965	Novel	English
Aidoo, Christina ca. 1942–	Ghana	The Dilemma of a Ghost	1965	Play	English
Akpan, Ntieyong Udo ca. 1942–	Nigeria	The Wooden Gong	1965	Novel	English
Apronti, Jawa 1940–	Ghana	poetry in Transition magazine, mid 1960's	1965*	Verse	English
Arkhurst, Frederick S. ca. 1920–	Ghana	"Renascent Africa"	1965	Essay	English
Ashenafi, Kebede 1937–	Ethiopia	Confession	1965	Novel	English
Brand, Dollar ca. 1935–	S. Africa	poetry in various journals	1965*	Verse	English
Chacha, Tom ca. 1940–	Tanzania	"The Road to Mara"	1965	Story	English
Egudu, Romanus ca. 1930–	Nigeria	poetry in various journals	1965*	Verse	English
Euba, Femi ca. 1935	Nigeria	The Game	1965	Play	English
Ijimere, Obotunde 1930–	Nigeria	Eda	1965	Play	Yoruba
Ike, Vincent C. 1931–	Nigeria	Toads for Supper	1965	Novel	English
Kimenye, Barbara ca. 1940–	Uganda	Kalasanda	1965	Stories	English
Komey, E. A. 1927–	Ghana	poetry in various journals	1965*	Verse	English
Kinyanjui, Peter ca. 1940	Kenya	Third Party Insurance	1965	Play	English
Lufti, Ali Sayed 1950–	Sudan	poetry in African/ English Literature	1965	Verse	Shukria-Arabic
M'Baye, Annette (Mme) ca. 1940–	Senegal	Poèmes africaines	1965	Verse	French
Motsisi, Moses 1931–	S. Africa	"Riot" in Pan African Short Stories	1965	Story	English
Nagenda, John 1938–	Uganda	"And This, At Last"	1965	Story	English
Nganthojeff, Job 1940–	Cameroon	Mélange	1965	Verse	French
Nicol, Abioseh 1924–	Sierra Leone	The Truly Married Woman	1965	Stories	English
Okafor-Omali, Dilim ca. 1940–	Nigeria	A Nigerian Villager in Two Worlds	1965	Folklore	English
Omara, Tom 1946–	Uganda	The Exodus	1965	Play	English
Parkes, Frank 1932–	Ghana	Songs from the Wilderness	1965	Verse	English
Taiwo, Oladele ca. 1935–	Nigeria	The King's Heir	1965	Stories	English
Tshakatumba, Matala M. ca. 1940–	Zaïre	poetry in Afrique journal and others	1965	Verse	French
Vaughan, J. Koyinda 1927–	Nigeria	"Africa and the Cinema"	1965	Essay	English

526

Author By Category

Author	Country	Work	Date	Genre	Language(s)
Amadi, Elechi 1934–	Nigeria	*The Concubine*	1966	Novel	English
Bunseki, A. Fukiau kia 1934–	Zaïre	*Dingo-Dingo*	1966	Verse	Kikongo
Dipoko, Mbella Sonne 1936–	Cameroon	*A Few Nights and Days*	1966	Novel	English
Dongmo, Jean ca. 1945–	Cameroon	poetry in various journals	1966	Verse	French
Fonseca, Mário A. 1939–	Cape Verde	"Quando a vida nascer"	1966	Verse	Portuguese
Gatanya, James 1945–	Kenya	*The Battlefield*	1966	Play	English
Guèye, Youssouf 1928–	Mauritania	poetry in various publications	1966	Verse	French
Henries, Mrs. A. Doris Banks ca. 1930–	Liberia	essays in various works and journals	1966	Essays	English
Higo, Aig ca. 1942–	Nigeria	poetry in various publications	1966	Verse	English
Hiheteh, R. K. ca. 1940?–	Ghana	*Painful Road to Kadjebi*	1966	Novel	English
Kachingwe, Aubrey 1926–	Malawi	*No Easy Task*	1966	Novel	English
Lopes, Henri 1937–	Zaïre	poems in *New Sum of Poetry from the Negro World*	1966	Verse	French
Menga, Guy ca. 1940–	Congo Braz.	*La marmite de Koka-Mbala*	1966	Play	French
Mezu, Sebastian 1941–	Nigeria	*The Tropical Dawn*	1966	Verse	English
Munonye, John 1929–	Nigeria	*The Only Son*	1966	Novel	English
Mwalilino, Katoki ca. 1942–	Malawi	"The Awakening Malawi on July 6th 1964"	1966	Verse	English
Nassir, Ahmad ca. 1890–	Kenya	*Poems from Kenya, Gnomic Verses in Swahili* (in trans.)	1966	Verse (published in English)	Swahili
Ndu, Pol N. 1940–	Nigeria	"Ritual Dance"	1966	Verse	English
Njoroge, James 1933–	Kenya	*Tit for Tat*	1966	Play	English
Nogar, Rui 1933–	Mozambique	poems in *Notícias de Bloqueio* and other journals	1966	Verse	Portuguese
Nwapa, Flora 1931–	Nigeria	*Efuru*	1966	Novel	English
Obenga, Théophile-Joseph	Congo, Braz.	poems in *New Sum of Poetry from the Negro World*	1966	Verse	French
Ogot, Grace 1930–	Kenya	*The Promised Land*	1966	Novel	English
Okpaku, Joseph ca. 1935–	Nigeria	*Born Astride the Grave*	1966	Play	English
Ologoudou, Emile 1935–	Dahomey	poems in *New Sum of Poetry from the Negro World*	1966	Verse	French
Osogo, John ca. 1930–	Kenya	*The Bride Who Wanted a Special Present*	1966	Stories	English
Pliya, Jean ca. 1935–	Dahomey	*Kondo le requin*	1966	Play	French
Ramala, Joseph 1915–	S. Africa	*Leeto la Mokriste*	1966	Trans.	No. Sotho

527

African Authors

Author	Country	Work	Date	Genre	Language(s)
Samkange, Stanlake 1922–	Rhodesia	On Trial for My Country	1966	Novel	English
Selormey, Francis 1927–	Ghana	The Narrow Path	1966	Novel	English
Sumaili, Gabriel ca. 1935	Zaïre	Aux flancs de l'équateur	1966	Verse	French
Ukoli, Neville 1940–	Nigeria	The Twins of the Rain Forest	1966	Novel	English
Valente, Malangatana 1936–	Mozambique	poems in Black Orpheus magazine	1966	Verse	Portuguese
Wade, Amadou ca. 1940–	Senegal	Présence. Poèmes	1966	Verse	French
Agunwa, Clement ca. 1940–	Nigeria	More Than Once	1967	Novel	English
Asalache, Khadambi 1934–	Kenya	A Calabash of Life	1967	Novel	English
Diallo, Assane Y. ca. 1940	Senegal	Leyd'am	1967	Verse	Peul/French
Djoleto, Amu 1929–	Ghana	The Strange Man	1967	Novel	English
Duodu, Cameron 1937–	Ghana	The Gab Boys	1967	Novel	English
Dzovo, Emmanuel 1915–	Ghana	Salami and Musa	1967	Novel	English
Kahiga, Samuel ca. 1940–	Kenya	Potent Ash	1967	Stories	English
Kibera, Leonard ca. 1940–	Kenya	Potent Ash	1967	Play	English
Kouadio-Tiacoh, Gabriel ca. 1920–	Ivory Coast	La légende de N'zi le Grand, Guerrier d'Afrique	1967	Folklore	French
Mutabaruka, Jean-Baptiste 1937–	Rwanda	poem in African Writing Today	1967	Verse	French
Nakasa, Nathaniel 1937–1965	S. Africa	stories in South African Writing and other publications	1967	Stories	English
Odinga, Ajuma Oginga 1912–	Kenya	Not Yet Uhuru	1967	Autobio.	English
Ogunyemi, Wale ca. 1932–	Nigeria	Born With Fire on His Head	1967	Play	English/ Yoruba
Oniororo, Niyi ca. 1942–	Nigeria	Lagos Is a Wicked Place	1967	Stories	English
Owuor, Henry ca. 1938–	Kenya	"Luo Songs" in an Introduction to African Literature	1967	Essay	English/ Luo
Rubadiri, James David ca. 1930–	Tanzania	No Bride Price	1967	Novel	English
Siriman, Cissoko ca. 1940—	Mali	Ressac de nous-mêmes	1967	Verse	French
Armah, Ayi Kwei 1938–	Ghana	The Beautyful Ones Are Not Yet Born	1968	Novel	English
Balogun, Ola 1945–	Nigeria	Shango and Le roi-éléphant	1968	Plays	French
Bebey, Francis 1929–	Cameroon	Embarras et Cie	1968	Verse	French
Bukenya, A. S. 1944–	Uganda	The Secret	1968	Play	English
Echeruo, Michael 1946–	Nigeria	Mortality	1968	Verse	English
Ikiddeh, Ime 1938–	Nigeria	Blind Cyclos	1968	Plays	English

Author	Country	Work	Date	Genre	Language(s)
Kay, Kwesi ca. 1940–	Ghana	*Maame*	1968	Play	English
Kayira, Legson ca. 1940–	Malawi	*The Looming Shadow*	1968	Novel	English
Kironde, Erisa ca. 1940–	Uganda	*The Shadow of the Glen*	1968	Play	English
Leshoai, Benjamin 1920–	S. Africa	*Masilo's Adventures* *The Wake*	1968 1968	Stories Play	English English
Maddy, Pat 1936–	Sierra Leone	*Yon Kon*	1968	Play	English
Mukasa-Balikuddembre, J. ca. 1943–	Uganda	*The Famine* and *The Mirror*	1968	Plays	English/ Luganda/ Runyoro
Oculi, Okello 1942–	Uganda	*Orphan* (in free verse) and *Prostitute* (prose)	1968 1968	Novel Novel	English English
Ofori, Henry 1925–	Ghana	*The Literary Society*	1968	Play	English
Ouologuem Yambo 1940–	Mali	*Le devoir de violence*	1968	Novel	French
Palangyo, Peter 1939–	Tanzania	*Dying in the Sun*	1968	Novel	English
Pieterse, Cosmo 1930–	South West Africa	"Ballad of the Cells"	1968	Verse	English
Rwakyaka, Proscovia ca. 1945–	Uganda	poems in *New Voices of the Commonwealth*	1968	Verse	English
Serumaga, Robert 1939–	Uganda	*A Play*	1968	Play	English
Tati, Jean-Baptiste 1938–	Congo, Braz.	*Poèmes de la mer*	1968	Verse	French
Tulya-Muhika, Sam ca. 1940–	Uganda	*Born To Die*	1968	Play	English
Wachira, Godwin ca. 1938–	Kenya	*Ordeal in the Forest*	1968	Novel	English
Willis, Jackson 1939–	Tanzania	"Les Rivaux," published in French in French anthology as an extract only	1968	Novelette	French/ English
Asare, Bediako ca. 1930	Ghana	*Rebel*	1969	Novel	English
Boetia, Dugmore ca. 1920	S. Africa	*Familiarity Is the Kingdom of the Lost*	1969	Autobio.	English
Head, Bessie ca. 1940–	Botswana	*When Rain Clouds Gather*	1969	Novel	English
Kgositile, W. K. 1938–	S. Africa	*Spirits Unchained*	1969	Verse	English
Kyei, Kojo G. 1932–	Ghana	*The Lone Voice*	1969	Verse	English
Liyong, Taban Lo 1938–	Uganda	*Fixions*	1969	Stories	English
N'Debeka, Maxime 1944–	Congo, Braz.	*Soleils neufs (Poèmes)*	1969	Verse	French
Ruhumbika, Gabriel 1938–	Tanzania	*Village in Uhuru*	1969	Novel	English
Salih, Tayeb 1929–	Sudan	*Season of Migration to the North*	1969	Novel	Arabic
Soyinka, Kayode ca. 1938–	Nigeria	various plays produced	1969	Plays	English
Taylor, W. H. 1940–	Sierra Leone	*A Poet's Palette*	1969	Verse	English
Umeasiegbu, Rems Nna 1943–	Nigeria	*The Way We Live*	1969	Stories	English

African Authors

Author	Country	Work	Date	Genre	Language(s)
Anozie, Sunday 1942–	Nigeria	*Sociologie du Roman Africaine*	1970	Schol.	French/ English
Farah, Nuruddin ca. 1945–	Somalia	*From a Crooked Rib*	1970	Novel	English
Ibukun, Olu ca. 1945–	Nigeria	*The Return*	1970	Novel	English
Johnson, Lemuel ca. 1935–	Nigeria	stories in various journals	1970*	Stories	English
Kayo, Patrice ca. 1940–	Cameroon	*Hymnes et sagesse*	1970	Verse	French
Mokgatle, Monyadice 1911–	S. Africa	*Naboth Mokgatle of Phokeng*	1970	Autobio.	English
Ndlovu, Joshua 1946–	Rhodesia	"Not Enough"	1970	Story	English
Okpewho, Isadore ca. 1942	Nigeria	*The Victims*	1970	Novel	English
Owomoyela, Oyekan ca. 1935–	Nigeria	*Candles and Incense*	1970	Film script	English
Quaye, Cofie ca. 1947–	Ghana	*Sammy Slams the Gang*	1970	Novel	English
Seruma, Enerico ca. 1940–	Uganda	*The Experience*	1970	Novel	English
Ulasi, Adaora Lily ca. 1945–	Nigeria	*Many Thing You No Understand*	1970	Novel	English
Aduamah, Enos ca. 1940–	Ghana	*Nothing Happens for Nothing*	1971	Novelette	English
Echeruo, Kevin 1946–	Nigeria	poem in *Okike* magazine	1971	Verse	English
Mubitana, Kafungulwa ca. 1930–	Zambia	"Wiko Masquerades"	1971	Essay	English
Mukasa-ssali, Paul 1946–	Uganda	poems in *Poems from East Africa*	1971	Verse	English
Mulaisho, Dominic 1933–	Zambia	*The Tongue of the Dumb*	1971	Novel	English
Obiechina, E. N. 1933–	Nigeria	"Song of a Madman"	1971	Verse	English
Okeke, Uche 1935–	Nigeria	*Ibo Folktales*	1971	Folklore	English
Sankawulo, Wilton ca. 1945–	Liberia	"The Evil Forest"	1971	Story	English
Sey, Kofi ca. 1925–	Ghana	poetry in *Messages: Poems from Ghana*	1971	Verse	English
Thage, Johannes 1950–	S. Africa	"It Came Like a Waterfall"	1971	Story	English
Winful, E. A. ca. 1920–	Ghana	poetry in *Messages: Poems from Ghana*	1971	Verse	English

N. B.

1. Abbreviations:
   Schol. (for scholarship: history, philosophy, political science, anthropology, ethnology, literary criticism, etc.)
   Autobio. (for autobiography)
2. The language or languages in which the author normally wrote or writes, published or publishes in, is (are) given in column 6, the language of the work here specified being cited first.
3. Number of authors in each chronological period:

Pre-18th Century:	9
1700–1799:	11
1800–1899:	34
1900–1919:	29
1920–1939:	64
1940–1959:	172
1960–1972:	261
	580

580 (of which 574 have separate entries; 14 authors merely cited in main text not included in table)

Appendix F

Authors, by Genre

This appendix lists authors by genre. Many authors will be listed under more than one of the headings, so the total will add to more than the number dealt with in this volume. The categories and author counts are as follows: Novelists—219; Storytellers—133; Poets—292; Playrights—106; Journalists—77; Autobiographers/Biographers—43; Scholars/Critics/Essayists/Translators/Folklorists/Letter Writers—149.

Novelists—219

Author	Country	Language(s)
Abdulla, Muhammed Said	Kenya	Swahili
Abrahams, Peter	South Africa	English
Abruquah, Joseph Wilfred	Ghana	English
Achebe, Chinua	Nigeria	English
Acquah, G. R.	Ghana	Fante/English
Aduamah, Enos Yao	Ghana	English
Afawark, Gabra Iyasus	Ethiopia	Amharic
Aguínwa, Clement	Nigeria	English
Akpan, Ntieyong Udo	Nigeria	English
Albasini, João	Mozambique	Portuguese
Alcântara, Osvaldo	Cape Verde	Portuguese
Aluko, Timothy M.	Nigeria	English
Amadi, Elechi	Nigeria	English
Ananou, David	Togo	French
Armah, Ayi Kwei	Ghana	English
Asalache, Khadambi	Kenya	English
Asare, Bediako	Ghana	English
Ashenafi, Kebede	Ethiopia	English
Assis Júnior, António de	Angola	Portuguese
Awoonor, Kofi	Ghana	English
Badian, Seydou Kouyate	Mali	French
Bahelele, Jacques N.	Zaïre	Kikongo
Bebey, Francis	Cameroon	French
Bediako, Kwabena Asare	Ghana	English
Bengani, Redvus Robert	South Africa	Zulu
Beti, Mongo	Cameroon	French
Bhêly-Quénum, Olympe	Dahomey	French
Blay, J. Benibengor	Ghana	English
Boetia, Dugmore	South Africa	English
Bolamba, G.	Zaïre	French
Bomela, Bertrand M.	South Africa	Xhosa
Boni, Nazi	Upper Volta	French

531

Novelists

Author	Country	Language(s)
Casely-Hayford, Joseph Ephraim	Ghana	English
Chafulumira, English William	Malawi	Nyanja
Chidyausiku, Paul	Rhodesia	Shona
Cissé, Emile	Guinea	French
Citashe, I. W. W.	South Africa	Xhosa
Cole, Robert Wellesley	Sierra Leone	English
Conton, William F.	The Gambia	English
Coulibaly, Augustin-Sonde	Upper Volta	French
Dadie, Bernard Binlin	Ivory Coast	French
Danzana, S.	South Africa	Xhosa
de Graft, Joe Coliman	Ghana	English
Dembele, Sidiki	Mali	French
Dhlomo, Herbert Issac	South Africa	Zulu/English
Dhlomo, Rolfus, R. R.	South Africa	Zulu
Diagne, Ahmadou Mapaté	Senegal	French
Diallo, Bakary	Senegal	French
Diop, Massyla	Senegal	French
Dipoko, Mbella Sonne	Cameroon	English
Djoleto, Amu	Ghana	English
Domingues, Mário	São Tomé	Portuguese
Duarte, Fauste	Cape Verde	Portuguese
Dube, John L.	South Africa	Zulu
Duodu, Cameron	Ghana	English
Dzovo, Emmanuel	Ghana	English
Easmon, Raymond Sarif	Sierra Leone	English
Egbuna, Obe Benue	Nigeria	English
Ekwensi, Cyprian	Nigeria	English
Fagunwa, Chief Daniel O.	Nigeria	Yoruba
Farah, Nuruddin	Somalia	English
Fula, Arthur Nuthall	South Africa	Afrikaans
Gicaru, Muga	Kenya	English
Gonçalves, António Aurélio	Cape Verde	Portuguese
Guma, Enoch Stephen	South Africa	Xhosa
Guma, Samson Mbizo	South Africa	English/Southern Sotho
Hazoumé, Paul	Dahomey	French
Head, Bessie	Botswana	English
Heruy, Walda Sellase	Ethiopia	Amharic
Hihetah, Robert Kofi	Ghana	English
Horatio-Jones, Edward B.	Nigeria	English
Ibukun, Olu	Nigeria	English
Ike, Vincent Chukwuemeka	Nigeria	English
Jabavu, Noni Helen Nontando	South Africa	English
Jeboda, Joshua Ofuwafemi	Nigeria	Yoruba
Johnson, Lemuel	Sierra Leone	English
Jolobe, James J.	South Africa	Xhosa
Jordan, Archibald Campbell	South Africa	Xhosa
Kachingwa, Aubrey	Malawi	English
Kane, Sheikh (or Cheikh) Hamidou	Senegal	French
Karlee, Varfelli	Liberia	English
Kayira, Legson	Malawi	English
Khaketla, Caroline N.	Lesotho	Southern Sotho
Kibera, Leonard	Kenya	English
Kitereza, Aniceti	Tanzania	Kikerebe/Swahili
Koffi, R. A.	Ivory Coast	French
Konadu, Samuel	Ghana	English
Koné, Maurice	Ivory Coast	French
La Guma, Alex	South Africa	English
Laye, Camara	Guinea	French
Lesoro, Ephraim A. S.	South Africa	Southern Sotho

Novelists

Author	Country	Language(s)
Liyong, Taban Lo	Uganda	English
Loba, Aké	Ivory Coast	French
Lomami-Tshibamba, Paul	Zaïre	French
Lopes, Manuel António	Cape Verde	Portuguese
Made, Emmanuel H. A.	South Africa	Zulu
Madiba, Moses Josiah	South Africa	Northern Sotho
Mahtama, Sellase Walda	Ethiopia	Amharic
Maile, Mallane Libakeng	Lesotho	Southern Sotho
Makonnen, Endalkacaw (or Makwannen)	Ethiopia	Amharic
Makouta-Mboukou, Jean-Pierre	Congo (Braz.)	French
Makumi, Joel	Kenya	English
Makwala, Silpha Phaladi Ngwako	South Africa	Northern Sotho
Malembe, Timothée	Zaïre	French
Malonga, Jean	Congo (Braz.)	French
Masondo, Titus Z.	South Africa	Zulu
Mathieu, Jean	Zaïre	French
Mathivha, Matshaya	South Africa	Venda
Matip, Benjamin	Cameroon	French
Matsepe, Oliver Kgadine	South Africa	Tswana
Mazrui, Ali Al'Amin	Kenya	English
Menga, Guy	Congo	French
Mensah, Toussaint Viderot	Togo	French
Mezu, Sebastien Okechukwa	Nigeria	English
Milheiros, Mário	Angola	Portuguese
Mncwango, Leonhard L. J.	South Africa	Zulu
Modisane, ("Bloke") William	South Africa	English
Mofolo, Thomas Mokopu	Lesotho	Southern Sotho
Moikangoa, Cornelius E. R.	Lesotho	Southern Sotho
Molefe, Arthur Ignatius	South Africa	Zulu
Moloto, Davidson Pelman	South Africa	Tswana
Mopeli-Paulus, Attwell Sidwell	Lesotho	Southern Sotho/English
Moroke, Samson Alexander	South Africa	Tswana
Moumouni, Abdou	Niger	French
Mpashi, Stephen Andrea	Zambia	Bemba
Mqhayi, Samuel Edward	South Africa	Xhosa
Mseleku, Malcolm Raymond	South Africa	Zulu
Mthembu, Robert Hiram	South Africa	Zulu
Mulaisho, Dominic	Zambia	English
Munonye, John	Nigeria	English
Mutombo, Dieudonné	Zaïre	French
Mvomo, Rémy Gilbert Médou	Cameroon	French
Mzamane, Godfrey I. M.	South Africa	Xhosa
Naigiziki, J. V. S.	Rwanda	French
Ndawo, Henry Masila	South Africa	Xhosa
Ndhambi, Etienne Penyisi	South Africa	Tsonga
N'Djok, Kindengve	Cameroon	French
Ngani, Marcus Aurelius	South Africa	Xhosa
Ngcobo, Moses John	South Africa	Zulu
Ngubane, Jordan Khush	South Africa	Zulu
Ngugi, James Thongio'o	Kenya	English
Nicol, Abioseh	Sierra Leone	English
Njau, Rebecca	Kenya	English
Nketia, John Hanson Kwabena	Ghana	Assante-Twi
Nkomba, Lester L.	Malawi	Nyanja
Nokan, Charles	Ivory Coast	French
Ntara, Samuel Yosia	Malawi	Cewi-Nyanja
Ntsane, Kemuele Edward	South Africa	Southern Sotho
Ntsanwisi, Hudson William	South Africa	Tsonga
Nwankwo, Nkem	Nigeria	English

533

Novelists

Author	Country	Language(s)
Nwapa, Flora	Nigeria	English
Nxumalo, James Alfred	South Africa	Zulu
Nxumalo, Natalie Victoria (neé Nxaba)	South Africa	Zulu
Nxumalo, Otty Exrom	South Africa	Zulu
Nyembezi, Cyril Lincoln	South Africa	Zulu
Nzekwu, Onuora	Nigeria	English
Nzouankeu, Jacques Mariel	Cameroon	French
Obeng, R. E.	Ghana	English
Obianim, Sam J.	Ghana	Ewe
Ogali, Ogali Agu	Nigeria	English
Ogot, Grace Akinye	Kenya	English
Okara, Gabriel Inomotimi	Nigeria	English
Okpaku, Joseph	Nigeria	English
Okpewho, Isadore	Nigeria	English
Olisah, Sunday Okenwa	Nigeria	English
Oniororo, Niyi	Nigeria	English
Ouologuem, Yambo	Mali	French
Owono, Joseph	Cameroon	French
Oyônô, Ferdinand Léopold	Cameroon	French
Palangyo, Peter K.	Tanzania	English
Paris, Prince Modupe	Guinea	English
p'Bitek, J. P. Okot	Uganda	Lwo/English
Peters, Lenrie	Gambia	English
Phatudi, Cedric Namedi	South Africa	Northern Sotho
Philombe, René	Cameroon	French
Plaatje, Solomon Tshekiso	South Africa	Tswana/English
Pliya, Jean	Dahomey	French
Quaye, Cofie	Ghana	English
Rajemisa-Raolison, Régis	Malagasy	Malgache/French
Rakoma, Joseph	South Africa	Northern Sotho
Ramaila, Epafras M.	South Africa	Northern Sotho
Ramathe, A. C. J.	South Africa	Southern Sotho
Randrianarisoa, Pierre	Malagasy	Malgache/French
Ribas, Oscar Bento	Angola	Portuguese
Rive, Richard	South Africa	English
Robert, Shaaban	Tanzania	Swahili
Robinary, Michel F.	Malagasy	French
Romano, Luís	Cape Verde	Portuguese
Rubadiri, James D.	Malawi	English
Ruhumbika, Gabriel	Tanzania	English
Sadji, Abdoulaye	Senegal	French
Sakubita, M. M.	Zambia	Lozi
Salih, Tayeb	Sudan	Arabic
Samkange, Stanlake	Rhodesia	English
Sankawulo, Wilton	Liberia	English
Seboni, Michael O. M.	Botswana	Tswana
Segoete, Everitt L.	Lesotho	Southern Sotho
Sellassie, Sahle	Ethiopia	Amharic/English
Selormey, Francis	Ghana	English
Sembéne, Ousmane	Senegal	French
Senyatsi, Charles P.	South Africa	Northern Sotho
Seruma, Eneriko	Uganda	English
Serumaga, Robert	Uganda	English
Sinxo, Guybon B.	South Africa	Xhosa
Sissoko, Fily-Dabo	Mali	French
Socé, Ousmane Diop	Senegal	French
Soyinka, Wole	Nigeria	English
Swaartbooi, Victoria	South Africa	Xhosa
Travele, Moussa	Mali	French

Novelists

Author	Country	Language(s)
Tsegaye, Gabre-Medhin	Ethiopia	Amharic/English
Tutuola, Amos	Nigeria	English
Ukoli, Neville M.	Nigeria	English
Ulasi, Adaora Lily	Nigeria	English
Uzodinma, Edmund C. C.	Nigeria	English
Vilakazi, Benedict	South Africa	Zulu
Wachira, Godwin	Kenya	English
Walda, Giyorgis	Ethiopia	Amharic
Weakly, John Marangwanda	Rhodesia	Shona
Yoftahe, Neguse	Ethiopia	Amharic

Poets—292

Authors	Country	Language(s)
Abdillaahi, Muuse	Somalia	Somali
Abedi, Sheikh Kaluta	Tanzania	Swahili
Abrahams, Peter	S. Africa	English
Abu Dulama Ibn Al-Djaun	Iraq	Arabic
Achebe, Chinua	Nigeria	English
Acquah, G. R.	Ghana	Fante/English
Adali-Mortty, Geormbeeyi	Ghana	English
Afawark, Gabra Iyasus	Ethiopia	Amharic
Aidoo, Christina	Ghana	English
Aig-Imoukhuede, Frank	Nigeria	English
Akinsemoyin, Kunle	Nigeria	English
Alcântara, Osvaldo	Cape Verde	Portuguese
Alegre, Caetano da Costa	São Tomé	Portuguese
Ali, Abdullah Gureh	Somalia	Somali
Anahory, Terêncio	Cape Verde/Guinea (Bissau)	Portuguese
Andrade, Costa	Angola	Portuguese
Antar	Arabia	Arabic
António, Mário	Angola	Portuguese
Apronti, Jawa	Ghana	English
Arkhurst, Frederick	Ghana	English
Armah, Ayi Kwei	Ghana	English
Armattoe, Raphael	Ghana	English
Asalache, Khadambi	Kenya	English
Awoonor, Kofi	Ghana	English
Azevedo, Pedro Corsino de	Cape Verde	Portuguese
Bâ, Oumar	Mauritania	French, Fulani
Badian, Seydou Kouyaté	Mali	French
Bahelele, Jacques N.	Zaïre	Kikongo
Bambote, Pierre Makambo	Central African Republic	French
Bankole, Timothy	Sierra Leone	English
Barbosa, Domingos Caldas	Brazil	Portuguese
Barbosa, Jorge	Cape Verde	Portuguese
Bart-Williams, Gaston	Sierra Leone	English
Bebey, Francis	Cameroon	French
Bessa Victor, Geraldo	Angola	Portuguese

African Authors

Poets

Author	Country	Language(s)
Blay, J. Benibengor	Ghana	English
Bognini, Joseph Miézan	Ivory Coast	French
Bokwe, John Knox	South Africa	Xhosa
Bolamba, Antoine-Roger	Zaïre	French
Brand, Dollar	South Africa	English
Brew, Kwesi	Ghana	English
Brutus, Dennis	South Africa	English
Bunseki, A. Fukiau kia	Zaïre	Kikongo
Burns-Ncamashe, Sipo	South Africa	Xhosa
Caluza, Reuben Tolakele	South Africa	Zulu
Cardoso, António	Angola	Portuguese
Cardoso, Pedro Monteiro	Cape Verde	Portuguese
Casely-Hayford, Gladys May	Ghana	English
Chitepo, Herbert	Rhodesia	Shona
Clark, John Pepper	Nigeria	English
Codjoe, Thomas A.	Ghana	English
Couchoro, Félix	Togo	French
Coulibaly, Augustin-Sonde	Upper Volta	French
Craveirnha, José	Mozambique	Portuguese
da Cruz, Viriate	Angola	Portuguese
Dadie, Bernard Binlin	Ivory Coast	French
da Matta, Joaquim Dias	Angola	Portuguese
Danquah, Joseph	Ghana	English
Dáskalos, Alexandre	Angola	Portuguese
da Silveira, Onésimo	Cape Verde	Portuguese
de Andrade, Mário Coelho	Angola	Portuguese/Kimbundu
de Graft, Joe Coliman	Ghana	English
Dei-Anang, Michael Francis	Ghana	English
Dempster, Roland Tombekai	Liberia	English
de Noronha, Rui	Mozambique	Portuguese
de Sousa, Noémia Carolina	Mozambique	Portuguese
Dhlomo, Herbert Isaac	South Africa	Zulu/English
Diakhaté, Lamine	Senegal	French
Diallo, Assane Y.	Senegal	Peul/French
Diallo, Bakary	Senegal	French
Diop, David Mandessi	Senegal and France	French
Dipoko, Mbella Sonne	Cameroon	English
Disengomoko, A. Emile	Zaïre	Kikongo
Djoleto, Amu	Ghana	English
Dogbeh-David, Richard	Dahomey	French
Dongmo, Jean Louis	Cameroon	French
dos Santos, Marcelino	Mozambique	Portuguese
Duodu, Cameron	Ghana	English
Duuh, Ali	Somalia	Somali
Echeruo, Kevin	Nigeria	English
Echeruo, Michael J. C.	Nigeria	English
Egharevba, Chief Jacob U.	Nigeria	Edo/English
Egudu, Romanus	Nigeria	English
Ekwere, John	Nigeria	English
Epanya-Yondo, Elolongué	Cameroon	French
Espirito Santo, Alda de	São Tomé	Portuguese
Faarah, Nuur	Somalia	Somali
Ferreira, António Baticã	Guinea (Bissau)	Portuguese
Ferreira, José da Silva Maia	Angola	Portuguese
Fonseca, Aguinaldo B.	Cape Verde	Portuguese

536

Poets

Author	Country	Language(s)
Fonseca, José Mário Alberto	Cape Verde	Portuguese
Freire, Albuquerque	Mozambique	Portuguese
Fula, Arthur Nuthall	South Africa	Afrikaans
Gabra, Egzi 'abeher	Ethiopia	Amharic
Gbadamosi, Bakare A.	Nigeria	English
Germacaw, Takla Hararyat	Ethiopia	Amharic
Gqoba, William W.	South Africa	Xhosa
Guèye, Youssouf	Mauritania	French
Guma, Samson Mbizo	South Africa	Southern Sotho/English
Hardallo	The Sudan	Arabic
Henries, Mrs. A. Doris B.	Liberia	English
Higo, Aig	Nigeria	English
Ilmi, Bownderi	Somalia	Somali
Jabavu, Davidson Don T.	South Africa	Xhosa/English
Jacinto, António	Angola	Portuguese
Joachim, Paulin	Dahomey	French
Johnson, Lemuel	Sierra Leone	English
Jolobe, James James	South Africa	Xhosa
Jordan, Archibald C.	South Africa	Xhosa
Kabbada, Mika'el	Ethiopia	Amharic
Kagame, Abbé Alexis	Rwanda	Rwanda/French
Karim, Ahmed Awad	Somalia	Shukria-Arabic
Kariuki, Joseph	Kenya	English
Kayo, Patrice	Cameroon	French
Kayper-Mensah, Albert W.	Ghana	English
Keita, Fodeba	Guinea	French
Kgositsile, William K.	South Africa	English
Khaketla, Bennett Makalo	Lesotho	Southern Sotho
Khaketla, Caroline N.	Lesotho	Southern Sotho
Komey, Ellis Ayetey	Ghana	English
Koné, Maurice	Ivory Coast	French
Kumalo, Peter E.	South Africa	English
Kunene, Mazisi Raymond	South Africa	Zulu
Kyei, Kojo Gyinaye	Ghana	English
Lara Filho, Ernesto	Angola	Portuguese
Latino, Juan	Guinea and Spain	Latin
Lemos, Virgílio de	Mozambique	Portuguese
Lesoro, Ephraim A. S.	South Africa	Southern Sotho
Lima, Manuel	Angola	Portuguese
Liyong, Taban Lo	Uganda	English
Lopes, Henri	Zaïre	French
Lopes, José da Silva	Cape Verde	Portuguese
Lopes, Manuel António	Cape Verde	Portuguese
Lufti, Ali Sayed	The Sudan	Arabic/English
Machaka, Samson R. M.	South Africa	Northern Sotho
Maddy, Pat Abisodu	Sierra Leone	English
Made, Emmanuel H. A.	South Africa	Zulu
Madiba, Moses Josiah	South Africa	Northern Sotho
Mahammed, Sheikh 'Abdille	Somalia	Somali
Maimo, A. O.	Cameroon	English
Malutama, Rémy	Zaïre	Kikongo

African Authors

Poets

Author	Country	Language(s)
Mama, Goodwill Soya	South Africa	Xhosa
Mangoaela, Zakea Dolphin	Lesotho	Southern Sotho
Margarido, Maria Manuela	Príncipe	Portuguese
Mariano, Gabriel	Cape Verde	Portuguese
Markwei, Matei	Ghana	English
Martins, Ovídio de Sousa	Cape Verde	Portuguese
Massaki, André	Angola	Kikongo
Matip, Benjamin	Cameroon	French
Matsepe, Oliver K.	South Africa	Tswana
Maunick, Edouard J.	Mauritius	French
M'Baye, Annette (Mme.)	Senegal	French
Mbiti, John Samuel	Kenya	Kikamba/English
Medeiros, António A. T.	São Tomé	Portuguese
Mensah, Toussaint Viderot	Togo	French
Mezu, Sebastien O.	Nigeria	English
Milheiros, Mário	Angola	Portuguese
Miranda, Nuno de	Cape Verde	Portuguese
Mire, Ismaa'iil	Somalia	Somali
Modisane, "Bloke"	South Africa	English
Mohapeloa, Josias M.	Lesotho	Southern Sotho
Mohapi, Michael M.	Lesotho	Southern Sotho
Moiloa, James Jantjies	South Africa	Southern Sotho
Molefe, Arthur I.	South Africa	Zulu
Moore, Bai Tamia(h) J.	Liberia	English
Mopeli-Paulus, Attwell S.	Lesotho	Southern Sotho/English
Moroke, Samson A.	South Africa	Tswana
Mpashi, Stephen A.	Zambia	Bemba
Mqhayi, Samuel Edward	South Africa	Xhosa
Mseleku, Malcolm R.	South Africa	Zulu
Mubitana, Kafungulwa	Zambia	English
Mukasa-ssali, Paul	Uganda	English
Musa, Hajji Ismail G.	Somalia	Somali
Mutabaruka, Jean B.	Rwanda	French
Muyaka (Haji al Ghassaniy)	Kenya	Swahili
Mvomo, Rémy Gilbert M.	Cameroon	French/English
Mwalilino, Katoki	Malawi	English
Mwana, Kupona	Kenya	Swahili
Nagenda, John	Uganda	English
Nassir, Ahmad	Kenya	Swahili
Ndao, Cheik A.	Senegal	French/English/Wolof
Ndawo, Henry Masila	South Africa	Xhosa
N'debeka, Maxime	Congo (Braz.)	French
Ndhambi, Etienne P.	South Africa	Tsonga
Ndu, Pol N.	Nigeria	English
Nénékhaly-Camara, Condetto	Guinea	French
Neto, António A.	Angola	Portuguese
Ngangu, Jackson	Zaïre	Kikongo
Ngani, Alfred Z.	South Africa	Xhosa
Nganthojeff, Job	Cameroon	French
Ngidi, Andreas Henry	South Africa	Zulu
Nicol, Abioseh	Sierra Leone	English
Nogar, Rui	Mozambique	Portuguese
Nokan, Charles	Ivory Coast	French
Nortje, K. Arthur	South Africa	English
Nsimba, Samuel A.	Zaïre	Kikongo
Ntloko, President M.	South Africa	Zulu
Ntsane, Kemuele Edward	South Africa	Southern Sotho
Ntsikana	South Africa	Xhosa

Poets

Author	Country	Language(s)
Ntsiko, Jonas A.	South Africa	Xhosa
Nunes, António	Cape Verde	Portuguese
Nxumalo, Otty Ezrom	South Africa	Zulu
Nyembezi, Cyril L.	South Africa	Zulu
Nyunaï, Jean-Paul	Cameroon	French
Obenga, Théophile-J.	Congo (Braz.)	French
Obiechina, Emmanuel	Nigeria	English
Oculi, Okello	Uganda	English
Odeku, Emmanuel L.	Nigeria	English
Okara, Gabriel I.	Nigeria	English
Okeke, Uche	Nigeria	English
Okigbo, Christopher	Nigeria	English
Ologoudou, Emile	Dahomey	French
Opara, Ralph C.	Nigeria	English
Osadebay, Dennis C.	Nigeria	English
Osório, Ernesto Cochat	Angola	Portuguese
Ouologuem, Yambo	Mali	French
Parkes, Frank Kobina	Ghana	English
p'Bitek, J. P. Okot	Uganda	Lwo/English
Pederek, Simon	Ghana	English
Peters, Lenrie	The Gambia	English
Pieterse, Cosmo G.	South West Africa	English
Qamaan, Bulhan	Somalia	Somali
Raage, Ugaas	Somalia	Somali
Rabéarivelo, Jean-J.	Malagasy	French/Malagasy
Rabémananjara, J.-J.	Malagasy	French
Rabu, Wad Hasad	The Sudan	Shukria-Arabic
Raditladi, Leetile	Botswana	Tswana
Rajemisa-Raolison, R.	Malagasy	French/Malagasy
Ramaila, Epafras M.	South Africa	Northern Sotho
Ramananato	Malagasy	Malagasy
Ranaivo, Jacques F.	Malagasy	French/Malagasy
Randrianarisoa, P.	Malagasy	French/Malagasy
Ransome-Kuti, Rev. J. J.	Nigeria	Yoruba
Ribas, Oscar Bento	Angola	Portuguese
Rive, Richard	South Africa	English
Robert, Shaaban	Tanzania	Swahili
Robinary, Michel F.	Malagasy	French
Romano, Luís	Cape Verde	Portuguese
Rubadiri, James D.	Malawi	English
Rukn Al-din	Egypt	Arabic
Rwakyaka, Proscovia	Uganda	English
Saiyid, Abdallah	Tanzania	Swahili
Saiyid, Abu Bakr	Kenya	Swahili
Saiyid-U'mar	Kenya	Swahili
Salaan, Arrabey	Somalia	Somali
Sancho, Ignatius	born on shipboard, lived in England	English
Saoli, Jacob R.	South Africa	Southern Sotho
Seboni, Michael	Botswana	Tswana
Segun, Mabel J.	Nigeria	English
Sengat-Kuo, François	Cameroon	French
Senghor, Léopold S.	Senegal	French
Sentso, Dyke	South Africa	Southern Sotho

Poets

Author	Country	Language(s)
Sey, Kofi	Ghana	English
Shaikh, Muhyi	Tanzania	Swahili
Shembe, Isaiah	South Africa	Zulu
Sinda, Martial	Congo (Braz.)	French
Sinxo, Guybon B.	South Africa	Xhosa
Siriman, Cissoko	Mali	French
Sissoko, Fily-Dabo	Mali	French
Socé, Ousmane Diop	Senegal	French
Soga, John Henderson	South Africa	Xhosa
Soga, Tiyo	South Africa	Xhosa
Soga, Tiyo Burnside	South Africa	Xhosa
Sontonga, Mankayi E.	South Africa	Xhosa
Sow, Alpha	Guinea	French
Soyinka, Wole	Nigeria	English
Stephen, Felix N.	Nigeria	English
Sumaili, Gabriel	Zaïre	French
Sutherland, Efua	Ghana	English
Syad, William	Somalia	French/English
Tati, Jean-Baptiste	Congo (Braz.)	French
Tavares, Eugénio	Cape Verde	Portuguese
Taylor, W. H.	Sierra Leone	English
Tenreiro, Francisco	São Tomé	Portuguese
Tiendrébéogo, Yamba	Upper Volta	French
Touré, Sadan-Moussa	Guinea	French
Traoré, Mamadou	Guinea	French
Travele, Moussa	Mali	French
Tsegaye, Gabre-Medhin	Ethiopia	Amharic/English
Tshakatumba, M. M.	Zaïre	French
U Tam'si, Tchicaya	Congo (Braz.)	French
Valente, Malangatana	Mozambique	Portuguese
Vieira, Luandino	Angola	Portuguese
Vilakazi, Benedict	South Africa	Zulu
Vingadio, Timotéo	Zaïre	Kikongo
Wade, Amadou Mustapha	Senegal	French
Walda, Giyorgis	Ethiopia	Amharic
Wheatley, Phillis	Senegal and U.S.A.	English
Winful, E. A.	Ghana	English
Wonodi, Okogbule	Nigeria	English
Yoftahe, Neguse	Ethiopia	Amharic
Ziryab	Iraq and Islamic Spain	Arabic

Scholars/Critics/Essayists/Translators/ Folklorists/Letter Writers—149

Author	Country	Language(s)
Achebe, Chinua	Nigeria	English
Acquah, G. R.	Ghana	Fante/English
Ademola, Frances	Ghana	English

540

Scholars/Critics/Essayists/Translators/
Folklorists/Letter Writers

Author	Country	Language(s)
Aduamah, Enos Yao	Ghana	English
Afawark, Gabra Iyasus	Ethiopia	Amharic
Aggrey, James	Ghana	English
Akpan, Ntieyong Udo	Nigeria	English
Amo, Antonius G.	Ghana	Latin
Anozie, Sunday A.	Nigeria	French/English
Armattoe, Raphael	Ghana	English
Ashenafi, Kebede	Ethiopia	English
Bâ, Mallam Amadou	Mali	French/Bambara/Fulani
Ba, Oumar	Mauritania	Fulani/French
Bába, Ahmad al Tinbukhti	Mali	Arabic
Bankole, Timothy	Sierra Leone	English
Bessa Victor, Geraldo	Angola	Portuguese
Bunseki, A. Fukiau	Zaïre	Kikongo
Busia, Kofi Abrefa	Ghana	English
Capitein, Jacobus	Unknown, lived in Holland	Latin
Cardoso, Pedro	Cape Verde	Portuguese
Casely-Hayford, J. E.	Ghana	English
Chum, Haji	Kenya	Swahili
Coulibaly, Augustin	Upper Volta	French
da Matta, Joaquim	Angola	Portuguese
Danquah, Joseph B.	Ghana	English/ Akuapem-Twi
da Silveira, Onésimo	Cape Verde	Portuguese
de Andrade, Mário	Angola	Portuguese/ Kimbundu
Desewo, P. M.	Ghana	Ewe
Disengomoko, A. E.	Zaïre	Kikongo
Dube, John L.	South Africa	Zulu
Egharevba, Jacob	Nigeria	Edo/English
Egudu, Romanus	Nigeria	English
Fuze, Magema	South Africa	Zulu
Gonçalves, António	Cape Verde	Portuguese
Hazoumé, Paul	Dahomey	French
Henries, A. Doris B.	Liberia	English
Hinawy, Sheikh M. A.	Kenya	Swahili
Ikiddeh, Ime	Nigeria	English
Ishak	Ethiopia	Amharic
Jabavu, Davidson D. T.	South Africa	Xhosa/English
Jabavu, John Tengo	South Africa	Xhosa
Jolobe, James J.	South Africa	Xhosa
Jordan, A. C.	South Africa	Xhosa
Kagame, Abbé Alexis	Rwanda	Rwanda/French
Kati, Mahmud	Mali	Arabic
Kayo, Patrice	Cameroon	French
Keita, Fodeba	Guinea	French/Malinké
Kenyatta, Jomo	Kenya	Kikiyu/English
Khaketla, Bennett	Lesotho	Southern Sotho
Kitereza, Aniceti	Tanzania	Kikerebe/Swahili
Latino, Juan	Guinea/Spain	Latin
Lemos, Virgílio de	Mozambique	Portuguese
Lufti, Ali Sayed	The Sudan	Arabic/English
Lutuli, Chief Albert	South Africa	English
Maboko, F. M.	South Africa	Tsonga
Macauley, Jeannette	Sierra Leone	English
Mahtama, Sellase Walda	Ethiopia	Amharic
Maile, Mallane L.	Lesotho	Southern Sotho

Scholars/Critics/Essayists/Translators/
Folklorists/Letter Writers

Author	Country	Language(s)
Makiwane, Tennyson X.	South Africa	English
Makouta-Mboukou, J.-P.	Congo (Braz.)	French
Mama, Goodwill	South Africa	Xhosa
Mangoaela, Zakea Dolphin	Lesotho	Southern Sotho
Mariano, Gabriel	Cape Verde	Portuguese
Massaki, André	Angola	Kikongo
Masondo, Titus Z.	South Africa	Zulu
Mazrui, Ali Al'Amin	Kenya	English
Mbelle, Isaiah B.	South Africa	Xhosa/English
Mesatywa, Ezra W.	South Africa	Xhosa
Mezu, Sebastien	Nigeria	English
Milheiros, Mário	Angola	Portuguese
Miranda, Nuno de	Cape Verde	Portuguese
Mockerie, Parmenas	Kenya	English
Mofokeng, Sophonia M.	South Africa	Southern Sotho
Mokgatle, Monyadice M.	South Africa	English
Mokone, Nowen G.	South Africa	Tswana
Molefe, Arthur I.	South Africa	Zulu
Molema, Moliri S.	Botswana	English
Moore, Bai Tamiah	Liberia	English
Mopeli-Paulus, Attwell	Lesotho	Southern Sotho/ English
Moumouni, Abdou	Niger	French
Mphahlele, Ezekiel L.	South Africa	English
Mqhayi, Samuel E.	South Africa	Xhosa
Mubitana, Kafungulwa	Zambia	English
Muhammad wad Daif Allah	The Sudan	Arabic
Mukasa, Ham	Uganda	Luganda
Musa, Hajji Ismail G.	Somalia	Somali
Mzamane, Godfrey	South Africa	Xhosa
Nagenda, John	Uganda	English
Ndawo, Henry M.	South Africa	Xhosa
Ndhambi, Etienne P.	South Africa	Tsonga
Nénékhaly-Camara, C.	Guinea	French
Ngani, Alfred Z.	South Africa	Xhosa
Nkabinde, Abram C.	South Africa	Zulu
Nketia, John H. K.	Ghana	Assante-Twi
Nkosi, Lewis	South Africa	English
Nkrumah, Kwame	Ghana	English
Nokan, Charles	Ivory Coast	French
Ntara, Samuel Yosia	Malawi	Cewa-Nyanja
Ntloko, President M.	South Africa	Zulu
Ntsanwisi, Hudson W.	South Africa	Tsonga
Nxumalo, James Alfred	South Africa	Zulu
Nxumalo, Otty Ezrom	South Africa	Zulu
Nyabongo, Prince Akike	Uganda	Swahili/English
Nyembezi, Cyril L.	South Africa	Zulu
Nyerere, Julius K.	Tanzania	Swahili/English
Obiechina, Emmanuel N.	Nigeria	English
Odinga, Ajuma Oginga	Kenya	English
Ogbalu, Fred Chidozie	Nigeria	Ibo/English
Ojike, Mazi Mbounu	Nigeria	English
Okafer-Omali, Dilim	Nigeria	English
Okeke, Uche	Nigeria	English
Okpaku, Joseph	Nigeria	English
Osogo, John	Kenya	English
Owuor, Henry	Kenya	Luo
Paris, Prince Modupe	Guinea	English

Scholars/Critics/Essayists/Translators/ Folklorists/Letter Writers

Author	Country	Language(s)
p'Bitek, J. P. Okot	Uganda	Lwo/English
Phatudi, Cedric N.	South Africa	Northern Sotho
Philombe, René	Cameroon	French
Plaatje, Solomon T.	South Africa	Tswana/English
Quénum, Maximilien P.	Dahomey	French
Rajemisa-Raolison, Régis	Malagasy	Malagasy/French
Rakoma, Joseph	South Africa	Northern Sotho
Ramaila, Epafras M.	South Africa	Northern Sotho
Ranaivo, Jacques F.	Malagasy	Malagasy/French
Randrianarisoa, Pierre	Malagasy	Malagasy/French
Reindorf, Rev. C. C.	Ghana	English
Ribas, Oscar Bento	Angola	Portuguese
Romano, Luís	Cape Verde	Portuguese
Rubadiri, James D.	Malawi	English
Sadi, Abdurahman as-	Mali	Arabic
Sancho, Ignatius	Unknown/lived in England	English
Sarbah, John Mensah	Ghana	English
Seboni, Michael O. M.	Botswana	Tswana
Segoete, Everitt L.	Lesotho	Southern Sotho
Sekese, Azariele	Lesotho	Southern Sotho
Sengat-Kuo, François	Cameroon	French
Senghor, Léopold Sédar	Senegal	French
Sidahome, Joseph E.	Nigeria	English
Soga, John Henderson	South Africa	Xhosa
Soga, Tiyo	South Africa	Xhosa
Sow, Alpha	Guinea	French
Sutherland, Efua	Ghana	English
Taiwo, Oladele	Nigeria	English
Tiendrébéogo, Yamba	Upper Volta	French
Traoré, Mamadou	Guinea	French
Vaughan, J. Koyinda	Nigeria	English
Vilakazi, Benedict	South Africa	Zulu
Vimbe, John M.	South Africa	Xhosa
Vingadio, Timotéo	Zaïre	Kikongo
Yilma, Darasa	Ethiopia	Amharic

Storytellers—133

Author	Country	Language(s)
Abubakar, Imam	Nigeria	Hausa
Abubakar, Sir Tafawa Balewa	Nigeria	Hausa
Achebe, Chinua	Nigeria	English
Adoki, G. E.	Ghana	English
Aidoo, Christina	Ghana	English
Akar, John Joseph	Sierre Leone	English
Akinsemoyin, Kunle	Nigeria	English
Armah, Ayi Kwei	Ghana	English
Bahelele, Jacques N.	Zaïre	Kikongo
Bamboté, Pierre Makambo	Central African Republic	French
Barbosa, Jorge (Vera-Cruz)	Cape Verde	Portuguese
Bart-Williams, Gaston	Sierra Leone	English
Bebey, Francis	Cameroon	French
Bemba, Sylvain	Congo (Braz.)	French

Storytellers

Author	Country	Language(s)
Bessa Victor, Geraldo	Angola	Portuguese
Beti, Mongo	Cameroon	French
Bhêly-Quénum, Olympe	Dahomey	French
Brew, Kwesi	Ghana	English
Chacha, Tom	Tanzania	English
Chidyausiku, Paul	Rhodesia	Shona
Clark, John Pepper	Nigeria	English
Codjoe, Thomas A.	Ghana	English
Conton, William F.	The Gambia	English
Craveirnha, José	Mozambique	Portuguese
da Matta, Joachim Dias	Angola	Portuguese
Danquah, Mabel (née Dove)	Ghana	English
da Silveira, Onésimo	Cape Verde	Portuguese
de Almeida, José Maria	São Tomé	Portuguese
de Andrade, Mário Coelho	Angola	Portuguese/Kimbundu
de Graft, Joe Coliman	Ghana	English
Dei-Anang, Michael Francis	Ghana	English
·Dias, João	Mozambique	Portuguese
Diop, Birago Ismail	Senegal	French
Easmon, Raymond Sarif	Sierra Leone	English
Egbuna, Obe Benue	Nigeria	English
Ekwensi, Cyprian	Nigeria	English
Ekwere, John	Nigeria	English
Farah, Nuruddin	Somalia	English
Gbadamosi, Bakare A.	Nigeria	English
Gonçalves, António Aurélio	Cape Verde	Portuguese
Heruy, Walda Sellase	Ethiopia	Amharic
Honwana, Luís Bernardo	Mozambique	Portuguese
Horatio-Jones, Edward B.	Nigeria	English
Hutchinson, Alfred	South Africa	English
Iroaganachi, J. O.	Nigeria	English
Itayemi, Phebean	Nigeria	English
Johnson, Lemuel	Sierra Leone	English
Jordan, Archibald Campbell	South Africa	Xhosa
Kagara, Malam Abubakar Imam	Nigeria	Hausa
Kagara, Malam Muhammadu Bello	Nigeria	Hausa
Kahiga, Samuel	Kenya	English
Kakaza, Lillith	South Africa	Xhosa
Kibera, Leonard	Kenya	English
Kimenye, Barbara	Uganda	English
Konadu, Samuel	Ghana	English
Kouadio-Tiacoh, Gabriel	Ivory Coast	French
Kumalo, Peter E.	South Africa	English
La Guma, Alex	South Africa	English
Laye, Camara	Guinea	French
Leshoia, Benjamin	South Africa	English
Lesoro, Ephraim A. S.	South Africa	Southern Sotho
Liyong, Taban Lo	Uganda	English
Machado, Pedro Felix	Angola	Portuguese
Maimane, J. Arthur	South Africa	English
Makonnen, Endalkacaw	Ethiopia	Amharic
Makouta-Mboukou, Jean-Pierre	Congo (Braz.)	French
Mariano, Gabriel	Cape Verde	Portuguese
Matthews, James	South Africa	English
Mbiti, John Samuel	Kenya	Kikamba/English
Milheiros, Mário	Angola	Portuguese
Miranda, Nuno de	Cape Verde	Portuguese
Modisane, ("Bloke") William	South Africa	English
Moikangoa, Cornelius E. R.	Lesotho	Southern Sotho
Mokone, Nowen Godratius	South Africa	Tswana

Storytellers

Author	Country	Language(s)
Motsamai, Edward	Lesotho	Southern Sotho
Motsisi, Moses Casey	South Africa	English
Mpashi, Stephen Andrea	Zambia	Bemba
Mphahlele, Ezekiel L.	South Africa	English
Mqhaba, Alton A. M.	South Africa	Xhosa
Mseleku, Malcolm Raymond	South Africa	Zulu
Mulikita, Fwanyanga Matale	Zambia	English/Lozi
Musa, Hajji Ismail Galaal	Somalia	Somali
Nakasa, Nathaniel Ndzivane	South Africa	English
Ndlovu, Joshua	Rhodesia	English
Ngango, Jackson	Zaïre	Kikongo
Ngugi, James	Kenya	English
Niane, Djibril Tamsir	Mali	French
Nicol, Abioseh	Sierra Leone	English
Njoroge, James Kingangi	Kenya	English
Nkosi, Lewis	South Africa	English
Ntantala, Phyllis P.	South Africa	English
Ntuyahaga, Mgr., Lord Bishop of Usumbura	Rwanda	Ruanda
Nxumalo, Henry	South Africa	English
Nyabongo, Prince Akike K.	Uganda	Swahili/English
Obiechina, Emmanuel N.	Nigeria	English
Odoi, Nicholas Akrong	Ghana	Ga
Ofori, Henry	Ghana	English
Ogot, Grace Akinye	Kenya	English
Okara, Gabriel Inomotimi	Nigeria	English
Okeke, Uche	Nigeria	English
Oluwa, I. I.	Nigeria	English
Osogo, John	Kenya	English
Osório, Ernesto Cochat	Angola	Portuguese
Owoyele, David	Nigeria	English
Oyono, Ferdinand Léopold	Cameroon	French
Pliya, Jean	Dahomey	French
Quaye, Cofie	Ghana	English
Ramalia, Epafras M.	South Africa	Northern Sotho
Ramokgopa, Herbert D.	South Africa	Northern Sotho
Ribas, Óscar Bento	Angola	Portuguese
Rive, Richard	South Africa	English
Sadji, Abdoulaye	Senegal	French
Salih, Tayeb	Sudan	Arabic
Sam, Gilbert A.	Ghana	English
Sankawulo, Wilton	Liberia	English
Segun, Mabel J. (née Imoukuede)	Nigeria	English
Seid, Joseph Brahim	Chad	French
Sekese, Azariele	Lesotho	Southern Sotho
Sellassie, Sahle B. M.	Ethiopia	Amharic/English
Sembène, Ousmane	Senegal	French
Senghor, Léopold Sédar	Senegal	French
Sentso, Dyke	South Africa	Southern Sotho
Seruma, Eneriko	Uganda	English
Sissoko, Fily-Dabo	Mali	French
Taiwo, Oladele	Nigeria	English
Thage, Johannes R.	South Africa	English
Themba, Daniel C. D.	South Africa	English
Tutuola, Amos	Nigeria	English
Umeasiegbu, Rems Nna	Nigeria	English
Uzodinma, Edmund C. C.	Nigeria	English
Vieira, Luandino	Angola	Portuguese
Vingadio, Timotéo	Zaïre	Kikongo
Willis, Jackson A. M.	Tanzania	English

545

Playwrights—106

Author	Country	Language(s)
Aidoo, Christina	Ghana	English
Aig-Imoukhuede, Frank	Nigeria	English
Akar, John Joseph	Sierra Leone	English
Babalola, Solomon A. Q.	Nigeria	Yoruba
Badian, Seydou Kouyaté	Mali	French
Balogun, Ola	Nigeria	English/French
Bart-Williams, Gaston	Sierra Leone	English
Bukenya, Augustine S.	Uganda	English
Chidyausiku, Paul	Rhodesia	Shona
Clark, John Pepper	Nigeria	English
Dadié, Bernard Binlin	Ivory Coast	French
de Graft, Joe Coliman	Ghana	English
Dei-Anag, Michael Francis	Ghana	English
Dembele, Sidiki	Mali	French
Dhlomo, Herbert Isaac	South Africa	Zulu, English
Diakhaté, Lamine	Senegal	French
Disengomoko, A. Emile	Zaïre	Kikongo
Easmon, Raymond Sarif	Sierra Leone	English
Edyang, Ernest	Nigeria	English
Egbuna, Obe Benue	Nigeria	English
Ekwere, John	Nigeria	English
Euba, Femi	Nigeria	English
Farah, Nuruddin	Somalia	English
Gatanyu, James	Kenya	English
Germacaw, Takla Hawaryat	Ethiopia	Amharic
Henshaw, James Ene	Nigeria	English
Hutchinson, Alfred	South Africa	English
Ijimere, Obotunde	Nigeria	Yoruba
Ikiddeh, Ime	Nigeria	English
Jolobe, James J.	South Africa	Xhosa
Kabbada, Mika'el	Ethiopia	Amharic
Kay, Kwesi	Ghana	English
Kayper-Mensah, Albert	Ghana	English
Keita, Fodeba	Guinea	French
Khaketla, Bennett Makalo	Lesotho	Southern Sotho
Kibera, Leonard	Kenya	English
Kinyanjui, Peter	Kenya	English
Kironde, Erisa	Uganda	English
Koffi, R. A.	Ivory Coast	French
Ladipo, Duro	Nigeria	Yoruba
Leshoia, Benjamin	South Africa	English
Lesoro, Ephraim A. S.	South Africa	Southern Sotho
Maddy, Pat Abisodu	Sierra Leone	English
Maile, Mallane Libakeng	Lesotho	Southern Sotho
Maimane, J. Arthur	South Africa	English
Maimo, A. O.	Cameroon	English
Makgaleng, Mamagase Macheng	South Africa	Northern Sotho
Makwala, Silpha Phaladi Ngwako	South Africa	Northern Sotho
Mal'aku, Baggosaw	Ethiopia	Amharic
Mathivha, Matshaya	South Africa	Venda
Matip, Benjamin	Cameroon	French
Matshikiza, Todd	South Africa	English
Menga, Guy	Congo (Braz.)	French
Mncwango, Leonhard L. J.	South Africa	Zulu
Mofokeng, Sophonia Machabe	South Africa	Southern Sotho
Mohapi, Michael Molelekoa	Lesotho	Southern Sotho
Moiloa, James Jantjies	South Africa	Southern Sotho
Mopeli-Paulus, Attwell	Lesotho	Southern Sotho/English

Playwrights—106

Author	Country	Language(s)
Moroke, Samson Alexander	South Africa	Tswana
Mukasa-Balikuddembre, Joseph	Uganda	Luganda/Runyoro-Rutoro/ English
Mulikita, Fwanyanga Matale	Zambia	English/Lozi
Nagenda, John	Uganda	English
Naigiziki, J. V. Savério	Rwanda	French
Ndao, Cheik A.	Senegal	French/English/Wolof
N'Debeka, Maxime	Congo (Braz.)	French
Ndebele, Nimrod	South Africa	Zulu
Nénékhaly-Camara, Condetto	Guinea	French
Ngani, Marcus Aurelius	South Africa	Xhosa
Ngugi, James Thongio'o	Kenya	English
Niane, Djibril Tamsir	Mali	French
Njau, Rebecca	Kenya	English
Nketia, John Hanson Kwabena	Ghana	Assante-Twi
Nkosi, Lewis	South Africa	English
Nokan, Charles	Ivory Caost	French
Ntloko, President Nthetho	South Africa	Zulu
Nwankwo, Nkem	Nigeria	English
Nzouankeu, Jacques Mariel	Cameroon	French
Odoi, Nicholas Akrong	Ghana	Ga
Ofori, Henry	Ghana	English
Ogali, Ogali Agu	Nigeria	English
Ogunde, Hubert	Nigeria	Yoruba
Ogunmola, Elijah Kolawole	Nigeria	Yoruba
Ogunyemi, Wale	Nigeria	Yoruba
Okpaku, Joseph	Nigeria	English
Olagoke, David Olu	Nigeria	English
Opara, Tom	Uganda	English
Opara, Ralph C.	Nigeria	English
Owomoyela, Oyekan	Nigeria	English
Oyônô-Mbia, Guillaume	Cameroon	French/English
Phatudi, Cedric Namedi	South Africa	Northern Sotho
Rabemananjara, Jean-Jacques	Malagasy	French
Raditladi, Leetile	Botswana	Tswana
Ranaivo, Jacques F.	Malagasy	Malgache/French
Randrianarisoa, Pierre	Malagasy	French/Malgache
Ribas, Oscar Bento	Angola	Portuguese
Rotimi, Olawale	Nigeria	English/Yoruba
Senyi, Kobina	Nigeria	English
Serumaga, Robert	Uganda	English
Sinxo, Guybon B.	South Africa	Xhosa
Soyinka, Kayode	Nigeria	English
Soyinka, Wole	Nigeria	English
Sutherland, Efua Theodora	Ghana	English
Takla, Hawaryat	Ethiopia	Amharic
Tsegaye, Gabre-Medhin	Ethiopia	Amharic/English
Tulya-Muhika, Sam	Uganda	English
Yoftahe, Neguse	Ethiopia	Amharic

Journalists—77

Author	Country	Language(s)
Aig-Imoukhuede, Frank	Nigeria	English
Akar, John Joseph	Sierra Leone	English
Albasini, João	Mozambique	Portuguese

Journalists

Author	Country	Language(s)
Arkhurst, Frederick S.	Ghana	English
Armah, Ayi Kwei	Ghana	English
Asare, Bediako	Ghana	English
Awolowo, Abafemi Awo	Nigeria	English
Azikiwe, Benjamin N.	Nigeria	English
Bankole, Timothy	Sierra Leone	English
Bhêly-Quénum, Olympe	Dahomey	French
Bokwe, John Knox	South Africa	Xhosa
Bolamba, Antoine-Roger	Zaïre	French
Cardoso, António	Angola	Portuguese
Casely-Hayford, Joseph E.	Ghana	English
Codjoe, Thomas	Ghana	English
Coulibaly, Augustin-Sonde	Upper Volta	French
Craveirnha, José	Mozambique	Portuguese
da Cruz, Viriate	Angola	Portuguese
Danquah, Joseph B.	Ghana	English
Dhlomo, Rolfus R. R.	South Africa	Zulu
Diop, Massyla	Senegal	French
Duodu, Cameron	Ghana	English
Espírito Santo, Alda de	São Tomé	Portuguese
Fafunwa, Babs	Ghana	English
Fonseca, Mário Alberto	Cape Verde	Portuguese
Gqoba, William W.	South Africa	Xhosa
Honwana, Luís Bernardo	Mozambique	Portuguese
Horton, James Africanus	Sierra Leone	English
Jabavu, Davidson Don Tengo	South Africa	Xhosa/English
Jabavu, John Tengo	South Africa	Xhosa
Kachingwe, Aubrey	Malawi	English
Kagara, Malam Abubakar	Nigeria	Hausa
Khaketla, Bennett Makalo	Lesotho	Southern Sotho
Kimenye, Barbara	Uganda	English
Komey, Ellis Ayetey	Ghana	English
Lemos, Virgílio de	Mozambique	Portuguese
Maimane, J. Arthur	South Africa	English
Makiwane, Tennyson Xola	South Africa	English
Margarido, Maria Manuela	Príncipe	Portuguese
Mariano, Gabriel	Cape Verde	Portuguese
Massaki, André	Angola	Kikongo
Matthews, James	South Africa	English
Modisane, "Bloke"	South Africa	English
Mohapi, Michael Molelekoa	Lesotho	Southern Sotho
Morel, Marion	South Africa	English
Mphahlele, Ezekiel L.	South Africa	English
Nakasa, Nathaniel N.	South Africa	English
Ngubane, Jordan K.	South Africa	Zulu/English
Ngugi, James Thongio'o	Kenya	English
Nkabinde, Abram Charles	South Africa	Zulu
Nkosi, Lewis	South Africa	English
Ntantala, Phyllis P.	South Africa	English
Nxumalo, Henry	South Africa	English
Oculi, Okello	Uganda	English
Ofori, Henry	Ghana	English
Ogali, Ogali Agu	Nigeria	English
Okpaku, Joseph	Nigeria	English
Opara, Ralph C.	Nigeria	English
Opara, Ralph C.	Nigeria	English
Parkes, Frank Kobina	Ghana	English
Pereira, José de Fontes	Angola	Portuguese
Rabémananjara, Jean-Jacques	Malagasy	French/Malagasy

Journalists

Author	Country	Language(s)
Rajemisa-Raolison, Régis	Malagasy	Malagasy/French
Rammala, Joseph L.	South Africa	Northern Sotho
Ramokgopa, Herbert D.	South Africa	Northern Sotho
Ranaivo, Jacques F.	Malagasy	Malagasy
Rubusana, Walter B.	South Africa	Xhosa
Sarbah, John Mensah	Ghana	English
Segun, Mabel J.	Nigeria	English
Sellassie, Sahle B. M.	Ethiopia	Amharic/English
Senghor, Léopold Sédar	Senegal	French
Soga, Tiyo	South Africa	Xhosa
Themba, Daniel C. D.	South Africa	English
Vaughan, J. Koyinda	Nigeria	English
Vieira, Luandino	Angola	Portuguese
Vimbe, John M.	South Africa	Xhosa
Wachira, Godwin	Kenya	English
Walda, Giyorgis	Ethiopia	Amharic

Autobiographers/Biographers—43

Author	Country	Language(s)
Ademola, Frances	Ghana	English
Akiga, Benjamin	Nigeria	Tiv
Awolowo, Obafemi Awo	Nigeria	English
Azikiwe, Benjamin N.	Nigeria	English
Bokwe, John Knox	South Africa	Xhosa
Bonne, Nii Kwabena III	Ghana	English
Casely-Hayford, Adelaide	Sierra Leone	English
Casely-Hayford, Joseph Ephraim	Ghana	English
Cugoana, Ottobah	Ghana	English
Gatheru, Reuel John Mugo	Kenya	English
Gicaru, Muga	Kenya	English
Henries, Mrs. A. Doris Banks	Liberia	English
Hutchinson, Alfred	South Africa	English
Kagara, Malam Muhammadu Bello	Nigeria	Hausa
Kayira, Legson	Malawi	English
Lutuli, Chief Albert John	South Africa	English
Made, Emmanuel H. A.	South Africa	Zulu
Mahtama, Sellase Walda	Ethiopia	Amharic
Makonnen, Endalkacaw	Ethiopia	Amharic
Massaki, André	Angola	Kikongo
Matip, Benjamin	Cameroon	French
Modisane, ("Bloke") William	South Africa	English
Mokgatle, Monyadice Moreleba	South Africa	English
Molema, Moliri Silas	Botswana	English
Moore, Bai Tamia (h)	Liberia	English
Mpashi, Stephen Andrea	Zambia	Bemba
Mphahlele, Ezekiel L.	South Africa	English
Mqhayi, Samuel Edward	South Africa	Xhosa
Ngani, Alfred Zwelinzima	South Africa	Xhosa
Nkrumah, Kwame	Ghana	English
Ntara, Samuel Yosia	Malawi	Cewa-Nyanja
Ntsanwisi, Hudson William	South Africa	Tsonga
Nyabongo, Prince Akike	Uganda	Swahili/English
Odinga, Ajuma Oginga	Kenya	English
Ojike, Mazi Mbounu	Nigeria	English

Autobiographers/Biographers

Author	Country	Language(s)
Okafor-Omali, Dilim	Nigeria	English
Paris, Prince Modupe	Guinea	English
Philombe, René	Cameroon	French
Ramaila, Epafras M.	South Africa	Northern Sotho
Robert, Shaaban	Tanzania	Swahili
Sinxo, Guybon B.	South Africa	Xhosa
Umeasiegbu, Rems Nna	Nigeria	English
Vassa, Olaudah Gustavus	Nigeria	English

Appendix G

Authors, by Country of Origin

Number of Authors Cited from Each Country

Angola—22
Botswana—4
Cameroon-19
Cape Verde Islands—18
Central African Republic—1
Chad—1
Congo, Brazzaville—9
Dahomey—7
Ethiopia—15
The Gambia—2
Ghana—55
Guinea, Bissau—1
Guinea—9
Ivory Coast—7

Kenya—29
Lesotho—15
Liberia—5
Malagasy—7
Malawi—7
Mali—11
Mozambique—11
Mauritania—2
Mauritius—1
Niger—1
Nigeria—87
Príncipe (Island of)—1
Rhodesia—5
Rwanda—4

São Tomé (Island of)—6
Senegal—17
Sierra Leone—12
Somalia—13
South Africa—124
Southwest Africa—1
Sudan—6
Tanzania—10
Togo—3
Uganda—15
Upper Volta—3
Zaïre—16
Zambia—5
Other—7

Total: 594, of which 574 are dealt
with in separate entries in the text

Author List, by Country of Origin
Number of authors indicated after name of country

ANGOLA—22

Andrade, Costa
António, Mário
Assis Júnior, António de
Bessa Victor, Geraldo
Cardoso, António
da Cruz, Viriato
da Matta, Cordeiro
Dáskalos, Alexandre
de Andrade, Mário
Ferreira, José da Silva Maia
Jacinto, António
Lara Filho, Ernesto
Lima, Manuel
Machado, Pedro
Massaki, André
Milheiros, Mário
Neto, António A.
Osório, Ernesto Cochat
Pereira, José de Fontes
Ribas, Óscar Bento
Roberto, Alvaro H.
Vieira, Luandino

BOTSWANA—4

Head, Bessie
Molema, Moliri Silas
Raditladi, Leetile
Seboni, Michael

CAMEROON—19

Bebey, Francis
Beti, Mongo
Dipoko, Mbella
Dongmo, Jean Louis
Epanya-Yondo, Elolongué
Kayo, Patrice
Ikello-Matiba, Jean
Maimo, A. O.
Matip,. Benjamin
Mvomo, Rémy Gilbert
N'djok, Kindengue
Nganthojeff, Job
Nyunaí, Jean-Paul
Nzouankeu, Jacques
Owono, Joseph
Oyono, Ferdinand Léopold

Oyônô-Mbia, Guillaume
Philombe, René
Sengat-Kuo, François

CAPE VERDE ISLANDS—18

Alcântara, Osvaldo
Anahory, Terêncio
Azevedo, Pedro
Barbosa, Jorge
Cardosa, Pedro
da Silveira, Onésimo
Duarte, Fausto
Fonseca, Aguinaldo
Fonseca, Mário A.
Gonçalves, António A.
Lopes, José da Silva
Lopes, Manuel
Mariano, Gabriel
Martins, Ovídio
Miranda, Nuno de
Nunes, António
Romano, Luís
Tavares, Eugénio

African Authors

Motsamai, Edward
Segoete, Everitt Lechesa
Sekese, Azariele M.

LIBERIA—5

Dempster, Roland
Henries, Mrs. A. Doris Banks
Karlee, Varfelli
Moore, Bai Tamiah
Sankawulo, Wilton

MALAGASY (MADAGASCAR)—7

Rabearivelo, Jean-Joseph
Rabemananjara, Jean-Jacques
Rajemisa-Raolison, Régis
Ramananato
Ranaivo, Jacques F.
Randrianarisoa, Pierre
Robinary, Michel F.

MALAWI—7

Chafulumira, English W.
Kachingwe, Aubrey
Kayira, Legson
Mkomba, Lester L.
Mwalilino, Katoki
Ntara, Samuel Yosia
Rubadiri, James D.

MALI—11

Bâ, Mallam Amadou Hampaté
Bâba, Ahmad
Badian, Seydou
Dembele, Sidiki
Kati, Mahmud
Niane, Djibril Tamsir
Ouologuem, Yambo
Sadi, Abdulrahman as-
Siriman, Cissoko
Sissoko, Fily Dabo
Travele, Moussa

MOZAMBIQUE—11

Albasini, João
Craveirinha, José
de Noronha, Rui
De Sousa, Noémia
Dias, João
dos Santos, Marcelino
Freire, Albuquerque
Honwana, Luís
Lemos, Virgílio de
Nogar, Rui
Valente, M. G.

MAURITANIA—2

Bâ, Oumar
Guéye, Youssouf

MAURITIUS—1

Maunick, Edouard J

NIGER—1

Moumouni, Abdou

NIGERIA—87

Abubakar, Imam
Abubakar, Tafawa Balewa
Achebe, Chinua
Adoki, G. E.
Agunwa, Clement
Aig-Imoukhuede, Frank
Akiga, B. Akiga Sai
Akinsemoyin, Kunle
Akpan, Ntieyong
Aluko, Timothy M.
Amadi, Elechi
Anozie, Sunday
Awolowo, Obafemi Awo
Azikiwe, Benjamin
Babalola, Solomon
Balogun, Ola
Clark, John Pepper
Echeruo, Kevin
Echeruo, Michael
Edyang, Ernest
Egbuna, Obi B.
Egharevba, Chief Dr. J.
  Uwadiae
Egudu, Romanus
Ekwensi, Cyprian
Ekwere, John
Euba, Femi
Fagunwa, Chief Daniel
Gbadamosi, Bakare A.
Henshaw, James Ene
Higo, Aig
Horatio-Jones, Edward B.
Ibukun, Olu
Ijimere, Obotunde
Ike, Vincent Chukwuemeka
Ikiddeh, Ime
Iroaganachi, J. O.
Itayemi, Phebean
Jeboda, Femi
Kagara, Malam Abubakar
  Imam
Kagara, Malam Muhammadu
  Bello
Ladipo, Duro
Mezu, S. Okechukwu
Munonye, John
Ndu, Pol N.
Nwankwo, Nkem
Nwapa, Flora
Nzekwu, Onoura
Obiechina, Emmanuel N.
Odeku, E. Latunde
Ogali, Ogali Agu

Ogbalu, Fred Chidozie
Ogunde, Hubert
Ogunmola, E. Kolawole
Ogunyemi, Wale
Ojike, Mazi Mbounu
Okafor-Omali, Dilim
Okara, Gabriel I.
Okeke, Uche
Okigbo, Christopher
Okpaku, Joseph
Okpewho, Isadore
Olagoke, David
Olisah, Sunday Okenwa
Oluwa, I. I.
Oniororo, Niyi
Opara, Ralph C.
Osadebay, Dennis Chukude
Owomoyela, Oyekan
Owoyele, David
Oyelese, J. O.
Ransome-Kuti, Rev. Canon
Rotimi, Olawale
Segun, Mabel
Senyi, Kobina
Sidahome, Joseph E.
Soyinka, Kayode
Soyinka, Wole
Stephen, Felix
Taiwo, Oladeli
Tutuola, Amos
Ukoli, Neville
Ulasi, Adaora, Lily
Umeasiegbu, Rems Nna
Uzodinma, Edmund
  Chukuemeka
Vassa, Olauday Gustavus
Vaughan, J. Koyinda
Wonodi, Okogbule

PRINCIPE (Island of)—1

Margarido, Maria Manuela

RHODESIA—5

Chidyausika, Paul
Chitepo, Herbert Wiltshire
Ndlovu, Joshua
Samkange, Stanlake
Weakl/, John Marangwanda

RWANDA—4

Kagame, Abbé Alexis
Mutabaruka, Jean-Baptiste
Naigiziki, J. V. Saverio
Ntuyahaga, Mgr.

SAO TOME (Island of)—6

Alegre, Caetano, da Costa
de Almeida, José Maria
Domingues, Mário

553

African Authors

Espírito Santo, Alda de
Medeiros, António A. T.
Tenreiro, Francisco José

SENEGAL—17

Diagne, Ahmadou Mapaté
Diakhaté, Lamine
Diallo, Assane
Diallo, Bakary
Diop, Birago
Diop, David
Diop, Massyla
Ka, Abdou Anta
Kane, Cheikh Hamidou
M'Baye, Annette (Mme.)
Ndao, Cheik A.
Sadji, Abdoulaye
Sembène, Ousmane
Senghor, Léopold Sédar
Socé, Ousmane Diop
Wade, Amadou Mustapha
Wheatley, Phillis
  (wrote in English in U.S.A.)

SIERRA LEONE—12

Akar, John Joseph
Bankole, Timothy
Bart-Williams, Gaston
Casely-Hayford, Adelaide
Cole, Robert W.
Easmon, Raymond
Horton, James A. B.
Johnson, Lemuel
  (b. in Nigeria)
Macauley, Jeanette
Maddy, Pat
Nicol, Abioseh D.
Taylor, W. H.

SOMALIA—13

Abdillaahi, Muuse
Ali, Abdullah
Duuh, Ali
Faarah, Nuur
Farah, Nuruddin
Ilmi, Bownderi
Mahammed, Sheikh Abdille
Mire, Ismaa'iil
Musa, Hajji Ismael Galaal
Qamaan, Bulhan
  (also lived in Ethiopia)
Raage, Ugaas
Salaan, Arrabey
Syad, William Joseph
  (originally from Terr. of
  Affars-Issas)

SOUTH AFRICA—124

Abrahams, Peter Lee
Bengani, Reduus

Boetia, Dugmore
Bokwe, John Knox
Bomela, Bertrand
Brand, Dollar
Brutus, Dennis
Burns-Ncamashe, Sipo
Caluza, Reuben
Citashe, I. W. W.
Dazana, S.
Dhlomo, Herbert
Dhlomo, Rolfus
Dube, John
Dube, Violet
Fula, Arthur
Futshane, Zora Z. T.
Fuze, Magema ka Magwaza
Gqoba, William
Gulube, D. N.
Guma, Enoch
Guma, Samson
Hutchinson, Alfred
Jabavu, Davidson
Jabavu, John Tengo
Jabavu, Noni Helen
Jolobe, James
Jordan, Archibald C.
Kakaza, Lillith
Kgositsile, William
Khumalo, J. M.
Kumalo, Peter E.
Kunene, A. A. S.
Kunene, Mazisi Raymond
La Guma, Alex
Leshoai, Benjamin
Leshoro, Ephraim Alfred G.
Lutuli, Chief Albert John
Maboko, F. M.
Machaka, Samson
Made, Emmanuel
Madiba, Moses
Maimane, J. Arthur
Makgaleng, Managase M.
Makiwane, Tennyson Xola
Makwala, Silpha Phaledi
Mama, Goodwill Soya
Mangoaela, Gideon
Masondo, Titus Z.
Mathivha, Matshaya
Matsepe, Oliver Kgadime
Matshikiza, Todd
Matthews, James
Mbebe, A. Z. T.
Mbelle, Isaiah Budlwana
Mesatywa, Ezra Whillemus
Mkhize, C. S.
Mkize, E. E. N.
Mncwango, Leonhard L. J.
Modisane, William
Mofokeng, Sophonia Machabe
Moiloa, James Jantjies
Mokgatle, Monyadice M. N.
Mokone, Nowen Godratius
Molefe, Arthur Ignatius

Moloto, Davidson Pelman
Morel, Marion
Moroke, Samson Alexander
Motsisi, Moses Casey
Mphahlele, Ezekiel L.
Mqhaba, Alton A. M.
Mqhayi, Samuel Edward K.
Mseleku, Malcolm Raymond
Mthembu, Robert Hiram
Myeza, M. D.
Mzamane, Godfrey
Nakasa, Nathaniel Ndzivane
Ndawo, Henry Masila
Ndebele, Nimrod Njabulo
Ndelu, B. Z. B.
Ndhambi, Etienne Penyisi
Ngani, Alfred Z.
Ngani, Marcus A.
Ngidi, Andreas Henry
Ngubane, Jordan Kush
Ngubeni, M. M.
Nkabinde, Abram Charles
Nkosi, Lewis
Nortje, K. Arthur
Ntantala, Phyllis P.
Ntloko, President Mthetho
Ntsanwisi, Hudson
Ntsane, Kemuele
Ntsikana
Ntsiko, Jonas
Nxumalo, Henry
Nxumalo, James
Nxumalo, Natalie Victoria
  (née Nxaba)
Nxumalo, Otty Ezrom
Nyembezi, Cyril Lincoln
Nzimande, A. M.
Phakathi, A. B.
Phatudi, Cedric Namedi
  Makepeace
Plaatje, Solomon Tshkisho
Rakoma, Joseph Ramathea
Ramaila, Epafras
Ramathe, A. C. J.
Rammala, Joseph Lesibe
Ramokgopa, Herbert Daniel
Rive, Richard
Rubusana, Walter Benson
Saoli, J. Russell
Sentso, Dyke
Senyatsi, Charles Phuti
Shembe, Isaiah
Sinxo, Guybon Budlwana
Soga, John Henderson
Soga, Tiyo
Sontonga, Mankayi Enoch
Swaartbooi, Victoria N. M.
Thage, Johannes Ralakiti
Themba, Daniel Canadoise
Vilakazi, Benedict
Vimbe, John Muir

SOUTHWEST AFRICA—1

Pieterse, Cosmo

SUDAN—6

El Hardallo
Karim, Ahmed Awad
Lufti, Ali Sayed
Muhammad wad Daif Allah
Rabu, Wad Hasad
Salih, Tayeb

TANZANIA—10

Abedi, Sheikh Kaluta
Chacha, Tom
Kitereza, Aniceti
Nyerere, Julius K.
Palangyo, Peter K.
Robert, Shaaban
Ruhumbika, Gabriel
Saiyid, Abdallah
Shaikh, Muhyi
Willis, Jackson A. M.

TOGO—3

Ananou, David
Couchoro, Félix
Mensah, Toussaint Viderot

UGANDA—15

Bukenya, Augustine S.
Kimenye, Barbara

Kironde, Erisa
Liyong, Taban Lo
Mukasa, Ham
Mukasa-Balikuddembre,
  Joseph
Mukasa-ssali, Paul
Nagenda, John
Nyabongo, Prince Akiki
Oculi, Okello
Omara, Tom
p'Bitek, J. P. Okot
Rwakyaka, Proscovia
Serumaga, Robert
Tulya-Muhika, Sam

UPPER VOLTA—3

Boni, Nazi
Coulibaly, Augustin-Sonde
Tiendrébéogo, Yamba

ZAIRE—16

Bahelele, Jacques N.
Bolamba, Antoine
Bolamba, G.
Bunseki, A. Fukiau kia
Disengomoko, A. Emile
Lomami-Tshibamba, Paul
Lopes, Henri
Malembe, Timothée
Malutama, Rémy
Mathieu, Jean
Mutombo, Dieudonné

Ngangu, Jackson
Ntsimba, Samuel A.
Sumaili, Gabriele
Tshakatumba, Matala
Vingadio, Timetéo

ZAMBIA—5

Mpashi, Stephen Andrea
Mubitana, Kafungulwa
Mulaisho, Dominic
Mulikita, Fwanyanga
Sakubita, M. M.

OTHER—7

Abū Dulāma Ibn Al-Djaun
  (b. Badhdad (?), wrote
  in Arabic)
Antar (b. Arabia, wrote
  in Arabic)
Barbosa, Domingos Caldas (b.
  on shipboard, wrote in Por-
  tuguese)
Capitein, Jacobus (b. West
  Africa, wrote in Latin and
  Dutch)
Rukn Al-Dīn Baibars al-Bun-
  duqdari (wrote in Arabic)
Sancho, Ignatius (b. on ship-
  board, wrote in English)
Ziryāb (b. probably near
  Baghdad, wrote in Arabic)

Appendix H

Authors, by African Language or Languages Employed

For approximate location of these language areas, see the maps on the end papers in the front and back of this volume, and the map on page 493.

Amharic (Ethiopia)--16
Afawark, Gabra Iyasu
Ashenafi, Kebede
Gabra, Egzi'abeher
Germacaw, Takla H.
Heruy, Walda Sellase
Ishak
Kabbada, Mika'el
Mahtama, Sellase Walda
Makonnen, Endalkacaw
Mal'aku, Baggasaw
Sellassie, Sahle (also English)
Takla, Hawaryat
Tsegaye, Gabre-Medhin
(also English)
Walda, Giyorgis
Yilma, Darasa
Yoftahe, Neguse

Arabic (Mali, Sudan, Iraq, Egypt, Arabia)--14
Abu Dulama (Iraq)
Antar (Arabia)
Baba, Ahmad al Tinbukhti (Mali)
Kati, Mahmud (Mali)
Mahammed, Sheikh 'Abdille Hassan
(Somalia and also used Somali language
Muhammad wad Daif Allah (Sudan)
Rukn Al-Din (Egypt)
Sadi, Abdulrahman as-(Mali)
Salih, Tayed (Sudan)
Ziryab (Iraq)

Shukria or Butane-Arabic (eastern Sudan)
El Hardallo
Karim, Ahmed Awad
Lufti, Ali Sayed (also English)
Rabu, Wad Hasad

Bambara (Mali)--1
Bâ, Mallam (also French and Fulani)

Bemba (Zambia)--1
Mpashi, Stephen Andrea

Edo (or **Bini**) (Nigeria)--1
Egharevba, Chief Dr. Jacob Uwadiae
(also English)

Ewe (Ghana)--2
Desewe, P. N.
Obianim, Sam J.

Fante or **Fanti** (Ghana)--1
Acquah, Gaddiel Robert (also English)

Fulani or **Fulbe, Fulfulde, Peulh** (Senegal, Guinea, Mali)--3
Bâ, Mallam (Bambara and French)
Bâ, Oumar, (also French)
Diallo, Assane Y. (also French)

Ga (Ghana)--1
Odoi, Nicholas Akrong

Hausa (Nigeria)--4
Abubakar, Imam
Abubakar, Sir Tafawa Balewa
Kagara, Malam Abubakar Imam
Kagara, Malam Muhammadu Bello

Ibo or **Igbo** (Nigeria)--1
Ogbalu, Frederick C. (also English)

Kikamba or **Kamba** (Kenya)--1
Mbiti, John Samuel (also English)

Kikerebe (Tanzania)--1
Kitereza, Aniceti (also Swahili)

Kikiyu, Kikuyu or **Gicuyu** (Kenya)--1
Kenyatta, Jomo (also English)

Kikongo (Zaïre, Angola)--8

Bahelele, Jacques N.
Bunseki, A. Fukiau kia
Disengomoko, A. Emile
Malutama, Rémy
Massaki, André
Ngangu, Jackson
Nsimba, Samuel
Vingadio, Timotéo

Kimbundu (Angola)--2
de Andrade, Mário (also Portuguese)
Vieira, Luandino (also Portuguese)

Lozi (Zambia)--2
Mulikita, Fwanyanga M. (also English)
Sakubita, M. M.

Luganda (Uganda)--2
Mukasa, Ham
Mukasa-Balikuddembre, Joseph
(also Runyoro-Rutoro and English)

Luo, Lwo or **Acoli** or **Acholi** (Kenya and Uganda)--2
Owuor, Henry
p'Bitek, J. P. Okot (also English)

Malagasy, Malgache, or **Madagascan** (Malagasy)--5
Rabéarivelo, J. J. (also French)
Rajemisa-Raolison, Régis (also French)
Ramananato
Ranaivo, Jacques F. (also French)
Randrianarisoa, Pierre (also French)

Nyanja or **Cewa-Nyanja** (Malawi)--3
Chafulumira, English William
Nkomba, Lester L.
Ntara, Samuel Y.

Ruanda, Rundi, Rwanda (Rwanda)--2
Kagame, Abbé Alexis (also French)
Ntuyahaga, Mgr. Lord Bishop

557

African Authors

Runyoro-Rutoro (Uganda)--1
Mukasa-Balikuddembre, Joseph
  (also Luganda and English)

Shona (Rhodesia)--3
Chidyausika, Paul
Chitepo, Herbert
Weakly, John Marangwanda

Somali (Somalia Republic, Ethiopia,
  and Kenya)--11
Abdillaahi, Muuse
Ali, Abdullah
Duuh, Ali
Faarah, Nuur
Ilmi, Bownderi
Mahammed, Sheikh 'Abdille
  (also Arabic)
Mire, Ismaa'iil
Musa, Hajji Ismail Galaal
Qamaan, Bulhan
Raage, Ugaas
Salaan, 'Arrabey

Sotho, Southern or Sesotho
  (Lesotho and South Africa)--24
Guma, Samson M. (also English)
Khaketla, Bennett Makalo
Khaketla, Caroline N.
Lesoro, Ephraim A. S.
Maile, Mallane Libakeng
Mangoaela, Zakea Dolphin
Mangoaela, Gideon
Mofokeng, Sophonia Machabe
Mofolo, Thomas M.
Mohapeloa, John
Mohapeloa, Josias M.
Mohapeloa, Joshua P.
Mohapeloa, Moeketsa D.
Mohapi, Michael
Moikangoa, Cornelius F. R.
Moiloa, James J.
Mopeli-Paulus, Attwell S. (also English)
Motsamai, Edward
Ntsane, Kemuele E.
Ramathe, A. C. J.
Saoli, Jacob R.
Segoete, Everitt
Sekese, Azariele
Sentso, Dyke

Sotho, Northern or Sepedi
  (South Africa)--10
Machaka, Samson Rasebilu Mfoka
Madiba, Moses Josiah S.
Makgaleng, Mamagase M.
Makwala, Silpha P. N.
Phatudi, Cedric Namedi M.
Rakoma, Joseph R. D.
Ramaila, Epafras M.
Rammala, Joseph L.
Ramokgopa, Herbert D.

Senyatsi, Charles P.

Swahili (Tanzania, Kenya)--15
Abdulla, Muhammed Said
Abedi, Sheikh Kaluta
Chum, Haji
Hinawy, Sheikh Mbarak
Kitereza, Aniceti (also Kikerebe)
Muyaka (Haji al-Ghassaniy)
Mwana, Kupona
Nassir, Ahmad
Nyabongo, Prince Akike
  (also English)
Nyerere, Julius Kambarage
Robert, Shaaban
Saiyid, Abdallah
Saiyid Abu Bakr
Saiyid-Umar
Shaikh, Muhyi

Tiv (Nigeria)--1
Akiga, Benjamin

Tsonga (South Africa)--3
Maboko, F. M.
Ndhambi, Etienne P.
Ntsanwisi, Hudson W.

Tswana (Botswana and
  South Africa)--7
Matsepe, Oliver Kgadine
Mokone, Nowen Godratius
Moloto, Davidson P.
Moroke, Samson A.
Plaatje, Solomon T. (also English)
Raditladi, Leetile
Seboni, Michael

Twi-Assante (Ghana)--2
Nketia, John
Danquah, Joseph B. (Akuapem-Twi)

Venda (South Africa)--1
Mathivha, Matshaya

Wolof (Senegal)--1
Ndao, Cheik (also French and English)

Xhosa or Xosa
  (South Africa)--33
Bokwe, John Knox
Bomela, Bertrand
Burns-Ncamashe, Sipo
Citashe, I. W. W.
Dazana, S.
Futshane, Zora Z. T.
Gqoba, W. W.
Guma, Enoch S.
Jabavu, Davidson Don Tengo
  (also English)
Jabavu, John Tengo
Jolobe, James J.
Jordan, A. C.

Kakaza, Lillith
Mama, Goodwill Soya
Mbebe, A. Z. T.
Mbelle, Isaiah Budlwana
  (also English)
Mesatywa, Ezra W.
Mqhaba, Alton A. M.
Mqhayi, Samuel E.
Mzamane, Godfrey
Ndawo, Henry Masila
Ngani, Alfred A.
Ngani, Marcus Aurelius
Ntsikana
Ntsiko, Jonas
Rubusana, Walter B.
Sinxo, Guybon
Soga, John H.
Soga, Tiyo
Soga, Tiyo Burnside
Sontonga, Makayi E.
Swaartbooi, Victoria
Vimbe, John M.

Yoruba (Nigeria)--12
Babalola, Solomon
Fagunwa, Chief Daniel O.
Gbadamosi, Bakare A.
Ijimere, Obotunde
Jeboda, Joshua Ofuwafimi
Ladipo, Duro
Ogunde, Hubert
Ogunmola, Elijah Kolawole
Ogunyemi, Wale
Oyelese, J. O.
Ransome-Kuti, Rev. J. J.
Rotimi, Olawale (also English)

Zulu (South Africa)--35
Caluza, Reuben T.
Dhlomo, Herbert (also English)
Dhlomo, Rolfus R. R.
Dube, John L.
Dube, Violet
Fuze, Magema ka Magwaza
Gulube, D. N.
Khumalo, J. M.
Kunene, A. A. S.
Kunene, Mazisi Raymond
Made, Emmanuel
Masondo, Titus Z.
Mkhize, C. S.
Mkize, E. E. N.
Mncwango, Leonhard L. J. (also English)
Molefe, Arthur I.
Mseleku, Malcolm R.
Mthembu, Robert H.
Myeza, M. D.
Ndebele, Nimrod W.
Ndela, B. Z. B.
Ngcobo, Moses J.
Ngidi, Andreas H.

558

Ngubane, Jordan
Ngubene, M. M.
Nkabinde, Abram C.
Ntloko, President M.

Nxumalo, James A.
Nxumalo, Natalie V. (née Nxaba)
Nxumalo, Otty Ezrom
Nyambezi, Cyril Lincoln

Nzimande, A. M.
Phakathi, A. B.
Shembe, Isaiah
Vilakazi, Benedict

Total Using African Languages: 233

Appendix I

Authors, by European Language or Languages Employed

Writers Using English: 238

Abrahams, Peter
Abruquah, J. W.
Achebe, Chinua
Acquah, G. R. (also Fante)
Adali-Mortty, G.
Ademola, Frances
Adoki, G. E.
Aduamah, E. Y.
Aggrey, James
Agunwa, C.
Aidoo, Christina
Aig-Imoukhuede, F.
Akar, J. J.
Akinsemoyin, K.
Akpan, N. U.
Aluko, Timothy
Amadi, Elechi
Anozie, Sunday (also French)
Apronti, Jawa
Arkhurst, F. S.
Armah, A. K.
Armattoe, R.
Asalache, K.
Asare, B.
Awolowo, O. A.
Awoonor, Kofi
Azikiwe, B. N.
Babalola, S.
Balogun, Ola (also French)
Bankole, T.
Bart-Williams, G.
Bediako, K. A.
Blay, J. B.
Boetia, D.
Bonne, N. K. III
Brand, Dollar
Brew, Kwesi
Brutus, S. A.
Bukenya, A. S.
Busia, K. A.
Casely-Hayford, Adelaide
Casely-Hayford, Gladys
Casely-Hayford, Joseph E.
Chacha, Tom

Clark, John P.
Codjoe, Thomas A.
Cole, R. W.
Conton, W. F.
Cugoana, Ottabah
Danquah, J. B.
    (also Akuapem-Twi)
Danquah, Mabel
de Graft, J. C.
Dei-Anang, M. F.
Dempster, R. T.
Dhlomo, H. I. (also Zulu)
Dipoko, M. S.
Djoleto, Amu
Duodu, Cameron
Dzovo, Emmanuel
Easmon, R. S.
Echeruo, Kevin
Echeruo, Michael
Edyang, Ernest
Egbuna, O. B.
Egharevba, J. U. (also in Edo)
Egudu, Romanus
Ekwensi, Cyprian
Ekwere, John
Euba, Femi
Fafunwa, Babs
Farah, Nuruddin
Gatanyu, James
Gatheru, R. J. Mugo
Gbadamosi, B. A.
Gicaru, Muga
Guma, Samson (also English)
Head, Bessie
Henries, Mrs. A. Doris B.
Henshaw, James E.
Higo, Aig
Hihetah, R. K.
Horatio-Jones, E. B.
Horton, James A. B.
Hutchinson, Alfred
Ibukun, Olu
Ike, Vincent C.
Ikeddeh, Ime

Iroaganachi, J. O.
Itayemi, Phebean
Jabavu, Davidson D. T.
    (also Xhosa)
Jabavu, Noni H. N.
Johnson, Lemuel
Kachingwe, Aubrey
Kahiga, Samuel
Kariuki, Joseph
Karlee, Varfelli
Kay, Kwesi
Kayira, Legson
Kayper-Mensah, A. W.
Kenyatta, Jomo (also Kikiyu)
Kgositile, W. K.
Kibera, Leonard
Kimenye, Barbara
Kinyanjui, Peter
Kironde, Erisa
Komey, Ellis A.
Kumalo, Peter E.
Kyei, Kojo
La Guma, Alex
Leshoia, Benjamin
Liyong, Taban Lo
Lufti, Ali Sayed (also Arabic)
Lutuli, Chief Albert
Macauley, Jeanette
Maddy, Pat
Maimane, J. A.
Makwane, T. X.
Maimo, A. O.
Makumi, Joel
Markwei, Matei
Matshikiza, Todd
Matthews, James
Mazrui, Ali Al'Amin
Mbiti, John S. (also Kikamba)
Mezu, S. O.
Mncwango, L. (also Zulu)
Mockerie, P. G.
Modisane, "Bloke" William
Mokgatle, M. M.
Molema, M. S.

561

African Authors

Writers Using English:

Moore, Bai Tamiah
Mopeli-Paulus, A. S.
Motsisi, Moses
Mphahlele, Ezekiel L.
Mubitana, K.
Mukasa-Balikuddembre, Joseph (also
   Luganda and Runyoro-Rotoro)
Mukasa-ssali, Paul
Mulaisho, Dominic
Mulakita, F. M. (also Lozi)
Munonye, John
Mvomo, Rémy (also French)
Mwalilino, Katoki
Nagenda, John
Nakasa, N. N.
Ndao, Cheik A. (also French and
   Wolof)
Ndlovu, Joshua
Ndu, Pol N.
Ngubane, Jordan
Ngugi, James
Nicol, Abioseh
Njau, Rebecca
Njoroge, James
Nkosi, Lewis
Nkrumah, Kwame
Nortje, K. Arthur
Ntantala, Phyllis
Nwankwo, Nkem
Nwapa, Flora
Nxumalo, Henry
Nyabongo, Prince Akike
   (also Swahili)
Nyerere, Julius K. (also Swahili)
Nzekwu, Onuora
Obeng, R. E.
Obiechina, E. N.
Oculi, Okello
Odeku, E. L.
Odinga, A. O.
Ofori, Henry
Ogali, Ogali A.
Ogbalu, Fred C. (also Igbo)
Ogot, Grace A.
Ojike, M. M.
Okafor-Omali, Dilim
Okara, Gabriel
Okeke, Uche
Okigbo, Christopher
Okpaku, Joseph
Okpewho, Isadore
Olagoke, David
Olisah, S. O.
Oluwa, I. I.
Omara, Tom
Oniororo, Niyi
Opara, Ralph
Osadebay, Dennis
Osogo, John
Owomoyela, Oyekan
Owoyele, David
Palangyo, Peter K.

Paris, Prince Modupe
Parkes, Frank K.
p'Bitek, J. P. Okot (also Lwo)
Pederek, Simon
Peters, Lenrie
Pieterse, Cosmo
Plaatje, Solomon T. (also Tswana)
Quaye, Cofie
Reindorf, Rev. C. C.
Rive, Richard
Rotimi, Olawale (also Yoruba)
Rubadiri, James
Ruhumbika, Gabriel
Rwakyaka, Proscovia
Sam, Gilbert
Samkange, Stanlake
Sancho, Ignatius
Sankawulo, Wilton
Sarbah, John M.
Segun, Mabel J.
Sellassie, Sahle B. M. (also Amharic)
Selormey, F.
Senyi, Kobina
Seruma, Eneriko
Serumaga, Robert
Sey, Kofi
Sidahome, Joseph E.
Soyinka, Kayode
Soyinka, Wole
Stephen, Felix N.
Sutherland, Efua T.
Syad, William (also French)
Taiwo, Oladele
Taylor, W. H.
Thage, Johannes
Themba, Daniel
Tsegaye, Gabre-Medhin
   (also Amharic)
Tulya-Muhika, Sam
Tutuola, Amos
Ukoli, Neville
Ulasi, Adaora
Umeasiegbu, Rems
Uzodinma, Edmund
Vassa, Olauday G.
Vaughan, J. K.
Wachira, Godwin
Wheatley, Phillis
Willis, Jackson
Wonodi, Okogbule

Writers Using French: 100

Ananou, David
Anozie, Sunday (also English)
Bâ, Mallam A. H. (also Bambara and
   Peulh)
Bâ, Oumar (also Peulh)
Badian, Seydou
Balogun, Ola (also English)
Bamboté, P. M.
Bebey, Francis

Bemba, Sylvain
Beti, Mongo
Bhêly-Quénum, O
Bognini, J. M.
Bolamba, A. R.
Boni, Nazi
Cissé, Emile
Coulibaly, A. S.
Couchoro, Félix
Dadie, B. B.
Dembele, Sidiki
Diagné, A. M.
Diakhaté, Lamine
Diallo, A. Y. (also (Peulh)
Diallo, Bakary
Diop, Birago
Diop, David
Diop, Massyla
Dogbeh-David, Richard
Dongmo, Jean L.
Epanya-Yondo, Elelongué
Guèye, Youssouf
Hazoumé, Paul
Ikelle-Matiba
Joachim, Paulin
Kagame, Abbé Alexis
   (also Rwanda)
Kane, Cheikh H.
Kayo, Patrice
Keita, Fodeba
Koffii, R. A.
Koné, Maurice
Kouadio-Tiacoh, Gabriel
Laye, Camara
Loba, Aké
Lomami-Tshibamba, Paul
Lopes, Henri
Makouta-Mboukou, J. P.
Malembe, Timothée
Malonga, Jean
Mathieu, Jean
Matip, Benjamin
Maunick, Edouard
M'Baye, Annette
Menga, Guy
Mensah, Toussaint V.
Moumouni, Abdou
Mutabaruka, Jean-Baptiste
Mutombo, Dieudonné
Mvomo, Rémy G. M. (also English)
Naigiziki, J. V. S.
Ndao, Cheik A. (also English and
   Wolof)
N'debeka, Maxime
N'djok, Kindengve
Nénékhaly-Camara, Condetto
Nganthojeff, Job
Niane, Djibril Tamsir
Nokan, Charles
Nyunaï, Jean-Paul
Nzouankeu, J. M.
Obenga, T. J.

Author By Category

Writers Using French

Ologoudou, Emile
Ouologuem, Yambo
Owono, Joseph
Oyono, Ferdinand
Oyônô-Mbia, Guillaume
Philombe, René
Pliya, Jean
Quénum, M. P.
Rabéarivelo, Jean-Joseph (also Malgache)
Rabémananjara, J. J.
Rajemisa-Raolison, R. (also Malgache)
Ranaivo, Jacques (also Malgache)
Robinary, Michel F.
Sadji, Abdoulaye
Seid, Joseph B.
Sembène, Ousmane
Sengat-Kuo, François
Senghor, Léopold Sédar
Sinda, Martial
Siriman, Cissoko
Sissoko, Fily-Dabo
Socé, Ousmane Diop
Sow, Alpha
Sumaili, Gabriel
Syad, William (also English)
Tati, J. B.
Tiendrébéogo, Yamba
Touré, Sadan-Moussa
Travele, Moussa
Tshakatumba, Matala
U Tam'si, Tchicaya
Wade, Amadou

Writers Using Portuguese: 58

Albasini, João
Alcântara, Osvaldo
Alegre, Caetano
Anahory, Terêncio
Andrade, Costa
António, Mário
Assis Júnior, António de
Azevedo, P. C. de
Barbosa, Domingo Caldas
Barbosa, Jorge
Bessa-Victor, Geraldo
Cardoso, António
Cardoso, Pedro M.
Craveirnha, José
da Cruz, Viriate
da Matta, Joaquim
Dáskalos, Alexandre
da Silveira, Onésimo
de Almeida, José Marie
da Andrade, Mário (also Kimbundu)
de Noronha, Rui
De Sousa, Noémia C.
Dias, João
Domingues, Mário
dos Santos, Marcellino
Duarte, Fausto
Espírito Santo, Alda de
Ferreira, António B.
Ferreira, José da Silva Maia
Fonseca, Aguinaldo B.
Fonseca, Mário Alberto
Freire, Albuquerque
Gonçalves, A. A.

Honwana, Luís B.
Jacinto, António
Lara Filho, Ernesto
Lemos, Virgílio de
Lima, Manuel
Lopes, José da Silva
Lopes, Manuel António
Machado, Pedro Felix
Margarido, Maria
Mariano, Gabriel
Martins, Ovídio
Medeiros, António Alves T.
Milheiros, Mário
Miranda, Nuno de
Neto, António A.
Nogar, Rui
Nunes, António
Osório, Ernesto
Pereira, José
Ribas, Oscar B.
Romano, Luís
Tavares, Eugénio
Tenreiro, Francisco
Valente, Malangatana
Vieira, Luandino

Writers Using Afrikaans (South Africa)—1

Fula, Arthur Nuthall

Writers Using Latin: 3

Amo, Antonius G.
Capitein, Jacobus
Latino, Juan

Total Using European Languages: 400

563

Appendix J

Authors, Female

Name	Country
Ademola, Frances	Ghana
Aidoo, Christina	Ghana
Casely-Hayford, Adelaide	Sierra Leone
Casely-Hayford, Gladys	Ghana
Danquah, Mabel	Ghana
De Sousa, Noémia Carolina	Mozambique
Dube, Violet	South Africa
Espírito Santo, Alda de	São Tomé
Futshane, Zora Z. T.	South Africa
Head, Bessie	Botswana (b. S. Africa)
Henries, A. Doris Banks	Liberia
Itayemi, Phebean	Nigeria
Jabavu, Noni Helen Nontando	South Africa
Khaketla, Caroline	Lesotho
Kimenye, Barbara	Kenya
Macauley, Jeanette	Sierra Leone
Margarido, Maria Manuela	Príncipe
M'Baye, Annette	Senegal
Morel, Marion	South Africa
Mwana, Kupona	Kenya
Njau, Rebecca	Kenya
Ntantala, Phyllis	South Africa
Nwapa, Flora	Nigeria
Nxumala, Natalie Victoria	South Africa
Ogot, Grace Akinye	Kenya
Rwakyaka, Proscovia	Uganda
Segun, Mabel	Nigeria
Sutherland, Efua T.	Ghana
Swaartbooi, Victoria	South Africa
Ulasi, Adaora Lily	Nigeria
Wheatley, Phillis	Senegal and U.S.A.

PART III
PUBLISHERS, JOURNALS, BOOKSHOPS

Appendix K

Major Publishers of African Literature

The United States

Africana Publishing Corporation
101 Fifth Avenue
New York, N. Y., 10003

African Studies Association
218 Shiffman Humanities Center
Brandeis University
Waltham, Mass., 02154

Andronicus Publishing Co., Inc.
666 Fifth Avenue
New York, N. Y., 20019

Astor-Honor, Inc.
114 Manhattan Street
Stamford, Conn., 06904

Atheneum Publishers
122 East 57th Street
New York, N. Y., 10017

Black Academy Press
Box 366, Ellicott Station
Buffalo, N. Y., 14205

Black Orpheus Press, Inc.
322 New Mark Esplanade
Rockville, Md., 20850

Cambridge University Press
32 East 57th Street
New York, N. Y., 10022

John Day Company
200 Madison Avenue
New York, N. Y., 10016

Dodd, Mead and Co.
79 Madison Avenue
New York, N. Y., 10016

Doubleday and Company, Inc.

277 Park Avenue
New York, N.Y., 10017

E. P. Dutton and Co., Inc.
201 Park Avenue South
New York, N. Y., 10016

Fawcett World Library
67 West 44th St.
New York, N. Y., 10036

Farrar, Strauss and Giroux, Inc.
19 Union Square West
New York, N. Y., 10003

Grosset and Dunlap
51 Madison Avenue
New York, N. Y., 10010

Grove Press, Inc.
214 Mercer Street
New York, N. Y., 10012

Harcourt, Brace and World, Inc.
757 Third Avenue
New York, N. Y., 10017

Harper and Row, Publishers
19 Union Square West
New York, N. Y., 10003

Hill and Wang, Inc.
141 Fifth Avenue
New York, N. Y., 10010

Houghton Mifflin Co.
2 Park Street
Boston, Mass., 02107

Humanities Press, Inc.
303 Park Avenue South
New York, N. Y., 10010

Indiana University Press
Tenth and Morton Streets
Bloomington, Indiana, 47401

Johnson Reprint Corporation
111 Fifth Avenue
New York, N. Y., 10003

Alfred A. Knopf, Inc.
501 Madison Avenue
New York, N. Y., 10022

Kraus Reprint Corporation
16 East 46th Street
New York, N. Y., 10017

Liveright
386 Park Avenue South
New York, N. Y., 10016

Little, Brown and Co.
34 Beacon Street
Boston, Mass., 02106

McGraw-Hill Co., Inc.
330 West 42nd Street
New York, N. Y., 10036

Macmillan Co.
866 Third Avenue
New York, N. Y., 10022

Meridian Books
The World Publishing Co.
2231 West 110th Street
Cleveland, Ohio, 44102

Negro Universities Press
(and Greenwood Press)
51 Riverside Avenue
Westport, Conn., 06880

African Authors

New American Library, Inc.
(and Signet)
1301 Avenue of the Americas
New York, N. Y., 10019

Northwestern University Press
1735 Benson Avenue
Evanston, Ill., 60201

October House, Inc.
55 West 13th Street
New York, N. Y., 10010

Odyssey Press, Inc.
55 Fifth Avenue
New York, N. Y., 10003

Oxford University Press
200 Madison Avenue
New York, N. Y., 10016

Penguin Books, Inc.
7110 Ambassador Road
Baltimore, Md., 21207

Pergamon Press, Inc.
Maxwell House, Fairview Park
Elmsford, N. Y., 10523

Praeger Publishers, Inc.
111 Fourth Avenue
New York, N. Y., 10003

G. P. Putnam's Sons
200 Madison Avenue
New York, N. Y., 10016

Random House, Inc.
457 Madison Avenue
New York, N. Y., 10022

The Third Press
444 Central Park West
New York, N. Y., 10025

Twayne Publishers, Inc.
31 Union Square W.
New York, N. Y., 10003

University of California Press
2223 Fulton Street
Berkeley, Calif., 94720

University of Wisconsin Press
P. O. Box 1379
Madison, Wisconsin, 53701

Vanguard Press, Inc.
424 Madison Avenue
New York, N. Y., 10017

Walker and Company

720 Fifth Avenue
New York, N. Y., 10019

Great Britain

International African Institute
St. Dunstans Chambers, 10–11 Fetter Lane
London E. C. 4, England

George Allen and Unwin Ltd.
Ruskin House
40 Museum Street
London W. C. 1, England

E. J. Arnold and Son Ltd.
Butterley Street
Hunslet Lane
Leeds 10, Yorkshire, England

Associated Book Publishers Ltd.
11 New Fetter Lane
London EC4P 4EE, England

Cambridge University Press
Bentley House
P. O. Box 92
200 Euston Road
London N. W. 1, England

Frank Cass and Co. Ltd.
67 Great Russell Street
London W. C. 1, England

The Clarendon Press
Walton Street
Oxford OX 2 6DP, England

Collier-Macmillan Ltd
10 South Audley Street
London W. 1, England

Rex Collings Ltd.
6 Paddington Street
London, W. 1, England

Rosica Colin Limited
4 Hereford Square
London SW 7 4TU, England

William Collins, Sons and Co. Ltd.
14 St. James's Place
London S. W. 1, England

André Deutsch Ltd.
105 Great Russell Street
London WC1B 3LJ, England

Evans Brothers Ltd.
Montague House
Russell Square
London, W.C.1, England

Faber and Faber Ltd.
3 Queen Square
London W. C. 1N 3AU, England

Fontana Books (see William Collins, Sons)

Ginn and Co. Ltd.
18 Bedford Row
London W.C.1, England

Victor Gollancz Ltd.
14 Henrietta Street
Covent Garden
London W.C.2, England

George G. Harrap and Co. Ltd.
182 High Holborn
London W. C. 1, England

Heinemann Educational Books Ltd.
48 Charles Street
London W1X 8AH, England

Hutchinson Publishing Group Ltd.
178–202 Great Portland Street
London, W.1, England

Longman Group Ltd.
Longman House, Burnt Mill
Harlow, Essex, England

Lutterworth Press
Luke House
Farnham Road
Guildford, Surrey, England

Macmillan and Co. Ltd.
Little Essex Street
London W.C.2, England

Methuen and Co. Ltd.
11 New Fetter Lane
London E. C.4, England

Frederick Muller Ltd.
Ludgate House
110 Fleet Street
London E.C.4, England

Thomas Nelson and Sons Ltd.
36 Park Street
London W.1, England

Peter Owen Ltd.
12 Kendrick Mews
Kendrick Place
London S.W. 7, England

Oxford University Press
Ely House, 37 Dover Street
London W.IX 4AH, England

Publishers, Journals, Bookshops

Panaf Books
89 Fleet Street
London E.C.4, England

Panther Books Ltd.
3 Upper James Street
Golden Square
London W.1, England

Penguin Books Ltd.
21 John Street
London WC1N 2BT
England

Pergamon Press Ltd.
Headington Hill Hall
Oxford OX3 OBW, England

Routledge and Kegan Paul Ltd.
68–74 Carter Lane
London EC4V 5EL, England

Arthur H. Stockwell Ltd.
Elms Court, Torrs Park
Ilfracombe, Devonshire
England

University of London Press Ltd.
St. Paul's House
Warwick Lane
London E.C.4, England

Writers Forum
262 Randolph Avenue
London W.9, England

France

Afrique
21, rue Barbet de Jouy
Paris VII

Edit. Caractère
40, rue de Collisée
Paris, VIII

Edit. Gallimard
5, rue Sébastien-Bottin
Paris VII

Edit. Jean Grassin
50, rue Rodier
Paris IX

Edit, René Julliard
8, rue Garancière
Paris VI

Edit. Renée Lacoste
121, Avenue de Villiers
Paris XVII

Edit. Robert Laffont
6, Place Saint-Sulpice
Paris VI

Edit. Albin Michel
22, rue Huyghens
Paris XIV

Edit. Nalis
65, rue de Courcelles
Paris VIII

Edit. Pierre-Jean Oswald
7, rue d'Ecole Polytechnique
Paris 75005

Edit. Séghers
3 Bd. de la Tour Maubourg
75007 Paris

Edit. du Seuil
27, rue Jacob
Paris VI

Edit. Sociales
168, rue du Temple
Paris III

Edit. Stock
6, rue Casimir Delavigne
Paris VI

L'Afrique Littéraire et Artistique
Société Africaine d'Edition
32, rue de L'Echiquier
Paris X

Libraire Flammarion et Cie.
26, rue Racine
Paris VI

Libraire Hachette
79, Boulevard Saint-Germain
Paris VI

Libraire Fernand Nathan et Cie.
9, rue Méchain
Paris XIV

Libraire Plon
8, rue Garancière
Paris VI

François Maspero
1, Place Paul Painlevé
Paris V

Nouvelles Edit. Debresse
17, rue Duguay-Trouin
Paris VI

Nouvelles Edit. Latines
1, rue Palatine
Paris VI

Présence Africaine
25 bis, rue des Ecoles
Paris V

Les Presses Universitaires de France
49, Boulevard Saint-Michel
Paris V

Belgium

Edit. Gérard and Cie.
65, rue de Limbourg
Verviers

Institut de Sociologie Solvay
Université Libre de Bruxelles
44, Avenue Jeanne
Brussels 5

Portugal

Minerva, Editorial, Manuel Rodrigues
Sucrs, Lda.; Rua Luz Soriano 31–33
Lisbon 2

Pax Editora
Rua do Souto 73 a 77
Braga

Portucalense Editora, S.A.R.L.
Prace
Guilherme Gomes Fernandes 45,1
Porto 34

Seara Nova
Emprensa de Publicidada
Rua Bernardo Lima 23–1 Esq.
Lisbon 1

The Netherlands

N. V. Brill
Oude Riyn 33a
Leiden

Mouton Publishers
5 Harderstraat
P. O. Box 1132
The Hague

Germany

Moritz Diesterweg
Hochstrasse 31
6000 Frankfurt (M) 1

African Authors

German Democratic Republic

Seven Seas Books
Seven Seas Publishers
Glinkastrasse 13–15
Berlin W 8
 (orders taken by:
 Deutsche Buch
 Export und Import GmbH
 Leninstrasse 16
 Postfach 160
 601 Leipzig)

Liechtenstein

Kraus-Thomson Organization, Ltd.
FL–9491
Nendeln

Africa

African Universities Press
P. O. Box 1287
Lagos, Nigeria

Anowuo Educational Publishers
2R McCarthy Hill
Accra, Ghana

A. A. Balkema
P. O. Box 3117
93 Kerom St.
Cape Town, South Africa

Al Bashir Bookshop
P. O. Box 1118
Khartoum, Sudan

Benibengor Book Agency
P. O. Box 40
Aboso, Ghana

East African Literature Bureau
P. O. Box 30022
Nairobi, Kenya

East African Publishing House
Uniafric House
Koinange Street
P. O. Box 30571
Nairobi, Kenya

East Africa's Cultural Heritage
African Contemporary Monographs
East African Institute of Social and

Cultural Affairs
Nairobi, Kenya

Editions C.L.E.
B.P. 4048
Yaoundé, Cameroon

Editions Nationales Algériennes
88, rue Didouche-Mourad
Algérs, Algiera

Evans Brothers (Nigeria Publishers), Ltd.
Rational Bldg.
6 Lagos By-Pass
P.M.B. 5164
Ibadan, Nigeria

Ghana Publishing Corp.
P. O. Box 4348
Accra, Ghana

Ibadan University Press
Ibadan University
Ibadan, Nigeria

Institute of African Studies
University of Ibadan
Ibadan, Nigeria

Institute of African Studies
University of Ife
Ile-Ife, Nigeria

Librairie Clairafrique
2, rue Sandiniéry
B.P., 2005
Dakar, Senegal

Lovedale Press
Lovedale (Alice)
Cape Province
South Africa

Mambo Press
P.O. 779
Gwelo, Rhodesia

Mbari Club
P.O. Box 1463
Ibadan, Nigeria

Moxon Paperbacks, Publishers
P.O. Box M. 160
Accra, Ghana

National Educational Company of
 Zambia, Ltd.
P.O. Box 2664
Lusaka, Zambia

Nwankwo-Ifejika and Co., Publishers
26 Ogui Commercial Layout
P. O. Box 430
Enugu, Nigeria

Nasionale Boekhandel
P.O. Box 122
Parow, Cape Town, South Africa

Orisun Acting Editions
P.M.B. 3079
Ibadan, Nigeria

Oxford University Press
P.O. 1141
Cape Town, South Africa

Pilgrim Books Ltd.
305 Herbert Macaulay Street
P.O. Box 3560
Lagos, Nigeria

Shuter and Shooter (Pty.) Ltd.
P.O. Box 109
Pietermaritzburg, South Africa

Sudan Bookshop
P.O. Box 156
Khartoum, Sudan

Uganda Publishing House Ltd.
P.O. Box 2923
Kampala, Uganda

University of the Witwatersrand
Dept. of Bibliography, Librarianship and Typography
Jan Smuts Avenue
Johannesburg, South Africa

J. L. van Schaik,
P. O. Box 724
Pretoria, South Africa

Witwatersrand University Press
Milner Park
Jan Smuts Avenue
Johannesburg, South Africa

Appendix L

Journals Specializing in African Literature

This appendix first discusses the early journals that were the forerunners of contemporary African literature. It then devotes separate subsections to a discussion of the two most influential journals in French-speaking and English speaking worlds respectively, *Présence Africain* and *Black Orpheus*. Another subsection gives an overview of African literary journals in Portuguese. Finally, three subsections organized by language category list with addresses journals now publishing in the Africana field. For more details on each journal, consult *Ulrich's International Periodicals Directory*.

Early Journals

Possibly the very first journal in French to specialize in African and Afro-American culture and literature was the *La Revue du Monde Noir* (The Review of the Black World), published in Paris from 1930 to 1931 in six numbers. The Haitian editor, Dr. Sajous, and Mlle. Andrée Nardal from Martinique, were prime movers in this venture. Inspired by the upsurge of black writing in Harlem during the 1920's in New York and the growing clamor for recognition and respect on the part of the black world, they brought together writers from Africa, the Caribbean, and North and South America at soirées and meeting in Paris. This activity was an important factor in the growth of the movement which would find its name in Césaire's neologism, *négritude*.

In 1932 a small group of West Indians in Paris published the inflamatory journal *Légitime Défense* (Legitimate Defense) which drew heavily on Marxist and Freudian thought and the esthetics of André Breton, the French Marxist-surrealist poet. Etienne Léro, the leader of the circle, further denounced the corruption and callousness of the ruling elites in the colonial world, and decried the gross poverty and spiritual sickness of the peoples of the colonialized world everywhere. Quickly suppressed by the French authorities, the 20-page pamphlet got into enough hands to assure its message—cultural independence for all blacks—would never be lost again.

Three young students two years later issued a modest news-sheet, *L'Etudiant Noir* (The Black Student) which widened the attack on cultural assimilation of blacks by whites and called for a serious study of African culture in all of its manifestations as a source of strength with which to withstand the all-encompassing culture of Europe. The thinking here had moved beyond the complaints of the alienated "colored" elites of the Caribbean to express a mystique of race and shared history. Aimé Césaire, who, with Léon Damas and Léopold Senghor had organized and published the journal, first used the term *négritude* in its pages. All three young poets were to become in time members of the French National Assembly and persistent advocates of the struggle for political and cultural independence.*

During the Second World War, Césaire was a teacher in Martinique and there he published for five years (1941–1945) his own journal, *Tropiques,* with René Ménil and Aristide Maugée. Along with the short-lived Haitian journal, *Revue Indigène,* published in Port-au-Prince from July 1927 to February 1928, *Tropiques* was the first sign of changing times in the Antilles and a harbinger of events to take place in Africa after the war. A similar development in the British Caribbean was the establishment of the Barbados journal *Bim* in 1943. It began as the magazine of a small group called the Young Men's Progressive Club, but Frank Collymore, an English teacher in a Barbados Grammar School, expanded the journal to the entire island of Barbados, and with the help of George Lamming, then a young poet, to Trinidad and other islands. Early writers contributing to *Bim* in the early days were Samuel Selvon, V. S. Naipaul, Edgar Mittelholzer, Harold Telemaque and Clifford Sealy. The BBC Overseas Service in 1944 with "Caribbean Voices" made known the *Bim* writers throughout the Caribbean. *Bim* had been issued in 43 numbers through 1966

and the English language review *Kyk-Over-All* also published 28 numbers in Georgetown, British Guiana from 1945 to 1962. Since the 1940's many other journals and reviews have sprung up in the area, in England and France, and of course in Africa and the United States, devoted to black culture and literature.

Présence Africaine

The most significant publishing event in the francophone cultural area was the establishment in 1948 of *Présence Africaine,* a magazine and a book publishing house which for a quarter of a century

nouvelle série trimestrielle   2ᵉ trimestre 1965

L. V. THOMAS : Senghor à la recherche de l'homme Nègre.
MALCOLM X : La Communauté Noire Américaine et la Révolution Africaine.
J. P. CLARK : Thèmes de la Poésie Africaine d'expression anglaise.
Pathé DIAGNE : Royaumes Serères.

★

POEMES
PALABRES — NOTES

now has published hundreds of works in African literature, general history,

*See Appendix D

politics, ethnography, and allied subjects. *Présence Africaine* also operates a bookshop where African works in whatever language are on the shelves and where writers come to pick up their mail, to talk, and hold meetings.

The name "Présence Africaine" was first employed by Alioune Diop in 1942 or 1943. Owner and publisher of the journal and its press since its inception, Diop intended the term to signify the manifestation of African sciences and arts, and the African experience, on the world stage. The African "presence" was to be felt. The first, auspicious issue of November, 1947 was a large volume of 198 pages, and, though it had little financial support, its importance was clear because of the encouragement of such notable French writers as Albert Camus, Jean-Paul Sartre, André Gide, and such leading black American authors as Langston Hughes, Richard Wright, and Mercer Cook. At first, from 1947 to 1957, *Présence Africaine* was exclusively a French-language journal though it had special issues in English and in Portuguese, but, from 1957 on, it often carried articles and works of literature in languages other than French as a regular practice. "L'Orphée Noir," Sartre's now famous though still controversial preface to the journal's first anthology, *Anthologie de la nouvelle poésie nègre et malgache de langue française,* collected and edited by Senghor, gave the collection a prestigious push. Césaire and Damas, and other Antillean writers continue to contribute to the journal but today it is by and large a showplace for African writers.

A few major events in the journal's history deserve special mention: from 1950–1954 special issues were produced devoted to carefully selected topics. The first International Conference of Negro

Alioune Diop

Writers and Artists, held in Paris, September, 1956, and the second Conference in Rome, March–April, 1959, were organized by *Présence Africaine* and reported in special numbers of the journal; in 1956, Diop and others organized the Society of African Culture with the journal becoming its official organ. Since 1965 the journal has been issued in English as well as French and carried articles or creative works in at least one language other than French. In 1966, Presence Africaine published its very broad and multi-lingual anthology, *Nouvelles somme de poésie du monde noir* (New Sum of Poetry from the Negro World), the largest book of its kind yet to appear. Selections are from almost every area of the world with all texts in the original French, English or Portuguese. (The

575

book publishing house of Présence Africaine was founded in 1956.)

It is hard to imagine what African and black cultural studies in general would be without *Présence Africaine*. Once obscure writers who graced its early pages are now major figures in the black cultural world, and indeed in the intellectual world in general. For hundreds of scholars, writers, critics, historians, and readers in the general public, the journal has provided a voice and a supporting "presence" for the African experience in our time.

Black Orpheus and the Mbari Club

Stimulated by the example of the French-language review, *Présence Africaine,* and the first congress of black writers and artists, (Paris, 1956), Ulli Beier, Jahnheinz Jahn, and gifted young students at the University of Ibadan published the first number of *Black Orpheus* in September, 1957. Represented in early issues were many writers who were to become leaders of the new African literature: Gabriel Okara, Léopold Senghor, David Diop, Wole Soyinka, and Ezekiel Mphahlele. Senghor and Diop, of course were already well known in francophone Africa but were getting their first important exposure in an English-language journal. *Black Orpheus* also carried work by pan-African writers from North and South America and from the Caribbean: Aimé Césaire, Paul Vesey, Langston Hughes, Léon Damas, and others were represented.

Jahn relinquished his editorial functions after issue 6, and Wole Soyinka, joined by Mphahlele, newly arrived from South Africa, picked up the reins still partially held by Beier for the next six

issues. During this period, Nigerian writings predominated and francophone writings tapered off in the journal's offerings. New writers considered important today who first appeared in *Black Orpheus* at this time were Dennis Brutus, Lenrie Peters, John Pepper Clark, Kofi Awoonor (then George Awoonor-Williams), Christina Aidoo, and Grace Ogot.

Soyinka severed his full-time editorial connection with the journal in 1964 and Mphahlele his in 1966. With support of the Congress for Cultural Freedom and the Nigerian branch of Longman Green, *Black Orpheus* was able to pay for contributions for the first time from issue 12 onwards. Abiola Irele, Ronald Dathorne, Ulli Beier, and Mphahlele came and went as co-editors during the issuance of numbers 13 to 21. These early volumes are now collector's items.

In 1968, John Pepper Clark and Abiola Irele accepted editorial responsibility, and Volume II, numbers 2–7 were published for the Mbari Club by the *Daily Times of Nigeria* Ltd.

Bernth Lindfors in his "A decade of *Black Orpheus* (*Books Abroad*, October, 1968) summed up the first ten years by noting that the last three years of the journal were broader in their range than the earlier issues and more cosmopolitan in their styles and treatment of themes. Some 25 writers of fiction from 16 countries were contributors in this period, along with many poets and artists in other genre. Lindfors found that also during this period the work of 224 writers and visual artists from 26 African states and 14 Caribbean and Latin American nations had appeared in the review. Writers from the United States, England, and other nations also were represented.

Longmans of Nigeria Ltd published in 1964 a paperback anthology of some of the better items. Such writers as Christina Aidoo, Cyprian Ekwensi, Alex La Guma, Bloke Modisane appeared in the section "New Realities." Mallam Hampaté Bà of Mali, Birago Diop of Senegal, Andrew Salkey of Jamaica and D. O. Fagunwa of Nigeria were in the "Tradition" section. Okara's story "Okolo" and Laye's "The Eyes of the Statue" appeared in the section "Experiment."

The Mbari Club of Ibadan for writers and artists was, particularly in its early years in the late 1950's and early 1960's, a remarkable association of talented individuals who soon blossomed into Africa's most dynamic group. *Black Orpheus* magazine was only one recipient of this creativity and energy, for plays, art shows, craft exhibits were produced out-right by members of the circle or stimulated by its example.

A few of the very attractive Mbari Club publications are: Soyinka's *Three Plays*, J. P. Clark's *Song of a Goat*, Ladipo's *Three Yoruba Plays*, La Guma's *A Walk in the Night*, Léon Gontran Damas' *African Songs*, Okigbo's *Heavensgate* and *Limits*, Rabéarivelo's *24 Poems*, Brutus' *Sirens · Knuckles · Boots*, and U Tam'si's *Brush Fire*. All of the publications have illustrations by African artists and are in attractive typography and in unusual format. They are now considered collectors items.

In 1972 the University of Ife Press of Ile-Ife, Nigeria took over the distribution of all Mbari titles and the publication of *Black Orpheus*. Abiola Irele of the University of Ibadan and Ime Ikiddeh of the University of Ife became the editors of the journal. Black Orpheus Press, Inc. an American book publisher took over the publication and distribution of *Black Orpheus* in the United States, Canada, and the rest of the Western Hemisphere. The first issue in the spring of 1973 reflected a renewed interest in the inter-relationship of African and Afro-American concerns.

African Literary Journals in Portuguese

Although Portugal established presses in India and Japan as early as the 16th century, it waited until 1842 to set up the first one in Africa. In 1842 in Praia, the capital of the Cape Verde Islands, the first journal published was the *Boletim Oficial*. A journal of the same name started up three years later in Luanda, Angola, the first Portuguese journal on the mainland. The Angolan press-shop published in 1850 what is believed to the first work of Portuguese verse to be printed in Africa: *Espontaneidades da minha alma* (Spontaneous Outpourings of My Soul) by José da Silva Maia Ferreira who was probably the son of an African woman.

Most of these early bulletins and others established elsewhere in the Portuguese empire have not yet been thoroughly researched to see what literature they may have contained. The *Almanach de Lembranças* (est. 1851 in Lisbon), however, was studied in detail by António Fernandes de Oliveira. His research showed that the major portion of the literary contributions, primarily of Angolan origin, appeared in the fourteen year period 1879–1893.

The first purely literary review anywhere in Portuguese Africa appears to have been the Luandan journal, *A Aurora*, which probably had only one or two issues in 1856–57. From 1866 to 1869, there was a literary section in the political paper, *A Civilisação da África Portuguêsa*. With the growth of a middle class of mestiço and Africans during the last decades of the 19th century, other reviews were published, a few in Kimbundu, the African language of the Angolan capital. *O Futuro d'Angola* (founded 1882) was the most important of these. In 1901 another literary African journal in Portuguese appeared, *Ensaios Litterarios* (Literary Essays), edited by Francisco Castelbranco, and the next year Pedro da Paixão Franco began publishing *Luz e Crença* (Light and Faith), both in Luanda. Another review carrying a great deal of literature was the *Almanach Luso-Africano*, published in the Cape Verdes by the Catholic Seminary of São Nicolau beginning in 1894. Such important early writers as Eugénio Tavares (1867–1930) and José Lopes (1872–1962) contributed their verse to it.

In Mozambique the first journal was the *Boletim Oficial* (est. 1854). It was not until 1918, however, that the first literary journal appeared in Mozambique. This was *O Brado Africano,* edited by black African and mestiço journalists, led by João Albasini and his brother José. A bi-weekly, it was published in Xironga and Portuguese. *Itinerário* appeared from 1940 to 1942 in Lourenço Marques. In 1971, J. P. Grabato Dias and Rui Knopfli, both poets, issued the first two numbers of *Caliban,* called an "antologia" to mitigate censureship, but carrying critical articles—all on poetry.

In Guinea (Bissau), a dependency of Cape Verde until 1879, the first journal was the *Boletim Oficial* (est. 1880), and there was no literary activity which called for any more specialized, or less official, magazine.

In 1936, Jorge Barbosa of the Cape Verdean island of Santiago was a leader in the establishment of the cultural review *Claridade* (Clarity) whose motto was, "Let's plant our feet on the soil." Leading writers of the islands coming to the fore in this review were A. A. Gonçalves, Baltasar Lopes who sometimes wrote under the name of Osvaldo Alcântara, and Manuel Lopes from Santo Antão. After a long life it was no longer published after the early 1960's. Its demise was probably the result of the pressures from Portuguese authorities against journals expressing separatist or nationalist sentiments in the empire.

Convivium, Boletim Cultural, edited by a group centered around António Filipe Neira in Benguela, Angola, began in the late 1960's as African nationalism was driven underground. Carrying poetry, stories, book reviews and short articles it issued its sixth number in December, 1971. Another Angolan journal of recent vintage is *Vector, Cadernos de Poesia,* first published in 1971 in Nova Lisboa,

Angola, by the poet António Bellini Zara. The Luandan newspaper, *A Província de Angola*, publishes a literary supplement which is of modest interest.

One key place for young Portuguese Africans to publish was in Portugal itself. After many years of stagnation since the *Almanach de Lembranças* had failed, a new school of writers sprang up in 1945 in Lisbon to call itself the "Estudantes do Império." It came to publish the important journal, *Mensagem* (Message) in Lisbon and Luanda, Angola—and eventually—many works of poetry, folklore, and fiction by young Africans. The group also collected and published pioneering anthologies of creative writing by authors of each region overseas. This same circle was a transmitter of the negritude ideas of Césaire, Senghor, and Damas throughout the intellectual world of Portuguese Africa. Its very effectiveness and the African nationalism it stirred in the empire no doubt contributed to its difficulties. *Mensagem* ceased in 1950 after only five years of activity and the Casa dos Estudantes do Império, the publishing house of the group, ceased publishing works in 1965. Authors closely associated with *Mensagem* and the Casa dos Estudantes were Agostinho Neto, Mário António, António Jacinto, and the women poet, Alda Lara of Benguela (1930–1962) who, though European, was closely identified with African literature.

To some extent a spiritual descendant of the Angolan version of *Mensagem* was the Luandan review *Cultura* which was established in 1957; it published the poet, Arnaldo Santos and the story teller, Luandino Vieira.

Other journals which have published literature and/or criticism by Portuguese-African writers were:

In Lisbon: *Humanidade, As Farpas, Seara Nova, O Diabo, Bulletin des Etudes Portugaise, Estudos Ultramarinos, Colóquio* (published in 1950's and early 1960's), *Jornal da Tarde, Diário Popular,* and *A Noite;*

In Coimbra, Portugal: *Presença,* and *Revista de Portugal;*

In Luanda, Angola: *Diário de Luanda, Jornal de Angola, Arquivos de Angola;* and *Boletim do Instituto de Investigação Científica de Angola;*

In Porto, Angola: *O Primeiro de Janeiro,* and *Notícias do Bloqueio* (published in 1950's and 1960's);

In Lourenço Marques, Mozambique: *Revista Africana* (published in the 1880's);

In Rio de Janeiro, Brazil: *Dom Casmurro;*

In São Paulo, Brazil: *O Estado de S. Paulo;*

In Paris: *Révolution*, edited by Portuguese exiles.

African Authors

English-language Journals

Africa
10–11 Fetter Lane
London EC 4, England

Africa Report
866 United Nations Plaza
New York, N. Y., 10017

Africa Today
c/o Graduate School of Inter-
   nationalStudies
University Park Campus
Denver, Colo., 80210

African Abstracts
A Quarterly Review of Ethno-
   raphic,Social, and Linguistic
   Studies Appearing in Current
   Periodicals
International African Institute
St. Dunstans
Dunstans Chambers,
10 Fetter Lane
London EC 4, England

African Affairs
Oxford University Press
Press Road
Neasden, London, N.W. 10
England

African Arts/Arts d'Afrique
African Studies Center
University of California at Los
   Angeles
Los Angeles, Calif., 90024

African Literature Today
Distributors:
   Heinemann Educational Books Ltd.
   48 Charles Street
   London W. 1, England,
and
   Africana Publishing Corporation
   101 Fifth Avenue
   New York, N. Y., 10003

African Notes
Institute of African Studies
University of Ibadan
   Distributor:
   University Book Shop
   Nigeria Ltd
   Ibadan, Nigeria

African Digest Ltd
2 Arundel Street
London, England

African Studies
Witwatersrand University Press

Jan Smuts Avenue
Johannesburg, South Africa

African Studies Bulletin
African Studies Association
Brandeis University
218 Shiffman Humanities Center
Waltham, Mass., 02154

African Studies Review
African Studies Center
Michigan State Center
Michigan State University
East Lansing, Michigan

Africana Library Journal
A quarterly bibliograpahy and news
   bulletin
Africana Publishing Corporation
101 Fifth Avenue
New York, N. Y. 10003

Afro-Asian Theatre Bulletin
American Education Theater
   Assoc., Inc.
John F. Kennedy Center
726 Jackson Place
Washington, D. C., 20566

Afro-Asian Writings (see Lotus)

Ba Shiru
Department of African Languages
   and Literature
1450 Van Hise Hall
University of Wisconsin, Madison,
   Wisconsin, 53706

Black Academy Review
Black Academy Press, Inc.
3296 Main Street
Buffalo, New York, 14214

Black Images
P. O. Box 280
Station F
Toronto 5, Ontario
Canada

Black Lines: A Journal of Black Studies
Black Studies Dept., University of
   Pittsburg
P.O. Box 7195
Pittsburg, Penna., 15213

Black Orpheus
University of Ife
Ile Ife, Nigeria
In the Western Hemisphere—dis-
   tributed by:
      Black Orpheus Press, Inc.

322 New Mark Esplanade
Rockville, Maryland 20850

Black Theatre
200 West 135th Street
New York, N. Y., 10030

Black World
(formerly *Negro Digest*)
The Johnson Publishing Co., Inc.
Rockefeller Center
1270 Avenue of the Americas
New York, N. Y., 10020

Books Abroad
University of Oklahoma Press
Norman, Oklahoma, 73069

Black Theatre Bulletin
American Theatre Association
1317 F. Street N.W.
Washington, D. C., 20004

Busara (successor to *Nexus*)
East African Publishing House
P.O. Box 30571
Nairobi, Kenya

Cahiers d'Etude Africaine (publishes
   in French and English)
(see listing under French language
   journals)

*Canadian Journal of Black Studies
   in Canada*
Loyola College
Montreal 262
Quebec, Canada

The Conch
c/o Department of English
University of Texas
Austin, Texas, 78712

Contrast
211 Long Street
Cape Town, South Africa

*A Current Bibliography on African
   Affairs*
Greenwood Periodicals, Inc.
51 Riverside Avenue
Westport, Conn., 06880

Cultural Events in Africa
The Transcription Centre
84c Warwick Avenue
London, W. 9, England

Darlite
The University College
P.O. Box 35041

580

English-language Journals

Dar es Salaam, Tanzania

Drum
Drum Publications (Pty) Ltd.
62 Eloff Street Ext.
P.O. Box 3413
Johannesburg, South Africa

East Africa Journal
East African Publishing House
P.O. Box 30571
Nairobi, Kenya

English Studies in Africa
University of the Witwatersrand
Press
Milner Park
Johannesburg, South Africa

Ethiopia Observer
P.O. Box 1896
Addis Ababa, Ethiopia

Grass Curtain
The Southern Sudan Assoc. Ltd.
Room 19, Ludgate Hill
London EC4, England

Ibadan
Ibadan University
Ibadan, Nigeria

The Jewel of Africa: A Literary and Cultural Magazine from Zambia
Mphala Creative Society
University of Zambia
Box 2379
Lusaka, Zambia

Jonala (Journal of the New
African Literature and
the Arts)
The Third Press
444 Central Park West
New York, N. Y., 10025

Journal of Commonwealth Literature
Heinemann Educational Books Ltd.
48 Charles Street
London W. 1 (No. 1–8), England or:
Oxford University Press
Ely House, Dover Street
London W1, England

*Journal of the Nigerian English Studies
Association*
c/o B. Smith
The British Council
Dugbe, Ibadan, Nigeria

Journal of Ethopian Studies
Box 1176 Addis Ababa, Ethiopia

or: Subscriptions: Oxford University Press
Box 12532, Church House Government Road,
Nairobi, Kenya

Journal of Modern African Studies
Cambridge University Press
32 E. 57th Street
New York, N.Y., 10022

Journal of West African Languages
Institute of African Studies
University of Ibadan
Ibadan, Nigeria

Leeds African Studies Bulletin
University of Leeds
Leeds, England

The Literary Review
Fairleigh Dickinson University
Teaneck, New Jersey, 07666

Literature East and West
Carney 446
Boston College
Chestnut Hill, Mass., 02167

Lotus (formerly *Afro-Asian Writings*)
Permanent Bureau of Afro-Asian
Writers
104 Kasr El-Aini Street
Cairo, U.A.R.

Makerere Journal (see *Mawazo*)

Mawazo (succeeded *Makerere
Journal*)
Makerere University
Box 7062
Kampala, Uganda

Mila
Cultural Division
Institute for Development Studies
University College
Nairobi, Kenya

Moran
Department of Literature
Morogoro's Teacher's College
Morogoro, Tanzania

The New African
2 Arundel Street
London W.C. 2, England

New Writing from Zambia
The New Writers' Group
Box 1889, Lusaka, Zambia

Nexus (see *Busara*)

Nigeria Magazine
Exhibition Centre
Marina, Lagos, Nigeria

Nommo
77 East 35th Street
Chicago, Illinois, 60616

Odu (succeeded *Journal of Yoruba,
Edo and Related Studies*)
Oxford University Press Warehouse
State Highway, Ilupeju Industrial
Estate
P.M.B. 1003
Oshodi, Lagos, Nigeria

Okike: A Nigerian Journal of New Writing
Nwankwo-Ifejika & Co. Publishers
26 Ogui Commercial Layout
P.O. Box 430
Enugu, Nigeria

Okyeame
Writers' Workshop
Institute of African Studies
University of Ghana, Legon
Legon, Ghana

Ophir
P.O. Box 3846
Pretoria, South Africa

*Ozila: Cameroon
Literary Workshop*
B.P. 73
Yaoundé, Cameroon

*Panafrica. A monthly journal of African
life, history and thought*
58 Oxford Road
Manchester, England

Penpoint
Dept of English
Makerere University College
Kampala, Uganda

Phylon
Atlanta University
223 Chestnut Street
Atlanta, Georgia

The Purple Renoster
87 Roberts Avenue
Kensington, Johannesburg, South
Africa

Research in African Literatures
English Department

581

African Authors

English-language Journals

University of Texas
Austin, Texas 78712

South Africa: Information and Analysis
Lewis Nkosi, editor
104 Boulevard Haussemann
Paris 8, France

South African Outlook
Box 363
Cape Town, South Africa

South African Pen Yearbook
c/o Lewis Sowden
Rand Daily Mail
174 Main Street
Johannesburg, South Africa

Studies in Black Literature

University of Virginia, Dept. of
English
Box 3428, Fredericksburg, Virginia

Sub-Saharan Africa: A Guide to Serials
The Library of Congress, Reference
Dept.
General Reference and Bibliography Division
African Section
Washington, D. C., 20540

Ufahamu. Journal of the African Activist Association
African Activist Association
African Studies Center
University of California
Los Angeles, Calif., 90024

The Uganda Journal

Uganda Society
Private Bag
Kampala, Uganda

World Literature Written in English
Dept. of English
The University of Texas at Arlington
Arlington, Texas

Zambezi
University College of Rhodesia
P.O. box MP 45
Mount Pleasant, Salisbury,
Rhodesia

*Zuka. A Journal of East African creative
writing*
P.O. Box 12532
Nairobi, Kenya

French-language Journals

Abbia
Centre de Littérature Evangelique
B.P. 4048
Youndé, Cameroon

Africa (formerly *Afrique au Sud du
Sahara*)
Agence France-Press
13 Place de la Bourse
Paris, France

Africa
B.P. 1826
Dakar, Senegal

African Arts/Arts d'afrique
African Studies Center
University of California at Los
Angeles
Los Angeles, Calif., 90024

Africa-Turvuren
Amis du Musée Royal de l'Afrique
Centrale
13 Steenweg op Leuven
Turvuren, Belgium

Afrique
21 rue Barbet de Jouy
Paris 7, France

L'Afrique Actuelle
19, rue Greneta

Paris 2, France

*L'Afrique Littéraire
et Artistique*
32, rue de l'Echiquier
Paris 10, France

Afrique Nouvelle
B.P. 282
Dakar, Senegal

Art et Littérature
Les Presses Universitaires de France
49, Boulevard Saint-Michel
Paris, France

Bingo
B.P. 176
Dakar, Senegal
or: 11, rue de Teheran
Paris 8, France

Cahiers d'Étude Africaines
Edit. Bd. Moutons et cie.
5 Herderstraat,
The Hague, Netherlands

*Canadian Journal of Black Studies in
Canada*

(see listing under English-language
journals)

Congo Magazine
Ministère de l'Information
Section Presse Ecrite

2, Avenue Lippens
B.P. 8246
Kinshasa, Zaïre

*Dombi: Revue Congolaise des Lettres et
des Arts, Creation et Critique*
B.P. 3498
Kinshasa-Kalina, Zaïre

Poésie Vivante
11, rue Hoffmann
Geneva, Switzerland

Jeune Afrique
51, Avenue des Ternes
Paris 14, France

Le Livre Africaine
13, rue de Sevres
Paris 6, France

*Ozila: Forum littéraire Camerounais
(Cameroon Literary Workshop)*
B.P. 73
Yaoundé, Cameroon

Portuguese-language Journals

A Província de Angola (newspaper which carries literary supplement)
Luanda, Angola

Caliban (for poetry only: began in 1971)

Editors: J. P. Grabato Dias and Rui

Knopfli
Livraria Texto
Caixa Postal 4030
Lourenço Marques, Mozambique

Convivium, "Boletim Cultural" (poetry, literary news, reviews)
Redaccto de "Convivium"
Caixa Postal 168
Benguela, Angola

Vector, Cadernos de Poesia (poetry only)
Nova Lisbon, Angola

A Civilização da África Portuguesa, Luanda, Angola

Almanach Luso-Africano, S. Nicolau, Cape Verde

Angola, Luanda, Angola

A Noite, Lisbon, Portugal

Arquivos de Angola, Luanda, Angola

As Farpas, Lisbon, Portugal

Boletim do Instituto de Investigação de Angola, Luanda, Angola

Claridade, S, Vicente, Cape Verde

Colóquio, Lisbon, Portugal

Cultura, Luanda, Angola

Diário de Luanda, Luanda, Angola

Estudos Ultramarinos, Lisbon, Portugal

Humanidade, Lisbon, Portugal

Itinerário, Lourenço Marques, Mozambique

Jornal de Angola, Luanda, Angola

Jornal da Tarde, Lisbon, Portugal

Luz e Crença, Luanda, Angola

Mensagem, Luanda, Angola

Notícias do Bloqueio, Porto, Angola

O Brado Africano, Lourenço Marques, Mozambique

O Futuro d'Angola, Luanda, Angola

Revista Africana, Lourenço Marques, Mozambique

Revista de Portugal, Coimbra, Portugal

Révolution, Paris, France

Seara Nova, Lisbon, Portugal

Appendix M

Bookshops and Book Distributors Specializing in African Literature

The United States

Academic Library Service
6489 Sould Land Park Drive
Sacramento, Calif., 95831

Africana Center
International University Booksellers, Inc.
101 Fifth Avenue
New York, N.Y., 10003

The Cellar Bookshop
Box 6, College Park Station
Detroit, Mich., 48221

Chatham Bookseller
38 Maple Street
Chatham, New Jersey, 07928

Drum and Spear Bookstore
1371 Fairmont Street, N.W.
Washington, D. C., 20009

Humanities Press, Inc.
303 Park Avenue South
New York, N.Y. 10016

The More Bookstore
855 Divadero Street
San Francisco, Calif., 94117

National Memorial Bookstore
101 West 105th Street
New York, N. Y.

Northwestern University Press
1840 Sheridan Road
Evanston, Illinois, 60201

University Place Bookshop
821 Broadway
New York, N.Y., 10003

Canada

Third World Books and Crafts
70, Walton Street
Toronto, 2

Great Britain

B. H. Blackwell Ltd.
48–51 Broad Street
Oxford, England

Dillon's University Bookshop Ltd.
1 Malet Street
London WC1E 7JB, England

Francis Edwards Ltd.
83 Maylebone High Street
London W.I., England

W. Heffner and Sons Ltd.
3–4 Petty Curry
Cambridge, England

Heinemann Educational Books Ltd.
(for East African Publishing House titles)
48 Charles Street
London W1X 8AH, England

Kegan Paul, Trench, Trubner and Co.
43 Great Russell Street
London WC1B 3LJ, England

University Press of Africa
1 West Street
Tavistock, Devon, England

Ginn and Co., Ltd
(for African Universities Press titles)
18 Bedford Row

London W.C.1, England

France

Librairie du Camée
3, rue de Valence
Paris V

Librairie Orient
17, rue de l'Odéon
Paris VI

Librairie Présence Africaine
25 bis, rue des Ecoles
Paris V

Michèle Trochon
76, rue du Cherche-Midi
Paris VI

Belgium

Librairie Africaine Hubaut
10, rue Stevin
Brussels 4

Le Livre Africaine
35, rue Van Elewyck
Ixelles, 1050
Brussels

Italy

Libreria Paesi Nuovi
31, 33, 35 Via Aurora
Rome

Portugal

Livraria Portugal
Rua do Carmo 70–74
Lisbon

African Authors

Livraria Historica e Ultramarina
Travessa da Queimade 28
Lisbon 2

Africa

Cameroon

Centre de Littérature Evangélique
(CLE)
B.P. 4048
Yaoundé

Librairie Aux Frères Réunis
B.P. 5346
Duala

Papeterie Moderne
B.P. 495
Yaoundé

Central African Republic

Librairie Hachette
B.P. 823
Bangui

Chad

Librairie Mauclert
B.P. 337
Niamey

Ethiopia

Birhan Bookshop and Stationery
Box 302
Addis Ababa

G. P. Giannopoulos
P.O. Box 120
Addis Ababa

Menno Bookstore
P.O. Box 1236
Addis Ababa

Gabon

Librairie Hachette du Gabon
B.P. 121
Libreville

Ghana

R. J. Moxon
The Atlas Bookshop
P.O. Box M160
Accra

University Bookshop
University of Ghana
P. O. Box 1, Legon

Ivory Coast

Bibliothèques Universitaires de
l'Afrique
Immeuble C.I.C.A.
Avenue de Gaulle
Adidjan

Librairie Africaine
B.P. 328
Abidjan

Librairie Carrefour
B.P. 8326
Abidjan

Librairie générale Mme. E. Pociello
B.P. 1757, et 587
Abidjan

Kenya

The East Africa Literature Bureau
(see The Textbook Centre)

S. J. Moore Bookshop
P.O. Box 31062
Nairobi

The Textbook Centre
P.O. Box 7540
Nairobi

University College Bookshop
University College
Nairobi

Malagasy

Librairie de Madagascar
B.P. 402
Tananarive

Malawi

The Times Bookshop
P.O. Box 445
Blantyre

Mali

Librairie Deves et Chaumet
B.P. 64
Bamako

Librairie Populaire du Mali
B.P. 28
Bamako

Mozambique

Minerva Central
C.P. 212
Lourenço Marques

Nigeria

Nigerian Book Suppliers of Ibadan
(and Lagos)
P.O. Box 3870
Lagos

Northern Nigerian Publishing
" Corp.
Gaskiya Corp.
Zaria

University Bookshop Nigeria Ltd
University of Ibadan
Ibadan

University of Ife Bookshop Ltd
University of Ife
Ile-Ife

Rhodesia

Mambo Press Bookshop
Parthenon House
7th Street
P. O. Box 779
Gwelo

Senegal

La Maison du Livre
13, avenue Roume
Dakar

Librairie Clairafrique
B.P. 2005, Place Protet
Dakar

Sierra Leone

Fourah Bay College Bookshop Ltd
University of Sierra Leone
Freetown

Somalia

The New Africa Booksellers
P.O. Box 897
Mogadishu

South Africa

Exclusive Books
Kotze Street
Hillbrow, Johannesburg

Fort Hare University Press

586

University of Fort Hare
P.O. Fort Hare
Fort Hare

Lovedale Press
Alice, Cape Province

C. Struik
P.O. Box 1144
Cape Town

Frank R. Thorold (Pty.) Ltd
Raines Bldgs.
54 Eloff Street
Johannesburg

Sudan

Sudan Bookshop
P.O. Box 156
Khartoum

South West Africa

Swakopmunder, Munder Boek-
handlung
P.O. Box 500
Swakopmund

Tanzania

The Cathedral Bookshop
P.O. Box 2381
Dar es Salaam

Dar es Salaam Bookshop
P.O. Box 9030
Dar es Salaam

University Bookshop
University College
Dar es Salaam

Uganda

Makerere University Bookshop
Makerere University College
Kampala

Zaïre

Librairie Congolaise
B.P. 2100
Kinshasa

Librairie St. Paul
B.P. 2447
Lumbumbashie

Zambia

University of Zambia Bookshop
The University of Zambia
Lusaka

PART IV
BIBLIOGRAPHIES, CRITICAL STUDIES, ANTHOLOGIES

Appendix N

Bibliographies and Critical Studies on African Writing

Bibliographies

Abrash, Barbara. *Black African Literature in English Since 1952: Works and Criticism*. New York: Johnson Reprint Corp., 1967. Very useful when published, the large volume of new work by African writers and the criticism and discussion of that writing has quickly dated this still useful study. However, the 463 items provided for period 1952–1966 are quite adequate.

Afro-American and African Films, 1970 revised catalogue. African Studies Program, Indiana University, Woodburn Hall 223, Bloomington, Ind., 47401.

American University and Research Library Holdings in African Literature. *African Studies Bulletin*, XI, 2, September 1968, pp. 286–311.

Baratte, Thérèse. *Bibliographie: Auteurs africaine et malgache de langue française*, second revised edition. Paris: Office de Co-operation Radiophonique, 1966, 1968. This work is very useful in its specialized area of concern.

Black Literature in Paperbound Books. New York: R. R. Bowker Co., 1180 Avenue of the Americas, 10036, 1970.

Cesar, Amandio and Mário António. *Elementos para una bibliografia da literatura e cultura portuguêsa ultramarina contemporânea*, Lisbon, 1968.

East, N.B. *African Theatre: A Checklist of Critical Materials*. New York: Africana Publishing Co., 1970.

Gérard, Albert S. "Bibliographic Problems in Creative African Literature." *Journal of General Education*, XIX (167), 25–35.

Ghana in Print, semi-annual catalogue (The Atlas Bookshop, P.O. Box M, 160 Accra, Ghana).

Hamner, Robert D. (ed.). *Literary Periodicals in World English* (Commonwealth and Former Commonwealth Countries): *A Selective Checklist*. Supplement to WLWE Newsletter No. 14, November 1968 (published by Department of English, the University of Texas at Arlington, Arlington, Texas, 76010).

International African Bibliography of Current Publications on Africa. London: International African Institute, St. Dunstans Chambers, 10/11 Fetter Lane, London, E.C. 4, 1971 and 1972.

Jahn, Jahnheinz. *Neo-African Literature*, translated from the German by Oliver Coburn and Ursula Lehrburger. New York: Grove Press, 1968. This is an important source for early works by African writers and the information on oral, pre-colonial aspects of the continent's literature in Hausa, Swahili, Sotho, Xhosa, and Zulu is useful indeed.

Jahn, Jahnheinz and Claus Peter Dressler, *Bibliography of Creative African Writing*. Nendeln, Liechtenstein: Kraus Thomson, 1971. This new work offers 2176 titles in the up-dating of the authors' earlier *A Bibliography of New-African Literauure: from Africa, America, and the Carib ean* (New York, Praeger, 1965 and London, Andre Deutsch, 1965), but here only African works are dealt with. The only important omissions for students of Black African literatures are the writings in Amharic from Ethiopia, and the relatively incomplete coverage of work in Kikiyu and the lesser known vernaculars of South Africa. This new work also offers some data concerning biographical and/or critical studies of many of the authors and reviews of their work. Of special interest are the lists of translations of African works and the bibliography on Negritude which offers 47 titles. This compilation in an indispensable tool to the serious student of African writing.

Lindfors, Bernth (compiler). "A Preliminary Checklist of English Short Fiction by Non-Europeans in South Africa, 1940–1964," *African Studies Bulletin*, XII, 3, December 1969.

Moser, Gerald M. *A Tentative Portuguese-African Bibliography: Portuguese Literature in Africa and African Literature in the Portuguese Language*. Bibliographical Series No. 3. University Park, Penna.: The Pennsylvania State University Libraries, 1970. This is a unique study of the writers and works in this virtually ignored field in the United States. Some biographic date is offered. A second edition, much augmented from the first, is planned for publication in 1973.

Murphy D. and Harry Goff. *A Bibliography of African Languages and Linguistics*. Washington D.C.: The Catholic University of America Press, 1969.

Paden, John N. and Edward Soja. *The African Experience*, Volume III (Bibliography). Evanston, Illinois: Northwestern

African Authors

University Press, 1970. (Volume I and II of this work offer an encyclopedia treatment of all aspects of African studies. The section on literature, though of interest, is not extensive.

Research Services in East Africa. Nairobi: East African Publishing House, 1971. This is a guide to research institutions and available services for scholars.

Sheub, Harold. *Bibliography of African Oral Narratives.* Occasional Paper No. 3, African Studies Program. Madison, Wisconsin: University of Wisconsin Press, 1972. This is the definitive work in English in this area: 2373 entries.

Stevens, W. D. *African Film Bibliography.* New York: African Studies Association, 1966.

Tooley, R. V. *Collectors' Guide to Maps of the African Continent and Southern Africa.* London: Carta Press, 1969.

Varley D. H. *African Native Music: An Annotated Bibliography* (reprint of 1936 edition). London: Dawson's, Pall Mall, 1970.

Zell, Hans and Helene Silver. *A Reader's Guide to African Literature.* New York: African Publishing Corp., 1971. Helpful information on 654 works of creative literature, 67 anthologies of African writings in English or French, 23 bibliographies, and 40 works of criticism. All in all, some 776 works are described and an additional 44 mentioned which are of very recent publication. The one or two-page biographies, with photos of the authors in most cases, of 53 of the leading authors in French and English provide some important information and short discussions of the authors' works; they offer interesting quotations concerning the artists' general problems, publishing histories, and early literary influences. On the negative side one notes that only eleven of the 53 authors dealt with write in French, none in Portuguese, and there are no writers whose major work is in any of the African languages. Very useful, however, are the lists, with addresses of magazines and reviews, of journals devoted to African writing, and the annotated bibliography of recent periodical articles.

Critical Studies

General

Anozie, Sunday Ogbonna. *Sociologie du roman Africaine.* Paris: Aubier-Montaigne, 1970. (A "structuralist" approach to African creative writing in English and French.)

Atkinson, Brian Hebbelewhite. *Fiction Writing for West Africans.* London, New York: Macmillan, 1962; and New York: St. Martin's Press, 1962.

Beier, Ulli. *Introduction to African Literature.* London: Longmans, 1967. (A collection of essays edited by Beier.)

Belinga, Enos M. S. *Littérature et musiques populaire en Afrique noire.* Paris: Ed. Cujas, 1965. (African music and literature in the context of the traditional arts of Africa.)

Cartey, Wilfred. *Whispers from a Continent: the literature of contemporary black Africa.* New York: Random House, 1969; in paperback: New York: Vintage, 1969; London: Heinemann, 1971.

Chome, Jules. *Le drame du Nigeria.* Brussels: Tiers Monde, 1969.

Cook, Mercer, and Stephen E. Henderson. *The Militant Black Writer in Africa and the United States.* Madison: University of Wisconsin Press, 1969.

Gleason, Judith. *This Africa: Novels by West Africans in English and French.* Evanston, Illinois: Northwestern University Press, 1965.

Graham-White, Anthony. "West African drama: folk, popular, and literary." Unpublished doctoral dissertation, Stanford University, Stanford, Calif., 1969.

Henries, A. Doris Banks. "Surveys of Liberian Literature," in *Liberian Writing: Liberia as seen by her own writers as well as by German authors.* Tübingen: Erdmann, 1970.

Heywood, Christopher. *Perspectives on African Literature.* New York: Africana Publishing Corporation, 1970.

King, Bruce. *Introduction to Nigerian Literature.* New York: Africana Publishing Corporation. 1972. (The broadest treatment thus far of Nigerian writing, including that in Yoruba, Hausa, and Edo, provided in a general work.)

Klimá, Vládimir. *Modern Nigerian Novels.* London: C. Hurst (Dissertations orientalis, volume 18), 1970.

Knappert, Jan. *Traditional Swahili Poetry. An investigation into the concepts of East African Islam as reflected in the Utenzi literature.* Leiden: Brill, 1967.

Krog, E. Walter (ed.). *African Literature in Rhodesia.* Gwelo, Rhodesia: Mambo Press, 1966.

Larson, Charles. *The Emergence of African Fiction.* Bloomington, Indiana; Midland Quality Paper Series, Indiana University Press, 1972.

Laurence, Margaret. *Long Drums and Cannons: Nigerian dramatists and novelists 1952–1966.* London: Macmillan, 1968.

Lindfors, Bernth Olof. "Nigerian fiction in English, 1952–1967." Unpublished doctoral dissertation, University of California, Los Angeles, 1969.

Makouta-Mboukou, J. P. *Black African Literature: An Introduction.* Washington D. C.: Black Orpheus Press, 1973. (Emphasis on francophone literature.)

Makward, Edris and Leslie Lacy. *Contemporary African Literature.* New York: Random House, 1972.

Moore, Gerald. *English Writing in the Tropical World.* London and Harlow: Longmans, 1969.

———. *Seven South African Writers.* London: Oxford University Press, 1962.

Mphahlele, Ezekiel. *The African Image.* London: Faber, 1962.

Pieterse, Cosmo and Donald Munro (eds.). *Protest and Conflict in African Literature.* London: Heinemann, 1969; New York: Africana Publishing Corp., 1969.

Bibliographies

Pieterse, Cosmo and Dennis Duerden (eds.). *African Writers Talking: a collection of radio interviews*. New York: Africana Publishing Corp., 1972.

Povey, John F. "Canons of Criticism for Neo-African Literature" *African Proceedings*, III (1966), 73–91.

Ramsaran, J. A. *New Approaches to African Literature. A Guide to Negro-African Writing and Related Studies*, second edition. Ibadan: Ibadan University Press, 1970. (Sketchy in part and unreliable for some of the publishing information, this work yet gives a general overview of African writing rare in other works.)

Roscoe, Adrian A. *Mother is Gold: A Study in West African Literature*. London: Cambridge University Press, 1971. (This work is of particular interest for its treatment of political prose and journalism. Its discussion of Nigerian drama, particularly that in Yoruba, is excellent.)

Shore, Herbert L. *Africa on Stage*. London: Oxford University Press, 1969.

Taiwo, Oladele. *An Introduction to West African Literature*. London: Nelson, 1967.

Tibble, Anne. *African/English Literature*. London: Peter Owen, 1965. (Though basically an anthology, this work provides useful analysis of writing by region and of each of the works anthologized. There is also useful field research with oral poets collected and commented upon for the first time.)

Tucker, Martin. *Africa in Modern Literature: A survey of contemporary writing in English*. New York: Ungar, 1967

Wright, Edgar. "African Literature I: Problems of Criticism." *Journal of Commonwealth Literature* (Leeds University, Leeds, England), II (December 1966), 103–112.

On African Writing in French

Brench, A. C. *The Novelists' Inheritance in French Africa: Writers from Senegal to Cameroon*. London, New York: Oxford University Press, 1967.

———. *Writings in French from Senegal to Cameroon*. London, New York: Oxford University Press, 1967.

Colin, Roland. *Littérature africaine d'hier et de demain*. Paris: A.D.E.C., 1965.

———. *Les contes noirs de l'Ouest Africain, témoins majeurs d'un humanisme*. Paris: Présence Africaine, 1957. (The preface is by Léopold Senghor.)

Jadot, J. M. *Les écrivains Africains du Congo-Belge et du Ruanda-Urundi*. Brussels, 1959.

Kennedy, Ellen Conroy. *The Negritude Poets*. New York: Richard Seavers-Viking, 1973.

Kesteloot, Lilyan. *The Intellectual Origins of the African Revolution*. Washington, D.C.: Black Orpheus Press, 1972.

———. *Les écrivains noirs de langue française: naissance d'une littérature*. Brussels, Université Libre de Bruxelles, 1965; English translation by Ellen Conroy Kennedy as *Negritude is Born*, Philadelphia, Temple University Press, 1973. From today's vantage point this work is most useful for its pioneering effort to understand the sociological-esthetic experiences which helped produce original new literatures in French-speaking Africa and the Caribbean. The bibliographies of even major writers are incomplete, however, and relatively few authors are discussed. There is a serious need for a new over-all study of francophone literature in Africa, author by author, and major work by major work, similar to the treatment of A.S. Gérard in his *Four African Literatures*.

Loufti, Martine Astier. *Littérature et colonialisme*. Paris, The Hague: Mouton, 1972.

Melone, Thomas. *De la négritude dans la littérature négro-africaine*. Paris: Présence Africaine, 1962.

Pagéard, Robert. *Littérature négro-africaine: Le mouvement littéraire contemporaine dans l'Afrique noire d'expression française*, second edition. Paris: Le Livre Africain, 1966.

Premier congrès international des écrivains et artistes noirs (Compte rendu complet, 2 volumes). Paris: Présence Africaine, 1956–57. (First issued in *Présence Africaine* magazine, Nos. 8, 9, 10, 14, and 15.)

Sartre, Jean-Paul. "Black Orpheus," introduction to *Anthologie de la nouvelles poésie nègre et malgache* by Léopold Sédar Senghor, Paris: Presses Universitaires de France, 1948, 1969. First published as "Orphée noir," this famous essay has seen several English translations, the first by Samuel W. Allen. Paris: Présence Africaine, 1963.

Société Africaine de Culture (Colloque sur l'art nègre: 1er Festival mondial des arts nègres, Dakar—1-24 avril, 1966). Paris: Présence Africaine, 1967. (Published in English as *Society of African Culture*, Paris: Présence Africaine, 1968.)

Traoré, Bakary. *Le théâtre négro-africain et ses fonction sociales*. Paris: Présence Africaine, 1958. Only francophone plays are discussed in this now quite dated work.

von Grunebaum, G.E. *French African Literature: some cultural implications*. The Hague: Mouton, 1964.

Wauthier, Claude. *L'Afrique des africains: inventaire de la négritude*. Paris: Seuil, 1964. Translated from the French by Shirley Kay as *The Literature and Thought of Modern Africa: a survey*. London: Pall Mall, 1967, and New York: Praeger, 1967. This is one of the finest treatments of its subject, but literature is only one of several subjects. It is most useful for francophone literature.

On African Writing in Portuguese

Andrade, Mário. "Littérature et nationalisme en Angola." *Présence Africaine*, Vol. 41, (1962), 91–100.

António, Mário. (Fernandes de Oliveiro). "African Writers in Portuguese." *African Arts* (Winter 1970), 80–84.

———. "Colaborações angolanas no *Alamanach de Lembranças*, 1851–1900," *Boletim do Instituto de Investigação Científica de Angola*, III, 1 (1966), 75–85.

———. "Influência da literature brasileira sôbre as literaturas portuguesas do Atlântico Tropical," mimeographed lecture, Lisbon, 1967.

African Authors

Araujo, Norman. *A Study of Cape Verdean Literature.* Boston: Boston College Press, 1966. (This is the first study of the literature of the Islands.)

Cesar, Amândio. *Parágrafos de literature ultra marina.* Lisbon, 1967.

Ervedosa, Carlos. *A literature angolana.* Lisbon: Casa dos Estudantes do Império, 1963.

Ferreira, Manuel. *A aventura crioula, ou Cabo Verde, uma síntese, etnica e cultural.* Lisbon, 1967.

Lopes, Manuel. "Reflexões sobre a literatura cabo-verdiana ou A literatura nos meios pequenos." in *Colóquios cabo-verdianos.* Lisbon: Centro de Estudos Politicos e Socias, Junta de Investigações do Ultramar, 1959.

Lopo, Júlio de Castro. *Para a história do jornalismo em Angola.* Luanda, 1952.

Margarido, Alfredo. "Incidence socio-économique sur la poésie noire d'expression portugaise," *Diogène,* Vol. 37 (1962), 53–80.

———. La littérature angolaise de la découverte au combat." *L'Afrique Littéraire et Artistique,* Paris (December 1968), 8–17

Montenegro, José. *A negritude. Dos mitos às realidades.* Colecção Metropole e Ultramar, 31. Braga, Portugal: Pax, 1967.

Moser, Gerald M. *Essays in Portuguese-African Literature.* Penn State Studies 26. University Park, Penna.: The Pennsylvania State University, 1969. A break-through in the study of African works created in Portuguese, this slim volume offers the first important information in English of this usually neglected area. The first three chapters are of particular importance: "The Origins of an African Literature in the Portuguese Language," "The Social and Regional Diversity of African Literature in the Portuguese Language," and "Africa as a Theme in Portuguese Literature." There is also a brief "anthology" of Portuguese texts with English translations, an index of authors' names and pseudonyms (very common) and a short index of titles of works and periodicals. Consulted with Moser's *A Tentative Portuguese-African Bibliography* this work makes possible an adequate acquaintance with writing generally poorly known, if known at all.

Oliveira, José Osório de. *Poesia de Cabo Verde.* Lisbon, 1944.

Randles, W. G. L. *L'image de Sud-Est Africain dans la littérature africaine au XVIe siecle.* Lisbon: Centro de Estudo Históricos Ultramarinos, 1959.

Rodrigues, Júnior José. *Poetas de Moçambique (Contribuição para um júzo interpretivo).* Lorenço Marques: Africa Editôra, 1965.

———. *Para uma cultura moçambicana.* Lisbon, 1951.

Soromenho, Castro. *Contribuição portuguêsa para o conhecimento da alma negra.* Lisbon, 1952.

On African Writing from Malagasy

Andrianarahinjaka, Lucien. "Ramanato: An Early 19th Century Malagasy Poet." *Présence Africaine,* 55 (1965), 45–73.

Gérard, Albert S. "La Naissance du theatre à Madagascar." *Bulletin d'Information* CEDEV, 8 (1967), 28–35.

Houlder, J. A. *Ohabolana or Malagasy proverbs* (with Malagasy proverbs in original text and French translation). London: Foreign Missionary Association, 1916, new edition with French and Malagasy texts only. Antananarivo, Imprimerie Luthérienne, 1960.

Koshland, M. "The Poetry of Madagascar." *Africa South,* 4 (1960), 114–119.

"La Nostalgie dans la poésie malgache," *Revue de Madagascar,* 3 (1948), 67–75.

Mondain, G. "Note sur les tout premiers débuts de la littérature malgache avant l'arrivée des Européens." *Bulletins de l'Académie Malgache,* XXVI (1944–45), 43–48.

Poulhan, Jean. *Les hain-teny.* Paris: Gallimard, 1939 (first edition, 1913).

Wake C. and J. O. Reed. "Modern Malagasy Literature in French." *Books Abroad* 38 (1964), 14–19.

On African Writing from Ethiopia

Cerulli, Enrico. *Storia della letteratura etiopica,* third edition. Florence, 1968.

Comba, Pierre. "Le roman dans la littérature Ethiopienne de langue Amharique," (a paper read at the second International Conference of Ethiopian Studies, Manchester University, July 1963). *Journal of Semitic Studies,* IX (Spring 1964), 173–186.

Gérard, Albert S. "Amharic Creative Literature: The Early Phase." *Journal of Ethiopian Studies,* VI, 2 (1968), 39–59.

———. *Four African Literatures: Xhosa, Sotho, Zulu, Amharic.* Berkeley and Los Angeles: University of California Press, 1971.

Leslau, Wolf (ed.). *Ethiopians Speak: Studies in Cultural Backgrounds.* Berkeley: University of California Press, 1965.

Levine, Donald N. *Wax and Gold: Tradition and Innovation in Ethiopian Culture.* Chicago, 1965.

Messing, Simon D. "A Modern Ethiopian Play—Self-Study in Culture Change." *Anthropological Quarterly,* XXXIII, 3 (1960), 149–157.

Pankhurst, Richard. "The Foundations of Education, Printing, Newspapers, Book Production, Libraries and Literacy in Ethiopia," *Ethiopia Observer,* VI, 3 (1962), 241–290.

Riad, Zaher, "The Foundation of the Ethiopian Theatre." *Bulletin de l'Institute des Etudes Coptes* (1958), 72–7.

Ricci, Lanfranco. "Canti imperiale amarici." *Rivista degli studi orientali,* XXXV (1960), 179–189.

———. "Romanzo e novella: due esperimenti della letterature amarica attuale." *Journal of Semitic Studies,* IX (1964), 144–172. (Some detailed analysis of particular works is provided; unfortunately, there is not enough bibliographic detail to provide an over-all view of the subject.)

Bibliographies

On African Writing from Southern Africa

Astrinsky, A. *South African Novels, 1930–1960*. Cape Town: University of Cape Town, 1965.

"The Brief Search for an African Hero: The Chaka Mzilikazi Story in South African Novels." *Discourse*, XI (1968), 276–283.

Doke, Clement. "The Basis of Bantu Literature." *Africa*, XVIII (1948), 284–301.

——. "A Preliminary Investigation into the State of the Native Languages of South Africa with Suggestions as to Research and the Development of Literature," *Bantu Studies*, VII (1938), 1–98.

——. "Scripture Translation into Bantu Languages." *African Studies*, XVII (1958), 82–99.

Davis, John A. and James K. Baker. *Southern Africa in Transition*. New York: Praeger, 1966.

Ellenberger, Victor. *A Century of Mission Work in Basutoland: 1833–1933*. Morija, Morija Press, 1936.

Franz, G. H. "The Literature of Lesotho." *Bantu Studies*, LV (1930), 145–180.

Gérard, Albert S. *Four African Literatures: Xhosa, Sotho, Zulu, Amharic*. Berkeley and Los Angeles: University of California, 1971. An indispensable study of the four literatures concerned, this work provides a rich narrative of pre-colonial literatures, the arrival of missionary schools, their presses and publishing programs, and the gradual development of writers who learn to exploit the European forms with the traditional, oral patterns and preoccupations of their own cultures.

The notes are excellent, the bibliographies less so, for many authors treated in the main text fail of adequate coverage in the bibliography of the language concerned and some authors are scanted entirely. On occasion the bibliographies offer variant titles or typographically inaccurate versions of works discussed in the text. There are also some serious errors of fact or contradictions of fact between the notes and the texts on given matters. All in all, however, Gérard's work has exploited most of the available bio-bibliographic information on the four literatures dealt with.

Guma, S. M. *The Form, Content and Technique of Traditional Literature in Southern Sotho*. Pretoria: van Schaik, 1967.

Inauen, Beatrice. "Dix ans de littérature Shona." *Bethléem*, V (May 1967), 154–157.

Jabavu, D. D. T. *The Influence of English on Bantu Literature*. Lovedale, South Africa: Lovedale Press, 1944.

Kunene, Daniel P. and Randal A. Kirsch. *The Beginnings of South African Vernacular Literature*. Los Angeles: University of California Press, 1967.

Kunene, Mazisi. "Portrait of Magolwane—the Great Zulu Poet." *Cultural Events in Africa*, XXXII (July 1967), 1–14.

Miller, G. M. and H. Sergeant. *A Critical Survey of South African Poetry in English*. Cape Town: Balkema, 1957.

Morris, Donald R. *The Washing of the Spears: A History of the Rise of the Zulu Nation Under Shaka and Its Fall in the Zulu War of 1879*. New York: 1965.

Perrat, Claude-Hélène. "Premières années de l'implantation du Christianisme au Lesotho (1833–1847)." *Cahiers d'Etudes Africaines*, IV, 1 (1963), 97–125.

Shepherd R. H. W. *Bantu Literature and Life*. Lovedale, South Africa: Lovedale Press, 1955.

——. *Lovedale and Literature for the Bantu: A brief history and a forecast* (reprint of Lovedale edition of 1945). Westport, Conn.: Negro Universities Press, 1970.

——. *Lovedale, South Africa: The Story of a Century: 1841–1941*. Lovedale, South Africa, Lovedale Press, 1942.

Sundkler, G. Bengt M. *Bantu Prophets in South Africa*. London, 1948.

Wilson, Monica and Leonard Thompson (eds.). *The Oxford History of South Africa*. Oxford: Oxford University Press, 1969.

595

Appendix O

Anthologies of African Writing in English, French, and Portuguese

Anthologies of African Writing in English

Ademola, Frances (ed.). *Reflections: Nigerian Prose and Verse.* Lagos: African Universities Press, 1962.

Allen, J. W. T. (trans. and notes). *Six Examples of a Swahili Classical Verse Form.* New York: Africana Publishing Corporation, 1971.

Andrzejewski, B. W. and Lewis, I. M. (eds.). *Somali Poetry.* Oxford: Clarendon Press, 1964.

Angoff, Charles and Povey, John (eds.). *African Writing Today.* New York: Manyland Books, 1969.

Awoonor, Kofi and Adali-Mortty, G. (eds.). *Messages: Poems from Ghana.* London: Heinemann, 1970.

Banham, Martin (ed.). *The Horn. Nigerian Student Verse 1959.* Ibadan: Ibadan University Press, 1960.

Banks-Henries, A. D. (Comp.). *Poems of Liberia (1836–1961).* London: Macmillan, 1966.

Barker, William Henry (coll. and tr.). *West African Folk Tales.* London: George G. Harrap and Co., 1917.

Barra, G. *1,000 Kikuyu Proverbs.* London: Macmillan, 1960.

Bassir, Olumbe (comp.). *An Anthology of West African Verse.* Ibadan: Ibadan University Press, 1957.

Beier, Ulli. *African Poetry: An Anthology of Traditional African Poems.* London and New York: Cambridge University Press, 1966.

——. *Introduction to African Literature: An Anthology of Critical Writings from Black Orpheus.* London: Longmans, 1967

—— (ed.). *The Origin of Life and Death: African Creation Myths.* London: Heinemann, 1966.

—— (ed.). *Political Spider and Other Stories.* London: Heinemann, 1969.

—— (ed.). *Three Nigerian Plays.* London: Longmans, 1967.

—— (comp.). *Yoruba Poetry: An Anthology of Traditional Poems.* New York and London: Cambridge University Press, 1970.

—— (ed.). *Black Orpheus: An Anthology of African and Afro-American Prose.* London: Longmans, 1964.

Beier, Ulli and Gbadamosi, Bakare (comps.). *Ijala: Animal Songs by Yoruba Hunters.* Port Moresby: Papua Pocket Poets, 1967.

—— (Comps.). *The Moon Cannot Fight: Yoruba Children's Poems.* Ibadan: Mbari Publications, 1964.

—— (Comp. and tr.). *Yoruba Poetry.* Ibadan: General Publications Section, Ministry of Education, 1959.

Berry, John P. *Africa Speaks: A Prose Anthology with Comprehension and Summary Passages.* London: Evans, 1970.

Bleek, Wilhelm Heinrich Immanuel (comp.). *Specimens of Bushman Folklore.* London: G. Allen and Co., Ltd., 1911.

Bloomhill, Greta. *The Sacred Drum: a collection of stories based on folklore of Central Africa.* Cape Town: Timmons, 1960.

Brench, Anthony Cecil (comp.). *Writings in French from*

Senegal to Cameroon. London: Oxford University Press, 1967.

Burlin, Natalie [Curtis] (ed.). *Songs and Tales from the Dark Continent.* New York and Boston: G. Shirmer, 1920.

Butler, Guy (ed.). *A Book of South African Verse.* London, Oxford University Press, 1959.

Cartey, Wilfred (comp.). *Palaver. Modern African Writings.* New York: Thomas Nelson, 1970.

Cendrars, Blaise (comp.). *The African Saga.* Tr. by Margery Bianco [L'Anthologie Nègre]. New York: Payson and Clark, 1927. (Original French edition: 1921.)

Chatelain, Heli. *Folk-Tales of Angola.* Boston and New York: Houghton, Mifflin and Co., 1894.

Clark, Leon E. (ed.). *Coming of Age in Africa: Continuity and Change.* 6 vols. New York: Praeger, 1969.

Cook, David (ed.). *Origin East Africa: A Makerere Anthology.* London: Heinemann, 1965.

Cook, David and Lee, Miles (comps.). *Short East African Plays in English.* London: Heinemann, 1968.

Cook, David and Rubadiri, David. *Poems from East Africa.* London: Heinemann, 1971.

Cope, Jack and Krige, Uys (eds.). *The Penguin Book of South African Verse.* Baltimore: Penguin Books, 1968.

Cope, Trevor (ed.). *Izibongo: Zulu Praise Poems.* Oxford: Clarendon Press, 1968.

Courlander, Harold (comp.) *The King's Drum, and other stories.* London: Hart-Davis, 1963.

Creel, J. Luke, with Bai Gai Kiahon. *Folk-tales of Liberia.* Minneapolis: T. S. Denison, 1960.

Dathorne, Oscar Ronald (ed.). *African Poetry for Schools and Colleges.* London: Macmillan, 1969.

Dathorne, O. R. and Feuser, Willfried (eds.). *Africa in Prose.* Baltimore: Penguin Books, 1969.

Dei-Anang, Michael F. *Africa Speaks: A Collection of Original Verse with an Introduction on 'Poetry in Africa'.* Accra: Guinea Press, 1959.

Denny, Neville. *Pan African Short Stories.* London: Thomas Nelson and Son, 1965, 1967.

Dick, John B. *African Forum.* London and New York: Cambridge University Press, 1968.

——. *The Cambridge Book of Verse for African Schools.* London and New York: Cambridge University Press, 1966.

Doob, Leonard W. (ed.). *Ants Will Not Eat Your Fingers–a Selection of Traditional African Poems.* New York: Walker and Co., 1966.

Drachler, Jacob (ed.). *African Heritage.* New York: Collier Books, 1964.

Edwards, Paul G. (ed.). *Modern African Narrative.* London: Nelson, 1966.

597

African Authors

———. *Through African Eyes*. 2 Vols. Cambridge: The University Press, 1966.

———. *West African Narrative*. Edinburgh: Thomas Nelson, 1963.

Evans-Pritchard, E. E. (ed.). *The Zande Trickster*. London and New York: Oxford University Press, 1967.

Farsi, S. S. *Swahili Sayings from Zanzibar*. Dar es Salaam: East African Literature Bureau, 1958.

Feldman, Susan. *African Myths and Tales*. New York: Dell, 1963.

Finnegan, Ruth (ed. and tr.) *Limba Stories and Storytelling*. London and New York: Oxford University Press, 1967.

———. *Oral Literature in Africa*. London: Oxford University Press, 1970.

Fisher, Ruth B. *Twilight Tales of the Black Baganda*. Rev. ed. London: Cass, 1970.

Forrest, R. *An African Reader*. London: Longmans, 1965.

Fouda, Basuke-Juleat *et al* (eds.). *African Poems in French*. Rev. ed. Nendeln, Lichtenstein: Kraus Reprint, 1970.

Fox, Doreen (ed.). *East African Childhood: Three Versions*. London and New York: Oxford University Press, 1967.

Frobenius, Leo and Fox, Douglas C. *African Genesis*. New York: Stackpole Sons, 1937.

Fuchs, Peter. *African Decameron*. Tr. by Robert Meister. New York: I. Obolensky, 1963, 1964.

Fuja, Abayomi (ed.). *Fourteen Hundred Cowries: Traditional stories of the Yoruba*. London and New York: Oxford University Press, 1962.

Gbadamosi, Bakare and Beier, Ulli (eds.). *Not Even God is Ripe Enough*. London: Heinemann, 1968.

Gordimer, N. and Abrahams, L. *South African Writing Today*. Harmondsworth, Engl: Penguin, 1967.

Green, R. *An Anthology of Prose Verse from East Africa*. Nairobi: East African Literature Bureau, n. d. [1970].

Gresshof, N. M. *Some English Writing by South African Bantu*. Capetown; University School of Librarianship, 1943.

Hansen, J. (ed.). *One Voice*. London: Arnold. Ltd., 1966.

Harries, Lyndon (ed. and tr.). *Swahili Poetry*. Oxford: Clarendon Press, 1962.

———. (ed. and tr.). *Swahili Prose Texts*. London: Oxford University Press: 1962, 1965.

Henries, A. Doris Banks. *Liberian Folklore*. New York: Macmillan, 1966.

———. *Poems of Liberia*. London: Macmillan, 1966.

Hollo, Anselm (ed.). *Negro Verse*. London: Vista Books, 1964.

Hooper, Alfred G. (comp.) *Short Stories from South Africa*. Cape Town, New York: Oxford University Press, 1970.

Hughes, Langston (ed.). *An African Treasury: Stories, Poems and Essays by Black Africans*. New York: Pyramid Books, 1961.

——— (ed.). *Poems from Black Africa*. Bloomington: University of Indiana Press, 1963.

Huntington, G.W.B. (Tr. and ed.). *The Glorious Victories of 'Amda Seyon, King of Ethiopia,' together with the history of the Emperor and Ceon, otherwise -Called Gabra Mazcal*. London and New York: Oxford University Press, 1965.

Ikiddeh, I. (ed.). *Drum Beats: an Anthology of West African Narrative Poems*. Leeds: E. J. Arnold, 1968.

Irele, Abiola (ed.). *Lectures Africaines. A Prose Anthology of African Writing in French*. London: Heinemann, 1969.

Jabavu, Davidson Don Tengo. *Bantu Literature*. Lovedale: Mission Institution Press, n. d.

Jablow, Alta (comp.) *An Anthology of West African Folklore*. London: Thames and Hudson, 1961, 1962.

Johnston, H. A. S. *A Selection of Hausa Stories*. London and New York: Oxford University Press, 1966.

Kennedy, Ellen Conroy. *The Negritude Poets*. New York: Richard Seaver, Viking, 1973.

Knappert, Jan (ed.). *A choice of flowers. Swahili love poems with translations*. London: Heinemann, 1971.

——— (ed.). *Myths and Legends of the Congo*. London: Heinemann, 1971.

——— (ed.). *Myths and Legends of Swahili*. London: Heinemann, 1970.

———. *Traditional Swahili Poetry: An investigation into the concepts of East African Islam as reflected in the Utenzi Literature*. Leiden: Brill, 1967.

Koelle, Sigismund Wilhelm. *Africann Native Literature: or Proverbs, Tales, Fables, and Historical Fragments in the Kanuri or Bonuri Language*. 2d ed. Graz, Austria: Akademische Druk-und Verlagsastalt, 1968. Reprint (From 1854 edition).

Komey, E. A. and Mphahlele, Ezekiel (eds.). *Modern African Short Stories*. London: Faber and Faber, 1964.

Kunene, D. P. *Heroic Poetry of the Basotho*. London: Oxford University Press, 1971.

Krige, Uys and Cope, Jack (see Cope and Krige)

Larson, Charles (ed.). *African Short Stories. A Collection of Contemporary African Writing*. New York: Macmillan, 1970.

——— (ed.) *Prejudice: 20 Tales of Oppression and Liberation*. New York: Macmillan, 1970.

Litto, Frederick M. *Plays from Black Africa*. New York: Hill and Wang, 1968.

Manley, Deborah (ed.). *Growing Up*. Lagos: African Universities Press, 1967.

Marland, M. (ed.). *The Experience of Colour–an Anthology of Prose, Verse and Pictures*. London: Longman, 1970.

Mbiti, John S. (ed. and tr.). *Akamba Stories*. Oxford: Clarendon Press, 1966.

Miller J. E. et al. *Black African Voices*, Glenview, Ill: Scott, Foresman and Co., 1970.

Moore, Gerald and Beier, Ulli. *Modern Poetry from Africa*. Rev. ed. London: Penguin, 1968.

Morris, Henry F. *The Heroic Recitations of the Bahima of Ankole*. Oxford: Clarendon Press, 1964.

Mphahlele, Ezekiel. *African Writing Today*. Harmondsworth: Penguin, 1967.

Nassir, Ahmad: *Poems from Kenya, gnomic verses in Swahili* (L. Harries, tr.). Madison: University of Wisconsin Press, 1966.

Njururi, Njumbj (comp.). *Agikuyu Folk Tales*. London: Oxford University Press, 1966.

Nolen, Barbara (ed.). *Africa is People: Firsthand accounts from Contemporary Africa*. New York: Dutton, 1967.

Nwoga, D. T. (ed.). *West African Verse*. London: Longmans, 1967.

Nyembezi, C. L. S. *Zulu Proverbs*. Johannesburg: University of Witwatersrand Press, 1945.

O'Connell, Ruby M. Agar. *Sintsomi: Bantu folk stories*. Lovedale: Lovedale Press, 1938.

Okala, L. (ed.). *Drum Beat: East African Poems*. Nairobi: East African Publishing House, 1967.

Okeke, Uche. *Ibo Folktales*. Garden City, N. Y.: Doubleday, 1971.

Okpaku, Joseph (ed.). *New African Literature and the Arts*. 2 vols. New York: Thomas Crowell, 1970.

O'Sullivan, Rev. John (ed.). *The New Generation: prose and verse from the secondary schools and training colleges in Ghana*. Accra: State Publishing Corp., 1968.

Pieterse, Cosmo (ed.). *Eleven Short African Plays*. London: Heinemann, 1971.

——— (ed.). *Seven South African Poets*. London: Heinemann, 1970.

——— (ed.). *Ten One Act Plays*. London: Heinemann, 1968.

Présence Africaine. *An Anthology of New Verse from the Negro World in Four Languages*. Paris: Imprimerie Dessaint, 1966.

Radford, W. L. *African Poetry for Schools*. Nairobi: East African Publishing House, 1970.

Radin, Paul (ed.). *African Folktales*. Princeton, Princeton University Press, 1970.

Rattray, Robert S. *Akan-Ashanti Folk Tales*. London: Oxford University Press, 1930.

———. *Ashanti Proverbs*. London: Oxford University Press, 1916.

——. *Hausa Folklore, Customs, Proverbs, etc.* London: Oxford University Press, 1913.

Reed, John and Wake, Clive (eds.). *A Book of African Verse.* London: Heinemann, 1964.

Ridout, R. and Jones, E. (eds.). *Adjustments: an anthology of African and Western Writing.* London: Edward Arnold, 1966.

Rive, Richard (ed.). *Modern African Prose.* London: Heinemann, 1964.

—— (ed.). *Quartet.* London: Heinemann, 1965.

Robinson, C. H. *Specimans of Hausa Literature.* Farnborough, U. K.: Gregg International Publishers, 1969.

Robinson, William H. *Nommo: An Anthology of Modern Black African and Black American Literature.* New York: Macmillan, 1972.

Rutherfoord, Peggy (ed.). *African Voices.* New York: Vanguard Press, 1960. [Published in 1958 as *Darkness and Light: An Anthology of African Writing,* London: Faith Press.]

Sangster, E. G. and Quashire, C. K. A. (eds.). *Talent for Tomorrow: An Anthology of Creative Writing from the Training Colleges of Ghana.* Accra: Published for the Ghana University of Education by the Publishing Division of the State Publishing Corp., 1968.

Schapera, I. (ed. and tr.). *Praise Poems of Tswana Chiefs.* Oxford: Clarendon Press, 1965.

Sergeant, H. (ed.). *Poetry from Africa.* Oxford: Pergammon, 1968.

Shapiro, Norman (ed.). *Negritude: Black Poetry from Africa and the Caribbean.* (trans. from the French). New York: October House, 1970.

Shelton, Austin J. *The African Assertion.* New York: Odyssey Press, 1968.

Shore, H. I. and Shore-Bos, Megcheline (eds.). *Come Back, Africa: Fourteen Short Stories from South Africa.* New York: International Publishers Co., 1968; Berlin, Seven Seas Books, 1968.

Skinner, Neil (ed. and tr.). *Hausa Readings: Selections from Edgar's 'Tatuniyoyi.* Madison: University of Wisconsin Press, 1968.

——. *Hausa Tales and Traditions.* 3 vols. London; Cass, 1969.

Soyinka, Wole (ed.). *Plays from the Third World. An Anthology.* New York: Doubleday, 1971.

St. John-Parsons, Donald. *Legends of North Ghana.* London: Longmans, 1958.

—— (ed.). *More Legends of North Ghana.* London: Longmans, 1960.

—— (ed.). *Our Poets Speak: An Anthology of West African Verse.* London: University of London Press, 1966.

Swanzy, Henry (ed.). *Voices of Ghana.* Accra: Ministry of Information and Broadcasting, 1958.

Taiwo, Oladele. *Introduction to West African Literature.* London: Nelson, 1967.

Tibble, Anne (ed.). *African-English Literature.* New York: October House, 1965.

Torrend, J. (ed. and tr.). *Specimans of Bantu Folklore from Northern Rhodesia.* New York: E. P. Dutton and Co., 1921.

Tracey, Hugh. *Lalela Zula: 100 Zulu Lyrics.* Johannesburg: Africa Music, 1948.

——. *The Lion on the Path and other African Stories.* New York: Praeger, 1968.

Tucker, A. N. (ed.). *The Disappointed Lion and other stories from Central Africa.* London: County Life, 1937.

Turner, D. T. et als (eds.). *Voices from the Black Experience (African and Afro-American Experience).* New York: Ginn and Co., 1971.

Wake, Clive (ed.). *An Anthology of African and Malagasy Poetry in French.* London: Oxford University Press, 1965.

Walker, B. K. and Walker, W. S. (eds.). *Nigerian Folktales.* New Brunswick, N. J.: Rutgers, 1961.

Walker, Joseph A. *Drum Say, Be! An Anthology of African Literature.* New York: Fawcett, 1971.

Watts, Margaret E. (ed.). *The New Generation: Prose and Verse from the Secondary Schools and Training Colleges of Ghana.* Accra: State Publishing Corp., 1967.

Whitely, W. H. (comp.). *A Selection of African Prose.* 2 vols. Oxford: Clarendon Press, 1964.

Yassin, Mohammed. *Tales from Sierra Leone.* London: Oxford University Press, 1967.

Young, T. Cullen (ed.). *African New Writing. Short Stories by African Writers.* London: Lutterworth Press, 1947.

Anthologies of African Writing in French

Amon d'Aby, François Joseph, ed. *Le théâtre populaire en République de Côte d'Ivoire.* Abidjan: Cercle Culturel et Folklorique de la Côte d'Ivoire, 1965.

Ayissi, Léon-Marie. *Contes et berceuses Beti.* Yaoundé: Ed. CLE, 1966.

Bâ, Amadou-Hampaté. *Kaidara.* Paris: Juillard, 1969. (long oral poem from Peul with original Peul text and literal French transcription)

Belinga, Enos M. S. *Littérature et musique populaire en Afrique noire.* Paris: Ed. Cujas, 1965.

Bol, V. P. and Allary, J. *Littérateurs et poètes noirs.* Léopoldville: Bibliothèque de l'Etoile, 1964.

Caverhill, Nicholas, ed. *Recueil des textes africains: an anthology of modern African writing in French.* London: Hutchinson, 1967.

Cendrars, Blaise. *Anthologie nègre.* Paris: Corêa, 1947, (the definitive, corrected edition), in paperback, 1972.

Colin, Ronald. *Littérature africaine d'hier dt de demain.* Paris: Association pour le développement Educatif et Culturel, 1965.

——. *Les contes noirs de l'Ouest Africain, témoins majeurs d'un humanisme.* Paris: Présence Africaine, 1957.

Copans, Jean. *Contes Wolof du Baol.* Dakar-Hann: Centre O.R.S.T.O.M., 1948.

Coupez, A. and Kamanzi, Thomas, eds. *Littérature courtoise (ou de cour) du Rwanda.* London, New York: Oxford University Press, 1969.

Dadié, Bernard. *Légendes africaines.* Paris: Seghers, 1954. Preface by Alioune Diop.

——. *Le pagne noir: contes africains.* Paris: Présence Africaine, 1955.

Damas, Léon Gontran. *Poètes d'expression française d'Afrique noire, Madagascar, Réunion, Guadeloupe, Martinique, Indochine, Guyane.* Paris: Seuil, 1947.

Diabate, Massa M. *Janjon et autres chants populaires du Mali.* Paris: Présence Africaine, 1970. Preface by Djibril T. Niane.

Diop, Birago. *Contes et lavanes.* Paris: Présence Africaine, 1963.

——. *Les contes d'Amadou Koumba.* Paris: Présence Africaine, 1965. (Translation by Dorothy S. Blair: *Tales of Amadou Koumba.* London, New York: Oxford University Press, 1966)

——. *Les nouveaux contes d'Amadou Koumba.* Paris: Présence Africaine, 1967.

Diop, O. S. *Contes et légendes d'Afrique noire.* Paris, 1962.

Eliett, Edouard. *Panorama de la littérature négro-africaine (1921–1962).* Paris: Présence Africaine, 1965.

African Authors

Evans-Pritchard, E. E. ed. *The Zande Trickster*. London, New York: Oxford University Press, 1967. (stories and comments on folktales from the Central African Republic in francophone africa)

Fouda, Basile-Juléat et als. *Littérature camerounais*. Cannes: Impr. Aegitna, 1961, and Liechtenstein, Kraus Reprint, 1970.

Hama, Boubou. *Contes et légendes du Niger*, 2 vols. Paris: Présence Africaine, 1972.

Hughes, Langston and Reynault, Christiane, eds. *Anthologie africaine et malgache*. Paris: Seghers, 1962.

Hutchinson, Joyce A. (comp.). *Voix d'Afrique: A French Reader for and About Africa*. New York: Cambridge University Press, 1967.

Irele, Abiola, ed. *Lectures africaines: a prose anthology of African writing in French*. London: Heinemann, 1969. (text extracts in French, notes and commentary in English)

Issak, Tchoumba Ngouankeu. *Autour du lac Tchad (contes)*. Yaoundé: Ed. CLE, 1969. (folktales from N. Cameroon and The Chad)

Jadot, J. M. *Les écrivains africains du Congo Belge et du Ruandi-Urundi*. Brussels, 1959.

Justin, André. *Anthologie africaine des écrivains noirs d'expression française*. Paris: Institut Pédagogique Africaine, 1962.

Kagame, Alexis. *Bref aperçu sur la poésie dynastique du Rwanda*. Brussels: Ed. Universitaires, 1950.

———. *Introduction aux grands genres lyriques de l'ancien Rwanda*. Butare, Rwanda: Ed. Universitaires du Rwands, 1969.

———. *La poésie dynastique au Rwanda*. Brussels, Inst. Royal Congo Belge, 1951.

Kane, M. *Les contes d'Amadou Coumba*. Dakar, 1968.

Kesteloot, Lilyan. *Anthologie négro-africaine: panorama critique des prosateurs, poètes et dramatourges noirs du XXème siecle*. Verviers, Belgium: Gérard, 1967.

———. *Les écrivains noirs de language française: naissance d'une littérature*, 3rd edition, revised. Brussels: Université Libre de Bruxelles, Institut de Sociologie, 1965.

———. *Neuf poètes camerounais*. Yaoundé: Eds Abbia and CLE, 1965.

Matip, Benjamin. *A la belle étoile. Contes et nouvelles d'Afrique*. Paris: Présence Africaine, 1962.

Mohamadou, Eldridge and Mayssal, Henriette. *Contes et poèmes Foulbés de la Bénoué*. Yaoundé: Ed. CLE, 1965.

Mushiete, Paul. *Littérature française africaine: petite anthologie des écrivains noirs d'expression française*. Leverville, Zaïre: Bibliothèque de l'Etoile, 1957.

———. *Anthologie des écrivains congolais*. Kinshasa: S.N.E.C., Ministère de la Culture, 1969.

Niane, Djibril Tamsir. *Soundjata ou l'épopée mandingue*. Paris: Présence Africaine, 1960. (Translated into English by G. D. Pickett: *Sundiata: an epic of old Mali*. London: Longmans, 1965)

Nouvelle somme de poésie du monde noir. Paris: Présence Africaine, 1966. (also separate English titled edition as *New Sum of Poetry from the Negro World*, Vol. 57, Présence Africaine, 1966)

Packman, Brenda, ed. *Étoiles africaine: morceaux choisis de la littérature de l'Afrique noire*. London: Evans, 1968.

Pagéard, Robert. *Littérature négro-africaine: le mouvement littéraire contemporaine dans l'Afrique noire d'expression française*. Paris: Le Livre Africain, 1966.

Poètes d'Afrique. La Courneuve (Seine), France: Eds. de l'Académie Populaire de Littérature et de Poésie, 1956.

Raponda-Walker. A. *Contes gabonais. (nouvelle édition revue et augmentée de Roger-L. Sillans)*. Paris: Présence Africaine, 1971.

Sainville, Léonard, ed. *Anthologie de la littérature ne-gro-africaine; romanciers et conteurs négro-africains*, 2 vols. Paris: Présence Africaine, 1963, 1968.

Senghor, Léopold Sédar. *Anthologie de la nouvelles poésie nègre et malgache*. Paris: Presses Universitaires de France, 1948, 1969. Preface by J.-P. Sartre: "Orphée noirs."

Shapiro, Norman R., ed. and trans. *Négritude: Black poetry from Africa and the Caribbean*. New York: October House, 1970. (original texts in French of early négritude writers: Césaire, Damas, Senghor, U Tam'si, B. Dadié, Bognini, etc.)

Sissoko, Fily-Dabo. *Sagesse noire, sentences et proverbes malinkés*. Paris: Ed de la Tour du Guet, 1955.

Socé, Ousmane. *Contes et légendes d'Afrique noire*. Paris: Nouvelles Editions Latines, 1962.

Towo-Atagana, Gaspard, and Towo-Atagana, Françoise. *Nden-bobo, l'araignée toilière (conte béti)*. Yaoundé: Ed CLE, 1966.

U Tam'si, Tchicaya Gérald Félix. *Légendes africaines*. Paris: Seghers, 1969.

Vally-Samat, Renée. *Contes et Légendes de Madagascar*. Paris: Fernand Nathan, 1962.

Wake, Clive, ed. *An Anthology of African and Malagasy Poetry in French*. London, New York: Oxford University Press, 1965. (extracts in French of most important early writers and notes and comments in English on authors)

Warner, Keith Q. *Voix Françaises du Monde Noir*. New York: Holt, Rinehart, 1971.

Anthologies of African Writing in Portuguese

A. Folklore

Almeida, António de. *Sôbre o ciclo do lobo em Cabo Verde e na Guiné Portuguesa*. Lisbon: Junta de Investigações do Ultramar, 1965.

Archer, Maria (Emília). *Africa Selvagem, Folclore dos negros do grupo "bantu."* Lisbon: Guimaraes and Cie, n. d. but c. 1935.

Chatelain, Héli, trans. *Contos populares de Angola by M. Garcia da Silva*. Lisbon: Agência Geral do Ultramar, 1964.

———. *Folk-tales of Angola*. New York: Negro Universities Press, 1969. (a re-issue of 1894 original edition)

Diogo Júnior, Alfredo. *Angola na tradição e na lenda*. Luanda: 1963.

Estermann, Carlos. *A mulher e dois filhos. Conto com diversos elementos aculturados*. Luanda: 1964. (offprint: *Boletim do Instituto de Angola*, no. 17).

Ferreira, José Gomes and Carlos de Oliveira. *Contos tradicionais portugueses*. Lisbon: Iniciativas Editoriais, 1957, 2 vols.

Ferreira, Manuel. *Fabulário do Ultramar*, in *Grande Fabulário de Portugal e Brasil*. Lisbon: 1962. 2 vols.

Folk-tales of Angola. Memoirs of the American Folk-Lore Society, 1. Lancaster, Penna.: 1894. (50 tales in Ki-mbundu, with literal English translations)

Lambo, Gonzaga. *Cancioneiro popular angolan. Subsidios*. Série etnografica, 1. Lisbon: Casa dos Estudantes do Império, 1962.

Margarido, Alfredo. *Canções populares de Novo Lisboa*. Lisbon: Casa dos Estudantes do Império, 1964.

Nascimento, Hermínio do. *Doze canções da Luanda. Comentarios, transcrições e harmonização*. Lisbon: Diamang, 1962.

Oliveira, José Osório de. *Literatura Africana*. Lisbon: Agência Geral das Colónias, 1944. 2nd ed., Lisbon: Sociedad de Expansão Cultural, 1962.

Reis, Fernando. *Soiá. Literatura oral de São Tomé*. Colecção Metropole e Ultramar, 9. Braga: Pax, 1965.

——. *Povô flogà: o povo brinça. Folclore de S. Tomé e Príncipe*. São Tomé, 1969.

Ribas, Oscar (Bento). *Ilundo. Divindades e ritos angolanos*. Luanda: Museu de Angola, 1958.

——. *Missoso. Literatura tradicional angolana*. 3 vols. Luanda, 1961–64.

——. *Sunguilahdo. Contos tradicionais angolanos*. Lisbon: Agência-Geral do Ultramar, 1967.

Romano (Madeira de Melo), Luís. *Cabo Verde: Renascenca de uma civilização no Atlântico mèdio*. Lisbon: Ocidente, 1967.

Tadeu, Viriato Augusto. *Contos do Caramô. Lendas e fábulas mandingas da Guiné portuguêsa*. Lisbon: Agência-Geral das Colónias, 1945.

Soromenho, Castro. *Lendas negras*. Lisbon: Cosmos, 1939. 4th ed., 1965.

B. General and Literary:

Abranches, Henrique (Moutinho). *Diálogo. Contos*. Colecção Autores Ultramarinos, Série literatura, 12. Lisbon: Casa dos Estudantes do Império, 1963.

Albuquerque, Orlando de. *Cidade do Indico*. Angola: Aos 4 Ventos, 1962, 2nd ed., Agência-Geral do Ultramar, 1963.

——. *De Manhã cai o cacimbo. Contos*. Colecção Ultramar, 3. Porto, Angola: Portucalense Editôra, 1969.

——; and Evaristo, Victor. *Poesia de Moçambique*. Lisbon: Casa dos Estudantes do Império, 1951 (offprint from *Mensagem* magazine, No. 12)

Andrade, Mário (Pinto) de. *Antologia da poesia negra de expressão portuguêsa*. Paris: P. J. Oswald, 1958.

——. *Literatura africana de expressão portuguêsa. Antologia temática*. 2nd ed. Algiers, 1967.

Cabral, Alexandre. *A fula. Contos*. Colecção Imbondeiro, 51. Sà da Bandeira: Imbondeira, 1963.

——. *Contos da Europa e da Africa*. Lisbon: Edições Expansão, 1947.

Casimiro (dos Santos), Augusto. *Portugal atlântico. Poemas da Africa e do mar*. Lisbon: Agência-Geral do Ultramar, 1955.

César (Pires Monteiro), Amândio. *Algumas vozes líricas de Africa*. Lisbon; 1962.

——. *Contos portugueses do ultramar. Antologia*. Colecção Ultramar, 2, Vol II. Porto, Angola: Portucalense Editôra, 1969.

——. *Parágrafos de literatura ultramarina*. Lisbon: Sociedade de Expansão Cultural, 1967. (collection of review articles on many authors)

—— and António, Mário Oliveira, M. A. Fernandes de. *Elementos para uma bibliografia de literatura e cultura portuguêsa ultramarino contemporânea*. Lisbon: Agência-Geral do Ultramar, 1968.

Colecção Hoje e Amanhã, No. 1. Lisbon: Orion, 1958.

Conceição Nobre, Maria da (ed.) *Antologia de poesias angolanas*. Novo Lisboa, Angola: Câmara Municipal de Nova Lisboa, Serviços Culturais, 1957.

Contos d'Africa. Antologia de contos angolanos. Introduction by Mário de Andrade and Leonel Cosme. Sà da Bandeira: Publicações Imbondeiro, 1961.

Cunha, Manuel Barão. *Aquelas longas horas. Narrativas sôbre a actual epopéia africana*. Lisbon, 1968.

Ervedosa, Carlos (Eduardo). *A literatura angolana. Rèsenha histórica*. Colecção Autores Ultramarinos, Série Ensaio, 1. Lisbon: Casa dos Estudantes do Império, 1963.

——. *Poetas angolanos*. Preface by Mário António. Lisbon: Casa dos Estudantes do Império, 1959. (this essay is a reprint from the *Boletim da Casa dos Estudantes do Império*.

Figueiredo, Jaime de. *Modernos poetas cabo-verdianos*. Praia, Cape Verde: Imprensa Nacional, 1961.

I (primeiro) encontro de escritores de Angola, held in Sà da Bandeira, January 19–27, 1963. Published in Sà da Bandeira, Edição de "Publicações Imbondeiro" e dos Serviços Culturais do Município da Sà da Bandeira, 1963.

Mákua. *Antologia poética*. 3 vols. Sà da Bandeira: Imbondeiro, 1962–1963.

Margarido, Alfredo. *Poemas para uma bailarina negra*. Lisbon: Fôlhas de Poesia, 1958.

——. *Poetas moçambicanos*. Lisbon: Casa dos Estudantes do Império.

——. "Incidences socio-économiques sur la poésie noire d'expression portugaise." *Diogènes*, No. 37, Paris, Jan–Mar. 1962, pp. 53–80.

——. "La littérature angolaise de la découverte au combat," *L'Afrique Littéraire et Artistique*, No. 2, Paris, Dec, 1968, pp. 8–17.

Mariano, Gabriel (Lopes da Silva). *Poetas de Cabo Verde*. Lisbon: Casa dos Estudantes do Império, 1960 or 1961.

Maurão, Fernando. *Contistas angolanos*. Lisbon: Casa dos Estudantes do Império, 1960.

Montenegro, José. *A negritude, Dos mitos às realidades*. Colecção Metropole e Ultramar, 31. Braga: Pax, 1967.

Moser, Gerald M. *Essays in Portuguese-African Literature*. Penn State Studies 26. University Park, Penna: Pennsylvania State University, 1969. (a small anthology of Portuguese-African works and English translation is at end of volume)

Nèves, João Alves da. *Poetas e contistas africanos de expressão portuguêsa*. São Paulo: Editôra Brasiliense, 1963.

Nobre, Maria da Conceição. *Antologia de poesias angolanas*. Novo Lisboa, Angola: Câmara Municipal, 1957.

Paço d'Arcos, Joaquim (Belford Correia da Silva). *Poemas imperfeitos*. Lisbon, 1952. (contains poems from S. Tomé, Angola, and Mozambique)

Polanah, Luís. *Poetas moçambicanos*. Introduction by Alfredo Margarido. Lisbon: Casa dos Estudantes do Império, 1960.

Rodriques Júnior, José. *Poetas de Moçambique*. Lourenço Marques: Africa Editôra, 1960.

Tavani, Guiseppe. *Poesia africana di rivolta*. Coll. Tempi Nuovi, 31. Bari, Laterza, 1969. (this work is in Italian, but has useful items on Portuguese Africa)

Tenreiro, Francisco and Andrade, Mário de, eds. *Poesia negra de expressão portuguêsa*. Lisbon: Livraria Escolar Editôra, 1953.

Trigueiros, Luís Forjaz, ed. *Cabo Verde, Guiné, S. Tomé e Príncipe, Macau e Timor*. Lisbon: Livraria Bertrand, 1963.

Appendix P

Anthologies of African Writing
Analytical Table

This table gives a detailed breakdown of the features of fifty-nine anthologies of African writing. The numbers in the last eight columns on the right represent the number of pages within the anthology devoted to the genre listed at the top of the columns.

Editor	Short Title	No. of Pages	No. of Authors	No. of Selections	Essays-Articles	Autobio. or Biog. Items	Plays	Folklore & Legends	Novels	Poetry (oral)	Poetry (written)	Short stories, tales**
Ademola	Reflections	123	13	34	20	20					25	30
Andrzejewski	Somali Poetry	167	9	30	60					80	20	
Angoff and Povey	African Writing Today	304	28	44	18				70		60	124
Awoonor and Adali-Mortty	Messages	190	14	115							175	
Banham	Nigerian Student Verse 1959	33	13	27							24	
Bassir	An Anthology of West African Verse	68	14	35							68	
Beier	African Poetry	80		54						70		
Beier	An Introduction to African Literature	272	22	27		20			80	50	100	
Beier	Political Spider	118	16	17					15			100
Beier and Gbadamosi	The Moon Cannot Fight	44		33						44		
Beier	Three Nigerian Plays	89	3	3			85					
Beier	Yoruba Poetry	126		123						123		
Cartey	Palaver: Modern African Writings	183	27	31	115	12	42	115			11	
Cendrars	The African Saga	378		103					340	8		
Cook	Origin East Africa	188	25	42		50					16	120
Cook and Lee	Short East African Plays in English	148	9	10			140					
Cook and Rubadiri	Poems from East Africa	206	50	131							186	
Cope	Izibongo Zulu Praise Poems	230	26	26	86					155		

African Authors

Editor	Short Title	No. of Pages	No. of Authors	No. of Selections	Essays-Articles	Autobio- or Biog. Items	Plays	Folklore & Legends	Novels	Poetry (oral)	Poetry (written)	Short stories, tales**
Doob	Ants Will Not Eat Your Fingers	127		100						100		
Denny	Pan African Short Stories	223	16	16								215
Drachler	African Heritage	285	34	71	123	11		30	34		18	
Edwards	Modern African Narrative	196	14	14	155				155			35
Edwards	Through African Eyes, I.	102	18	20	47		3		34			
Edwards	West African Narrative	252	15	21	200				200			45
Gordimer and Abrahams	South African Writing Today	264	42	44	130	20					30	130
Harries	Swahili Poetry	326		86				150		100		
Harries	Swahili Prose Texts	298		50				145				
Hollo	Negro Verse	48	17	26						7	32	
Hughes	An African Treasury	192	35	46	72			3			19	60
Hughes and Reynault	Anthologie africaine et Malgache (anglophone writers are translated into French)	312	38	81		80			120		80	
Hughes	Poems from Black Africa	160	38	86						12	133	
Ikkideh	Drum Beats	155	10	10					125			
Justin	Anthologie Africaine (francophone writers only)	190	20	28	175	10			175			175
Knappert	Myths and Legends of the Congo	218		102				217				
Komey and Mphahlele	Modern African Stories	227	25	25					55			165
Leslau and Leslau	African Folk Tales	62		25				55				
Litto	Plays from Black Africa	317	6	6			300					
Moore and Beier	Modern Poetry from Africa	268	47	145							242	
Morris	The Heroic Recitations of the Bahima of Ankole	143		7	60					64		
Mphahlele	African Writing Today	347	41	47		9			73			
Nwoga	West African Verse	243	20	71	120						115	
Okpaku	New African Literature and the Arts, I	359	32	44	90		60		35		40	80
Okapku	New African Literature ..., II	251	20	40	100	50					40	35
Pieterse	Seven South African Poets	132	7	93							120	
Pieterse	Ten One Act Plays	309	10	10			300					

Editor	Short Title	No. of Pages	No. of Authors	No. of Selections	Essays-Articles	Autobio. or Biog. Items	Plays	Folklore & Legends	Novels	Poetry (oral)	Poetry (written)	Short stories, tales**
Présence Africaine	*New Sum of Poetry from the Negro World* (all works are in original language)	574	146	383							544	
Rattray	*Ashanti Proverbs*	190		830						174		
Rattray	*Hausa Folk-Lore, Customs, Proverbs*	305		100				305				
Rideout and Jones	*Adjustments*	164	9	9								164
Senghor	*Anthologie de la nouvelle poésie nègre et malgache* (francophone only)	227	16	119							210	
Sergeant	*Poetry from Africa*	101	4	50							95	
Shelton	*The African Assertion*	273	36	49				13	11	18	96	52
St. John-Parsons	*Our Poets Speak*	64	21	26	7						28	
Tibble	*African-English Literature*	304	41	54		10		100			27	179
Trask	*Classic Black African Poems*	61		39						45		
Walker and Walker	*Nigerian Folk Tales*	113		37				66				
Whiteley	*A Selection of African Prose, I*	200		46					180			
Young	*African New Writing*	126	7	14								115
Miller, O'Neal, & McDonnell	*Black African Voices*	431	31	60	70	50	33	45			39	83

N.B. Some items counted have been included in two or more categories, and not all items fit the categories used: total number of pages therefore of the work often are not clearly reflected in type of literature covered.

This table based on research of David L. Ganz

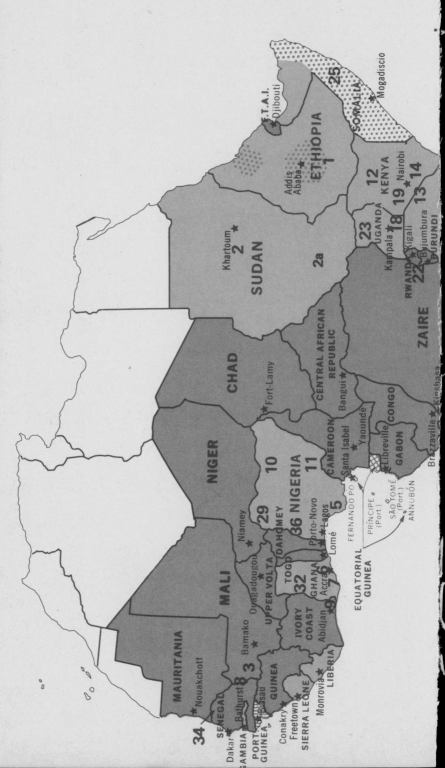

The Languages of Black Africa